The Great Train Race

THE GREAT TRAIN RACE

Railways and the Franco-German Rivalry, 1815–1914

By
Allan Mitchell

Berghahn Books
NEW YORK • OXFORD

Published in 2000 by

Berghahn Books

www.berghahnbooks.com

© 2000 Allan Mitchell
First paperback edition published in 2006

All rights reserved.
Except for the quotation of short passages
for the purposes of criticism and review, no part of this book
may be reproduced in any form or by any means, electronic or
mechanical, including photocopying, recording, or any information
storage and retrieval system now known or to be invented,
without written permission of the publisher.

Library of Congress Cataloging-in-Publication Data

Mitchell, Allan.
　The great train race : railways and the Franco-German rivalry, 1815–1914 /
by Allan Mitchell.
　　p. cm.
Includes bibliographical references and indexes.
ISBN 1-57181-166-4 (hbk) — ISBN 1-84545-136-8 (pbk)
　1. Railroads–France–History.　2. Railroads–Germany–History.
3. Railroads and state–France–History.　4. Railroads and state–Germany–
History.　5. World War, 1914–1918–Transportation.　I. Title.
HE3065.M58—2000
385'.0943—dc21　　　　　　　　　　　　　　　　　　　　　00-034266

British Library Cataloguing in Publication Data

A catalogue record for this book is available from the British Library.

Printed in the United States on acid-free paper.

Contents

List of Illustrations — vii
Preface — viii
Introduction: The Conundrum of Comparative History — x

Part I: Launching the Railway Age

1. **France, 1815–1870** — 3
   Liberalism and the Legrand Star, 4
   The Emergence of the Great Railway Companies, 8
   The Surge of the Second Empire, 18
   Trains and Free Trade, 24
   The Military Implications, 31

2. **Germany, 1815–1870** — 37
   The Dilemmas of Political Diversity, 38
   Particularism Unbound, 43
   Prussia and the Push for Unification, 50
   Before the Take-Off, 54
   Strategic Thought and Military Action, 60

3. **Comparisons, 1815–1870** — 68
   Administrative Organization, 69
   Economic Competition, 75
   Military Strategy, 79

Part II: The Signals Are Set

4. **France, 1870–1890** — 85
   After the Fall, 86
   The Counterattack of the Companies, 90
   The Failure of Centralism, 99
   A Condition of Troubling Inferiority, 104
   Railways and the Republican Army, 112

5. **Germany, 1870–1890** — 120
   Bismarck's Railroad Policy, 121
   The Reassertion of States' Rights, 129
   Germany Transformed, 136
   The Age of St. Gotthard, 141
   The Consolidation of Military Predominance, 149

6. Comparisons, 1870–1890   156
Administrative Organization, 157
Economic Competition, 164
Military Strategy, 168

PART III: INTERNAL AND INTERNATIONAL TENSIONS

7. France, 1890–1914   175
Recovery and Controversy, 176
The Companies Face Nationalization, 182
Private Enterprise or Public Service? 190
The Long Stagnation, 197
France Prepares for War, 204

8. Germany, 1890–1914   213
The Specter of Prussification, 214
Flirting with Unification, 220
Low Expectations and High Finance, 228
Railroads and the German Take-Off, 234
The Consequences of Escalation, 241

9. Comparisons, 1890–1914   248
Administrative Organization, 249
Economic Competition, 255
Military Strategy, 259

Epilogue: From Trains to Trenches   265

List of Abbreviations   270
Notes   272
Bibliography   307
Name Index   316
Subject Index   322

List of Illustrations

TABLES

1.	Northern Railway Company: Gross Income from Freight, 1852–1857	19
2.	Track Length of French Railway Companies, 30 September 1857	19
3.	French Railway Investments, 1823–1856	20
4.	Northern Railway Company: Gross Annual Income, 1860–1868	27
5.	Completed Railroads in France and Germany, 1850–1869	70
6.	Shipping Tonnage: Entrance and Exit, 1860–1873	79
7.	Total Railroad Investments by German Medium States, 1870–1880	143
8.	Kilometric Tonnage of German Railway Freight, 1870–1879	143
9.	German Commerce with Italy, 1881–1883	147
10.	Heavy Freight Carried by National Rail Networks, 1880–1893	163
11.	Transfer of Funds between the French State and the Eastern Railway Company, 1899–1910	184
12.	Total Production of German Light and Heavy Industry, 1880–1913	235
13.	Total Value Created in German Transportation, 1880–1913	235
14.	Total Gross Income from German Railway Freight, 1880–1913	236
15.	Track Length of Major State Railway Companies, 1880–1913	237
16.	Total Gross Income from German Passenger Fares, 1880–1913	238
17.	Comparative Growth of National Railway Systems, 1830–1910	253
18.	Total Rolling Stock, 1914	253
19.	Tonnage Entering North European Ports, 1891–1896	257
20.	Imports of Perishable Foods, 1897–1907	258
21.	Merchant Steamships, 1899–1914	259
22.	Annual Average Real Military Expenses, 1880–1910	262

MAPS

(between Chapters 2 and 3)
1. Main Railways in France, 1850
2. Main Railways in Germany, 1850
3. Main Railways in France, 1860
4. Main Railways in Germany, 1860

(between Chapters 5 and 6)
5. Major French Railway Companies, 1880
6. Major German Member States, 1880

(between Chapters 8 and 9)
7. Main Railways in France, 1914
8. Main Railways in Germany, 1914

Preface

When I was a boy, I went every Friday evening with my mother to the railway station in Ashland, Kentucky, to meet my father, who was arriving from across the state. Tiny and terrified, I stood there on the platform as the train crept in to a halt, heaving, scraping metal, and hissing steam. That gigantic engine right next to me was a monster, huge and alive, more frightening than any other creature extant. No less clearly I recall the exhilaration of my first train ride, moving over rails at speeds faster than I had ever known: the big cars, the people seated or milling about, the scenery racing by, the steady clatter and occasional whistles on the outside, the destination ahead. Those were thrills never to be forgotten, and probably they count as explanation enough for this book.

Yet there is another reason for such a volume. Later, by inadvertence, I became a comparative historian. It was not America but Europe (where my parents were born, in Scotland) that always fascinated me. Through a series of chances I ended by dividing nearly half of my adulthood between France and Germany. They became the focus of my studies, my research, my professional career, my private life. It seemed only natural, then, that I should eventually complete my historical work by attempting to compare them, and for that purpose the train was an ideal vehicle. A single technology, developed of course in Great Britain, arrived on the European continent at the same time in the 1830s. But within the French and German realms it evolved in quite disparate fashions during the nineteenth century. How and why was that so, I wondered? It was the normal question of any historian, a curiosity that led in my case to this scholarly enterprise.

Along the tracks I was aided and guided by many individuals who personally or professionally crossed my path. There is no way for me to thank them except to remember some of their names here in a list much too short: my mother, who kept matters of life and death in perspective; Catherine and René, Alex and Bob, Alena, Erica, Julian, and Melanie, a family whose love was all that anyone could want; Larry Joseph, the best of friends and of hosts; Hannes Siegrist and Lilli Sprecher, who kept a warm spot for me in Berlin; Josef and Ruth Becker, whose home near Augsburg was my beachhead in southern Germany; Jim Harrison, president of the

Bogliasco Foundation, who provided a delicious respite at the Centro Studi Ligure near Genoa; Jenefer Shute, who shared my taste for good writing, Gorgonzola, and the Cinque Terre; David Luft, the smartest and warmest of alter egos; Kevin McAleer, Eileen DeMarco, and Paul Dutton, students who became colleagues and friends; Belinda and Marc and Isabel, just adorable; Evelyn and Horst Wittmann, Old World charmers, along with Rebecca, who allowed me to be her sometime mentor; Chantal Bamberger, ever knowledgeable and always gracious; Karen Bowie, who knows about train stations and much more; Jürgen Kocka, who offered a chance to try out my tentative ideas at his Arbeitsstelle für Vergleichende Gesellschaftsgeschichte in Berlin; Patrick Fridenson, who sneaked me in the side door of the Ecole des Hautes Etudes and found lodging at the Maison Suger in Paris; Peter Hennock, who personified the English connection; François Caron and Georges Ribeill in France, Rainer Fremdling and Hans-Ulrich Wehler in Germany, whose writings set the standard; the German Marshall Fund of the United States, which provided financial support; Anne Liisa Harris, whose efficient and charming editorial assistance was invaluable; Shawn Kendrick, who was my extraordinarily thorough and thoughtful copy editor; Marion Berghahn, who took this project on and saw it through; and the many wonderfully patient archivists, who somehow tolerated my pestering.

A.M.
Boulder, Colorado

INTRODUCTION

The Conundrum of Comparative History

There were three basic models of a national railroad system developed in nineteenth-century Europe. From the outset, after 1815, Britain became an embodiment of the first: unfettered private enterprise with a minimum of direct state regulation. Beginning in the 1830s Belgium devised a second model, the opposite: a unified and tightly controlled state network suitable for a small fledgling nation struggling to establish an identity and to survive amid its imposing neighbors. Located on the spectrum between these poles were the systems usually designated as "mixed," including those in both France and Germany, which were similar at first in combining private and public interests. In a host of important respects, however, the mixture in the two national instances proved to be quite different. To define such similarities and differences is the purpose of this book.

Very early in my research of nineteenth-century European rail transportation I began to conceive of this work in terms of a juxtaposition between center and periphery. For me that notion was not necessarily weighted with soaring theoretical implications, although I remained aware that those abstractions exist. Rather, such a distinction provided a practical division of labor—here the advocates of centralism, there the opponents—which proved useful for both the French and German circumstances.[1]

The long-standing etatist tradition of France guaranteed that state regulation would be a conspicuous feature in the development of railways there, and the principal institutions of control were already in place: the restored monarchy, the Ministry of Public Works (Travaux Publics), the parliamentary committees, and, above all, the powerful state engineering corps of Ponts-et-Chaussées. Yet in the 1830s and 1840s the French, eager to avoid a huge public debt while sustaining the growth of commerce and industry, chose to concede railway operations to private joint-stock companies. In time, as is well known, the number of such major enterprises devolved to six. Two of them are of only marginal interest here: the Southern Railway Company (Compagnie du Midi), which was small, relatively insignificant, and confined to a remote corner of France without access to Paris; and the Western Railway Company (Compagnie de l'Ouest), which soon proved to be a proverbial one-trick pony because only its Paris-Le Havre line was profitable, and which perpetually ran a deficit that led to its absorption by the French state well before the First World War. Thus it seemed legitimate for me to focus on the four main business firms that formed the bulwark of the railroad industry in France: the Eastern Railway Company (Compagnie de l'Est), the PLM (Paris-Lyon-Méditerranée), the PO (Paris-Orléans), and the Northern Railway Company (Compagnie du Nord). The recurrent tensions between agencies of state control and representatives of these four large private enterprises necessarily comprise a central theme of any history of nineteenth-century French railways.

The conflicts of center and periphery were somewhat different in Germany, but they were no less pronounced. In the absence of a national state at the outset of the railway age, the Germans at first lacked the alternative of centralism. But the push toward national unification could not ultimately fail to affect the railroad industry, and once the German nation-state approached reality, the inherent contradictions of centralism and federalism were bound to appear. At its center, the new Reich after 1870 was a hybrid of Prusso-German institutions with its Kaiser-king and its chancellor-premier, the Prussian Ministry of Public Works (Ministerium der öffentlichen Arbeiten), a bicameral national parliament seated in Berlin, and a freshly minted national railway office (Reichseisenbahnamt). Attached to this complex structure, though separate and often opposed to it, were the regimes of the most prominent member states (Bundesstaaten) of the Reich: Saxony, Bavaria, Württemberg, and Baden. Of the many other smaller member states, only Hesse deserves mention; but its eventual integration into a railway union with Prussia enables us to regard the Hessian case in that context. Thus, as in France, the main constituent elements of the German periphery may logically be limited to four, thereby creating—without forcing—an analogous configuration for the purposes of comparative analysis.

Once this fundamental conception of the topic became clear, the itinerary of my research was fixed. Yet completing it proved to be much more of an athletic event than I had initially imagined. Conducted in the immediate wake of the Cold War, my investigation of the relevant archives occurred during a time of transition and confusion. The demise of the former DDR and the dismantling of the Berlin Wall left a totally chaotic landscape for the wandering scholar. The good news for me personally was free access to East German archives (to which, apparently on the false assumption of the infamous Stasi that I was a CIA agent, I had been denied entry for over two decades). But the bad news was that I was obliged to leave Berlin for several long stays in Potsdam, Coswig (near Wittenberg), and Merseburg, where lodging and cuisine were frankly less than ideal. Before the completion of my volume, moreover, nearly all of the collections I consulted during this initial research were relocated and reclassified, requiring another round of visits. So much for the German center. As for the periphery, my assignment was scarcely less strenuous, albeit more pleasant, because my methodology dictated long sojourns in Dresden, Munich, Stuttgart, and Karlsruhe. Whether such an exertion was justified is something that readers must judge. For me, at least, it provided an extensive primer in the geography of Central Europe.

The corresponding work in France began more comfortably. It started at the musty library of the Ecole des Ponts-et-Chaussées in downtown Paris and then moved conveniently across the city to the new ultra-modern surroundings of the Archives Nationales. There, once more, I first approached the center (i.e., the French state) through a steady diet of ministerial papers, memoranda, minutes, and statistics. As all habitués of the AN know, the slow pace there demands more endurance than athleticism, since the lengthy history of centralized bureaucracy in France is all too well reflected in its archival structure. Or so I thought until one day, having turned to the papers of the private railway companies (the analogue of my circuit in southern Germany), I was dismayed to learn that they had been removed to the Centre des Archives du Monde du Travail (CAMT) in Roubaix, a bleak outpost where I had thereafter to continue my investigation. Thus any researcher who wishes to explore matters concerning French private enterprise, including railroads, will henceforth need to do so literally out on the periphery, just a few kilometers from the Belgian border.

* * * * *

So it was that I experienced the best of times (Paris, Berlin) and the worst of times (Roubaix, Merseburg), as well as much in between. During that process I came to realize that the book I hoped to write could not simply report the forced march of my research. The nagging problem was that I had not one story to reconstruct but four:

Local. While in the archives, much of my attention was naturally consumed by the details of a particular public or private railway concern. How was it financed and organized? What were its special political and economic circumstances? How was it administered and operated, and by whom? Such specific questions do not permit vague answers. Generalities about national railway systems, it became clear, would be of little value without a firm grasp of their component networks.

Regional. The interaction of various individual railway enterprises inescapably constituted a second theme. For one reason or another, they tended to cluster and to combine their efforts, sharing routes, stations, or rolling stock. Common rates required mutual negotiations, frequently conducted outside of direct central control. In France, the large private companies often sought each other's advice and consent, at least when they were not quarreling among themselves, and after 1870 they began to meet regularly in the guise of a syndicate for the "great beltway" (Grande Ceinture) of railroads around Paris. In Germany, most regional railway business was usually conducted as a kind of formal diplomacy among governments: Prussia dickered with Saxony, Bavaria dealt with Württemberg, and so on. Thus the internecine disputes of the southern states as well as their erratic opposition to the prussification of railway politics became factors of considerable importance in Germany's internal affairs.

National. At this third level, the concept of center and periphery gained an obvious utility for my analysis. The French state was forever attempting to regulate transportation in the form of unified rates, safety regulations, health-care plans, military construction, and much more. These efforts were frequently resisted, deflected, or ignored by the private railway companies, which offered only grudging compliance whenever they judged their autonomy to be threatened by excessive administrative or legislative intrusions. Likewise, in Germany such tension became immediately evident once the Reich was unified and Otto von Bismarck began to attack the particularism of the member states in railway politics. Although his initial attempts to consolidate a national rail system were thwarted, pressure from Berlin for conformity remained a source of contention within the German nation, and the other state capitals continued to resist further encroachment on their rights.

International. In addition to comparing and contrasting two national railway systems, this study attempts to chart their commercial and military competition. In this regard, one generalization stands out: a railway network could not outperform the national economy of which it was an integral part. Hence, the remarkable and sustained growth of Germany in the late nineteenth century could not fail to benefit its railroads, whereas, without an economic take-off of equal dimension, French industry lagged in some respects, as consequently also did its commerce via rail. But these developments were not entirely one-sided, and a careful analysis of them merits our attention. Needless to insist, a natural closing theme of the book is how this international trade rivalry was gradually displaced by the approach and outbreak of the Great War, the military planning of which was essentially a contest between the French and German railways leading to the front.

* * * * *

The central problem in drafting this book has been how to fit all of the foregoing complexity into a single comprehensive format. Searching for a suitable outline, I initially drafted three alternate schemes of organization, then rejected two of them before settling on a third. My first notion was to write a long foreword covering the period up to 1870 with the intention of treating the rest thematically: French and German administration, personnel, finance, commerce, rolling stock, military strategy, etc. As a test, I composed separate essays on specific topics such as ports, tunnels, and locomotives during the development from 1870 to 1914. But I found in these trials that there was too much back-and-forth between

French examples and German variants. The peculiarity of the two national contexts tended to blur, and the comparisons became arbitrarily scattered. Thereupon, a second possibility suggested itself: to divide the volume into equal halves on France and Germany, with parallel chapters recounting the two national stories throughout the nineteenth century, which could then be compared in a general conclusion. But this arrangement would have had the contrary effect of dwelling unduly on the national trends while deferring likenesses and contrasts between them to some grand finale. This, I feared, would not result in a genuine comparative history but instead in a pair of separate chronicles, placed side by side, much in the manner of a conventional textbook.

Accordingly, I turned to another option, adopted here, which is to divide the subject into three chronological periods: 1815-1870, 1870-1890, and 1890-1914. Each of these, as I will attempt to demonstrate, had a distinctive character. Without excessive rigidity, it is possible to repeat within these successive epochs a simple procedure: first France, second Germany, and third comparisons. This neat grid provides two serious advantages over the discarded schemes: it maintains a coherent sense of time, which is after all the basic mode of historical explanation, without losing sight either of national particulars or of international comparisons; and it allows a convenient division of the whole into three manageable sections, each with three chapters. If this structure now appears obvious, I can only say that it was not inherent in the research nor patent to me from the start.

Withal, one matter was manifest from the beginning: my goal was to write a comparative history. Most of my previous work had concentrated on the "influence" exercised by imperial Germany in France after 1870. Although comparisons were sometimes explicit, and always implied, the archival research for the resulting trilogy was conducted largely in Paris, with only occasional excursions across the Rhine.[2] This new effort was to be different because, I believe, comparatists must always maintain a sense of symmetry. They should conduct their research on both components equally and attempt to keep them in balance. Yet we know that real life is not symmetrical, and comparatists cannot of course avoid fundamental discrepancies in sources or in substance. Indeed, their task will eventually become to identify such marked distinctions and to insist on them—though not before an effort to achieve symmetry. If we do not first search for similarities, we shall never discover the extent of differences.

Comparative analysis of the national data could take several forms. For the sake of consistency, it seemed essential here to retain three principal criteria of comparison: (1) administrative organization, (2) economic competition, and (3) military strategy. These general rubrics, tracked through each of the three chronological periods, should allow sufficient flexibility and still provide a framework for comparing the French and German railway systems: how they functioned, how they meshed, and finally how they clashed. The epilogue of this volume is intended to draw these elements together and to address the question implicitly posed in its title: after all who won the Great Train Race?

One final point. This book does not represent an attempt, strictly speaking, to compare two large technological systems. A certain body of historical literature has adopted this terminology, which is certainly relevant to my project. But it is crucial to stress that we are dealing here with two *national* technological systems, that is, with formations in which many other factors besides technology played a significant and often predominant role. As one comparative historian has commented: "Technological affairs contain a rich texture of technical matters, scientific laws, economic principles, political forces, and social concerns. The historian must take the broad perspective to get to the root of things and to see the patterns."[3] Probably we need a neologism to indicate a comparison of two "technonational" systems, thereby making an essential distinction. We would otherwise be at a loss, for example, to understand why technological superiority ceased to be the paramount concern of French and German railway managers on the eve of the First World War. There were, as always, many other matters at stake for nations locked in a rivalry that lasted throughout the nineteenth century and, in a more muted form, exists to this day in a Europe transformed.

Part I

Launching the Railway Age

Chapter 1

FRANCE, 1815–1870

In many ways, France was well prepared for the railway age. Among its durable traditions, dating far back into the national past, was an extensive state bureaucracy that maintained coherence while rulers came and went. Even the cataclysms of the Great Revolution and its Napoleonic aftermath did not shake the grip of French administration; indeed, as Alexis de Tocqueville so ably showed, it was the Old Regime that finally triumphed after all. The monarchy of the Restoration years after 1815 could therefore count on a firm institutional base upon which to found a new government. Notably this included a Ministry of Commerce and Public Works, which oversaw an existing system of transportation that already contained a network of highways and canals. Such matters were the special domain of the famous Ecole des Ponts-et-Chaussées in Paris, where France's prestigious corps of civil engineers received training and from which they then fanned out to supervise the construction and maintenance of the nation's transport facilities. The appearance of railroads during the three decades before 1848 was thus to augment but not fundamentally to alter centralized arrangements of long standing.[1]

One might prepare an ample list of other factors that favored the growth of a railway industry. For example, France was blessed with fertile lands that could support a multitude of agricultural enterprises, large and small, whose abundant products awaited wider distribution. The beginnings of industrialization were meanwhile becoming evident, although the era of revolution had been a major setback in that regard, and the countryside was dotted with urban centers begging for better connections. Moreover, France possessed an intelligent population of cultural elites and skilled artisans, just the sort of persons suited to conceive, manage, and operate a huge conglomeration of tracks and trains.[2]

That said, there were certain handicaps to consider. For all its advantages, France did not yet have a confidently prosperous middle class comparable to that of England and Scotland. Nor, accordingly, was its commerce developed to the same magnitude. Large houses of private banking and international business were also wanting. In short, unlike their British contemporaries, the French lacked deep concentrations of liquid wealth necessary for launching capitalist ventures on a vast scale.[3]

Liberalism and the Legrand Star

The origins of French railways were inauspicious. Built for horse-drawn carriages, the earliest lines connected hills to valleys, thus linking mines to towns or factories to waterways. They were constructed without a sense of network and certainly with little premonition of a grand future. If there was any underlying assumption about the utility of fixed wooden or iron tracks, it was simply that better transportation meant greater prosperity. And the potential advantages of speed and regularity by rail were plain to see. Hence there was nothing remarkable about the first concession by royal decree in 1823 of a railroad between the city of St.-Etienne and the river port of Andrézieux on the Loire, where a regular service began in 1828. Besides such limited connections for the purpose of hauling freight, generally coal and ore, a few of the initial projects were basically people-movers, like those that brought passengers from St.-Germain-en-Laye and Versailles to Paris. But let it be noted that none of these original tracks proved to be of much significance in the long term, and they are properly consigned to a murky prehistory of the huge industry that was to be.[4]

The first attempts of traction by steam locomotive in France can be dated in 1832. We have all seen pictures of those wondrous contraptions, usually of English design, that caused greater curiosity for their fumes and noise than for any rapid motion. By the late 1830s, nonetheless, a number of projects were under construction or consideration that might have more enduring economic impact: Epinal to the Burgundy canal, Strasbourg to Basel, Montpellier to the Mediterranean port of Cette, Paris to Rouen and Le Havre. Unfortunately the last of these became embroiled in an investment crisis, requiring it to be delayed and renegotiated, all of which served as a disconcerting example for available capital. Rather than a steady march of success, the early progress of French railways was often impeded by hesitations and failures. One must therefore record not only the list of new concessions before 1840 but also the lack of confidence and coherence in planning, the reluctance of state officials to assume direct responsibility for rail projects, and a notable shortage of local investors willing to risk large sums on a primitive and unproved technology.[5]

Among the greatest impediments to the development of a unified railway system in France was liberalism. Without entering here into any elaborate definition of the liberal creed, we may at a minimum assume that this pervasive ideological tendency of the early nineteenth century espoused individualism and, consequently, a curtailment of direct state intervention into the private sphere. If so, when transposed into business terms, such a doctrine represented a consensus favorable to the freedom of capitalistic enterprise. It goes without stressing that these general principles were all too likely to be ignored whenever sizeable profits were at stake, but surely one should not underestimate the power of ideas in the marketplace. In any event, the attraction of liberal dogma can be documented a thousand times over.[6] Specifically, it was well articulated after 1830 by one of the two or three most influential politicians of the July Monarchy, Adolphe Thiers, who happened to be the French Minister of Commerce and Public Works at the very moment when the extent of the state's role in railways first became a public issue. Thiers was less than an ideal spokesman for liberalism, because his doctrinal proclivities were always clouded by personal ambition. Yet, with respect to rails, his opinion arguably carried more official weight than any other before 1848, and we would do well to take particular note of it.

Speaking to the Chamber of Deputies on 27 June 1833, Thiers was quick to delimit the intentions of his government. "I do not come to propose to you the creation of railways at the expense of the state; such a thought would not enter either your mind or ours." He allowed that state engineers might be called upon to establish routes, estimate expenses, and in a general way "direct the efforts of capitalists," but his declaration explicitly supported the establishment of railroads in the form of a private industry. On that basis he requested and received from the Chamber an allocation of 500,000 francs with which to finance a study of plans for the future. The adoption of this measure, one must add, in fact deferred any real action by the state. Meanwhile, Thiers, who was not devoid of imagination, could elaborate his own vision of a magistral north-south rail axis from Le Havre to Algiers that would, he claimed, bring untold commercial and military advantages to the nation. The main line would attract a dominant share of European trade, thus "preventing this transit from falling into the hands of Germany," and at the same time would provide an avenue for French troop movements everywhere from the Belgian frontier to North Africa.[7]

From the outset, then, it was clear that France would adopt a "mixed" system of railroads, in which the operations of private enterprise would be subject to some government supervision. The only question was the extent of state control. Whereas liberals hoped to hold administrative regulation to a minimum, the leadership of Ponts-et-Chaussées soon came to the view that central planning and thus a considerable degree of state involvement were essential for the common good. This was the position adopted and vigorously advocated by Alexis Victor Legrand, who guided the Corps after 1832 for the next fifteen years. Although his persuasiveness became legendary—he even tutored Adolphe Thiers on the evils of unregulated capitalism—Legrand's lead pipe certainty about the virtue of bureaucratic controls was bound to provoke controversy.

An extraparliamentary committee convened in 1837 was the first public forum to hear a proposal for what became well known as the Legrand Star. Its fundamental notion was simply that Paris was the capital of Europe. The main railway lines should radiate from this center to major French cities and borders in every direction: to Lille and Belgium in the north, to Strasbourg and Germany in the east, to Marseille and the Mediterranean in the south, to Bordeaux and Spain in the southwest, to Le Havre and England in the west. It is easy to perceive how the configuration of France's railway future was already predicted in this bold program. Yet it also contained implications not to everyone's liking. According to Legrand, the government must seize the initiative by granting concessions to private enterprises, which would then be constrained to accept the state's intervention as "master of rates" and as arbiter of disputes. A single rational scheme in the national interest could be secured only through the application of strict regulatory standards set by Ponts-et-Chaussées. The Corps, as the chief advisory body to the Ministry of Public Works, would thereby become the key. No one could miss the self-serving nature of Legrand's corresponding legislative concept, a bill formally submitted to the Chamber of Deputies in 1838, but who could gainsay its logic?[8]

Therewith began an internal struggle that was to last for the balance of the century. Legrand was far from conquering everything in his path. Symptomatically, to the contrary, 1838 was also the year in which a billion-franc appropriations bill for railway construction was defeated in the French parliament. Distinctive elements of the Star—Paris to Orléans, Lyon to Marseille, a line to the Belgian border—were temporarily blocked; and, more enduringly, the principle of massive state participation in the funding of construction suffered a rude setback.

Bit by bit, nevertheless, projects were approved, concessions were granted, building was started in the early 1840s. There was still a willy-nilly quality to such activity, especially when it was disrupted by acrimonious disputes over routes. Metz was disappointed, for instance, when a more direct *tracé* via Nancy was selected for the Paris-Strasbourg line. Likewise, the connection between Dijon and Mulhouse was hotly contested, whether by the valley of the Doubs or the Saône, with both sides claiming that military and commercial advantages made their choice imperative. These cases were fairly typical of the hundreds of dossiers accumulating in the Ministry of Public Works in which local and departmental officials conjured sprawling geopolitical scenarios to justify a case for extending tracks through one region (obviously their own) rather than another.[9]

There is no reason to resist the conventional *terminus ad quem* of this early history of French railroads, namely the law of 11 June 1842. Although it by no means settled the many issues raised in the preceding decades, the new legislation did provide a sturdy platform for future development. The keynote was sounded by Minister of the Interior Duchatel in May, when he pointed out that the English model—with its multiple concessions, lack of state subsidies, and unbridled competition—was unsuitable for France. Fiascos such as the first attempts to link Paris with Rouen and with Orléans showed that French private capital was insufficient without official assurances to investors. If the parliament decided to leave railroads to enterprises without state support, Duchatel warned, "I guarantee that the system will arrive at a total abortion," because "capitalists do not want to risk their funds on hazardous ventures." Accordingly, he concluded, it was necessary to reach "a kind of alliance, a sort of marriage as one says, between the state and the companies." It would be difficult to imagine a more apt expression of the spirit of the 1842 law, which thus codified the "mixed" governance of French railways.[10]

One thing was certain: if France intended to remain in the vanguard of civilization, it would need to compete effectively with other nations by creating railway networks. To that end, the Legrand Star would serve to make Paris "the rendez-vous of all Europe."[11] The rail system was conceived much like the existing French hierarchy of admirable roadways, with their royal routes, regional highways, and local capillaries. To implement this grand design would require the cooperation of the state, along with its departments or communes, and private industry. Perhaps it is best to describe the putative division of labor by distinguishing infrastructure from superstructure. The state would assume responsibility for the former by determining routes, confiscating property when needed, surveying and laying roadbeds, and designing bridges and tunnels. Private companies would then provide the rest by acquiring rolling stock, hiring personnel, operating and maintaining regular service. But there is danger in making this arrangement sound too neat; it was not. Many ambiguities in fact remained, and they were to be a constant source of friction well into the twentieth century.

Besides, not everyone was pleased. Adolphe Thiers predictably appeared in parliament to register liberal dissent. Others raised further objections, but an amendment to incorporate some of the proposed alterations went down 222 to 152, and the government's bill—essentially the Legrand Star—was adopted in the Chamber by a vote of 255 to 83.[12] Verdicts on the law have varied. One notable nineteenth-century contemporary, Alfred Picard, called it "an immense progress" that permitted France to enter "a new and prosperous era." Another railway expert of the time, Edmond Teisserenc de Bort, was less sanguine, acknowledging the superiority of Legrand's conception over that of other nations but complaining about the "onerous" concessions to private capital required by a mixed system. At least, Teisserenc added, the 1842 legislation terminated an era of indecision that had made France "the laughing-stock of Europe."[13] Later commentators have tended to celebrate, as one of them has flatly put it, the "victory" of Ponts-et-Chaussées. If so, it was at best a partial success that left liberalism intact and permitted the formation of large private railway companies dedicated to the principle and practice of free enterprise.[14]

The Emergence of the Great Railway Companies

Fundamentally, the law of 1842 meant that France would follow the British example of soliciting investment capital to finance the construction of railroads by granting concessions to private firms. The difference would be in the much more stringent controls exercised by the French state through its Ministry of Commerce and Public Works, with the advice and consent of Ponts-et-Chaussées. Thus the number of concessions and companies would presumably be limited to avoid rampant competition and to encourage the formation of viable enterprises that would be both dynamic and stable in developing the railway industry.

So much for lofty intentions. As for the reality, trial and error would decide the outcome amid the chronic political and economic instability that characterized nineteenth-century France. The actual number of private railway companies was conspicuously left unspecified by the 1842 law. Many years would pass before the identity of the major players was securely defined in the untidy process of absorbing smaller ones. The period before 1870 must therefore be regarded as a virtual free-for-all dominated by regional and local rivalries. National considerations, despite repeated admonishments from the central administration, played a relatively minor part in the proceedings. Yet a certain rationale of unified standards was never totally ignored, and the pattern that was prefigured by the Legrand Star did emerge. To comprehend this evolution of French railroads we therefore need to examine in closer detail the fate of the four most significant concessions granted by the state to private firms.

The Eastern Railway Company (Compagnie de l'Est)

The main railway routes of eastern France were determined early and without much ambiguity. The private Paris-Strasbourg Company obtained a concession in 1845 for what was manifestly to be the principal artery, passing via Nancy, with one spur track to Reims and another to Metz, whence extensions would then reach Luxemburg via Thionville and Saarbrücken via Forbach. In addition, although it would take another decade to negotiate and execute, a second main line from Paris to Mulhouse (and on to Basel) was already on the drafting board of Ponts-et-Chaussées.[15] Logical as this scheme may seem in retrospect, at the time it left two obvious anomalies. First, as noted, the important cities of Reims and Metz received no direct connection to Paris, provoking their respective municipal and departmental representatives to complain vociferously about the resulting commercial disadvantages.[16] And second, the tracks of the rebaptized (in 1855) Eastern Railway Company conspicuously failed to penetrate the majestic ridge of the Vosges Mountains, which thus constituted an imposing north-south barrier of 120 miles between the frontier cities of Strasbourg and Mulhouse. Much of Alsace-Lorraine thereby remained in reality a distant and forbiddingly Germanic territory. Truth to tell, the much vaunted integration of that region into France because of improved rail transportation was never more than a precarious gain, later to be all but vitiated by the Franco-Prussian war. One must wonder how many patriotic tears were shed after 1870 for the "lost provinces" by persons who actually had little or no contact with them.[17]

Be that as it might, from a national standpoint, a potentially no less significant function of the Eastern Company was to provide connections to Germany. Vigorous construction of railroads beyond the Rhine was greeted with considerable enthusiasm in Paris because, it seemed, "all [tracks] are converging toward France."[18] Besides the dazzling prospect of easy commercial access to the Rhine Valley, there were visions of metal ribbons stretching across southern Germany to Austria, linking Paris to Vienna and beyond (a romantic notion that later helped to sell countless passages on the Orient Express). But in fact such international connections still had relatively little to do with the fortunes of French railway companies. A journey from Paris to Munich in the 1850s lasted over twenty-six hours, and there was no direct or regular service to Vienna. Likewise, in the days before transalpine tunnels, a trip from Paris to Milan took sixty hours—two days and a half! In the foreseeable future, under these circumstances, the Eastern would surely need to look closer at hand for serious profits.[19]

The Eastern Company's internal organization was rather typical of French railway enterprises. At its core was an Administrative Council (Conseil d'administration), composed of about twenty members with personal wealth, social connections, and presumably some business acumen. The minutes of this group—which usually met weekly or fortnightly, according to the season—are our most regular and reliable source on quotidian operations. Less useful, except as a barometer of broad policy and financial statistics, are annual reports made by the Council to the General Assembly of major stockholders. Day-to-day matters were handled by a director, more or less powerful as his personal charisma permitted, who was assisted by a small staff (housed in or near the Company's main railway terminal in Paris) and by an Executive Committee (Comité de direction) that ordinarily discussed routine questions and avoided politically sensitive issues.[20]

At some risk of simplification, we may say that the bulk of the Eastern Company's administrative deliberations concerned four categories:

1. *Rolling stock.* Given the uneven nature of the terrain within its territory, which included both river valleys and rugged hillsides, the Eastern required a variety of locomotives, passenger cars, and freight wagons. These were supplied either by the Company's own workshops (*ateliers*) or by private contractors, of whom Creusot (Schneider), Cail, and Koechlin were the most active in sales before 1870. We should particularly note that the practice was firmly established for the Company to consider sealed bids from industrial

firms for vehicles and rails, without prior consultation with the Ministry of Public Works, and to place orders accordingly.[21]
2. *Personnel.* The Company usually took direct charge of hiring and firing employees, without consulting state officials, and it also decided on their wages and social benefits, if any. Top administrators aside, many of whom were large stockholders, the Eastern's annual salary scale in the 1850s ranged from over 3000 francs for stationmasters in major cities to 140 for women hired as gatekeepers at level crossings across the countryside. Between these extremes, ever pushing for increases, were the locomotive engineers (*mécaniciens*) and firemen (*chauffeurs*) who piloted trains day and night.[22]
3. *Rates.* It was here that the latent conflict between state control and private enterprise became most apparent. From the Company's perspective, the government was forever hectoring it about the need for lower passenger fares and freight rates, whereas the vitality and autonomy of the Company hinged on its flexibility to fix such charges according to the market. Specifically, in the case of the Eastern, special rates for international shipments were deemed indispensable in order to compete with the various neighboring state companies of Belgium and Germany. "The favor accorded in such cases," the Company argued, "would benefit the general interest of the nation."[23]
4. *Routes, stations, and schedules.* These practical considerations were, after the 1842 law, legally in the province of the state. Yet they were also deeply implicated in the daily operations of the rail companies. The Eastern's records are therefore filled with references to ministerial decisions accepted, disputed, or rejected by the current director or the Administrative Council. Such conflict between the companies and the cabinet was an essential element of the French railway industry throughout the nineteenth century.[24]

Issues were, of course, complicated by personalities. A case in point was a proposal for the construction of a rail line from Reims via Soissons to Paris. This matter was first brought to the attention of the Eastern's Administrative Council in June 1855, when it was revealed that a new railway firm—the Compagnie des Ardennes, headed by the powerful Pereire banking family—would be awarded the coveted concession. Awkwardly, this line would skirt the border between the Eastern and Northern companies, raising a question as to whether its traffic would enter Paris at the Gare de l'Est or the Gare du Nord. "One member" of the Council—unidentified by name in the minutes but surely none other than James de Rothschild himself—argued that cooperation between the two established companies could, in effect, freeze the Pereires out. But other members objected that the interests of the companies were not identical and that a decision on the entry to Paris was unavoidable. By a "great majority" the Council thereupon chose a separate course, agreed to a compromise with the Ardennes Company, and turned its back on the Northern. Hence, Rothschild resigned from the Council, never to return, and was shortly to be replaced by Emile Pereire.[25]

Less than a decade later, in 1863, the Ardennes Company was annexed by the Eastern, enabling the latter to establish operations in all of eastern France. Thereafter, the Pereire influence quickly waned, and the practice of a monopoly by one large rail company in the region was ensconced. But, apart from the clash of ambitious personalities, two lessons were not lost: first, that the state retained the power to prod the great railroad companies by threatening to allow the creation of smaller ones within their territory; and second, that the indistinct boundaries between the companies remained a confounding legacy of the 1842 law and an unresolved source of conflict.[26]

The PLM (Paris-Lyon-Méditerranée)

The railway situation in southeastern France was less settled than elsewhere, and it took many years to arrive at a coherent solution. An initial concession to the Paris-Lyon Company in 1852 was backed by "precious guarantees" from the state, meaning that the government agreed to protect the fledgling PL against its older and stronger neighbors. The first problem was to arrest the menacing expansion of the Eastern Railway Company, whose Paris-Mulhouse route already entered the valley of the Saône. Thus it became essential for the new Company to acquire rights to the Dijon-Besançon-Belfort arc along the Doubs River, thereby erecting a barrier to serve as a boundary against any intrusion from the northeast.[27]

To the west, meanwhile, a region in dispute with the Paris-Orléans Company was the so-called Bourbonnais, south of Bourges and Nevers, north of Clermont-Ferrand, including the triangle of Montluçon, Moulins, and Vichy. Once again it was necessary for the PL to move aggressively in carving out a monopoly, and, without pausing here for the details, we may confirm that it did so. Securing this second enclave ensured the integration of other lines just north of Lyon, such as Bourg to Chalon-sur-Saône and to Dôle. Obviously, more connections would follow: to the industrial center of St.-Etienne, to the Jura and Geneva, and into the rich wine regions of Burgundy.[28]

This hectic activity in the mid-1850s, however, left open the most intriguing of all possibilities. What of an extension to the south with access to Marseille and the Riviera? Not only was this question complicated by a separate concession to an adjacent Lyon-Mediterranean Company, there also existed another firm with as yet undefined aspirations south of Clermont, the Grand Central Company. It was the avowed intention of the latter to create a vast network, to be called the Southwestern Railway Company, that would establish a second north-south expressway between Paris and Marseille. Patently, such far-flung ambitions could only be realized, as a report by the PL's Administrative Council noted, "at the expense of neighboring companies." An unruly scramble thereupon ensued in which each contestant sought to gain an advantage through government patronage. The end came suddenly in 1857 with the fusion of the PL and LM into the PLM (Paris-Lyon-Méditerranée) and the dissolution of the Grand Central, which was divided between the PLM and the Paris-Orléans Company. The French state had thereby fashioned "two great networks perfectly delimited." With the concurrent addition to the PLM of the Bourbonnais, the connections to St.-Etienne and Switzerland, plus the concession of several secondary lines, the largest of the major French railway companies was virtually complete.[29]

All of the above, let it be stressed, could only have been achieved through "a veritable association of interests with the state," as the PLM's Administrative Council put it.[30] Incidentally, this ostensible harmony included an arrangement whereby the Company operated French railways in Algeria, for which it received from the government a tidy annual subsidy of about 3 million francs. Other subsidies were forthcoming to encourage the construction of more secondary lines. And, most significantly, the PLM could and did call upon "guarantees of interest," which were in essence state loans to reassure investors that any temporary losses incurred by the enterprise would not significantly curtail dividends. These inducements were of course offered to all of the major companies.[31]

Although the PLM's corporate image was thus firmly etched, the fusion of 1857 in reality masked a residual duality. For several years thereafter, the Administrative Council remained divided into northern and southern sections. In 1862 the annual report to the General Assembly contained for the first time a combined alphabetical list of the Council's thirty members; and a single director, Paulin Talabot, was appointed to head the Company's bureaucracy. But there were still two presidents and two vice-presidents until the following year, when a reorganization abolished the north-south distinction altogether and substituted, according to function, two separate divisions for construction and operations. At last the Administrative Council could boast that "there is only one Company, one administration." A final consolidation occurred in 1864 with the absorption of the Dauphiné Company located in the alpine region around Grenoble.[32]

These details well illustrate the slow institutional evolution of the large French railway companies, which came haltingly and uncertainly to a clear self-definition. Their emerging identity was not prescribed by any decree, law, or foresighted vision of a national railway system. Rather, it was forged both by the fierce local competition among private businesses and by a testy symbiotic relationship between those commercial enterprises and the central state.

The PO (Compagnie Paris-Orléans)

The eldest sister among the great French railway enterprises, the Paris-Orléans Company could trace its origins as far back as the first General Assembly of its stockholders in 1838. Basically, the PO's self-appointed assignment was to link the Seine and Loire valleys, as well as to provide further connections to southwestern France, Bordeaux and beyond. It also obtained a direct line to Nantes and southern Brittany. This brief enumeration is sufficient to suggest two characteristics that clearly distinguished the PO from the PLM and the Eastern Railway Company: first, most of its terrain was relatively flat, without the Vosges or the Alps to cross; and second, its commerce was, much more than the others, dependent on agriculture.[33]

An internal power struggle nearly wrecked the Company at its inception. A challenge by François Bartholony to the PO's first president, the headstrong and authoritarian Comte Pillet-Will, quickly turned to acrimony and personal insults. To be sure, some general principles of management were at issue: the procedures and prerogatives of the presidency, whether the Administrative Council could risk investment capital without formal approval from stockholders gathered in a General Assembly, the advisability of guaranteed interest in the form of loans from the state, and so on. But ultimately it was style rather than substance that mattered. Bartholony vehemently attacked the "false and dangerous" tactics of an arbitrary executive whom he accused to his face of "a lack of dignity and morality." Finally, it was Bartholony who prevailed. In December 1839 he became the PO's "definitive" president, a post he was henceforth to hold for the next three decades.[34]

Thus the 1840s began for the PO with a brief if somewhat forced optimism, as Bartholony boasted of a future "more secure than ever," and there was talk of "a new liberal era."[35] The Company had ambitions that included extending tracks not only southward to Toulouse but also eastward to Geneva and the Rhine. Yet, in truth, the PO never completely escaped from a fear of "strong hostility" in the French parliament, and in its Administrative Council some complaints were heard that Company representatives were "treated almost like enemies" by local and government officials.[36] Perhaps it was precisely because of its insecurities that the PO was the most adamant among major railway companies defending their autonomy as private businesses. In January 1842, its Council unanimously adopted a resolution "that the Company has the most absolute right of administration [and] that the state may not under any pretext intervene in its operations."[37] This became a theme often repeated as, for example, when the Ministry of Public Works pressed for the prior submission of an annual budget requiring government approval. The Company retorted that such a procedure would allow the French cabinet to intervene in private financial affairs and to control expenditures, with the inevitable result that "all liberty of action would be taken from the Company." By means of such practical matters, in other words, the principle of liberalism was being tested. Typically for a mixed system like the French, a compromise was soon found when the PO agreed to submit a provisional budget—"nothing definitive"—that could always be modified by its Administrative Council during the course of the year in question.[38]

Meanwhile, the atmosphere of the July Monarchy remained favorable. King Louis Philippe himself displayed "the most benevolent intentions," and the Company was able to reap windfall profits after the opening of its Paris-to-Orléans service in 1843. One telling measure of prosperity was an increase in the locomotive fleet: from 22 in 1840, to 52 in 1845, and to 88 by 1848. Earnings were likewise rising at an annual rate of about one million francs, although with expansion, of course, so were costs.[39] The PO agreed to a fusion with the struggling Compagnie du Centre, an omen of its true vocation, especially when the government announced in 1845 that access to Lyon across the plains of Brie was being granted to the new PL firm. This news meant that the PO could forget about dreams of direct connections to Switzerland and Germany, instead confining itself to the southwest, a delimitation that was probably a blessing in disguise in view of future developments.[40]

In 1847 the French economy began to falter, causing severe repercussions for the railway companies. Traffic slowed, and the PO entered into what its own records termed "a financial crisis." The Company's vulnerability coincided with, and perhaps encouraged, a visible discontent among its employees, who began to organize and to present demands for higher wages, better hours, and a reform of supervisory personnel. Although the Council called "inadmissible" a petition to dismiss several unpopular Company officials, it worried that agitation might permanently damage the fragile administrative structure and therefore decided "to make the Company safe from such consequences" by granting concessions.[41]

This was the disturbing scene when news broke of the February Revolution in 1848, the flight of Louis Philippe, and the collapse of the liberal Orleanist cabinet, whose final premier was Adolphe Thiers. PO director Antoine Banès hurried to the Hôtel de Ville to confer with the new Lamartine government, pointing out that uninterrupted service by his Company would assure that Paris was adequately supplied with foodstuffs from the provinces. The response was positive, and the National Guard was dispatched forthwith to guard the PO's main railroads. But labor unrest threatened to implode, especially when a group of locomotive engineers demanded—vaguely but emphatically—"some amelioration of their social position." Badly shaken, the Administrative Council decided to negotiate and, if necessary, to capitulate. However, the provisional government, dreading a total collapse and a consequent disruption of provisions for the capital, ordered that the Company be "sequestered" and placed under the command of two republican commissars. Meanwhile, plans for a *rachat*, a complete takeover of the PO by the state, were being prepared for submission to the National Assembly, which began to debate such a bill in mid-May. President Bartholony protested this "dictatorial act" and was awarded a vote of confidence by his Administrative Council, but in truth he was left with little room to maneuver. All of which came to an abrupt halt with the infamous June Days of 1848, when a full-scale insurrection in Paris was decisively crushed by the French army. In August the sequestration of the PO was lifted, and all pending confiscatory legislation was annulled.[42]

Louis Bonaparte's election to the presidency of the Second Republic in December 1848 signaled a return to normalcy. The PO took its cue by streamlining operations to be "simpler and more economical," which meant that it could move to lay off "all the useless workers"—not to mention those charged with disloyalty during recent events. This time of retrenchment also allowed the PO to complete its acquisition of the Compagnie du Centre as well as the private companies of Nantes and Bordeaux. Once again minutes of the Administrative Council announced a "new era."[43] And indeed it was: that of the Second Empire. Under imperial patronage the PO initially enjoyed a "remarkable increase" in business. During 1853 gross receipts rose by 10 million francs, passengers were up 50 percent, and the volume of freight grew by 32 percent in tonnage, 42 percent in net income. By the end of that year, the PO had 250 locomotives in operation on a network approaching 1500 kilometers.[44]

In effect, then, Napoleon III made the PO and other companies an offer they could not refuse. As the Administrative Council asked rhetorically: "How can we not be struck by such advantages?" Loans and subsidies were readily available, stockholders' interest on investment was guaranteed, profits were booming in the early 1850s. True, the PO failed in its efforts to secure a separate Paris-Avignon right-of-way, which fell to the PLM, but it did gain access to the Mediterranean via a more circuitous westerly route. Thus, the Company's concerns about its borders were refocused in that direction, and the Council became alerted to the probable need "to struggle energetically … against competition from the Western Railway Company." That unwieldy corporation, however, proved to be a far less formidable opponent than the PLM. Despite its lack of an industrial base, the PO managed to solidify its position among the major railway companies.[45]

The Northern Railway Company (Compagnie du Nord)

The compactness and homogeneity of its terrain helped to place the Northern Railway Company among the most prosperous of French firms in the nineteenth century. It also had other distinct advantages. A location adjacent to the Lowlands afforded easy access across the Belgian frontier to rich coal fields and international ports. Thus the entire region became one of Europe's industrial crossroads, for which metal tracks provided ideal linkages. The Northern Company could even count on some agriculture, since more than 80 percent of France's sugar beet production developed within its territory.[46]

Yet surely its most significant and distinguishing trait was the paramount influence of the fabulously wealthy Rothschild family. Usually three Rothschilds, sometimes as many as five, sat together on the Company's Administrative Council. Moreover, a major share of the Northern's financial transactions was handled directly by the Rothschild Bank, whose fathomless resources ensured solvency even in the leanest of times. Hence, during the 1850s and 1860s, when the other rail companies were forced to seek government loans to cover the guaranteed interest of their stockholders, the Northern alone was able to forego further borrowing. Investors could trust the bank instead. The Company's administrative procedures reflected this vital difference, because the political role of its Executive Committee (Comité de direction), presided over by James de Rothschild, was incomparably greater than elsewhere. As founder and principal financier of the Company, James exercised unmatched authority over its business policies, virtually without challenge. A single instance of dissent was recorded in the minutes of the Administrative Council: "One member raises some objections to the preponderance accorded to the voice of the president in the [Executive] Committee." Yet a decision to refer any split vote in the Committee to the Council did nothing to alter the reality of Rothschild's domination of both. For that reason, it should be added, records of the Northern Company are often less revealing than those of the other railway firms. In the absence of a resident stenographer at the Rothschild breakfast table, we shall probably never know how most crucial decisions were reached.[47]

Constituted in 1845, the Northern Company had already acquired the essential contours of its network by 1850. The main line, of course, ran from Paris to Lille, whence on to Roubaix, Tourcoing, and the Belgian border. East-west branches extended to the ocean: from Lille to Dunkerque and from Hazebrouck to Calais. A third coastal port would be serviced by the Paris-Amiens-Boulogne tracks. Finally, a separate line was stretched from Paris to St.-Quentin, which—in order to meet competition from the Paris-Strasbourg connection for a share of trade with Germany—was soon to be continued in the direction of Cologne via the Meuse Valley through the Belgian cities of Charleroi, Namur, and Liège (a route well known ever since to tourists between France and Germany).

Like other railroad companies, the Northern suffered from a variety of childhood ailments, including numerous conflicts with the Ministry of Public Works. We may leave the details aside, except to note that the Company insisted on its prerogatives to order rails and rolling stock without government interference, and it especially chafed at the presumption of the state to impose uniform security measures (such as signals at level crossings), the installation of which was costly. This latter issue arose notably in 1847 when the French economy entered "difficult circumstances" that cut into railway profits, leading to the first formal meeting of officials from all of the major firms at the headquarters of the Paris-Orléans Company, where they drafted a joint complaint about "bothersome incoherences" in the enforcement of ministerial decrees. The companies, nevertheless, were still far from creating an effective lobby for private railway enterprise, and this initial gathering remained for the time being an isolated incident.[48]

Like the Paris-Orléans Company, the Northern endured some tumultuous events in 1848. And like the PO, it was forced to wage a two-front campaign: attempting to avoid expropriation by the provisional government while also contending with clamorous employees in an effort "to calm this effervescence." James de Rothschild took the lead in both negotiations, meeting with republican ministers as well as delegations of workers. Despite his willingness to make concessions, he succeeded in neither. As we saw in the case of the PO, plans for a *rachat* of the railway companies by the state went to parliament; and, after a breakdown in the bargaining, the Northern Company's workshops went out on strike. Units of the National Guard then occupied the Gare du Nord, and Rothschild began personal discussions with the Prefect of Police about "measures to restore tranquility." But we know that order was imposed otherwise—brutally, by military force, in the June Days.[49]

Thereafter little remained of the agitation. Some employees were welcomed back, albeit without the "onerous conditions" they had demanded. The Company's workforce was substantially reduced, allowing an annual savings of half a million francs. Although this "reorganization" (so the minutes read) was ostensibly effected as a measure of rationalization, it was surely not without a motive of political revenge. The number of workmen heretofore employed in Company workshops at La Chapelle, close to Paris, was reduced from 1300 to 400, and the main activity of the *ateliers* was transferred to Amiens and Lille. Beyond that, the Administrative Council was persuaded by the sobering experience of past months that the Company's future could only be assured by financial independence. A debt of 60 million francs left from the Northern's earliest days would be retired by regular annual installments, and no further loans or guarantees of interest from the state would be accepted. The Northern thereby set itself apart from the other competing railway companies, for which it eventually came to serve as a model of sound management.[50]

The transition from Second Republic to Second Empire was largely uneventful for the Northern Company. Business resumed in an apparent era of prosperity. The largest competing private railway firm within its territory, the Boulogne Company, was absorbed without undue friction.[51] Meanwhile, a new organization was conceived that was later to prove of significance in the relationship between the private and public sectors: the syndicate of the Paris beltway (Ceinture), an interior rail system circling nearby the capital's main terminals. It should be stressed, however, that this project of linking the companies both physically and politically was not primarily the result of a farsighted intention on the part of the companies. Rather, the Ministry of Public Works was particularly keen to establish a single administrative channel through which it could treat with the companies as a group instead of separately. In fact, the records of the Northern Company demonstrate that attempts to coordinate the policies of the companies produced "no result" during a gathering in 1853: "It is well understood that, whatever opinion prevails within the conference, the liberty of the Company remains totally intact." Furthermore, it will be recalled that this was precisely the period when the Eastern and Northern companies became entangled in a bitter struggle over their common borders and when James de Rothschild finally stalked out of the Eastern's Administrative Council. Not cooperation but rather competition thus predominated in this phase of the railroad industry.[52]

Statistics of the Northern were no less spectacular for that. In the years from 1851 to 1854, the Company's passenger travel rose from 3.9 to over 5 million fares. Freight increased in the same period by 29 percent, and growth continued through the mid-1850s, nearly trebling before the end of the decade (see Table 1). By the beginning of 1857, the Northern had 328 steam locomotives circulating on French tracks, another 42 in Belgium (to facilitate imports of coal), and 112 more on order.[53]

Perhaps it is fitting to round out this overview of the private French railway firms by citing a document sent to the Northern's main office in the autumn of 1857 by the Ministry of Public Works, which listed the total number of kilometers of track in operation and under concession at that time. These data clearly demonstrate that six large rail companies had emerged in France (the four discussed here plus the Western and Southern lines). In addition, there were two medium-size enterprises, the Ardennes and Dauphiné companies, which were already in a process of assimilation by, respectively, the Eastern Railway Company and the PLM. Of the remaining six railroad societies, five were minuscule local trunk lines of no consequence, and the sixth was the Paris beltway, just beginning its service under the control of the large companies. To be sure, there are other criteria by which to measure the size and importance of transportation facilities, but Table 2 offers an illustration of the shape of France's railway networks at the height of the Second Empire.

The Surge of the Second Empire

France had entered the railway age hesitantly. Hopes aroused by the 1842 law were hardly wafted above Paris before the placid demeanor of the July Monarchy was broken by the boisterous events of 1848. The Second Republic—after the June Days, a relatively calm transition, as it happened, from Louis Philippe to Louis Bonaparte—offered a respite for reorganization, whereupon the scene was set for a sustained spurt by the French railway industry. The 1850s thus proved to be a decade of thriving commerce and unprecedented economic prosperity. Presumably, one

TABLE 1: Northern Railway Company: Gross Income from Freight, 1852–1857 ("Petite Vitesse")

Year	Francs
1852	10,740,000
1853	14,401,000
1854	18,660,000
1855	23,541,000
1856	25,252,000
1857	27,462,000

Source: "Rapport," 28 April 1858, CAMT Roubaix, 48 AQ, 570.

TABLE 2: Track Length of French Railway Companies, 30 September 1857 (kilometers)

Company	In Operation	Under Concession	Together
1. Nord	855	503	1358
2. Est	1342	525	1867
3. Ardennes	55	367	422
4. Ouest	949	829	1778
5. Orléans (PO)	1465	1745	3210
6. PLM	1841	1403	3244
7. Midi	727	765	1492
8. Dauphiné	89	165	254
9. Ceinture	17	—	17
10. Graissessac à Béziers	—	52	52
11. Bessèges à Alais	—	30	30
12. Anzin à Somain	19	—	19
13. Hautment à la frontière	—	9	9
14. Carmaux à Albi	—	18	18
Totals	7359	6411	13,770

Source: "Chemins de fer français: situation approximative au 30 septembre 1857," CAMT Roubaix, 48 AQ, 3590.

might summarize the onset of the Second Empire in these simple terms. But they disguise some unresolved conflicts and deep-set problems that could not fail to reappear, no matter how auspicious the beginning.

First, the question of finances. A report sent by the current Minister of Public Works, Eugène Rouher, to his emperor in 1856 deserves our close attention. It contained a detailed account of the total funds expended until that time for railroad construction (see Table 3).

TABLE 3: French Railway Investments, 1823–1856 (francs)

	Expenses by the State	Expenses by the Companies	Totals
1823–1829	—	3,300,000	3,300,000
1830–1841	3,228,740	172,097,753	175,326,493
1842–1847	278,553,677	509,411,555	787,965,232
1848–1851	298,417,147	198,711,088	497,128,235
1852–1854	51,187,751	646,690,064	697,877,815
1855	55,200,000	430,406,485	485,606,485
1856	20,286,000	458,569,713	478,855,713
1823–1856	706,873,315	2,419,186,658	3,126,059,973

Source: E. Rouher to Napoleon III, 30 November 1856, AN Paris, F[14] 8508.

The pattern indicated here reveals a number of fundamental facts about the growth of the French rail system. The state's direct participation in funding construction was obviously belated and, except for the atypical era of the Second Republic, far inferior to that of private enterprise. Indeed, the companies invested well over three times more than the state, nearly 2.5 billion francs of the 3.1 billion total. Judging by the figures for the early 1850s, that trend was reestablished under the Bonapartist regime, although state loans to the companies were not included. In sum, France was developing a very costly new technology without depleting the public treasury. If one seeks a basic reason for maintaining a mixed system of the private and public sectors, it is here. Hence, the French solution for financing the railroads seemed to most contemporary observers to be both logical and economical.[54]

This consideration was compounded by another. Even though initially unperceived, there was in reality a glass ceiling for the expansion of French railways, given the system of administration adopted. This was so because once the main rail lines had been constructed and the grand design of the Legrand Star was realized, the private companies had a sharply diminishing interest in further building. The records of more than one Administrative Council contained remarks like this: "Our network is virtually complete."[55] Yet meanwhile the Ministry of Public Works was besieged by myriad projects, schemes, and requests of all manner from local and regional politicians, who gathered in the Corps Législatif as representatives of a population eager for better transportation. The original principle of railways was still valid: good trains meant greater prosperity. A town or countryside that was not well connected to some company's network was sure to stagnate, whereas the commerce of those located on main lines or convenient spurs was certain to succeed.

Typical was a protest from one of the by-passed towns, Mayenne, whose municipal council deplored the lack of a local railway "without which neither progress nor prosperity is any longer possible."[56]

A major test of these axioms came late in the 1850s. As we saw, the companies were able early in that decade to realize a statistical bonanza: receipts soared, new tracks were laid, more powerful locomotives were purchased, and so forth. These advances were sustained. Just to cite one example, the Northern Railway Company's gross annual income in the years 1854–1860 rose from 38.5 to 60 million francs, an increase of well over 50 percent. By any standard, French industry lifted and was lifted by the growth of railways, all of which was possible under the astute patronage of the imperial state. Thanks largely to Bonapartist policies, especially when compared to the bygone days of the July Monarchy, credit was more available and investment capital abundant.[57]

This was the economic situation when a temporary crisis suddenly erupted in late 1857. Railroad stocks dropped, money markets tightened, companies reduced service, and new construction came to a virtual halt. Fully recognizing the essential role of railways for recovery, the imperial regime determined to draft new conventions with the companies, which were signed in 1859. Neither this settlement nor the negotiations that led to it were one-sided. True, the large companies were under attack in the parliament and press, widely blamed for the slump because of alleged mismanagement of their regional monopolies. But they shook off these charges and took their case straight to Napoleon III, who, during a series of meetings in his residence at St. Cloud, became personally involved as an arbiter. In essence, company spokesmen—notably from the Paris-Orléans—sought the emperor's agreement that France should definitively settle on the priority of the six largest private companies (while not entirely precluding the formation of smaller ones) in a system of regional "networks" (*réseaux*), which would of course be coordinated and supervised by the state. Bonaparte, as a consultant from the PO observed, "did not reject these ideas."[58] Predictably, as the months passed, a dispute arose between company officials and the Ministry of Public Works over the balance of power in the proposed agreement. If their autonomy were seriously compromised, the companies argued, it would mean their "discredit and ruin." To the contrary, the emperor's advisers counseled that the time had come for a crackdown on the companies. How much Napoleon III was actually swayed by dire prophecies of doom and how much he leaned toward the entreaties of his cabinet, one cannot say. In any event, by the summer of 1858 his patience had snapped and he ordered "an immediate solution." Early in the following year a deal was struck.[59]

The pivotal stipulation of the 1859 conventions between the French state and private companies was a separation of railroads into "old" and "new" networks. More feasible for bookkeeping than for daily operations, this distinction separated the lucrative main tracks from secondary byways, thereby allowing the companies to retain their considerable profits from the former while receiving protection against undue deficits on the latter. In these paragraphs there was something for both sides. The companies acquired greater security through added subsidies and guarantees of interest for their stockholders. They were also able to quiet some of the "erroneous or false doctrines" of detractors in the public arena. At the same time, the government avoided the astronomical expense of confiscating the companies and was able to revitalize the faltering economy by reassuring anxious investors. As a result, railway expansion would continue into the 1860s.[60]

Attempting to put as positive a face on these accords as possible in a report to its General Assembly, the Administrative Council of the PO characterized them with some accuracy as "an association of the state and the companies, not the substitution of the former for the latter."[61] It would probably be fatuous to reformulate that judgment or to designate one side or the other as a victor in the outcome. Rather, it is more appropriate to regard the 1859 conventions as an element of continuity in French history, confirming the 1842 railway law and laying the foundation for a future settlement in 1883. They enabled the nation to move on with a mixed yet coherent system of networks. Henceforth the companies might be subjected to stricter control by the central state, but they would also be strengthened in their function as private regional enterprises. One crucial consequence, however, was left unstated: in order to sustain their end of the bargain, most of the companies (the Northern excepted) would be dependent on massive state loans, estimated in the aggregate by one commentator at no less than 3 billion francs.[62]

After 1859 the companies were thus forced into a flight to the fore. That is, they were again submitting to the first iron law of expansion: increasing receipts also mean rising expenditures. To preserve their autonomy and their income, the companies had agreed to do the bidding of the state in building costly secondary lines on the "new" networks. They had at least four pressing motivations for adopting such a policy of escalation. First, they still had to worry about the state's undiminished authority to grant concessions to smaller rogue companies within their respective territories, a right the Ministry of Public Works would not hesitate to exercise when faced with a firm's reluctance to obey. Second, despite the recent conventions, harsh criticism of the companies was not entirely muffled, and they still had reason to fear that discontent with their performance might be converted into demands for more stringent controls. Third, they were constantly forced to adapt to the exigencies of improved technology—stronger engines, steel rails, air brakes, automatic signals, etc.—which spurred competition and increased expense. Finally, they needed to create and sustain a clear superiority over other modes of transportation, notably waterways, which often required them to modulate their rates and hence to shave their profit margins. In each of these regards there was pressure to build now, ask questions later, and accept additional obligations in the meanwhile.

Many data support these generalizations. In 1864, for instance, the PLM received from the state a whopping subsidy of 8.4 million francs to encourage construction (including 3.6 million for Algeria), but it was nonetheless obliged to borrow another 10 million in order to balance the difference between gross income and elevated costs.[63] Even the Northern Railway Company, although possessing the means to avoid such indebtedness, felt the squeeze in coal and coke imports from Belgium. Competing with the extensive canal system of that region kept its rates well below the level commanded by other companies. Thus in 1864, after a round of rate reductions, the Northern's Administrative Council boasted of a "fortunate result," by which it referred to a rise in tonnage, not profits, because greater volume meant more trains in circulation, more engines to pull them, and more personnel to operate them. In effect, there was a second iron law of escalation: increased activity requires greater investment. And one may add a corollary that the growing importance of railroads as ligaments of industry enhanced the state's tendency to supervise and coordinate them. In no uncertain terms, the Ministry of Public Works informed the companies in 1864 that it henceforth intended, "without aspiring to absolute uniformity," to enforce governmental regulations to the letter.[64]

Beyond these economic and political aspects, the railroads were of course becoming a social phenomenon of immense stature. By employing thousands of technicians, office personnel, and manual workers, the companies could not avoid deep involvement in the labor history of the nineteenth century. That several of them had experienced social turbulence in 1848 was warning enough of things to come. As always, the most immediate issues were wages and hours. Every concession on them had unavoidable ramifications throughout the railway industry. One might wonder why so much was often made of a mere 50–centimes raise for employees of a single firm, but any such adjustment was likely to have a ripple effect involving thousands of workers and ultimately millions of francs. Meanwhile, prudence and perhaps social conscience led to a concern for employees' health. Most companies began to maintain their own medical staff and pharmaceutical outlets. Initially, the Paris-Orléans Company constituted an exception, preferring to sponsor and subsidize a mutual aid society (*société de secours mutuel*) for its workers and offering them a primitive scheme of profit-sharing. Early pension plans also reflected uncertainties about policy. Most of the companies affiliated with the national retirement fund (*caisse de retraite*) founded by the imperial state, but misgivings were manifest that they were thereby inviting further government interference in personnel matters best left to the private sphere.[65]

It is appropriate in this context to mention the employment of women. At first glance, the railways appeared to be entirely a man's world. Yet, even if virtually invisible, women were soon employed in considerable numbers by the French companies, most often in the menial tasks of cleaning passenger cars, attending toilets, and selling tickets in stations. Frequently, wives of employees were also engaged to serve as assistant gatekeepers (*aides-garde-barrière*) at level crossings across the countryside, where they usually lived with their family in tiny *maisons de garde* on the main lines. Although this practice, including the cost of constructing such housing, was not inexpensive for the companies, it was still cheaper than the alternative of building more viaducts or tunnels. Records show that the average wage of women gatekeepers, representing perhaps 50 percent of the female labor force before 1870, ranged between only 120 and 180 francs a year, and they, unlike the males, had little or no prospect of a raise or a bonus. By 1860 the entire French railway industry employed over 21,000 persons, of which fewer than 1500 were women, about 7 percent. To these facts we may safely append the remark that women's presence on the roster of the rail companies was primarily an economy measure to slow the steady rise of personnel costs.[66]

The 1860s ended much like the previous decade, with rumors and symptoms of an economic crisis that were almost identical: a flurry of panic on the Paris Bourse, renewed strain between the imperial government and the private companies, and a move to draft another revision of the conventions between them. These changes do not merit much attention, because they only reaffirmed earlier accords without altering their character. There was simply more of everything: details, assurances, and controls ("increasingly strict," the Eastern Company complained). Not for the first time nor the last, the most vexing issue was finances. Who was to pay for what? "Serious difficulties" arose over matters such as the enlargement of railway stations and the purchase of new engines. Were these expenses to be reckoned as a necessary part of the maintenance of the original infrastructure or, rather, as optional improvements of the superstructure? More bluntly put, the dispute was over the share of costs to be assumed by the state or at least covered by its loans. When times were good, as they had been for most of the Second Empire, such considerations seemed less troublesome. But once the economy noticeably began to sputter in 1868, they soon became "a question of principle" for the companies.[67] Even if a decisive solution were possible at the time, which was unlikely, the increasingly embattled regime of Napoleon III was in a poor posture to impose one. Hence the year 1870 began badly, and it would not improve.

Trains and Free Trade

The ability to move a large mass rapidly over long distances was unique to railroads. The proper cost of doing so was less clear. The central issue of commerce by rail, in other words, was rates, and there was scarcely any aspect of transportation not directly related to it. This was particularly so in the French scheme because of the primary role allotted to private enterprise. For the companies it was self-evident that their existence depended on, and could solely be justified by, profit. It followed that they would seek to charge whatever the freight would bear: the highest possible rates should be adapted to specific circumstances of trade. Agencies of the state understandably took a contrary view. They tended to conceive of the companies as public servants whose task it should always be to provide cheap and efficient transportation for the population, to assist the development of agriculture and industry, and thereby to ensure the competitiveness of the French economy among European nations: the lower and more uniform their rates, therefore the better. Even when formulated in this way, verging on caricature, these two positions display an inherent logic expressed a thousand times over in the documentation of the period. They were bound to clash.

We recall Alexis Legrand's aspiration that the state become "the master of rates." In a sense that was so, at least insofar as each concession granted to a private company was accompanied by a *cahier des charges* stipulating hypothetical maxima that could be collected for transporting goods over a given distance. But this arrangement manifestly remained very general and could not possibly account for every contingency. It meant, in effect, that the companies could lower their rates but not raise them beyond a limit, which left them in reality with a considerable latitude. Whenever the government insisted on its prerogative to enforce restrictions, as in 1847, the companies promptly accused it of an "excess of power" (in specific cases this allegation was several times upheld by the Conseil d'Etat), and they continued to maintain that the functioning of free enterprise in the railway industry was incompatible with the state's presumption to dictate rates.[68]

Any detailed study of French commerce in the 1840s and 1850s will show the inability of the state to hold a tight rein on the companies. Perhaps the best example was the Northern Railway Company's coal trade with Belgium, which was hard to gainsay for sheer complexity. In 1849 a table of transport prices proposed a schedule to carry loads from three Belgian mines to forty French cities, each with a different rate! Furthermore, the weather was a factor. If there was a warm winter, the Northern needed to reduce its rates in order to compete with canals. But if temperatures dropped far below freezing and the canals were clogged, it only made sense for the Company to raise the rates and gain better profit. In this instance and many like it, the obvious difficulty for the state was the same: initiative invariably lay with the companies, which attempted to mount a sensible response to market conditions. The state could not regulate the rates until they were fixed, and the elaborateness necessary to do so was beyond the capacity of existing bureaucracy.[69]

If the interregnum of the Second Republic produced no lasting effects, it nonetheless placed these early assumptions about the railroads into question. There was every reason to suppose that the advent of the Second Empire might bring about more stringent state regulation of commerce, and so it initially appeared. By the mid-1850s the battle lines were drawn. Here some thick description will be useful to explain the evolution of imperial railway policy and to pull together various strands of analysis. Although this story involved all of the major French firms, it centered on the Paris-Orléans Company, whose records are our best source.

By 1855 the PO was embroiled in a dispute with the current Minister of Public Works, Eugène Rouher, over both Brittany (how it should be divided with the Western Company) and the Bourbonnais (concerning a connection to Vichy). The PO's complaints to the cabinet were expressed "in an absolute manner," while the equally unyielding Rouher brought the matter to Napoleon III himself, who ordered an immediate inquiry.[70] During the ensuing months small issues were swallowed by larger ones, as when the Vichy question came to depend on the fate of the entire Grand Central Company. Other specific differences were subsumed under general propositions; this, as we saw, occurred notably at the 1856 conferences in St. Cloud between PO President Bartholony and the emperor, which hinged on the state's recognition of the regional monopolies of the large company networks (*réseaux*). Precisely this principle was now at stake in the gathering altercation over rates. It was Bartholony's contention that the Ministry of Public Works was seeking, as part of the Grand Central settlement and the merger of the PLM, to establish the government's authority to establish railway rates. This would be tantamount, he argued, "to nothing less than an abdication by the companies of their rights, even of their property, an abdication impossible for them to accept."[71] Such was the case presented in person by Bartholony during an audience with the French emperor in January 1857. By then the question of drafting new conventions with the companies was already before the cabinet, and Bonaparte was concerned to reach a viable compromise. He allowed that the companies were obliged to honor the interests of their stockholders, whereas the government also had to meet the needs of the public—each faced a demanding constituency. But Bartholony persisted, and after an hour of intense discussion, Napoleon III finally uttered these critical words: in the soon forthcoming treaty "the Company would remain master of its rates." Transcripts do not ordinarily record deep feelings; consequently, one cannot fathom Bartholony's immediate reaction of relief. We do know, however, that he later tended to exaggerate his own triumph and to insist that he had actually obtained the "complete freedom" of the companies in setting rates. Yet if the companies had not abdicated, neither had the state.[72]

One concluding episode needs to be related here. It revolved around that forever ambiguous notion of *homologation*, which remained the last sticking point before the signing of the 1859 conventions. Did it mean that the Minister of Public Works merely accorded his *ratification* of decisions on rates after they were fixed by the companies? Or did they require his *prior approval*? On this, the most fundamental of issues, there was an "almost total disaccord" between Bartholony and Rouher. An attempt to mediate was undertaken by Alexis Legrand's most illustrious successor at Ponts-et-Chaussées, Ernest de Franqueville. But neither side would budge. Rouher proposed that the lapidary term *approbation* be substituted, but that change was "completely" rejected by the PO, speaking for the companies. Finally, it was Rouher who blinked. After Bartholony's threat to inflate their controversy into a constitutional issue before the Conseil d'Etat, the Minister agreed to return to the original terminology of *homologation*. The now discarded alternative, said Bartholony as he proudly announced the verdict to a special session of PO stockholders, "seemed to imply that the state had a right to interfere in the regulation of rates, which the companies justifiably rejected." Again, we may fairly charge him with an overstatement, but the outcome was undeniably to maintain the status quo in language and in practice. Within the limitations set by their concessions, the companies would continue to establish the rates for railroads, the state to ratify them.[73]

Therewith the way was open to the 1859 conventions and another round of commercial prosperity in the early 1860s. Records of all the major railway companies tell an identical story of unbroken expansion until the autumn of 1867, when "serious difficulties" began to overtake them. Annual gross income rose on average between 10 and 15 percent, the result of heavily increased freight and passenger traffic on the "old" lines, whereas the "new" tracks generally operated at a gnawing deficit. But such was precisely the circumstance foreseen in the conventions signed by the French companies with the state, which continued to supply generous loans to them as well as subsidies to spur further building.[74]

As the most secure and least vulnerable of the French firms, the Northern Company could legitimately boast of its "constantly progressive march" through the decade.[75] Table 4 tells the story.

TABLE 4: Northern Railway Company: Gross Annual Income, 1860–1868

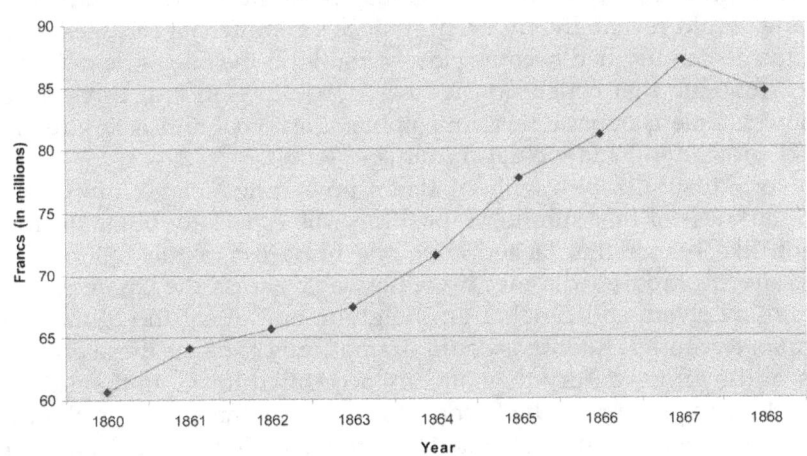

Source: "Rapport présenté au nom du Conseil d'administration," 26 April 1869, CAMT Roubaix, 48 AQ, 570.

The Eastern Company fared somewhat less well, bothered as it was by persistent government demands (often for faintly disguised military reasons) to construct more commercially unproductive connections in the frontier areas. Company officials were thus forced to issue a timid disclaimer to stockholders that "we have not at all sought the concession of the new lines we are going to undertake."[76] Likewise, reluctant or not, the PLM experienced the greatest boom in its history, doubling the length of its network in the dozen years after the corporate fusion of 1857.[77] For its part, the PO displayed the same pattern of expansion, which its self-satisfied leadership vaunted as clear evidence of "the strength of private enterprise in our country," thereby muttering once more the liberal mantra of opposition to excessive state control. Hence another "happy" year was reported to PO stockholders at the end of 1866, although trouble was already in sight that would soon affect all the companies: a civil war in Germany that hampered commerce, the outbreak of a cholera epidemic, severe flooding in central France, and consequently what was called in the winter of 1867–68 the worst grain harvest of the century.[78]

These were the years following the so-called Cobden Treaty of 1860, an Anglo-French trade agreement that lowered tariff barriers and was then extended to the German Zollverein. An incipient Common Market? Without diminishing the salutary effects of this arrangement for the expansion of railways, it would surely be a mistake to become rhapsodic about a triumph of liberalism and of laissez-faire economics. Insofar as the French companies were concerned, there was no lopsided victory over the imperial state, whose patronage remained so essential to them. Rapid growth came at a cost that only easy credit could meet. By the late 1860s the major companies were in effect borrowing about 40 million francs a year from the state.[79] Their prosperity was therefore less splendid and much less secure than it seemed, as the slump at the end of that decade would reveal. In any event, France's commercial fortunes in the nineteenth century had become closely bound to the fate of its railroads. To corroborate that conclusion we need only to glance at three of the nation's staple economic sectors: combustibles (coal and coke), textiles (wool and cotton), and victuals (grain and wine).

No industrialization without steam power; no steam without coal. The starkness of that simple proposition was especially poignant for a nation like France that lacked adequate resources of fuel. At first the necessity of imports was met by waterways: across the Channel from Britain, by rivers and canals from Belgium, and along the Rhine from German territories. Railroads could dramatically enhance these possibilities, and by mid-century they already accounted for more than a third of coal tonnage. During the Second Empire that share was on the rise. But growth was not unproblematic, as the experience of the Northern Railway Company illustrated. Coal and coke shipped by the Company increased in 1859 by over 160,000 tons, an extra income of more than

70,000 francs. Fully 68 percent of this bulk was imported from Belgium, with most of the rest supplied by French mines. But the Northern had to contend with both stiff competition from Belgian suppliers and the cheaper rates for long distances offered by canals. By 1862 tonnage was still rising but income was declining: the trade in combustibles had actually become deficitary for the Company because more of its business was dependent on short hauls from French mines. Obviously, the problem was how to sate the ever more voracious appetite of French industry while yet turning a profit. The Northern was therefore moved in September 1863 to make a drastic reduction in its rate schedule. The effects quickly became apparent as long-distance shipments from Belgium returned to French rails. During the first half of 1865, coal tonnage handled by the Company rose 25 percent, and its trade balance tipped back into the black. Unfortunately, due to this higher density of traffic, expenses increased along with receipts. Lower rates inevitably meant a narrowed profit margin, and the Northern's "coefficient" (the relative amount of gross income consumed by operating costs) became far less favorable: from only 36 percent in 1864, it climbed for the first time to over 50 percent in 1868.[80] From such plain numbers we can draw three uncomplicated conclusions: railroads both reflected and boosted France's economic growth; they were relentlessly forced by commercial pressures into escalation; and they remained forever susceptible to market fluctuation, of which they were an integral part.

Textiles had, of course, been a basic commodity in the first wave of the Industrial Revolution during the late eighteenth century. But that wave scarcely touched French shores, as the wool trade remained largely an affair between the British Isles and Flanders. The expansion of revolutionary France under Napoleon Bonaparte brought such enterprise within the realm, but it was lost again at the Congress of Vienna and then awarded to Belgium in 1830. Hence, apart from luxury items of lace or silk, the growth of the French textile industry depended on the development of railways. Most of the new factories were located along the northeastern border, especially in Alsace, where only railroads could draw together all the elements necessary for industrialization: raw materials, steam power, artisanal skills, and regular conduits of rapid distribution into a broad domestic market. The last factor was critical, since it was clearly useless to produce cloth and apparel in quantity if those goods could not be conveniently dispensed throughout the land.

To expedite this entire process railways were perfectly suited. Many of the rail lines in the vicinity of the Vosges, for example, were in effect connectors from factory to farm or, more likely, to urban centers. The appearance in mid-century of several large Parisian department stores, such as the Bon Marché, must be understood in this context, as terminals for French textiles that were transported by rail. The key was cotton, mostly imported from the United States until the Civil War in the 1860s, when shipments were more likely to arrive from India at Le Havre. Railroads did the rest as they moved bales of raw cotton to places of production, thread between spinners and weavers, and then cloth or clothing from manufacturer to market. Though French textiles never attained the sheer quantity of the English and a large share of the industry was lost to Germany by the war of 1870, this sector of the national economy nonetheless highlighted the crucial role of railways in the erratic but positive evolution of French commerce after 1815.[81]

French agriculture constituted by its nature a more sprawling platform, albeit an indispensable one, upon which most industrial progress rested. One may generalize that, before 1870, production and consumption of foodstuffs were local or regional; a national agriculture hardly existed. Yet the gradual advance of railways caused a leveling of the price structure among the fertile areas and others. Grain, to be specific, became much cheaper and more available in sections of France where it was scarcely grown. Moreover, many perishables like fruits and vegetables could for the first time be transported by rail (just as oysters were being rushed daily from Brittany to fancy Paris restaurants), adding quality and variety to the French diet. From a business standpoint, however, the effects were not consistent. In the same manner, for instance, that the shipment of coal was essential to the Northern Company and textiles to the Eastern, grain trade was critical for the Paris-Orléans. Thus, when flooding struck central France in the mid-1860s, poor harvests cost the PO dearly. But at the same time they actually benefited the PLM, because the recently expanded grain market required an increase of imports from Russia, which arrived from the Black Sea at Marseille, whence they were routed northward on PLM tracks.[82] The scenario for wine was similar. Before the first linkage of railway networks, consumption of beverages was ordinarily in the region of production. By the 1860s, however, new conduits were available for distribution, and railway company records became rife with elaborately negotiated agreements on common rates for sending many thousands of hectoliters of wine across the country. Slowly the sluices were also being opened for champagne, cognac, and calvados to become national drinks. Peasants into alcoholics? It seems a bit much to blame every social ill of the nineteenth century on railroads; still, the lively trade in beverages that we now take for granted would not have been possible without them.[83]

It is important not to exaggerate the rapidity of these economic and commercial developments, nor their uniformity. After all, France possessed a huge land mass, much of which had little or no regular rail service. Many towns and regions were simply left aside by the commotion elsewhere. The French state had deliberately chosen to decentralize its railways by encouraging the major private companies to create regional monopolies. No wonder, then, that it was premature before 1870 to speak of a national railway system. Perhaps it is fair to suggest that France had developed the concept of a unified railway pattern but not the reality. And in 1870 it was the reality that counted.

The Military Implications

The defeat of Napoleon Bonaparte at Waterloo brought the pre-railway age of warfare to a close. Within a few years thereafter, the notion of sending troops and supplies into combat without adequate rail transportation had become obsolete. Well before the end of the nineteenth century, the logistics of every European army became largely dependent on tracks and trains. A technology that did not exist at the beginning of the century thus came to dominate military strategy by its end. On the ground, however, change was slower. The great Bonaparte had been dead for over a decade before the first railroad was opened in France, and it was not until the reign of his nephew after 1850 that the military utility of rapid movement by rail was actually demonstrated.

The potential of railroads to alter the nature of warfare was quickly recognized. Unfortunately, our sources for the earliest strategic thinking—one cannot yet speak of planning—are fragmentary, but they are fairly consistent. The first reflex in the 1830s was to assume that railways would bring a decisive edge for the defense: interior connections would enable a national army to concentrate its forces swiftly against any offensive thrust by an invading foe.[84] A decade later, however, worries were being expressed that the French pattern of main lines leading from the frontiers to Paris might provide corridors all too convenient for an invasion. In any case, there was unanimity that steam power, especially when harnessed with instant communication by telegraph, was bound to transform the conduct of armed combat. As one French military expert wrote in 1842: "It should produce, quite soon, a veritable revolution in the art and science of warfare."[85]

One striking feature of these initial speculations was the frequency with which Germany was identified as "the enemy." But which Germany? The settlement at the Congress of Vienna in 1815 had granted the Rhineland to Prussia, which now became France's most proximate and potentially formidable eastern neighbor. A memo in the Ministry of War on German politics in the 1830s raised the possibility of an eventual national unification, commenting that "only Prussia could assume leadership of this vast operation," and, if so, "she would become a power of the first order."[86] Yet that, admittedly, was a reading of tea leaves. For the time being, French observers generally posited that the Habsburg monarchy represented the preeminent military force of Central Europe, while, as one officer put it after an extensive tour of the member states and free cities in the German Confederation, the Prussian army remained "in reality a composite of militias." The author of this account was also prescient enough to discern "seeds of discord" already evident in strained relations between Prussia and Austria.[87]

Of all the military authorities posting watch on his country's military posture relative to Germany, the most knowledgeable was Paul de Bourgoing, who served with the French legation in Munich throughout the 1840s. His voluminous reports and miscellaneous writings left no question about the "military advantages" of railroads. He personally witnessed tests conducted in Bavaria that dispelled certain doubts, expressed in France, concerning the capacity of trains to transport not only infantry but also cavalry and artillery. Bourgoing was one of those who spotted the potential of railways for offense as well as defense, but he was uncommonly sanguine about their likely impact: "Let us thank heaven that we are situated as neighbors of this calm and good German nation that will in the future be, more than ever, indifferent to any thought of aggression." His undue optimism was somewhat unsettled, however, by the events of 1848, and thereafter he took careful note of the rapid extension of railroads in the German territories, "a vast ensemble that today offers such facilities for the transport of troops." Bourgoing therefore urged his superiors in Paris to press forward with strategic countermeasures such as the direct line to Strasbourg.[88]

We may sum up these scattered "memoirs and reconnaissances" (as they are aptly classed in the military archives at Vincennes) by saying that French experts recognized early on that railways might enhance the threat of a German invasion but they tended to discount it for the foreseeable future. "Nothing indicates an offensive attitude, nothing that is hostile to France," reported the French consul at Mainz in 1849, echoing the views of his colleague in Munich.[89]

As in other regards, the Second Empire brought a new impetus to military affairs. Twice during the 1850s France effectively deployed railroads for strategic purposes: once in mid-decade to expedite troops via Marseille to embark for the Crimea, and again in 1859 to join in the Italian campaign against Austria. Both appeared to be an enormous success. Rails enabled the French army to move huge quantities of men and materiel southward in short order. This feat earned France the reputation as the leader among European nations in the military exploitation of railroads. It also prompted the most recondite appraisal of pre-1870 railway technology in warfare by Pierre Charié-Marsaines, a leading engineer and inspector general at Ponts-et-Chaussées. After reviewing several previous theoretical treatments of his topic, Charié-Marsaines dwelled on the recent French successes in the use of transportation and communications, which had "profoundly changed ... the art of war." He made short work of the old debate between the relative advantages of railways for offense or defense, contending that France must anticipate both by proceeding to build a system of transversals to connect its main routes. In essence, he was thereby proposing the construction and coordination of a fully integrated national rail system of star lines and concentric circles, providing the flexibility necessary to confront any military contingency. Also, he did not fail to note that such a pattern of transportation would enable the imperial government to meet domestic emergencies by what he termed "an interior strategy [of] rapid concentration." It all made perfectly good sense, yet for a Bonapartist regime that was already distracted and beginning to falter, as we can now see, Charié-Marsaines's treatise read like a charter of unrealized ambitions. His projects would have to await another day.[90]

Measuring the thrust of military considerations in the rise of French railways cannot be an exact science. To do so, we must enter into the details of dozens of practical problems that had to be resolved as time passed. It is very instructive to examine two related issues much debated since the 1840s: on which side of a waterway should the rail line be constructed? And how close to the German frontier? With its eye ever on "the enemy," the French army habitually favored a location on the opposite bank of a river or canal, preferably far from the border. But the surprise is how often other factors overshadowed strictly military logic. While planning the Paris-Strasbourg line, for example, French army engineers (collectively known as the *Génie*) successfully defended a route via Lunéville, south of Nancy, on the grounds that the tracks would be protected by a fort and would pass behind a canal. But on another stretch along the Zorn River, military authorities favored the right bank (predictably, away from Germany), whereas Ponts-et-Chaussées preferred for technical and commercial reasons to build on the left bank. A decision for the latter was rendered by a "mixed committee" (*commission mixte*) of civilian and military engineers, a common procedure of arbitration.[91]

Sometimes the Minister of War, when faced with strong opposition from his colleague at Public Works, opted not to lobby for a particular solution even if it was militarily preferable. That instance occurred when parliamentary deputies from the Saône Valley vainly protested the choice of a shorter *tracé* along the Doubs River via Besançon, which they called "impractical and infeasible" because its proximity to the frontier would allow an invader to cut the connection "in the blink of an eye." Yet no official support for the Saône was forthcoming. Even when military authorities did take a stand, they were not certain to have their way. Appeals to utilize the "mighty natural barrier" of the Loire by building a line on the left bank were rejected in favor of one on the right bank after Ponts-et-Chaussées determined that grading problems with unstable soil would otherwise create "excessive difficulties and expenses."[92] From these and many similar instances we can gather at least two generalizations: first, that civil-military relations were always complex and often strained; and second, that the French state was frequently torn by internal divisions that pitted one political faction or cabinet minister against another.

There is no difficulty in demonstrating that many other decisions about the construction or location of railroads had a distinctive military component. When the current Minister of Public Works, Pierre Magne, pleaded the "utility and urgency" of building an interior beltway (*petite ceinture*) of rails about Paris in 1851, he pointed out the commercial advantage of reducing the number of wasteful freight transfers (*transbordements*); but he also added: "The strategic importance of the belt railway is no less evident." Accordingly, the state provided nearly half of the 9 million francs in funding originally allocated for the project, and in return it obtained free military transportation on the beltway for army personnel. Later a trunk line was added to link the arsenal at Vincennes directly with it to facilitate the shipment of munitions.[93] A set of general regulations for military transportation provided by the private companies was first codified in the mid-1850s and then renewed in 1861. In this revised version the companies received firm assurances that the reimbursement of their expenses by the Ministry of War would henceforth be more prompt, and reciprocally they accepted further obligations to cooperate in military training and mobilization procedures. In these complex arrangements there was ample room for ambiguity and conflict; hence, the private companies usually designated a member of their administration to oversee relations with the military. The Eastern Company added a senior officer, General de Noizet, to its Administrative Council specifically for that purpose, hoping thereby to avert "serious difficulties" with army engineers.[94]

A list of minor civil-military crises over railways could be extended almost indefinitely. As a rule they concerned finance. If the rationale of a given construction was primarily military, the state was likely to incur a higher liability for its expense, because the companies could justifiably claim that they were being burdened with operating costs without offsetting commercial profits. For obvious reasons, the records of the Eastern Company are particularly rich in this sort of documentation. As a supplement to the Paris-Strasbourg route, the military value of the Paris-Mulhouse line via Belfort was hardly to be denied, and the Ministry of War did not hesitate in 1856 to arrange a handsome subsidy for its fortification. Likewise, in 1863 the state signed a special convention with the Eastern for the creation of a "third network," in reality intended to become a complex of debarkation facilities for military convoys, for which the Company was to receive a total recompense of 62,800,000 francs in semi-annual installments. Several other projects, such as the establishment of a major depot at Châlons-sur-Marne and the extension of capillary lines in the Ardennes region, were similarly negotiated at the behest of the army.[95]

Commercial and military interests were ordinarily assumed to be compatible, because a main rail line could presumably serve either. Yet there were problems at both ends. On the frontier a proliferation of spur tracks could hasten the passage of freight and perhaps assist local industry, but they made the border more porous. More than a thousand kilometers stretched along France's northeastern rim from Dunkerque to Longwy and on to Mulhouse. As the webbing of rails thickened, the possibilities for by-passing the few serious defensive forts necessarily grew. And once advanced beyond the frontier, an enemy might cross over to a main line and hasten toward the capital. In Paris there was another obvious military liability of the emergent French rail system. The tracks of all the major companies, save the Southern, now converged on one tiny beltway. What was true of French commercial transactions was certain to be no less characteristic of military operations: they were all based on the regional networks of the private companies, which the state was attempting—with more or less success—to regulate. And all railroads led to Paris, where congestion was already a way of life.

In retrospect, of course, we are well aware of the ineluctable military consequences. For years the French had been uneasy about Germany, but it was an attitude born less of fear than of curiosity. Once Paris was linked by rail to Alsace, France had a manifest stake in the Rhineland, and Napoleon III did nothing to discourage talk of Strasbourg as the *plaque tournante* of European railways. Then Bismarck brought matters to a head. The war against Denmark in 1864 was notable for the use of railroads, especially by the Austrians, to invade Schleswig-Holstein—though reports from the French military attaché in Berlin to the Minister of War, Marshal Randon, boasted that the performance in Germany was less impressive than the Italian campaign by France seven years earlier.[96] The subsequent defeat of the Habsburg monarchy by Prussia in 1866 came as a shock. At least the old question about which Germany the French might have to face had now found a definitive answer.

French military affairs from 1867 to 1870 were dominated by Randon's successor, Marshal Niel, who pushed reforms in an attempt to prepare for a possible showdown with Prussia. Looking over the record of those years from the standpoint of railways, one cannot fail to be struck by the helter-skelter tenor of Niel's efforts. Rail networks, it seems, are not susceptible to sudden change. To his credit, Niel spurred more construction in border areas, particularly the northeastern corner near Longwy. He helped to create a new civil-military committee in 1869 that was assigned to treat "diverse questions" that had arisen. And he tried to update the regulations for troop transports by rail, a final draft of which appeared in February 1870 just after Niel's untimely death. Meanwhile, the Ministry of Public Works was busy with implementing these and other measures, always hampered by the need to negotiate agreements with the private companies. They had to be requested to train engineers of the *Génie* to drive locomotives, and they were asked for permission to allow artillery officers to assist in loading cannons onto freight wagons at company stations. A decree to install a special military unit, separate from company *ateliers*, to repair and maintain rolling stock in wartime, was not issued until 19 July 1870, a few hours before the beginning of combat.[97]

The collage of such fragments of evidence forms a convincing portrait of last-minute innovation. With one foot of their mixed railway system heavily planted in private enterprise, the French were unprepared in the prewar years to produce a unified and tightly coordinated railway strategy. There is no reason to contradict the crushing judgment of François Jacqmin, director of operations at the Eastern Railway Company, that in 1870 France possessed "no serious organization of military transportation."[98] Without it, the war was lost. Viewing this spectacle of confusion, we can only recall one of the most powerful images in French literature—at the conclusion of Zola's novel *La Bête Humaine*—when a driverless French troop train hurtles eastward in the night while inside the drunken soldiers insouciantly sing and laugh and swear.

Chapter 2

GERMANY, 1815–1870

In the early stages of the railway era, the absence of a German national state had both advantages and disadvantages. With no central regulatory agencies to worry about, investors were free to pursue one project after another in search of profits. The first railway construction in Germany therefore tended to be rapid and relatively cheap; and if the industry were measured solely on the basis of track length, we might say that the German territories quickly assumed leadership on the European continent.

Until about 1840 German railway investments were virtually all by private capital. And, of course, they were ordinarily local, within discrete boundaries: Nürnberg-Fürth and Munich-Augsburg in Bavaria, Leipzig-Dresden in Saxony, Berlin-Potsdam in Prussia, etc. But inevitably two mutations occurred that brought permanent change. The first was a growing concern of the various states to acquire their own rail lines, to regulate them, and to retain their financial gains. Therefore, seen as a whole, the German railroad map soon came to resemble that of traditional *Kleinstaaterei*, a jumbled potpourri full of vitality but also internecine rivalries. The second development was closely related and equally fundamental. As railroads were extended, they were bound to cross state frontiers, thereby creating instant ambiguities and conflicts. Interstate commerce soon became a commonplace. Hence, some institutional means had to be conceived to coordinate and regulate the burgeoning railway industry on a regional, national, and international scale. Rail transportation thus became an integral part of the general tendencies of nineteenth-century Germany.

In their fashion, the Germans thereby arrived at a mixed system of railways. Their particular mixture contained at least three basic elements that simultaneously constitute major themes of the period before 1870. There was, first of all, an inherent discord between the private and public sectors—with a trend usually, but not always, toward the latter. Second, the competition among states was especially stark in Germany, such that differences over rates, rights-of-way, and regional interests deeply marked the evolution of railways. Finally, in a peculiarly German form, a clash between center and periphery was sure to flare once aspirations for national unity became pitted against the entrenched forces of particularism embodied by the regimes of the individual states.

The Dilemmas of Political Diversity

By the time the first primitive steam locomotive on German soil laboriously made its way across the six kilometers between Nürnberg and Fürth in December 1835, there was already much speculation about the future constitution of a national railway system. The only problem was that a German nation-state was lacking to realize such schemes. By far the most famous of these was propagated by Friedrich List, the legendary godfather of all German railroad planners. Although his perspective was clearly affected by an evident pride in his adopted homeland of Saxony, List's thinking was largely formed by his experience abroad in America, England, and France. This enabled him to grasp an essential truth: that the backwardness of the Germanic territories in highway and canal transportation, relative to the Western nations, might be a boon to the new railway industry. The key, he thought, would be a main thoroughfare from Hamburg over Berlin to Leipzig, which would then be linked for both commercial and military reasons to the East, the South, and the Rhineland. A sketch map of this vision remains one of the most frequently reproduced documents of European history. Considerably less well known is a characteristic essay published in French during List's two-year stay in Paris from 1837 to 1839, which he dramatically entitled *Le monde marche*. From a commercial standpoint, he wrote, the chief profiteer of the nineteenth century was likely to be France because of that country's geopolitical centrality; but of course Germany could not fail to benefit from railroads as well. As for the military effect, List went so far as to declare that war would eventually become impossible, given the decisive advantage of rapid transport for the defense. Yet he was uncertain about the proper balance between the public and private sectors. List tended to believe that private ownership should predominate, with the state being restricted to a regulatory role. But the latter would surely have an important if still indeterminate part to play.[1]

Nationalism and liberalism were the two most conspicuous themes of early German writings about railways. A vast national network, to quote one statement in 1834, would promote "the great general commercial interests of the entire German Fatherland."[2] From Munich, Prussian Minister August von Dönhoff meanwhile reported the interest there in extending a line from Hamburg all the way to Lake Constance, a connection that would have military as well as industrial and commercial importance. Above all, it would, unlike a railroad in the Rhineland, be well protected from outside incursion, "a route that is all German, all national, and independent of foreign influence." Dönhoff later expanded on the superiority of north-south tracks over east-west insofar as the latter would only increase contacts between the southern states and France, whereas the former could advance "purely national, purely German relations and rapprochements." He reiterated his worries about the Rhine corridor, which might be disrupted by "the enemy."[3] Similar utterances abounded, indicative of an unsurprising tendency among post-Napoleonic German authors to regard their nation as an emergent anti-France. It followed that railways might be viewed as the mortar of national unification.

Liberals, as one would expect, looked more often to Great Britain, and much more positively. In advocating construction of a line from his city of Cologne to Antwerp, for example, Ludolf Camphausen cited the model of Manchester-Liverpool as a salutary linkage between industrial and commercial centers. Like others, he admired the economy, rapidity, and regularity of railroads. But he insisted on a clear priority of private enterprise, ordinarily the liberal trademark.[4] With far more ambiguity, David Hansemann also foresaw some limitation to the state's role as a concessionaire: it should maintain the right to repurchase a rail company but should not exercise it for at least thirty years, thus encouraging capital ventures in the meantime to take their course. Hence he criticized the recent Prussian railway legislation of 1838 as excessively etatist.[5] Manifestly, such general essays tended to be imprecise about the minutiae of policy. Nationalism and liberalism were therefore not mutually exclusive, and it is useless to draw the distinction too finely. These few instances should be sufficient, however, to suggest that the onset of railways in Germany provoked an outpouring of theoretical tracts that owed much of their interest to the political chaos in which they appeared.

After 1815 this scene was at least nominally presided over by the Federal Diet of the German Confederation (Bund), which gathered intermittently in Frankfurt. Alas, that assembly's reputation will never fully recover from Heinrich Heine's acerbic bon mot for it: "O Bund, Du Hund, Du bist nicht gesund" (Oh Confederation, you dog, you're sick)—though it should be noted that many contemporaries took it quite seriously. In railway affairs, the Diet had more symbolic presence than political clout. That is, it basically made proposals to the states rather than laws, hoping to exercise a certain moral suasion. Above all, the Diet provided a forum of discussion about common problems. But the majority of delegates could properly be described as diplomats, professional or amateur, without the necessary qualifications to formulate realistic policy for business and technology. Railway trade was consequently never regulated by the Bund. Besides, as everyone knew, it was a house badly divided, a fact embarrassingly exposed by the turmoil of 1848. A resolution in the Diet during that time dilated on the urgency of a "close, essential, necessary linkage among railways in the various states of Germany," which of course identified precisely what was wanting. A telltale circumstance was that the federal army had no generalissimo (one might be designated in case of war) and was fully dependent on the mutual cooperation of the two German superpowers and the smaller states. When that did not materialize in 1849, the influence of the Confederation waned.[6]

For rather different reasons, the German Customs Union (Zollverein) was no better suited to regulate the railroads. Founded in 1834, just a few months before the inauguration of Nürnberg-Fürth passenger service, the Zollverein was to gain an unquestionable significance in promoting interstate commerce by lowering tariff rates. But the absence of Austria in these arrangements still posed an insuperable problem for the railway industry, because the Habsburg monarchy's political and military power had seemingly been enhanced by railways. It remained a force to be reckoned with, especially since Austrian tracks before 1870 provided the German territories with their only direct access to the Mediterranean via Trieste. Moreover, the Prussian predominance within the Customs Union in many regards weakened it because the fear of *Verpreussung*, an excess of economic control by Berlin, dissuaded the other German states from committing their rail networks to supervision by the Zollverein. Accordingly, it makes more sense to describe the Customs Union as a bundle of local and regional commercial interests rather than as a platform for national unity. It has been plausibly argued that the Zollverein finally achieved greater political than economic significance; certainly, in any event, it could not be considered as the primary underpinning of a national railway system.[7]

The complementary deficiencies of the German Bund and the Zollverein largely explain the creation in 1847 of the Association of German Railway Administrations (Verein Deutscher Eisenbahn-Verwaltungen). Although the initiative for this organization also originated in Prussia, it incorporated a widespread need to cope with questions raised by interlocking private and state railway networks, to establish technological norms for them, and thereby to promote safe and profitable rail traffic across intra-German boundaries. In this grouping we can see the beginnings of a truly national German railway system that, in addition, attracted the participation of adjacent administrations throughout Central Europe from the Netherlands to the Balkans. Notably, the VDEV included Austria yet deliberately sought to avoid the overt political overtones of the Frankfurt Diet and the Customs Union. Wisely, Prussia made a conscious effort, at first, to maintain a modest profile. The founding plenary session of the Association was convened in Vienna in 1849; not until 1853 did it meet in Berlin. Likewise, its journal began regular publishing during the 1840s in Stuttgart; the editorial office was then moved to Leipzig in 1862 and only later to Berlin.[8]

That said, one should by all means avoid exaggerating the authority of the Association. It is somewhat misleading to suggest, as has one historian, that "the VDEV could have made adoption of its policies mandatory for all members, but it declined to do so."[9] In truth, governments of the individual states at no time contemplated any such action, loath as they were to cede their political autonomy to an amorphous conglomerate of public and private railway administrations. What held them together was a frank recognition that common standards, starting with the same track gauge, were indispensable to mutual economic prosperity. Given Germany's lack of political unity and therefore of any central regulatory agency, only a voluntary cooperative effort could assure the norms for signals, brakes, weights, rates, and the like, which were necessary to take advantage of the possibilities of commerce by rail. In the absence of coercion, these needs were imperfectly met before 1870. The wonder is how well the VDEV worked to standardize the operations of more than sixty members whose tracks covered over 15,000 kilometers.[10]

We must briefly observe another peculiarity of the German railway industry, one that perhaps merits a full-scale study: the "leagues" (Verbände) of railway companies that proliferated in the 1850s and 1860s. These unsteady alliances emerged in a bewildering variety of combinations, frequently overlapping and often competing. In an unregulated national market economy, they sought to establish regional groupings to set rates and exchange rights-of-way. Doubtless, they thereby reflected a disorderly adolescence of German railways, and their very existence indicated the inability of the Association of German Railway Administrations to provide a sufficient basis for commercial activity. As the Association's own journal commented, the leagues were a "necessity" for the free development of the German railroads.[11] Among the more important leagues were the North German (linking Leipzig and Berlin to Cologne), the Middle German (successor to a failed clique of private Prussian companies), and the South German (originally combining Bavaria's and Württemberg's state systems with five private companies, while curiously excluding Baden). But there were also the Southeastern (which did include Baden), the Rhenish (meant to deal with French companies), the Westphalian, and so on. Nine such leagues were listed in 1864; three years later, a Bavarian legate in Stuttgart itemized Württemberg's affiliation with seventeen of them![12] By that time, however, military and political events had already overtaken the leagues. Before the end of the decade, the Middle German League was dissolved, essentially giving way to the North German Confederation of 1866, and a general shakeup followed. The leagues would not survive the 1870s. Although these ephemeral organizations probably had a minimal effect on the ultimate course of Germany's development, to their credit they did perform a useful function in facilitating regular consultations among public and private companies. And, on the margin of these meetings, railroad men from the state networks could gather for confidential talks, free of the usual diplomatic constraints at formal conferences.

In this administrative strudel of German railway networks, several structures of enterprise were possible. Some states had only private ownership: mostly small principalities in the north such as Mecklenburg, Holstein, Lauenburg, Nassau, and Anhalt. Others possessed exclusively state railroads: Braunschweig and Hanover in the center, Württemberg and Baden in the south. But most represented a mixture of the public and private sectors: Prussia, Saxony, Bavaria, the two Hessian states, and also Austria. In the early 1850s it appeared that the trend toward outright state control would prevail. Of the forty-nine companies joined in the Association of German Railway Administrations at that time, only thirty-four were still private, fifteen state-owned. Both Saxony and Bavaria were consolidating their networks by acquiring more private holdings, and Prussia assumed direct responsibility for three major lines: the Ostbahn (Berlin to Königsberg) plus two formerly private firms in Westphalia and the Saarland.[13]

Of course Prussia was crucial. And of all the large German states, Prussia was the least inclined to espouse state ownership, notwithstanding the long and expensive Ostbahn, which was largely a concession to the military establishment. Hence, twenty of the thirty-four private companies in the VDEV were on Prussian territory, whereas in the mid-1850s its state railroads measured barely more than Bavaria's and exceeded Hanover's by only a third. The origins had been humble, starting in the 1830s with small coal lines bearing the name of their pioneer Friedrich Harkort. For once Prussian conservatives and liberals saw eye-to-eye: there should be no state funding for these tiny local businesses. Yet greater intentions, such as a linkage between the Rhine and Weser rivers, meant larger companies, and with them came an inducement for the state to arrange loans and offer guarantees to investors. Thus the Prussian regime became increasingly engaged, for instance, in encouraging a connection from Cologne via Minden to Hanover, completed in 1847. Still, it was the usual Prussian way to attract private capital in the form of joint-stock companies (Aktiengesellschaften) rather than through credit banking or government subsidies. The state should participate, but how much? That was the central issue of the 1850s, when August von der Heydt used his authority as Prussian Minister of Commerce to promote more rapid expansion through direct state involvement. His ambitions were blocked, however, by the equally formidable Minister of Finance, Karl von Bodelschwingh, who championed the interests of a bureaucratic apparatus dedicated in Prussia to opposing a spiral of public investments, debts, and risks. If Heydt briefly held the initiative—in addition to the three state lines mentioned, we may add his sponsorship of the Berlin Ringbahn, an interior beltway connecting the capital's main rail terminals—he was finally thwarted by a combination of budgetary restraints, stock market fluctuations, and political maneuvers. Prussia thereupon entered the decade of the 1860s with a hotchpotch railway network tilted toward private enterprise.[14]

Particularism Unbound

Seen from the vantage of Germany's southern rim, the railroads were a godsend. The troubles of 1848 and the frustrations of 1849, when the Frankfurt Diet was unceremoniously disbanded, revealed the vulnerability of ruling houses throughout the land. Already shaken by the Napoleonic incursion before 1815, the institution of monarchy was in serious difficulty, and it became amply clear that a retrenchment would not be possible without firm economic footing. That was exactly what railways could provide. They represented not only a fitting symbol of *Kleinstaat* autonomy (whenever a ruler's coat of arms was emblazoned on the door of a train's passenger compartment), they also became its financial substance. Commerce by rail could turn a handsome profit, and with it a state might underwrite all the other trappings of its independence, including a suitably elegant royal court life and a diplomatic corps dispersed across Europe.

It is therefore appropriate to regard the new rail industry as a critical component in the consolidation of German particularism. Anyone could see some possible advantages to be gained through a unified national railway system, but the special interests of the separate states posed a countervailing force of considerable dynamism. The tension between these poles was quintessential to Germany's emergence as a powerful nation-state in the nineteenth century, just as it is necessarily at the core of its railway history. For better or worse, the federal character of German polity was to be perfectly mirrored by the configuration of its railroads.

In retrospect, if the Prussian state was somehow predestined to participate in a national solution—a vocation that it accepted but grudgingly until the 1860s—it is arguable that four other major German principalities were no less certain to uphold the dogma of states' rights and to favor the decentralization of any such political entity: the kingdoms of Saxony, Bavaria, and Württemberg, and the Grand Duchy of Baden. An overview of these regimes is thus indispensable for our understanding of the German evolution and for any comparisons with France that are thereby suggested.

Saxony

Geography may not be destiny, but it tells us much about rail connections. Because the modern kingdom of Saxony was situated snugly between Prussia and Bavaria, its landscape was bound to contain vital junctions of a lively north-south trade. There was consequently good reason to consider Saxony, as had Friedrich List, as the hub of a putative German railway system—and, in fact, by 1870 it ranked second only to Belgium among the most dense networks of track in Europe. But as a rail power, Saxony had the fault of its virtues: the close proximity of two powerful neighbors. The annexation of some Saxon territory by Prussia in 1815 had left a legacy of tension, which helps to explain the episodic recurrence of what came to be known as the "railway war" (*Eisenbahnkrieg*) between the two states. Relations with Bavaria were little better, constantly marred by mutual suspicions that the other was deviously plotting with Prussia. So it went, a tale of territorial rivalries that changed in form over time but lost little intensity as the century progressed.[15]

The linchpin of Saxony's rail network was the Leipzig-Dresden Company, which began construction of a main line in 1836 and completed it three years later. Founded by a group of independent stockholders, it was at once immensely successful and therewith assured that private enterprise would be the foundation of Saxon railway politics (it was not acquired by the state until 1876). In the elaboration of a network, the role of the regime was restricted to offering temporary guarantees of interest to investors and purchases of up to one-third of company stocks. On that basis, new rail lines radiated to Berlin, to Bavaria via Hof, to Poland via Görlitz, and from Dresden to Prague. Like the other states of Europe, however, Saxony soon had to deal with diminishing returns. Once the main lines had been spoken for, investors became reluctant to part with their capital in order to promote ancillary projects that promised little profit. As in Prussia, a move toward the creation of state-owned railroads therefore began in the 1840s and reached a peak in 1854, when an open bid was made to take over the Leipzig-Dresden line. After an aroused opposition of Saxon stockholders stood firm in the breach, that attempt was abandoned, and official policy reverted by 1859 to moderate state support for private initiatives.[16]

This bare outline should not suggest a total absence of state regulation. Any modern visitor to the capital of Dresden will not fail to notice a huge administrative edifice perched on the right bank of the Elbe, directly across from the famous silhouette of the inner city. This commanding view was altogether appropriate for the Ministry of Finance, core of the Saxon cabinet and eventual master of its railway bureaucracy. Initially located in Leipzig, the supervisory agencies of the state's rail system were gradually consolidated in Dresden, where the Minister of Finance became the key figure in the Saxon regime. During this lengthy process, stretching over decades, the extensive administrative structure of a state railway network was thus set in place. In the meanwhile, as a memorandum from the Finance Ministry in August 1859 made clear, Saxon railway employees were to be organized like postal workers and placed under uniform rules applying to all state functionaries. Saxony thereby began the 1860s, parallel to Prussia, with a mixed organization of private and public elements held in precarious balance.[17]

Bavaria

In the question of private versus public ownership of the railroads, Bavaria was the German state to make the most abrupt volte-face. All of its early lines, from the tangential Nürnberg-Fürth to the crucial Munich-Augsburg, were initially built with private joint-stock investment capital. But King Ludwig I and his cabinet had other ideas, attracted as they were to a Belgian model of centralized state control—and to profits. Like Saxony, Bavaria came to regard the railways as analogous to the postal service, a public institution under governmental aegis in which employees would wear Bavarian uniforms, drive Bavarian engines (from the Maffei locomotive plant near Munich), punch Bavarian tickets, and speak with a strong Bavarian accent. Private lines were allowed, and indeed for special purposes encouraged, but the main arteries belonged to the Bavarian Staatsbahn. With the government's purchase of the Munich-Augsburg Company in October 1844, the cornerstone of that state network was firmly planted.[18]

The Bavarian railway bureaucracy was bounced around from one state ministry to another until it finally came to reside in the Ministry of Foreign Affairs, perhaps betraying an ambition that the Wittelsbach dynasty should cut a figure on the international stage, well beyond its borders. Three examples may help us to define what was particular about Bavaria's circumstances. First was the priority ascribed to the major north-south trade route that passed from Hof on the Saxon frontier through Augsburg to Lindau. In a broad vision this route—of course, with several connections to Munich—began and ended with access to waterways: from the North Sea at Hamburg stretching down through Bavaria to Lake Constance in the south, whence on to Switzerland, Italy, and the Mediterranean. Even on a less grand scale the intra-German link among Bavaria, Saxony, and Prussia was in itself of vital commercial importance, nor was it ignored by military planners. Any analysis of Bavarian railway politics must therefore keep the primacy of this main line in view.[19]

A second international consideration derived from Bavaria's possession of the Rhenish Palatinate. Reacquired from France for services rendered during the Napoleonic empire, this small but strategic left-bank territory gave Bavaria a stake in the other great north-south trade avenue from the Netherlands to Switzerland. In supervising the Palatine railways, left mostly in private hands, Munich proved to be cautious. When consulted in 1838, Ludwig said that he preferred to permit a line on neither side of the Rhine, but if Baden and Prussia built a railroad on the right bank (as surely they would), then Bavaria should support one on the left bank as well. The latter project, however, unavoidably raised issues of another dimension because of the French presence in Strasbourg and Mulhouse, which were soon joined by rail to Paris. True, Bavaria had assumed obligations to the German Bund, but the allure of a closer French connection was beckoning.[20]

A third issue subsumed the first two and prefigured their relative weight in the balance of Bavarian history. By the early 1840s there was already talk of a great east-west railway that would ultimately connect Paris and Vienna. What could be more logical, then, than to construct a route straight from Augsburg to Ulm as the vital link between Munich and Stuttgart? That question became acute once the Bavarian state purchased the Munich-Augsburg Company in 1844. It was soon evident, however, that the cabinet had no interest in extending those tracks directly westward. Rather, "the most natural connection," argued the Ministry of Foreign Affairs, would be northward from Augsburg via Donauwörth and Nördlingen. The rationale for this considerable detour was no mystery: Bavaria wished above all to defend its north-south monopoly from Munich and Augsburg to Lake Constance at Lindau without fear that traffic might be diverted to a shorter trajectory on Württemberg's tracks over Ulm to the port of Friedrichshafen. In sum, Bavaria's policy was particularism incarnate.[21]

By 1848 there were three major gaps remaining in the projected itinerary from Paris to Vienna: Strasbourg-Karlsruhe, Ulm-Augsburg, and Munich-Salzburg. Until the other two were filled, Munich let it be known, a direct link across its territory would be "of secondary importance." The 1850s were therefore consumed with dozens of diplomatic conferences at which participants solemnly agreed on the importance "for all of southern Germany" of completing "the southern German railway network."[22] But such appeals to regional pride bogged down in rhetoric, and a railroad map of Germany in 1860 still displayed the same three gaps. As a consequence, passengers traveling between Paris and Vienna were better advised to book their tickets via Frankfurt, Dresden, and Prague. As for freight, it apparently occurred to no one to bother with recording the meager statistics. In 1861 a curious treaty was finally concluded whereby Württemberg agreed to a twelve-year delay in shipping transit goods from the north to Friedrichshafen in return for an agreement with Bavaria opening the way at last to Ulm. The details of this episode form a delicious story of political hypocrisy and, what is more, a perfect example of the continuation of German *Kleinstaaterei* into the railway age.[23]

Württemberg

The perennial weakling of southern German railway networks was Württemberg. Mountainous, rocky, and heavily wooded, its terrain was less suited than others for rail transportation. It also lacked proximity to industrial areas and large urban markets. Perhaps most importantly, Württemberg was squeezed between two jealous neighbors, Bavaria and Baden, each of which tenaciously guarded major north-south trade corridors to which they sought to prevent easy access from Stuttgart.

After a decade of dithering, Württemberg did not open its first railway until 1845. A joint-stock company had been formed in 1835 to construct a line from Stuttgart to nearby Cannstatt, yet at first nothing came of it but conferences and resolutions. Meanwhile, the other southern states made a start with their own north-south connections, which took priority despite oratory by Württemberg's diplomatic representatives in Munich and Karlsruhe about the "European significance" of a great east-west railroad.[24] We have already alluded to Stuttgart's travails with Bavaria about Ulm. With Baden the difficulties were hardly less troublesome. Forlorn, Württemberg naturally coveted an entrance to the Rhineland and envisioned one northwest line to Mannheim, another to the southwest that would lead—"as soon as conditions permit"—over Karlsruhe to Strasbourg and Basel. That was 1840, five years before any building was completed. At least it was possible to legislate a basic law on 18 April 1843, which set guidelines for a mixed system of state railways and concessions to private companies. In fact, however, that intention was never realized, since Württemberg soon began to develop a rail network exclusively under state ownership.[25]

A bureaucratic quirk is noteworthy. Like Saxony, Württemberg initially conceived of trains as vehicles of domestic economic policy, placing the railway directorship under the Ministry of the Interior in September 1844, then transferring it to the Ministry of Finance a month later. Yet the interminably confounding dealings with Bavaria, Baden, and later Prussia were such that the state's entire railway administration was finally moved to the Ministry of Foreign Affairs in 1864. In this respect, Württemberg's administrative history closely resembled that of Bavaria.[26]

By 1850 Württemberg was busy with building a rail link from Stuttgart via Ulm to Friedrichshafen on Lake Constance. But this line would languish without proper approaches; and these, as we have observed, were effectively blocked for years by Bavaria and Baden. Negotiations were conducted with both, and bargains struck, without any immediate action. Moreover, a new issue arose in the late 1850s that was to complicate matters still further. Talks began among Bavaria, Switzerland, and Austria about construction of an international line along the northeastern shore of Lake Constance. This "Bodensee beltway" would stop at Lindau, however, thus maintaining the isolation of Friedrichshafen and perpetuating the quarantine of the entire Württemberg railway network. Anguished pleas from the regime in Stuttgart were to no avail. Württemberg continued to be excluded from the sporadic discussions, and when a treaty eventually emerged in the mid-1860s, Stuttgart was again shut out. So much for southern unity and European significance.[27]

Baden

Advantageously located in Germany's southwestern corner, Baden could not avoid a dual role in the nation's railway affairs. First, of course, it oversaw the entry from Switzerland to the right bank of the Rhine and thus the most active north-south trade route in Europe. Second, Baden's proximity to France placed it at the railheads of both Strasbourg and Mulhouse, through which commerce was sure to pass from Paris and the French plains to southern Germany. This double assignment was clearly indicated by a decree of Grand Duke Leopold in 1838, which outlined a project for the state to construct a Rhenish line between Basel and Mannheim with a spur track to Kehl, opposite Strasbourg.[28] At least two caveats, however, are in order. First, Baden was painfully slow to realize these intentions. Hampered by budgetary constraints, the main line took nearly seventeen years to build. Second, France notwithstanding, the priority of a north-south orientation was never questioned. Such was the recommendation of a special administrative panel that had deliberated on the state's railroad policies since 1833. And such was still the conclusion of Rüdt von Collenberg, Minister of the Interior in 1841, who advised Leopold that Baden should respond to Württemberg's entreaties about an east-west connection by stating that "an obligation cannot be assumed *for the time being*." Presumably the italics were intended to suggest that some favorable action might be forthcoming in the future, as eventually it was. But priorities remained priorities.[29]

Leopold's decree, to repeat, stipulated that Baden's network was to be constructed and operated at state expense. In fact the government was quite willing to dispense concessions for ancillary track to private companies, but there was insufficient demand and the entire network became, like Württemberg's, a public enterprise. Its administration, however, was unique. A single directorship for the railway and postal services was at first inaugurated. In 1854 postal affairs were separated, and a sole directorship for transportation was instituted. That agency was then transferred in 1860 to a newly created Ministry of Commerce. Hence this bureaucratic structure resembled none of the others we have examined, reflecting Baden's tendency to remain a loner among the major German states.[30]

No aspect of Baden's early railway history more neatly illustrates that trait than the adoption of a broad track gauge. This matter is actually much less of a mystery than some writers have assumed. One must recall that what became the standard European gauge (outside of Russia and Spain) of 4 feet 8 1/2 inches was also controversial in England from the start. Many British engineers preferred a broader gauge, and when Baden's envoys were negotiating the purchase of two locomotives and tenders with Robert Stephenson and Company in 1842, they received assurances from their London counterparts (in English) about "all the advantages which this greater width affords with regard to being able to give greater strength in general as well as in detail." In adopting a track gauge of virtually 5 feet 3 inches (1.6 meters), furthermore, Karlsruhe had reason to believe that such alleged technological superiority would everywhere prevail. The same width was being utilized by several Dutch lines—Amsterdam-Arnhem and Amsterdam-The Hague-Rotterdam— and the late-starting Württemberg might soon follow.[31] Later this proved to be an expensive miscalculation, as Baden's railway officials already admitted in 1846, when, even before the founding of the Association of German Railway Administrations, there could no longer be doubt of "the general German track gauge." Nonetheless, it required another seven years before Baden finally agreed to act. Rüdt von Collenberg conceded in 1853 that Karlsruhe now stood alone, and he gained the unanimous consent of the cabinet and parliament for the huge appropriations necessary to convert all of the state's tracks and rolling stock to the German standard. Simultaneously, Baden also shifted from longitudinal to lateral railroad ties (*Längsschwellen* to *Querschwellen*) and thereby, too, adopted the German norm. Otherwise the lucrative advantages of a favorable geographic location would have been forfeited.[32]

Meanwhile, as already documented, Baden's altercations with Württemberg continued. Political leaders in Karlsruhe were not insensitive to the entreaties from Stuttgart for east-west lines, which were "not to be dismissed out of hand." In 1843 Minister of the Interior Marschall von Bieberstein submitted over forty pages of glowing prose to the cabinet in which he unveiled his vision of a "railway network not only of Germany but Europe" that would reach from the Black Sea to the Atlantic and from northern Germany to the Adriatic. But Baden's paramount concern was to protect its watch on the Rhine—specifically, the rail center and inland port of Mannheim—against Württemberg's intrusion. This objective was the basis of a long and frustrating (for Stuttgart) debate on whether to favor a connection via Bretten and Bruchsal or Pforzheim and Durlach. Württemberg wanted the former; Baden insisted on the latter. Stalled by the popular uprisings in Baden during 1848, Württemberg's legates returned to the fray thereafter "with strengthened resolve" and obtained a treaty for Bretten-Bruchsal at the end of 1850. In due time, of course, both lines were built.[33]

One final issue deserves our attention: the railroad bridge at Kehl, which was implicit from the beginning of Baden's planning. After all, why lay tracks to Kehl if not to cross over to Strasbourg? And of what value was Marschall's visionary scheme (not to mention that of Napoleon III) unless the French Eastern Railway Company became attached to Baden's state network? Karlsruhe consequently decided to move ahead with the bridge project in 1844. Yet many years would again pass before the deed was done. The Diet of the German Bund, which held a hypothetical veto, approved construction of the bridge in 1858 with the sole provision that the German half be mined for self-destruction in case of war. The work was completed three years later, and for Baden another historical phase seemed to be opening after decades of defending its own narrow interests. The new Minister of Commerce, Gideon Weizel, confidently wrote in 1862 of the "*necessity*" of expanding his state's contacts with its neighbors.[34] Was the man in charge of Baden's railway network thereby announcing an end to particularism and the beginning of an era of international trade? Perhaps that was his intention, but first there was the nagging question of Germany's national unity.

Prussia and the Push for Unification

When Otto von Bismarck became the prime minister of Prussia in September 1862, he had little acquaintance with the world of German railways. He would soon learn. For the time being he inherited a regime that had, after a flirtation with interventionist policy in the 1850s, virtually renounced altogether any state control of the private railroad companies. An official census of such enterprises counted twenty-two of them located at least partially on Prussian soil. The government's ownership was meanwhile confined to the original three state lines plus a more recent connection in Lower Silesia and the Berlin beltway, five in all.[35]

After a brief pause at the conclusion of the previous decade, expansion of the Prussian railways resumed in the 1860s. It would continue into the early 1870s, during which time twenty-seven new private companies received concessions from the Prussian state.[36] This spectacular boom of private railway enterprise in northern Germany now spawned a number of moral equivalents to the American "robber barons" of the late nineteenth century. The most notorious of them was Bethel Henry Strousberg, the so-called "railroad king" of the period. Not coincidentally, this phenomenally clever financier reached the apex of his success in the late 1860s. His many projects included a cluster of tracks around Hanover, the lines from Berlin to Halle and Görlitz, Frankfurt-an-der-Oder to Posen, and Breslau into the Balkans. But like many a German capitalist, to finish the story, Strousberg became overextended in the rampant speculation that followed the war of 1870. He also had to suffer charges of corruption in his dealings with banks and politicians, including the Prussian Minister of Commerce Itzenplitz, who was forced to resign in 1872 under suspicion of scandal. By 1873 Strousberg's star had fallen.[37]

These details were characteristic of Bismarck's first decade in office, which was marked by laissez-faire liberalism in Prussian railway politics. In fact, of the major German states, Prussia was the least prone to regulation. Elsewhere, especially in Saxony and the South, the functioning of state networks was a steady preoccupation of the highest authorities. Judging by the plethora of relevant dispatches to be found in the archives, railways always commanded the close attention of statesmen and politicians. By contrast, as we know, Bismarck had other things on his mind after 1862, and his government made a studious effort (Itzenplitz aside) to stay out of railway affairs, apart from routinely granting concessions to private companies. Hence we cannot argue, in Prussia's case, that such matters prefigured the path to national unity. Political issues are best understood in other terms, not as a result of economic necessity.[38]

The year 1866 altered nearly everything in Germany, notably including the railroad map. We may confine ourselves here to listing four principal changes that occurred before 1870, although their ramifications are beyond counting. Our purpose cannot be a lengthy narrative of German political history but a brief analysis of how these events affected the railway picture.

First, Austria was excluded. Among the manifest consequences of Prussia's swift military victory over the Habsburg monarchy (about which more later), this was perhaps the least important for the annals of transportation. That was so because, though abruptly separated from Germany, Austria nonetheless remained a member of the Association of German Railway Administrations, and its trains continued to roll much as before. True, the VDEV's newspaper henceforth relegated reports from the Habsburg realm to the rubric of foreign affairs—"Vienna letters," as they were charmingly called—but Central European timetables and freight schedules scarcely reflected the sensational turn of events in 1866. The Prussian decision not to enter Vienna nor to annex Habsburg territory was tantamount to leaving the Austrian railway system intact. Commercial relations with the two closest German states, Bavaria and Saxony, both of which had sided with Austria against Prussia in the recent conflict, were effortlessly restored. While Berlin's attention shifted westward, therefore, the Austrian frontier was virtually as active as ever.[39]

Second, the southern German states were cut adrift. Had a single block been thereby formed and if something approaching a unified transportation system had emerged south of the Main, the entire scene would have been transformed by the creation of a third Germany. But we have seen how deeply particularism was entrenched in the southern states and how north-south trade routes had long taken precedence over east-west passages. Habits and roadbeds were not easily repositioned, nor was political leadership suddenly emboldened by a military conflict most southerners deplored. To the contrary, caution and hesitation became more than ever the prevailing mood in Munich, Stuttgart, and Karlsruhe alike. We may take as typical a set of instructions sent in February 1867 by the Bavarian premier, Chlodwig von Hohenlohe, to his legation in Berlin. Prussia's dominance of Germany, he wrote, was now a fact of life. The Prussian state commanded a population of 30 million and a victorious army of 800,000. It would therefore be desirable to arrange some sort of "international" alliance with Berlin in order to strengthen Munich's position against (unspecified) dangers that threatened. If Bavaria were an independent political entity, like Switzerland or Belgium, an autonomous course might be proper. But the historical, national, and commercial ties to the rest of Germany did not allow the luxury of isolation. Hence Bavaria should seek "participation in the material advantages of a greater collectivity." Hohenlohe assumed, however, that "the independence and integrity of the southern states" as well as the sovereignty of their dynasties would be preserved. In these elegant phrases we find a dollop of realism mixed into an immense brew of ambiguity. The future may have been uncertain, but it was most unlikely to contain a resolution unconnected to the colossus of the North.[40]

Third, a North German Confederation was founded. After 1866 the existence of the German Bund in Frankfurt had to be terminated. The stage for so many rhetorical duels between Prussia and Austria in the past, the former Diet became instantly defunct once this contest was moved onto the battlefield. As for the Zollverein, it had also been made obsolete by the events of 1866 and needed to be reconstituted to conform to the new circumstances. In addition, the relationship between the new Confederation and the southern states required clarification. All of this agenda went into the brief, complex, and inglorious history of the German Zollparlament, founded by Bismarck in July 1867. Suffice it to say that this body furthered neither the cause of southern cooperation nor that of national unity. Yet perhaps the biggest loser of 1866 was Saxony. Militarily occupied within three days after the outbreak of armed hostilities, then allowed to preserve its ruling house if not its dignity, the kingdom on the Elbe was inexorably drawn into the Prussian orbit and left dangling indecorously from the underbelly of the North German Confederation. This posture was rendered all the more uncomfortable by a paragraph about railways in the 1867 constitution. According to Article 41, any railroads deemed necessary for the defense or general commerce of the Confederation might be constructed at its expense "even against the objection of member states." If taken seriously and strictly enforced, the basic law of the Confederation would have ended any pretense of Saxon autonomy. Little wonder that Dresden and the southern capitals were appalled at the prospects for their independent railway networks or that a resurgence of particularism soon became evident in popular elections for the Zollparlament. By 1869, as a result, Bismarck had largely lost interest in it. National unity, if it came, would now have to be achieved by other means.[41]

Fourth, Prussia was enlarged. The list of Berlin's principal annexations included Schleswig-Holstein, Hanover, Hesse-Kassel, Nassau, and the city of Frankfurt. By far this was the most important consequence of 1866. Prussia thereby added more than four million souls to its populace and, simultaneously, a host of railroads to its network. Many of these lines were state-owned, the number of which in Prussia increased from five to twelve. It should be added that such aggrandizement was not regarded by contemporaries as solely a Prussian grab for power, though many Saxons and southerners thought so. Across northern Germany some people welcomed their new citizenship in the expectation that they would henceforth benefit from the largess of the Prussian crown. Petitions began to pour into Berlin from localities in the annexed territories that supported a railroad project in their vicinity. A bloated Prussia was arguably better than a voracious Prussia.[42]

The extreme complexity of events just prior to the war of 1870 precludes a detailed reconstruction here of their chronology. Nor can we be absolutely certain about the intentions of Bismarck, ever the master at keeping his options open. Yet a few observations are permissible. Within the Reichstag of the North German Confederation, growing support for a more unified railway network was beginning to coalesce. In March 1869 a motion was brought to the floor for the creation of a "special committee" to study the "entire transportation system." Despite an explicit assertion that this action was not politically motivated, it is impossible to mistake its thrust. The most arresting aspect of such parliamentary agitation was the support it received from those Reichstag deputies who could loosely be grouped as liberals—including fabled names like Miquel, Bennigsen, and Lasker—who saw in expansion of the Confederation's prerogatives a chance to limit those of the Prussian monarchy. Barely a year later, in April 1870, another motion from that quarter urged the chancellor to develop "common guidelines" for the administration of the north German railroads.[43]

Apparently Bismarck was willing. His extensive correspondence in the prewar period indicated a drift in his attitude toward a greater centralism that would not be confined to Prussia. In December 1869 he lamented to Minister of Commerce Itzenplitz the "difficulties" (*Übelstände*) caused by the scattered patchwork of state and private railways in Prussia. What was needed, he wrote, was the creation of a more coherent system so that "the railroads in the territory of the [North German] Confederation might actually be administered as a single network." A Prussian conservative to the core, Itzenplitz was not convinced that the Confederation, even while moving toward obligatory rules, should force the individual states into measures such as lowering rates. After all, he pointed out in a memo to Bismarck, the states always had to worry about "profitability" (*Rentabilität*). In his customary scrawl with a blunt black pencil, the chancellor jotted a response in the margin: "Profitability is not the sole interest of the state; the needs of the populace are at least equally valid." Bismarck as the champion of popular opinion? Minimally, we may conclude that he was becoming skeptical about the narrow claims of Prussian particularism.[44]

This supposition is corroborated by another exchange in the spring of 1870 between Bismarck and Theodor Weishaupt, current director of the Prussian railway administration within the Ministry of Commerce. Weishaupt obviously shared Itzenplitz's concerns, and he therefore cautioned the chancellor against the inception of a "special organ" (meaning a central committee) for the regulation of railroads by the North German Confederation; rather, he contended, it would be advisable to strengthen the authority of the existing Prussian bureaucracy—ergo, himself. To this modest proposal Bismarck's reply was cool and somewhat enigmatic: "But it is important in my opinion to bring into harmony the interests of the public and the railway administrations." With all due caution in interpreting Bismarck's habitually sphinxlike pronouncements, we may nevertheless note two things: the contradiction implied by the word "but" and the reiterated invocation of the public interest. At the very least, his statement displays a recognition of an existing dichotomy between centripetal and centrifugal forces. Less clear was how they were to be reconciled.[45]

In sum, it is not fanciful to imagine Bismarck—and with him the German nation—consciously poised in early 1870 on the threshold of a new era. Since 1866, a victorious and expanded Prussia had indisputably been the base of Bismarck's power, but the final solution of his political problems might yet lie in transcending the limits of the Prussian state and embracing a unified German Reich. Between the tendencies of centralism and those of its opponents, a tug of war had begun in earnest.

Before the Take-Off

Amusing as it might be to speculate about how the German economy would have developed after 1815 had there been no railways, the fact remains that trains and tracks did appear. True, the marketplace would not have remained static without steam engines, and some economic development would have occurred in any case. And true also, we cannot precisely measure the effect of railway transportation on German commerce, given the multiplicity of factors to be weighed in the total. Yet such counterfactual propositions are finally a tease, and we had best get on with what actually happened, when, and why.[46]

Most economic historians have done exactly that and have concluded that railway engines provided the elemental force of Germany's extraordinary growth in the nineteenth century. What we are observing, several of them have concluded, was one grand take-off from an agricultural to an industrial society. There is much to recommend this view, and the statistics of German industrial expansion are not easily gainsaid. But there is an obvious danger of exaggerating and of allowing the known outcome—Germany's indisputable industrial preeminence in Europe at the end of the century—to color our interpretation of its origins. Perhaps it is wise not to push the take-off theory too far back in time and instead to allow the period before 1870 to have its own history.[47]

We are better advised to stake out a middle ground. There are persuasive reasons for doing so. For one, the vaunted statistics of industrial growth are only crude approximations and must, especially when attempting to draw national comparisons, be treated with caution and some skepticism. For another, it is quite impossible to disaggregate the impact of railways from the rest of industrial enterprise. We know that they were important, but no one has ever devised a formula to quantify that importance with any precision. Raw figures are fine, and some will be cited here, but they do not a certainty make. Finally, as the consultation of a railroad atlas will confirm, we are dealing before 1870 mainly with local interests and fragmentary patterns. There were until that date few regional networks and no national systems in sight. We are observing, in short, only the beginnings of a nexus of technological innovation and economic growth, the erratic construction of a platform for what might later be justifiably termed a take-off in Germany. But there is little evidence within the given chronological framework for a full-blown notion of an Industrial Revolution, which may be overwrought and misleading when applied to railroads. The circumspect phrase of one expert is more nearly on the mark: these years were a time of "technological maturation" in which "the railroad was basic."[48]

Germany entered the post-Napoleonic era with three commercial handicaps, for each of which railroads provided an offset. As so often emphasized here, the first was traditional *Kleinstaaterei* that created a need to cross borders and create regional networks. If Germany had consisted of a few large states, things might have been different. But geography and political frontiers were often at odds, and commerce by rail was intolerant of long detours. To be sure, there were some curious instances of lines purposely skirting boundaries to avoid negotiation of interstate treaties; but many barriers were soon breached. The first German railway to cross a domestic border was the Magdeburg-Leipzig line in 1840, and the first international connection led from Cologne into Belgium just three years later. Although particularism often delayed this process, as in the case of Ulm, the pressure to elevate railway construction to a regional level was inexorable. Realization of the recurrent fantasy of an Orient Express was hence only a matter of time, albeit a time that came after 1870.[49]

Germany's second lack was a linkage among regional networks. The very mention of Ulm evokes that problem, and we have naturally dwelled on the historical disunity of the southern states nakedly revealed in their railway politics. A narrative of the diplomacy of the Paris-Vienna connection would read like a Feydeau comedy, with doors opening and slamming while various actors stalk on and off the stage. Again, one cannot fail to underscore the obstacles along the way and to observe that the significance of interstate commerce in the South remained minimal before 1870. If the North was more successful, it was not only because the need was more urgent but also that Prussia was simply larger. To put this matter into perspective, it should be recalled that Prussia's past had to do primarily with Poland and Russia, Sweden, and of course Austria. Seen from Berlin, the Rhineland was a recently acquired and distant colony that needed to be attached to what was now called the "motherland," meaning Brandenburg and East Prussia. Because Germany's main rivers—the Rhine, Weser, Elbe, and Oder—run northward to the sea, railroads might well perform this task. And so they did, eventually, with stunning results. By 1870 the Ruhr had become the industrial heartland of Europe, and Prussia's new horizons stretched westward on metal tracks.[50]

The third handicap was a need for outlets. Germany lacked what only its neighbors could supply: saltwater seaports. Early in the century Hamburg alone, confined within the choppy North Sea, counted as a major German harbor. German commerce required access to Antwerp and Rotterdam, which treaties and trains could provide. Let it be said that these commercial arrangements were reciprocal and that the small lowland countries were eager to have Germany's business. But it was axiomatic that the full potential of German industry could only be realized through the pursuit of international trade. Germany was thus condemned to be an expansive European power or none at all. The same was true when facing south, where the impediments for commerce were still more formidable. Austria was connecting Vienna to Trieste; France, Paris to Marseille. And Germany? More than one writer pointed to Genoa as Germany's natural port on the Mediterranean, and talk of a transalpine tunnel to make that possible was already heard before 1848. Railroads on this scale required large visions and huge capital investments, both of which were scarce before 1870. Slowly, very slowly, plans began to take shape that would bond Germany and Italy. Although these were not realized until later, the smart money was already speculating on Switzerland.[51]

In all of the foregoing we can perceive a gradual unification of the German economy in which the development of railway networks was both cause and effect. The improving technology of rail transportation tended in two regards to level the price structure across the land: by hauling goods from one region to another and by lowering the rates for doing so. Sales rose, costs declined. Canals were still a factor, especially in northern Germany, and the competition from waterways kept railroad officials on their toes. Actually it worked both ways. In 1860, for instance, the Bavarian Minister of Commerce expressed concern that the increase of freight on the Nürnberg-Regensburg rail line was hurting the region's canal trade; he thereupon intervened to lower canal rates. But in the following year he complained that Hungarian grain was being shipped in larger quantities via Trieste rather than on Bavarian tracks between Salzburg and Mainz; he then ordered steps to lower railway rates. This kind of downdraft was evident everywhere in Germany and was felt by state and private companies alike.[52]

Uniquely, the railway companies were at once purveyors and consumers of products within the leading sectors of heavy industry, including iron and later steel rails. The metal industry, including such emerging family dynasties as the Krupps and Wendels, flourished because thousands of tons of track were needed to build networks that could then carry more tons of track. The statistics show what an incentive this became for German firms: in 1843 fully 88 percent of the rails used in German construction were imported from Great Britain; a decade later it was only 50 percent; and by 1863 the figure was under 15 percent. We must surmise that railways were both stimulating the growth of domestic industry and laying the groundwork for a national economy.[53]

The same was true of the German locomotive industry. As the century moved past its midpoint, railway engines became larger and more powerful. That is, they both consumed and pulled more metal. By 1855 the various German rail administrations (including that of Austria) were operating over 2000 locomotives built by forty-six different firms, of which the most important were Borsig in Berlin (630), Wien-Raab in Vienna (207), Maffei in Munich (183), and Kessler in Stuttgart (165). Foreign imports were still a factor, especially from Stephenson in Newcastle (145), but falling. By 1860 Borsig's total production had surpassed

1000 engines, and the relative share of English, Belgian, and American manufacturers continued to decline. As of 1865, so the Association of German Railway Administrations said, exactly 4768 locomotives were in service on its lines, of which only 574 were imported; in addition, sixteen German firms had meanwhile exported over a thousand engines.[54] The need for new locomotives and replacements for those retired had reached an annual average of 580, with the level of exports at about 120 a year. Hence, the total of German (still including Austrian) locomotive production was 700 per annum and, the VDEV proudly announced, "this number will doubtless increase very soon."[55] We know, because of the wars of 1866 and 1870, that the "doubtless" in this statement reflected a misplaced optimism, but the expanding German locomotive industry had unquestionably become a juggernaut.

For good measure, we may include the coal industry. During the first half of the nineteenth century, when the railways were in their infancy, Germany needed little coal and produced little. But one thing inevitably led to another as big enterprises interlocked. In order to manufacture the engines that burned huge quantities of coal and the rails that carried them, the metal trades needed vast supplies of coal for smelting. Before 1848 German mines extracted barely three million tons of coal a year. By 1860 that amount had nearly quadrupled, and by the end of that decade, Germany's annual production of coal reached almost 30 million tons.[56] In other words, commerce in coal increased approximately ten-fold in the two decades before 1870, and a rising percentage of that freight was simultaneously carried and consumed by trains. Although exact calculations are admittedly impossible, one must also attempt to conceive of this remarkable expansion in terms of the people involved: the hundreds of thousands of individuals—executives, employees, workers, miners—whose lives were thrust into the maelstrom of industry, all of whom needed to be housed, clothed, and nourished. Ideally, then, our account should go on to analyze the statistics of growth in the building trades, the textile industry, and agriculture. But this exercise is best left to the econometricians. Whatever their reckoning, they would surely agree that railways in every instance played a stellar role, whether in the more rapid distribution of cement and wood, of wool and cotton, or of wheat and wine.[57]

Three caveats must be registered here. The first, as noted, concerns the unreliability of numbers. We are faced, as one authority has gloomily stated, with "the virtual impossibility of proving anything about theories of growth through the use of history, and the propensity of economic historians, with rare exceptions, to overgeneralize."[58] The problem begins with data-gathering. In Germany dozens of public and private railway administrations kept their separate financial records, each with an idiosyncratic system of bookkeeping. The same was true of manufacturing firms, many of which had a checkered history full of erratic financial transactions. To take just one outstanding example, the infamous Lahusen dynasty in Bremen helped to make that city into a center of the textile industry in Germany. But eventually its affairs became embroiled in family and political disputes, its office files were scattered or confiscated, and its records left in disarray. Scholars therefore rely at their peril on the neat rows of official numbers published regularly by government bureaucracies, and readers must beware.[59]

A second limitation is that evidence of the impact made by railways on the general economy becomes less and less distinct as one moves away from the enterprises most directly affected, such as metals, locomotives, and coal. In the textile industry, for example, it became common in the nineteenth century to build spur tracks right into the factory grounds, thereby facilitating the movement of raw materials in and finished products out. But who is to measure the precise difference that they made in the development of German manufacturing or to separate the exact share of commerce owing to rails from that of waterways, which brought the bales of raw cotton from America or India to the railheads of northern European ports? Multiply these complications by several thousand and one would begin to address the problem of statistical accuracy.

Finally, it follows that the influence of rail transportation on German localities and regions was very uneven. Some places were clearly benefited, others left as economic backwaters. The Ruhr, the Saar, and parts of Silesia became industrial giants, but that mattered little to villagers in Schleswig-Holstein, the Bavarian Alps, or the Black Forest. Once more, the statistical evidence is suspect, but the overall pattern of German economic growth suggests that railways usually worked in favor of the consolidation of large businesses, without precluding the commerce of many smaller ones, especially those near city stations and rural stops where shops tended to cluster.[60]

In lieu of a summary, we may conclude this overview of some commercial aspects of German railways before 1870 by considering the steps leading to completion of the St. Gotthard Tunnel, which proved to be incomparably the greatest economic coup of nineteenth-century Europe. With hindsight, it is not difficult to reconstruct the evolution of this mighty project in four distinct phases. By doing so, we may recall several of the central themes of the time during which Germany began rehearsing for its role as the dominant economic power on the Continent.

In the first phase, interest arose in the late 1840s about the feasibility of a direct rail link between southern Germany and northern Italy by means of a railway tunnel through Switzerland. The chambers of commerce of Milan and Genoa were especially keen about the prospect of easy access to the rich German market, and, accordingly, they offered tidy subsidies to study the likely costs and alternative routes. They were joined by three Swiss cantons, which in turn addressed inquiries to the three major south German states about their participation. When everyone's attention was suddenly diverted by the stirring events of 1848, however, momentum was lost and the matter languished.[61]

A second phase, the decade of the 1850s, was long on speculation but short on concrete proposals. The German press was replete with articles and editorials about various possibilities, and the Swiss names that would preoccupy European planners for years to come became familiar: Lukmanier, Splügen, Simplon, St. Gotthard, and Mt. Cenis. Each had its advocates. Mt. Cenis concerned only Italy and France as a link from Milan and Turin to Grenoble, Lyon, and the Rhône Valley. St. Gotthard was central and would lead from Genoa and Milan northward to Bern and Basel, whence into the Rhine corridor via Baden on the right bank or Strasbourg on the left. Lukmanier was much farther east and, because it would better serve Constance and Lindau, was attractive for Bavaria. Splügen was supported by the Rothschilds for financial reasons of their own. Simplon's time had not yet come, because its utility would depend on prior decisions about the others.[62]

The penultimate phase began with a treaty signed in June 1862 between Italy and France to begin the Mt. Cenis project. Adored by the francophone western cantons of Switzerland, it left no alpine rail freight route between there and the Brenner Pass, controlled by Austria, at the country's extreme eastern flank. To many German Swiss, including the current president of the Helvetic Confederation Emil Welti, it therefore seemed that a central rail passage was imperative. Subsidies for engineering studies were forthcoming from Lucerne and Bern, and the response from Italy was positive. And Welti felt encouraged to renew contacts with the German South. There, however, he quickly encountered the ensconced particularism that we know. Baden wanted only St. Gotthard and was more than willing to offer a subsidy to ensure its selection. To the contrary, Bavaria had no interest in a route that would draw trade away from its own north-south artery. Württemberg, as always, hesitated and attempted to bargain: it would support Baden only if progress were assured on its east-west connections, thereby securing for Stuttgart a portion of increased Rhineland commerce. Preliminary discussions in 1865 established that both Italy and Switzerland were likely to grant large subsidies. The rest would be up to the German states. But how would they ever agree?[63]

By 1866, in a fourth phase, the issue awaited a German reaction. But in Berlin the prospect of constructing a tunnel in central Switzerland appeared remote and relatively inconsequential when compared to an imminent conflict with Austria. Not until that was settled and the North German Confederation was founded could the question regain the surface. As twenty years earlier, the impulse originated in Italy, where the new national regime decisively threw its support to the choice of St. Gotthard. That unsubtle signal was received most clearly in Karlsruhe, the German capital that had the most to gain. The central route through Basel would obviously bring "not insignificant advantages" for Baden, observed its current Minister of Commerce. The Italian announcement thus required a "rapid decision" in Germany to subsidize that project if it were to be realized.[64]

The crucial new factor was that Otto von Bismarck was now prepared to place the substantial weight of the North German Confederation behind St. Gotthard. A month-long conference in the Swiss capital of Bern in September and October 1869 worked out the details. Of an estimated total expense of 187,000,000 Swiss Francs, most of which would be financed from the sale of stocks, the sum of 85 million was to be collected in the form of state subsidies: 45 million from Italy, 20 million from Switzerland, and another 20 million from the German states.[65] The only problem was to gather it. Without resorting here to a lengthy narrative, we may record that Bismarck's consummate skills as a unifier of the German nation were sharpened to achieve a positive outcome. In the spring of 1870 he assembled delegates from the states (Bavaria declined to attend) at a conference in Berlin. There, interestingly, Baden agreed to a contribution of 3 million Swiss Francs, Prussia only 1.5.[66] But in the meantime, at the chancellor's behest, Prussian Minister of Commerce Itzenplitz was soliciting the large private railway companies in northern Germany, three of which pledged a million SF each. Once the German quota was reached, the formal signature of a tripartite international treaty on 20 June 1870 was a conclusion foregone. Only weeks before the outbreak of a war with France, Bismarck thus successfully completed negotiations for the commercial agreement that would help to sustain a German economic take-off in the decades ahead.[67]

Strategic Thought and Military Action

Few subjects have attracted more scholarly attention than German military organization. Many excellent histories have plotted its progress in greater or lesser detail and with more or less admiration. All agree that railways played an increasing part in German strategic thinking in the nineteenth century. Indeed, they became central to military planning everywhere in Europe.[68]

The peculiarity of the German circumstance, of course, lay in facing two fronts. At the very beginning, even before the first steam engine rolled on Bavarian tracks, a Hanoverian mining engineer by the name of Grote balanced his prediction that the railroads would soon bring a stimulus to the general commercial interests of the German nation with a warning about the strategic threat posed by the "two great militant and potentially dangerous neighboring states, France and Russia."[69] Virtually the same vocabulary was used during the ensuing decade by more widely cited writers, such as Friedrich List and Carl Eduard von Pönitz, who attempted to define the German geopolitical situation.[70] Clearly, what most interested these early commentators was the defensive capability of railways to transfer combat troops from east to west or vice versa.

The focus in the 1840s, however, was on France. With its wastelands and wide track gauge, Russia was too distant, too plodding, to constitute an immediate threat. On the contrary, the French were busily augmenting their offensive prowess by extending rail lines to their eastern frontier. Prussia's man in Frankfurt, Count Dönhoff, reported Bavarian worries that the French army could amass 100,000 troops on the Rhine within a week.[71] Josef Maria von Radowitz complained that a connection between Strasbourg and the left-bank fortress at Germersheim might prove "useful to the French."[72] The current Prussian Minister of War, General von Canitz, likewise admonished in 1846 that east-west transportation in Germany was "completely underdeveloped" and that hence the French army might "suddenly intrude" without fear of serious opposition.[73] In the same year, while presiding over the Diet in Frankfurt, Dönhoff summed up the concerns of these and other military critics: "North, middle, and south Germany are consequently very threatened." The Bund responded in 1847 with a resolution that six new east-west lines should be prepared to counter France.[74]

If such a rhetorical splurge went unheeded, it was primarily for two salient reasons that we have already examined. One was a lack of coordination, especially in the North, among private and state railway companies. Already in 1839 David Hansemann raised the issue of how private companies could be strategically integrated in case of war. Would they simply be taken over by the state, used for military purposes as long as needed, and then reimbursed for their services? In 1841 the Prussian cabinet forwarded an *aide mémoire* to the monarch that pointed out this problem and recommended that steps be taken to increase government control over private companies.[75] A second hindrance, particularly in the South, was the inveterate particularism of the states. In Bavaria, for example, military commanders were always more amenable than the political leadership to cooperation with other states in opening strategic rail conduits, mindful as they were of the Palatinate's vulnerability. But when pressure was applied in 1846 by the military committee of the Bund to hasten completion of a main route across southern Germany to the Rhine, Bavarian Prime Minister Karl von Abel sniffed that such strategic arguments were "scarcely a justification" for altering his state's priorities.[76]

Because Germany's railway administrations were scattered among more than thirty states and dozens of private companies, the total of their construction boom in the 1840s was difficult to gather. At the beginning of the decade the German territories had only 469 kilometers of track; by the end, nearly 6000.[77] To that extent the competition among smaller firms and states was salutary. But amid all this activity there was no denying a tacky incoherence to which the founding of the Association of German Railway Administrations in 1847 was an initial response. From a military standpoint, the lack of any large-scale planning became shockingly apparent in 1848. During that spring, democratic stirrings in Baden erupted into insurrection, and some Prussian troops were called in to quell the populace. But the soldiers had to move mostly by highways—we remember that Baden's track gauge was still anomalous—and, as the moderate liberal Cologne banker Gustav Mevissen later remarked, it was doubtful that such popular uprisings could have been contained had they occurred under transport conditions of winter.[78] Hardly less unsettling was the specter of an invasion by fanatical republican troops from France. An excited statement of alarm from Baden to the military committee of the Confederation in March 1848 conjured the scenario of an incursion by "huge masses of hungry [French] laborers," followed by the assault of "thousands of armed workers from Paris across the German frontier."[79] These hyperbolic fantasies soon dissipated, but they epitomized a heightened awareness of German incapacity to deal with domestic or foreign violence. Thereupon, Prussia's diplomatic humiliation by Austria at Olmütz in 1850 only underscored the point: in railway affairs, as in other regards, German national unity was far from a reality.[80]

So the Germans returned in the 1850s to the *status quo ante*, a retrenchment of ruling houses that deserved any label but that of a liberal New Era. It was also a time for countless studies by various state administrations of the potential military deployment of railroads. A lengthy list of such reports and memoranda could be compiled, the cumulative effect of which was to confirm just what 1848 had already revealed. If the German Bund were to be militarily viable, it would need a much tighter regulation of its several railway networks. One of the few practical restrictions on the autonomy of the states, dating back to a resolution adopted by the Diet in 1832, was an agreement that no bridges could be built to cross borders without permission from Frankfurt. In only two instances, however, did this issue come to serious debate. One concerned a route in the Palatinate that might, with access to Baden's main north-south lines, connect Neustadt to Strasbourg. Completion of the project would require a bridge over the Lauter River near Weissenburg, to which Bavaria raised a question about its potential military use by the French. But an investigation showed that the proposed structure would span the Lauter at a point where the water was only 8 meters wide and less than 2 meters deep. Since the stream could thus be easily forded, Munich's objection was waived.[81] A second instance, already mentioned, was far more consequential for strategic reasons: the broad rail link across the Rhine between Strasbourg and Kehl. Both Baden and the regime of Napoleon III were eager to complete the bridge, but the Bund had to be persuaded. The matter dragged on for a year after the early summer of 1857, during which time construction proceeded from both ends, even though the railway administration in Karlsruhe could not technically allow any operations on it without formal consent from Frankfurt. Faced with a fait accompli—a bridge virtually completed, aside from the mining of its pillars—the German Diet acquiesced and a treaty was signed in June 1858 that finally opened the way for a Paris-Vienna railway across southern Germany.[82]

In standard military histories one ordinarily hears at this juncture a loud drumroll heralding the appearance of Count Helmuth von Moltke, who was appointed chief of the Prussian General Staff in 1858. Yet there are three compelling reasons to mute that sound here. First, at the time of his selection by Prince Wilhelm of Prussia, Moltke was still unknown and inexperienced, without any previous service in the field. He initially took his place in a tiny suite of offices at the Ministry of War, where his modest duties consisted mostly of topographical studies and data-gathering about lines of communication with neighboring states, notably including railways. To say that Moltke at first ran a slightly glorified map room might be too severe, but certainly the concept of a General Staff did not yet have the glowing luster that it later acquired.

Second, Moltke's reputation as a military genius, in the words of a circumspect biographer, emerged only "very gradually."[83] Though a North German (from Mecklenburg), the son of a Danish officer, he was not to the manor born a Prussian. After several years of obscurity as a military consultant in Turkey, he returned to Germany in the early 1840s. If anything distinguished him from his contemporaries, it was a precocious recognition of the strategic importance of railways. He gained some practical experience (one wonders how much?) by joining the board of directors of the new Hamburg-Berlin rail company. But his military career remained mediocre until a fortuitous personal encounter with Wilhelm, who became regent, then king, in the mid-1850s. Though Moltke had caught his monarch's eye, he did not yet have his ear. Direct access (*Immediatverkehr*) to the throne and to Prussian field commanders was not granted to him until a decade later. Meanwhile, he was overshadowed by Prussia's dominant military personality of that era, General Albrecht von Roon, the ultra-conservative Minister of War during the 1860s. Not until the Prusso-Danish conflict of 1864, when his advice proved sounder than that of Roon's other advisers, did Moltke gain prominence.[84]

Third, for all of his renowned cultivation and philosophical bent, Moltke was above all a military technician, trained in a cadet school like the majority of his fellow officers. He had climbed slowly through the ranks, loyal to his calling and his king. He was decidedly not, as some historians would have it, the representative of a new anti-authoritarian wave of the future—liberal, bourgeois, or whatever—not someone determined to challenge the absolutist traditions of the Hohenzollern crown. Moltke fit the existing mold of a Prussian career officer perfectly well; it was just that he was better at his chosen profession than others. He also had a king who trusted him and, in Bismarck, a brilliant, if bullying, accomplice.[85]

The relevance of these biographical details is easy to spot. As Moltke rose to greatness, so did the General Staff, which was expanded and reorganized in 1864 when a special Railway Section was installed in Berlin. Thereby, very late in the day, railways became institutionally pivotal in Prussia's military planning. What gave this significance, of course, was the impending collapse of the German Bund. The success of the French expeditionary force in Italy had further increased apprehensions in Germany about the Rhenish frontier and Napoleon III's manifest ambitions there. The Bavarian regime continued to worry about "an eventual enemy takeover" in the Palatinate. Baden prepared measures against "an intruding opponent." A Hessian representative pointed out the "absolute necessity" of more double tracks in Germany, which had only 25 percent compared to France's 62 percent.[86] Yet the Bund's attempts to assuage these cares brought only criticism, because everyone knew that its pretensions were the fig leaf of impotence. In 1861 Bavarian Prime Minister Ludwig von der Pfordten objected that the efforts of the Confederation's military committee in Frankfurt, which aspired to be a national war ministry, were producing nothing but friction, whereas what Germany needed was more construction and coordination among the states if railways were to become useful "during a future mobilization."[87]

We know where this was leading. The German Civil War of 1866 followed hard upon its American counterpart. The great military spectacle of two large federated states locked in a struggle between North and South had a number of striking differences and similarities. Apart from the length of combat and the toll in casualties, the main distinction was that the North fought in the United States to preserve the union; in Germany, to divide it. It has also been said, with far less justification, that both conflicts were among the first major railroad wars. Many comparatists agree that the American armies better exploited railways in the field.[88] Indeed, that conclusion deserves to be regarded as an understatement. The Prussians made relatively poor use of military transportation by trains and only very marginally owed victory to them.

Newly established in his revamped General Staff headquarters and still unsure of his triangular relationship with Wilhelm and Bismarck, Moltke was in no position to take charge. The hesitation in Berlin lasted longer than he had hoped, and hence his projection of a quick thrust into Bohemia was barely salvaged since Prussia was able to employ five rail lines toward the combat zone versus Austria's one. Yet these tracks diverged widely and thus presented the Prussians with two intractabilities. Although 200,000 men could be swiftly moved southward by rail within twenty-one days, they were widely dispersed along a 250-mile front once they arrived. Without being able to concentrate by means of transversals, they were therefore extremely vulnerable to a breakthrough by Habsburg troops, had Vienna's commanders but summoned the agility and wit to mount it. Moreover, Moltke's plans had provided for bringing troops to railheads but not for supplying them once they fanned out onto the battlefields. Backed-up boxcars and shortages of food and munitions were the inevitable result. Neither problem was solved and, famously, the decisive battle at Königgrätz became something of a fluke when one Prussian unit stumbled onto the enemy and was saved by the arrival of another—on foot. The conflict, in short, was decided by horses, infantrymen, and the needle gun.[89]

Apart from military operations, we must evaluate the political implications of 1866. One historian acknowledges the advantages gained by Prussia through improved transportation in Germany, then adds: "But it is by no means clear that the railroad made the Bismarckian Reich a natural or necessary political formulation. If one studies a map of the Central European rail system in 1860, any number of political, social, economic, and cultural connections seem possible."[90] Any number? The reality, so often placed in evidence here, was a clear priority accorded to north-south lines in which nearly all of the German states had an important stake. Within Prussia, of course, east-west railroads were crucial bonds between the Rhineland and Berlin, but elsewhere they counted far less. These facts of life help to explain why the southern states offered but token opposition to Prussia's aggression, despite their expressions of sympathy for the Habsburg cause. We are all free to speculate about what the consequences might have been in the hypothetical event of an Austrian triumph in 1866. Nonetheless, the actual outcome was arguably the one most compatible with the existing lay of the land and of its fixed metal tracks.

Even more so, these observations apply to Prussia's relations with France between 1866 and 1870. Napoleon III's hope to coax the southern German states into some kind of coalition with Catholic France and Austria, and thus to prevent their unification with Protestant Prussia, rested on nothing more substantial than the Strasbourg-Kehl bridge. Although the South clearly did not wish to be abjectly absorbed into the North German Confederation, there was no serious question after 1866 about where its real interests were. Properly, most historians tend to dwell on Bismarck's astute outmaneuvering of the "Caesar on the Seine."[91] But his task was surely eased by a frank recognition throughout Germany that present and future commercial links were likely to function best on the basis of a national railway system, no matter what form of federal political structure came to be imposed on it.

In any event, the impression was widespread in Germany that the solution of 1866 was temporary and that a showdown with "the enemy" was inevitable. Certainly that was the view of Helmuth von Moltke, whose immense prestige after Königgrätz—deserved or not—was now secure. While Bismarck was busy fending off French advances to acquire Luxemburg, Moltke prepared almost unnoticed a reform that became essential to the German system of military transportation. Attached to his railway office in Berlin, a central committee of civil and military officials was founded to coordinate mobilization procedures. For every major east-west railway across the territory of the North German Confederation, a so-called "line commission" was created, each of which reported to the General Staff through the central committee. This arrangement removed the principal obstacle to rapid troop movement: the necessity, in many cases, of crossing several state borders or of using the tracks of private companies. Henceforth, soldiers could be moved in one swoop from, say, Berlin to Mainz without changing engines or personnel. In peacetime the borders would remain intact, but in the event of war, civilian authorities would promptly cede their place to military officers. In effect this measure instituted in northern Germany a shadow government, which would assume command in case of conflict. By 1870 six such lines were already operational. Accordingly, in 1869 the schedule projected by Moltke for moving troops to the French frontier was reduced from twenty-four to twenty days. And in the summer of 1870 that feat, transporting over 400,000 men by rail, was actually accomplished in eighteen.[92]

Detailed and explicit regulations for military transportation were drafted for the North German Confederation (including Saxony) and summarily adopted by its legislature. In the chancellor's office, however, that action was deemed insufficient. The new rules still had no application in the southern states, which lacked any strategic norms, and Bismarck's subalterns dutifully launched a campaign to have them adopted below the Main.[93] Baden posed no real problem, since Karlsruhe had abandoned much pretense of military independence and was frankly counting on Prussian aid against a menace from France.[94] Württemberg's legendary ambivalence was again on display, its relations with Baden and Bavaria complicated by cutting a deal on the St. Gotthard Tunnel.[95] In Munich the cabinet was divided. The Bavarian Minister of War favored negotiations with Berlin, and he was weakly seconded by Prime Minister Hohenlohe, who was forced to contend with powerful opposition from particularists fearful that an unwanted war with France would be decided in Berlin without consultation in the South.[96] They were not far wrong. Withal, after hundreds of anxious memos and dispatches, on 26 June 1870 a set of mutual rules was agreed upon, scheduled to go into effect three weeks later.[97] But by that date, 16 July, the diplomatic crisis over the Ems dispatch had reached a boiling point, and a French declaration of war was in all the newspapers. Like the St. Gotthard agreement, the belated adoption of common procedures for wartime military transportation was an improvisation under mounting pressure. It had no effect on the course or outcome of the conflict in 1870, which was thus as properly advertised a Franco-Prussian war.[98]

Postscript: hours after the commencement of hostilities, orders were issued in Baden to destroy the Strasbourg-Kehl railway bridge across the Rhine. Therewith, literally and figuratively (as one says in both French and German), Napoleon III's ambitions fell into the water.

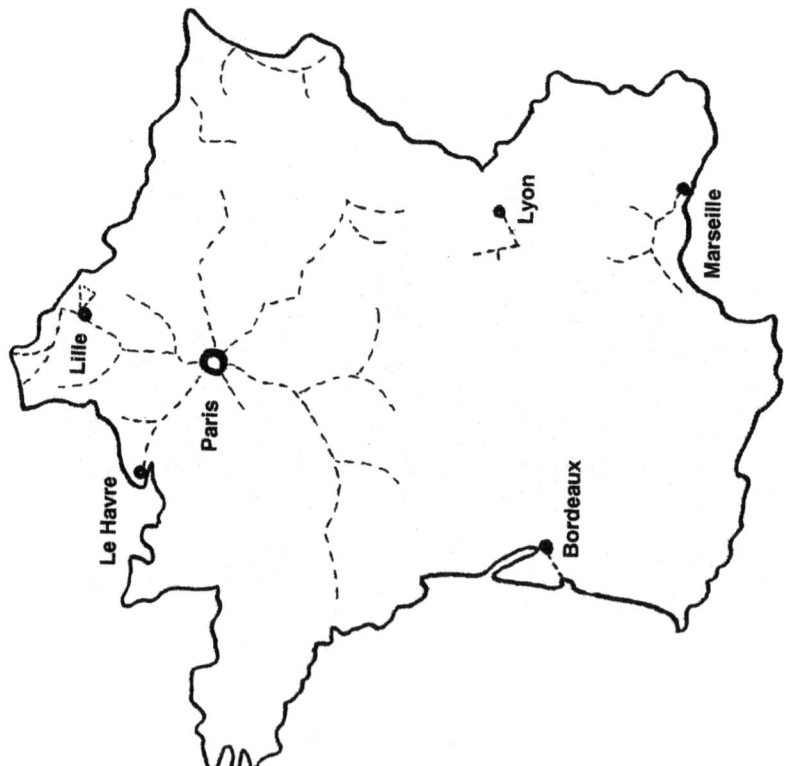

MAP 1: Main Railways in France, 1850

MAP 2: Main Railways in Germany, 1850

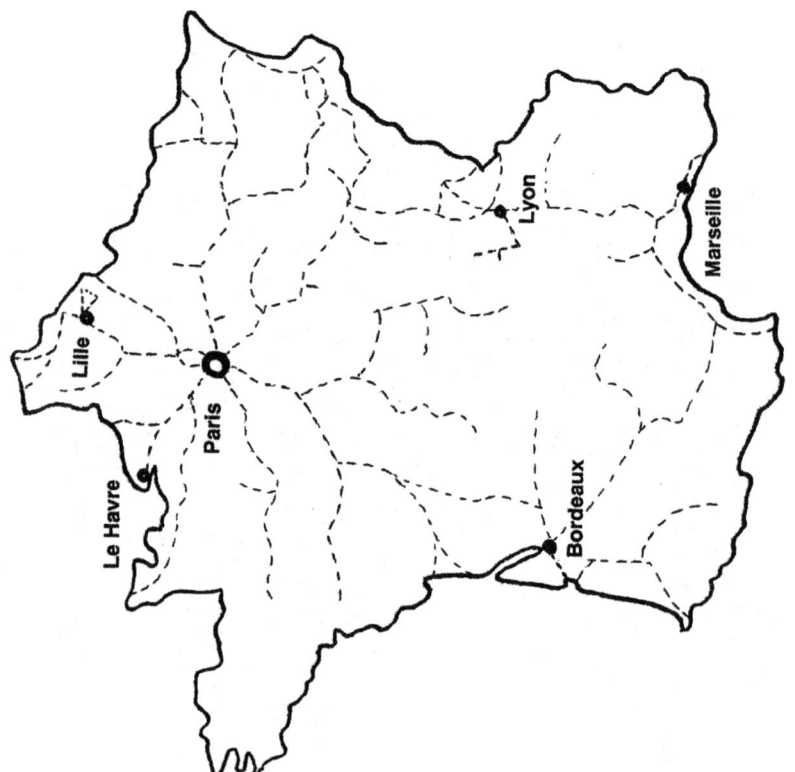

MAP 3: Main Railways in France, 1860

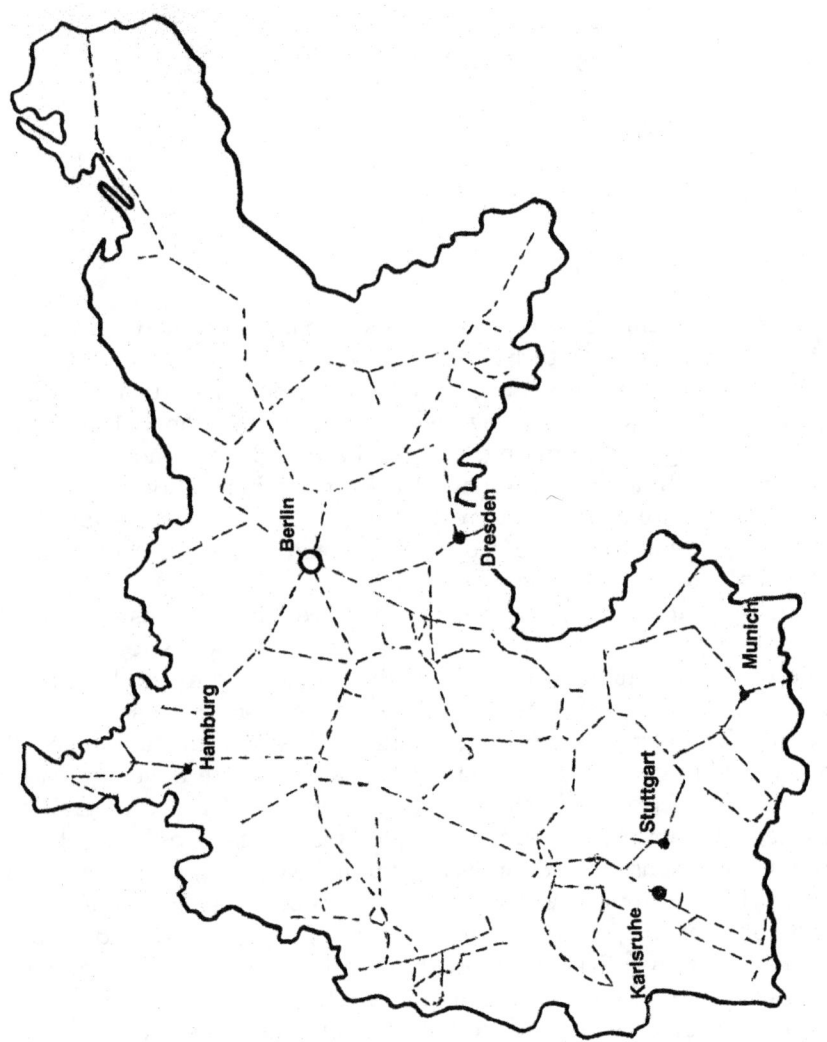

MAP 4: Main Railways in Germany, 1860

Chapter 3

COMPARISONS, 1815–1870

After attempting to treat France and Germany separately, each in its own terms, we may turn now to an explicit comparison of their railway histories from post-Napoleonic origins to the war of 1870. The first thing that strikes the observer is an elemental phenomenon that we might call a technological swamping. Once Britain took the lead in putting steam-powered engines onto metal tracks, the other nations of Europe were bound to follow. The innovation of railways was irresistible, and no European people could afford to ignore them. It soon became simply unthinkable to miss the train.

This assumption implies a second: the advent of railroads stimulated competition among European nation-states. Even in the case of Germany, as we have seen, there was an immediate tendency to think in these global terms, though the institutions to realize them were still lacking. Local interests were initially paramount, to be sure, but the nineteenth century was to be the age of the nation-state, and the development of railways can best be understood by taking that framework for granted. Because British tracks remained separate, unconnected to the Continent without an expensive and time-consuming sea passage, the principal rivalry within Europe was certain to develop between France and Germany. Politicians, diplomats, entrepreneurs, military officers, and railway administrators on both sides of the Rhine anticipated such an eventuality, which surely verged on a self-fulfilling prophecy.

Nothing could be more natural, then, than a comparison of the French and German railway systems, a basic subject close to the core of nineteenth-century European history. Precise statistical measurements may be impossible, or at least dubious, but gaining a sense of similarities and differences is within our capability. To do so, it will be useful to adopt three essential criteria of comparison: administrative organization, economic competition, and military strategy. Each provides a complementary perspective on our topic, and together they should enable us to comprehend it.

Administrative Organization

In one regard, the problem of building railroads was everywhere the same: they would require copious infusions of capital. Yet if investment needs were great, profit motives were correspondingly strong. It is therefore no surprise to note that the first railway patrons in both France and Germany were private financiers, wealthy men who seized an opportunity to enhance their personal fortunes by forming small joint-stock companies to develop a new and more rapid mode of transportation. Before the 1840s this primitive form of capitalism was the rule, resulting in a few scattered rail lines of as yet limited consequence.

Railroad technology never had a tabula rasa. Highway and canal systems already existed and were more or less strictly regulated by the governments of Europe. The integration of rail traffic with other modes of transport was an unavoidable issue, and the role of the state thereby automatically became a question posed. From the beginning, accordingly, technological and political matters were intertwined. Again the rule was clear: the state granted concessions to private companies, which would then—under certain restrictions stipulated in their charter—be free to operate their business. Unclear, however, was the actual degree of state regulation or the subsequent extent of direct state participation. Such general terms describe equally well the early circumstances of the railway industry in the French and German territories.

Some scholars have concluded from their study of this early history that the state actually had a "restraining influence" on the investment and construction of railroads by private enterprises.[1] But the notion that state intervention was a negative factor appears in a comparative view to be simplistic. In the first place, any hindrance due to government interference was surely more prevalent in France than in Germany. An established tradition of etatism, institutions such as Ponts-et-Chaussées that embodied it, and the stoutly conditioned reflexes of centralism made it all but impossible for the French to proceed in creating railway networks without first devising a national scheme of administration for them. Meanwhile, the German states lacked all of the above—or at least they knew such characteristics only as fragments of an inchoate national identity—so that neither the Bund, nor the Zollverein, nor the sprawling Association of German Railway Administrations could remotely attain a level of control possible in France. These obvious distinctions were reflected in the far more rapid tempo of early track-building in the German lands (see Table 5), where standards were less uniform and usually less severe, permitting flimsier and faster construction.

Waiving any suspicions about the utter reliability of such textbook figures, we can fairly assume that in a general way they confirm the more timorous entry of the French into the railway age. That fact qualifies without altering the partial truth that in Germany, too, the state did sometimes constrain private initiative. Better said, political interests

TABLE 5: Completed Railroads in France and Germany, 1850–1869 (kilometers)

	France	Germany		France	Germany
1850	2915	5856	1860	9167	11,089
1851	3248	6143	1861	9626	11,497
1852	3654	6605	1862	10,522	12,048
1853	3954	7147	1863	11,533	12,651
1854	4315	7571	1864	12,362	13,114
1855	5037	7826	1865	13,227	13,900
1856	5852	8613	1866	13,915	14,787
1857	6868	8991	1867	15,000	15,679
1858	8094	9650	1868	15,835	16,316
1859	8840	10,593	1869	16,465	17,215

Source: Michael Stürmer, *Das ruhelose Reich. Deutschland 1866–1918* (Berlin, 1983), p. 76.

occasionally outweighed financial or technological advantages. We have several times alluded to the most egregious instance of this disruption, Bavaria's refusal before 1870 to permit direct rail traffic on a line from Augsburg to Ulm. But this example suggests further complications. In Germany, namely, competition among the member states of the Confederation, which spurred construction, was a no less significant factor than government restrictions that sometimes inhibited private investment. A state's action might hasten as well as hinder the rapid development of new rail connections.

Essentially, we are confronted here with another counterfactual proposition. What might have happened if the state had stayed entirely out of the railroad industry? What, in other words, would have occurred if liberalism had invariably prevailed over etatism by reducing government regulation to an insignificant minimum? The answer, of course, is that we cannot know. Certain is only that, beside controls and restraints, the state in both France and Germany also provided loans, subsidies, guarantees, and assurances. Whether private investors would have so readily come forth with their funds in the absence of such inducements is beyond reckoning. In the statistics previously cited we can see how the French began in the 1850s to catch up with Germany and how they attained virtual parity by the late 1860s. It appears less than coincidental that this advance happened under the Second Empire, when France created the institutions of credit banking and government support that stimulated the nation's general economic growth through increased private investment. The Prussian state, in the meantime, returned to a more liberal stance and lost some of the dynamism that had vaulted Germany to an early statistical lead. Thus observed in the round, a categorical judgment that "the state" negatively influenced the development of railways during the first part of the nineteenth century appears too narrow to describe a more complex reality.

A proper sense of complexity need not preclude some valid generalizations. One common denominator of the emerging French and German railway systems was a tension between center and periphery. These terms may be defined variously—as opposition between the forces of centralism and federalism, regulation and deregulation, nationalism and particularism, government intervention and local autonomy, etatism and liberalism—but they were by some token applicable to France and Germany alike. The no less manifest difference was that the two nations came to this confrontation, so to speak, from opposite directions. As the railway age began, France had a distinct center and a vague periphery. That is to say, as to the former, the French state possessed a monarchy, a national parliament, a unique corps of state engineers, and a single Ministry of Public Works, whereas the latter was represented by the newly created railway companies whose slow and uncertain formation stretched over decades. In Germany, however, it was the center that lacked firm contours before 1870 as the national cause struggled toward self-definition, whereas the particularistic interests of the periphery were well established within the member states and free cities of the Confederation. What France and Germany shared in the decades after 1815, given these divergent geneses, was a movement toward the middle ground of a mixed system.

Despite the danger of exaggerating specific comparisons, one cannot fail to remark the parallel roles of Alexis Legrand and Friedrich List. Personal differences aside, their pioneering visions of national rail systems were astonishingly similar. When placed side by side, if the viewer squints just a bit, sketches of the Legrand star and List's first railway map might easily be confused. On both, tracks can be seen radiating from a capital city located centrally in the northern half of the nation while ancillary networks extend southward. Still more hallucinatory, even under sharp focus, are the nearly identical urban plans of Paris and Berlin in the 1860s. Both were divided by east-west rivers, the Seine and the Spree, on the left and right banks of which several railheads were located. Neither capital had a central station; hence travelers necessarily arrived at a northern or southern terminal within the city limits and, in order to continue their journey, were forced to proceed on foot, by horse-drawn carriage, or in a beltway railcar. Although we lack any method to evaluate the significance of visions and maps, there is no question that railways helped to promote the national identities of France and Germany as well as the rivalry between them. Doubtless, in the years before the war of 1870, Paris deserved to be called (in Walter Benjamin's famous phrase) the capital of the nineteenth century. But a worthy challenger was created in Berlin, among other reasons, because it became the rail hub of a powerful nation.

The relative weight of liberalism in the two nations is no easier to measure, but it should not be underestimated. We tend to forget how pervasive this political ideology proved to be not only in France but also throughout Germany, especially in Prussia, in the decades before 1870. If ever ideas can be said to bolster economic practice, it was here. French and German private railway enterprises repeatedly invoked a widespread assumption that state budgets should be balanced, public agencies should not unduly interfere with individual rights, and government regulation of business should be restricted. Thus intellectually armed, robber barons or not, entrepreneurs and large investors rallied most of the risk capital required to build the railroads. We can round up the usual suspects—Bethel Henry Strousberg in Germany, Emile and Isaac Pereire in France, the Rothschilds—but they only stand in for the dozens of other stockholders without whom the inception of a flourishing railway industry in a large nation would be hard to imagine. At least, few persons in France or Germany imagined it seriously at first, with an exception perhaps made for a few troubled months in 1848. True, the advocates of state ownership seemed to make headway in the 1850s, but during the final decade before 1870 Germany saw a liberal comeback, notably in Prussia and Saxony, and somewhat the same occurred in imperial France where Napoleon III's grip was gradually weakened by folly and foreign adventure.

Although there were evident similarities between France and Germany in the opening phase of railroad development, as both nations struggled to assimilate a new technology, it is impossible to dwell upon them without suggesting some fundamental differences. The mutual invention of mixed systems, as we noted, came about in disparate fashions. Germany had no counterpart to the Corps of Ponts-et-Chaussées, a fact of administrative life with extensive ramifications. Records of the Corp's directorate attest the thoroughness with which all aspects of railway construction and operation were examined by central agencies of the French national administration. The corresponding minutes of the Association of German Railway Administrations appear almost frivolous by comparison, being essentially transcripts of diplomatic gatherings in which delegates from various states express opinions, cast non-binding votes, and promise to consult with their regimes before the next meeting. Fortunately for the German nation, these exercises nonetheless produced extraordinarily uniform results before 1870, though Central Europe was still far from becoming a homogeneous entity in railroads or otherwise.

Just as the centers began as binary opposites, so did the peripheries. German *Kleinstaaterei* remained very much a reality. States with their own long-standing ruling houses such as Saxony, Bavaria, Württemberg, and Baden had been fixtures on the European scene for centuries. Each responded to the appearance of steam locomotives by establishing independent railway administrations that were fitted into existing bureaucratic structures. These agencies were not to be easily dislodged, and they quickly became adamant defenders of states' rights. The extant archives of all the peripheral German states show them to be ever anxious about outside tampering with their internal affairs and, as nationalism loomed nearer, always fearful of *Verpreussung*. But Prussian domination of the German nation, it must be stressed, was never unproblematic in Berlin itself, where particularism was no less ferocious. Bismarck's policies, not only regarding the railroads, were thus drenched in ambiguity, and we should also keep in mind that a salient outcome of the victory over Austria in 1866 was a vast increase in Prussia's stake in owning and operating its own state railway network.

For all of these considerations, to reverse the perspective, there was no French equivalent. The evolution of the large private railway companies—and therewith the formation of a French periphery—was tantamount to creating a federal system of governance where none had existed. For railroads, in essence, the French induced artificially what came naturally to the Germans: decentralization. Arguably, the French state thus gained more than it bargained for, as we are reminded by Napoleon III's grudging consent to company officials that they—not the state—might remain "the master of rates." Hence, while Germany drifted toward a more unified polity with potentially greater state control of the railroads, France was forced to reconfirm prerogatives of private enterprises upon which its mixed system was partially based.

We have noted how liberalism was an important element of the ideological landscape in both France and Germany. But we can also perceive, without getting too far ahead of the story, why their respective trajectories were beginning to part. Although lacking a coherent political movement to represent it, French liberalism was in fact the more pervasive and would prove the more durable of the two. And in France liberalism specifically meant deregulation, in opposition to the state controls imposed by the Bonapartist regime of the Second Empire. Expressions of liberal doctrine were therefore common in the corporate sessions and annual reports of private railway companies, whose devotion to the regular dividends of their stockholders was often pitted against governmental demands to provide a public service of transportation to the populace. German liberalism was more complex, differing from state to state within the Bund, and it was less likely to justify particularistic interests of the periphery. Indeed, a distinctive current of National Liberalism was jelling into an identifiable political party that contested the authority of ruling establishments and challenged states' rights. As we saw, some German liberals actively supported Bismarck's incipient *dirigisme* of the railroads in the late 1860s, hoping that the North German Confederation would afford them a chance to supersede the conservative monopoly of the Prussian monarchy. There were thus aspects of the German liberal tradition that were totally unknown in France, where the historic provinces (Normandy, Brittany, Burgundy, etc.) retained no political clout whatever, unlike the member states of the German Confederation. In truth, the only geographic boundaries that really mattered within the French state were those rather indistinct ones that separated the private railway companies. In their fashion, these firms had become by 1870 the true champions of federalism and liberalism in France.

In his discussion of French centralism and its survival under the Restoration monarchy after 1815, Tocqueville went so far as to say that

"Paris was France."[2] Given some intended hyperbole, this statement came close to describing French railway administrations. All of the five largest companies (the four examined here plus the Western) had their headquarters in the capital. Structurally, in many ways they resembled political units, small independent states with their titular rulers, prime ministers, bureaucracies, and budgets. And they gained virtual hegemony within a designated portion of the national territory. Accordingly, it is not far-fetched to portray them as defenders of a kind of regional particularism analogous to that of several member states of the German Bund. A peculiarity of the French circumstance, however, was that this defense occurred almost exclusively in Paris, where company administrators might encounter one another daily and could meet with cabinet ministers (or, on occasion, a monarch or emperor) on short notice. We may safely assume that such contacts were frequently arranged but rarely recorded. French railway archives are filled with references to some tête-à-tête of which no transcript or further trace is to be found because such private conferences were considered as confidential administrative business. In Germany, by contrast, railway affairs more nearly resembled formal diplomacy and were indeed very often conducted by trained diplomats who filed extensive reports of their rather stiff conversations. Saxony and the southern states, of course, kept envoys in Berlin and sent delegates to national administrative and legislative gatherings, but (Prussia excepted) the basics of the railway business were managed in provincial capitals far removed from extraneous personal contacts. Berlin was not Germany. Thus the propinquity of French railway managers and the dispersion of their German counterparts explain a difference in administrative methods as well as the historical records of them.

National idiosyncrasies in railway administration were to some extent reflected also in the status of railway workers. In France the employment of engineers, firemen, conductors, office personnel, stationmasters, gatekeepers, ticket sellers, construction workers, watchmen, and others was exclusively in the province of the private companies. They were in charge of hiring and firing employees, disciplining them, providing rudimentary medical care and welfare programs, sometimes constructing housing (for guardians at level crossings), and so forth. These arrangements came under challenge in 1848 but were not fundamentally altered thereafter. Correspondingly, French railway workers were like the laborers in other private industries. They may have aspired to a special status, like coal miners, on grounds that their work was both dangerous and indispensable to the national economy, but such pretensions could still be coolly ignored by the companies before 1870. Since trade unions were no factor in early nineteenth-century France, the companies clearly held the upper hand over a labor force that was undeveloped and underrepresented. Meanwhile, in Germany the status of railway employees was no more exalted but somewhat different—a difference that derived largely from the considerable number of them who were, in effect, functionaries of the state. As we noticed earlier, even in those German states with mixed railroad systems, such as Saxony and Bavaria, there was a habitual tendency to treat railway labor much the same as postal workers. Every indication is that this arrangement was mutually consensual. Most German railway administrators as well as workers could agree that together they were, by and large, employees of the state, an attitude that can only be labeled as a kind of corporatism. Presumably, because a substantially larger portion of its agents was directly responsible to private railway firms, Prussia again stands out as an exception. Yet even there, as many a traveler had occasion to observe, employees in uniform were much in evidence, as if the state's tradition of military discipline had been carried over to its railroads.

An observant reader will be aware that the employment of women has previously been mentioned in regard to France but not Germany. The reason is simple. French women were widely engaged in the railway industry before 1870; German women, much less. In both countries their tasks were menial, their hours long, and their wages derisory. This job description well suited the private French railway companies, which were forever trying to hold down payroll costs while coping with expanded traffic. Besides helping around stations or cleaning passenger cars, many women were hired to assist their husbands in gatekeeping chores at level crossings. But in Germany this assignment was still thought to be a man's work, essentially the function of traffic police. Besides, state railroads were less overtly driven to turn an immediate profit and were more likely to boast of the greater efficiency and safety of their services. Be that as it may, the massive employment of female labor in the German industry would await another day.[3]

All in all, perhaps the main lesson to be learned from a comparison of early railway administrations in France and Germany is that there can never be a purely technological innovation. The same British know-how was imported almost simultaneously to several parts of the European mainland. Despite some apparent similarities that we have suggested, the fundamental differences between the two major continental states are conspicuous, a divergence largely to be explained by the varying national contexts into which that new technology was absorbed.

Economic Competition

Economic growth is much like a ballroom dance contest with its intricate patterns and rhythms, its movements fast and slow, its syncopations, sways, and swoons. To an impartial judge observing their performances from the sidelines, France and Germany probably deserved similar marks in the early nineteenth century. For both there were three distinct phases between 1815 and 1870. First came the economic recovery of the post-Napoleonic decades—just as railroads were making their initial (and commercially still insignificant) appearance—a relatively tranquil time terminated by the boisterous uprisings of 1848. This period was followed by the salutary boomlet of the 1850s, when European nations enjoyed the benefits of improved transportation encouraged by governments eager to promote fledgling industrial firms. After another brief pause during the crisis between 1857 and 1859, a third phase of expansion began in the early 1860s with renewed economic confidence and the further extension of railway networks until late in that decade, when political upsets, diplomatic maneuvers, and military conflicts announced *l'année terrible* of 1870.

The fact that this schema can be applied equally well to France and Germany raises several questions of interpretation. Can we, for example, accept the notion of so-called *Kondratieffs*, which posits one long swing of economic prosperity from 1848 to 1873? Certainly it did not appear so to contemporaries. Records from the railway industry suggest instead a succession of stops and starts, scant evidence for a tidy theory of perpetual upward motion. The long term was a series of short terms, each of which produced its unique set of circumstances, problems, personalities, and tensions. Historians are, of course, paid to generalize, but a global thesis that railroads everywhere helped to inspire a sustained industrial growth across a thirty-year span is of doubtful utility for either the French or the German case, still less for both.[4]

Striking parallels between the French and German patterns of economic growth before 1870 also cast suspicion on this categorical opinion: "The rise of Germany to an industrial nation was more closely attached to the railroad than in other countries."[5] When comparing Germany with Great Britain, this statement may be counted as a virtual truism, simply because the much earlier English industrialization was technologically linked with textiles. But in their timing and sectorial emphasis, the developments in France and Germany were more nearly identical. Both were retarded in contrast to Britain, and they consequently expended the early decades of the nineteenth century in "closing the gap."[6] Both did so by adapting British technology to their respective political systems. It can be argued that the German effort was initially more intense, but that was a difference of degree rather than of kind. We would hardly want to contend that the heart of a large man is more essential to his body than that of a smaller woman to hers on the grounds that it must pump more blood for him to survive. Magnitude alone is not determinant. On what scale shall we measure the "close attachment" of Belgian coal for the business of France's Northern Railway Company and presume to declare it less crucial than, say, Prussian fuel imports from Silesia? The closer the comparison, it seems, the less convincing the proposition becomes.

Nor is the foregoing an isolated instance of terminology that applies equally well to France and Germany after 1815. In fact, it is remarkable how accurately some of the fashionable vocabulary now employed by economic historians can describe the railways of both. They constituted a "leading sector" of the national economy and were thus an example of "unbalanced growth" that had "linkage effects" back to the coal industry and forward to the steel industry.[7] Also, as noted, in their mutual relationship to Britain, France and Germany in like manner suffered and ultimately benefited from economic "backwardness."[8] Both experienced a fitful growth that indisputably created a mighty European triumvirate of industrial superpowers with extensive rail systems. Maybe it is fair to suppose that "Germany is the best illustration of the generous yield of systematic investment in a backward economy of high potential."[9] Yet France ran a close second and surely deserves to be counted in the same category.

Still, we cannot ignore the Achilles' heel of France's economy: the inadequacy of its combustibles for heavy industry. Coal statistics are again our best indicator, and we may summarize them with stark simplicity: France had no Ruhr. Whereas the analogous Pas-de-Calais was able before 1870 to raise its annual production to only about 2 million tons, extractions in the Ruhr basin increased from 1.6 million to nearly 12 million tons during the two decades after 1850. Altogether, German mines supplied almost twice as much coal as the French and also yielded much larger quantities of coke, which, because it burned cleaner, was more useful for blast furnaces and passenger locomotives. This relative French disadvantage had to be offset by imports from Belgium, Britain, and Germany, thus representing a permanent drag on the national growth rate in comparison to the less encumbered German progress.[10]

We have no infallible means to measure the total impact of railroads on European economies because it is impossible to disaggregate railway statistics from other indicators. Even when certain numbers can be separated, they do not provide unambiguous proof. One historian has calculated, for example, that the growing legion of railway workers was still only a tiny percent of the entire German labor force before 1870.[11] On that basis, one could scarcely contend that railroads played a decisive economic role, but such figures must be weighed against numerical evidence that no other commercial sector attracted such a quantity of investment capital during the nineteenth century.[12] To reiterate an earlier observation, the most that one can safely conclude is that railways developed a reciprocal relationship with the general economy, lifting as well as being lifted by the existing flow of commerce.

All the while that flow was becoming measurably more rapid. The increased pace of European traffic was already evident soon after 1815, well before the introduction of railroads, which thus came to sustain rather than to create an upward trend.[13] Basic to this development was the correlation dear to all capitalists between greater volume and lower prices. There was consequently a natural deflation of railway rates on the principle of shipping more and charging less per ton. We saw examples in both France and Germany of how stiff competition with canals affected the level of commercial rates. With their alacrity and reliability, whatever the weather, trains held a decisive edge over plodding barges. But if railways were winning the race against waterways, they were doing so at a cost, required as they were to adjust their fares whenever challenged. One can speculate that improved technology always promotes deflation through increased speed, precision, or quantity of production. In any event, that is what occurred in the early railway age.

In this stage of development, economic competition was largely on a local scale. Railways did not suddenly change that fact, though the possibilities of international trade were immediately apparent. As happens so often, potential far exceeded performance. Hypothetically, the decade of the 1860s, and on into the 1870s, comprised a time of free trade for the three major commercial nations of Europe. Yet that opening came before the railways were able to take full advantage of it, because national rail systems (except in Belgium) did not exist on the Continent. Moreover, the free trade era proved to be an anomalous episode when Germany, followed by France, reverted to protectionist tariffs after 1870. Within this general economic context, the concept of center and periphery is useful in comparing the French and German railroads. No analysis can overlook the intense internal rivalry among private companies (in France) or federated states (in Germany). Each of these peripheral entities developed its own politics and protected its own financial interests. Meanwhile, appeals for national unity—established but unstable in France, idealistic and emerging in Germany—remained to a greater or lesser extent frustrated by such overt particularism. Any economic history of trains told strictly from the vantage of a central nation-state therefore risks missing the essence of the matter.

Did railways finally bolster one national economy more than another? Although this rhetorical question does not admit an exact answer, we may cautiously venture a somewhat premature response. Accumulating trade statistics tended to favor Germany. One of the manifest criteria for measuring the difference with France was the total amount of freight transferred between trains and ships in the port cities on the European mainland. By that standard Germany was beginning to assert its superior economic prowess even before 1870. Earlier we took note of a fundamental distinction: whereas France had an embarrassment of riches in regard to ports—Marseille and Cette on the Mediterranean and a host of harbors along the Atlantic Coast from Bordeaux to Dunkerque—Germany needed to develop international shipping in order to compete. Hence, while French ports vied for government subsidies and advantageous deals with their domestic railway companies, German firms diligently sought new outlets to the sea and lower railway rates to exploit them. "This loathsome state of things," as Jules Siegfried later wrote, resulted in a greater inefficiency and relatively excessive expense of the French system. Consequently, Siegfried added for instance, Swiss businesses often preferred to trade through non-French ports.[14] Freight statistics (see Table 6) tend to corroborate these

TABLE 6: Shipping Tonnage: Entrance and Exit, 1860–1873

	Le Havre	Antwerp	Hamburg
1860	1,642,934	1,087,506	1,688,000
1869	2,179,411	2,529,764	2,844,230
1873	2,419,626	3,940,257	3,370,740

Source: Jules Siegfried, *Quelques mots sur la question des chemins de fer en France* (Le Havre, 1875), p. 11.

observations and to confirm a tilt away from France before 1870 that became still more accentuated thereafter. If such numbers seem less than conclusive, they were nonetheless a strong hint of things to come. "From the viewpoint of international commerce," as the most knowledgeable of current French authorities has commented, railway firms in France found themselves "in a position of inferiority."[15]

As the summer of 1870 approached, however, the dominant mood throughout Europe was optimism. Hundreds of letters and dispatches to be found today in the archives testify to a belief that both France and Germany stood on the threshold of a prosperous era of peace. The imagination of Europeans everywhere was stirred by the opening of the Suez Canal. Given the completion of the Mt. Cenis tunnel and a secure prospect of St. Gotthard following within a decade, the way was now open for unobstructed commerce between Asia and the Atlantic. Was, as Leopold von Ranke had dreamed, a higher European unity soon to emerge from the competition among states? There were unfortunately those with other ideas.

Military Strategy

The new age of warfare had to wait a while. True, there was no shortage of speculation in Europe about the changes that might occur because of improved transportation by rail—particularly, it was thought, in buttressing a nation's defenses by enabling its armies to concentrate at the point of attack. But there was also some understandable skepticism. To comprehend it, one needs only to glance at sketches of the first steam locomotives. It was hard to imagine that such contraptions could alter the face of battle; they had neither the capacity nor the rapidity nor the flexibility to make much difference. After all, the armies of Bonaparte, Wellington, and Blücher had not done too badly without them. So trains offered no instant military success, and they did not immediately revolutionize strategic thinking. It would therefore be mistaken to suppose that, because of railways, warfare took a sudden leap into the future.

Yet second thoughts came quickly enough. As rail lines were extended, networks thickened, and speeds increased, the logistical potential of railroads became evident to all. No less clearly, they might well serve to mount an offensive campaign. Much consideration was consequently devoted in France and Germany to the location and protection of main rail lines. Military advisers spoke up in favor of building them under the surveillance of nearby fortresses, at a safe distance from frontiers, and on the opposite side of waterways—opposite, that is, from "the enemy," an oblique designation very early reserved by the French for the Germans, and vice versa.

In the 1850s France proved that theory could be put into practice. Thousands of French troops with their equipment were moved southward during the Crimean and Italian wars, much to the self-satisfaction of commanders in Paris. But in the long run they were actually victims of their own success because of the optical illusion that trains could easily deploy armies. Their failing was to give insufficient weight to the fact that French military planning (such as it was) was based on the nation's private railway companies. The tracks of the PLM were superbly suited for the purposes of that decade, capable of shipping men and supplies from Paris to Marseille. Yet suppose France should be called upon to transfer military forces across the country, say, from Bordeaux to Sedan? For that eventuality, as it happened, the French Etat-Major had no ready solution.

Most early railway construction was for commercial rather than military reasons. Still, in Germany, too, strategy was not neglected, especially in view of the patent need to defend two fronts. Much of the Prussian state's direct involvement in the new railway industry must be explained in these terms, notably its sponsorship of the Ostbahn, which could ferry troops to and from the northeast. There were also political and economic rationales for attaching the sugar beets and grain fields of East-Elbian Junker estates to the Berlin and Brandenburg markets. But in fact the state undertook the project at the urging of the military only after it became clear that private investment sufficient to finance it was lacking.

Germany had other special problems in adapting railways to warfare. As always, particularism raised its princely head, exposing the bald spot of the German Bund. The absence of political unity that became so painfully apparent in 1849 remained an impediment for military strategy thereafter, which was no secret either in Frankfurt or Paris. This disability was compounded by the difficulties of integrating private railway companies into state planning. This was primarily an issue for Prussia, but it was likewise evident in other monarchies that had mixed systems, such as Saxony and Bavaria. We recall, for instance, that most of the Bavarian lines in western frontier areas of the Palatinate were left in private hands.

These complications were of course not unknown in France, where the archives of the major railway companies contain ample evidence of civil-military strife. French circumstances were likely to match engineers of Ponts-et-Chaussées against those of the military *Génie*. They ordinarily faced off in the so-called *commissions mixtes*, the transcripts of which reveal that military leaders did not invariably have their way. As in Germany, disputes over railway projects often centered on finance. Whereas private companies strained for profits, the state sought a balanced budget. Meanwhile, within the government, disputes arose between the Ministries of Finance or Public Works and the Ministry of War. In style and substance, the stenographic reports of such altercations in France and Germany are virtually interchangeable.

In the 1860s two military personalities stood out: Adolphe Niel and Helmuth von Moltke. Historians generally love a winner, and it is admittedly difficult not to award the first prize to Moltke. Still, Marshal Niel's intentions were quite similar and his vision no less lucid. He believed that central military planning and a simple strategy were necessary to make optimal use of more rapid transportation by rail. To those ends the Etat-Major must be reformed with the addition of a special railroad bureau. Like Moltke, Niel had the support of his sovereign. Napoleon III, no stranger to Germany or the German language, was, if anything, more enthusiastic than his senior officers about creating a more Teutonic military establishment and altering France's conservative professional army procedures. But his star was sinking just as Wilhelm's was rising. More than Bonaparte probably realized, his foolhardy expedition to Mexico had cost him a chance to compete on the Rhine. While Niel's ambitions were thus thwarted, it was Moltke who prevailed. His reform solution of military line-commissions, which were to take over from civilian officials in wartime, had a certain air of improvisation. Yet it was sufficient unto the day in late July 1870 when Prussian troop trains began rolling toward the Rhenish frontier. Thirteen German army corps therefore arrived within little more than a fortnight, whereas at that critical moment Niel's nascent reforms only added to French confusion.[16]

The war of 1870 has been refought over and over in detail. There is no reason to repeat it here. We may simply observe that these battles comprised the first and only major railway war of nineteenth-century Europe. By comparison, French campaigns in the 1850s were only forays abroad that finished with skirmishes. The same was true of the Austro-Prussian expedition of 1864 into Schleswig-Holstein. Railways mattered more in 1866, but for reasons cited in Chapter 2, they were less crucial to the outcome than often assumed. In 1870 railroads became unequivocally essential to the course of the conflict by enabling Moltke's forces to outman and outmaneuver the French during the war's opening phases. Combat thus occurred on French rather than German soil, contrary to most expectations in Paris. Certainly 1870 was no 1940, but the term *Blitzkrieg* scarcely seems misplaced. Meanwhile, the bulk of French reserves remained backed up in the Paris bottleneck. Rather than relieving the inherent flaws of the French military system, railways tended to compound them.[17] Within a matter of weeks, the French resistance was disorganized and dispirited. Some of the same problems that had plagued Moltke's men in 1866 recurred; principally, the wide dispersion of units for which supplies were often stalled in the rear. But it was early autumn in France, harvest time in one of Europe's richest agricultural belts. Besides, the hostilities were mercifully brief. Already at the beginning of September, MacMahon's army was forced to capitulate near Sedan, and the other main French force under Marshal Bazaine was trapped at Metz. Efforts by Léon Gambetta to organize a national militia in western France were heroic but futile, and the same can be said of the Paris Commune. Never, in sum, was the military result in doubt once the initial encounters had been decided on the Franco-German border. German victory was sealed by superior rail transportation.[18]

The Franco-Prussian war taught one lesson, and it required no military genius to grasp it: in future warfare, rapid transit would be decisive. Such was to be the dominating notion of European strategy for decades to come, the basic concept of the Schlieffen Plan, and the primary motive of all French preparations to counter it. In this respect, among others, the railway age had arrived.

Part II

The Signals Are Set

Chapter 4

FRANCE, 1870–1890

The Franco-Prussian war brought only woe to France. The most acute pain blessedly ended with an armistice in January 1871, but the discomfort continued throughout the immediate postwar years. After investing Alsace and Lorraine, German troops occupied the adjacent French provinces, thereby temporarily taking control of the entire Eastern Railway Company as well as other lines leading to Paris. The capital was surrounded, while all of its main transportation arteries to the outside were cut. The government of the infant French republic was thus divided between Paris and Bordeaux, with only carrier pigeons for communication until rail traffic could be restored. That event was delayed by the outbreak in March of the Paris Commune, which provided a dose of reality to all but those blinded by idealism or frustration. The truth was that for the moment Germany held the fate of France in a tight clinch, and the provisional government was consequently forced to conclude the onerous terms of the Treaty of Frankfurt on May 20. Only then were the railways opened, prisoners of war and chassepots returned, and an assault mounted that crushed the insurrection within a week.

French troubles were by no means at an end. Besides the loss of territory and the damage of conflict, the nation was saddled with a huge public loan required to acquit a reparations settlement of 5 billion francs. The total cost of putting France's house back in order was at least three times that sum. Public bond issues to meet these debts brought welcome cash but also mortgaged the state for a decade, consuming nearly half of its annual budget.[1] Meanwhile, the Eastern Company was effectively sliced in half, and the other companies suffered severe disruptions. Irregular passenger service and infuriating freight blockages were the result, lasting well into 1872. The inadequacies of the French railway system and its lack of sufficient equipment, first revealed by the war, were now plain for all to see.

After the Fall

Altogether it was appropriate that the first president of the Third Republic was Adolphe Thiers. For the job he possessed two indispensable qualifications: he could not be blamed for the imprudences of Napoleon III, and he was acceptable to Otto von Bismarck.[2] He also had an immense ego and was visibly flattered to become the first citizen of the land. As we saw much earlier, when Thiers first became involved in railway affairs as Minister of Public Works in the 1830s, his liberalism was limited while his etatist tendencies were held in check. In that regard, at least, he represented a political balance. It is therefore mistaken to portray him as a closet Bonapartist, as if he were at heart an incurable advocate of centralism. In fact, his roots remained deeply planted in Orleanism and thus, specifically, in a conception of railways formed before 1848 under the July Monarchy. If he now harked back to 1859, it was because he assumed, correctly, that the conventions of that year reinforced the legislative settlement of 1842. In short, Thiers embodied the principles of a mixed system of public and private enterprise, an equilibrium of liberalism and etatism for which he fancied himself the supreme arbiter.

Accordingly, it was quite in Orleanist character for Thiers to reassure the representatives of France's major railway firms in January 1872 that he had decided "to defend passionately the interest of the companies."[3] Yet, lacking any large party or popular movement behind him, his stance was insecure—all the more so once the schedule of reparations was finally met, under constant hectoring from Bismarck, and the German occupation drew to a close. In late May 1873, only weeks after the last Prussian grenadier had departed French soil, Thiers was abruptly ousted in a coup that brought the so-called "government of moral order" under Marshal MacMahon and Albert de Broglie. If the nation's morality was thus put into order, one must add, precious little was done to restore political stability. Hence all questions as to the constitution of the new republic and its railway system were reopened.

The search for scapegoats is doubtless part of every lost war. In France the favorite, of course, was Napoleon III. He was closely followed by the professional army, the public schools, and the private railway companies, not necessarily in that order. Criticism of the companies came at once and emanated from various quarters. Perhaps the politically most significant source was within parliament, where a republican consensus was supposedly to be formulated and legislated. Chief there among detractors of the existing system was a royalist deputy, Claude-Marie Raudot, elected in December 1871 as chairman of the Chamber's special committee on railroads. His was a flagrant liberal view; that is, he wished the transportation industry to be rid of state controls, giving rein to free enterprise and eliminating what he viewed as the debilitating influence of Ponts-et-Chaussées, whose directorate he considered "a hindrance, a cause of delays and useless expenses...." Meanwhile, amid a hail of complaints about disjunctures in railway service, one of Raudot's colleagues on the committee regretted "to see commerce in the hands of the companies."[4] Such comments were explicitly intended to discredit prewar arrangements and to propose a nationwide deregulation that would dismantle the regional monopolies of the six main companies while also restricting government interference.

Although not a unanimous opinion within the Thierist regime, this contention had vigorous boosters at cabinet gatherings in the persons of Minister of Public Works Roger de Larcy and Minister of Finance Auguste Pouyer-Quertier, both of whom likewise took aim at the major firms and favored a proliferation of smaller ones. Meanwhile, several harsh disquisitions about the ubiquitous chaos in freight yards and train stations arrived as petitions from various chambers of commerce—Montpellier, Avignon, Nimes, and Amiens notable among them—which attributed the unacceptable conditions on France's main lines to the inability of the companies to cope with the needs of the nation's industry and agriculture. These conclusions were collected by a special parliamentary committee of inquiry, whose report was eventually published in 1874. As one member commented in summarizing its findings: "Absolute liberty cannot be left to the [major] companies."[5]

Thus, already stirred in the late 1860s, a resurgence of small companies gathered momentum in the early 1870s. Mostly these were sponsors of local projects awarded to private investors for specific purposes, such as spur tracks connecting industrial plants and rail lines. But some, like the Company of the Charentes, grew to considerable size and strength, especially in that area of southwestern France where ambiguous boundaries and wobbly companies (the PO, Southern, and Western) converged. This activity also spawned a generation of latter-day robber barons, two of whom stood out: Simon Philippart and Dominique de Beaurepaire. The dealings of the former must be mentioned subsequently. As for the Comte de Beaurepaire, a loose cannon among French entrepreneurs, he became notorious for his persistent efforts to acquire the concession for an Amiens-Dijon thoroughfare. Seen in a larger context, this campaign was part of a series of projects, variously designated, the ultimate objective of which was the same: to provide France with a sweeping transversal from Calais or Dunkerque to Marseille, by-passing Paris by a northerly route through the rich industrial belt near the Belgian and German borders, a solution obviously desirable for commercial and military purposes alike in order to avoid clogged approaches to the capital.

Characteristic though it was of the 1870s, this movement on behalf of smaller railway companies was already losing steam by mid-decade. Such ventures were possibly too risky and untidy to begin with, and they were certainly incompatible with the usual procedures of France's railway networks. A first drastic blow was dealt to this ultra-liberalism by the reconstitution of the Eastern Railway Company after 1872, at a time when the very existence of that firm swayed in the balance. But the unkindest cut of all was a decision by the Broglie cabinet in 1875 to reject Beaurepaire's bid and to award the Amiens-Dijon concession to the Northern and Eastern companies. Embarrassingly, even Claude-Marie Raudot had to concur with this action because of an excessive subsidy (39 million francs) demanded by Beaurepaire and his partners. Attempts to plead the case for the advantages of a new small company in the region failed to budge the government from its course.[6] Handwriting appeared on the walls of the Palais Bourbon, where it was read out by Minister of Public Works Charles Christophle in December 1876 before a session of the Chamber's railway committee. He was concerned, Christophle said, to prevent an uncontainable wave of bankruptcies among smaller companies. The existence of the six major private monopolies was an accomplished fact of the French rail system. It would be an error to encourage competition between them and smaller firms having connections neither to ports nor to Paris. Therefore, the committee's minutes continued, "he believes that it is necessary to consolidate the regime of the large companies."[7]

Not that attacks on the French system thereby subsided. To be reckoned with was another form of protest from the opposite flank, etatism, where critics of the companies rallied once more under the durable banner of *rachat*. Perhaps it is an exaggeration to speak of a tradition in this instance, but proposals for a Belgian style of national railway system, owned and operated by the state, were as old as the industry itself. Heretofore the one shining moment in that long story had been the sequestration of 1848, but that episode was short-lived and may well have collapsed in any event, even if not eradicated by the military reaction of the June Days. Subsequently, the Second Empire had buttressed the mixed system of administration by sustaining the major companies while attempting to tighten the state's supervision of them. The ensuing defeat and disgrace of the Bonapartist regime could thereupon be seen as reason enough to reject that arrangement of regional monopolies and to move on to a genuine nationalization.

This was precisely the rationale behind a parliamentary motion submitted by the deputy Clément Laurier and thirty-three colleagues, notably including Léon Gambetta, on 3 February 1872: a total confiscation of the private railway companies. Led by Pouyer-Quertier, liberal opposition was prompt and categorically negative, pointing out that the current financial quandary of the young republic made such a gigantic transaction unthinkable. Faced with this basic truth, the Gambettists dropped their demands a fortnight later.[8] For a short while, as we have just established, initiative therefore passed to the proponents of small companies—who were no less hostile to the existing system but were convinced that they offered a better alternative to it. Once that agitation began to falter, however, the etatists soon reappeared, led by one of Gambetta's most trusted lieutenants, François Allain-Targé. A direct confrontation became imminent in 1876 when the latter presented an amendment to a bill in the Chamber of Deputies, the effect of which would have been a virtual takeover of the PO: the company would ostensibly be left in place but stripped of such essential prerogatives as the right to set rates. However, this motion became bogged down in more far-reaching disputes about the principles of republican governance. Conservative opposition to basic reforms was centered in MacMahon's presidential office and in the Senate, agents powerful enough to block any measures originating from the Chamber, where Allain-Targé's amendment passed by a vote of 231 to 192. But dismissal of the cabinet by MacMahon in the spring of 1877—provoking the so-called "*seize mai* crisis"—led to hotly contested parliamentary elections in which Gambettist republicans (aided by Thiers until his death during the campaign) prevailed, albeit not overwhelmingly, against conservative supporters of the president. Thus defeated but not deposed, MacMahon stubbornly held on until January 1879, thereby prolonging a twilight period in which any further radical initiatives could be prevented, although the tired conservative leadership had lost its mandate to rule. Moral order had now turned into manifest dysfunction.[9]

It was in the midst of this complex transition that the figure of Charles de Freycinet emerged. He soon proved to be, along with Léon Gambetta and Jules Ferry, one of the outstanding French politicians of the postwar era. An engineering graduate of the illustrious Ecole Polytechnique and a former aide-de-camp of Gambetta during the militia phase of the Franco-Prussian war, Freycinet was now called to the cabinet as Minister of Public Works. Within the context presented above, his appearance was a conscious rejection of the two problematical alternatives of extreme liberalism and etatism. He incarnated the intention to maintain a mixed system of French railroads while increasing the state's control over the private enterprise of the major companies. By avoiding deregulation and yet stopping well short of Draconian confiscation, Freycinet offered a compromise suitable for many Gambettists, unopposed by the majority of MacMahonian conservatives, supported by the Corps of Ponts-et-Chaussées, and capable of mustering a favorable vote in both houses of parliament. On the basis of this new orthodoxy Freycinet was empowered to launch a bold undertaking to revitalize the railway industry through massive state financial support for public transportation facilities. The Freycinet Plan became a household word in France, conjuring visions of longer tracks, wider canals, and greater harbors. True, to realize this vast project would require the expenditure of at least 5 or 6 billion francs, but the enthusiasm of the moment was such that virtually any sacrifice was imaginable that would allow France to break its present impasse and to escape the postwar doldrums.

The Freycinet Plan seemed to be the most startling volte-face of the nineteenth century. But we must take care not to overlook its fundamentally cautious purpose with regard to railway administration. Despite the still insistent demands for a *rachat*, Freycinet firmly opposed that measure, which, if adopted, would truly have been a revolutionary innovation. Instead, he hoped to preserve the private companies, confident that he could persuade them to accept a "considerable extension of the role of the state."[10] Perhaps the most telling phrase to epitomize the motive of the Freycinet Plan was coined by Daniel Wilson in an address to the Chamber of Deputies: what France needed, he said, was "distributive justice." To spread the benefits of modern transportation to all of the republic's citizens throughout the nation meant an accelerated expansion. If the private companies were reluctant, the state would take matters into hand by funding a huge program of public works. To be sure, there must be limits. As the report of a Senate committee stated simply: "The state cannot do everything." Yet this served only to reinforce Freycinet's own disinclination to back confiscatory legislation, which was sure to arouse hostility in the Senate and which, the report concluded, could only bring "disastrous consequences."[11]

Reform, then, but not revolution—all of which, Freycinet presumed, would enhance the grandeur of France. In the short term, that happy result would occur by reaffirming the established administrative principles of 1842 and 1859, perpetuating the mixed system of the past. As for the long term, if successful, the platform adopted in 1879 would surely have strengthened claims for a stricter state control of the private sector, thereby tilting the balance toward centralism and a conception of the railways as a public service. Such was the apparent drift of things as the decade of the 1880s began.[12]

The Counterattack of the Companies

The end of the Franco-Prussian war brought a noteworthy change of guard in the administration of the French companies. Indeed, this period might well be termed the great age of directors or, better said, the age of great directors. Of course, there had been some eminent predecessors—Clément Sauvage (Eastern), Charles Didion (PO), and above all Paulin Talabot (PLM)—but the new generation of directors was the most formidable of the century: François Jacqmin of the Eastern, Gustave Noblemaire at the PLM, and Antoine-Emile Solacroup of the PO. Their capabilities and personal charisma went far to explain the survival of the companies in the difficult decades before 1890. As usual, because of the always abundant supply of male heirs in the prolific Rothschild family, the Northern Company was somewhat exceptional, but it, too, produced an able cadre of administrators to carry on.

Did this mean that the companies thereby came increasingly under the sway of engineers more notable for their technical than political acumen? That view is tempting but, for two reasons, misleading. First, both the state and the companies had long boasted strong corps of engineers who, even though not perpetually in the public spotlight, had provided the underpinning of the railway industry. A distinctive feature of French administration was to allow state engineers to take leave from government employment and to serve for years or sometimes decades with the companies before returning to their posts—a practice known as "slipperage" (*pantouflage*) in reference to the cozy though often conflictual relationship between the company engineers and the Corps of Ponts-et-Chaussées. The difference was simply that the more prominent company directors now emerged directly from this tradition: Jacqmin and Noblemaire, for instance, had been close friends since attending the Ecole des Ponts-et-Chaussées. Thus, as before, the status and skill of engineers trained in elite French schools remained basic to the railway industry. Second, as we shall see, the political involvement of railway officials was just as urgently required as ever. Jacqmin and Solacroup conferred frequently with cabinet ministers and parliamentary leaders; Noblemaire moved easily in Parisian ballrooms and international diplomatic circles; and gala receptions given by the Rothschilds became legendary. The companies were thus guided by men who acted much like any heads of state, as in a sense they were. The challenge after 1870, however, was to keep their own dominions intact.

The Eastern Railway Company

Rail service on the Eastern was disrupted in 1870–1871 for seven months at an estimated loss in revenue of 38 million francs. So read the Company's records. But how can a disaster be calculated? All of the tracks in Alsace-Lorraine, over half of the entire Eastern network, were gone. Much of the rest remained de facto under German control, even when operated by a French administration. This "deplorable situation," as the Administrative Council described it, was financially eased by an indemnity of 325 million francs received from Germany under terms of the Treaty of Frankfurt, which was supposed to compensate for the rails, stations, and equipment claimed in the annexed territories by the new Reich. Yet, of course, this sum was actually part of the total reparations settlement, being less than one-fifteenth of the funds extracted by Bismarck from the French republic.[13]

During this period of "altogether exceptional gravity," Company officials were admonished by the Administrative Council to exercise the "strictest moderation." Necessarily they did. But a more basic issue was how and, in fact, whether the Eastern's network would be reconstituted. Entirely new rail patterns needed to be plotted, crossings and stations rebuilt or replaced, and "very delicate" problems resolved about border connections to the detached provinces henceforth under German rule.[14] The list of military damage was extensive, nearly half of it self-inflicted by French efforts in the autumn of 1870 to stem the enemy's advance by destroying tracks, tunnels, and bridges. Estimates were initially set at about 15 million francs; later they rose to 20 million and more. During the conflict, moreover, the Germans had seized 169 of the Eastern's locomotives. Most of them were returned right after the war, thus leaving the Company with a surplus of engines for its reduced service, but the condition of the machines was "seriously deteriorated." Because such rolling stock was "not at all in a normal state of maintenance," Company workshops needed to be expanded and refurbished for repair work at an additional cost of 6.3 million francs.[15]

We are able to fit this *cahier de doléances* into a context of demands in parliament and the press to break up the monopoly of the major companies. The curiosity was that the Eastern Company, having born the brunt of the German assault and thus having become associated with the loss of Alsace-Lorraine, had to endure less of this wrath than the others; instead, it could be considered a pitiable victim of Bismarck's persecution of France. And the new republican government was quick to reassure the Eastern's director that the Company's survival was a national priority. In a meeting with Clément Sauvage in September 1871, President Thiers pledged that he would "energetically" support a new convention between his government and the Eastern, personally denying that he would permit smaller companies to intrude: "You can place your confidence in me." With his customary rhetorical flair, Thiers also explicitly rejected any proposals for a confiscation of the large companies: "I would rather be crushed under a millstone than fail to maintain respect for their treaties and established rights."[16] Tenuous as the Thierist regime was, such fragile sentiments could offer only limited security. Still, there is no question that the Eastern Company enjoyed a special status among French railway firms because of both its recent past and its future commercial and military potential.

Apparently for the same reasons, the Eastern was almost unscathed by the Paris Commune. There was something downright churlish about making still more trouble in the spring of 1871 for the beleaguered Company, which reported little internal strife. One illicit organization of engineers (drivers) and firemen did briefly appear, a movement reminiscent of 1848, and disciplinary measures were duly imposed on them thereafter: seven were fired, thirteen demoted, and eleven reprimanded. But no further labor conflicts with its workers bothered the Eastern's administration before 1890.[17]

Since the late 1860s François Jacqmin had progressively assumed more directorial responsibilities from Sauvage, whose death in November 1872 completed that transfer of political authority. It was therefore Jacqmin who conducted negotiations with the Broglie cabinet for a new convention, which was signed in 1873. By then an atmosphere of normalcy had returned, and the Company was able to deal with such loaded issues as the Amiens-Dijon dispute with the Comte de Beaurepaire and his colleagues. Eager as the Eastern Company's Administrative Council was to regain strength through expanded service, however, it was not always prepared to do the state's bidding in constructing lines of dubious profitability. Because of its strategic location on the German border, the Company remained more than the others under inordinate pressure to comply with the wishes of military planners. Commercial interests counted as well, leading the Eastern to conduct regular negotiations and to conclude "treaties" with its powerful neighbors, the Northern Company and the PLM, just as sovereign states are wont to do.[18]

Often debilitated by attacks of asthma and gout that forced him to remain in his Paris residence or country estate far away from the Company's main administrative offices at the Gare de l'Est, Jacqmin daily sent batches of memoranda to his subalterns with instructions to resist efforts of the state bureaucracy to impose uniformity on the railway firms. He sought, as he wrote, to "thwart with absurdity the notion of a single [national] network" by raising objections and delaying compliance.[19] Given the chronic instability of French cabinets during the early Third Republic, these tactics were well suited to blunt the practical effect of state controls and to preserve a measure of autonomy in the conduct of the Company's business. Hence, by resuscitating the Eastern Company after the debacle of 1870, the French state helped to ensure the survival of the traditional form of private enterprise in the railway industry.

The PLM

The conflict of 1870 and the ensuing German occupation naturally had more immediate impact on the Eastern Railway Company than on the PLM. These events were nonetheless perceived by the latter's officials as a series of "terrible crises" that resulted in a chaos of "stoppages and disorders." The PLM managed in August to transport over 200,000 troops with their steeds and supplies toward the front, but with rail lines severed north of Lyon, its efforts failed to avert a capitulation at Sedan. The Germans temporarily occupied about one-quarter of the PLM's network. Service from Paris to Burgundy was not restored until mid-March 1871, only to be cut once more by the Commune. Company reports on the civil insurrections in Paris, Lyon, and Marseille recounted in lurid detail "the gangs that everywhere sow disorder," the fires set in railway offices destroying precious archives, and the employees held at gunpoint while demonstrators paraded their "exaggerated pretensions." After it was all over, seventeen workers were dismissed and deprived of their pensions, while several others were demoted or reprimanded. We should note that later protests by some engineers and firemen about the harshness of these penalties went unheeded; the guilty were not reinstated.[20]

Compared to the Eastern Company, physical damage of the PLM's facilities was minimal. By one reckoning the final bill came to this:

Damage caused by German hostilities	1,270,000 francs
Damage caused by French defense	1,150,000 francs
Damage caused by the Commune	945,000 francs
Total	3,365,000 francs

Referring to these losses, Paulin Talabot admitted "the impossibility of satisfying the needs of industry and commerce." Recovery, as a consequence, was likely to be "rather slow," as the Administrative Council cautioned, and so it was. The need for repairs, the shortage of rails and rolling stock, and the necessary enlargement of stations kept the Company's understaffed workshops behind schedule until mid-decade.[21]

The PLM did gradually rebound. At the end of 1875 the Administrative Council had to concede that "the general movement of business has remained weak." But income began to rise irregularly thereafter, and expenses, thanks largely to a decline in coal prices, held steady or fell. The acquisition of new locomotives, always a good indicator of progress, increased. Steel rails and electric signals made their appearance, while the installation of heating units and cushions (even in third class) were the first beginnings of more comfortable passenger service, which the Company liked to think of as the expression of its "humanitarian sentiment"—not to mention its greater profits.[22] Yet a certain unsteadiness in the Company's leadership was detectable. Several times the administrative structure was reshuffled. Talabot was awarded a new title as General Director, but he was suffering from poor health and perhaps not unrelated legal problems (in 1872 he disappeared for a month in prison). Although his authority was officially reaffirmed by the PLM's Administrative Council in late June 1873, it was surely not coincidental that Gustave Noblemaire was appointed to his staff a few weeks later. Previously chief of the PLM's affiliate in Algeria, Noblemaire now became the Company's assistant director of operations in Paris. A man endowed with worldly sophistication and flamboyant style, Noblemaire quickly became Talabot's heir apparent and, to no one's surprise, succeeded him in 1881, thereby gaining a post he would hold until 1907.[23]

Noblemaire's aggressiveness can be amply documented in Company records, whether it was a question of lowering rates to attract Spanish wines onto PLM tracks or aiding coal mines of the Gard and Loire to counter English competition. As his reputation grew, other companies often looked to him for leadership in defending their rights against state intrusions. This struggle—always latent, occasionally explicit—resurfaced in the late 1870s over the issue of rates, déjà vu, and the meaning of ministerial control. Whereas the companies, and Noblemaire foremost, worried about "the absolute domination of the state," the new Minister of Public Works Charles de Freycinet complained of "the excessive power of the companies," which he accused of becoming "a state within a state." These were the lines drawn that were to be tested as the Freycinet Plan went into effect.[24]

The PO

"Everything changed." So a detailed report by the Administrative Council of the Paris-Orléans Company described events in the summer of 1870.

The railways became "a veritable machine of war," although most of the actual fighting occurred well beyond the PO's borders. Its trains brought troops from the south and returned the wounded, while its stations were flooded with refugees fleeing battle (scenes we ordinarily associate with 1940). Company headquarters had to be moved first to Tours, then on to Bordeaux as the German encirclement of Paris encompassed Orléans and the Loire Valley. Nine of the Company's bridges and tunnels were destroyed, all of which was euphemistically recorded in PO documents as part of "exceptional circumstances." They were followed by another euphemism called "the events," meaning the Paris Commune, during which only minor fire damage reached the Company's offices. Although gasoline was brought in by the rebels, it was explained, invading government troops arrived in time to prevent a major conflagration. Nevertheless, a hiatus in regular service lasted from mid-September 1870 until the following 19 June, when normal operations resumed.[25]

Compared to the Eastern Company or the PLM, the PO thus emerged relatively unscathed, though the three immediate problems of recovery were the same. First, there was a bill to pay, estimated by the Company as follows:

Damage caused by German hostilities	1,080,000 francs
Damage caused by French defense	420,000 francs
Damage caused by the Commune	65,000 francs
Total	1,565,000 francs

Second, there were employees to discipline or dismiss. Because such cases were erratically entered into minutes, an exact count for the PO is impossible, but the aggregate was presumably similar to the other companies. Also identical was the reaction of the Administrative Council to protest over the summary firing of dissident workers, who were ignored. Third, there were freight blockages to be dealt with, especially barrels of wine, which had stood on the PO's loading docks for months. The endless difficulties of relieving such *encombrements* were compounded by large German requisitions of freight wagons, thereby exacerbating the postwar shortage of rolling stock in most of France.[26]

The financial troubles of the PO were particularly acute. It had neither the indemnities (from Germany) and subsidies (from the French government, often for military construction) of the Eastern Company, nor the size and strength of the PLM, nor the deep Rothschild pockets of the Northern. The Company was therefore forced to borrow heavily from the state in the usual form of "guarantees of interest" inherited from the Second Empire, which the Thierist regime—likewise strapped for cash—was reluctant to award. Moreover, the PO was meanwhile squeezed by state levies added onto passenger fares and freight charges, a kind of value-added tax that imposed an "enormous burden" on all of the companies. Friction over finances was evident in the Company's frequent refusal to grant requests from the Ministry of Public Works for special fare reductions. Two clear exceptions, however, were made for travelers attending major annual horse races, such as the Grand Prix de Paris, and for French pilgrims to Lourdes and Paray-le-Monial, which soon became, with new rail connections, among the most celebrated religious shrines of Europe. These were the PO's early contributions to the origins of tourism by railway.[27]

The Company's outstanding administrator of the time was Antoine Solacroup, a personality less expansive and dominating than François Jacqmin or Gustave Noblemaire but a tenacious defender of the Company's rights. It was Solacroup who became active in resolving the PO's most crucial political issue in confrontation with the Ministry of Public Works. This matter centered on the future of the Company of the Charentes, a conglomerate of small firms within or bordering the putative territory of the PO, which was now presented with some unpalatable alternatives. One was to expand the Charentes, adding the Company of the Vendée on the Atlantic Coast south of Nantes, and thereby to create a seventh large private railway enterprise. Or the state might acquire these companies and establish its own railroad network under direct government operation. Or, finally, the entire southwestern region of France might be integrated through a gigantic *rachat*, likely including the PO itself. Each of these proposals had its advocates in parliament, and when Didion and Solacroup appeared before a committee in the Chamber of Deputies to testify against them in favor of strengthening the PO, they were met with "profound silence."[28] Once Charles de Freycinet arrived as Minister of Public Works in December 1877, however, he and Solacroup became engaged in a series of conferences to thrash out a solution. Nearly a full year of deadlock ensued before Freycinet finally conceded that the extremes of a seventh large private system or a total confiscation by the state would be "inopportune." The two sides agreed that a Compagnie de l'Etat should be formed by a redistribution of several rail lines, without which such a state-owned enterprise could not be viable. Specifically, the new state company would acquire all connections west of the Paris-Bordeaux tracks. Most of the Company of the Charentes would then be absorbed by the PO, which, ever suspicious of assuming unprofitable operations, demanded "serious guarantees" from the state.[29]

These circumstances are recounted here in some detail because they best illustrate, from the vantage of the companies, how the balance of power between them and the state remained precarious. If the companies succeeded in warding off the worst—either a proliferation of smaller firms or a complete takeover by the state—they still had to face Freycinet and Ponts-et-Chaussées, both determined to expand government control of the nation's railroads. Although a deal on the redistribution of routes was closed in early 1879, as the PO's Administrative Council warned, there would yet be "painful" adjustments while the Company attempted to defend its autonomy "to the degree possible."[30]

With the French economy improving in the late 1870s, then, the PO entered the next decade with caution and some confidence. But such optimism was undercut in February 1880 by Solacroup's sudden death, leaving the Company with unstable leadership during the crucial years to come.

The Northern Railway Company

When the war of 1870 started on France's eastern front, the Northern Company reacted at first as if it were a distant and temporary disturbance. Regular service was continued on its network with some special trains added for military transport. But once the German armies had advanced to encircle Sedan at the beginning of September, there was no more business as usual. Delays and disrupted connections became the rule, as bridges and tunnels were blasted to impede the enemy's progress; and, of course, the Germans did their part as well. In all, forty-five structures were destroyed on Northern lines. The Company also lost 472 freight wagons to the invaders, some of which later straggled back in disrepair. Workshops at La Chapelle were temporarily converted to the production of rifles and cannons, and Company workers were armed to protect vital rail installations. Yet these measures did little to forestall the "unfortunate events" that followed.[31]

After the armistice, the Northern Company attempted, "with the consent of the Prussian administration," to restore some semblance of service beyond the perimeter of the Paris siege, and trains began to roll intermittently from Paris to Lille and Calais. But the onset of the Commune put an abrupt stop to that activity, while the Company's administrative functions had to be transferred to Amiens and Lille. Only one adjective seemed appropriate to describe the total result—"disastrous."[32]

Yet, after all, the Northern Company recovered more quickly than the others for the obvious reason that it possessed more available cash and credit, due in large measure to the Rothschild Bank. Besides, some of its most important economic assets and a sturdy fleet of its locomotives were secure behind the Belgian border, untouched by the conflict in France. By late 1872 the Northern's gross receipts had regained the prewar level, and the Company could begin again to place orders for rails, locomotives, and other rolling stock. The Administrative Council was able to report that finances were "much more satisfactory than we could have hoped." Notwithstanding its advantages, however, the Company could not avoid the freight blockages that plagued others. Nor did its rapid recovery come cheaply. Repairs, purchases of vehicles, replacement of rails (now often of steel), and rising personnel costs all put a strain on the budget.[33]

During the mid-1870s the Northern was locked into two types of conflictual relationship, akin but not identical. The first directly involved the state, whose demands might take the form either of parliamentary legislation or of ministerial decrees. In addition to the taxes on passenger fares, baggage, and packages imposed by the fiscally embattled Thiers regime in 1871, another 5 percent surcharge on heavy freight (called "Petite Vitesse") was enacted into law on 12 March 1874, cutting still more sharply into Company profits. Possibly worse, from the Northern's perspective, was the government's subsidization of canals in its region, which forced the Company to lower its rates for the transportation of coal and coke. In 1875, for example, the six major rail firms carried a total of over 14 million tons of combustibles, of which the Northern accounted for 36.5 percent and the PLM 34 percent. Yet the Northern earned only 34.6 percent of its gross receipts from such shipments, whereas the PLM gained 40 percent.[34] Consequently, it was not difficult for the Northern Company to cast state agencies in the role of vampires, draining the blood of their victims through misguided policy and excessive control. These allegations also pertained to technological improvements, sometimes gladly adopted by the companies but frequently prescribed by the state over their objections. If it is proper to speak of "a sort of miracle" in regard to the introduction of more efficient railway technology in the 1870s, records of the Northern and the other companies show that their implementation of it was somewhat grudging and not without overt resistance to the state's imposition of expenses unspecified in their original concessions. "The French companies," as one of their mutual resolutions stated in 1876, "protest energetically against the imposition of such measures."[35]

A second source of altercation was the Northern's dealings with other companies. As usual, there were border disputes and difficult negotiations with the Eastern Company and the PLM. The best example was a flurry about connections to Paris from Reims, the Ardennes, and southeastern Belgium. The Eastern Company's route via Epernay came under challenge from the Northern's line via Soissons, threatening to rupture a treaty of two decades standing. According the Northern's version, in 1875 the Eastern suddenly presented "unexpected demands," against which the former was forced to seek a means of defense "and if necessary of attack." In this instance, the Ministry of Public Works attempted to placate both sides by not entirely satisfying either. It was a draw.[36]

A more serious affair concerned one of the smaller companies, formed in the late 1860s, that now threatened the Northern's monopoly in its territory. The Northeastern Company (Compagnie Nord-Est) was a creature of the infamous Belgian financier Simon Philippart, who sought to integrate his holdings in the coastal region west of Lille with those in the vicinity of Maubeuge, east of Valenciennes. Philippart could plausibly argue that he had merely acquired some 300 kilometers of noncontiguous track in which the Northern had no manifest interest; furthermore, his holdings lacked access to Paris and therefore presented no threat to the Northern's monopoly. Yet the latter's leadership suspected much more sinister motives in the ambitions of such smaller firms. The showdown came at a meeting of the Northeastern's Administrative Council in December 1875. During a "lively debate" over a proposed compromise with the Northern Company, Philippart was attacked by Emile Erlanger, a rival banker at the Crédit Mobilier and a crony of James de Rothschild. After the discussion became "very passionate and very confused," Erlanger demanded that Philippart be removed from the Council. Thereupon, "general tumult [and] violent protests" followed. When Erlanger declared himself Philippart's successor as president of the Northeastern, police intervened and "in the name of the law" cleared the meeting room. His pride and reputation badly wounded, Philippart never fully recovered, and, as we saw, the cause of the small companies quickly began to decline.[37]

This brief glimpse into the Northern's internal history is sufficient to document the ferocity with which the future of the French railway system was contested in the 1870s. If the self-defense of the Northern and the other major companies was successful, it was primarily for two reasons. One was the lack of feasibility of the alternatives: neither were the politically and financially unstable cabinets of the early Third Republic capable of a total confiscation of the whole railway industry, nor were the smaller companies able to sustain themselves against the clout, administrative tradition, and entrenched positions of their large competitors. The second explanation was a fortuitous economic upturn at decade's end that helped to restore the confidence and fiscal viability of the major companies. A marked improvement in its revenues was noted by the Northern's Administrative Council for the final quarter of 1877. The following year proved to be "exceptionally favorable." In part, these increments could be attributed to a salutary bump by the Paris Exposition of 1878, but the "remarkable increases" continued into the early 1880s, abetted by the state's implementation of the Freycinet Plan. The Northern Company's records of such items as the soaring orders for new locomotives and other rolling stock leave no doubt that French railway executives presumed themselves to be on the crest of a promising expansion. Seemingly, they had survived the storm.[38]

The Failure of Centralism

The end of the Freycinet Plan came suddenly. Panic struck the Lyon stock exchange on 21 June 1882 and soon spread to Paris. Banks and businesses quickly found themselves on the brink of bankruptcy, and some plunged over. Such episodes had occurred in the past, but this time was to be different: "The depression which began in 1882 lasted longer and probably cost France more than any other in the nineteenth century."[39] Explanations for the crash range from the general to the specific, that is, from a long-term structural weakness of the French economy (a sagging demographic curve meant reduced demand) to the particular *conjoncture* of the moment. Already in 1881 there were warnings of hyperextension. The Northern Railway Company reported that its gross income during that year was "very satisfactory" but that expenses—for laying tracks, purchasing rolling stock, and hiring new personnel—were "excessive," producing an "unfavorable result." Yet it seemed that the craze for construction had become insatiable.[40]

The brief period of prosperity from 1879 through 1881 must therefore be seen as a raising of the guillotine. When the blade fell, it decapitated the Freycinet Plan in a stroke. Within a month the Ministry of Public Works began consultations with the large private companies about the possibility of drafting new conventions, an obvious purpose of which would be to salvage whatever was possible of the grand hopes that were now dashed. Among them were the demands, still heatedly expressed at the end of 1881, for a confiscation of the Paris-Orléans Company, possibly as the first step in a reconfiguration of the entire French railway system. But the state was no longer in a condition for such drastic change. The strongest attack on the strident *rachat* proposals now came from Léon Say, a sometime cabinet member and long-standing administrative officer of the Northern Railway Company, who did not shy from calling the Freycinet Plan a "disaster." He also went on to say that seizure of the large private companies would be an irreparable error, a crippling blow to the public treasury. Moreover, he added, it was absurd to confiscate the PO unless the real intention were to restructure the French rail system as a whole, which was well beyond the capability of the present republican government.[41] Instead, what the new Minister of Public Works Henry Varroy proposed was "a truce of fifteen years." In other words, France's mixed railway system would be retained with its uneasy balance between the state and the private companies. The latter would be free of any fear of confiscation, in return for which they would agree to at least a modicum of expansion foreseen in the Freycinet Plan. Once an accord was reached on these general propositions, bargaining on the details could begin.[42]

It is important to distinguish what the conventions of 1883 accomplished from what they did not. In the first place, we should note the plural form. Although sometimes referred to in the singular, they in fact comprised six separate accords. The state was obliged to come to terms with each of the private companies individually. Second, though the companies remained under attack from some members of parliament as "enemies of the Republic," they were in a relatively strong position because of their newly won immunity from confiscation. The critical issue in negotiations was therefore the perennial one of the extent of state control over commerce. That matter came to a head in April 1883, when the current Minister of Public Works David Reynal demanded that the state henceforth exercise an "absolute right" to establish rates. He was promptly opposed by Gustave Noblemaire, speaking for the companies, who flatly asserted that in this matter they could not compromise without a loss of independence. After three weeks of altercation, Reynal finally relented and his pretensions were "definitively abandoned."[43] With that sticking point removed, a final version of the conventions could be drafted in June. For good reason Reynal was less than ecstatic—"the state is always the dupe," he sighed—but his government was willing to come to terms.[44] Accordingly, it is quite dubious to portray the 1883 conventions as a turning point of French railway history or to suppose that this date signaled the end of one era and the beginning of another. One should emphasize, rather, the continuity from 1842 and 1859 to 1883 and beyond. In reality, the traditional mixed system of public and private enterprise was thereby left intact, and the state's power to regulate the industry remained limited regarding such essential functions as the fixing of rates, even if it was still free to exert increased pressure to reduce them. Hence, the conventions of 1883 marked no watershed.

Once the Freycinet Plan was abandoned, the republican government's main concern was to ensure a suitably rapid pace of rail construction. Every region wanted its railways and every town, no matter how remote, coveted its own station. The Ministry of Public Works therefore sought a "third network" (*troisième réseau*) throughout the land, which meant an agreement by each of the companies to undertake the construction of hundreds of additional kilometers of ancillary track. Much of the cost would be borne by the state treasury, but the means and credit of the companies would be deployed. Their continued existence was an essential component of the scheme. The distinction between "old" and "new" routes was now erased (requiring a baffling change in bookkeeping procedures), and state guarantees for all rail lines would become available. The state would thus carry greater risks but also claim a greater share of profits, if any, beyond a subsistence level. This much deeper involvement of state agencies implied potential restrictions on the freedom of the companies: their finances might be more tightly controlled, their rates reduced and unified, their orders of rolling stock closely watched, their safety measures regulated. If fully implemented, as one historian has concluded, such imperatives would mean that "the state had obtained great advantages."[45] But the actual impact was still undetermined, a significant matter we shall later need to address.

For the French state, after the high expectations aroused by the Freycinet Plan, the conventions of 1883 were something of a comedown, the best available compromise under distressing economic circumstances. The companies, on the other hand, accepted them with a certain relief. In December each of them convoked their current stockholders for a special session at which the respective administrative councils had no difficulty in obtaining unanimous approval. Those present at the Eastern Company's meeting heard that demands for state confiscation of the companies were defeated, and that the regime's ambition to become "absolute master" of rates had been thwarted. Similarly, at the PLM there were boasts of "the triumph of true economic principles" because the proponents of a *rachat* had been routed, their errors and sophisms exposed. In return for a reduction in state taxes on freight, the Company would consent to lower rates, all the better to meet foreign competition. And it would also agree to construct 2000 kilometers of new track, while mutually acknowledging "the principle of the association of the state with the great companies." The Paris-Orléans Company was more concerned with the "revision of frontiers" in western France, which would henceforth be divided among the PO, the Western Company, and the newly consolidated state network (Compagnie de l'Etat), whose existence was in effect ratified. Despite some unavoidable problems of redistribution, at least the new convention put an end to the "veritable danger" of creating small companies within the PO's domain. Investors of the Northern Company were meanwhile reassured by their Administrative Council that finally the threats of proliferating smaller firms and of outright confiscation by the state were terminated: "Today all these dangers have disappeared." The Company could therefore resume its regular operations with the confidence that challenges to the French railway system raised since 1870 had been vanquished by the new convention. "It puts an end to a period of sterile and dangerous struggles."[46]

These brave words were spoken before the depth of France's depression was known. We need to measure that phenomenon in concrete terms in order to illustrate the devastating impact that the decade of the 1880s had on the French economy and on the railway industry in particular. To do so, it will again be useful to return to the records of the private companies, whose individual performances after 1883 provide the best criteria with which to frame a composite picture. First, however, a word of caution is in order. The statistics that follow, though drawn straight from transcripts and memoranda of the time, should be treated solely as approximations. Part of the problem, as mentioned, was a necessary alteration in accounting by the companies to conform with the 1883 conventions, which ended separate bookkeeping for different categories of railway lines. Furthermore, the hand-written ledgers of company finances were compiled through a myriad of notes and slips from hundreds of administrative officials, a procedure never exact and always in flux. An unusually frank admission of fiscal confusion within the Northern Company described how information was gathered from various train stations throughout the network. Given that these reports were fragmentary and often tardy, accountants at the Paris headquarters would habitually estimate (not to say falsify) the likely results and then later alter some numbers to approach the assumed correct totals: "We rectified our error by increasing or decreasing … the figures [as if] we had adhered to the information sent by the stations." Although this deliberate obfuscation may have arrived at reasonably accurate tabulations in the end, it could admittedly give "an erroneous impression of the situation of current traffic." Presuming that such statistical legerdemain was common among the companies, we stand forewarned.[47]

The general pattern of the Eastern Company was fairly typical of the French railway firms. Turbulence on the stock exchange that had started in the summer of 1882 resulted by the beginning of 1884 in what the Administrative Council called a full-blown "industrial and commercial crisis." During that year the Company's income fell by 4 million francs, and in 1885 by another 7 million. Reports were that the Eastern's entire business operation declined by 16 percent in 1885 and by 18 percent in the next year. Because income was sharply down, with no apparent means to increase it, the Company's only recourse was to reduce service, curtail schedules, and lay off personnel—measures for which later historians would adopt a term unknown in the 1880s: downsizing. Implementation of this policy, however, was made more difficult by administrative orders from the Ministry of Public Works about enforcing nationwide safety measures for the industry, much to the exasperation of François Jacqmin. More feisty than ever in his dotage, Jacqmin repeatedly challenged such decrees ("there are some questions for which no solution is possible") and supported collective efforts by the companies to appeal for arbitration by the Conseil d'Etat on charges of an "excess of power." By decade's end the Eastern had regained its financial equilibrium and was able to benefit from a boost through the Paris Exposition of 1889. Yet the losses were severe, and whether they could soon be recovered remained unsure.[48]

The impact of the economic slump on the PLM was immediate and drastic. Whereas the Company's gross income increased 14 million francs in 1881, it was deficitary by 4.7 million in 1882. In 1883 the network's traffic fell by 7.3 percent and its net product was down more than 9 million francs. Expenses of that year increased by over 5 million francs, which included an average raise of 8 percent in salary awarded to the Company's employees during the preceding flush period from 1879 to 1882. As a consequence, the workforce would need to be "considerably reduced." Yet an upturn was long in coming. For 1885, the PLM's Administrative Council reported a drop of another 9.5 million francs in income and "a reduction of traffic beyond all expectations." The same was true of 1886: "a serious and persistent decline in earnings beyond what could ever have been feared." Not only was French industry lagging, but agriculture as well. The Company's grain shipments were off by 9 percent in 1885, while wine and spirits plummeted 6 percent that year and again the next. By 1887 signs of recovery became apparent as gross income rose back to an annual level of 8 million francs, yet the total volume of the PLM's operations in 1888 was still below that of 1882. The improvement was thus "a good omen but too slow."[49]

Less dependent on the condition of industry, the Paris-Orléans Company experienced a slower but equally certain decline. From 1884 to 1887, the Company's income was shaved by 11 percent and its expenses, in a "spirit of economy," were reduced by 13 percent. In addition to the generally morose state of French commerce, specific hardships also struck the PO: the widespread phylloxera epidemic in its region, troubles in the grain market, competition from waterways, and wildcat strikes in the minefields of the Gard and the Loire. Never financially secure, the Company was thereby forced deeper into debt, resorting to larger state loans in the guise of guaranteed interest: 9 million francs in 1883, 15.5 million by 1886, another 16.2 million in 1887, "only" 8 million during the Exposition year of 1889. Tellingly, in 1890 the gross income of the PO was 15.5 million francs below the level of 1884. These were patently the statistics of depression.[50]

The Northern Railway Company was the champion of downsizing. In 1882, for instance, the Northern added 144 locomotives to its fleet and signed contracts for 148 more; in 1886 only six engines were acquired and none was ordered. Indications of trouble appeared in 1883 when the rise in expenses far outstripped that of income, meaning that the Company's "coefficient" (the portion of costs to credits) climbed to 54 percent. The recent conversion of accounting to a new format made comparisons difficult, and Northern officials freely conceded that "real" losses exceeded published numbers: the decline of earnings in 1884 was actually 8 million francs rather than the 6.5 million reported to stockholders. Remarkably, despite these setbacks, the Northern's coefficient fell back to nearly 46 percent by 1888, thanks to such cost-cutting measures as ceasing orders for rolling stock. Toward the end of the decade, a resurgence of coal and coke shipments allowed the Administrative Council to classify the Company's financial status as "very satisfactory," although it once more admonished that an alleged curtailment of expenses was "more apparent than real." Despite the lack of exact accounting, it seems likely that in 1890 both income and outlay of the Northern remained below the levels of 1884. Better than the other companies, the Northern thus managed to maintain its fiscal balance, but it did so only by seriously restraining its investments and operations.[51]

So many statistics tell the single tale of a contracting French economy and, with it, of a diminished railway industry. Unsatisfactory though it may appear, the conclusion must be repeated that cause and effect were inseparable. The private companies were participants and not merely spectators in the national economic debacle of the 1880s. Above all, they suffered along with other French enterprises from the excessive ambition and insufficient self-discipline of the Freycinet Plan, the failure of which left both the state and the private companies in a prolonged fit of depression.[52]

A Condition of Troubling Inferiority

France's economic performance after 1870 was mediocre at best. The slow postwar recovery and the ensuing rush of the Freycinet Plan proved to be only a temporary reprieve. During most of the 1880s, French commerce shriveled, railway networks contracted, and industrial growth stagnated. These unfortunate circumstances occurred during what some contemporaries called the "Suez revolution." Until the approach of the centennial year 1900 at the much celebrated *fin de siècle*, probably no single event of the nineteenth century stirred the imagination of Europeans so much as the opening of that great canal in 1868. The exotic appeal of Suez and the romantic notion of linking Asia to Europe helped to propel a whitecap of enthusiasm in France and elsewhere, contributing emotionally to the exploits we vaguely classify as imperialism.

Not coincidentally, the inauguration of the Suez Canal was closely followed by the completion of the Mt. Cenis Tunnel, conceived as the natural extension of one engineering marvel by another. The new interlocking systems of water and rail transportation, it was thought, would hasten the global economy and commerce toward an era of prosperity. Even though these grand visions were short-lived and soon replaced by more sober evaluations, a trace of them remained in the minds of railway planners who supposed that Europe was now poised for a season of increasingly intense international competition. This development, in fact, became one of the distinguishing characteristics of the period from 1870 to 1890, lending it a commercial profile markedly different from the preceding years of more provincial concerns. Not that local or regional problems were suddenly gone and forgotten. But national and international perspectives grew conspicuously more evident.[53]

Although the Mt. Cenis Tunnel linking northern Italy to France was actually completed during the Franco-Prussian war, formal ceremonies for its opening were delayed until the autumn of 1871. The French were hardly in a celebratory mood, however, and the nation's railway networks were already overburdened. As a result, the initial impact of the Mt. Cenis was negligible, both psychologically and economically. Moreover, the specter of St. Gotthard was meanwhile haunting Europe. It was plain to see that this Italo-Swiss-German project, to be completed within a decade, would be more central and crucial for international trade. Consequently, a clamor soon arose in the French parliament for a third tunnel, located somewhere between Mt. Cenis and St. Gotthard, that would restore a commercial advantage to France. Several conservative senators and deputies circulated a petition favoring a subsidy of 4 million francs to prepare a rail passage via the Simplon through Switzerland. This solution, assured Claude-Marie Raudot, among others, would complete the "Suez revolution"; but it could only be accomplished with strong state assistance, since the French companies were incapable of mounting such an effort. In the mid-1870s, however, the Broglie government was still uncertain, and it was above all reluctant to squander its limited funds on a project situated well beyond French borders. The Ministry of Public Works thus balked and ordered instead a study of another possibility at Mt. Blanc, where a tunnel would presumably be closer and cheaper. But when this project, too, was deferred, a third faction appeared to oppose both proposals and to argue that France would be better served by further developing its existing facilities, especially navigation on the Rhône. This contention was seconded by a special review committee appointed by Ponts-et-Chaussées, whose preemptory conclusion was that the third alternative would be "more simple, more certain, and less expensive."[54]

Inconclusively, the debate lingered on into the 1880s, while the St. Gotthard opened and threatened to draw French passenger and freight traffic eastward. In France all parties could agree that some attempt must be made "to parry competition of the St. Gotthard and to repair the damage that it will not fail to cause." But what should it be? After a series of disputatious hearings, the majority of a parliamentary committee voted in July 1881 to support a transalpine tunnel project, "especially Mt. Blanc."[55] Yet public opinion remained divided, if we judge from proclamations released by French business interests. For example, the Paris Chamber of Commerce demanded a new tunnel, fearing that traffic via Mt. Cenis would otherwise be "gravely compromised" by St. Gotthard, whereas the Marseille Chamber of Commerce contended that the Rhône corridor was the key and that another tunnel would fail to divert much transit from the St. Gotthard. Impasse and inaction resulted, the ultimate consequence of which was cogently stated by one member of an extraparliamentary committee in 1883: "The respective situations of France and Germany vis-à-vis Italy have thus entirely changed."[56]

A different but equally noteworthy tunnel proposal deserves a brief mention here: a rail link under the English Channel, which could also be viewed as the logical complement to Suez. Glancingly discussed before 1870, this enticing mirage gained a more concrete status when the former Bonapartist economic adviser and famed free trade advocate Michel Chevalier applied for a special concession for it in 1874. Not only was his group of potential investors encouraged by Ponts-et-Chaussées, it had the backing of wealthy Rothschilds on both sides of the Channel. Records of the Northern Railway Company reveal that, at the time, this project was already considered both technologically feasible and extremely desirable. "A big step forward" in 1875 was followed with "the most lively interest" by Company officials, especially when a geological survey confirmed that an Anglo-French railroad tunnel was within existing engineering capabilities. After Chevalier's death in 1879, leadership passed to Léon Say, who in 1880 offered "the most reassuring guarantees" while obtaining the approval of Ponts-et-Chaussées for a three-year extension of the concession. As we know, these ambitions would require another century to realize. Prohibitive costs in a period of economic weakness and the reluctance of the British government to cooperate were impeding factors sufficiently weighty to sink the initiative well before 1890. All that remained were large cartons of documents now on deposit in the French National Archives.[57]

If France wanted to compete in international commerce, it would need better rail connections to other countries, not only by land but also by sea. Hence ports were no less significant, or controversial, than tunnels. By mid-century all of Europe's main ports had become railheads, and France if anything had a plethora of them. Indeed, the unremitting competition among them must be counted as one reason for the impairment of French trade after 1870. Government allocations to improve one harbor facility invariably provoked demands from others for equal treatment. Throughout the 1870s state funds were in short supply, and the Executive Council of Ponts-et-Chaussées could only lament that "our ports are not completed, our canals and navigable rivers remain in distress." Furthermore, divided as it was into separate private companies, the entire French rail system was ill suited to connect the Atlantic to the Mediterranean. Only one line stretched from Le Havre to Paris, where transfers and delays occurred before goods could be moved to Marseille or points between. This peculiarity explains a push within the Chamber of Deputies in 1873 for an alternative route from coast to coast: "Without a direct line from Calais to Marseille," said one speaker, "the traffic between England and the Orient will be lost by France and gained by Germany." Yet the expense of such construction at a time of penurious state budgets was simply beyond the Republic's capacity, and, to reiterate, the very conception of it ran contrary to the structure of the French railway industry. The Chamber's railway committee therefore rejected the initiative by a vote of 17 to 4.[58]

Nevertheless, the correspondence of the Ministry of Public Works, Ponts-et-Chaussées, and parliamentary committees was repeatedly filled with references to "the national interest" and "the great national importance" of improving French ports as well as railway access to them. These pleas were tinged with dark hints of French decline, all the more so once the completion of the St. Gotthard approached. As Le Havre and Dunkerque were losing ground to Antwerp, and Marseille to Genoa, it seemed obvious enough that St. Gotthard was deliberately "an enterprise directed against French commerce."[59] We need look no further for a rationale of the Freycinet Plan, with its vast outlays projected for harbors and rails. As Ponts-et-Chaussées commented in 1878: "The competition of neighboring ports makes great works necessary." Likewise, speaking in 1882 for the Comité consultatif des chemins de fer (CCCF), a main advisory body in the Ministry of Public Works, Alexandre Gottschalk expanded on the struggle to compete with Belgian and German railroads for transit via St. Gotthard to and from the Atlantic ports: "There is reason to hurry, because the present situation is not without danger." By assuring cheaper rates and fewer delays, he added, lowland harbors were gaining a decisive lead over the French. No wonder that the 1873 project of an uninterrupted railway between Calais and Marseille was revived during the early euphoric days of Freycinet's ministry. Because of St. Gotthard, as a bill presented to parliament stated, this undertaking should be launched "as soon as possible." But, along with the rest of the Freycinet Plan, these hopes were soon doused with depressing economic data.[60]

As ever, the central issue for the French railway industry was not structures—tunnels, bridges, or harbors—but rates. We have seen how the immediate postwar years were marked by hefty recriminations against the private companies and by their rebuttal. Particularly harsh in that regard was the so-called Dietz-Monnin report, presented to parliament in 1872 and later amplified by its author, who charged that the multitude of special rates set by the companies was merely an elaborate means to evade the terms of their concessions from the state. Accordingly, the companies were accused in the Chamber of Deputies of wielding "excessive power," an allegation vehemently denied by François Jacqmin and other railway executives, who pointed out *au contraire* the "enormous burden" imposed by governmental taxes on freight and passenger fares. Such polemics tended to balance out and create a permanent oscillation of opinion in which all could faintly concur that there were just too many separate rates; and yet, as one deputy said, to be profitable the companies would require "a little liberty."[61]

The five-year period from 1878 to 1882 can be seen as a kind of heyday for the Ministry of Public Works. This stretch of relative prosperity and promise opened a window of opportunity for the state to press its case for greater control of railway rates and, at long last, to redefine that venerable and always vague notion of *homologation*. At the time, four capable and vigorous men served successive terms as minister: Charles de Freycinet, Henry Varroy, Sadi Carnot, and David Reynal. Each attempted to curtail arbitrary abuses of the rate structure by the companies and to insist that increases or alterations necessarily required prior approval of Public Works, not simply a ratification after the fact. Needless to elaborate, the companies responded by denouncing any attempt to enforce "the absolute domination of the state" and by claiming that they were in fact at pains to promote "national industry," albeit within a flexible pattern of rates of which they were the proper judge.[62] The climax of this altercation occurred in 1883 when Reynal, after returning to the ministry for a second term, tried to establish a board of rate arbitration, a move with which the major private companies refused to cooperate. Once more the outcome was inconclusive. Reynal's proposal was quietly dropped, despite the unambiguous recommendation of a parliamentary investigation headed by Richard Waddington that the state would be justified to "reassert the authority that should never have been allowed to escape."[63] But escape it had. In view of this deadlock, the declining fortunes of French industry, and the impact of St. Gotthard on international trade, an extraparliamentary committee of deputies and departmental officials drew in March 1883 this pessimistic conclusion: "Compared to other foreign nations, France is today in a condition of troubling inferiority."[64]

The difficult situation of the French nation as a European railway power was well illustrated by international conferences held in the Swiss capital of Bern between 1878 and 1886. The fear of the private companies was that such gatherings might result in resolutions that could then be exploited by the French government to impose on them uniform regulations or policies, particularly in regard to rates. That danger was called to the attention of the Ministry of Public Works by Alphonse de Rothschild as early as 1874. A joint communiqué by the companies in 1877 reiterated their reservations, shortly before preliminary meetings convened in Bern during the following year.[65] Nothing came of them. Instead, the French companies continued their usual practice of negotiating with one another and, either individually or in unison, with the state. An example was a treaty between the Northern and Eastern companies to divide commercial prerogatives in Germany: the former assumed primacy in the northern regions (Cologne, Hamburg, Berlin, and beyond), whereas the latter took the south (Frankfurt, Munich, and Vienna)—an arrangement still reflected in train schedules today.[66]

When the first major international convocation assembled in Bern in 1882, the ostensible focus was a question of technological standards: should all nations agree to a maximum track gauge of 1435 millimeters, as was already the case in Germany and most of northern Europe (clearly a legacy of the Association of German Railway Administrations), or might the limit be stretched to 1465 millimeters, as was sometimes the practice in France, Italy, and Belgium? When polled by Ponts-et-Chaussées, most French administrators and engineers expressed support for maintaining the existing circumstances and thus refusing to adopt German norms. But the actual issue was not purely technological. Internal correspondence shows that the principal objection of the major railroad firms was that the enforcement of international conventions would in reality "modify the contract concluded between the French companies and the state." A joint declaration by their representatives therefore bluntly repulsed the recommendation of the Bern majority for stricter standards: "A diplomatic convention should not have that effect."[67] That viewpoint was later adopted by the Comité de l'exploitation technique des chemins de fer (CETCF), another important advisory board for the Ministry of Public Works. For once, the public and private sectors in France stood firm together. The only problem was, as David Reynal worried in 1884, that France risked isolation as the only country unwilling to accommodate itself to a concerted attempt to promote commerce through technological consensus. Yet a subsequent Bern conference in 1886 laid the matter to rest by adopting a Swiss compromise motion to admit the possibility of track gauges, at least in sharp curves, anywhere between 1435 and 1465 millimeters. If such a convenient resolution gave satisfaction to the French delegation, it also exposed two glaring features of this protracted negotiation: the secondary importance of its technological aspect and the dogged inflexibility of French railway management.[68]

A new factor of commercial, military, and political importance was the formation of a large beltway (Grande Ceinture) of railroads around Paris. The inadequacy of the existing smaller beltway within city limits had been embarrassingly displayed by the war and the freight blockages thereafter. Besides, the Ministry of Public Works—ever eager to curb the excessive power of the companies as well as to facilitate trade across the land—preferred to deal with one administrative organ of private railway enterprise rather than several. The establishment of a beltway syndicate thus actually originated from an initiative by the state, not as part of some clever plot by the companies. Because the Western Company at first chose not to become involved, the Syndicate was initially composed of the Big Four (Eastern, PLM, PO, and Northern), a tight circle from which the Trojan horse of the State Company—on grounds that it had no access to Paris—was excluded. Beginning its formal meetings in 1876, the Syndicate soon became a champion of the private companies' autonomy and a master of studied delay, repeatedly prompting individual responses by them to governmental instructions or inquiries. Did the state have a right to impose on them expenses beyond the explicit terms of their concessions? "We think not," was the curt reply of the companies.[69] When the Bern conferences began, the Syndicate warned that no binding international treaty would be possible before national uniformity was first achieved, which did not obtain in France. Understandably, the Ministry of Public Works was appalled by this Frankenstein's monster, sheepishly intoning that "the great companies have a certain power, but it is not unlimited."[70] The inception of new regulatory agencies like the CCCF and the CETCF can thus been seen as efforts by the government to tighten its grip on commercial and technological standards in face of the Syndicate's obstinacy. It has been asserted that these fledgling governmental bodies succeeded in imposing regulations on the companies that "severely limited their freedom of action."[71] But evidence for the effectiveness of the state's restraints is in fact scanty for the period before 1890. Neither the records of the Syndicate, nor of the companies, nor of Public Works itself provide much basis for such a claim. As for later decades, we shall see.[72]

Two of the most indicative criteria for gauging the effectiveness of state regulation before 1890 were locomotives and finances. As for the former, we have seen that precedents about the right of the private companies to determine their purchases of rolling stock had a long history dating back to the earliest days of railroads. Orders for new engines were steeply up during the Freycinet years. A single noteworthy change was the unusual frequency with which the companies began looking abroad to acquire new locomotives, particularly in Belgium and Britain, once it became clear that neither their own workshops nor other French manufacturing firms had the capacity to meet immediate needs. While this practice raised some administrative eyebrows in Paris, it ended abruptly with the ensuing economic crisis. Whereas the French railway companies acquired a record 741 locomotives in 1882, they bought only 44 in 1888. Cutbacks in the domestic locomotive industry were accordingly drastic. Company *ateliers* all but abdicated from construction, delivering a grand total of five engines in 1888. Other French industrial plants did little better, producing altogether only 51 locomotives in 1887, 39 in 1888, and 26 in 1889.[73] These paltry numbers indicate that there was in fact not much for the government to regulate. Hence, a special committee on rolling stock, appointed by Ponts-et-Chaussées, returned a recommendation in July 1889 that the companies be left "a certain latitude" in meeting the fluctuating market prices and their individual needs. In return, they should merely be admonished to report more regularly to the Ministry of Public Works.[74]

One innovation of the 1883 conventions was the creation of a special corps of "general commissars" to inspect the financial operations of the companies. This novelty was thought necessary in view of the increased practice of cost-sharing between the state and the companies, notably when it came to military construction. Public Works and parliament were also concerned to enforce safety requirements, such as electric signals and air brakes, in order to avert "a veritable field of carnage" from railway accidents. With their habitual reluctance to comply, the companies responded with evasions and excuses to the government's pleas that they provide statistical data *"with the least possible delay."*[75] Meanwhile, as mentioned, a move by Charles de Freycinet to require the companies to present an annual budget for prior approval by Public Works was vigorously protested by the companies, which charged that the minister had "exceeded his authority." Back and forth the argument went, with the companies conceding only that they would submit their financial projections for government inspection "insofar as possible." For its part, the directorate of Ponts-et-Chaussées—with a risible display of bureaucratic circumlocution—claimed that state agencies must exercise ultimate control over all matters financial "except those modifications that particular circumstances might justify."[76] In short, the recently installed cadre of *inspecteurs des finances* was making little or no headway. This was the nub of an official report in June 1890, which deplored the inability of state officials to obtain sufficient information from the companies. To this effect it quoted (future President of the Republic) Félix Faure: "The organization of this special control ... has not given the results expected.... It is indispensable that the control be exercised with more authority." Further reform was nevertheless deferred.[77]

Is it permissible, then, to greet "the birth of a new railway" and to hail a "France transformed" after the conventions of 1883? To be sure, a case for that conclusion can be made and has already been skillfully constructed.[78] Yet a patient reading of the various archival records we have examined does not strongly support it. Rather, a more familiar and disabused expression seems to be appropriate here: "plus ça change, plus ça reste la même chose." The essential feature of the French railway system remained unaltered: it was, as before, mixed between the public and private sectors. Although threatened from all sides with more stringent controls or even by outright confiscation, the major companies still managed to maintain their integrity. The collapse of the Freycinet Plan meant a failure of centralism and a reversion to the established nineteenth-century balance of liberalism and etatism. Not a watershed in France but rather the lack of it was the dominant fact of the period after the war of 1870.

The date 1883 thus deserves to be located in the middle of this chapter, not at its end. Both the French economy and the railway trade on which it depended were damaged by the recession of the mid-1880s. Thereafter, neither state officials nor company administrators could throttle—or transform—the other. France did not emerge in 1890 with a newly conceived railway system but with a severely chastened version of the old.

Railways and the Republican Army

Whereas the German Empire was proclaimed in Versailles, it is arguable that the French Third Republic was founded in Frankfurt. The title of the provisional "government of national defense," established in Paris on 4 September 1870, was appropriately chosen. But as such it was a failure. It could neither avert defeat nor create a stable regime. Above all, it could not dominate the Paris Commune—not, that is, until Adolphe Thiers came to terms with Otto von Bismarck, who then gave orders permitting French troops and trains to close in on the capital. Thereupon, and not before, the Republic was in business. Yet the new state was now stripped of its eastern frontier and thus shorn of its exterior defenses. Militarily as otherwise France needed to rebuild, to start again. Gone was Napoleon III and with him the professional army that had fared so miserably against Moltke's invading forces. Railroads had manifestly made the difference, and therefore it became an unchallenged purpose of French strategic planning to develop a national system of networks that would enable the Republic to defend itself with equal or superior alacrity (as always, compared to Germany) whenever the occasion should arise.

A number of specific lessons were learned from the lost war. The future mobilization of a great million-man army would require careful planning; one could no longer count on improvisation or a blind faith that somehow the *furia francese* was sure to prevail. Moreover, such plans would require the construction of strategic lines across company boundaries. In order to avoid the "enormous delays and dreadful scenes of disorder" in Paris, as one eye-witness recalled, it would also be necessary to build a beltway beyond the city limits. Existing and projected rail connections should be more fully integrated into military preparations to ensure prompt execution of mobilization procedures. These were some of the basic notions that, if implemented, would enable the republican army to turn back any future German assault.[79]

In practice, of course, these were not trivial matters. The military record of the early Third Republic was consequently pockmarked with disputes. We may group the most prominent of these under three topics: costs, priorities, and command structures. The first stemmed directly from the peace settlement, its staggering reparations bill, and the resulting need to meet interest payments on a huge public debt. Within the confines of a tight budget, the government was forced for years to economize at every turn. To rebuild a defensive perimeter on the new Franco-German frontier—with major bastions at Verdun, Toul, Epinal, and Belfort—would require extravagant appropriations. The infantry also needed to be completely rearmed and re-equipped, while the cavalry wanted fresh horses and the artillery steel cannons. It followed that funding for strategic railway construction was limited and contested. The relative commercial or military value of a given line was always debatable, and conflicts abounded between state officials and the private companies over their respective share of the expenditures. Likewise, inside the government, dissension arose between the Ministry of War and the Ministry of Public Works, usually with Ponts-et-Chaussées attempting to mediate as an honest broker. Reassurances from the state administration that "everything possible" was being done to satisfy civilian as well as military demands did not deter the "systematic hostility" of the companies whenever they felt that some strategic purpose was being fulfilled at their expense. Nor, as a contributor to the *Journal des sciences militaires* observed, did these altercations hasten the day when France would match Germany's "gigantic works," which represented an "immense danger" that must be countered "at any price." But the price seemed prohibitive, as the failure of the Freycinet Plan confirmed.[80]

Differences over spending for expanded railway facilities were often accompanied by questions about their location. Which rail lines were to be built where? Again, such issues of priority can be documented from the transcripts of various committee hearings. Most of these naturally concerned frontier areas, where the danger was greatest of inadvertently providing the enemy with a convenient by-pass or easy lateral access to the French interior. The Ministry of War demanded to be consulted about the construction of every connection. That military prerogative was established in 1872 only for the "frontier zone," but a disagreement promptly arose as to its extent. Left to their own designs, military leaders would probably have designated half of the country as frontier, thus including within the zone Paris and territory as far south as the Loire Valley. Public Works resisted undue extension of the military jurisdiction in an effort to retain control of railway building. As a rule, civilian officials supported commercial proposals marked on maps with a blue line, whereas military personnel indicated their alternatives with a red line. If no resolution were reached, as often occurred, the matter would go before a "mixed committee" (*commission mixte*) of arbitration, possibly to reach a settlement on the compromise of a green line. But the Ministry of Public Works and the directorate of Ponts-et-Chaussées complained, with considerable justification, that such bodies tended to be biased toward military solutions.[81] An example of these contentious procedures was the negotiation of a route for the exterior Paris beltway (Grande Ceinture), completion of which was delayed for several years while military men argued for sites in open terrain near fortresses and civilians defended commercially advantageous links between population centers. What emerged from these complex dealings was a triangular configuration of interests. In one corner was the military, ever insisting on its "absolute" priority, at least in the frontier zone, to determine the route, cost, and strategic viability of all railway projects. In another stood the companies (especially, for obvious reasons, the Eastern), always contending that the Minister of War should cover all of the investments for new construction whenever a line or second track was not indispensable for trade. And in the third was the Ministry of Public Works, abetted by Ponts-et-Chaussées, shifting from case to case, sometimes conceding "motives of a superior order" to the military but meanwhile scheming to limit its influence.[82] Despite the fragmentary nature of military records and the complicated and often hidden involvement of the French army in railway affairs, this aspect remains essential. No complete history of railroads in France can be written without reference to all of those red lines.

A third fundamental problem involved the position of railways in the military chain of command. There was certainly no shortage of possibilities. In the initial years of the Republic the focus of military decision-making was the Conseil supérieur de la guerre (CSG), a creature of Adolphe Thiers and his Minister of War, General Ernest de Cissey. But the membership of the CSG also included Marshal MacMahon, who briskly opposed what he considered the outdated military policies advocated by Thiers (who basically favored the restoration of a professional army) and who therefore joined a cabal to oust him in May 1873. Once MacMahon acceded to the presidency, the CSG soon relinquished its central role. Meanwhile, Cissey created another military advisory group, the Comité supérieur de défense (CSD), presided by Marshal François Canrobert. This organ's preoccupation was to establish a new system of fortifications on France's eastern frontier, a labor associated with the name of its most illustrious member, General Séré de Rivières. Yet it was never clear just what purpose the CSD might otherwise serve, and it too declined in importance. Some of the resulting void was filled by the Comité des fortifications, which frequently became involved in hearings over the location and cost of rail lines, their relative proximity to fixed defenses, and their protection by smaller redoubts (*forts d'arrêt*) designed to interdict any hostile incursion along French tracks.[83]

Uncertain was the relationship between these three bodies and the French General Staff (Etat-Major), whose officers commanded the peacetime army and would presumably lead it into war. To do so, they needed to ensure the operation of essential railways, for which their military corps of engineers (*Génie*) was directly responsible. That seemingly unassailable conception was undercut, however, by the fact that France now had a republican form of government in which an elected parliament and a civilian cabinet were supposed to have the final word. The Ministry of War—until the late 1880s always occupied by a senior military leader—was therefore putatively in charge of all strategic planning, and it is fair to conclude that the epicenter of the army's sprawling railway administration was located within it. Sixteen different ministers (two of whom served twice) attempted between 1870 and 1890 to bring some coherence to French military thinking and, specifically, to incorporating railways into the nation's strategy. Because of such manifest instability at the cabinet level, most of the actual development of French military plans, including the arrangements for railroads, occurred in the modest offices of the Ministry's Fourth Bureau, whose records are critical for our understanding of France's military preparations right up to 1914.

More exalted in title, but less crucial in planning, was the Commission militaire supérieure des chemins de fer (CMSCF), inaugurated in the early 1870s with the stated intention of raising the military use of railways in France "to the level of progress realized by neighboring countries." Behind this transparent reference to Germany was the hope of "concentrating in a single hand the direction of operations to be effected simultaneously on the entire national network." What the French needed, in short, was a Moltke. Failing that, the CMSCF never quite lived up to its billing, and in reality it remained, as a later staff memo accurately put it, "alien to the design of our transportation plans." Accordingly, the steady, practical work required for an effective mobilization of French troops finally fell to a small band of junior officers in the Rue St. Dominique: the Fourth Bureau.[84]

From a military standpoint, then, the decade of the 1870s may be described as a time when France slowly derived a strategic plan and developed the means to implement it. The scattered efforts of various military agencies mentioned above were pulled together as part of the Freycinet Plan, so that one could legitimately speak of a coherent program starting in 1877. Its terms were outlined in a report by General Andigné in the following year, as meanwhile the current Minister of War, General Borel, negotiated the details with the six large railway companies. In essence, the idea was to designate a certain number of tracks to create a "complementary network" that comprised railways of "general interest."[85] These euphemistic terms, always common in military parlance, signified an intention to form a standby system of major rail arteries that would enable the army to concentrate and mobilize rapidly in any national emergency. A legislative bill presented to parliament by Freycinet in November 1878 indicated that more than 230 individual lines would be included. For public (and foreign) consumption, the commercial utility of this selection was emphasized. But when, after the customary discussion in committees and subcommittees, Daniel Wilson addressed a session of the Chamber of Deputies in March 1879, the first rationale he frankly offered for the proposal was "its usefulness for the national defense."[86]

Military planning proceeded apace. Throughout the 1870s estimations by the Fourth Bureau were that a German offensive was likely to originate between Metz and Strasbourg, south of Verdun. A violation of Belgian or Swiss neutrality was thought unlikely. Since the French army itself was in no condition to launch an assault—the alleged "war scare" of 1875 had been nothing more than a German hoax—its preparations were purely defensive. To that end, the Fourth Bureau took charge of extending platforms in railway stations: *quais d'embarquement* in the West, *quais de débarquement* in the East. Top secret rail schedules were drafted, and the completion of new lines and second tracks was pushed. These measures were pronounced of "capital importance" by a new Minister of War, General Farre, who disclosed that his objective was to increase the number of possible daily train convoys to the front from thirty-six to forty-eight.[87]

All of this activity occurred before the collapse of the Freycinet Plan, and it, of course, produced the usual conflicts. In choosing certain routes for their military advantage and imperiously rejecting others because they might assist an enemy advance, military leaders had to face charges that they would only "sterilize" the countryside by depriving farms and rural businesses of commercially essential tracks.[88] Yet military planning had its own momentum, and one must conclude that the generals more often than not had their way. To what did it all add up? The best answer to that question is provided by a gorgeous map prepared by the Fourth Bureau and approved by the CMSCF in July 1882. It shows three main corridors of military transportation by rail: (1) a northern cluster with lines converging from Lille, Amiens, Rouen, and Rennes into the Seine Valley toward Paris and then eastward; (2) a central complex with connections from Nantes, Bordeaux, and Limoges along the Loire to Orléans and points northeast; and (3) a Rhône-Alp conduit from Marseille, St.-Etienne, Clermont-Ferrand, and Grenoble to Lyon and whence to the north. Bearing in mind that French military planning continued to be based on the existing administrative structure of the large private railway companies, we may translate this scheme into simpler terms: the networks of the Northern Company, the PO, and the PLM would forward troops and supplies to the region of the Eastern, where they would be gathered and distributed for combat.[89]

The late 1880s were marked by the appearance of two distinctive personalities in the Ministry of War: General Georges Boulanger and, no less, Charles de Freycinet. Of the two, Boulanger was the more colorful but less effective. In his behalf, however, it must be said that he brought to the post an energy and determination heretofore lacking. He deplored the "lassitude" (*sommeil*) of his predecessors and attempted to raise the level of French military preparedness by adopting the concept of "political tension." Before actual mobilization procedures were officially set in motion, during which the major railway companies would in effect be requisitioned by the army, a period of political tension was to be quietly signaled by the Minister of War. Without alarming the public—or, one must add, alerting foreign governments—the French could begin to concentrate troops and provide cover for vulnerable defensive positions on the frontier. These operations would require the assistance of the companies, which they indicated a willingness to provide. Perhaps, Boulanger mused, it might even be possible to commence rail transportation for some units before the period of political tension, "properly speaking." Yet he worried about the capability of the companies to transfer large numbers of troops safely and he openly harangued a parliamentary committee about the need for more uniform regulations on the railroads to overcome "the spirit of doubt that currently exists." As the chairman of that committee added in concurrence: "The question is posed; it must be resolved."[90]

But Boulanger displayed little patience with railway matters and, in fact, he failed to resolve the problems he exposed. Instead, Boulanger began what can only be described as a vicious campaign of xenophobia, which led him to have much more contact with the Second Bureau (in charge of counterespionage) than with the Fourth. The difficulty, as he saw it, was simply that railroads and fortifications could not be hidden from view. Thus, in a time of political tension when the French would be trying under his scheme to hide initial troop deployments, spies might be able to tip off the enemy. Boulanger therefore conspired with Colonel Jean Sandherr, head of the Second Bureau, to draft lists of aliens residing in France as well as French citizens of dubious reliability, especially German-speaking Alsatians. Such "suspects," duly inscribed on *Carnet A* and *Carnet B*, as the lists were called, could then be apprehended, imprisoned, and eventually removed to internment camps in the southwest, far from the French rail network on the borders of Germany. All of this was to be executed, we note, before a formal declaration of war and without any trials. It was not, in view of subsequent French history, a splendid precedent: we know that the arrest of Alfred Dreyfus would occur within a few years, then the razzias and deportations under the Vichy regime several decades later. Manifestly, such outbursts of French anti-Semitism had their origins here.[91]

One other aspect of Boulanger's tenure in the Rue St. Dominique must attract our attention. Although the minister himself devoted only sporadic notice to the details of strategic planning, his subalterns continued to do so. In August 1886, a proposal emerged with support of the Fourth Bureau to convert French mobilization procedures to the German model. In technical terminology, this meant that the army would thereby abandon its *commissions de réseau* in favor of *commissions de ligne*. If so, the current system based on the large railway companies would be replaced by a structure analogous to Moltke's pre-1870 reform, which was intended to expedite troop movements across internal borders and which, according to the Fourth Bureau, provided Germany with "an incontestable superiority." This opinion did not go unchallenged. One military committee, assigned to study the new proposal, found that Moltke's innovation was no more than "a simple palliative for bad organization" resulting from the multiplicity of German railway administrations. By contrast, the committee report continued, all of the major French companies had their headquarters in Paris, permitting "a centralized system in which the advantages outweigh the inconveniences." With these lines drawn, the argument raged into 1887 while Boulanger's own fancy drifted toward the political affair that later bore his name. Nothing was decided before a shift of cabinets in May terminated his stay in office. Whether from conviction or inertia, a radical change in France's method of mobilization was never effected. As before, the basis of French strategic planning remained the private railway companies.[92]

Thereupon, after a brief and inconclusive interim, Charles de Freycinet entered the Ministry of War in April 1888 as its first civilian head, a cabinet position he was to hold for nearly five years. Without a military career, he was nonetheless accustomed as a graduate of the Ecole Polytechnique to wearing a uniform, and he had professional training as a civil engineer. His experience as Léon Gambetta's young man during the war of 1870 still lent him a certain military aura, and his dedication to defending the Republic was not in doubt. Above all, it was he who had set in motion the 1877 program for the construction of a national network of military rail lines. Now he was awarded a chance to complete as Minister of War what he had earlier begun as Minister of Public Works.[93]

Freycinet assumed the task with his usual vitality. We may summarize his efforts by saying that he introduced a new sense of realism, which dictated some retrenchment and certain innovations. First, he consolidated the military command structure, fusing the Conseil supérieur de la guerre with the Comité supérieur de défense (actually abolishing the latter) while explicitly assigning to the Fourth Bureau the primary responsibility for strategic planning. Second, he obtained from the French parliament a three-year recruitment system, thus bringing the Third Republic at last closer to its professed ideal of a citizen army. Third, he adopted a scheme of *gares régulatrices* (called "GRs"), which were staging areas at railway stations well behind the front from which troops could be deployed by local commanders as circumstances might require—thereby inserting a welcome measure of tactical flexibility into otherwise highly centralized strategic planning. Fourth, in view of confirmed reports and simulated tests of terrifying advances in German artillery, Freycinet ordered an extensive refurbishing of France's major eastern fortifications and, meanwhile, a "declassification" of smaller bastions and *forts d'arrêt* along the Belgian border. This impressive ledger of achievement added up, as General Miribel put it, to nothing less than "a general revision of our defensive system."[94] Unfortunately, we must place one additional item on Freycinet's record: at the urging of the Second Bureau's Colonel Sandherr, the man who was soon to frame Captain Dreyfus, he also approved several arrangements to enlist corps commanders and departmental prefects in the project first envisaged by Boulanger for the incarceration of suspected spies and enemy sympathizers.[95]

Freycinet's thinking, it should be emphasized in conclusion, was deeply influenced by his understanding of the impact of railways on military affairs. He remained well aware of Germany's ability to strike suddenly by exploiting the increasingly thick webbing of European railroads.

"Profound modifications," as General St. Germain told the CSG, were therefore necessary. In the unrealistic French visions of mounting brilliant counteroffensives, added General Billot, there was too much emphasis on martial music and drawn bayonets, more suitable for "theatrical presentations." Hence, the plans adopted in 1887 were "generally inapplicable, often dangerous," the CSG decided, and it would be advisable to revert to the purely defensive mode of 1884.[96] In this spirit Colonel Leplus, head of the Fourth Bureau, requested that the railway companies submit revised versions of their putative mobilization procedures; he set a deadline for submission at mid-December 1889.[97] Thereby, in effect, the false enthusiasm stirred by Boulanger's man-on-horseback leadership was exposed and abandoned by Charles de Freycinet. His more sober approach demanded important strategic readjustments and continued the interminable tinkering that had characterized French military affairs ever since the defeat of 1870. As we have repeatedly noted, however, one basic reality was unchanged by 1890: the bedrock of France's existing system of military transportation, and therefore of its strategic planning, was still the private railway companies.

Chapter 5

GERMANY, 1870–1890

The creation of the German Kaiserreich was no accident. Other outcomes might have been possible, of course, but the political resolution of 1871 hardly seems the least probable. After all, Prussia had long been part of the European pentarchy of major states, possessing a distinguished monarchical tradition, a stable administration, and a strong army—all key elements in the victories over Austria and France. Hegel might have said that by 1870 the Zeitgeist was already resident in Berlin. Meanwhile, the southern German states became reluctant allies, but allies nonetheless, attracted to the solar plexus of Central European power and attached to it by economic interests as well as cultural affinities. That union was not automatic or unproblematic, yet it suddenly made perfect sense and could even be imagined as the inexorable culmination of longstanding aspirations for German nationhood: at long last, a Second Reich. Now Wilhelm was the German Kaiser, Bismarck the imperial chancellor, Moltke the military commander, and Berlin the capital. Obviously lacking, however, were the institutions of a national bureaucracy. These would require decades to create, and it was self-evident in this regard that the Bismarck era would be decisive. After being ambiguous for so long, the German center could now assume a concrete form, to which the periphery—Saxony and the southern states—would need to adjust. That formation and that adjustment were the twin main themes of German history before 1890.

Railroads were an essential component of this development, both binding the nation economically and, through a succession of controversies, often dividing it politically. Much was at stake, not least the character of German federalism. If the Prussian monarch was recognized as *primus inter pares*, in other words, it remained unclear what sovereignty would be left to the *pares*. In the railway industry, that matter depended on practical measures, not legal abstractions. The recent constitution stipulated only that the regime of the Reich should exercise supervisory authority over Germany's railroads "in the interest of national defense and general transportation." The crucial problem of the two decades between 1870 and 1890 was to translate that Delphic phrase into reality.[1]

Bismarck's Railroad Policy

Sometimes victory produces nearly as much chaos as defeat. So we might conclude, at least, from the improvised quality of political activity in Germany during the year 1871. At Dresden, a hastily summoned conference in early March gathered delegates from eighteen separate railway administrations "within the territory of the German Reich." Without established leadership, bureaucracy, program, or agenda, they could scarcely hope to avoid confusion. Virtually the only topic on which a formal resolution was concluded concerned the disposition of French rolling stock confiscated in the war and indemnities to be awarded to French railway companies. Even these harmless agreements elicited some reservations from Saxony, Bavaria, and Württemberg, a harbinger of times to come.[2]

The imperial constitution was not ready for ratification until the month following. Many of its provisions were adopted almost verbatim from the charter of the North German Confederation. They made no mention of a national railway administration. In one regard, the document was indeed a step backward, since it contained an explicit exemption for Bavaria's "special privileges" (*Reservatrechte*), which excluded Munich from Berlin's putative control over the railroads. This extraordinarily juicy apple of discord contained the seeds of particularism not only for Bavaria but, implicitly, for other member states of the Reich as well. For the time being, such issues were relegated—where else?—to the office of the imperial chancellor (Reichskanzleramt or RKA), which meant that Bismarck and his already overworked staff assumed day-to-day direction of the railroads. For Rudolf Delbrück, to whom the major responsibility temporarily fell, this task represented a distraction to which he inadequately attended. His reflex was to regard the national railway system as a natural extension of the North German Confederation, though that entity was defunct. The unsurprising result was that controversy and disorganization continued into 1872.[3]

To describe Otto von Bismarck's frame of mind as displeased would be tepid. Even a person of lesser genius could have perceived the political, economic, and military advantages to be realized by a unified national railway administration, analogous to the Reich's postal service. Earlier we saw how Bismarck's reckoning before 1870 led him to contemplate a single rail system throughout northern Germany. Now, like Delbrück (whom he was doubtless prompting), the chancellor assumed that the best solution would be simply to assimilate the networks of the southern states. Let there be no mistake: throughout the 1870s Bismarck actively sought to create a uniform national railway system for the new Reich—and he failed.⁴

The first symptom of serious dissonance was exposed by a memo, sent from Delbrück in January 1872 to the various member states, in which he instructed them to report to the RKA any new projects to construct or modify railway connections. Such prior notification, as he later explained, was not intended to throttle the initiative of the states but to enable his office to acquit its constitutional duty and thus "not to be confronted with faits accomplis."⁵ This demand touched off a flurry of activity outside of Berlin. Diplomatic representatives of Saxony and Bavaria consulted on the likelihood of a "categorical refusal." Within the Bavarian administration, a legal expert professed to be "astonished" at Delbrück's orders, for which he found "not a trace" of support in the German constitution. Besides, any rules applicable to the other states would be "non-binding" for Bavaria. Saxony also expressed "substantial doubts" about Berlin's pretensions, while Württemberg was slightly more reserved in finding that a preemptory check on its rail projects by Reich officials "does not seem absolutely required." Alone Baden raised no pointed objection.⁶ Accordingly, as the months rolled by, Delbrück obtained little acknowledgment and less cooperation from points south. In exasperation, he finally proposed in October 1872 to create a "Central Committee" in Berlin to rule on all railway projects in the Reich, but his suggestion fizzled and was soon forgotten.⁷

The foregoing established the background for a debate in the Prussian Chamber of Deputies at the outset of 1873. This occasion provided Bismarck with an initial opportunity to grumble darkly about the wretched condition of railroads in Prussia and the Reich. Most of his complaints concerned the mixed system of private and public rail enterprises within the borders of Prussia. But he also had in view the "inconvenience" (*Übelstand*) of having to coordinate so many different state networks in all of Germany.⁸ Thus, in ideological terms, his targets were both liberalism and particularism. From this acute displeasure emerged the impetus to found an imperial railway office (Reichseisenbahnamt or REA) charged with supervision of the entire national system. The title of the new bureau, advisory to the chancellor, was an agenda in itself that openly advertised Bismarck's ambitions for more centralism. He originally intended to bring a founding legislative act to the Bundesrat, but, fearing further protests from state delegations there, he chose instead to move the bill first through the Reichstag, where southern opposition would be limited to a negative vote by Catholic deputies from the Center Party. This ploy might actually have had a clear political advantage in the early days of the anti-Catholic Kulturkampf, because it was sure to promote the majority support of northern conservatives and National Liberals. Conveniently, Bismarck found a southerner from Württemberg to present the motion, as if it were not primarily at his own behest. With the Reichstag vote overwhelmingly favorable, the Bundesrat submitted, and a law creating the REA was passed on 27 June 1873. Bismarck now had an imperial railway office without an imperial railway.[9]

The initial choice for president of the REA was unfortunate. Because he was a noted banking executive with the famous Disconto Gesellschaft, Friedrich Wilhelm Scheele was eminently vulnerable to charges of conflict of interest. His troubles began with the Prussian cabinet, which contained several advocates of states' rights, starting with those of Prussia. Minister of Commerce and Public Works Heinrich von Achenbach frankly revealed his own particularistic inclinations to Scheele, stating that he did not read the mandate of 27 June to mean that the REA was henceforth empowered to tell the states "that you must do this or that, or not," a presumption that would only lead to a "disturbing dualism." All questions affecting Prussian railways, he added in secret, should be channeled through his ministry.[10] Scheele received the same cool treatment from the Association of German Railway Administrations (VDEV), whose current chief declined a request to supply the REA with statistical data on the grounds that the VDEV was an international organization that must avoid suspicion of favoritism toward Germany.[11] Apart from the already apparent reticence of Saxony and the southern states, then, Scheele had his problems with securing status for the REA in Berlin. Internal correspondence of the Prussian cabinet shows that state officials there carried out their post-1870 reforms without consulting the REA. It was Achenbach who proposed a revised bureaucracy of regional directorates for the railways in northern Germany, with a central bureau in Berlin, after acknowledging that the original administrative structure provided by Prussia's 1838 legislation was "no longer adequate." He also found it necessary to divide the railway department of his ministry into one section for the state network and another for private companies "because of frequent cases when the interests of state railroads clash with those of private railroads."[12]

A playwright might consign these events before the spring of 1874 to a prologue and then present the ensuing drama in three acts. The first began in March with a presentation to the Prussian cabinet of an REA plan to create a national railway system under central direction, notably including a unified structure of rates (a pivotal issue that will occupy us subsequently). In the usual Bismarckian fashion, rumors of an impending major reform were leaked to the press, setting in motion a wave of public speculation. Far more significant was the categorically negative reaction of the member states, to which Scheele sent multiple copies of the proposed "draft of an imperial railway law" (*Reichseisenbahngesetzentwurf*).[13] Without disguise, its purpose was to transfer all authority over construction and operation of German railroads from the individual states to the national regime. As a result, the reactions to Scheele beyond Berlin were even more hostile than to Delbrück in months past. The most aggressive of them was a scathing 41-page memorandum prepared by Württemberg's ranking railway administrator, Friedrich von Dillenius, who castigated the initial draft as "highly undesirable" and predicted that excessive intervention by the Reich was bound to provoke "unpleasant contradictions." Thereupon, the government in Stuttgart, typical of the others, concluded that its policy in future railway negotiations among the member states would be "as far as possible to hold off any intervention by a third party," namely Berlin.[14] For its part, the Prussian cabinet decided not to decide, thereby masking for a time its internal divisions. Once this circumstance became clear, Scheele submitted his resignation from the REA and in the summer of 1874 disappeared.[15]

His successor was Albert Maybach, a shrewd career bureaucrat and former president of the Prussian railway directorate in Hanover, who became one of the few persons to maintain Bismarck's unwavering trust and support. Maybach opened a campaign of charm to allay what he openly conceded were serious "doubts and reservations" emanating from Germany's provincial capitals. He recommended, and Bismarck approved, three changes in approach. First, a revised "provisional draft of an imperial railway law" (*Vorläufiger Entwurf eines Reichseisenbahngesetzes*) was circulated in April 1875. The revision moved paragraphs ensuring states' rights to the front of this much briefer document and emphasized that it was designed merely as the basis for discussion among member states, private companies, and the Reich. Second, a conference would be convened in Berlin at which state delegates would be able to present and, it could be hoped, resolve their grievances. Finally, after some indecision, Maybach chose (like Delbrück before him) to steer the resulting legislative bill toward the Reichstag rather than the Bundesrat. We may record in advance that it never reached that destination.[16]

A full debate occurred during five sessions of the conference held from 5 to 12 June 1875. The official transcript covers precisely 102 tightly printed pages and documents in excruciating detail the disintegration of Maybach's initiative. The climax may be easily spotted on page 96 when Maybach addressed a plenary assembly of state and Reich delegates: "Gentlemen, I cannot avoid describing the current result of our consultations as largely negative."[17] Little else needs to be reiterated or added. The collusion of liberalism and particularism was fatal to Bismarck's hopes. The private companies and provincial states were united in resisting his overtures, wishing together, as the president of the Rhenish Railway Company put it, to guard the freedom to operate their networks "without the continual interference of central supervisory agencies." Increasing the chancellor's distress, moreover, was his inability to hold the Prussian cabinet together. A lack of consensus within Bismarck's inner circle became painfully evident, and an obituary for the Berlin conference and the two drafts of an imperial railway law was spoken by Achenbach, who pronounced a Prussian legislative resolution offered in support of them to be "ambiguous, partly incomprehensible, and scarcely acceptable."[18]

A second phase began with Bismarck's withdrawal in the late summer of 1875 to his East Prussian estate at Varzin, where he licked his wounds and reconsidered his options. In October he conferred with Maybach, and the two men decided to attempt another alternative. It is unclear which of them was first to formulate the proposal; perhaps the idea was obvious to both. Under the terms of the new plan, Prussia would sell all of its railroads to the Reich. As a consequence—it is important to make this distinction—the Reich and not Prussia would purchase the private companies in northern Germany and, just possibly, elsewhere. In December, at a parliamentary soirée of Reichstag deputies (rather than Bundesrat delegates, who were more likely to be directly concerned), the chancellor then launched a trial balloon, teasing his listeners with his latest scheme, which as customary was also tipped to the press. A few weeks later, the Kaiser was formally notified that the Prussian cabinet favored "a transfer of the entire Prussian rail network to the Reich." Ominously, Wilhelm was in addition informed that this "preliminary step" would lead to a gradual concentration of German railways "in the hand of the Reich." Although we must allow some room for interpretation of these remarks, they surely suggest that Bismarck had by no means abandoned the prospect of an eventual nationalization but that he now intended to seek it by another means.[19]

There were two difficulties. First, staying in character, some members of the Prussian cabinet raised objections to what they saw as a threat to their state's autonomy. None of them wished to contradict Bismarck openly, but Achenbach and Minister of Finance Otto Camphausen both worried about the future legal status of Prussia's private rail companies, and they expressed doubts about abandoning the mixed system that had served the state treasury so long and successfully. In these concerns we can detect a certain complicity of traditional Prussian conservatism and a liberal business ethic, each of which was able to strike a noble pose in defense of the Hohenzollern crown. Bismarck's irritation with them was palpable. At a cabinet meeting he retorted that "the most important thing is the implementation of the Reich's constitution, and that is impossible without concentration of the railroads in the Reich." To this end, Prussia's action would be a beginning, he added, whereupon the other German states might follow.[20]

About their inclinations we do not need to speculate. The assault on Bismarck's plan was led by the Saxon prime minister Richard von Friesen. He did not wish to interfere with Prussia's domestic affairs, Friesen claimed, but any purchase of railroads by the Reich automatically became a matter for its member states. Such action, he believed, could not be accomplished without a change in the legal framework of 1871—a barely veiled accusation that Bismarck's new policy was unconstitutional. In a raging rebuttal, Bismarck noted that Saxony had relatively few private railway firms and was therefore spared the "regrettable disunity" faced by Prussia. "For now," Bismarck emphasized, "it is a matter of preliminary discussion on an internal matter of *Prussia*." Should Prussia choose to act, Saxony might express an opinion about legal propriety. Until then, no constitutional issue was raised, no legal change was required.[21] This exclamation can fairly be described as a statement of strict constructionism, and Bismarck was technically correct. Yet the potential ramifications were too transparent to be ignored by Friesen and his political counterparts in the southern states, who had reason to suspect the chancellor's motives and ultimate ambitions. Nationalization, as they were perfectly aware, would above all mean prussification. It was certainly no coincidence that, just at this time, Saxony and Bavaria moved to purchase the remaining private companies in their territory, with the manifest objective of precluding the direct acquisition of them by the Reich.

Public agitation continued, and Albert Maybach found repeated occasions to deplore the role of private railway companies. When a newspaper editorial appeared favoring expansion of holdings by the Reich, he had 500 copies printed (at the expense of the RKA) and distributed to parliamentary deputies. Bismarck meanwhile lobbied for the Kaiser's support, never an insuperable problem, and he repeatedly intervened to defend his project in debates at the Prussian Chamber of Deputies. Yet Bismarck was in fact thwarted again, and Maybach admitted as much in a 58-page memorandum in May 1876, when he reluctantly concluded that "no prospect exists" for the unification of German railways by continuing the course pursued throughout the past year. In June, both houses of the Prussian parliament passed a motion approving the sale of Prussian railroads to the Reich. But the bill was stillborn, just as Maybach had conceded, and for a second time in the decade Bismarck had reached an impasse.[22]

Nothing was altered in this outcome by Maybach's various attempts during 1877 to stiffen the authority of the REA through implementation of uniform regulations for the nation's railways. He proposed to create a nationwide administrative system for all German railroads with a central directorate in Berlin and "district councils" (Bezirksräte) in the provinces. However, as Maybach was well aware, to legislate such a structure and to impose it from the nation's capital would have encountered fierce resistance and likely rejection. He was consequently left with the weak hope that regimes of the member states might be coaxed into implementing the intended reform if reassured that the new district councils would "hardly be distinguishable from the previous state administrations."[23] This marked no advance toward centralism in Germany. Nor did Bismarck suppose any such thing when Friesen, his nemesis in Saxony, offered his own version of a national railway law, which the chancellor summarily dismissed as "a Magna Charta of particularism." Never one to mince words, though as in this instance he often kept them confidential, Bismarck informed his personal staff in December 1877 that he now considered his second attempt to consolidate railways under the Reich to be "failed" (gescheitert).[24]

At the end of the 1870s, faute de mieux, Bismarck moved to a third option. He did so with some disappointment but also in a spirit of defiance: if it was particularism the member states of the Reich wanted, Prussia would show them how it was done. First, a charade was played out. In February 1878 the chancellor instructed Achenbach—who, in effect, had betrayed him—to attempt passage of a reform of the Reich's railway administration through the Bundesrat and, if possible, the Reichstag during the current legislative session. Unquestionably they both knew that such an effort was certain to falter. In reality, Bismarck had decided on a quick and efficient purge of the Prussian cabinet. On 23 March Camphausen was dismissed from the Ministry of Finance, and five days later Achenbach submitted his resignation. With his principal antagonists in Prussia thus removed, Bismarck would have his way in forcing further changes. Achenbach was replaced by a compliant and faithful civil servant, Karl von Hofmann, from the staff of the RKA. The Ministry of Commerce and Public Works was divided, with Albert Maybach assuming the duties of the latter plus the directorship of the imperial railways in Alsace-Lorraine. In accepting his new ministerial position, Maybach abandoned the REA, leaving it without a president or much prestige for the balance of Bismarck's chancellorship. These alterations signaled a strong determination of the two men to leave their failures behind them. They could agree that allegations of unconstitutionality were "unacceptable," but there was nothing to be gained by pursuing further stratagems with the alerted and adamant regimes of the other states. Rather, Prussia would henceforth go it alone.[25]

Within the boundaries of the Prussian state, and therefore without any need to consult Saxony and the South, Bismarck was henceforth free to prepare a law expediting the purchase—not to say confiscation—of private railway companies in the North. Some of them, in the wake of a strong tremor in the stock market after 1872, were financially shaken, and it was a good time for shopping. Negotiations were already underway in 1878 for the state to buy out four of the companies, and more would surely be absorbed once the state parliament adopted a firm policy of *Verstaatlichung*, meaning in this case the acquisition of private firms by the Prussian state.[26]

There remained some pockets of opposition, or at least token reluctance, of which three deserve mention here. Within the Prussian cabinet, little static was any longer detectable except from Camphausen's successor in the Ministry of Finance, Arthur Hobrecht, whom Bismarck distrusted as a purveyor of "passive resistance." The chancellor's marginalia on ministerial correspondence displayed his steady support of Maybach, who often clashed with Hobrecht. A showdown came in the spring of 1879 when Hobrecht argued that financial constraints should prohibit the state's takeover of the Berlin-Stettin Railway Company. With an imperious tone, Maybach immediately pounced on him: "I, for my part, have been unable to share these reservations"—to which Bismarck dryly commented: "Ich auch." Other issues followed, such as Hobrecht's objection to Prussia's payments for the construction of parallel tracks, thought necessary for military purposes. But in the cabinet he was usually defeated and effectively neutralized. As a consequence, Bismarck and Maybach, despite their previous setbacks on the national scene and their persisting inability to squeeze legislation through the Bundesrat, could share a confidence that "we shall *with time* achieve our desired goal."[27]

Uncertainty about precisely what that goal entailed explains a second source of negativism centered in the Budget Committee of the Prussian Lower House. Nearly two-thirds of its members, Maybach complained, were composed of liberals of various stripes. To open and untangle this political can of worms would be complex beyond words, but we may simply observe that the general tendencies of the 1870s were not propitious for those political factions on Maybach's list of the Reich's enemies. In particular, the banner of the National Liberal Party was beginning to droop noticeably after the economic slump of 1873, and Germany's shift to a protectionist tariff policy by the end of the decade sealed the defeat and fragmentation of the liberal cause at the national level. These overarching factors, often chronicled elsewhere, were relevant to railway development insofar as they removed a major impediment to Bismarck's assertion of Prussian particularism.[28]

Another veteran champion of a mixed system of railroad governance was the Association of German Railway Administrations. Once settled into his office as Prussian Minister of Public Works, Maybach took increasing umbrage at the VDEV's constant pestering about railway standards and norms. To be sure, as he confided to Bismarck in April 1879, that organization had performed admirably to encourage some necessary technological uniformity in the past. But it now comprised sixty separate German rail companies, public and private, along with forty-one others. Its value for the future was moot: the VDEV was too broadly based to administer solely German railways and yet too narrowly focused to be truly international. Maybach favored the creation of an entirely new railway league for strictly German matters and perhaps another to treat international affairs, thereby including Italy, Switzerland, Belgium, and France, none of which belonged to the VDEV. In a terse confidential memo, Bismarck concurred with Maybach's proposal. Although nothing immediately came of this initiative (Bismarck did not wish to undercut negotiations in Bern, where the VDEV was simultaneously involved), skepticism remained in Berlin about the compatibility of the VDEV with the railway policy of Prussia and the Reich. Another star began to wane.[29]

As for the transfer of Prussia's railroads to the Reich—voted with fanfare months before by the Prussian parliament—it was now silently ignored. Maybach put the entire question into its proper perspective in October 1879 when he urged Bismarck to offer such a motion to the Bundesrat or at least formally solicit a statement of opinion from the regimes of the other member states: "If, *as expected*, the response is negative," he wrote, then the path would be clear for legislation in Prussia to sanction further sales of private rail companies to the state. That consummation, devoutly wished by the chancellor, was reached shortly before the conclusion of the decade. On 12 December 1879, a bill permitting an extensive *Verstaatlichung* of Prussian railways was passed into law.[30]

In view of these events, it is appropriate here to correct a pair of closely related errors that have crept into the lore of German railway history. The first is an improper translation of the German term *Verstaatlichung* by the English concept of nationalization. This equation is obviously false, because a national system of railway networks is exactly what did *not* emerge in the 1870s. The use of "nationalization" is misleading and quite simply mistaken as a description of the railway policy finally adopted by Bismarck after 1877. Clearly, the *Verstaatlichung* legislated in 1879 was a Prussian phenomenon, which was in its essence an assertion of that state's rights. In the German railway industry, particularism, not nationalism, was triumphant before 1890. To speak of "the nationalization of the Prussian railways from 1879 onwards" is perfectly oxymoronic.[31] The second blunder is to suppose that Bismarck's railway policy was a success. This erroneous assertion apparently derives from the logic: the chancellor wanted *Verstaatlichung*, and, well, he obtained it.[32] In such reasoning there is an evident short-circuit. Anyone who carefully examines the documentation concerning the evolution of German railroad administrations in the 1870s must conclude that Bismarck's efforts, even by his own admission, had failure written all over them. Before 1877 he sought to promote the politics of nationalization. Only after his attempts repeatedly came to grief did he and Albert Maybach devise a strategy of Prussian *Verstaatlichung*. These two notions should be separated and evaluated in a dynamic context of historical development, not confused or treated as a static verity. Demonstrably, the railroads of the new German Reich after 1870 were in a state of flux that cannot be summarized as a straight march to success.

The Reassertion of States' Rights

A curiosity was that the national unification of 1871 in some ways strengthened German particularism, which could thereafter be securely wrapped in a blanket of federalism guaranteed by the new imperial constitution. The inaugural ceremony of the Reich in the Hall of Mirrors at Versailles was a celebration of German princes, not of their administrations. A collaboration between national and state governments was assumed but not stipulated. The degree of harmony between the national bureaucracy, still in its first stages of formation, and those of the member states had yet to be determined. In negotiations, the latter often held a distinct advantage because of their long-standing traditions and unflinching loyalty to the established ruling houses they represented. "Reichsrecht bricht Landesrecht," the constitution proclaimed: the law of the central state takes precedence over that of a member state. Yet, as we have just seen, even in Prussia that principle remained far from infrangible.

Outside of the North, away from the seat of the central regime, claims for the dominance of the Reich in railway matters had a more distant and even less persuasive ring. Because the decade of the 1870s was a time for the improvisation of a national policy, Saxony and the southern states could take advantage of fluid circumstances to reaffirm their autonomy within an emergent and still amorphous federal structure. Yet a word of caution is appropriate. True, the non-Prussian "medium states" (Mittelstaaten, referring to their size) were usually unanimous in resisting the overreaching pretensions of Berlin, but they were not so coherent as to present a southern front. We have already gathered how their reactions to nationhood, and specifically to Bismarck's aspirations for a unified German rail system, were not sung in chorus like some barbershop quartet. Their quarrels, too, had a venerable tradition that continued as before. To unravel these differences and to see the subject as a whole, we must therefore return to the provinces and evaluate each circumstance in turn.

Saxony

Among the medium states Saxony was an anomaly. In 1866, we recall, it was absorbed into the improvised North German Confederation, where it was dominated by the imposing presence of neighboring Prussia. But the war of 1870 and the founding of the German Reich induced a reversal of fortune, because the North German Confederation was abolished and Saxony was cut loose. The neophyte imperial state was not, constitutionally speaking, an expansion of the Confederation but its replacement, so that Saxony reverted to its previous status as an independent kingdom—much like Bavaria or Württemberg—now within a federal union. These altered legal circumstances help to explain the eagerness there after 1870 to reassert the state's independence from Prussia. Geographically, Dresden remained the same number of kilometers away from Berlin, but emotionally, the distance had never been greater.

We have examined an initial instance: in 1872 Rudolf Delbrück's orders for prior inspection by the Reich of any planned railway project in Saxony drew not only an outraged reaction from across the border, but they also prodded Prime Minister and Minister of Finance Richard von Friesen to set off sirens of alarm. In the 1870s Saxony became the Cassandra of German particularism. Although Saxon delegates did not vigorously oppose Bismarck's innovation of a Reichseisenbahnamt, their suspicion of it was well advertised at the time and continued thereafter. Saxony learned to stall: memos from Berlin went months without an answer, statistics were supplied incompletely or not at all, and solicitations from the REA for input on matters of policy were ignored. An example was the response to the first draft of a national railway law. A copy was sent by the REA to Friesen on 13 March 1874 with a request for comment. By the beginning of September no reply was forthcoming, though one was promised soon. On 16 November Dresden noted rumors that Bismarck was contemplating a revision of the draft and, if so, no purpose would be served by an appraisal of it. In December Albert Maybach reiterated a plea for some official evaluation, but by the following March—fully a year after Berlin's initial contact on the question—the appearance of a second draft rendered any obedience to the REA's previous directives totally superfluous.[33]

The scenario was similar for the second stage of Maybach's campaign, that is, the auction of Prussia's rail network to the Reich. Once again Friesen was bluntly hostile to Bismarck and industrious in rallying the minions of opposition. His efforts were still more successful this time, since both Württemberg and Bavaria pledged to vote against the proposed measure. But the problem, as Friesen expressed it, was that no matter how "monstrous" the Prussian project, Bismarck's intimidating pressure might be sufficient to bully a majority in the Bundesrat. Accordingly, Friesen did not favor bringing the issue to a ballot in the national parliament, which could produce a "moral defeat" for states' rights. A better strategy would be to make the intransigence of the medium states unmistakably clear by eliciting a vote of rejection in their legislatures. Then adopting his own policy, Friesen steered Saxony's Chamber of Deputies to a 66 to 7 defeat of a motion on the Reich's purchase of Prussian railways.[34]

A renewal of the so-called "railway war" between Prussia and Saxony was an almost inevitable consequence. Principally at stake was the fate of private companies, whose days were now numbered. For reasons already stated, acquisition of the major Leipzig-Dresden line by the Saxon state railway system was, after long preparation, brought to completion. Perhaps an argument could be made that such action simply made good business sense, but it is impossible to overlook Friesen's ulterior motive—to contradict Bismarck. At the same time, the two also became entangled in a controversy over the Berlin-Dresden line, one of Germany's main thoroughfares, of which two-thirds was located on Prussian territory. This fact, so Berlin emphatically claimed, meant that *"the Prussian state has a predominant interest"* and, in buying out the company, should rightfully obtain control over its entire operation. To the contrary, Saxony supported a division of the company's holdings, thus ensuring its own operation on the third of tracks within the state's borders; locomotives should be exchanged at the frontier. When no compromise could be reached, the dispute was referred to a court of appeals in Lübeck, which in September 1877 handed down a decision in favor of Prussia. By then, however, Friesen had inflicted severe damage to Berlin's aspirations for nationalization of the railways. His retirement changed nothing in Saxony's determination to contain the threatening tide of prussification.[35]

Bavaria

As Bavarians were always quick to point out, the status of their state was special. Its *Reservatrechte*, allowed in the 1871 constitution as a result of confidential deals between Bismarck and King Ludwig II, granted

Bavaria legal immunity from imperial controls over railroads that were applicable to other states of the union. Its privileged position meant that the Bavarian monarch, not the Kaiser, should possess the ultimate sanction of railway projects, and that solely the Bavarian Minister of War should issue orders within the state during peacetime. So the constitution was generally interpreted and so, certainly, it was understood in Munich.

When Rudolf Delbrück's directive about new construction arrived at his desk in 1872, the Bavarian regime's chief legal expert declared it "unfounded" (*nicht begründet*) and added: "The supervisory authority of the Reich in the interest of national defense and general transportation has ... *absolutely no* application to Bavaria." In nearly identical terms, the Bavarian premier Adolf von Pfretschner communicated the same message directly to Bismarck in March 1873. Responding to a request from the chancellor (who invoked his constitutional duty) to delay a building project until Reich officials could verify its suitability for strategic planning, Pfretschner stated that a legal provision for such action was "inapplicable" (*nicht anwendbar*) for Bavaria. To place his government's decision in doubt would leave it in an "untenable posture."[36] Later Bismarck capitulated, withdrew his objection, and approved the construction with a proviso that bridges and tunnels be mined for defensive purposes. To this admonition Pfretschner coolly rejoined that the mining had been executed long before and that Berlin would assuredly be informed of any future projects after they were approved in Munich, which was of course to say that no prior notification would be forthcoming. Bismarck's parting shot, in turn, was that there seemed to be "a divergent conception in principle." Therewith, as so often, the chancellor demonstrated his mastery of understatement.[37]

The divergent principles of centralism and particularism remained on display throughout the balance of the 1870s while Bismarck attempted in vain to win Bavaria for his successive projects of nationalization. When the initial draft of a Reich railway law appeared, Pfretschner first consulted with his Ministry of Justice, then sent Bismarck a 16-page memorandum recalling the settlement of 1871 and its award of an "exceptional status" to Bavaria. One may well guess, incidentally, that the chancellor did not deeply appreciate Pfretschner's elevated tone of a law professor instructing his pupil. A certain smugness was also evident in the Bavarian reaction to the revised "provisional" draft and Maybach's accompanying invitation to a conference in Berlin to discuss it. Munich's representatives were sent to the nation's capital with orders to demand a full airing of their state's special privileges; but that proved unnecessary when, in effect, the entire matter was dropped.[38]

We can readily discern that Bavarian policy was not far removed from Saxony's, except that Pfretschner—resting more comfortably on the laurels of constitutionality—lacked Friesen's vehemence. He was, however, equally concerned about Bismarck's sudden shift to a proposal that the Reich acquire private railway companies in Prussia and, presumably, elsewhere. While Hesse supported this move and Baden maintained a discreet neutrality, Bavaria joined Saxony and Württemberg in opposing it. All three were convinced, as the Bavarian envoy Pergler von Perglas reported from Berlin, that Bismarck's ultimate intention was "to damage badly, virtually to destroy the autonomy and sovereignty of the separate German states."[39] Urged by Ludwig to learn the truth of such an allegation, Pfretschner found reason to worry about Bismarck's objectives but remained confident that "the nearly unrestricted control over railways" granted to Bavaria at Versailles in 1871 was inviolable. Still, Bavaria would need to avoid isolation from its natural allies and must therefore cultivate its relations with Saxony and Württemberg. All things considered, the chancellor's annoyance with Pfretschner was only slightly less acute than with Friesen. In a letter to Munich, which he was careful to sign as "the Royal Prussian Minister of Foreign Affairs," Bismarck claimed to be surprised by Pfretschner's insistence on Bavaria's *Reservatrechte* in view of the fact that his current policy involved "exclusively internal decisions by the Prussian regime." Again (as in the case of Saxony) we may question whether such an expression was not completely disingenuous.[40]

Long before the end of the decade, then, the differences between Munich and Berlin were sharply drawn. Yet one conclusion based on Saxony's archives is corroborated by Bavaria's: the mutual resistance of the medium states to Bismarck's railway policy stopped well short of a united front. Disputes about border crossings and access of one state's rail company across the territory of another were endemic, as before 1870. With all the publicity about national issues, these local matters remained a constant irritant. A conspicuous example was the altercation between Bavaria and Württemberg about a stretch between Memmingen and Leutkirch, south of Munich. Writ large, at issue was another struggle over a right-of-way for traffic to Lake Constance. Not only would this track affect the flow of rail freight through Württemberg's port at Friedrichshafen, it was also prized in Berlin for military reasons. Prodded by Maybach in April 1876, the two southern states began negotiations that ended in bitter disagreement. Stuttgart's demands were deemed "completely unacceptable" in Munich and, as we shall see, vice versa. Bavarian particularism, it appears, was a practiced reflex with many useful applications.[41]

Württemberg

The head of Württemberg's railway administration, Friedrich von Dillenius, posed a rhetorical question about the founding of an imperial railway bureaucracy: was it to be greeted or feared? He had no difficulty in answering. The Reichseisenbahnamt would surely be bound to "mix into many things" in an effort to force uniformity among the state networks. Such interference "must have a limit."[42] In the Bundesrat, alone among the medium states, Württemberg voted against creation of the REA, and thereafter no love was lost between them. While REA president Scheele maintained that the constitution awarded the Reich "control over railway rates" and issued regulations for "the German railroads," Dillenius expressed "very substantial reservations" and declared Württemberg's dutiful compliance "impossible."[43] The conflict sharpened to such a point in early 1874 that the REA formally threatened legal action unless its directives were promptly executed. Scheele personally visited the residence of Württemberg's envoy in Berlin, Baron von Spitzemberg, telling him that Bismarck was "especially sensitive" about the matter and was consequently prepared to invoke "the most extreme constitutional measures." Only an adroit intervention at this juncture by premier Heinrich von Mittnacht avoided court action. Delays had been created because Württemberg's railway administration was understaffed, he claimed, but after some adjustments of personnel more regular responses would be assured.[44]

At the same time, Mittnacht was repeatedly irritated by Bavaria's self-satisfied insistence on its special privileges; and he considered Saxony's jousting and unbridled criticism of Bismarck to be "unfortunate," because "the impression will be created of a contradiction between particularism and the unity of the Reich"—as indeed it was.[45] Nonetheless, Mittnacht's instructions to his diplomatic corps were to leave not "the slightest doubt" about Württemberg's rejection of Bismarck's various plans to assimilate the southern states into a national railway system.[46]

A parting glance at the sporadic negotiations between Bavaria and Württemberg in the 1870s will serve to illustrate the nagging issues of southern particularism. The twelve-year embargo on freight traffic from Bavaria's main north-south lines via Ulm to Friedrichshafen was due to elapse in 1872. Meanwhile, as a counter, Bavaria hoped to construct a shorter connection to Lindau via Memmingen and Hergatz, which would have the inconvenience of passing through a corner of Württemberg at Leutkirch. Perhaps a deal could be struck in return for a concession from Heidenheim to Ulm? But Stuttgart balked and urged instead that the two states review network links "in their entirety." This, in turn, did not suit Munich, which hinted at the possibility of some monetary compensations. "Dubious" and "infeasible," responded Württemberg. And so on. All of this apparently petty detail began to acquire its basic meaning in 1873 when the long-deferred question of a beltway along the northern shore of Lake Constance was opened. Now larger geopolitical considerations came into play, and Berlin's keen interest in them gave contacts among the southern states a rough edge, leading Mittnacht to warn that this might be "a first attempt [by Bismarck] to intervene in pending issues of railway connections between the two states."[47]

As it happened, Stuttgart and Berlin had a mutual interest in east-west tracks, the former for commercial and the latter for military reasons: two new lines crossing Württemberg's territory would increase freight traffic and facilitate more rapid access of Bavarian troops to the Rhineland.

Bavaria's regime evinced little interest in these connections but sought completion of a direct Munich-Memmingen-Leutkirch-Lindau line. Without tracing all of the twists and turns of this dispute, we can note the passions that it generated, such as Mittnacht's unbuttoned charges about Munich's "unscrupulous" (*prinziplos*) behavior and his bitterness over Bavaria's "preponderance" (*Übergewicht*) in the South. Complexities notwithstanding, any analysis of Germany's railway history must take into account these reverberations, which help to explain both the conflicts among the medium states and their collective relations to the Reich.[48]

Baden

Perhaps Baden deserves no more than a postscript. As the state most beholden to Berlin for commercial reasons (thanks to the St. Gotthard Tunnel), Baden was also the most vulnerable militarily, with its long border on the Rhine across from France. Karlsruhe therefore had less pretension to stubborn independence than the other non-Prussian capitals, a condition signified by the abolition in 1872 of a state Ministry of War and the acceptance, in effect, of the full integration of Baden's troops into the German army under a central command.

Yet railway administration was another matter. Delbrück's proposal to extend national regulations to the South gained a reception in Baden only marginally less cool than in Württemberg. True, Prime Minister Julius Jolly assured Bismarck of Baden's willingness to collaborate on several construction projects, and within the state's railway bureaucracy no strong protest arose against the Reich's stipulation of prior notice. But Baden's stated policy was to remain in step with the other medium states and thus to wait and see how they reacted. Consequently, debate was certain to erupt in Karlsruhe about the "extension of the Reich's competence over the railroads" versus the "fragmentation of the German railway system." It might therefore have seemed at least faintly ominous when Baden sent representatives to Stuttgart to confer with Dillenius, of all people, on mutual rail projects and policies.[49] By the time that a proposal from the REA for a joint rate system for the German railroads failed to gain adoption in the Bundesrat in June 1874, early enthusiasm in Baden for the benefits of national unification had clearly begun to wane. Writing to Baden's ruling Archduke Friedrich a year later, in reference to Bismarck's plans for nationalization, Minister of Commerce Ludwig Turban characterized the issue of rates as "totally muddled." While he did not oppose the chancellor in principle, Baden's regime must ensure that Berlin's initiative "does not damage the legitimate interests of the member states."[50]

Like other southern statesmen, Jolly was meantime harangued from Dresden by Heinrich von Friesen, who posed a loaded question: did he favor an alteration of the constitution? Jolly responded, somewhat evasively, that Baden held "similar reservations" to those of Saxony. But on the margins of a conference in Berlin during June 1875, Turban found an opportunity for secret talks with other delegates from the medium states and agreed with them that "direct supervision" of the railroads by the Reich was "not acceptable." Bismarck's clever divide-and-conquer tactics (for example, in an attempt to discredit Friesen he sent to Karlsruhe copies of Saxony's secret correspondence) did not dissuade Baden from a guarded neutrality that may be described as a correct form of German federalism. Appropriately, Baden proved to be pliable in negotiations with Württemberg on a westward rail extension from Friedrichshafen, later to be part of a Bodensee beltway, and it could also boast of "very cordial" relations with Bavaria.[51]

So far as Berlin was concerned, Baden drew the line on two issues: rates and rolling stock. When Maybach, acting as Prussian Minister of Public Works, pressured the states to adopt a more unified and simplified rate structure for freight shipments, Turban told Mittnacht that the maneuver "greatly surprises and repulses me." Similarly, although he conceded that the Reich might conduct regular military inspections and rule on the suitability of certain arrangements, Turban boggled at restraints on Baden's right to purchase any engines deemed necessary for efficient service. Karlsruhe chose simply not to respond.[52]

These details are sufficient to confirm that the decade of the 1870s ended rather badly for Bismarck. The effort to achieve an imperial railway system had foundered on the rocks of German particularism. Far from quelling the cause of states' rights, national unification had effectively enhanced it. Saxony, Bavaria, Württemberg, Baden, and, not least of all, Prussia—each for its own reasons and in its own style—remained defenders of their respective state autonomy, of which the railroad was now the quintessence.

Germany Transformed

It is no exaggeration to say that Germany underwent a railway revolution before 1890. The circumstances of the 1870s were drastically altered in the following decade, when Otto von Bismarck and Albert Maybach moved to enlarge the Prussian state network. Laws passed by the Prussian legislature on 20 December 1879 and 14 February 1880 empowered the state to proceed with the purchase of private companies throughout northern Germany. From a total of forty-four firms Maybach drafted an initial agenda in which thirteen major rail companies were to be acquired. His orders were emphatic: they should be captured "not one by one, with long intervals, but rapidly with broad strokes." Questioned by the Prussian Ministry of Finance about the likely success of such abrupt action, a confident Maybach responded that it was "fully assured."[53] Implementation of the new policy actually proved to be more troublesome than he supposed, but the final result was to create the largest single industrial enterprise in the world. This was *Verstaatlichung* on a grand scale.

Some private railway firms quietly acquiesced. Two examples were the Berlin-Potsdam-Magdeburg line and the Cologne-Minden Company, annexed to the state system in 1881 for about 240,000,000 Marks. Others were less pliable and, one must say, were in reality confiscated under duress. One of these was the Bergisch-Märkische Company, connecting Hanover to the Rhineland, which was defended in vain from a state takeover by the powerful Disconto Gesellschaft. The bank's "ruthless" behavior was denounced in the Prussian cabinet, where allegations were hurled against its selfish profit motives, such that it had been "scarcely patriotic" in the war of 1870.[54] Similarly, the Rhine-Nahe Company linking Bingen to Saarbrücken was recalcitrant, denying appeals to construct a second parallel track deemed necessary by the Prussian General Staff for its mobilization plans. Maybach was particularly incensed about this firm's reluctance to provide "the necessary security and rapidity" of transportation to the French border. Under pressure, it capitulated.[55]

A detailed enumeration of railroad purchases by the Prussian state dates from 1885. By that time, the government had already allocated nearly 900 million Marks to acquire fourteen private companies and had definite plans to fund over 550 million to assume public ownership of five more—a tidy sum of more than 1.4 billion Marks![56] Understandably, there were murmurs about overspending, and Bismarck had to apply the financial brakes, although his extravagance continued sporadically thereafter. To Maybach fell the job of organizing the vast new Prussian network, which he did through revisions of regional directorates north of the Main (excepting Saxony) in 1881 and again in 1887. Some of these offices, especially that in Cologne, retained considerable administrative discretion in their operations, but Prussia's railway policy was decided in Berlin. These structural adjustments reflected the fact that private railway ownership in Germany was fast disappearing as Bismarck succeeded in breaking the political spine of liberalism. The obvious question remaining, however, was how he would fare with particularism.[57]

In reality, not very well. Two ostensible reasons could be advanced by Berlin to boost new legislation by the Reich to regulate the railroads. The first was the existence of interstate lines. Prussia was free within its own borders to do as it pleased. But what of private companies whose tracks straddled state frontiers? We saw that this issue, regarding the Berlin-Dresden route, had soured relations between Prussia and Saxony in the 1870s. Now the medium states were quick to make their negativism known. Saxony claimed to have too few private lines to require any Reich law. And Bavaria, as usual, rather pompously restated its constitutional immunity: "a necessity ... for Bavaria cannot be regarded as a given." Baden, meanwhile, expressed vague reservations, and Württemberg was silent.[58] Since he had seen it all before, Bismarck decided not to risk another debacle and notified his subalterns that "pressure is to be avoided." The other justification was military, always a trump card in Bismarck's hand. But how should he play it? Apparently unsure, he had the REA prepare two separate legislative bills for a Reich law, one to establish national rules only for private companies and another that would cover both state and private rail operations. Without following this story, we can again record a notable lack of success. Only the first of the two REA drafts ever came into circulation, and it was promptly opposed on well-rehearsed grounds by the medium states.[59]

The ambiguity of Bismarck's intentions caused another storm of speculation in the newspaper press that he was belatedly attempting to force an imperial railway law after all, this time by deploying the intimidating weight of the Prussian state railway system for leverage. Confronted with these rumors, Maybach acted surprised by the implication that Bismarck intended a nationalization of the German railroads; actually, he claimed, the chancellor sought only a sort of "financial unity" in which all the states would cooperate in cost-savings by avoiding duplication and economizing on personnel and materiel. So far as Berlin was concerned, Maybach concluded, the recent consolidation of the Prussian state railway network and its "brilliant financial results" precluded a return to the conceptions (meaning the nationalization plans) of the 1870s. This frank interview with Maybach, conducted by Bavaria's envoy to Berlin, Count Lerchenfeld, probably came as close as possible to a definition of Bismarck's railway policy in the 1880s, and it vaguely foreshadowed the objectives to be pursued by his successors after 1890.[60]

Such is the proper context into which to place a visit in December 1883 by Württemberg's premier Mittnacht to Berlin, where he conferred with Maybach, and to Bismarck's private estate at Friedrichsruh near Hamburg. In Mittnacht's version, he was there to explain particularism, not to weaken it by cutting a sweet deal for his own state. Yet the medium states had reason to fear that their mutual, if often incoherent, opposition to Bismarck's aggrandizement might crumble. Nothing concrete came of all the fluster and the dozens of dispatches exchanged among provincial capitals, although this activity doubtless persuaded the Bavarian cabinet in 1884 to make a vigorous reassertion of its state's rights, including those of its railway administration. Insisting that putative laws and regulations by the Reich would be "inapplicable" for Bavaria, Prime Minister Krafft von Crailsheim claimed "a nearly total exemption in railway matters" for his regime and criticized the "deplorable tendency" of Berlin to by-pass the member states. For his part, at closed sessions of the Prussian cabinet, Bismarck attempted to put Bavaria in its constitutional place, theorizing that all of the German states were obligated to acknowledge the general authority of the Kaiser and the Reich's administration—that should be the rule, not the exception. These sharply divergent pronouncements from Munich and Berlin served only to harden the lines between particularism and centralism.[61]

Maybach's reforms of the national bureaucracy included an attempt to neutralize or perhaps abrogate the Association of German Railway Administrations (VDEV). In a confidential memo, he advised that in balloting for the chairmanship, the representatives of Prussia's regional directorates should vote as a block for a German candidate to prevent the leadership of the VDEV from slipping "outside of the borders of the German Reich." If a non-German won the election, he added without subtlety, "the existence of the Association in its current form could easily be placed into question." As it turned out, there was little reason for Bismarck to boycott or abolish the VDEV, whose future irrelevance had already been sealed by national unification. Hardly anyone would later notice when the Association quietly celebrated its fiftieth anniversary in 1896.[62]

The declining significance of the VDEV created a void that might logically have been filled by the Reichseisenbahnamt. Yet without Albert Maybach's powerful influence and immediate access to Bismarck, the REA lacked enough respect to exercise much authority. It was not for want of trying. The archives of all medium states of the Reich are choked with correspondence between their railway administrations and REA headquarters in Berlin. In the application of national standards, it seems, no problem was too great or too small for the REA: every local trolley line should be reported and reviewed before construction; the departure of a train should be announced by the stationmaster with two long blasts of his whistle; maximum hours should be enforced for all German railroad employees; compressed-air brakes should be uniformly installed, preferably Westinghouse; and so on.[63] No single issue of this kind caused so much friction, however, as the hectoring from Berlin for the states to construct more parallel second tracks. This demand, usually requested for military reasons and invariably championed by the REA, raised the most fundamental of considerations: who was to pay? Much of the tension during the 1880s between the national state and its constituent federal members came to center on this elemental question.

It was a problem, let it be specified, that primarily concerned the southern states. Unlike Saxony, which still boasted the densest rail network in Germany, the South had long stretches of single-track lines through sparsely populated rural areas. Prussia's interest in doubling some of those tracks was mainly military (with an exception made for a connection to Sigmaringen, which also had sentimental value as the legendary homeland of the Hohenzollerns). A good example was the hardest of southern chestnuts to crack: the dispute between Bavaria and Württemberg over a Memmingen-Leutkirch railway to Lake Constance. Attempts to reopen negotiations in 1884 stalled. But after Berlin prodded the two parties, Bavaria's premier Crailsheim composed a 28-page memorandum in which he made a thorough review of the conflict that had hung "in suspension" (*in der Schwebe*) for the past twenty years. Vigorous bargaining followed, finally culminating in a treaty in February 1887. But the completion of a Bodensee beltway, which would provide Württemberg with a new trade lane to Austria and Switzerland, remained blocked as before.[64]

At least the southerners were talking again. And they were also reasoning together: if parallel tracks had little commercial value in peacetime, given that Berlin urgently wanted them for military purposes, why should the states bear an inordinate share of the costs? Let the Reich pay. Armed with this very simple rationale, Mittnacht once more undertook in December 1886 to bell the imperial cat in Berlin. At no time before 1890 were the southern states closer to a common front. And they chose their moment well, because of Bismarck's simultaneous agitation over the martial appearance of General Georges Boulanger at parades in Paris and the chancellor's eagerness to obtain a new military septennate (an increased and guaranteed seven-year budget for the army). For once negotiations were not protracted. By mid-January 1887 a formula was devised by which the expense of future railroad construction having military implications (such as second tracks) would fall mostly on the Reich: Bavaria would ordinarily assume only 25 percent, Württemberg 20 percent, and Baden 15 percent. In the immediate vicinity of the French border, moreover, the Reich would be held accountable for 95 percent of the costs. Separately, Prussia and the Reich meanwhile agreed to a 40/60 split. On this basis, agreements on a number of delayed projects were soon concluded. Controversies over cost-sharing were by no means ended, because none of the states—neither Prussia nor the southern regimes—wished to forfeit every right to negotiation or any opportunity for maneuver. Yet, at a minimum, guidelines were thereby established that institutionalized a fiscal modus vivendi between center and periphery.[65]

This reconstruction of the conflicts that swirled around the German railway industry during the decade of the 1880s may be drawn to a close by considering a memo drafted by Bismarck for the new Prussian Minister of War, General Verdy de Vernois, on the first day of May 1889. Verdy's predecessor, faced with alarming reports from Paris about the French building strategic rail lines, had already raised a proposal with the recently elevated Kaiser Wilhelm II for correspondingly increased appropriations by the Reich. The issue, in a word, was escalation. Wilhelm apparently intended to take the matter personally in hand and, in effect, to encourage a greater military influence on the construction and operation of German railroads. This situation now motivated Bismarck to explain to Verdy the background of his "efforts energetically pursued for many years" to increase the competence of the Reichseisenbahnamt. That attempt, as the chancellor conceded not for the first time, had "failed" (*gescheitert*): initially because of "the opposition of my Prussian colleagues" and then, after the appointment of Alfred Maybach, because of "the constitutionally justified resistance of the associated regimes," meaning those of the member states that "decisively rejected any limitation of the autonomy of their railway jurisdiction (*Eisenbahnhoheit*)." This antagonism was certain to be sharpened by the proposal at hand. "From a resumption of these struggles," Bismarck admitted, "I can promise myself no success." Rather, they would lead to a "serious worsening" of relations between the Reich and the member states. The chancellor therefore declared that he was "not currently disposed to assume the responsibility for a new initiative." He urged instead that the military leadership desist and thus avoid raising "deeply embedded constitutional issues" with the Kaiser. Otherwise, the loyalty of the member states to the Reich would be shaken, and the chancellor himself would be forced into an "untenable position."[66]

Such a concentrated summary cannot hope to convey all of the nuances and allusions intended by the practiced hand of a master politician. Yet three essential elements of Bismarck's message were revealed by his lucid prose. First, a gathering crisis—created in 1888 by the disappearance of Kaiser Wilhelm I and the subsequent succession of the upstart Wilhelm II—was all too apparent. The chancellor was clearly embattled; his dominance over Kaiser, cabinet, and (at least in the North) railway policy was spinning out of control. Second, he was prompted to save the situation by a frank admission of past disappointments. Bismarck has rarely been commended by historians for his accurate self-portrayals, but in this instance he offered Verdy a reasonable facsimile of events since 1870: he and Maybach had fallen short of their purpose, the nationalization of the German railway system, and had been forced to recalibrate their policy. Divisions within Prussia as well as hostilities between the Reich and the medium states had stymied their ambitions. Finally, Bismarck's true confessions betrayed some weariness of an aging statesman whose goals remained unrealized. His reference to an "untenable position" may be taken as a recognition that he might soon be outmatched by a vigorous young Kaiser. But there was also a larger sense of resignation before the facts of life in imperial Germany. The regrettable truth was that the Reich was in some ways misbegotten—and one of them, in Bismarck's view, was a federal system that left considerable administrative authority to the individual states. Their staunch particularism, notably in regard to the railroads, he had been unable to budge.

The Age of St. Gotthard

The pattern of Germany's economic growth after 1870 was irregular but impressive. It began with a postwar boom, incomparably the greatest spurt of the nineteenth century, which lasted from early 1871 well into 1873. All economic historians agree on this phenomenal boost, although they have evaluated its significance variously. The statistics of growth, in any event, were stupendous. In just this three-year span, 2.7 billion Marks were invested while 928 new joint-stock companies (Aktiengesellschaften) were created. That sum exceeded by nearly 500 million Marks total investments for the entire period from 1850 to 1870, during which a mere annual average of about twenty-five joint-stock companies had been founded.[67] Several explanations have been offered for this extraordinary leap after the Treaty of Frankfurt, most of them quite obvious: the euphoria of military victory and political unity, the availability of plentiful capital and easy credit terms, the infusion of 5 billion francs in French reparations, the absence of strict state licensing for fledgling business firms, and so on. In short, a climate of liberalism and optimism prevailed—conditions that were soon shattered under a wave of stock and bank failures throughout Central Europe. Germany was like an overly eager runner who begins a race too fast and, unable to sustain the swift opening pace, is forced to slow and catch a second wind. By 1874 a deceleration was punctuated by bankrupted business firms, collapsed joint-stock companies, and tightened credit. Recent wage increases were rescinded and prices receded. Speculation was out and austerity in, as the confidence of managers, bankers, and investors was badly shaken.

The differences of interpretation do not hinge on these generalizations, about which there is consensus, but on their context. The classical hypothesis of long swings (*Kondratieffs*) posits three distinct periods in Germany's economic development: an "Industrial Revolution" (1850– 1873), a "Great Depression" (1874–1894), and then an unlabeled resurgence in the two decades before the First World War. Unfortunately, the neatness of this scheme is undermined by data that indicate a substantial rate of growth during the entire late nineteenth century—although, of course, not at the accelerated tempo of the three-year *Gründerboom* immediately after the war of 1870. Moreover, there is a conceptual problem in arbitrarily awarding the unprecedented statistics from the years 1871– 1873 to the prewar economic phase, thereby inflating its averages and flattening those of the postwar era. The result is to distort the entire picture by exaggerating the contrast between the "Industrial Revolution" and the "Great Depression," sobriquets that are best discarded.[68]

The weight of evidence has thus forced a sensible revision. A more sophisticated version in effect slices the periodic cycles into smaller segments, a series of economic short-runs, allowing for sustained growth after 1873 despite sporadic palpitations in the marketplace. One historian has divided the period from 1850 to 1873 into five phases, and 1874 to 1894 into another five. This refinement enables him to confine the uncomfortable experience of falling profit margins, prices, and wages to the late 1870s, now rebaptized as the "Great Deflation." Yet even this constriction of the original notion of *Kondratieffs* must admittedly recognize the continuity of Germany's general economic growth: "There can be no question of stagnation, let alone an absolute decline of production, except for a relatively short time in only a few branches [of industry]."[69] The loss of confidence after 1873, in other words, was a psychological reaction that restrained but did not halt Germany's post-1870 surge. When we adopt a global perspective, without dubious monikers or preinclinations, the numbers are eloquent, such as the total of German investments between 1850 and 1895:

1850–1870	2.3 billion Marks
1871–1873	2.8 billion Marks
1874–1895	2.4 billion Marks

Here we perceive not only the altogether exceptional character of the postwar boom but also the remarkable similarity between the two decades preceding and the two decades following it. In reality, there was after 1873 a return to normalcy in which the turbulence of war, boom, and bust was overcome, its gains slowly restored and reabsorbed into a steadily expanding German economy. If indeed there was a "Great Deflation," it deserves to be folded into a pattern of general economic growth since 1850.[70]

These conclusions are substantiated by a closer analysis of the railway industry. Given that railroad investments constituted perhaps as much as 30 percent of the national total, it is virtually a truism that the progress of rail transportation reflected the global pattern and to a great extent determined it. Although no meaningful statistical comparisons can be extrapolated for the Prussian state network during the transitional 1870s, figures from the four medium states offer convincing testimony (see Table 7). We see in the round a doubling—for Bavaria almost a tripling—of state allocations for the construction and operation of railway networks, and that during the depths of what was once called the Great Depression! Far less exact but nonetheless suggestive statistics have also been calculated for Germany's railway freight in the first postwar decade (see Table 8). Again, we note the incredible burst of the initial boom years. Yet all the more striking is that the gains of 1871–1873 were retained and in fact increased by 2 billion kilometric tons during the supposedly deflationary phase before 1880. If even remotely accurate,

TABLE 7: Total Railroad Investments by German Medium States, 1870–1880 (Marks)

	1870	1880
Saxony	211,779,000	567,416,000
Bavaria	338,537,000	1,006,088,000
Württemberg	238,419,000	441,885,000
Baden	215,012,000	393,295,000

Source: Fremdling et al., *Statistik der Eisenbahnen in Deutschland*, pp. 96–97, 126–32.

TABLE 8: Kilometric Tonnage of German Railway Freight, 1870–1879

1870	5.3 billion
1873	9.9 billion
1874	10.1 billion
1879	11.9 billion

Source: Wehler, *Deutsche Gesellschaftsgeschichte* 3: 556.

these data confirm that for the German railway industry the decade of the 1870s witnessed a tentative advance, which was to be continued in the 1880s. In retrospect, therefore, it appears certain that the commercial expansion from 1870 to 1890 represented a preparation of the platform from which a take-off of the German economy could be launched in the quarter century before 1914.

On a microeconomic scale, the central issue after 1870, as before, was rates. The detailed story of Bismarck's attempts to achieve a simplified and unified rate structure paralleled his failure to obtain an imperial railway law and partially explains it. The creation of a Reichseisenbahnamt (REA) in 1873 was specifically intended to resolve the rate question. Previous efforts by Rudolf von Delbrück to extend commercial parameters of the North German Confederation to the South had stalled. But the REA could initially do no better in combating the claims of states' rights, notably those of Bavaria, guaranteed by the constitution. By 1875, after Bismarck had seen enough, he called in Albert Maybach and entrusted him with herding a national rate plan through the Bundesrat. For reasons we know well, this initiative likewise bogged down in endless committee hearings, and Maybach was forced to concede that the constitution did not actually mandate national uniformity in setting railway rates; but it did provide a basis for the REA to encourage cooperation among the member states.[71] When the vanity of that hope became fully apparent, Maybach abandoned the REA, moved to the Prussian Ministry of Public Works, and again applied renewed pressure for a rate reform. In response the medium states drew a fine distinction between policy and practice: if it was the Reich's part to formulate general guidelines, the details of their application should be left to the states. As if to test that proposition, a series of conferences in Berlin drafted a national rate plan, which, after Bismarck's personal intervention in early 1879, was finally forwarded for legislative action to the Bundesrat. There thirty-five articles governing the rate policy of "the German railways" were adopted in June by a majority of thirty-two to twenty-five. But there was little cause for jubilation in the nation's capital. Among the twenty-five dissenting delegates were those of all four medium states as well as several smaller ones.[72] The manifest problem for the regime of the Reich, in the face of such opposition, was to enforce common standards throughout the land. When, for this purpose, Bismarck proposed to extend the authority of a special supervisory committee on rates seated in Berlin, he met a cold refusal. Württemberg's Friedrich von Dillenius undoubtedly spoke for the others: his administration, he said, would be "unable to support it."[73]

This brief sketch has a ring of familiarity. Nevertheless, it is imperative to examine more closely the cluster of issues that frustrated the implementation of a truly national rate structure. We can identify four of them. First, there was a disagreement about the method of fixing rates. Should it be done by value classification—that is, an appraisal of the relative worth of the goods to be shipped—as was traditional in both

Prussia and France? Or should a wagonload classification, which measured the usable capacity of freight vehicles rather than the units they transported, be adopted? In 1874, Bavaria and Württemberg adopted a mixed system, combining these procedures, and this method of computation became the national norm in 1876. Yet it is senseless to describe this action as a "breakthrough," as if the matter were thereby resolved.[74] Rather, adopting the term "mixed" was an admission that no clear settlement could be reached and that Germany would have to remain content with the confusion of general guidelines to be applied as individual railway companies saw fit.

A second problem was to designate a proper forum of rate arbitration. Regional leagues (Verbände) continued to be active in the 1870s, and the rate structure was often affected by bargains struck among their members. Yet their agreements were strictly voluntary, and if a member of some league felt disadvantaged, it could abstain or withdraw to avoid a majority decision. Albert Maybach's impatience with these unwieldy procedures led him to convene repeated conferences at the headquarters of the REA or the Prussian Ministry of Public Works in Berlin. But these gatherings always had an ad hoc character suitable for debating policy questions, not for determining a detailed schedule of rates.[75]

Intimately related was a third factor: the recurrent strain between North and South. The long-standing prejudices among the medium states toward Prussia had, through the creation of the Reich, acquired a new technical aspect because the taxation powers of the national regime were constitutionally limited to indirect domestic levies and international tariffs. Direct taxation was left to the states. Accordingly, as Bismarck came to realize and to advocate in the late 1870s, it lay in the Reich's interest to press for lower rates on Germany's internal transport of freight and for higher protective tariffs. Other terms may also be employed to explain the collapse of liberal principles and the turn toward protectionism in 1879, but a consideration of railway rates should be included among them.[76]

Finally, unlike the period before 1870, it followed that an international dimension would find a conspicuous place on this list. On the initiative of Switzerland, representatives of all the major continental European countries (Britain was excluded) met in the capital city of Bern in June 1878 to discuss making trade regulations more uniform among the nations. Initially, the most skeptical were the French delegates, who made it known that "their expressions of opinion are purely personal and cannot prevent further decisions by their government."[77] But the Germans, too, had serious reservations because of the unsettled condition of their own national rate policy. Above all, the question was whether an international arrangement should be binding for individual rail companies within the various states. Could a national regime negotiate obligatory terms for its several constituent parts? As this debate wore on into the 1880s, opposition grew more adamant and articulate. At another gathering in Bern in 1882, Bavaria was moved to make a categorical statement of its "special circumstances" and hence its right to fix rates that could not be abrogated by an international treaty. We need not chart the course of events that led to a third convocation in Bern in 1886, when a formal proposal was finally presented. After conducting secret talks with Austria-Hungary and the Netherlands, the German Foreign Office (in a word, Bismarck) suggested that the Reich's delegation should sign the accord. Not to do so would cast Berlin in a bad light; besides, it was dubious that regulations adopted in Bern would ever prove to be mandatory. Thereby relieved of any scruples, the German representatives could report back to Bismarck about their conciliatory stance, confident as they were that "the Reich is in no way bound by our signature." The conclusion is inescapable that this factor belongs with the previous three in any comprehensive explanation of the chaotic state of the German rate structure.[78]

Throughout the 1870s, in its commercial relations, Europe was meanwhile waiting for a very large shoe to drop: the opening of the St. Gotthard Tunnel. Only a few weeks after the Reich's founding, immediately upon his return from Versailles to Berlin, Bismarck had taken steps to resecure the financing for Germany's pledged (on 15 October 1869) subsidy of 20 million Swiss francs. Member states were solicited to make good on their earlier commitments, and, leaving nothing to chance, major banks were engaged to cover additional stock options: the Disconto Gesellschaft in Berlin, the Rothschild Bank in Frankfurt, and the Darmstädter Bank in Cologne.[79] Construction began and anticipation ran high. Until the inauguration of this new alpine passage through central Switzerland in 1882, the only arteries of rail trade from the Mediterranean were Brenner to the east and Mt. Cenis to the west. But with the completion of St. Gotthard, the face of European commerce changed. Since the opening of the Suez Canal, no single engineering feat had such a decisive impact.

The only question is whether German trade with Italy more nearly doubled or trebled between 1880 and 1885. In a secret memo to Bismarck in February 1884, Albert Maybach estimated that the Reich's total exports to Italy—measured in units of 100 kilograms (*Doppelzentner*)—had increased from 602,455 to 1,733,807. The gain, he noted, was mostly in heavy goods for which the railway was apt: no less than 89 percent of it could be attributed to coal and iron. Maybach therefore concluded that Germany might regard French efforts to counter St. Gotthard "without worry" (*ohne Sorgen*), because the superiority of the new trade route over its competitors "cannot yet be seriously threatened."[80] Subsequent statistical returns bore Maybach out. An analysis by the Prussian Ministry of Public Works, for example, made comparisons of German imports and exports with Italy (see Table 9). Manifestly, the early commercial advantage was all to Germany, though northern Italy was being provided with the raw materials to develop its industry and, eventually, to take advantage of rich markets in northern Europe. Furthermore, these spectacular and immediate results helped to sustain the Reich's economic vitality into the

TABLE 9: German Commerce with Italy, 1881–1883 (100 kilograms)

	1881		1883	
	Imports	Exports	Imports	Exports
Iron and iron products	67	383,284	213	847,366
Wood and wood products	8,356	9,815	9,183	29,433
Instruments and machines	139	56,816	257	83,924
Paper and paper products	291	3,069	199	14,861
Coal and coke	—	966	—	537,937

Source: "Einfuhr und Ausfuhr von und nach Italien," 29 April 1884, GStA PK Berlin, I. HA Rep. 93 E, Nr. 305 (M).

1880s and beyond, providing another example of the symbiosis between industrial growth and railway development.

To conclude this survey we need to return to the central theme of German particularism. Three apparently unrelated incidents of unequal significance may serve to illustrate various aspects of the Reich's conundrum after 1870, that is, how was it to impose greater unity on the nation's railroad networks? The first concerned rolling stock: the right of the states to acquire locomotives, passenger cars, and freight wagons to suit the individual needs of their rail networks. Germany already had a thriving locomotive manufacturing industry, which was not confined to the more industrial North. The Bavarian state railway system, for instance, habitually placed most of its orders with the Maffei firm near Munich, doing so on its own initiative.[81] But Maybach, once ensconced in the REA, promptly began to assert the proposition that the Reich had a constitutional responsibility to ensure that all German companies possessed enough locomotives for general transportation and national defense. He urged the states (with Bavaria ever the ticklish exception) to provide regular detailed reporting on available rolling stock and intended purchases. No exhaustive narrative is necessary to document the reaction of the medium states, each of which found reasons to demur. Even Baden, the least anti-Prussian of them, objected to this perceived interference in its internal affairs: although it was legitimate for the Reich to monitor the state's military expenditures, as Minister of Commerce Turban confided to the Württemberg regime in July 1879, "doubts arose" in Karlsruhe when it came to extending Berlin's prerogatives to rolling stock. Baden consequently chose to ignore Maybach's requests. Thereafter, in the major provincial capitals, the rest was silence.[82]

A second issue in the mid-1880s proved to be of less actual importance but disclosed a perpetual anxiety in high places about sustaining Germany's commercial superiority over France. It began with reports that the cosmopolitan director of the French PLM Railway Company,

Gustave Noblemaire, was exploiting his personal contacts during a voyage in northern Italy to make arrangements for channeling trade away from St. Gotthard onto his own firm's Mt. Cenis line. Maybach wasted no time in locating the villain in this piece, the international dispatching firm of Gondraud *frères*, which represented "French competition against German railway interests." Gondraud's thirty-six affiliates in Italy, Switzerland, and Germany, Maybach claimed in an outburst of hyperbole, "hold Germany's Italian trade to a great extent in their hands." He therefore issued instructions through the Reich's diplomatic corps—thus presumably with Bismarck's personal approval—secretly to withhold storage space for Gondraud's agents in or near German train stations. But Maybach's orders were never executed. Bavaria refused on grounds that such machinations would only divert its traffic eastward to the port of Trieste. Baden likewise saw "no justification" and Saxony "not the slightest reason" for measures to impede Gondraud's commercial activities. That was in 1887, just as the Boulanger affair was filling headlines of the European press, which was perhaps explanation enough for the undue excitement in Berlin. In any case, the intransigent response to Maybach provided yet another instance of German particularism in practice.[83]

A third incident at the end of the decade was far more fundamental and fairly epitomized the imbroglio over Germany's rate structure. In May 1888 Maybach quietly informed the Bavarian cabinet that the Reich's regime wished to lower rates on the nation's railways for all shipments to the northern German ports of Hamburg and Bremen. Surely it would be to everyone's advantage if trade were diverted from lowland harbors into the North Sea and onto German tracks. Munich answered that Bavaria's interests were in fact better served by the closer rail connections to the Rhineland, then on to Antwerp or Rotterdam. In return for the collaboration of his government, Bavarian premier Crailsheim demanded a substantial compensation. But what should it be? Negotiations ensued that, at Maybach's request, were to be held in secret between the two. When Maybach demanded proof that Bavaria's interest would be harmed by the proposed rate reductions, Crailsheim could only cite his state's increasing commerce with Belgium and Holland and reiterate fears that it would be diminished if the German ports were accorded more favorable terms. In the meantime, correspondence within the Bavarian administration revealed a bitter tone of recrimination against Berlin. At the risk of provoking an international rate war, it was alleged, Maybach was deliberating seeking to impose "dubious tariff regulations," the real purpose of which was to draw as much German and Austrian freight traffic as possible onto the lines of the Prussian state network. Cloaking its pretensions in patriotism, Prussia was in reality plotting to aid its own oversea harbors at the expense of Germany's inland river ports like Mannheim, Mainz, Frankfurt, and Passau. Bavaria could not be expected to support this maneuver without serious financial compensation from the funds that would surely fall to Prussia.[84]

In these three microcosms we see both the broad outlines and some of the minute intricacies of the German circumstance after 1870. By dint of repetition, if nothing else, the governments and railway administrations of the medium states had made a sustained pleading for states' rights. Under Prussian leadership the Reich had meanwhile been set into place, but, in economics as in politics, the Bismarckian regime fell far short of realizing its ambitions. St. Gotthard was a huge success, but a unified national rate system remained elusive. Germany's commercial history before 1890 thus displayed a record of unsteady growth and undiminished conflict.

The Consolidation of Military Predominance

Anyone who expected Germany to bask comfortably in the afterglow of victory did not understand Otto von Bismarck. True, the succession of military victories over Austria and France brought him and the General Staff an immense prestige. With its aura of invincibility, the German army became the envy of Europe. Yet the leadership of the new Reich was haunted by two disturbing and interlocking assumptions. The first was the inevitability, sooner or later, of facing a two-front military challenge. We have seen that this notion can be traced far back into the nineteenth century and was widely regarded as a geopolitical given. Bismarck's unstinting efforts after 1870 to isolate France were based on the premise that the Third Republic would not hesitate, whenever possible, to secure an eastern ally, and Germany would eventually need to confront them both. There was also a second supposition—that the maintenance of German superiority constituted the only certain way to guarantee the peace of Europe. Presumably all great powers are inclined to conceive of themselves in such self-serving terms. Germany, in any event, now did so. It hardly requires elaboration, when we lower these lofty axioms onto the level of available technology, to add that only the railways could render German aspirations possible. Only they could connect the two fronts and bring the weight of the Reich's military machine victoriously to bear. The centrality of the railroad in German military theory was thus self-evident. It is important, however, to delve into the practical problems that beset military planners as they sought the best means to implement what the German constitution blandly called "the national defense."

Although the documentation of this period is fragmentary—because much of it was destroyed by bombing raids in the Second World War—enough is extant to provide a consistent picture of internal conflicts. Even the virtually unchallenged authority of Helmuth von Moltke proved insufficient to prevent the disputes and tensions that occurred before 1890. And the basic reason is clear. The army was an instrument of war, and its preeminence in wartime was acknowledged on all sides. But what of peacetime? With that simple question the differences began and continued in a multiplicity of forms. Three stand out. First was the constant strain in German civil-military relations. Hypothetically the Kaiser was the supreme commander under whom the nation's military establishment was directly placed. Professional competence was always an issue, however, especially when designing mobilization plans or determining allocations for railway construction intended to realize them. The prominent role of the chancellor and his advisory Reichseisenbahnamt was bound to create friction with military experts for whom strictly political considerations mattered little. The same was true at an operational level. Peacetime railway administration was conducted by directorates (*Direktionen*), to each of which military plenipotentiaries (*Bevollmächtigten*) were attached. That the latter should assume full responsibility in case of war was agreed. But exactly when and how a transition could be effected from one to the other was less obvious. Meanwhile, there remained delicate questions of confidentiality about military planning and mobilization procedures. Despite the drafting of elaborate regulations and attempts to train military personnel to assume control over railway operations in a crisis, some uneasiness therefore persisted on both sides.

Hardly less bothersome were skirmishes over prerogatives within the military command itself. Under Moltke, the General Staff had its own railway section and frequently intervened to make its wants and wishes known. At the same time, the Ministry of War also represented military interests in the Prussian cabinet and imperial councils, dealing directly with various state and Reich officials on matters of finance and railway policy. It was all distressingly complicated and forever shifting, since so much depended on the relative gravitas of personalities that came and went. Any administrator—whether in the military, business, or academia—can instantly recognize this circumstance. At a lower level, the same ambiguity existed. Moltke's pre-1870 reforms had created so-called "line commanders" to expedite military transports in wartime, but it was uncertain what their capacity was in relation to the plenipotentiaries who, as their title stipulated, were supposedly to supplant peacetime civil authorities and direct the mobilization for war.

A third source of altercation, unavoidably, was the attempt of Reich bureaucracies to impose uniformity on the member states. Military interests were always served by standardization, whether of loading ramps, station designs, signals and brakes, locomotives and freight wagons, steel rails, or spurs and sidings. Ever eager to enhance its own status, the REA was in perpetual motion to champion military requests for compliance by the states. Most correspondence concerning military matters was consequently filled with pleas about the importance of such transactions for "the railroads of Germany" in behalf of the national defense. As we know, these supplications were not always well viewed in the South and were often ignored in Germany's provincial capitals. The same disharmony between center and periphery evident in other aspects of the railway industry thus appeared frequently in military records of the Bismarck era.[85]

Before moving on to examine the climactic events of the late 1880s, it is useful to review some specific instances to illustrate the general observations above. One of them concerned the alleged war scare of 1875. His suspicious gaze always focused on France, Bismarck wanted Germany to establish and sustain an overwhelming military strength on its western frontier. His personal influence after 1870 was therefore directed toward the integration of Alsace-Lorraine, and in March 1873 the chancellor categorically stated the "importance and urgency" of an appropriation by the Reich of over 100 million Marks to revamp the railroads in that sector to meet military needs. This action provoked the first of many sharp objections to the imposition of undue expense on the states, as well as their insistence on a right to negotiate railway treaties as they chose (such as Bavaria with Austria). It cannot be said that the medium states were altogether negative when it came to military cooperation: Bavaria, for example, signed an agreement for its staff officers to spend an eighteen-month tour of duty in Berlin to receive training—and no doubt indoctrination—in the Prussian way of army life. Yet they feared that Prussia could at any moment pull them into an unwanted war.

Precisely that anxiety was stirred in 1875 when Bismarck conjured an artificial diplomatic crisis with France in a transparent attempt to warn Paris against too rapid rearmament and rail construction on the German border. Probably at his suggestion, Albert Maybach then used the situation to conduct a kind of roadbed check on the medium states. Were they prepared to transport troops and cavalry steeds to the front, if need be? Particularly irritating was Maybach's solemn invocation of his constitutional prerogative to inspect the states. In Stuttgart Friedrich von Dillenius was peeved that Berlin had provided "no definite instructions." Nothing came of the false alarm except a hardening of already familiar rhetorical positions. Maybach began to insist on more regular reporting on military preparedness, and Bismarck reiterated the priority of extending the railway network in Alsace-Lorraine and connecting it to the German interior.[86]

A new theme was the unviability of private railway companies and the difficulty of incorporating them into the uniform procedures and mobilization plans so dear to the General Staff. As we have noted, this phase meanwhile saw the eruption of conflicts within the Prussian cabinet between those ministers who supported Bismarck's imperial schemes and others whose allegiance was more attached to their own state's monarchy. Clashes between Maybach and the current Minister of War, General von Kameke, echoed these disputes. At the same time, the "urgent need" to complete rail connections to the converted fortress at Metz and to bolster defenses on the Rhine became a stock phrase in the military vocabulary. Likewise, we should note, interest of the General Staff in Germany's eastern front increased. Construction of the French rail and fortification system west of the Vosges Mountains might make a quick incursion there less feasible and perhaps impossible. By 1879 Moltke consequently tended to favor a defensive holding operation in the West while an initial German offensive would point eastward. In that event, greater building costs must be expected, and louder differences over the military budget and the contribution of the states were to be anticipated.[87]

Reorganization of the Prussian railway system in the 1880s, by putting an end to private enterprise, resulted in yet another redefinition of military policy. By mid-decade Germany had a total track length almost double that of 1870. Moreover, the military was particularly keen to correct an earlier weakness of railway construction in much of the land: a lack of double lines, which were so much more flexible for logistic purposes. Expansion and improvement, in turn, created ever greater demands from Berlin for uniformity in equipment and operations, for which their military utility provided an ideal—because nearly incontrovertible—rationale. As in one case that we have observed, the Rhine-Nahe Railway, such reasoning sped Prussian *Verstaatlichung* to its conclusion. But regarding states' rights, of course, nationalization continued to founder. It is worthwhile in this respect to quote Bavarian Prime Minister von Crailsheim, who in April 1884 stiffly addressed his government's sentiments to one of Bismarck's close political associates: "The alleged notion that Bavaria's special rights cease at the point where the interests of national defense begin cannot be recognized from our standpoint."[88] This was not an isolated instance, and we can only conclude that the passions of southern particularism remained largely unbanked by repeated appeals to the higher national interest of military defense.

Slow and more subtle was a change at the top of the military hierarchy. Helmuth von Moltke was aging. After 1882 he was increasingly represented in official forums by the German Quartermaster General, Count Waldersee, an administrator who was competent enough but who could not possibly bring Moltke's prestige to the table. Accordingly, the late 1880s witnessed a temporary eclipse of the General Staff and a prominence of Prussian war ministers. One of the latter, General Bronsart von Schellendorf, was the first to cry wolf in a long secret memo to Bismarck in June 1885. This key document, because it raised the stakes considerably and thereby set a tone for the following years, deserves an extended summary. Its preamble began with the common assumptions that Germany faced a two-front military situation and that only railroads would enable the Reich to meet that dual challenge. Unfortunately, in recent preparations for a future conflict, "France has largely overtaken us—Russia threatens us likewise." Especially in the South, Germany's networks were now insufficient, wanting in density, too often having only single-track lines, and lacking adequate ramps. Hence, Bronsart argued, it had become obvious "that the circumstances … are tending more and more to our disadvantage." In 1870 the French had mustered only six direct lines to the German frontier. Already that figure had been increased to twelve, and by 1888 there would be fifteen main arteries of mobilization, nearly one for each army corps, all of them outfitted with double tracks. In case of war, France would therefore soon possess the capability of delivering 500 trainloads daily to the combat zone, and perhaps more.

In the meantime, Germany's military dominance was fast disappearing. For seventeen army corps the Reich could currently provide but five double-track lines, three single-track, and one mixed—an extent of construction "considerably behind the French network." Bronsart thereupon unveiled a proposal to execute no fewer than twenty-nine new building projects in the West. These were divided into three categories, for the first of which (thirteen projects) he estimated a total cost of 52 million Marks. Expenses for the second and third lists, he added, as if to spare Bismarck any further shock, had not yet been calculated. About the East Bronsart was less alarmist. But there, too, the balance was clearly tipping to a German debit, and the army must take care to guard against "surprises." It was therefore "absolutely necessary" to meet these escalating needs on the eastern front, which Bronsart briefly outlined in four categories requiring an additional expenditure of 18 million Marks. As for the immediate circumstance, he concluded with a short list of six projects in the West at 42 million Marks plus the entirety of his scheme for the East: in all 60 million Marks at once. This was a large round figure that would not easily slide down the parliamentary gullet. But surely no price was too high to avoid the national disaster of a foreign invasion. It was therefore a "duty" to adopt an appropriations bill "without delay." Bronsart closed by attempting to supply appropriate rhetorical grist for Bismarck's mill: "The security of the Reich rests in no small measure on the expansion of its railway network in the interest of national defense."[89]

In reading the official prose of a bureaucrat seeking funds for his favorite projects, one must always allow for a certain exaggeration. Waldersee was frankly skeptical and thought that the talk of an immediate military threat was "all a comedy."[90] Bismarck, nonetheless, took it quite seriously, resolved as he was to obtain a new military septennate that would increase the Reich's standing army by a tenth. The railway question thereby became a part of the larger issue of military expansion, which had all the makings of a constitutional crisis. All in all, two things are certain. First, Bismarck was determined after 1885 to throttle his opposition and was willing to take political risks to do so. Second, the well-publicized debut of General Georges Boulanger as French Minister of War and pretender to the Elysée palace suddenly made Bronsart's admonitions plausible.

If Bismarck had any reservations about supporting Bronsart, they were suppressed during a war scare in 1887 that seemed far more serious than that of 1875. Signs of nervousness were everywhere in Berlin. Confirmed in his mistrust of the French, Bronsart requested for his projects an immediate allocation of 90 million Marks, especially, as he said in obvious reference to Boulanger, because of "recent seemingly urgent circumstances." Bismarck meanwhile worried about rumors of French concentrations of rolling stock on the frontier (later declared false by

Waldersee), and he asked that Bronsart carefully check their stockpiling of coal supplies.[91] In a conversation with the Bavarian minister in Berlin, Count Lerchenfeld, Bismarck denied that he had deliberately inflated Boulanger's importance and said: "If France begins a war in the near future, given the relative state of armaments, this would be more favorable for Germany than if it should occur at a later date." Still, under his leadership Germany would undertake no preemptive military strike. There exists no golden scale upon which to weigh these words. We know only that the rattle of Bronsart's saber continued: more rapid construction of second tracks, greater pressure for financial contributions and closer cooperation from the member states, and more elevated allocation for strategic lines in the East had now become "urgently necessary."[92]

In 1888 Waldersee replaced the ailing elder Moltke (who died in 1891) as chief of the General Staff. It is likely that this led directly to Bronsart's resignation, and the story circulated that his replacement, General Verdy de Vernois, was handpicked by Waldersee in order to end strained relations with the Ministry of War. If so, the change made little difference for the Reich's railway policy. The alleged military threat from France was kept percolating even after Boulanger's disappearance and suicide: in his fashion, Charles de Freycinet, as a serious reformer, could be thought still more of a menace. We saw that Bismarck was forced in May 1889 to restrain Verdy's blustering attempts to override the reticence of the southern states to support a major escalation of strategic rail construction. Undeterred, in that summer Verdy pleaded for additional funding to build more bridges across the rivers Rhine and Weichsel, projects that would require many months to complete. From Varzin Bismarck replied: "I fear that a considerable part [of these projects] will need an interim for construction, during which the maintenance of peace is not likely. It is therefore questionable whether the allocations ... would not be better utilized for *direct* military purposes." Of course, no one will ever fathom all of Bismarck's motives and calculations. Did he actually believe that a war with France was imminent? Or did he merely find a convenient excuse to fend off Verdy's zealous demands? We cannot know for certain. Ambiguity had always been a way of political life for Bismarck, all the more so now that his chancellorship was in jeopardy. In the meantime, Verdy persisted. He assured that his proposals could be realized by April 1891 if they were budgeted at once. For his part, Bismarck continued to resist such action on grounds that it would not gain approval of the medium states. Verdy accepted a delay but prepared a draft of fifty-four rail projects of "special urgency" to be advanced at the earliest possible moment. "We have no excuse," he added in a covering letter, "to lose even the smallest amount of time."[93]

Without following this exchange any further, we can observe that Bismarck gradually gave ground to Verdy. In the end, appropriately, it was his long-time confidant Albert Maybach who persuaded him to do so. By way of a joint memo to the chancellor, Verdy and Maybach declared that the sustained building programs of the Reich's putative enemies left it no choice: "Especially, the extension and development of the French rail network in recent years is so advanced that the advantage possessed by Germany in this sector no longer exists." Finally, on 9 March 1890, Bismarck agreed to endorse a new railway appropriations bill of over 25 million Marks, for which the Reich would assume nearly two-thirds of the cost, Prussia the remainder.[94] It was one of his final acts as chancellor. Barely a week later Bismarck departed from Berlin and headed into retirement. He left for Friedrichsruh, of course, by train.

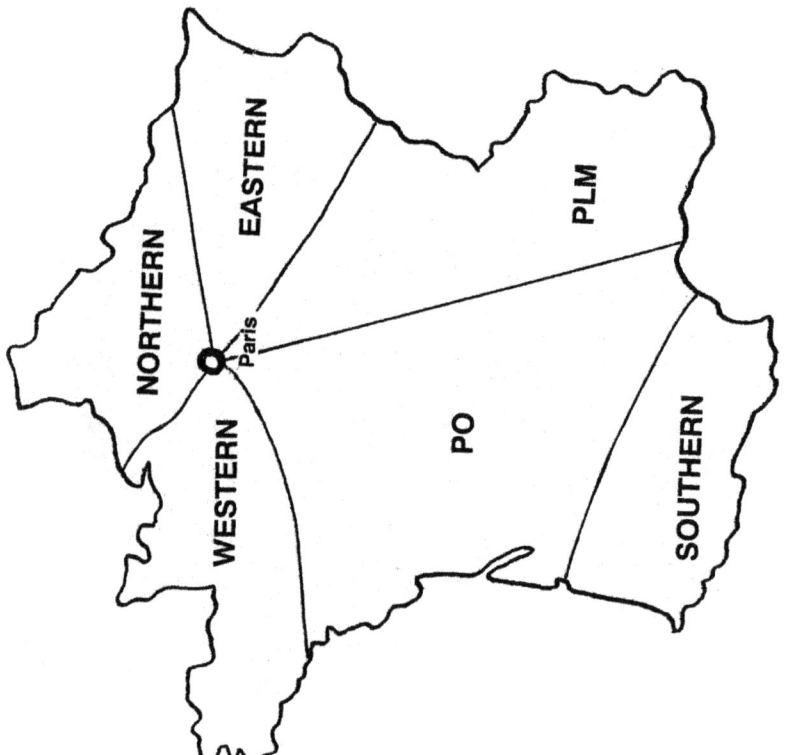

MAP 5: Major French Railway Companies, 1880

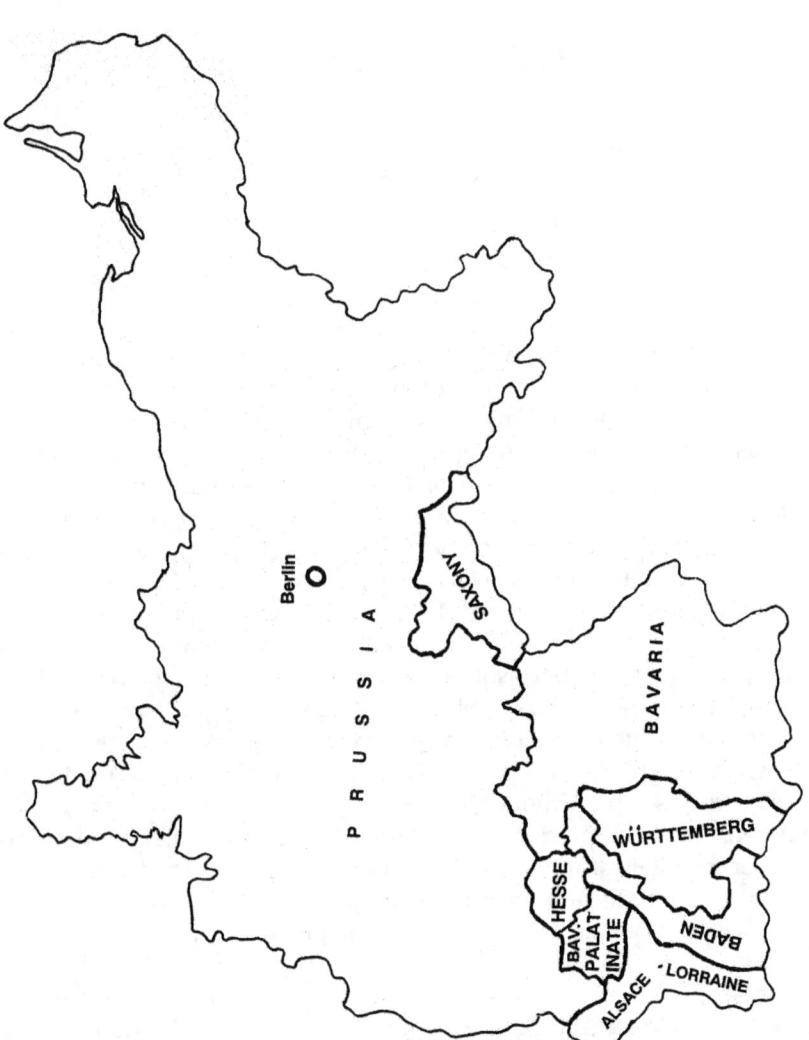

MAP 6: Major German Member States, 1880

Chapter 6

COMPARISONS, 1870–1890

After the Franco-Prussian War of 1870 there was in both countries a movement in favor of the nationalization of railways. Each was a failure. This is the basic premise with which any comparison of the two cases must begin. Another assumption is no less fundamental: confronted with their failure, the leadership of France and Germany responded in completely different fashions. Reduced to its most elementary terms, that difference resulted in the retrenchment of private railway enterprise in one case and its virtual abolition in the other. Whereas in previous decades they could both be appropriately classified as "mixed," now the two railroad systems parted company. In France, the new conventions adopted in 1883 perpetuated the supervisory power of the state; but the basis of the French railway industry nonetheless remained the major private companies, whose continued existence was likewise assured by the settlement. In Germany, meanwhile, a drastic change occurred that all but eliminated the private railroad sector. Although this was primarily a Prussian occurrence, the immense size and predominant political weight of that state could not fail to alter the total configuration of the German system. Thus, demonstrably, the national paths of France and Germany diverged by 1890.

As always, a certain danger lurks in the personalization of structural problems. Yet it is difficult to overlook a striking parallel in the public careers of Charles de Freycinet and Albert Maybach, whose names became so closely attached to the arrangements reached by their respective states. To mention them, however, is also to emphasize the obvious discrepancy between the political contexts within which they functioned. Behind Maybach loomed the domineering figure of Otto von Bismarck, avatar of the victorious German Reich and manipulator of an authoritarian regime that did not shrink from seeking (without always obtaining) radical solutions. Freycinet, by contrast, represented the defeated and chronically unstable French Third Republic, the character of which was in many respects ill suited to achieve sweeping and decisive reforms or concerted action. In analyzing the evolution of these two national railroad patterns, therefore, we need to keep the quite dissimilar configurations of Republic and Reich firmly in view. The range of possibilities was not identical nor, consequently, was the role of statesmen the same.

Administrative Organization

As France and Germany assumed new forms of government after 1870, both had compelling reasons to stress the unifying role of a national state. The necessities of economic and military competition on the European continent appeared to demand it. In respect to railroads, however, their constitutions were strangely imprecise, as if intentionally leaving the future administration an open question. Heretofore, there had been nothing but an improvised and haphazard accretion of laws, decrees, and conventions. Now was a time for definition, and it seemed that the most natural defining force was the recently conceived nation-state. Many of the French were led to this logical conclusion by tradition, the Germans by momentum.

Resistance to that centripetal pull was nevertheless powerful. In France, we saw, liberalism was still very much to be reckoned with. Respect for individual rights, private property, and free enterprise was no empty shibboleth. The French idiosyncrasy was that these principles were not espoused by a single political faction but spread generally throughout the nation's public life. Hence they constituted a pervasive emotional reality with which all republican reformers had to contend; accordingly, the private railway companies were to some extent protected by liberal predispositions. The same could not be said of Germany. The precipitous decline of liberalism there—specifically, of the National Liberal Party in the 1870s—left only one major opponent of Berlin's centralizing ambitions: particularism. Better said, the many interests of the Reich's member states could invoke a single federal principle, albeit in a confused and sometimes cacophonous fashion. Paradoxically, support for states' rights had been strengthened by the recent founding of an imperial regime, like the undertow of a cresting wave.

Such a brief summary of these familiar themes serves to settle the conclusion that France and Germany were simultaneously engaged in a process between 1870 and 1890 of redefining their respective center and periphery. Political ambiguities not withstanding, the names of the two national capitals became equally synonymous with the lure of centralism. For railway administrators the word Paris was shorthand for state regulatory agencies with long titles and strict intentions, such as the Comité consultatif des chemins de fer and the Comité de l'exploitation technique des chemins de fer. Similarly, the very mention of Berlin immediately called to mind the pretensions of the Reichseisenbahnamt. All such national administrative organs displayed a marked tendency to vaunt safety norms and military needs as justification for increased central control of the railroads. They did so, as we have observed, with only a modicum of success. Forever nagging and begrudging any limitation of their individual or collective autonomy were France's major private companies, tantamount (in their own view, at least) to independent states with their rulers, diplomats, bureaucracies, and budgets. These circumstances approximated those of Germany's long tradition of *Kleinstaaterei*, transposed into the nineteenth century and slowly transformed by the new tandem technologies of steam power and metallurgy. These generalizations make it fitting to evaluate the development of Franco-German railways not solely from the standpoint of the central states but also of their component parts. After 1870, more conspicuously than ever, the balance between them remained in tension.

When weighing these matters within the two national contexts, a basic distinction is at once apparent: the notion of *rachat* cannot be simply equated with *Verstaatlichung*. The French term comes much closer to the English concept of nationalization because it clearly implied the intent of a central government to acquire the holdings of private rail firms. Expressions of such a proposal in the past had been frequent and shrill, so that a recurrence after the war of 1870 came as no surprise. The defeat of the French armies could easily be blamed on the incompetence of the railway companies, reason enough to be rid of them. But public dissatisfaction with the division of French territory among six major rail enterprises also bred the opposite inclination: a total deregulation of the entire industry. In this perspective, it could be argued that the companies had become creatures of the previous Bonapartist regime, with its undue penchant for state regulation. If the problem was Napoleon, reject him, reject them. Moreover, this neat rationale accorded well with the broader tendencies of French republicanism, illustrated by the deregulation of alcoholic beverages in 1880. Yet these contradictory impulses tended to thwart one another, thereby creating an opening for the compromise of the Freycinet Plan, which promised a greatly enhanced participation of the state in railway affairs without its immediate and total acquisition of the companies. Unquestionably, then, Freycinet's grand vision embodied a trend in France toward etatism, the triumph of which would soon have consolidated centralism and severely curtailed the autonomy of the major railway firms. But we know the outcome was otherwise. A sudden collapse of this project in the early 1880s forced the French state to negotiate separate treaties with all six large rail companies, whose prerogatives to set rates, order rolling stock, and control their own finances remained largely intact.

The attraction of a nationalized railroad administration in Germany was altogether comparable and can be stated in nearly identical terms. By declaring railways to be a single public service, much like the postal system, the imperial regime hoped to cement the nation's political unification and to encourage more efficient deployment of rolling stock, more uniform specifications for locomotive construction, standardization of signals and safety regulations, better military utility, and above all greater profits for a Reich that was constitutionally restricted to indirect taxes. We have followed the tortuous efforts by Bismarck and Maybach to realize these benefits and, after repeated frustrations, their turn away from nationalization to the sweeping acquisition of private rail firms by the Prussian state. Furthermore, in order to avoid confiscation by the Reich of tracks within their borders, medium states like Saxony and Bavaria moved to do the same. The contrast with France could not be more stark insofar as the fate of private railroads was concerned. Yet the essential dynamic of the two fragmented national systems, namely the perpetual conflict between center and periphery, was remarkably alike. Complaints about encroachments in Paris on the rights of the large French rail companies had an eerily similar ring to those from the medium German states against the rude interventions of Berlin.

The eruption of national issues by no means crowded out regional concerns. Indeed, any number of the latter could be listed for purposes of a Franco-German comparison. For instance, there continued to be an intense rivalry between certain urban locales with aspirations to become major rail hubs: hence Amiens squared off against Lille in France (just as in the twentieth century over the location of Trains de Grande Vitesse), Bremen against Hanover in Germany. Likewise, disputes arose over certain rights-of-way, such as the proposal of a direct Amiens-Dijon connection that might penetrate the territory of the Northern and Eastern companies, much like the Bavarian projection of a rail passage to Lake Constance that would cross through a corner of Württemberg between Memmingen and Leutkirch. Rerouting freight traffic because of transalpine tunnels created some conflicts within both countries: the Mt. Cenis line, by directing Italian transit far north of Marseille, arguably hurt that port as well as its main rail carrier, the PLM; and the St. Gotthard Tunnel drew commerce via Switzerland to Basel, Baden, and the Rhine corridor, to the detriment of the Bavarian trade lane through Lindau. The construction of spur tracks was always controversial, tending as it did to favor some enterprises at the expense of others: good examples were the narrow-gauge lines that began to open the rich mine fields of the Briey basin in northeastern France or the indispensable rail link of a huge textile firm like the Nordwolle to the main thoroughfare between Bremen and Oldenburg, whence onto the Prussian network.[1] These specific cases represent many others that comprised the daily operation of regional and local railway administrations everywhere, irrespective of nation. Perhaps a positive symptom of increasing regularity on the railroads was a disappearance of the most infamous robber barons in France and Germany, as rogue entrepreneurs like Simon Philippart and Henry Strousberg had their last hurrah in the early 1870s.

At the same time, important European-wide (and American) innovations made their appearance after 1870. Most conspicuous, about which an extensive specialized literature exists, was a new generation of steam locomotives that replaced the single-axle Crampton type of engines previously dominant. A good example of the larger, faster, more powerful machines was the "Outrance," first adopted by the French Northern Railway Company, so-called because of its ability to run at full throttle without fatigue while pulling loads over 150 tons at speeds better than 90 kilometers an hour. No less significant were the four-cylinder "compound" locomotives, inaugurated in the 1870s, that made more efficient use of steam power by recuperating it to sustain constant pressure.[2] France and Germany simultaneously shared these gains, just as both increasingly adopted with variations the principle of the Westinghouse compressed-air brakes, permitting greater tempo with relative safety. These innovations were complemented by other technical improvements already mentioned: the block system to monitor the exact location of trains during their itinerary, electric signals to coordinate movements of rail vehicles and to warn road traffic of their approach at level crossings, telegraph and later telephone communication between stations, to iterate only the most obvious. Taken together as a cluster of invention, they vastly increased the speed and tonnage of freight transportation, therewith raising the economic potential—though not automatically the performance—of French and German railroads alike.

Passenger travel was also enhanced and increasingly democratized. Railway administrators took steps to expand their clientele by equipping cars with better lighting and heating, cushioned seats, and interior corridors and toilets. Private French rail companies as well as German state administrations kept close watch on their competitors, and their extant archival records contain numerous references to this or that amelioration by a rival that must be emulated to keep a competitive edge. The race among railway firms was equally stimulating for commerce and salutary for passenger service. Although a host of editorials in the newspaper press speculated about national differences—whether French trains were faster and more comfortable than German, or vice versa—the historian should desist. So many coaches traveling countless kilometers over such a long period of time under a wide variety of conditions do not permit a secure global judgment of that sort. We can merely observe that no earlier system of transportation had ever been remotely as easy and efficient as the railroad.[3]

Exact statistics on the total number of railway employees in the nineteenth century are impossible to assemble. We must be content with approximations and the certainty that the labor force was growing, somewhat more rapidly in Germany than in France. By the 1890s the aggregate of French *cheminots* working for the private companies was probably approaching 300,000. The German figure was closer to 400,000, and already—after its consolidation—the Prussian state network could boast of being "the largest technical enterprise in the world directed by government agencies."[4] Yet we are confronted here with a classic tale of the dog that did not bark. Labor organizations were weak and very little in evidence, partly due to the sprawling nature of the industry: in France workers were divided among the major railway firms and in Germany dispersed among state directorates.

Beyond that, between 1870 and 1890 both France and Germany underwent a period of political repression. Only the rhythm differed. Following the brutal elimination of the Paris Commune in 1871, a decade of arrests, trials, and legal harassment ensued in France. Amnesty for the communards was not granted by the republican government until the early 1880s, and only thereafter did the unionization of labor become feasible. French labor syndicates therefore tended to be small and scattered, with more than a dozen of them simultaneously claiming to represent the railway workers. In Germany, a labor movement likewise began to form, but it was suddenly undercut by the Bismarckian anti-Socialist legislation of 1878, which did not lapse until 1890.[5] Although these repressive measures affected all branches of the working class, they were consciously and perhaps especially aimed at employees of the railway industry, whose fidelity to the state was so crucial for obvious economic and military reasons. Albert Maybach said as much in 1878 when instructing his subalterns to call in police support without hesitation to defend railroads against "the danger ... of Social Democratic tendencies." His severity was seconded by Minister of the Interior Botho Eulenburg, who admonished state railway officials "to counter the pernicious agitation of Social Democracy in your administration with the maximum energy."[6] In the face of such menacing determination, the disorganized French and German labor forces had little choice but to remain quiescent for the time being.

The employment of women provided another point of comparison. We have noted that the French were the first to adopt this practice, especially by installing females as gatekeepers at level crossings. In doing so, as a contemporary remarked, the private railway companies "had given an example to all of Europe."[7] Between 1870 and 1890 a second wave of women employees began to appear in France in much greater numbers at stations and administrative offices as bookkeepers, secretaries, ticket-sellers, waitresses at buffets, shopkeepers, bookstall clerks, and newspaper vendors. German observers commented with approval on the "splendid results" of this development but expressed concern about mixing the sexes under crowded conditions. It would be better to arrange a separate room for females where they could be protected and their behavior controlled. "It has happened often enough," said one editorial with an unintended double-entendre, "that intelligent young girls had to be dismissed because their moral standards left something to be desired."[8] The great advantage of hiring women was obvious to private French companies and German state networks: they were cheap labor. A swift calculation showed that on a single line of the Eastern Railway Company, from Chalon-sur-Saône to Lons-le-Saunier, nearly half of the employees were females who had taken over a man's job at a fraction of the pay, thereby saving exactly 16,620 francs annually in operating costs, an average of 250 francs per kilometer of track.[9] For some types of office duties—tending petty cash accounts, checking statistics, sorting papers—women were credited by male supervisors with an "extraordinary cleverness," but a wall of benighted traditional attitudes stood in the way of a raise, promotion, or pension: "Women do not display the personal independence and the judgment that are necessary for some positions." Nevertheless, by 1890 females represented over 7 percent of the workforce on French railways and their ranks were growing. If Germany was slower to assimilate women, a rapid change would soon occur there with the introduction of the typewriter.[10]

However similar they were in certain respects, the French and German railway systems came to differ in magnitude. As a national entity, Germany's network became the largest in Europe. With more or less serious consequences, depending on the criteria applied, France lagged behind. In terms of track length, we saw that Germany took an early lead. But the significance of that fact is limited by the knowledge that French construction was generally more expensive and more solid because of the standards imposed on the private companies by the engineering corps of Ponts-et-Chaussées. Moreover, the gap was successfully narrowed somewhat by the enterprising regime of Napoleon III between 1850 and 1870. After the Franco-Prussian war, however, a newly united Germany surged forward once more and seemed to establish a durable advantage in size, a composite rail system roughly 25 percent longer than the French. Measuring track length, however, is only approximate. Should narrow-gauge railroads, spur tracks, and trolley lines be included? Should double tracks count the same as single? Should we give more weight to a measurement of network density in terms of track length per 100 inhabitants or per 100 square kilometers of territory (France led in the former but trailed Germany in the latter)? Ignoring these insoluble issues and employing very round figures, we can say that France increased its tracks between 1870 and 1890 from about 20,000 kilometers to nearly 35,000. The German total of rail lines in service meantime expanded from under 30,000 to over 40,000 kilometers.[11]

Yet it can be argued that track length was an unsuitable standard of measurement in the late nineteenth century. Most of the main rail lines had been completed by then, and, from a commercial viewpoint, many of the new railways built after 1870 had scant prospect of turning a profit. In both France and Germany, consequently, the rate of construction began to decline. France responded by negotiating a new round of conventions with the private companies in 1883; Germany, by disposing of the private sector altogether. Actually, many railway men had long denigrated the importance of track length anyway, often resisting governmental demands that commercial routes be determined by the shortest distance between supplier and consumer. Far more significant, they contended, was the "profile" of a rail line, which took into account the terrain, altitude, natural obstacles, grades, and curves through which it must pass.[12]

Perhaps a still better category is profitability, that is, the amount of income generated by a railway per kilometer of track. Although this standard, too, lacks the kind of precision that statisticians crave, we fortunately have an official French source from the mid-1890s that offers a global comparison of France and Germany in these terms (see Table 10). Despite all due reservations about the literal accuracy of these numbers, they disclose a distinct pattern that is undoubtedly valid and that permits us to draw three conclusions. First, the sheer volume of freight traffic on the German network was considerably greater than on the French. Even the boost of the Freycinet Plan, evident in the French figures for 1884, did not importantly alter the absolute dimensions. Second, whereas Germany displayed a steady growth of income in its commerce across the fourteen years in question, France suffered a notable setback in the late 1880s and did not regain its previous level until the next decade. As a consequence, the absolute difference widened to the degree that German receipts from railroads by the 1890s nearly doubled those of France. Finally, and significantly, the ratio of profitability (income per kilometer) shifted dramatically in Germany's favor. The French lead had evaporated by the mid-1880s, and a relative decline of the Third Republic continued thereafter.[13]

As far as we can tell, this change was profound and lasting. After the 1880s, Germany possessed a larger national economy with a longer, denser, and more profitable railway system. The fact that France could

TABLE 10: Heavy Freight Carried by National Rail Networks, 1880–1893

	Kilometers	FRANCE Income (francs)	Income/KM
1880	20,197	623,927,588	30,892
1884	26,375	631,185,846	23,934
1887	29,144	564,132,551	19,356
1891	30,442	660,704,640	21,704
1893	31,581	645,717,223	20,447
		GERMANY	
1880	33,646	717,511,847	21,325
1884	36,347	828,153,262	22,984
1887	39,157	938,416,000	23,965
1891	41,677	1,129,254,477	26,544
1893	42,736	1,186,408,730	27,827

Source: Chambre des Députés, "Proposition de loi tendant au rachat des réseaux des Compagnies de chemins de fer de l'Ouest et du Midi et à leur fusion avec le réseau actuel de l'Etat," 19 November 1895, AN Paris, F[14] 12122.

claim more kilometers of track per inhabitant than Germany only reflected a severe demographic crisis in the French nation, whose population growth was sinking to zero and below by century's end. Obviously, in an age of heavy industry and a rapidly expanding industrial labor force, the handicap of this negative development in France could not fail to affect the general economy and therefore the freight tonnage and gross income of railways. Furthermore, the growing discrepancy in performance may be attributed in part to a structural difference that favored Germany in the late nineteenth century. Government statistics from 1885 indicate that nearly two-thirds of the capital invested in French railroads up to that time came from the private sector.[14] It was therefore natural that stockholders should be rewarded, and the companies accordingly continued to withdraw large sums from their profit to pay out handsome dividends. With the partial and then virtually total exclusion of private funding in Germany, the various railway administrations of the Reich were under no such obligation. Insofar as state treasuries were concerned, the German system thus afforded instant fiscal gratification, whereas the French state was in effect counting on the long term. If all went well, France would allow the private companies to develop a prosperous industry, which at some later date (in the 1950s!) they would presumably turn over to the state once their concessions lapsed. But in the long term, as John Maynard Keynes reminded us, we are all dead.

Economic Competition

The patterns of economic growth in France and Germany during the railway age were remarkably similar before 1870. The industry and commerce of both marched briskly early in the three decades after 1840, only to stumble toward the end of each with the revolution of 1848, the recession of 1857, and the wars of 1866 and 1870. These lurches occurred almost simultaneously. Not so thereafter.

The period from 1870 to 1890 may be divided into three phases, the most striking aspect of which was the disparate economic performance of the two nations. In the immediate postwar years France suffered the consequences of a total military and political collapse, whereas a triumphant Germany underwent the greatest boom in its history. Then, in the late 1870s, the French economy displayed signs of recovery such that the republican regime was emboldened to launch the Freycinet Plan in an effort to sustain that boost; meanwhile, Germany's rampant stock market suddenly decelerated, exposing the Reich to what one historian has termed "the nasty six years."[15] A third stage ensued in the early 1880s when it was France that felt the effects of a serious deflation and commercial downsizing, although the Germans were able at the same time to renew their expansion and approach the astonishing levels of productivity established at the outset.

We are able to perceive and in part to measure the gap opening between France and Germany during this critical period. One contributing criterion was coal. France's lack of adequate fuel resources became magnified the more its national economy depended on rail transportation. By the end of the 1880s, the French annually consumed over 30 million tons of coal—double the amount of 1862—but produced only 20 million. Imports had therefore risen by 50 percent: five million tons a year from Belgium, four million from Britain, and 1.5 million from Germany in 1889.[16] Another indicator of French weakness, as we have noted, was the sharply declining and irregular demand for locomotives. Orders for new railway engines placed with the nation's manufacturers by France's private companies slacked off to 50 machines in 1888; yet Germany's annual production reached 700 locomotives, enough regular business to sustain sixteen large suppliers.[17] How did the French manage to keep their trains operating under such conditions? The simple solution was to retain old engines longer in service. By late century, the average age of rolling stock in France was 25 years; in Germany, 14 years. As one French expert has commented: "Certain [French] locomotives constructed in 1850 were still rolling in 1914. It was only after a minimum of 30 years' use, more usually after 40 years, that serious thought was given to replacing them."[18]

Not surprisingly, this period also saw a shift in the balance of trade between the two nations. From the mid-1870s to the mid-1880s, France slipped from an annual commercial surplus of more than 150 million francs to a deficit with Germany of 140 million, a difference of nearly 300,000,000 francs a year. This change in the economic relationship to Germany, much greater than with any of France's other trading partners, signaled more than a temporary statistical slump. There were already strong hints of a permanent structural transformation (which we must later examine) whereby the share of finished goods produced and exported by Germany grew, while the French percentage of manufactures in global European trade declined. As a leading sector of the economy, the locomotive industry was thus exemplary of a more general pattern.[19]

Neither in France nor in Germany were efforts by the national administration successful in imposing a more uniform rate system on the railroads. Despite repeated conferences in Paris and Berlin resulting in a seemingly infinite number of cajolements, decrees, and treaties, the reality was no centralization of commercial rates and not even a meaningful arbitration of them. Sensing that their very existence was at stake in the matter, French private companies and German medium states alike resisted encroachments on their prerogative to fix charges on freight. For the same reason, the attempt to negotiate international rate agreements at several conferences in Bern also failed to achieve any real uniformity or reduction: their constituent members would not cede to national governments the right to regulate the terms of trade in Europe. Claims by central states to be "the master of rates" fell without reverberation like trees in a vacant forest.

But pressure to reduce rates was permitted, and one may say that it was exercised more effectively in Germany, partially as a normal consequence of the higher volume of freight traffic there. The more goods were shipped, the less the cost per unit. The Prussian state railway system especially operated on that precept, and it thereby nudged the competing regimes of the other German states in the same direction. In France that sort of leverage seemed less forceful. The Northern Railway Company, because of rivalry from canals, ordinarily set its schedule of freight charges lower than the other firms, but they often declined to follow. In 1890 the French deputy Camille Pelletan recalled "old and persistent" criticisms of unduly high rates. He complained that "the companies actually have legislative power." According to his calculations, the average of German rates had decreased between 1875 and 1888 from 6.26 to 5.10 francs per kilometric ton, whereas the corresponding French drop was only from 5.99 to 5.94 francs.[20] This unflattering comparison of course drew a rebuttal from the companies, which presented their own figures, and produced a full-scale parliamentary inquiry led by Richard Waddington. His survey estimated that the averages should be lower: French rates were actually down between 1881 and 1888 from 5.89 to 5.66 francs per kilometric ton; equivalent German statistics, from 5.41 to 4.87. Yet it was a distinction without much difference. The three conclusions of Waddington's committee were like Pelletan's: French rates had been reduced less than the German; the private companies were responsible; and a more active intervention by central authorities was thus indispensable.[21] Such a statement was an admission that, on an international scale, Germany was gaining a competitive advantage while France was slow to respond. Commenting on French legislative delays, Pelletan was unsparing: "In effect, the state of affairs remains about the same."[22]

Contemporaries were unanimous in acknowledging another German advantage gained before 1890. The impact of the St. Gotthard Tunnel far exceeded that of Mt. Cenis. Symptomatic of that difference was the edgy debate in France about a third transalpine rail line via the Simplon, which contrasted with the smugness of German officials once the rising trade statistics with Italy began to roll in. As Count Münster, while ambassador in Paris, wrote to Bismarck in 1886, St. Gotthard had brought an "unexpectedly great advantage" to Germany, "mostly at the expense of French trade."[23] Among the strongest advocates of a Simplon counterstroke was the PLM's Gustave Noblemaire, who saw the project as necessary to aid French companies in their "struggle against the commercial progress of German railways." It would draw traffic back onto French tracks, he believed, and it would shorten the trajectory between Paris and Milan: 942 kilometers via Mt. Cenis, 891 via St. Gotthard, and only 835 via Simplon.[24] We know that not everyone was convinced, particularly after an investigative report in 1889 by the influential editor and journalist Edmond Théry, who concluded that (1) a Simplon Tunnel would provide no competition for St. Gotthard but would duplicate

Mt. Cenis; (2) it might bring some increase of transit to northern France but would certainly hurt the Midi; and (3) it would mostly benefit the port of Genoa at the expense of Marseille.[25] Consequently, French dithering continued. A self-satisfied comment by the journal of the Association of German Railway Administrations was near to the truth: St. Gotthard had provided the Reich with "a sharp weapon against French interests" and opened an "important new era" in European commerce.[26]

Ports were no less indicative than tunnels. In 1882 a special subcommittee of the Comité consultatif des chemins de fer, presided by the deputy (and the future president of the Third Republic) Félix Faure, prepared a composite statistical analysis of the harbors of northern continental Europe. It showed in detail, in terms of total tonnage, that Le Havre had begun the 1860s as the largest of these, soon to be overtaken in that decade by Hamburg and closely followed by Antwerp. During the 1870s Antwerp emerged as the leader, while Hamburg maintained its lead over Le Havre, which was also challenged by Rotterdam. In fifth place by the 1880s was Bremen, comfortably ahead of Dunkerque. Other French ports like Calais, Boulogne, and Dieppe lagged far to the rear.[27] Here was more than at once met the eye. If considered from the standpoint of connecting rail traffic, the numbers revealed that, of the five major ports in northern continental Europe, four were dominated by Germany. With few exceptions, merchant ships approaching the Continent had no reason to land their goods in Antwerp or Rotterdam if the destination was France. But they had every incentive, given the more favorable rates for freight by rail, to use these ports in commerce with Germany and Switzerland.

This observation was confirmed in a supplementary report drafted by a member of Faure's committee, a Ponts-et-Chaussées civil engineer named Alexandre Gottschalk, who examined facilities at Le Havre later in 1882 and learned, for example, that "shipments of cotton to Switzerland pass more and more via Antwerp" rather than by French ports and railways. The reasons, he explained, were that the Belgian and German railroads offered lower rates; their ports were better equipped and thus more efficient in loading and unloading at dockside; and they provided more rapid transportation, sometimes permitting a difference in time of delivery between five and eighteen days. Besides, the great textile mills of Alsace, under German management since 1870, had mostly abandoned French tracks for Rhineland routes.[28] Another official report in 1883 drove home the same point. A quarter of a century earlier Le Havre handled twice the tonnage of Antwerp, but it now had 50 percent less. Likewise, on the Mediterranean coast, Marseille had once commanded a volume of cargo seven times that of Genoa, but now only double; and that margin was likely to be further reduced by St. Gotthard.[29] Such visions of doom for the French republic may appear in hindsight to be overwrought. But there is no question that they had some statistical basis in an economic reality that was tilting in favor of the German Reich. For this fact of life, the French rail system was not entirely to blame, nor the German to credit. Still, by 1890 a distinct commercial imbalance was developing that was sufficient to feed French anxieties and German ambitions.

Military Strategy

The demonstration of Germany's military prowess in 1870 left France literally defenseless. Gone were the frontier installations in Alsace-Lorraine and gone, too, the mighty ridge of the Vosges Mountains. Where once the French had gazed down on the Rhine Valley, there now stood German troops and guns above the Moselle. At fortresses like Metz and Strasbourg the Germans merely needed to turn cannons about to face westward, whereas the French were forced to conceive new defensive positions, acquire new artillery pieces, design new command structures and cadres, develop a new strategy, and, in short, create an entirely new army.

One might therefore suppose that after 1870 the victors possessed every military advantage. But in three regards specific to railways, it was rather the French who held the upper hand. First, distance. The displacement of the Franco-German frontier meant that French trains required shorter lines to reach it. For better and for worse, the border was now much closer to Paris than to Berlin. A more compact rail network would serve French needs, while any future German offensive would demand a vast extension of connections across the Rhine. Second, all French planning could be predicated on a single front at the nation's northeastern fringe. Men and supplies would move in one direction with one goal: to halt a German advance. The logistics of Germany's awkward two-front circumstance were far more complex and the costs of construction much greater. Thousands of kilometers would separate Germany's strategic railheads; the French would be at most only a few hours apart. Finally, from the beginning, Germany's enormous rail system had a deficit in double tracks. Enforcement of the stricter building codes imposed by Ponts-et-Chaussées gave France's infrastructure of transportation this notable element of strength as well as greater uniformity, always a military virtue. Doubtless, the German army would have met no match in France between 1870 and 1890, yet this was not quite the open-and-shut case it seemed.[30]

One common feature of the French and German military establishments was internal conflict. It came in many forms, strikingly similar. There were disputes among cabinet members (the Ministry of War and the Ministry of Finance or Public Works), between ranking military officials (the French Etat-Major or German General Staff and their respective Ministry of War), and within the administration (civilian bureaucrats and military representatives). The nature of these altercations varied, usually involving financial allocations for construction, the relative competence of military men in the location of rail lines or the extension of frontier zones, and regulations for the implementation of any future transition from peacetime to wartime controls. In all of these, no case can be made for the story of a smooth evolution in France or Germany, nor for the notion that military planners invariably had their way. If there was a significant difference, it lay in the continuity and greater stability of the German high command under Helmuth von Moltke, which had no equivalent amid the fractured political conditions of republican France.[31]

The military issue that caused the most heartburn was the budget. The costs of the war and the payment of reparations to Germany threw the Third Republic (and its rail companies) into a deep financial slough. Because funds were scarce in the 1870s, military leaders constantly pressed government officials and company administrators to underwrite construction on their own. When, with the grand design of the Freycinet Plan, the French state attempted to take the matter in hand, a fiasco only provoked more bickering over the budget. At first, Germany's military condition appeared different because funding came easier in the flush postwar years. But the economic dip after 1873 and the alleged urgency of eliminating the deficit in parallel tracks soon produced strains over military allocations. The result, in both France and Germany, was an extended debate over cost-sharing, a question that posed in the most concrete form perplexities about the relationship of center and periphery. A good example was a deal, brokered by Ponts-et-Chaussées in 1886, between the Northern Railway Company and the French state: expenses for alterations in the line from Lille to Calais and Dunkerque would be split so that the Company's share was one-third. Such an arrangement exactly mirrored the general 1887 formula reached in Germany whereby the Reich agreed to a greater portion of outlays for strategically useful construction, whereas the member states assumed a lesser burden: Prussia 40 percent, Bavaria 25 percent, etc.[32]

No one will ever succeed in computing precisely the real military expenditures of France and Germany after 1870, nor consequently those for railways. Not only is much of the direct evidence scattered or lost, many extant documents were deliberately obfuscated and occasionally falsified. Nations had no interest in revealing their true military budgets or advertising the actual strategic value of railway construction. Rather than accepting official estimates, therefore, a thorough investigation would need to pry out the financial details of many thousands of individual allocations, a labor surely beyond the capacity of even the most dedicated researcher. We can cite one interesting if dubious memorandum from military archives that purported to compare the French and German budgets from 1882 to 1894. According to this source, France was spending more heavily than Germany throughout the 1880s and was not surpassed in military expenditures until the onset of the 1890s. But the memo also notes that the two bookkeeping procedures differed because many administrative items included by the French did not figure in the German totals, requiring a subtraction of at least 75 million francs from the former's tabulations for each fiscal year.[33] If so, the budgetary reality was far from published reports of it, and the discrepancy in favor of Germany occurred sooner than indicated. In military as in economic affairs, it appears, a financial gap was beginning to widen before 1890. Despite the confident assertions of certain historians that the republican army had reached virtual parity with the Reich's military machine by that time, Freycinet's conclusion as he surveyed the two decades since the war of 1870 seems to be more appropriate: Germany's "considerable augmentations" had left France "in a situation of inferiority too dangerous to accept with resignation."[34]

Whatever their estimation of the relative strength of France and Germany, all military leaders could agree on the need for central strategic planning based on the capability of railroads. Yet in at least four basic respects, the two nations departed from different premises. After all, France had lost the previous war, while Germany had won it. Again and again, French planners therefore combed through the inadequacies of their transportation system with an eye to improving its military utility, and they were beginning to make some progress. Although the Germans had been victorious, the logistical deficiencies already apparent in 1866 had recurred in 1870, and hence complacency was scarcely more appropriate in Berlin than in Paris. Second, it was only realistic for the French to assume a defensive stance, whereas German planning naturally stressed offense. Militarily defeated and diplomatically isolated, France could not hope after 1870 to mount an aggressive challenge on foreign soil to what everyone now conceded was the world's greatest army. At the same time, even if Bismarck formally declined to sponsor a preemptory strike against France, admittedly he remained aware that some moments for an offensive would be more propitious than others; and his military chieftains, should the occasion arise, would require little provocation or prompting to comply. Third, the administrative basis of mobilization plans was not the same. To reach the enemy's frontier, both French and German rail convoys faced the geographic imperative of crossing internal boundaries: those of the private companies in one case, member states in the other. To meet this problem the French designated a system of railroads "of general interest," but—despite a recommendation of the Fourth Bureau in the Ministry of War—they rejected a German model for mobilization and instead retained a procedure that depended on the coordination of the major companies. Germany's expectations were, in the meanwhile, pinned on Moltke's concept of strategic "line commissions," whose operation in wartime would be taken in charge by military plenipotentiaries. Let it be added, however, that the political reticence of the southern states was an acknowledged fact that strongly suggested a plan for a northerly thrust on Prussian tracks and a mere holding operation in the South. Fourth, we might say that the keynote of planning in France was elasticity, in Germany rapidity. Both general staffs were of course bending every effort to ensure swiftness of movement, but the direction of French motion would importantly depend on the route of a German invasion. The German priority must be to develop a first-strike capability, whereas France would need to prepare a quick response from several fixed points. Such were the elementary terms of two necessarily divergent strategic conceptions.

In ways concrete and abstract there were also similarities. Military authorities everywhere stressed technological uniformity: equipping national railway systems with nearly identical signals, brakes, switches, lights, and traffic rules would obviously expedite the movement of military convoys across the country. The fact that these intentions were imperfectly realized, however, produced a visible nervousness in France and Germany alike about unforeseen and potentially disastrous delays. A consequence was that both sides began to contemplate the need to anticipate a period of "political tension" or partial mobilization that would precede an actual declaration of war and allow more or less disguised troop movements by rail. These worries, in turn, encouraged a distinct rash of xenophobia among military men, ever suspicious that foreign agents were watching the construction of railroads that could not be hidden and might be sabotaged in a crisis. These not totally unfounded fears were perhaps more pronounced in France—and certainly under Boulanger they became more elaborately codified in enemies' lists—but contemporary German records contained the same mistrust of foreigners communicated among certain statesmen and railway administrators.[35] Finally, it followed that an aura of uncertainty surrounded military thinking, no better example of which was the doubt about Belgian neutrality and how far the Germans would extend their supply lines to circumvent the French system of fortifications.

Who held the lead? Because of the many imponderables, no definitive response is possible. The ultimate standard, a test of arms, was lacking. What is clear is that by 1890 both sides were still unsettled in their military planning and had a lengthy agenda of unfinished business. France was undergoing a major conversion of its entire defensive structure, requiring concrete and steel reinforcement of fortresses on the eastern frontier and the simultaneous declassification of indefensible redoubts on the Belgian border. These alterations, occurring as they did at the end of the Moltke era, were bound to encourage a reconsideration of Germany's offensive strategy. And we know well the identity of the man who would soon appear to recast it. Looking back, we can readily observe a kind of collusion that would eventually result between the Schlieffen Plan and the French measures to meet it. Both would be products of a mentality of escalation that had already begun. If the French were motivated by a sense of inferiority and a will to surmount it, the Germans were driven by a conviction of superiority and an urge to sustain it.

Part III

Internal and International Tensions

Chapter 7

FRANCE, 1890–1914

Following the splendid Paris Exposition of 1889, the French nation seemed more at ease with itself than at any time since the Great Revolution a century before. The shock of defeat in 1870 and the bitterness then engendered by the Paris Commune receded into the past, crowded aside by a growing prosperity and the unprecedented artistic and literary flourish that needs no introduction here. Social conflicts there were, of course, and political agitation that troubled the surface of public life, for which a mention of the Dreyfus Affair may stand for all the rest. Such dark shadings not withstanding, the dominant mood of the years before and after the turn of the century was optimistic. But we know that it did not last and that this reverie of *la douce France* would be utterly shattered in 1914. Consequently, looking back, historians can scarcely avoid the temptation to treat the time after 1890 as a prewar period. Yet it is important not to lapse into some teleological explanation of events that led to the First World War, nor to imagine that all things pointed to one inexorable fate.[1]

These familiar admonitions are particularly appropriate for the history of railways. It would be a distortion to suppose that the outcome of the twentieth century—nationalization of French rail networks—was predestined by developments of the nineteenth. Instead, the tensions between the central state and the private companies between 1890 and 1914, as earlier, should be evaluated in their own time and on their own terms. Only by doing so can we hope to gain a sense of the cataclysmic impact of the Great War on European society and polity. The conflict that finally erupted should not be recorded as the result of a steady evolution toward some *terminus ad quem*. It proved to be, rather, a jolting temblor that cracked the existing foundation of the entire French railway industry and permanently altered its structure.

Recovery and Controversy

After a disastrous slump during the 1880s, the French railway industry began a slow and uneven convalescence in the next decade. Gross receipts of the private companies remained sluggish in the early 1890s once the temporary heady effects of the Exposition year had worn off. Yet there were some encouraging signs. A few of the companies showed a surplus and accordingly attempted to reimburse the state for loans acquired in times past. But, the Northern Company excepted, all of them still had to request so-called guarantees of interest in order to sustain the dividends of their stockholders. By 1895, nevertheless, statistics were available indicating that the companies were operating in the black, though conducting their affairs with varying degrees of profit.[2]

Before 1900, the collective income of French railroads rose to unprecedented levels, but at the same time so did their annual expenditures. A major reason for both of these increases was a political bargain struck between them and the Ministry of Public Works: if the government rescinded the 10 percent tax on passenger fares imposed by Adolphe Thiers in 1871, the companies would agree to a corresponding reduction in ticket prices. The effects were remarkable. The Northern Company, for instance, boasted a 27 percent increment in passenger travel by the autumn of 1892. A greater occupancy of third-class carriages was especially noticeable, rising 32 percent by the year following. Since freight charges were (more slowly) also declining, the total volume of rail transit burgeoned. That was the good news. Less edifying for the companies—ever prodded by the state—was the necessity of providing more rolling stock, more equipment, more personnel, more safety measures, and more comfortable facilities. Democratization of railway travel thereby came at a heavy price for the companies, whose hectic existence after 1890 epitomized the crude dynamics of capitalism. Unable to raise fares or rates, yet forced to meet higher expenses, their only recourse was more growth.[3]

This resurgence of the regional companies and their constant need to economize on operations could not fail to produce strains in their relationship with the national state. Such altercations ranged from the trivial to the fundamental. We may arrange them here into five clusters, ascending in order of significance. First were some individual details of administrative decision-making. An example was a request by the Northern Company for the state to pay for a mobile loading crane (*grue roulante*) at a small provincial rail junction. Interestingly, this question was treated with full solemnity by the Executive Council of Ponts-et-Chaussées. As a committee report stated, the Northern's petition was "in itself without importance," but it was "fraught with consequences." If approved, even this paltry allocation might set an unfortunate precedent for the state's assumption of greater expenses for the expansion of all stations in the Company's network, contrary to the terms of its concession. In short, an administrative principle was at issue, namely the state's right to rule on the proper cost of railway construction: "It therefore retains the indisputable authority to limit these projects as it sees fit or even to postpone them altogether."[4] For their part, the companies were no less adamant. In the spirit of free enterprise they had concluded agreements with the publishing house of Louis Hachette to install bookstores in their main terminals (direct descendants of which, the "Relais-H," still exist today). Periodic renewal of their contracts often proved to be troublesome, however, and some disputes about the right of state censorship inevitably occurred. The Ministry of Public Works therefore sought to intervene as an arbiter in the negotiations with Hachette. To this advance, speaking in unison as the Syndicate of the Paris beltway, the companies gave a vigorous rebuff: if the stations were owned by the companies, which therefore assumed sole legal and financial liability for them, any "penetration" by the state into private business affairs conducted there would be unjustified. Incidents like these could be cited ad infinitum, and it is well not to neglect them when surveying the railroads.[5]

A second grouping may be classified as trial balloons. In early 1893 a proposal of this sort was brought to the floor of the Senate in the form of a motion that the state should name the directors of all French rail and mining companies, two industries essential for the national economy. Several senators immediately leaped to the defense of private enterprise, denouncing such "dangerous meddling," which was "inspired by the pure but false doctrine of state socialism." When the current Minister of Public Works Jules Viette expressed his own reservations about the motion, his confession was greeted with mock enchantment by the majority, and the motion was withdrawn. "Much ado about very little," commented the *Journal des Transports*, although it later happened that a nearly identical suggestion for state control of the appointment of all railway executives would reappear. Similarly, in May 1901 the Ministry of Public Works inquired tentatively whether it did not seem "rational" to the rail companies that the government directly supervise operations on those lines constructed at state expense. Once more company officials gathered in their Syndicate to draft a negative reply upon which each of them would base a separate response. When thus faced with five categorical refusals, the Ministry backed off.[6] We should not underestimate the significance of these inflated proposals, episodic as they were. They showed that the will of the companies to survive as autonomous concerns was constantly being tested and that after 1890 they were in peril at a weak moment of forfeiting their administrative independence. Whether they were to function in the future as private enterprises or public services was henceforth a perpetually open question.

A third flock of issues concerned technological innovations. Confronted with alarming statistics about the number of railway accidents, the Comité de l'exploitation technique des chemins de fer (CETCF) was especially keen to jettison older vacuum brakes (*freins à vide*) and to have the companies adopt the principle of continuous automatic compressed air (*freins continus automatiques*). The main difficulty was a multiplicity of designs: both the Westinghouse and Wenger systems had already been variously adopted or modified by the companies—despite their incompatibility—and a third brake firm, Lipkowski, was negotiating for a contract with the Northern Company. In addition to growing safety needs, military utility also represented a strong rationale for the state to seek a uniformity of type. But could the rail companies be forced to comply? Long debates in the CETCF failed to produce a solution in the 1890s. After the committee was reorganized and expanded in 1900, it was again presented with reports about "too frequent" incidents of brake failure. Another investigation concluded that most of the companies were sufficiently in conformity with the government's guidelines, although the split between Westinghouse and Wenger persisted. Only the Southern Company and the State Company still displayed serious defects, and hence for them "a more direct intervention by the administration would be justified." This conclusion, of course, also contained the inverse premise that interference by the state with the other major companies would be unjustified.[7]

Before moving on, it will be useful to glance at the issue of electrification. Tests on electrically powered engines were conducted in France, notably by the PLM, before the turn of the century. In 1900 the Ministry of Public Works created a special committee to investigate the question with the explicit motive of "not allowing ourselves to be farther outdistanced." That danger was quickened by reports in 1903 that the Germans had succeeded in operating experimental locomotives on straight and level military tracks at 220 kilometers an hour. The main technological obstacle for the French, it was thought, was to transmit electrical power far from its source; but the introduction of high-tension wires in 1904 seemed to clear the way for progress. As a coal-poor country, France had a clear and present incentive to develop the use of hydroelectrical energy. Yet the government's initiative continued to stall for years and was confined mostly to mountainous regions in the Alps and Pyrenees.[8]

Fourth were numerous and grating disagreements over budgetary matters. It had long been the ostensible policy of the republican government to oversee the finances of the large private companies, to require a regular accounting of their income and expenditures, and to demand a justification of any extraordinary projects. The difference after 1890 was a new determination to enforce it. For that purpose the Ministry of Public Works sought an allocation of 750,000 francs to recruit additional inspectors. But that vigilant self-appointed watchdog of free enterprise, the Senate Finance Committee, opposed the motion, and—despite a "vehement" defense by Jules Viette—the full Senate voted 144 to 109 to reject a reform of the state's inspection team, thus averting "the retention of supplementary if not useless functionaries." Yet undeterred, Viette persisted in persuading the Chamber of Deputies into adopting a similar measure. With the two houses of parliament deadlocked, he then attempted to proceed by ministerial decree, always easier to obtain than a law though harder to enforce. He took care to avoid a stance too radical, explaining his balanced policy to French President Sadi Carnot: "The railway companies are public services, but they nonetheless conserve in some regards the character of commercial societies"; they therefore retained a "mixed" personality—"at the same time commercial and public."[9]

Such dulcet reassurances obviously invoked the long tradition of French railroads dating back to 1842. They also accorded with one of the most popular and influential railway treatises of the era, written by the Berlin professor Richard von Kaufmann, which was published in 1896 and translated into French. Kaufmann's thesis, contrary to claims of Teutonic superiority advanced by some of his compatriots, was that both France and Germany had developed railway systems eminently suitable for their respective circumstances, and in many respects the French were better served by an adroit melding of private capital and state regulation. These were flattering words for the French ego. A chief engineer at Ponts-et-Chaussées, Henri Bonneau, restated Kaufmann's case for maintaining France's mixed system—situated midway between Germany's dominating state controls and the always assumed Anglo-American model of unfettered free enterprise—which had allowed the French to devise a transportation scheme "more appropriate than any other to the genius of our race." Kaufmann's translator, in a preface to the French edition of 1900, echoed these sentiments exactly in praising the nation's railway networks as an expression of "our own genius."[10]

Yet there were bound to be conflicts once the central state began to introduce laws and decrees that swelled the operating costs of the companies. Such was especially the case with social reforms passed into law after 1890. The private companies had actually pioneered this legislation by earlier creating medical services and pharmacies for their employees, sometimes helping to support mutual aid societies, and offering modest pensions. But now they found themselves outflanked by state requirements that were not railway-specific and that threatened significantly to raise the level of company expenses. Moreover, they claimed, with their former health and pension plans superannuated, rail workers would become confused and agitated, surely not in the state's best interest. The universal reaction of private management was well summarized by the *Journal des Transports*: "It is only belatedly, and not to innovate, to ameliorate, but perhaps to the contrary to impede [the companies] with constraining regulations, that the state has intervened in this question."[11]

All of the foregoing considerations culminated in the proposed *loi Bertaux* in 1901, a bill that fixed a daily limit of ten work hours for railroad employees and defined the terms of their pensions (after twenty years of service they were to receive one-half of their average annual wages during the final six). Representing the major companies, Gustave Noblemaire launched a biting counterattack, ridiculing the absurdities of strict enforcement of a ten-hour limit for engineers and firemen on lengthy round-trip runs and claiming that Bertaux's measure would elevate the annual operating budgets of the companies by 100 million francs. True, expenses did soon rise, though less ruinously than Noblemaire predicted. The main result was not to be measured in francs, however, but in the tensions and residual bitterness of the companies toward what they regarded as an oppressive state bureaucracy now bent on imposing "increasingly strict and onerous regulations."[12]

A fifth controversy surrounded the production and purchase of locomotives. Since 1842 it had been formally agreed that the private companies should acquire engines as needed in fulfillment of their concessions from the state. But the wish of the Ministry of Public Works after 1890 to tighten regulation of the railroads led it to insist on the prior notification of any such transaction, a proviso analogous to the rules for construction or modification of tracks and stations. Henceforth, the companies would be expected to report all estimated allocations for rolling stock and to provide "indispensable" justifications for any addition to their fleet of vehicles. There is ample evidence that the companies made some effort to comply with these instructions and that they frequently signaled when they were about to open bidding from locomotive construction firms. Did that mean, however, that the French state thereby succeeded in imposing "crushing" controls on the companies and that they were collectively reduced before 1914 to the status of a highly regulated public service?[13]

The complex answer to that question must begin by pointing out three loopholes in the government's stated policy. First, it was generally admitted that the companies could at any time carry out "regular maintenance" (*menus travaux*), although it was often problematic to distinguish between minor repairs of rolling stock and major replacements. Second, the companies claimed the right to act unilaterally in the event of emergencies, such as a sudden increase in freight or passenger travel caused by an unusually copious harvest or by public spectacles like the Paris Exposition. Third and most conspicuously, the companies were under no obligation to furnish the name of their suppliers. The understanding remained that they would announce their needs for locomotives to all interested construction firms, solicit bids from them, and then sign the most suitable contract. Furthermore, these three inherent limitations of state control were forever compounded by erratic reporting from the individual companies. There was consequently an evident discrepancy between claims by the Ministry of Public Works to exercise "unlimited power" over the supply of rolling stock and stubborn refusals by the companies to follow instructions promptly and fully by filling out standardized printed forms. The messy reality was that the companies did not challenge state regulations on principle so much as they resisted them in practice. They conceded little, biding their time while cabinets formed and fell, parliamentary committees met and adjourned, ministers came and went.[14]

It was under these circumstances that the Eastern Railway Company decided, almost unobtrusively, to test the waters with an announcement that it had accepted a bid for twenty locomotives from the Maffei plant near Munich, "one of the principal construction firms of Bavaria." Although Public Works did not intervene to forbid this purchase from a manufacturer in Germany (a term unspoken), such action did not go unnoticed. In mid-May 1901 a special parliamentary committee was founded to codify regulations on the acquisition of rolling stock and to hear complaints by French locomotive constructors about the dubious practices of the private rail companies. Within a fortnight the cabinet issued a ministerial decree requiring that the companies disclose the identity of all suppliers placing bids on contracts for locomotives, presumably so that the state could grant—or withhold—prior approval. We cannot fail to observe that the manner and tone of the government's pretension to dominate the companies in this fashion distinctly recalled the *homologation* debate of decades past. The issues were identical. Did policy decisions by the private companies require an explicit agreement of the state? Must the railway firms first obtain the assent of Public Works before acting? Was there, in effect, an official right of veto?[15]

It is fair to conclude that until the beginning of the twentieth century such questions were treated as internal affairs, a nexus of perennial French domestic problems recast after 1890 in a somewhat updated form. But the Eastern's deal with the Maffei factory and the state's swift reaction soon changed that. For the first time, charges of German "dumping" were heard in the Chamber's committee on railways, where it was revealed that German prices were nearly 29 percent below those in France because of mass production, cheaper labor costs, and the lower expense of primary materials, notably coal. As one prominent member of the committee, Henry-Louis Le Chatelier, lugubriously remarked: "Therefore, I do not believe that it would be possible for France to compete on the international market with Germany." Yet the immediate question was whether France could even maintain control of its own market. Nationalism was now an issue, forcefully brought to the public's attention on 7 January 1902 by a sensational headline in the Parisian daily *Le Matin*: "GERMAN LOCOMOTIVES IN FRANCE." The (inaccurate) report was that thirty engines with German drivers had just been delivered to the Eastern's workshops at Epernay. Quick rectifications were forthcoming: only twenty machines had arrived, and there were no German drivers who might, as *Le Matin* luridly suggested, later return to lead transports of German troops.[16]

The sequel was predictable. Embarrassed by stinging publicity about national impotence, the government issued another decree that reiterated the demand for prior notification of suppliers seeking bids from the companies for new locomotives. The companies replied by acknowledging the principle of compliance but contending that exceptions must be made in an emergency. To this the Ministry of Public Works responded that such extraordinary circumstances could be anticipated by careful planning, and each company was therefore directed to provide the government with its projected needs for rolling stock in the next ten years. Speaking for the others, the director of the Northern Company, Albert Sartiaux, scoffed at the notion of a decade's prediction. It was manifestly impossible, he argued, because of the "infinite facts" required to evaluate a railroad's performance in advance. Besides, he added (probably as a dig at the rival Eastern), his company had not placed orders abroad for over twenty years and had no plans to do so.[17]

By 1905, then, the French state and the private companies had reached a standoff on the issue of locomotives. Of the several altercations in which they were engaged, none better reflected the traditional conflict between etatism and liberalism. Old wine in new bottles? Instead, it seems that the season for a new vintage had arrived. Given its increasingly patriotic tinge, the nature of public discourse was changing. Every controversy was now becoming a national debate, framed in terms of a budding Franco-German rivalry, and the railroads could be no exception.

The Companies Face Nationalization

The private railway companies entered the 1890s meekly, their stature diminished and their resolve weakened by the recession of the previous decade. Nothing could have been more natural than a raft of new proposals for acquisition by the state of some or all of the French railroads: to a greater or lesser degree, in a word increasingly employed, nationalization. Paradoxically, it was just as the companies were beginning to show positive signs of financial recovery, about 1895, that a serious campaign for their disenfranchisement got underway. A bill presented to the Chamber of Deputies late that year by Gaston-Marie Guillemet and ninety-nine of his parliamentary colleagues advocated "radical reform" by seizure of the Western and Southern Companies and their fusion with the State Company. The idea was to found a great southwestern railway firm that could successfully compete with the Big Four, all of which would under the terms of this bill remain intact. A second motion by the deputy Léon Vacher foresaw a complete "nationalization" of the private companies that might, at long last, break their "exorbitant monopoly." Such a sweeping stroke was essential, Vacher contended, because there was no other way for the state to become the master of rates—or, he might have added, of engines. When the railway committee of the Chamber took up these two plans in the spring of 1899, a compromise emerged, sponsored by Jean Bourrat, that would have converted all of the companies except two, the Northern and the PLM, into state enterprises. Bourrat agreed with Vacher that it would be well to rid the French rail system of its "original sin," an excess of the companies' independence, but he was willing to settle for a tripartite division of the national networks, thus leaving two private firms at least temporarily in business to compete with a vastly expanded State Company. He professed confidence in the ultimate outcome because, when it came to the issue of private or public ownership, "the superiority of the state is clearly established."[18]

Which should it be: two, four, or six railway companies immediately confiscated by the state? For an entirely practical motive, that decision was delayed. Crowds flocking to the Paris Exposition of 1900 provided reason enough to avoid administrative disruptions, and the current Minister of Public Works Pierre Baudin therefore requested that all legislative action be deferred. Momentum stalled. Despite pleas for a resumption of parliamentary initiative, nothing further occurred until July 1903, when yet another special committee was formed, chaired by Alfred Picard, with the specific charge of restructuring all of the railroads in southwestern France, a measure that would directly affect the PO, the Western, and the State companies.[19] Now, in order to grasp these developments and to evaluate their results, we need to revisit individually France's major rail firms.

The Eastern Railway Company

Directorship of the Eastern Company passed in 1889 from François Jacqmin to Roger Barabant, who held that post until his retirement in 1905. The new director was a less contentious person than his predecessor, eager to cooperate with the other major rail companies and less obdurate in dealing with the Ministry of Public Works. Indeed, lest we think that the history of the companies was sheer negativism, one could compile a lengthy list of Barabant's successful negotiations on common rates, shared stations, mutual rights-of-way, joint construction projects, and the like. Still, there was certainly no shortage of conflicts. These were caused chiefly by parliamentary bills and administrative decrees that effectively raised operating costs for the companies, usually in the name of new safety regulations or social welfare. Barabant also had to contend with a few labor disputes that twice, in 1891 and 1899, erupted into strike attempts. In both instances the police stood by the company (once receiving a generous tip for their intervention), order was quickly restored, and several rail workers were dismissed without reinstatement.[20]

Yet Barabant's main worry, of course, was to restore the Eastern's financial viability and thereby to thwart those who urged nationalization of the companies while pointing to their deficits and reduced service in the late 1880s. In these efforts, albeit slowly, he succeeded. Although flat at first, the Eastern's gross income began to rise in 1895 at a steady rate of about 3 million francs annually. Such growth was unremarkable, but it enabled the Company's veteran president Henri van Blarenberghe to boast in 1898 of "very notable progress." He also correctly predicted that his firm would begin the twentieth century with a significant reduction of its debt to the state. Apart from a brief stumble (blamed by the Company on France's "economic crisis") just after the Paris Exposition of 1900, corporate profits were sufficient to allow huge transfers of capital to the

TABLE 11: Transfer of Funds between the French State and the Eastern Railway Company, 1899–1910 (francs)

Year	Loans from the State	Reimbursements to the State
1899	—	4,351,626
1900	—	10,568,247
1901	2,141,899	—
1902	2,971,552	—
1903	—	900,429
1904	—	2,890,260
1905	—	10,078,605
1906	—	18,303,333
1907	—	14,812,040
1908	—	8,702,111
1909	—	9,735,922
1910	—	17,952,747
Totals	5,113,451	98,295,320

Source: Compagnie de l'Est, Assemblée Générale, *Rapport*, 25 April 1911, CAMT Roubaix, 13 AQ, 2643.

national treasury, totaling nearly 100 million francs by 1910 (see Table 11). Therewith, as the *Journal des Transports* commented, the Eastern Company entered an "era of reimbursements" after the turn of the century.[21] These data of recovery demonstrate the dubiousness of an assertion that all of the private companies were condemned by the conventions of 1883 to losing their financial flexibility. The Eastern Company was in reality restoring its fiscal independence and becoming less beholden to the state than at any time since the reign of Napoleon III.[22]

A reliable means to check the Company's pulse is to chart its supply of locomotives. At Epernay the Eastern possessed one of France's most efficient railway workshops, which had a productive capacity of about thirty engines and tenders a year while employing a workforce of only 1500 men. During the 1880s, this rate was adequate to replace older locomotives and to sustain a relatively small increment of trade. With some evident pride the Eastern's Administrative Council reported in 1896 to the General Assembly of stockholders: "We are able to satisfy all the needs of current traffic." Yet we know that the 1900 Exposition created demands for increased passenger and freight service that led the Company to place orders with "private industry," including the infamous twenty locomotives from Bavaria. Once the economy resumed its upward course in 1905, the Eastern again had to solicit bids for locomotives from manufacturers beyond its Epernay workshops. Initially, these were accepted only from French industrial firms: Schneider at Creusot, the Société Alsacienne in Belfort, and Fives-Lille. But it soon became questionable whether that national line could be held.[23]

For all the improvements in his Company's fortunes, Roger Barabant terminated his career without shedding worries about administrative intrusions by the state, rising costs of operation, and the inherent risks of free enterprise in a volatile market. These were the "grave dangers" indicated by the Eastern's new president Charles Gomel in early 1906. The likelihood of nationalization appeared remote, but other troubles remained.[24]

The PLM

The stability and survival of the Paris-Lyon-Méditerranée Company owed much to Gustave Noblemaire. Director since 1881, he did not retire until the age of seventy-five in early 1907. This long tenure was no dance on roses. The Company's financial condition seemed chronically deficitary, mainly because its immense territory contained so many unprofitable rail links serving a rural population. Between 1884 and 1895 the PLM was forced to borrow some 28.8 million francs from the state in guarantees of interest. Noblemaire was determined to stop this financial bleeding and managed to reimburse 5.7 million in 1896 and another 10.3 in 1897. But that effort could not be sustained. After the "favorable circumstances" of the Exposition year 1900, red ink returned, and the PLM had to obtain from the state treasury a "rather important sum" of 10.5 million francs in 1901. At last in 1905 the Company was solvent enough to conclude a separate convention with a pledge to retire its accumulated debts in fifty-five annuities of 9 million francs. In short, the PLM shared the aim of the Eastern Company to regain its fiscal independence but was less rapid in doing so.[25]

Like the Eastern, too, the PLM had increasing problems with personnel. An abortive strike attempt in 1891 was serious enough to provoke the dismissal of 380 employees, none of whom was rehired. Like his colleague Roger Barabant, Noblemaire saw to it that police agents were offered a handsome *pourboire* for assuring the "right to work," meaning protection of the majority who stayed on the job. But behind the "usually rather vague and often unacceptable" demands of the strikers he sensed their legitimate concerns, commenting that "the current situation cannot remain as it is." Accordingly, Noblemaire set out to improve the lot of his workers, especially those at the bottom of the scale, by raising wages, supplying more health benefits, and (prodded by the state) reducing work hours. Likewise, he instituted a new program of family assistance (*secours*) and expanded the Company's retirement fund. Paralleled by similar arrangements in the other companies, these additional expenditures—invariably referred to as "sacrifices"—soon mounted into the millions. It is impossible to calculate such sums to the centime, but management estimated that burgeoning social costs had at least trebled by early in the new century. And yet, like the other rail firms, the PLM felt menaced by the state's penchant for passing additional social legislation that would induce "considerable expense" and might finally prove "ruinous."[26]

From the mid-1890s we are fortunate to have for the PLM very detailed statistics on the aggregate of capital invested in the firm (*dépense totale d'établissement*). They show that, from a bottom line of virtually 4.5 billion francs in total investments to date, private stockholders had accounted for about four-fifths. State contributions and subventions amounted to less than 20 percent, while French departments and communes had contributed no more than 1 percent. These data also disclose that the state had provided less than 10 percent of the funding for what was formerly known as the "old network" (that is, the main tracks), and that its part had slowly increased after 1870 to spur building of secondary and tertiary lines in the name of public service. Yet the bulk of the PLM's business was conducted on the original infrastructure, which generated the greater portion of its gross income. Generally, this pattern of investment was typical of the railway companies, though a complete profile of the variations among them would require a lengthy monograph in itself.[27]

It is useful to conclude this sketch by surveying the PLM's policy on locomotives. More frequently than the Eastern, the Company placed orders in the 1890s with "various French factories," thus relying less on its own already downsized *ateliers*. Expansion of the PLM's rolling stock represented the largest single item in its budget and of course contributed importantly to its deficits. After a splurge of purchases in 1900 and 1901, Noblemaire tried to cut back expenses: not a single new engine was acquired in 1903. Twenty remained on order, of which only three were added in 1904 to a total fleet of 2990 locomotives. Then came the economic upturn, with its abruptly increased requests by French industry for more railway service. The PLM responded by allocating 12,450,000 francs for rolling stock in 1906, including 100 new compound locomotives. Ostensibly, these bids were to be placed with French manufacturers. But what if the national locomotive industry lacked the capacity to supply them? To that question Noblemaire had a ready answer, but it was not one that state officials and parliamentary committees would want to hear.[28]

The PO

The Belle Epoque started badly for the Paris-Orléans Company. In 1890 its gross receipts stood at 15.5 million francs below their 1884 level. Meanwhile, expenses had shrunk by 11.5 million, indicating the magnitude of the PO's previous downsizing. We do not need to review the reasons for such weakness, except to recall that the Company was largely dependent on agriculture at a time when large stretches of French vineyards were still struggling to overcome the ill effects of a phylloxera epidemic. The difficulty was also partly structural, because more than half of the PO's income was derived from the Company's track between Paris and Bordeaux. Its territory thus lacked both industry and diversity.[29]

The decade began with a renewed downward spiral of deficits that required the Company to arrange for a series of state loans: 8 million francs in 1890, 8.9 million in 1891, 13 million in 1892, 11.8 million in 1893. The PO therefore had no alternative to maintaining a "spirit of strict economy," holding down track construction and locomotive contracts to virtually zero. Not until 1896 did the level of income surpass that of 1884, allowing a reduction of sums borrowed from the state to slightly under half a million francs. Although the *Journal des Transports* detected signs of a "renascent prosperity," it added that the PO remained saddled with an unduly large number of unprofitable railroads.[30]

Such a lackluster record lent weight to the parliamentary motion in 1894 for the state's acquisition of the PO. Given its bleak financial picture, the Company had every reason to fear this legislative threat. In evaluating the performance of its administration, we should keep the constant menace of nationalization in mind, as if observing the behavior of an inmate on death row. A most fitting description of the PO's capable director of this era, Charles Heurteau, would be as a master of crisis management. Like Roger Barabant and Gustave Noblemaire, he had to face down a strike attempt in 1891 that came sooner and proved more serious in the PO's case. For quelling it Heurteau gave full credit to the government's "energetic" measures to assure the right to work. Company records show that nearly half of the PO's labor force was involved and that many were ultimately dismissed. Though he rejected "certain unacceptable propositions" by the workers, Heurteau drew the same lesson as his fellow directors that the protests of PO employees merited more careful attention. Within its limited resources the Company set out to raise the wages of day laborers and women, offer extra financial assistance to families to offset high bread prices, support mutual aid societies, design a "very special" program of pensions, and allocate funds for cheaper staff housing and local cooperative stores. The downside of this largess was a significant rise in personnel costs, which added, the Company claimed, almost 26 percent of the total annual salary base before 1905. As in the case of the other companies, moreover, the amounts spent for social benefits were certain to be increased by impending parliamentary legislation on invalidity insurance and retirement pensions, adopted respectively in 1905 and 1909, though they both remained of limited impact before 1914.[31]

After the PO's lean years from 1884 to 1895, a phase of fiscal equilibrium ensued, permitting what the Administrative Council proudly called a "period of reimbursement." The Company returned 4 million francs to the state treasury in 1898, 3 million in 1899, lesser amounts for a few years, then 3.2 million again in 1904. Only in the years 1906 and 1907, however, did these repayments exceed the amount of interest due to the state for earlier loans. Still, the financial health of the PO unquestionably improved as revenue from passenger fares between 1895 and 1905 increased by 31 percent and freight shipments by 27 percent. We can also note that orders for new locomotives were slowly resumed and that they then trebled suddenly to 180 bids in the boom year of 1906.[32]

If these gains seem less than massive when compared to those of the Eastern Company or the PLM, they were adequate to earn the PO a reprieve from nationalization. Instead, as we saw, attention came to focus on a *rachat* of the Western Company, its fusion with the State Company, and a major restructuring of the railways in southwestern France. Dispute finally centered on the triangle of tracks connecting Nantes, Tours, and Le Mans, with their direct access to Paris. In return for the "painful sacrifices" of these lines, the PO was to receive some compensation of lesser connections south of the Loire Valley. At one point the Company balked when its Administrative Council decided to hold out for a fairer settlement and refused to accept, in effect, a "partial *rachat*." But it was finally a deal that the PO could not very well decline, lest it incur any further risk of nationalization. It therefore acquiesced after Georges Clemenceau became the French prime minister in October 1906 and gave stern orders that the matter be brought to closure. As Rilke once wrote: "Who speaks of victory? Survival is everything."[33]

The Northern Railway Company

No doubt the Northern was a jewel in the crown of French railway companies. But it could not hope to avoid being tarnished by the nation's economic troubles of the 1880s. Fortunately, as we have observed, the Company retained advantages that enabled it to ride out the worst and to recover with relative alacrity: a sound financial backing, a compact infrastructure, a broad industrial base, and a pivotal commercial location. These traits gave the Northern a greater potential for profitability than the other companies. Statistics from 1892 indicated that fourteen of the thirty-seven main lines of its "old network" were operating with gains, providing the Company a far greater consistency than its peers, though a lion's share of net income (slightly more than a third) was generated by the connections between Paris and Belgium. Caution was nonetheless a conditioned reflex of this conservative business firm, now securely in the hands of Alphonse de Rothschild, who presided over it until his death and the succession of his son Edouard in 1905. It was characteristic, therefore, when the Company's administration—under the astute direction of Albert Sartiaux—admonished in 1892: "We are entering, in effect, a period that may be difficult."[34]

So it was. True, the Northern's gross income began to rebound, but the rise of costs was "proportionately stronger." In the early 1890s, annual budgetary reports to the General Assembly of shareholders dripped with pessimism: 1891 was termed mediocre; 1892, "much less satisfactory"; and 1893, "even less satisfactory." The Northern thus needed to exercise "prudence" (a favorite word in its management's vocabulary), dictating that "we must delay all construction and all improvement of service," one result of which would be "an important reduction of passenger trains." Actually, the Company's passenger count had increased by 1895, a testimony to greater efficiency. Fewer trains were carrying more customers, notably in third-class carriages filled with season-ticket holders (*abonnements*) on short round-trip journeys (*aller-retour*). Such democratic trends were even more pronounced in the late 1890s. In the first half of 1898, for instance, the number of fares increased by 3.4 percent.[35]

We can extrapolate from these data a growth pattern that was paradigmatic for the entire French railway industry. After 1890 the private companies passed through three phases: a painfully slow retrenchment early in the decade; a marked improvement in the late 1890s that peaked with the Paris Exposition of 1900; then at the outset of the new century another disappointing spell that came to an end in 1905 when the national economy began to bolt upward. Whereas the Northern's income in the year 1899 was heralded "to far surpass our hopes," the gross receipts of 1901 fell by 17.6 million francs, and the first half of 1902 was "decidedly unsatisfactory." Indeed, the persistence of negative returns was such that the Company's Administrative Council began for the first time since 1870 to contemplate the possibility of requesting state loans as a guarantee of interest. That drastic step was not taken, however, and the Northern protected its reputation as the only rail firm to remain free of debts to the national treasury. Admittedly, not for the first time, the Northern Company's bookkeeping procedures were found defective, and an alleged surplus of earnings in 1903 hid a "real" deficit of at least one million francs. As late as the spring of 1905 a gloomy mood thus prevailed in the Gare du Nord: "Because current prospects are not more favorable, prudence is more than ever necessary for the Company." But within a few months there was already a "notable recovery" in sight, and by the end of the year Sartiaux confirmed a general increase of trade.[36]

As earlier, the acquisition of locomotives was usually a good indicator of a company's performance. The Northern's record before 1905 was generally like the rest, that is, modest and irregular. The Company added (mostly as replacements) only five steam engines in 1890 but forty-seven in 1891; sixty-one in 1898 but only one in 1899; forty-six in 1901 but only seventeen in 1902, four in 1903. Such numerical fluctuations are inconclusive, except to explain why company workshops were partially idled and to show that France's private locomotive construction firms had to contend with limited demand and unstable market conditions. Judged by this standard and not by the criteria of another day, such as track length, the French railway industry apparently lacked the dynamism to cope with a sudden spurt of the economy that was just around the next bend. In 1905 the Northern Company acquired not a single locomotive from French manufacturers, and only thirteen were built in its own *ateliers*. No wonder that Albert Sartiaux expressed apprehension that the Company might have reached the "reasonable limit" of its capacity.[37]

That said, the trajectory of the Northern Railway Company after 1890 was nevertheless upward. Its management was solid, its income growing, its traffic increasing, and its stockholders satisfied. With all of their unsteadiness, the same could be said of the Eastern Company, the PLM, and, to a lesser extent, the PO. Albeit erratic, the recovery of these firms provided little pretext to the advocates of their seizure by the state. The periphery held.

Private Enterprise or Public Service?

The final decade before the First World War presented a basic question. Should the French railway firms be instructed, indeed should they be required, to buy French? That issue was considered at length in February 1905 at a meeting of the Executive Council of Ponts-et-Chaussées, which ended by unanimously rejecting such a proposal. Not only could it hurt small manufacturers dependent on imports of certain materials unavailable in France, it might also provoke a protectionist retaliation abroad that would eventually harm French exports.[38] Actually, as it soon became evident, there were several other good reasons to avoid even the appearance of imposing an embargo, and nothing better revealed the unfeasibility of doing so than the locomotive industry. If the following description of this aspect of the railway industry is sufficiently detailed, we may be able to resolve the question as to whether the private companies had been so diminished by the conventions of 1883 and so shackled by government regulations thereafter that they fell under "the aegis of the state," submitting them before 1914 to "the needs of public service."[39]

Signs of economic resurgence became manifest by the spring of 1906. A "very prosperous" year was at hand, and, if so, there was an evident need for the companies to order more steam engines and to acquire them quickly. As months passed, the number of contracts rose accordingly, of which the great majority were concluded with French industrial suppliers. Records of the Eastern's purchases indicated that only a few of them were placed abroad (including the twenty locomotives delivered from Munich in 1902). Exceptionally, the PO accepted a bid for twenty machines from the United States, to which the Ministry of Public Works made no objection.[40]

The crisis arrived in 1907. Hackneyed though it may seem, the image most apt is a bursting dam. The trickle of 1902 became five years later an inundation of foreign locomotives. Already worried about this eventuality, the Comité de l'exploitation technique des chemins de fer (CETCF) took up the matter during closed sessions in February and March 1907. The consensus of its members was to encourage a policy of "prudence," that is, pressuring the private companies to plan ahead and thereby avoid any need for importing foreign engines. But doubts arose. The "weak production" of French factories might make it "absolutely indispensable" to place orders beyond the borders. The discussions thus ended with a pious motion that the nation's railway firms should turn abroad only if domestic suppliers demanded "unacceptable prices or delays."[41]

In the meantime, however, most of the companies were preparing to disobey this injunction. Their policy would be, as the Eastern's Administrative Council defined it, to accept bids from abroad "whenever necessary." To perceive such necessity did not take long. On 15 March 1907 the first major break occurred when Gustave Noblemaire announced an order by the PLM for 110 engines: 45 from Borsig in Berlin, 40 from Henschel in Kassel, and 25 from the Société Alsacienne, which straddled the Franco-German frontier at Belfort and Mülhausen. As Noblemaire explained, to the PLM's call for bids, five French suppliers had made no reply, while the others could not promise delivery before 1909. "Under these conditions, and to its great regret, the Company was obliged to turn abroad." He added: "Only the Germans offered proposals." The Ministry of Public Works accepted this transaction, merely stipulating that penalties should be imposed on the German manufacturers for any late deliveries. Two weeks later Noblemaire resigned from the directorship of the PLM and was elevated to the Legion of Honor. Quite deliberately he had launched a campaign of the companies to buy abroad, but he would not be present to see it through.[42]

The barriers soon began cracking. A few days after the PLM's announcement, the Eastern Company accepted a bid for forty German engines. Only the Northern pointedly resisted, declining a lower offer from Borsig to sign with a French firm. The PO meanwhile released an order for 180 locomotives and tenders, conspicuously leaving the identity of suppliers unspecified. Alarmed, the CETCF hastily reconvened on 6 April to hear a report from the Ministry of Public Works. It justified the PLM's purchase of foreign machines on grounds of "urgency and the impossibility of constructing them in France." The Company's chief engineer apologized for looking abroad, "and particularly to German firms," but to cope with expanded traffic more locomotives were necessary "as soon as possible," and they could be obtained more economically—at a savings of 1.5 million francs—by buying in Germany. A state inspector attached to the PLM reluctantly concurred: faced with a need to meet "tremendous difficulties," the Company had "obtained acceptable offers only from Germany." He was willing to approve the announced procurement "while regretting that the [PLM] has been obliged to turn abroad, and particularly to Germany." After another debate on these "serious and disturbing developments," the CETCF ratified the inspector's realistic conclusion that French industry "cannot at this time fill the orders currently demanded by the railroads."[43]

By the onset of 1908, pressure had mounted for a full parliamentary investigation, to be conducted by the newly rebaptized Committee on Public Works, Railways, and Roads in the Chamber of Deputies. Called to testify before this body, the current Minister of Public Works Louis Barthou was introduced under a cloud of criticism about the "lamentable effects" of government policy. He responded with statistics on orders of locomotives during 1906 when French rail companies had purchased 782 engines from domestic firms and 315 abroad. Barthou conceded that "a very considerable portion" of the orders for railway engines had been placed in Germany. But what did it mean for the state to possess a "right of control"? Even if that phrase implied an absolute veto on the purchase of foreign locomotives, it did not seem feasible to exercise it. If French industry has need, if the price is better, and if the delay is shorter, he said, "I will authorize a company to order abroad." Refusal to do so would be a "deviation" from the state's traditional policy that had permitted French companies to negotiate bids from private enterprises of their choice, whatever the nationality. And he then pronounced this clinching sentence: "I cannot forbid a company from turning abroad."[44]

The rest was anticlimactic. Whatever the public or political misgivings, French companies continued to acquire a significant number of locomotives in Germany. Even the expiring Western Company placed an order in 1908 with Henschel for sixty machines at an "extremely advantageous" price. Barthou's efforts to crack down on a requirement for prior approval by his Ministry went unheeded. When the PLM accepted bids for a new batch of engines in May 1908, the CETCF was curtly informed that "the Company has declined to reveal the name of the constructor." Likewise, the Eastern and Northern Companies placed orders later that year with "private industry," no identity specified. The PLM offered justification for its purchases, backed by precise statistics. In the years 1905–1908 it had ordered 357 locomotives in France (73 percent) and only 132 abroad, despite the lower cost of the latter. Thus "every contract awarded to French factories is a willing sacrifice in the interest of our national metallurgy." By acquiring so many French engines, the PLM had willingly forfeited 1,346,000 francs and also accepted longer delays of delivery, despite its "urgent needs," proof enough of the Company's "patriotic concerns."[45]

The Northern Company, alone among the private railway firms, continued to order exclusively from French suppliers. The others ignored the strictures of press, parliament, and Public Works by refusing to notify the government in advance of bids accepted abroad to meet the "constantly increasing needs of our operations." In July 1909, the PLM unilaterally purchased eighty-five new engines: twenty-five from Schneider at Creusot and sixty from Henschel in Germany. Even the small Southern Company imported machines from across the Rhine, despite the CETCF's complaint that this act was "deplorable for the good reputation of French industry." Official estimates were that of the 405 locomotives delivered to French companies in 1909, nearly two-fifths were of foreign origin, and more were needed. Just as these numbers became known, the Eastern Company announced another purchase of twenty engines from the Maffei factory near Munich—as if deliberately recalling the coup that had launched the entire matter. When challenged at a meeting of the CETCF, the Eastern's chief engineer coolly replied that it was "not a question subject to governmental action." And the state inspector attached to the Company, Paul Worms de Romilly, could not disagree. It was, as a member of the CETCF understated, "a very complex question," which became no simpler when the committee divided seven to seven over a motion to uphold the state's right to require prior approval of orders for locomotives. Given the deadlock that embarrassingly revealed the CETCF's ineffectuality, its only option was a reaffirmation that the companies might expect the state's concurrence with their acquisition of engines "on the condition that [they] make known to the administration at the proper time (*en temps utile*) the list of constructors … as well as the price and schedule of delivery."[46]

Taken as a whole, the archival records of the rail companies show conclusively that they did not yield to government pressure and that they persisted in affirming that "the proper time" for notification was after contracts had already been concluded. State agencies were thereby reduced to pleading, usually in vain, for the companies to identify their suppliers "as soon as possible." This frustrating circumstance induced another round of discussions by the CETCF in March 1911. As in years past, the ostensible subject was German dumping, for which exact statistics were now supplied by Henry-Louis Le Chatelier. At a time when the Prussian network was buying locomotives for 1.80 francs per kilo, German suppliers were selling them to French companies at 1.35. "Thus we find ourselves, without any possible doubt, facing a dumping operation." The basic problem was the inadequate capacity of French industry. While the Germans could produce 1500 locomotives annually, "a number very superior to their needs," French constructors provided only 450 in 1909, 350 in 1910, and a projected 500 in 1911. What should be done? To answer that awkward question a subcommittee of the CETCF under Clément Colson was assigned to study "operations of dumping."[47]

The last French pylon collapsed in early 1911 when the Northern Company released a statement that an order would be placed "abroad" for fifty locomotives: as it proved, ten in Belgium and forty in Germany. After so many concessions to the other companies, the CETCF could scarcely disapprove. Meanwhile, the Colson subcommittee, after its review, reported back to the CETCF in June 1911 with some further information about Germany's "obviously abnormal prices." The current rate for locomotives from suppliers in France was 1.57 francs per kilo; in Belgium, 1.49; and in Germany, 1.38 (including 23 centimes per kilo at customs). These were now the normal "conditions of the market," to which the French would need to adapt. With funereal certainty, as if speaking an epitaph, Colson concluded that it was "neither possible nor desirable to forbid the companies from turning abroad." So much for state regulation before 1914.[48]

A dramatic episode in the midst of these developments also revealed the limits of government control: the railway strike of 1910. Early that year, amid outbursts of protest by the companies about added costs arbitrarily imposed through state action, a new social welfare law of 21 July 1909 went into effect, establishing the principle of obligation for all workers and their employers to participate in a national pension fund. Objectively viewed, the situation of French labor was thereby improved. But long-standing dissatisfaction with the private rail companies over hours and wages nonetheless boiled over at a time when talk of a general strike was common. Ironically, it was the Northern, arguably the most prudent and progressive of the companies, that bore the brunt of this agitation. In mid-October traffic on the Company's main lines was severely disrupted, with less than 20 percent of trains leaving Paris. Stations and crossings were blocked at La Chapelle, Lille, Arras, Amiens, and Laon. Circulation remained normal only in the coastal regions near Dunkerque and Boulogne. Sabotage was reported at ten locations, telegraph and signal lines were cut, rocks hurled at engines, scraps of metal laid on tracks. "The crime is consummated," wrote the *Journal des Transports*.[49]

Reports meanwhile reached Paris from outposts of other firms. On the PO, about 700 employees—"non-commissioned" laborers mostly, rather than salaried personnel—staged a noisy walkout, but "numerous" were those who chose to return to work. Others who abandoned their posts could expect to be dismissed. The Eastern Company had the least trouble. None of its scheduled train departures was delayed or canceled, though in the border areas some freight connections with the Northern and the PLM were disturbed. A small minority of Eastern agents deserted, and the Administrative Council assured that they would not be rehired. Besides the Northern, the PLM experienced the most difficulty. "Agitators" (*meneurs*) appeared on 12 October and were joined on the next day by a growing squad of workers from stations, depots, and workshops, though many "visibly hesitated" to defect. The climax occurred on 14 October. "Nearly half" of the employees at one workshop went out on strike, while further commotion was evident in Paris, Arles, and Marseille. But normalcy was quickly restored in Paris on the following morning. The strikers were cowed after orders arrived from the Ministry of War to mobilize those of military age. This had an immediate effect, and by 18 October all was quiet.[50] In the wake of the upset, the PLM's directorate tried to draw a detailed profile of the protesters. Nearly 5000 of the Company's 78,500 employees had been implicated, two-thirds of them workers on daily wages. They were generally located in urban areas: 700 in Paris, 2000 around Lyon, 1500 at Marseille, and 600 near Geneva in the Savoy. There had been fifty acts of sabotage, "more or less serious," but no accidents. Eighty-one telegraph lines were cut, three attempts made to dynamite installations, plus a few incidents of revolvers drawn in trains. In all, 287 workers were discharged and perhaps as many as 200 other employees suspended or scolded. Such punitive action was "painful," the PLM contended, but it was "necessary for the maintenance of discipline."[51]

Not so much these incidents as such but their sequel should attract our attention. The shock of public violence on the railroads and the threat of their complete paralysis stirred both the private companies and the republican government to activity. Rail firms not only punished defectors, they rewarded the faithful. Within weeks following the crisis, for example, minutes of the Northern's directorate contained more than fifty pages of notices about "gratifications" for loyal employees, some of whom received a special bonus for the "distinction" of their service. The ensuing months saw more promotions, wage increases, and welfare benefits—but absolutely no reinstatement of pariahs, though some of them with long service records were granted modest indemnities. In the meantime, state officials prepared a parliamentary bill that would, in effect, declare strikes to be "altogether illicit" in a public service, as the railroads were henceforth to be designated. Prime Minister Aristide Briand also sought to institute some kind of labor arbitration. This measure was sponsored by the Socialist leader Jean Jaurès, who presented the Chamber of Deputies with a proposal for what he now designated as the Conseil supérieur de discipline. Suffice it to note here that this plan foundered on the uncertainty of two imponderables: how the membership of such an arbitration board would be chosen, and whether its judgments would be binding for both management and labor.[52]

The most pointed disagreements concerned the issue of amnesty. During initial discussions the companies remained categorically negative, just as they historically had been after insurrections in 1848, 1871, and the 1890s. Eugène Weiss, current director of the Eastern Company, instructed his administrative staff that all dismissals of employees should be considered "definitive," and it was therefore useless to grant them interviews about "irrevocable" measures.[53] His fellow directors concurred. When summoned to a meeting in October 1911 with Prime Minister Joseph Caillaux and Minister of Public Works Victor Augagneur, they refused to yield, declaring that "in the higher interest of order and discipline, it would not be possible to revoke the imposed sanctions." At most, they might consider some compensation for the aged among those released. While the pitch of vituperation rose on both sides, support gathered in parliament for a revision of the 1883 conventions, meaning that the companies should essentially be stripped of their autonomy. Caillaux remarked that this was in fact "a grave problem ... for which a solution cannot long be delayed." Yet it was.[54]

In March 1913 a new Minister of Public Works, Jean Dupuy, reopened the amnesty question by personally contacting Albert Sartiaux and requesting that sixty of the Northern Company's suspended workers be pardoned. Sartiaux did not flinch, again stating that such action would be "impossible." One month later, Caillaux's successor as prime minister, Louis Barthou, made a final attempt at reconciliation on the basis of a recent motion adopted by the Chamber in favor of an immediate amnesty. Despite Barthou's "very lively" entreaties at a meeting of all the presidents and directors of the companies, they unanimously reiterated a refusal to comply: "Their responsibilities and the necessity of discipline would not permit them to envisage any measures of this sort." For the companies, the amnesty issue was "definitively settled."[55]

Unable to impose its will on the companies to prevent their acquisition of foreign locomotives or to obtain an amnesty for their dismissed employees after the strike of 1910, the French government fared little better when it came to codifying a series of safety measures. Technological standardization was a specialty of the CETCF, which in turn advised the Ministry of Public Works. Part of the problem was that this committee, as if a microcosm of republican cabinets and parliaments, was often divided on questions of public policy. A fine illustration was the long debate in late January 1910 on the introduction of a uniform system of automatic coupling (*attelage automatique*) for freight cars. Already put into use in the United States (where, Worms de Romilly estimated, rail accidents had thereby been cut in half), such a device would need to be adopted on a European-wide basis to ensure the international circulation of rolling stock. But what system should France adopt and then recommend to other states? And how could the companies be persuaded to settle on a single technology, to test it, and to apply it throughout the nation? Members of the CETCF failed to agree: a decision between two coupling inventions (Moyet-Bouvier or Boirault) ended with a ballot of ten to eight.[56]

This outcome recalled the much earlier division of technical opinion on air brakes. In fact, that issue remained unresolved, as the CETCF learned in July 1911 when the Paris-Orléans Company announced the development of its own braking system for freight wagons. Its adoption was necessary, the PO's director explained none too convincingly, in order to meet the specific requirements of the Company's terrain. A young member of the CETCF (and later the president of the Third Republic), Paul Doumer, had strong objections: "What is needed is a common test, satisfactory for all needs [and] imposed on all networks." His formulation clearly rendered a politically correct impulse for the government to impose a technological uniformity on the nation's railroads. But the frank opposition of the companies was also represented on the committee, as one of Doumer's colleagues demonstrated by speaking in their defense: "A collective test may be as useless as it is dangerous." Another inconclusive ballot was accordingly entered into the CETCF's minutes: "The votes are divided." An alternative motion was thereupon adopted to the effect that each company should proceed separately with the testing of different brake procedures on freight trains. In reality, this measure confirmed the status quo and temporarily blocked stricter regulation by the state.[57]

A similar verdict concerned the utilization of electric signals. Called into joint session in the Ministry of Public Works, company representatives (except the PO, absent) offered differing accounts. The Northern had deployed a mechanical "crocodile" for the past thirty years and preferred to keep it. The PLM was experimenting with various electrical and mechanical devices without yet reaching a determination. The Eastern did not consider an innovation opportune at the present time. In the midst of this cacophony, Minister of Public Works Charles Dumont carried a small stick. He denied that the cabinet intended to impose any "injunctions" on the companies; he merely wished to hear them out in hopes that signal tests being conducted by the State Company might benefit from their experience. The muddled outcome of this discussion, like the previous two, suggested that before 1914 the CETCF was largely ineffectual in urging uniform technological standards on the private companies, which once again succeeded in evading mandatory state regulation.[58]

The same was true, finally, of the so-called Augagneur bill. We recall an earlier legislative initiative, unrealized, to grant the government authority to appoint the chief executive officers in the rail and coal-mining industries. In 1911 Victor Augagneur revived that motion in regard to senior railway officials, with the obvious intention of securing from them a more willing compliance with uniform policies. Unsurprisingly, a unanimous protest from company administrations was swift and unequivocal. As the PLM put it, Augagneur's proposal was "incompatible with our obligations" and could only have "disastrous" consequences. If the state should assume such power, the implication was, it would be tantamount to an outright confiscation of the companies and the obliteration of their independence.[59]

There was a manifest truth to this claim of the companies. By 1914 it had become clear that they must all be nationalized or not. And if not, they would continue to exercise their rights as private enterprises. To be sure, they were subject to a certain measure of regulation by the state. Yet the evidence is overwhelming that the railroads had not been reduced by crushing governmental controls to the diminished status of a public service. We scarcely need to add that no further action on the Augagneur bill was forthcoming.

The Long Stagnation

Several economic historians have agreed on the label of a "long stagnation" to describe France's economic performance in the late nineteenth century. They disagree only on its chronological limits. Had a certain lethargy already settled in during the late 1860s at a time when the nation faltered after two decades of sustained growth? Or was it an immediate consequence of the stock market collapse in 1882 that tolled the demise of the Freycinet Plan? And did this economic downturn effectively end in the mid-1890s? Or did it linger on until 1905, when a sudden economic upsurge swept the French into a decade of unprecedented prosperity?[60]

Various sets of statistics have been advanced to account for the pattern of France's economic growth between 1848 and 1914 without providing conclusive answers to the very large questions posed above. Here our much more specific task, in the shadow of such uncertainty, is to inquire whether the theoretical construct of a national economic stagnation can be confirmed or qualified by an analysis of French railroads. It is best to begin by admitting that the issue of chronology is not susceptible to definitive proof. Harkening back to the Second Empire seems far-fetched, although it is true that the Franco-Prussian War left the Third Republic with little chance of a brilliant recovery in the 1870s. Had it not been for Freycinet's overreaching ambitions, however, the budding developments around 1880 perhaps might have matured. We shall never know. As for a terminal date, likewise, no truth is self-evident. Records of the railway industry tend to bolster the hypothesis of an incipient recovery by 1896 but also a marked slump between 1900 and 1905. The data thus support a sense of complexity rather than of certainty, much like the diagnosis of a stroke: should a congenital weakness be emphasized or the traumatic event that leaves a patient partially disabled? In this instance, some case can surely be made for forty years of "stagnation" from 1866 to 1905; yet one might just as easily opt for a much stricter construction from 1882 to 1895 while positing unstable but not unproductive periods before and after.

Be that as it may, three observations must be added for which nineteenth-century railroads offer incontrovertible evidence. First, it is clear that stagnation is far too bland a term for the decade or so before 1895. We have observed that the French railway industry actually underwent a significant downsizing. The rate of growth did not merely oscillate; it dropped. The nation's demographic and economic curves were distressingly similar, even if the relationship of cause and effect remains a mystery. Second, a still more serious objection to the concept of stagnation is that the term falsely implies a lack of movement, as if we were watching a nearly motionless eddy trapped on the bend of a sluggish brook. In fact, from a detailed examination of French industry sector by sector, region by region, or—more to the point—rail network by network, the impression is unmistakable that the stream was flowing. On the Northern Railway Company alone, for example, the transportation of coal rose or fell depending on market conditions, strikes by miners in the Pas-de-Calais, demands of the metal industry, and so on. In the same region, too, the production of sugar beets fluctuated: down by 18.7 percent in early 1892, up by 35 percent in the second half of 1894, down again by 40 percent for the same period in 1895 (the lowest point since 1889), up once more by 55.5 percent in 1896. Such constant volatility of commerce is poorly translated by the idea that it was basically stagnant.[61]

Third, as we saw, through much of this time France was experiencing industrial growth, even when it was erratic and often obfuscated by aggregate statistics. By one global reckoning, rail traffic grew on an annual average of 4 percent from 1851 to 1913. But company expenses rose apace with gross income. Between 1898 and 1904, for instance, receipts of the Northern grew by 20 million francs, and allocations by

16.4 million; thus the average net income was barely a half million francs for each of those seven years. Yet that mediocre result was quite misleading as to the actual level of railway activity. True, the absolute number of locomotives in the Northern's fleet did not hugely increase, but many older models were retired and replaced by larger, more powerful engines that pulled heavier freight loads at higher speeds. Meanwhile, the volume of passenger travel vastly increased, a fact inadequately reflected in the profit column of the Company's ledgers because of wholesale fare reductions and season tickets. Cheaper and more efficient service does not make a strong case for stagnation.[62]

Since the earliest days of the railway age the defining economic issue had been rates, and that remained so in an era of increasing international competition. Articulate critics of the rail companies like Camille Pelletan continued to urge the complete uniformity of rates. He correspondingly presented a parliamentary bill that would have established nearly total state control of them. Meanwhile, the Ministry of Public Works in the person of Yves Guyot was less categorical, offering a milder version of regulatory legislation (which earned him a charge of collusion with Gustave Noblemaire). When directly confronted with the question if his Ministry in no case claimed the right to impose uniform rates on the companies, Guyot replied: "Precisely." Gridlock followed. By the end of 1893, Pelletan had to admit that, "in effect, the state of affairs remains about the same."[63]

The eventual success of the companies in fending off state regulatory agencies is confirmed by minutes of the Comité consultatif des chemins de fer (CCCF), whose chairman Alfred Picard fretted about the growing complexity of rates and the "accumulation of obstacles to a revision and a simplification of which everyone senses the need." In principle, Picard favored the application of state controls, from which the companies should be permitted to depart "only very exceptionally." Yet, as another prominent member of the CCCF, the free-trader Clément Colson, observed with disabuse, "it is always a question of fact and not of principle that dominates our discussions." On this, "the most delicate of all questions," Richard Waddington added, state regulation had encountered "absolute resistance."[64]

The economic stance of the companies was not only defensive. They also cooperated with one another in negotiating details of the rate structure. An extensive list of interregional consultations can be readily compiled from company records. Such commercial practice was especially notable among the PLM, the Eastern, and the Northern companies in whose territories most of French industry was located. Their initiatives involved fixing rates for goods moving on French tracks as well as frequent accords with Belgian, German, and Swiss railway organizations to facilitate international trade. Indeed, it is not an exaggeration to conclude that France's commercial structure, like its military planning, was essentially based on the private rail companies, which thereby gained yet another pretext to flaunt their indispensability. To hobble them by curtailing their rights to strike mutual bargains and to introduce special rates could only damage the national economy. The rising tensions of the prewar period were bound to strengthen this contention by the companies, because, as the director of railroads at Ponts-et-Chaussées said, "the state must above all take into account the competition that foreign lines might create for French lines." To be sure, he added a caveat: "The national interest should prevail over regional interests as well as over the special pleading of the railway companies." But that was only to state another principle to which they could easily accommodate.[65]

As in the past, international treaties—meaning such accords originating in diplomatic conferences—had little impact on the French companies. At an 1890 meeting in Bern, a general resolution was adopted in favor of setting standard rates for freight traded among the nations of continental Europe. Back in Paris this new convention was hailed in the Chamber's railway committee as a "fortunate transaction" between the French and German delegations, and the Ministry of Public Works proceeded to draft guidelines for application of the Bern resolution. But ever at the ready, Gustave Noblemaire challenged the Ministry's initiative, taken without consultation with the companies, "which seems to us exactly contrary to the harmony sought between domestic and international legislation."[66] Eventually this position gathered broad support even within the CCCF, where Alfred Picard expressed a commonly felt apprehension that rigid conformity with "Bern" (an identical scale of rates for every nation) would prove "unfavorable to [French] commerce." This discussion continued in much the same terms across two decades until, in 1911, a committee under Richard Waddington issued a summary report to the CCCF, which declared the Bern treaty to be incompatible with the commercial practices of France. Would it be opportune to adhere to regulations emanating "to a great extent from the German commercial code?" In an atmosphere now crackling with international tension, Waddington's group demurred. Instead, "there is reason to invite the French companies to seek with foreign companies some conditions of application [of rates] more in conformity with French legislation." In the end, the capital issue remained whether the state had a right to impose international accords on the private companies that might violate its conventions with them. Before 1914, the answer was decidedly negative.[67]

Parliamentary transcripts, committee minutes, ministerial reports, and memoranda may give us an impression of the public discourse about railroads and the decisions reached (or not) concerning them. But we need to delve further into the daily conduct of commercial transactions in order to locate the dilemmas faced by state administrators and company managers during the campaign for the unification and simplification of rates. To do so, it will be useful to catch a glimpse of French commerce product by product.

Coal and coke. "A unity of rates for all of France would be ideal," exclaimed a member of the CCCF in 1896. But would it? The problem was that French combustibles were in competition with English imports and, to a lesser extent, also Belgian and German. Besides, three different mining regions in the north, center, and south of France had to contend with one another. Flat rates on the railroads would favor the British, might help the north, but could have "fatal consequences" for the center and south. Northern coal was considered superior in quality to the rest of French products. Should rates therefore be lowered for the latter to enhance their competitiveness, thus in effect encouraging inferior grades of coal? Mines in the territory of the Northern Railway Company, including the Pas-de-Calais, were forced to compete with canals and needed lower rates (especially during mild winters) to do so. Special rates, at least in frontier areas, would presumably also motivate Belgian and German mines to send tons of heavy freight onto French tracks. Yet should the English enjoy the same rates, increasing their exports to France and thereby probably causing some mines to shut down operations? Protecting the French coal industry was an evident matter of "national interest," as the government repeatedly admonished the rail companies. But how were they going to respond? So many questions, so little consensus.[68]

Wool and cotton. In the post-Suez era, raw wool could be moved to France from Australia and Algeria by water, unloading either in Marseille or Antwerp and continuing by rail. Lower French railway rates favored Marseille in this competition, but they would also harm Algeria. Should regulation support one or the other? Similarly, bales of cotton heading for Alsatian textile mills generally arrived from the New World at Le Havre, Bremen, or Hamburg. Special import rates on French rails could encourage docking at Le Havre. Yet that advantage would come at the expense of other French ports. Should, in fact, the regulatory principle always be upheld that a national interest took precedence over local and regional considerations? A correct policy was not obvious to the CCCF, besieged as it was by petitions and complaints from chambers of commerce or departmental councils who felt slighted. As a member of the CCCF accurately noted during a dispute between Dunkerque and Le Havre, "in matters of commercial rates, the question is dominated by foreign competition." Yet the proper answer to that question was unclear.[69]

Grain and flour. Good harvests tended to benefit the PO and major wheat producers in its territory, but they actually disfavored the PLM because grain imports from Russia via Marseille might decline. The PLM wished to provide special rates to aid that port against Genoa, although that strategy drew protests from Switzerland, which counted on trade through the St. Gotthard Tunnel. There was also a question about whether flour should enjoy the same reduction in rates as unmilled grain, which would favor some routes over others and rails over the Rhône (presuming that bulk was easier to ship by water). The indecision of the CCCF was reflected in 1898 by a vote of twenty to nineteen, although after 1900 it did achieve some success in this matter by obtaining a more uniform railway rate for grain.[70]

Wine and spirits. During the phylloxera epidemic that lasted until 1890, importations of Italian and Spanish wines had compensated for the lower yields from southern France. Now the government aimed to recalibrate the rate structure to resuscitate French vintners in the Midi and also to aid those in Corsica and Algeria. But this policy, complained the PLM, was a form of protectionism against Italy and Spain and an illicit use of regulated rates as a substitute for tariffs. The Company could only hope that the regime would develop "a more exact appreciation of the true interests of our country" (and, we can add, of the PLM as the main carrier of imported wines). There were also complaints from the Eastern Company about the renewed influx of cheap wines from the South, profiting from lower rates, harming growers in its region, and stimulating alcoholism among its residents. Yet the circulation of wine and other beverages increased, for which trade by rail bore an unquantifiable share of the responsibility. If commercial rates were reduced and partially regulated, the flourishing business of French bars and bistrots was not.[71]

Stone and wood. Building materials were a staple of the French economy and subject to many of the familiar dilemmas in fixing rates for their transportation. Stones, in that regard, were like coal. Those from quarries in the Ardennes were of lesser quality than rock from the Vosges, but the former had close competition from Belgium. Reduced uniform rates might aid the Ardennes internationally, but they would also encourage the use of an inferior product within the domestic market. At the same time, an accord between the state and the Western Company for lower rates on imported lumber for construction was opposed by the Northern Company, drawing protests from the PLM and the Eastern, which supported them. The status quo unfortunately favored Antwerp over Dunkerque and other French ports. Among them, too, rates were often irregular and discriminatory: Bordeaux, for instance, was exploiting an advantage over Nantes. Which should it be, one rate or several? We cannot improve over a biting commentary by a member of the CCCF: "It is known that the slightest negotiation on this topic among the companies takes much more time than a discussion of the most complicated peace treaty by hostile nations. Thus, after so many years of talks, we almost always arrive at a negative result." In this instance, the outcome was a vote for uniform rates only on "exotic" wood, leaving the building trade in confusion about lumber.[72]

To extend this list would not alter the conclusion that we must draw from it: state regulation of transportation rates was imperfectly realized before 1914. That fact, as we have already begun to gather, was well illustrated by the rivalry among railheads at commercial ports. What suited one was sure to discomfort another. Ever since the opening of the St. Gotthard Tunnel, the commerce of France had been at a distinct disadvantage. The main continental trade route stretched from Belgian, Dutch, or German ports in northern Europe, along the Rhine corridor to Basel, then southward. Alone among French companies, the Eastern benefited from a piece of this action—a reason for its relative prosperity after 1890—yet it cooperated to some extent with the others in framing informal and sometimes confidential agreements on the division of traffic. Whatever harmony existed was soon upset, however, by a new shipping lane from Tilbury to Ostende in the mid-1890s. Though another agreement was cobbled at a conference in Rome in 1896, complaints were expressed in France about "a coalition of German and Belgian railroads," while it was crucial "to aid our factories to struggle victoriously against foreign competition." The French Ministry of Commerce ascribed part of the problem to the nation's lack of transversal rail lines (thus goods from Calais moved more easily via Brussels than into the French interior), but the main difficulty remained France's generally higher railway rates. There was another issue, recalled by the Northern Company and confirmed by the CCCF: the "well founded" protests of smaller ports against the government's preference for Le Havre. The desire of every region for its own railhead harbor remained at odds with the interests of the national economy.[73]

This self-contradiction was compounded by the inadequacy of French port facilities—which the ill-fated Freycinet Plan had intended to improve—to handle the new larger and faster transatlantic steam vessels coming into service. A report from Ponts-et-Chaussées lamented the "marked inferiority" of national ports and stressed the need to upgrade them in order "to fight against foreign competition." The quais of smaller commercial basins were too short, and even Le Havre suffered from a shallow harbor that would, without extensive dredging, remain unready to receive mammoth steamers. But should the state subsidize that port at the expense of Cherbourg, Brest, and Boulogne, where foreign ships were currently docking? This embarrassing question offered the Eastern Company an occasion to suggest that the real solution was to alter the rates for boats rather than trains, which in turn prompted an extraparliamentary committee to open an inquiry into "the causes of decadence" of the French merchant marine. Finally and inevitably, the entire matter landed back in the lap of the state's chief regulatory agency, the CCCF, where Alfred Picard threw up his hands. Perhaps, he speculated, it would after all be better to worry less about rails or ports and more about ships, which had become "a national political interest." Nonetheless, a formal vote by the CCCF in 1900 stipulated no general rates for French shipping. The rail companies could operate as before and, as Clément Colson remarked, "the game of rates" would continue.[74]

Yet we know the playing field was not level. Inauguration of the St. Gotthard Tunnel created an evident commercial imbalance. According to the *Journal des Transports*, the net income of the Mt. Cenis route in 1891 was only 1.8 million francs, whereas that of the St. Gotthard was more than triple that amount—about 6 million. French hopes to redress the situation were pinned on the Simplon, a project long discussed and delayed that was now prepared for execution. A special parliamentary committee assigned to study the problem of access to the proposed tunnel concluded that all of the likely alternatives would probably harm the port of Marseille and were therefore "scarcely favorable to French interests." Its report in 1901 to the Chamber of Deputies was appropriately evasive: "The divergence of views manifested within the committee does not permit it to arrive at a precise conclusion."[75] But there was no turning back, and soon the choices narrowed to two. The first was an improvement (including double tracks) of a circuitous route via Lausanne over Vallorbe and Frasnes. This rail line to French networks would be longer albeit much cheaper to accomplish than the second option, Faucille, which would provide a more direct connection from Geneva into central France, requiring the costly construction of a series of approach tunnels. Undecided, the access debate roiled French politics for years. As late as 1905, while plans were being finalized to open a first gallery of the Simplon, no course of action had yet been determined. The PLM laconically observed: "We are still at the same point."[76]

It took another five years for the stalemate finally to be broken. Initially, the government's support shifted to Faucille, as Minister of Public Works Armand Gauthier campaigned to rally the regime and to break opposition led by Gustave Noblemaire. He failed on both counts and was replaced in March 1906 by Louis Barthou, who announced that there was "no more time to lose." More time was thereupon lost with another special parliamentary committee (again chaired by Alfred Picard), another debate, another report. Picard frankly admitted that his group could reach no clear verdict and would have to face a "reproach of indecision." When requested at least to describe the committee's "tendencies," he cautiously indicated a tilt toward Frasnes-Vallorbe. But it was not until the summer of 1909 that this decision was adopted at an international conference in Bern. In the following year, upon approval of the French government, a concession for that line was awarded to the PLM. This northern access was to be complemented by a southern approach at the Lötschberg—none of which had any appreciable impact on European commerce before 1914.[77]

These details afford some notion of the reasons for a "long stagnation" of French commerce in the late nineteenth century. It was not simply a clash of blind economic forces in the night that could be reduced to a row of statistics. A study of the quotidian practice of railroads shows that France's rulers faced intractable political dilemmas and that they frequently experienced a failure of will. The rapid turnover of republican cabinets, ministers, and parliamentary committees abetted a pervasive atmosphere of indecision, and attempts to regulate the traditional modalities of rate-fixing by the rail companies fell short of the mark.

France Prepares for War

The earliest comprehensive scheme for the use of railroads in case of a major conflict with Germany was completed in 1888 and was simply called "the transportation plan." It lay in the nature of things that this document was conceived by the Fourth Bureau in the Ministry of War, overseen by the CMSCF (of which there is little trace), and executed by the companies, which, for want of their collective nationalization, remained the basis of peacetime rail operations and therefore of military planning. As elaborated in 1896, the transportation plan was divided into four phases:

couverture: the swift initial movement of troops into frontier zones to secure them against surprise attack;
mobilisation: the gathering of men, steeds, and equipment at specified points of debarkation in the interior;
concentration: the transfer of armed troops and supplies to designated railway stations near the front;
ravitaillement: the provisioning of the assembled army corps on the frontier from interior depots and armories.

For each of these phases, of course, the railroads would be fundamental. From the beginning they had been constructed with that purpose at least partially in mind. Now the challenge was to put them to use in as rapid and coherent a manner as possible in order to move French troops into position whenever circumstances required.[78]

To prepare a comprehensive program of national defense would be far easier were there a single state system of rail networks. We have already noted a military rationale of nationalization—so that in a crisis France's safety would not be "at the mercy of private interests," as one partisan stated—and we need not retrace here the long and thoroughly predictable debate from that standpoint.[79] Failing a total *rachat*, military planners would therefore need to negotiate with the companies. And just as one might expect, there is much evidence of such dealings. In a general sense, the problem was to coordinate the activities of army corps and rail companies, whose boundaries were not synonymous, and thereby to promote harmony between civilian officials and their military alter egos, who would presumably assume full command once a war was imminent. At issue were such vital questions as cost-sharing for construction of strategic lines and their location; compensation for military use of stations, tracks, and rolling stock; conduct of army maneuvers; distribution or supply of locomotives and freight cars; reserves of coal and water; and so on. From the specifics, a sort of grand settlement evolved in 1903 that was further amended four times before the war. It ensured that the companies would continue to conduct the railway business in peacetime, and that they would be requisitioned for military purposes on the first day of war.[80]

The gaze of military planners was naturally focused on the Eastern Railway Company, owner of nearly all tracks in the army's northeastern frontier zone. Many of its lines posed a hazard to defense by providing avenues of "penetration" for the enemy, which had to be mined for destruction. Disputes arose over proposals of new rail connections desirable for commerce, such as those leading from the recently exploited ore fields in the Briey basin. More than once the army's engineering corps registered an "absolute veto" that left proponents with "no illusion." Other projects were less categorically evaluated as "prejudicial to defense." They sometimes allowed hard bargaining with some prospect of success, provided that the Ministry of War could be persuaded that such projects created no threat to major fortifications such as Verdun. A related issue was the choice of track gauge, especially in the Ardennes region where narrow-gauge lines through rugged terrain were deemed both practical and defensible. But should they be set at 0.60 meters, 0.75, 0.80, or 1.0? Each had its advocates. After long insisting on a gauge of 0.80, the Ministry of War finally relented in 1908 and agreed to change all of the Ardennes tracks to a width of one meter, a solution that would unify railway equipment and yet offer sufficient safety from invasion. Withal, it must be said, the Eastern displayed a willingness to cooperate with military authorities and—aside from disputes over sharing the costs of construction—met its special responsibility for the national defense. When his company was rumored to be inadequately prepared for an outbreak of war, Director Roger Barabant angrily refuted such charges as "malevolent allegations." The Eastern stood ready on the firing line.[81]

Two other issues had national importance for the Company. One was a movement to pierce a tunnel through the Vosges Mountains, thereby reconnecting textile enterprises and other businesses that had been severed by the new boundaries of 1871. Spurred by an international lobby with headquarters in Paris and Berlin, the Comité commercial franco-allemand (CCFA), this cause gained some popular support in Alsace and Lorraine and backing among several deputies in the two national legislatures. A penny postcard was widely distributed on which a map displayed nine possible alternative routes. And there was also a tenth proposal, a tunnel through the so-called "Alsatian Balloon" at the southern tip of the Vosges. None of these gained favor with the Eastern Company, which considered them exorbitantly expensive and of limited commercial value. Also the French Ministry of War expressed its "most serious objections" to any weakening of the natural defensive barrier of the mountains. As for the Balloon, it was thought militarily insignificant due to its close proximity to the German border, where a railway could too easily be disrupted or captured by the enemy. When Lucien Coquet, president of the CCFA, visited Minister of War Jean Dupuy in 1910 to plead his case, he got nowhere.[82]

There was equal confusion about fortifications along the northern frontier from Luxemburg to the English Channel. Secret memoranda were circulated within the Ministry of War in 1899 that put this matter into troubling perspective. Artillery tests over a decade before had demonstrated that smaller forts could not hope to withstand a German bombardment. Moreover, the high density of rail lines in the region meant that isolated *forts d'arrêt*, intended to interdict traffic, could be readily by-passed. As a consequence, France had made a first priority of its four major eastern bastions at Verdun, Toul, Epinal, and Belfort. Despite large expenditures to modernize and reinforce them, they remained "quite insufficient" and (it was later calculated) would require a further allocation of 200 million francs. This necessity of "profound modifications," as a report by the Commission des places fortes stated, meant a prompt dispersal of all defensive equipment north of Verdun. Indeed, the French army could no longer count on a single fort "from the Sambre to the sea"—that is, west of Maubeuge—and others eastward might also become subject to "declassification": Hirson, Montmédy, and even Longwy. Finally, all of them were to be dismantled before 1914, without a shot being fired, already defeated by the improved technology of heavy artillery and railroads.[83]

There was perpetual disagreement about how much technological conformity should or could be imposed on the companies for military reasons. Army representatives on the CETCF—Colonel Michel in the 1890s, then Colonel Péchot—repeatedly pointed out the "great inconvenience" resulting from differences in the apparatus adopted by the companies for brakes, signals, switches, crossings, and the like, leaving the rolling stock of one railway firm "unsuited" to run on the tracks of another. But they were challenged, among others, by a young member of the CETCF, Emile Mayer (later the author of a critical study of the French high command), who called for the military to recognize that "conditions from one network to another are totally different" and that "a uniform regimentation would be nonsense." Invariably, these views tended to cancel each other out, as two examples will illustrate. When Péchot found a discrepancy in wheel rims (*bandages*) to be "altogether regrettable" for the national defense, an opinion "energetically" seconded by Ponts-et-Chaussées, the CETCF could muster nothing more than a vapid resolution drawing the attention of the companies to the military interest of achieving more uniformity. And another intermittent discussion over several years revealed that the types of stop signals employed by the Eastern and Northern companies were incongruous and could prove dangerous for military convoys. Yet the CETCF could reach no consensus about which of the two systems to recommend, given the enormous expense that would be imposed on one firm if forced to adopt the technology of the other.[84]

These practical issues pointed to a greater problem of the French military command structure. How much authority should be centralized and how much left to local initiative? A suggestion in 1892 that corps commanders obtain more responsibility for troop movements by rail in their area was sharply attacked by the Fourth Bureau, citing the unholy precedent of 1870, and was summarily rejected by the then Minister of War Charles de Freycinet as "neither justifiable nor desirable." But the question remained, especially after Freycinet's departure, who was in charge? By a "bizarre anomaly," the CMSCF lacked a military railway specialist for some years before 1898, when that deficiency was rectified. The Ministry of War meanwhile had two railway experts in the Second Bureau until their transfer around 1900; they were not replaced, and their function was soon absorbed into the "German section" of that Bureau. Railroads were also a frequent topic for the Commission des places fortes (revived by Freycinet in 1899), whose first reporter was a junior officer from the army's engineering corps, Joseph Joffre. But this body was only tangentially concerned with the strategy of movement by rail, and its competence overlapped with another planning group, the Commission d'études de la guerre de siège, founded in 1904.

Atop this heap of committees stood the Conseil supérieur de la guerre (CSG), which treated railway problems only episodically and always did so, of course, from a strictly military point of view.[85] This latter limitation drew the attention of General Billot, Minister of War in 1897, who urged the creation of a yet more exalted Conseil supérieur de la défense nationale (CSDN), which would include several ministers and other high civilian officials to confer with military leaders. Surely this supreme council would be able to gain a broader perspective on diplomatic, economic, commercial, as well as military factors. But no sooner had the CSDN met in December 1906 than the new Prime Minister Georges Clemenceau contemptuously dismissed a military memorandum that purported to analyze the strategic implications of another Franco-Prussian War on the European continent: "It is not possible," Clemenceau huffed, "to imagine that France would enter into conflict with Germany without having the support of England." After this inauspicious debut, the CSDN met once in 1907, once in 1908, and not again until October 1911.[86]

Much ultimately depended on anticipating the enemy. Long before the final reformulation of the Schlieffen Plan in 1905, the French correctly divined two of its fundamental premises: that German Reich would assume a defensive posture on its eastern front opposite Russia while throwing the bulk of its military might against France; and that the thrust of an initial German assault would fall on the French left flank. How did they know? The answer scarcely had to do with espionage. True, France deployed a cadre of diplomatic personnel, military attachés, and covert agents east of the Rhine, but they learned remarkably little. Commenting on Germany's likely intentions in 1902, the Second Bureau in the Ministry of War—center of French military intelligence—confidentially admitted that it had received "only a very small amount of reliable information" from its operatives, and consequently its prognoses "necessarily present a character purely hypothetical and lacking any precision." Five years later, when evaluating the German army's supposed schedule of mobilization, the Second Bureau again offered a disclaimer: "We possess no precise and certain information on the German plan of operations."[87]

What the French did acquire, however, was an extensive knowledge of German railway construction, which could not be hidden from even the most harmless tourist. By 1910 they could thus credit the Germans with completing five double-track rail arteries across the Rhine and recently developing an offensive potential in Alsace. Thus, it was the study of rail patterns that led the Second Bureau to a near certainty that a German attack could be expected north of the Moselle River through Luxemburg and a southern portion of Belgium. That conclusion would not otherwise have been self-evident. French war planners had long speculated on the sanctity of Belgian neutrality, though they did not seriously begin contemplating the contingency of its violation until after 1900. "Everything leads me to believe that the Belgian army will be prepared to offer a very serious resistance," wrote the French military attaché in Brussels in 1907. But he was still uncertain against whom. Belgium's close commercial ties with Germany had brought worries that Berlin was surreptitiously bargaining for more "lines of penetration," and suspicions grew on all sides. We can conclude that the French, despite the blindness of their spies, did nonetheless perceive the broad outlines of the Schlieffen Plan, yet they remained unsure of its northerly sweep, which they badly and almost disastrously underestimated.[88]

Because the French depended on their observation of enemy railroads for military intelligence, they correctly supposed that the Germans were doing the same. Accordingly, earlier measures to shield and, in a crisis, to cleanse frontier areas of foreigners were continued after 1890. Upon obtaining the confession of a German secret agent, Minister of War Freycinet ordered French border officials to "redouble efforts ... in the search for spies." Prefects were instructed to increase their surveillance of suspects and to report "their slightest movements." Hence, in 1893, the new Minister of War, General Mercier, and the chief of the Second Bureau, Colonel Sandherr, completed elaborate plans to round up nearly 100,000 foreigners (at least 32,000 in Paris alone) and to ship them by rail to detention camps in southwestern France. Undoubtedly, this pernicious atmosphere of xenophobia helps to explain the origins of the Dreyfus Affair, of which Mercier and Sandherr were the chief instigators. After 1900, let it be added, these extreme machinations fell into some disfavor with republican leaders, and less Draconian measures were envisaged, such as the house arrest of suspects or their surveillance by "community guards" composed of veterans' groups. Yet the principle remained that foreigners who failed to comply with regulations at the outbreak of war could be arrested and charged with spying.[89]

Attention meanwhile shifted to another security risk: the threat of a general strike. The greatest danger was known to exist among miners and railway workers, for whom the government at first made separate plans—including military force—to cope with a massive walkout. In 1902 the Fourth Bureau foresaw the need for a closer coordination of these preparations. After all, troops required to quell a coal strike would have to be transported by train, and a simultaneous rail strike would present more than a minor complication. After responding to numerous wildcat strikes in the mines and then the near insurrection of *cheminots* in 1910, the French regime had manifest reasons to fear the labor movement, and it consequently made a show of carrot and stick in hopes of averting further trouble. Yet we have seen that the state's ability to intervene with employees of private companies was in fact limited. Until the opening of the war and the assassination of the pacifist leader Jean Jaurès, therefore, unnerving doubts about the workers' loyalty to the nation's political establishment persisted.[90]

Rising apprehensions about France's unpreparedness and lack of a firm central command structure were fueled by the Second Moroccan Crisis in the summer of 1911. It was decided to unite the posts of generalissimo (who would assume full charge at the onset of war) and chief of the General Staff in the person of General Joffre. Soft-spoken but self-confident to the point of swagger, he was among those many senior officers and politicians convinced of the inherent superiority of offensive warfare. Indeed, at a meeting of the CSDN on 21 February 1912, Joffre advocated an initial French advance into Belgium and Luxemburg, violating their neutrality but catching the Germans off guard. Because the British shared the French desire to crush the Kaiserreich, he argued, they would "doubtless not be too scrupulous in the choice of means," and they would therefore accept "the solution that seems to us the most advantageous." For this astonishing proposal Joffre received support from Minister of War Millerand and Minister of the Marine Delcassé. But he was uncompromisingly opposed by Prime Minister (and soon President of the Republic) Raymond Poincaré, who contended that a preemptive strike would forfeit the support of both the British government and even the most francophile of Belgians.[91]

Extant records do not permit us to follow the political discussions and private conversations that ensued, but we know that Poincaré prevailed. He did so, it is permissible to speculate, not only for the diplomatic reasons stated but also because Joffre lacked any detailed agenda for transporting a huge French military force across the Belgian frontier. He was no Alfred von Schlieffen and, as far as we know, he had no great Joffre Plan. As one historian has aptly said: "Joffre did not lack character; he lacked ideas."[92] Perhaps an archival discovery will one day reveal that he did in fact conceive a precise scheme to utilize the railroads for his daring proposal, but it is most improbable. Heretofore, all French military planning, conducted essentially by the Fourth Bureau, had posited a movement on tracks leading onto the territory of the Eastern Railway Company. Altering these familiar assumptions in 1912 in order to base French operations at least partially on the network of the Northern Company would have been a pinnacle of folly. Reverting, as Joffre did, to the notion of an offensive thrust into Alsace was foolish enough. France can be grateful that the generalissimo did not have his way in 1914.

Instead, Joffre and his staff continued to tinker. He drafted Plan XVII, believing its predecessor was an "incomplete solution." The new strategic concept, not fully operational until mid-April 1914, did not afford greater rapidity because France's existing railway networks did not permit it. As a memo in the Ministry of War stated, "It seems we are near the limit." But Joffre hoped to achieve greater concentration in order to meet the expected "vigorous offensive" by more than a million Germans. The French should hold nothing back from their northeastern frontier zone, including alpine troops heretofore restrained by the possibility of an Italian intervention. Joffre also sought more flexibility, and for that purpose he studied the use of transversal lines and the relocation of *gares régulatrices*, frontier stations to which French units would be moved by train before proceeding on foot. Local commanders would have the authority to alter the length of railway transfers (closer or farther from the front, depending on the circumstances of battle) but not the route. Should entire rail lines become blocked, Joffre considered "alternates" (*variantes*), worked out by the Fourth Bureau, which might be adopted by field commanders in an emergency, if so ordered. "In principle," he said, no alternates should be necessary—which meant that he foresaw a need for exceptions and would probably grant them. In all of these fine adjustments we see Joffre straining to reconcile flexibility on the battlefield with the coherence of a single central command. Maintaining that balance was one of his best qualities. He did not want to deprive corps commanders of any sense of initiative, yet he refused to conduct war by telephone, insisting that every order be written and registered. We also note Joffre's frank recognition that French military planning depended on cooperation with the private rail companies. The *commission de réseau*, on which company representatives sat, remained the basic unit for execution of the "transportation orders" communicated to them in yellow envelopes, appropriately under the seal of the Fourth Bureau. A note to the military commissar attached to the Eastern Company succinctly summarized Joffre's intentions: army operations should be "elastic," yet they must be conducted with "all the order and method possible."[93]

The fear of being overmatched haunted French planning to the end, and many of the measures adopted during the final months before the war had a hint of desperation. Joffre's desire for "complementary construction" led the railway companies to demand 28 million francs in defrayment, more than the Minister of War's budget would allow. Likewise, as late as 25 May 1914, an expensive order was placed for 120 new pieces of heavy artillery (to be delivered within eighteen to forty-two months!). Another last-minute stopgap was a requested allocation of 5.5 million francs for the adequate provisioning of fortresses. The Fourth Bureau had determined that moving these supplies by rail would require the equivalent of 240 trainloads, which would obviously create a "grave inconvenience" at the time of mobilization for war. Such details betrayed the ambiance of improvisation so characteristic of Joffre's command.[94]

Was France prepared for war with Germany in August 1914? This review of Joffre's incomplete dossiers at that moment suggests not. But when is a nation ever ready to have its very existence tested in battle? At least Joffre could be certain that French army corps would move along double-track rail corridors to the front, that the private companies would cooperate in their transportation, and that specially constructed long platforms at stations throughout the northeastern sector would facilitate their debarkation. The railroads would do their part, and ultimately they—rather than taxi cabs rushing from Paris to the Marne—would save the French nation from another debacle.

Chapter 8

GERMANY, 1890–1914

Surely among the most significant developments of Bismarck's chancellorship was the expansion of the Prussian state railway network, which quintupled in size between 1870 and 1890. Thereby a unified company was created that stretched across all of northern Germany from Königsberg to Cologne. In railway politics this single administration henceforth functioned like a huge magnetic field, drawing inward toward itself the outlying metallic fragments on the national periphery—the other member states of the Reich. First the railroads of Hesse would become attached in 1895. Meanwhile, adjacent Saxony seemed possibly close to succumbing. And finally it was the southern states, especially Württemberg, that felt the powerful attraction of Prussia and indicated a new willingness to find some sort of accommodation. By 1900 the emergence of a national railway system appeared at hand. Precisely which steps were to be taken, and how one might lead to another, remained unclear. But a certain momentum was established.

At the same time, however, three familiar countervailing tendencies were regaining force, triggering a backlash. First was the old bugaboo of particularism, which continued to lock the large member states into competition and mutual suspicion. Second, hardly less serious, was Prussia's internal disharmony that had repeatedly pitted conservative defenders of the Hohenzollern monarchy against proponents of the Kaiserreich. Third came the clash between civilian and military interests, all the more fierce as Germany moved to construct a major battle fleet, thus conjuring fiscal problems literally beyond reckoning. As always, these strands were tightly interwoven, and it is unsurprising that many issues displayed more than one of them. As a bundle, in any event, they were fully capable of restraining the urge to unify the German railroads, and in the prewar decade they did just that. Therefore, the years before 1914 did not bring Germany appreciably closer to the goal Bismarck had once imagined when he innovated an imperial railway office in Berlin. Instead, it required the shattering impact of the Great War to accomplish what a century of political maneuvers failed to achieve.

The Specter of Prussification

Otto von Bismarck's resignation in 1890 left the future of German railroads in some uncertainty. Outside of military circles, the new chancellor, Leo von Caprivi, represented an unknown quantity. Furthermore, it was impossible to tell how the Prussian cabinet would react without Bismarck to prompt it. At least Albert Maybach was still in place at the Ministry of Public Works, and he initially attempted to keep matters in hand by drafting, with the Prussian Minister of Finance Johannes von Miquel, a plan for the "extension [and] completion" of the state railway system. In this effort there was considerable ambiguity, however, because their joint initiative could also be read as an intention to place a cap on spending. In addition, the usual bickering erupted over specifics: whether certain rail lines were essentially strategic or had real commercial importance, and consequently, in a given case, who was going to pay for them. Now bereft of Bismarck's support, Maybach soon discovered that he would be unable to have his way in such matters, and in the summer of 1891 he resigned.[1]

Caprivi's railway policy was ostensibly to shift the emphasis of his regime from Prussia to the Reich, thereby abetting Kaiser Wilhelm II in his loftier ambitions to be lord of the entire German nation. The Reichseisenbahnamt (REA), so long repressed by Bismarck and Maybach, finally acquired a new president, Friedrich Schulz, and Caprivi's purpose was clearly to upgrade it. Yet for his pains he quickly became boxed into a four-cornered controversy among the REA, the Ministry of War, the Ministry of Public Works, and the Office of the Imperial Treasury (Reichsschatzamt or RSA). This began with a proposal from the current Minister of War, General von Kaltenborn, to construct a new series of strategic rail projects at a cost of nearly 50 million Marks, immediately raising an obvious question about financing them. We recall, as did Kaltenborn's contemporaries, that a basic formula for cost-sharing had been devised in 1887. But there were now doubts about the agreement between the Reich and Prussia. Because many of the proposed lines were strictly strategic, the Prussian Ministry of Public Works suggested that the Reich should accept a greater share, with an exception being made for another connection to East Prussia (the Ost-Preussische Südbahn), considered to be of limited military value.[2]

These fiscal considerations were soon complicated by a political struggle between the REA and Maybach's successor at Public Works, Karl von Thielen. Each claimed to be the impresario of Berlin's railway planning and did not hesitate to belittle the competence of the other. Caught in the middle, Caprivi diffidently supported the REA but was unable to tamp down the dispute, which, in turn, was compounded by dissonance within the Prussian cabinet. Whereas Thielen described the state's financial picture as "not unfavorable" and therefore backed further building, Minister of Finance Miquel challenged that view and made a case for stringent economy. Given this standoff in the Prussian government, as the REA's Schulz brightly suggested, the sensible course was to solicit additional funds from the Imperial Treasury. But for Prussia to extract money from the RSA would automatically involve the Reich's other member states and, as Thielen noted, Bavaria was "little inclined" to pay more bills for strategic lines requested by the Prussian Ministry of War.[3]

This bewildering crossfire of irate memos among adversaries continued for months while Caprivi's arbitration was ineffectual. In May 1892, Kaltenborn expressed to the chancellor his "strongest reservations" about the REA's pretensions to become the hub of Berlin's entire railway administration, charging that its repeated intervention had caused "a considerable waste of time." He emphatically demanded that Schulz's office be subordinated to *"a military leadership."* In a pique, Caprivi commented: "I cannot accept that; it should have been done at the outset of the 1870s." The solution of the Bismarck years was settled, in other words, and all parties would have to comply.[4] But Caprivi's personal memoranda revealed his recurrent worries and self-doubts. Could he force the military? Should he bring the matter to the Bundesrat? What would be the effect on Bavaria and the other states? In the end he could do little more than implore Kaltenborn and the REA to work "hand in hand." Instead, the former resigned. Yet his successor, General von Gossler, was no better disposed to compromise with Schulz and archly told the chancellor so: "I do not find myself in a circumstance to agree with the assertions of the REA."[5]

Such detail is sufficient to draw the obvious conclusion that, when it came to railroads, Berlin was the scene of interminable infighting that virtually paralyzed Caprivi's disappointing regime. Two administrative changes were nevertheless instituted on his watch. One was the creation of a Central European time zone, ending countless local irregularities and enabling all the networks of the German states and Austria-Hungary to coordinate their schedules. Another was the adoption of a more centralized bureaucratic structure for the Prussian state railway system, eliminating dozens of local "operation offices" (*Betriebsämter*) and reinforcing the sway of a central directorate in Berlin with branches throughout northern Germany.[6]

The quarrels of the Caprivi years were unavoidably inherited by Chlodwig von Hohenlohe, who remained chancellor for the balance of the century. Although a Bavarian, having served long years as the Reich's governor in Alsace-Lorraine and then as the German ambassador to Paris, Hohenlohe was no narrow conservative advocate of particularism. Nor was he a Berlin insider. If he had any railway policy, it was to exercise budgetary restraint. He preferred to evaluate rail projects separately, to decide on the partition of costs in individual cases, and to defer additional allocations indefinitely. These modest intentions did not prevent him from becoming embroiled in another round of financial wrangles, which resulted when Miquel "unexpectedly" (so stated Hohenlohe) reopened demands that Prussia's share of spending for new rail construction be reduced from 40 to 20 percent. Miquel's most formidable opponent was Arthur von Posadowsky, a senior civil servant who spoke out effectively for the chancellor's office and the RSA with the argument that any reduction of Prussia's share was sure to be imitated by the other medium states, thereby placing an intolerable burden on the Reich's treasury. As an arbiter, Hohenlohe proved marginally more skillful than Caprivi. In cabinet meetings he pleaded for Prussia to maintain its quota of 40 percent "at least for now." Although Miquel grudgingly capitulated, he offered no guarantee for Prussia's financial participation in the future.[7]

The big news was elsewhere. After years of consultation, the state of Hesse decided in 1897 to join with Prussia in a railway consortium. It was a clear instance of the big fish swallowing a small one. For Prussia the advantages were considerable. Without a change of locomotives or personnel, its trains would henceforth be able to pass directly not only from Berlin via Hanover to Cologne but also from Berlin via Kassel to Frankfurt, and of course the main passage along the Rhine between Cologne and Frankfurt was open. Therewith Prussia gained complete dominance over the golden triangle in central Germany, a network of east-west connections of incomparable commercial and military utility. There were manifest rewards in the deal for Hesse as well: locomotives could be standardized and shared, fewer unladen freight cars would roll back and forth, personnel might be reduced, fares and rates lowered, volume increased, and cheaper fuel obtained from Prussian coal mines in the Ruhr. In short, both parties stood to realize lower overhead and higher income. All of which did not go unnoticed by the medium states that were meanwhile struggling to meet the budgetary demands of their own increased service and the consequent rising costs of operation. By 1900, employing over 325,000 persons and dispatching more than 11,000 locomotives on 30,000 kilometers of track, the Prussian-Hessian railway union became a dazzling bait for Berlin to dangle before southern statesmen.[8]

Precisely this apparent success, however, was bound to produce fears that Prussia now intended to move more aggressively to consolidate a national railway system: *Verpreussung* on the march. An old man nearing the end of his career, Württemberg's premier Mittnacht warned against prussification, taking exception to the opinion expressed in a Stuttgart newspaper that his state, through increased profits, could actually gain greater independence by joining in a union with Prussia. Such "illusions," Mittnacht told the Württemberg parliament, would not gain his support.[9] Likewise, Bavaria's veteran prime minister Crailsheim observed that no southern regime would deliberately choose to defy its dynasty or public opinion by "letting the railroads slip away." He was quoted in the Augsburg press as harboring "not the slightest inclination" toward closer ties with Prussia. This negativism was not confined to conservative elder statesmen. The Social Democratic Party, whose national leadership generally supported centralization, was also divided: southern and Rhenish Socialist leaders such as Georg von Vollmar in Munich and Eduard David in Mainz made their opposition to the prussification of railroads explicit.[10]

In Prussia, too, criticism remained vocal against any measures that might weaken the Hohenzollern monarchy's grip on northern railways. In the Lower House, conservatives in fact welcomed the reported apprehensions in Württemberg and Bavaria. It was not Prussia's responsibility, one of them declaimed, to bolster at its own expense the finances of other states; the more profitable Prussian network should protect its railway business and not allow its benefits to be dissipated throughout the Reich. Within the cabinet Minister of Public Works Thielen concurred by attacking the "intolerabilities" (*Unzuträglichkeiten*) created when the REA overstepped its competence by claiming prerogatives for the Reich that properly belonged to the individual states. Besides, Prussia could afford to bide its time without needlessly coercing the medium states toward unification. One of Thielen's close associates commented: "Prussia is in the fortunate circumstance of being able to observe the utmost patience." In the strictest secrecy, Thielen agreed and ordered that no further bargains be struck similar to that of the Prussian-Hessian union.[11]

Yet rumors continued to circulate that Württemberg wished to integrate its network into a national combine, and a favorable vote in the Stuttgart Chamber of Commerce showed that the business community supported such an arrangement.[12] This is the context in which to take special note of a report filed in April 1901 by the Prussian minister in Munich to the new German chancellor, Bernhard von Bülow. Its interest is heightened by careful annotations entered on the margins with the red ink of Kaiser Wilhelm II, who was now clearly excited and confident that an imperial railway system was finally close at hand. True, the dispatch read, southern fears of an intrusive Prussian bureaucracy were still rife, but the recently appointed successor to Mittnacht, Julius von Soden, was convinced that a closer national union was necessary [Wilhelm: "correct"]. Soden observed that Swabians can count and that they always have a healthy concern for material advantages [Wilhelm: "yes"]. The only real obstacle was Bavaria, which possessed a prosperous rail network four times the size of Württemberg's. Yet the Bavarian Palatinate was dependent on Prussian coal, and if the other medium states joined in a rail conglomerate, Munich would become isolated and suppliant [Wilhelm: "so it will come to pass"]. It might require some time, however, to shake Bavaria's special privileges [Wilhelm: "right"].[13]

This revealing document provides an insight into the collusion developing between Berlin and Stuttgart. With the weakest of the southern railway systems, Württemberg had the most to gain from following

Hesse's precedent, and Prussia had every reason to encourage such momentum without appearing overly eager to do so. Such a reading of the circumstances was confirmed in the autumn of 1902 when Thielen's successor at Public Works, Hermann Budde, dispatched Prussian representatives to meet discreetly with delegates from Württemberg and Baden in Lucerne, where all could agree that a stronger linkage of German railroads was "urgently desirable" but that Berlin would need to take a gradualist approach. Leaks of this gathering, which was followed by several more, began to appear in the Central European press with a convenient spin that the initiative for a wider railway union had originated in Stuttgart. Consequently, it was Württemberg that received full credit in November 1903 for a formal proposal for an accord among Prussia, Hesse, the Reichsbahn of Alsace-Lorraine, Württemberg, and Baden. In response, for once, Prussian and Reich officials in the nation's capital fell into step. REA president Friedrich Schulz conferred with the chancellor and expressed his support for a "more unified conception" of railway policy, while also pointing out to Bülow how this outcome would obviously differ from Bismarck's failed efforts in the 1870s: now it was Prussia's bargain to strike with the other states and not the Reich's. In the meantime, Budde and Soden conspired in secret to close the deal. Again, Budde reassured his interlocutor about "the national effort," although he explained that Berlin could not become too bold in asserting it lest the aversion of the other state regimes to prussification be unduly aroused.[14]

Ordinarily buried in bureaucracy, railroads now became a matter of *Grosse Politik*. As the Württemberg monarch grandiosely wrote to the Kaiser: "The great national idea to administer the German railways ... as a unified network still awaits its realization." The time had come to get on with it, he suggested, and his state was more than willing to take the lead. The Kaiser's reply graciously accepted support for widening the Prussian-Hessian union, and he thereupon instructed his underlings to take immediate steps to implement Württemberg's proposal of November 1903.[15] Bülow and Budde thus opened negotiations that led to a formal conference at Heidelberg in late September 1904. It was a gathering of federated states: Prussia, Hesse, Württemberg, and Baden, as well as an observer from Bavaria (to be identified shortly). Reich officials were also present to represent Alsace-Lorraine. The central item on the agenda was a proposed "operational association" (Betriebsgemeinschaft) that should expedite the circulation of locomotives, passenger cars, and freight wagons throughout Germany. It was agreed that this arrangement might be facilitated by a simultaneous reform of the national rate structure. The entire package would be presented for ratification by parliaments and public opinion as "the initiative of the southern German states," a half-truth at best. Summarizing the Heidelberg sessions for Chancellor von Bülow, Budde did not hide his elation and expressed his confidence that all formalities could be concluded by the first day of April 1906.[16]

Admittedly obstacles remained. Among the medium states, the attitude of Bavaria was indefinite, and Saxony was conspicuously absent. Another hurdle would be the Prussian cabinet and, behind it, the conservatives in parliament. To his fellow ministers in Berlin, Budde attempted to sell the proposal as an ideal solution for the practical problems of distributing the nation's rolling stock. He told his colleagues with more frankness than was feasible in public that a wider union would serve to strengthen "the leading position of Prussia in the Reich." It would be advantageous for the state both financially and militarily, whereas a failure to act was likely to encourage a resurgence of particularism in Saxony and the South. No full debate followed, but audible among the random comments was a prediction by Minister of Finance Georg von Rheinbaben that there were certain to be "difficulties and disputes." Bülow nonetheless closed by seconding Budde with an "agreement in principle." However, in light of circumstantial evidence and subsequent events, we are safe in presuming that Budde did not succeed in gaining the full consent of the Prussian cabinet.[17]

By the beginning of 1905, then, the swells of a new railway consortium reached high tide. An editorialist for the VDEV defined its objective as "the standardization of procedures with the maintenance of the autonomy of individual members." In this grand formulation there was no hint of self-contradiction. Rather, the paper struck a note of unrestrained optimism: "We are well underway!" So one might have gathered from reports of a second conference, this time convened in Berlin, to firm up the Heidelberg agreements. The gathering was joined by Saxony, Mecklenburg, and Oldenburg, thereby lending the appearance of a truly national assembly—albeit now more openly under Prussian aegis. The main topics of discussion were distribution of rolling stock, coordination of passenger and freight service, mutual operation of repair workshops, and rationalization of coal supplies. What had begun in secret became a subject of publicity. The prestigious *Frankfurter Zeitung* hailed the progress of the Berlin meeting, while taking care to ascribe special credit to Stuttgart's initiative.[18]

As could be expected, the voices of discontent were not quieted. "Deep reservations" among the southern states circulated in the newspaper press, where suspicions of Prussian motives and maneuvers were heard on all sides. Among the prominent personalities to speak out was the Württemberg Reichstag deputy Matthias Erzberger, who gave the new railway union qualified support while cautioning that the autonomy of its member states must be safeguarded. Meanwhile, the case for the project was strengthened by the publication of statistics on the increase of earnings, tracks, and locomotives on the Prussian-Hessian network. Armed with these numbers, Budde again rehearsed his arguments before the Prussian cabinet, claiming Rheinbaben's dark prognosis of impending conflicts was unfounded. Yet the latter restated it, stressing that a Betriebsgemeinschaft would require administrative institutions separate from and inherently rival to those of the Prussian state railway network, "whereas our principal duty must be to maintain the independence of the Prussian state."[19]

In this narrative lies enough evidence to corroborate that the opponents of a major interstate reorganization of German railroads were far from routed. Although the record of ensuing months is somewhat murky, because of a return to confidential and often intensely personal negotiations, neither the result nor the reasons for it can be in doubt. In November 1905 Julius von Soden remarked with unconcealed disappointment on Budde's "surprising and painful" withdrawal from the proposed railway union following "a change of opinion in Prussia."[20] This agonizing reappraisal may be attributed to four factors: widespread apprehension in the South about northern dominance, implacable resistance by particularist conservatives within Prussia, discord over the proportion of financial allocations for strategic rail construction, and the disinclination of all states concerned to relinquish control over their portion of the locomotive industry or the right to determine their orders of engines. To these we might perhaps add a fifth: Budde's debilitating illness and premature death in early 1906. But his demise occurred after the weakening and collapse of the attempt to reformulate German railway policy.

Flirting with Unification

After 1890 the other member states of Germany found themselves overmatched by Prussia. Until the 1880s the Prussian state railway system was relatively insignificant, its authority often challenged or thwarted by the many large private railroads that still existed in northern Germany. But henceforth, once the state's network had been consolidated and expanded, Berlin could ostensibly speak with one powerful voice on railway matters. The only problem for Prussia was to formulate a coherent policy, not a conclusion foregone. As before, the structural dichotomy of a Prusso-German regime in Berlin prevented any definitive clarification of the political basis for a unified rail system within the entire Reich.

Saxony and the South could take precious little comfort in the confusion emanating from Berlin. Although each had identifiably separate interests to defend, all of these states would have to confront the same complex problems of dealing with the North. Unavoidably, they would be buffeted somewhere between the poles of Prussian attraction and repulsion. How long or to what extent they could maintain a certain autonomy of action remained in doubt. The potential benefits of a national administrative and commercial unity were obvious enough. But at what price in a precipitous loss of independence? This central question would need to be posed and answered by every member state individually, according to its circumstances, in the knowledge that none of them could long resist the dominance of Prussia without continuing to exercise control of its own railway network.

Saxony

If the worst days of their "railway war" were seemingly in the past, Berlin and Dresden continued hostilities in the early 1890s by proxy. The Reichseisenbahnamt ordinarily spoke for the former, kibitzing on safety devices (brakes and signals), military needs (longer ramps and second tracks), or international freight agreements supposedly to be coordinated in the nation's capital. An attempt was mounted by the REA to codify such questions in a general set of "transportation regulations" (*Fahrdienstvorschriften*), but that effort sank in myriad details and did not resurface until a decade later. Within the Saxon administration, these matters were invariably handled by the Ministry of Foreign Affairs rather than the Ministry of Finance, where the actual seat of the state's railway bureaucracy remained. The two ministers frequently conferred, of course, and the latter advised his colleague with a wink to keep in mind that local problems often required local solutions. When first informed in 1896 of an impending Prussian move to conclude a "very advantageous" railway union with Hesse, Dresden responded with due caution and no overt bias. Undeniably, there was a strong economic appeal for Saxony to collaborate with Prussia, illustrated in 1900 by a conference in Potsdam at which a freight agreement was reached between the two states for the shipment by rail of fresh fruit from southern France.[21]

But these overtures were interrupted by rumors, very soon confirmed, that Prussia was conspiring with Bavaria to deprive Saxony of its pivotal role in north-south transit. For years the daily Berlin-Rome express had passed via Leipzig and crossed the Bavarian border at Hof on its way southward. Now word circulated of a deal between the regimes in Berlin and Munich by which the train would be rerouted via Halle and the frontier town of Probstzelle to Nürnberg, thus by-passing Saxony's major city. Although the new line must traverse the more wooded and mountainous terrain of the Thüringer Wald, time could be saved; and, as Bavaria pointed out, the heretofore neglected Franconian center at Nürnberg would be served.[22] At stake, as everyone knew, was not simply the schedule of an express passenger train but the path of a main European trade lane. Hence, Saxon Minister of Finance Paul von Seydewitz hastened to confer with Thielen in Berlin. There he complained that Saxony had been poorly treated: Prussia was ignoring the sacred principle of the shortest route and preferred instead the "most efficient," which was apparently whatever suited Berlin. For his part, Thielen denied that the two states were once more locked in combat, though he admitted to a conflict of interests. The matter unresolved, Seydewitz returned to the Saxon capital, where he claimed for public consumption that reports of a railway war were merely a "legend." Yet his blunter private thoughts were meanwhile confided to a colleague: in reality the Prussian railroad policy was always to require "the submission of one participant—the weaker—to the compulsion of the stronger."[23]

However attractive a union with Prussia may have appeared, therefore, Saxony's public stance was to deny any intention to pursue it. Indeed, if we are to believe the journal of the VDEV, Dresden's representatives at closed Reichstag committee hearings opposed a wider national association of state rail administrations "with hands and feet." Such was the widespread impression when Seydewitz was replaced in 1903 by Conrad Wilhelm Rüger. It was Rüger who would need to respond to the joint initiative for a Betriebsgemeinschaft by Soden and Budde. He began with a statement before the Saxon Upper House of his categorical opposition to a national consortium of railroads. We must note, however, that Prussia and Saxony were continuing to conduct negotiations on mutual freight arrangements. The truth was that they were like an elderly couple in a bad marriage that they could neither enjoy nor afford to dissolve.[24]

Saxon officials were not invited to the Heidelberg conference of September 1904 and were surprised to learn of it. The exclusion had been deliberate, they were told, because of an assumption that Saxony opposed the Württemberg proposal for a railway association. Dreading permanent isolation, Rüger promptly informed Soden and Budde that his state in fact hoped to participate. Soden was willing, provided Saxony approved the Heidelberg deliberations as a whole and did not set the negotiations back. Budde was likewise favorable, observing only that a Betriebsgemeinschaft would likely bring less benefit to Prussia and Saxony than to Württemberg and Baden. He added that discussions were still at the "very earliest stage," so that little time had been lost. Rüger assured them in turn that he would accept the Heidelberg accords on the premise that they were provisional and that "*all* further agreements" would be disclosed to Dresden. In secret, unknown to Soden or Budde, he appended a caveat: so far Saxony was "by no means inclined to enter a general railway association with Prussia."[25]

On balance, of the four medium states, Saxony was the most exposed to Prussian blandishments and the least inclined to them, as if the slightest shift might tip the scales. A Bavarian diplomatic dispatch correctly noted that Saxony had long and stubbornly maintained "a particularistic railway policy" at a time when the Prussian state network was gathering size and strength; but now Prussia no longer needed its closest neighbor, whereas Saxony would clearly profit from a broader association of transportation systems. Nonetheless, Dresden insisted all the more on flaunting its autonomy. This biting characterization was confirmed in 1905 by the deliberations of a special committee, chaired by the former Minister of Finance Seydewitz, which sought to rationalize the Saxon rail network, reduce personnel, and curb rising costs. Without a doubt, the common denominator of these measures was Saxony's intention to maintain an independent course, come what might.[26]

Bavaria

In the year 1895 Bavaria celebrated the fiftieth anniversary of its state railroads and did so with evident self-satisfaction. After all, Munich could boast the largest and most prosperous network among the medium states. The fabled "special privileges" (*Reservatrechte*), anchored in the imperial constitution of 1871, had withstood the tests of time and political stress. The only serious worry was isolation, which might occur if the other medium states were drawn too tightly into the Prussian orbit.

This threat was made all the more plausible by Bavaria's continuing friction with both Württemberg and Saxony. Stuttgart's pressure to complete a beltway around the northern shore of Lake Constance met Bavarian resistance until late 1895, when a treaty for the Lindau-Friedrichshafen line was finally adopted. Even then, recurrent disharmony was assured by related issues, such as Württemberg's plans to inaugurate a Berlin-Milan express that would pass through Stuttgart and Zürich, by-passing Munich and Augsburg.[27] As for Saxony, we saw how a similar proposal to alter established traffic patterns—namely, the Halle-Nürnberg connection—could inflame interstate relations as well. These sore points not withstanding, Bavaria's railway network experienced a period of financial recovery and expansion in the 1890s. By the turn of the century, it accounted for 39 percent of the state's gross revenue, thereby enabling the regime to finance its bureaucracy, retire its debts, and ease the growing burden of providing increased salaries and pensions for its employees.[28]

Understandably, Bavarian politicians were disquieted by rumors of an expanded Prussian-Hessian rail union to include Württemberg and Baden. They correctly surmised that Count Soden was a villain in this piece. Bavarian Prime Minister von Crailsheim shared worries that his colleague in Stuttgart lacked a necessary grasp of federalistic principles and that he would therefore not find it difficult to adopt a Prussian-Hessian model, an "undesirable" move that would entail "serious disadvantages" for Munich.[29] When quizzed on the subject, Soden was evasive: no deal had been concluded but one was not forever excluded. Yet we know that Soden was already pursuing his own course by opening talks with Thielen in Berlin. The Bavarians were kept uninformed, and their speculations began for the first time to give the term *Anschluss* a sinister connotation.[30]

Enter Heinrich von Frauendorfer as the Bavarian Minister of Transportation, a new cabinet post created in 1904 and intended to execute a reform of the state's railway administration. With his office now detached from the Ministry of Foreign Affairs, Frauendorfer promised a vigorous and independent course—"*sempre avanti*," he cried in tourist Italian to close his inaugural speech—that would notably include cost-cutting, reduction of personnel, and acquisition (*Verstaatlichung*) of remaining private rail companies in the Bavarian Palatinate. Certainly this was not the program of someone who could be expected to capitulate easily to Berlin. He was willing to consider some limited cooperation in national affairs but with no major concession and above all no sacrifice of the special status of his state's railroads. Accordingly, he prepared the Bavarian parliament for the possibility of some modest unitary measures, arguing that they would strengthen the state's finances and thus enhance rather than restrict its autonomy.[31]

In the short term, Frauendorfer's problem was to join in the political process already underway. Excluded from preliminary talks in Frankfurt, he approached Budde and Soden with a request to attend the Heidelberg conference, to which they agreed with the understanding that he would be present as a lone observer "to gather information." With one foot in the door, Bavaria then gained admittance in January 1905 as a regular participant at the ensuing Berlin conference, to which Frauendorfer ostentatiously led a delegation of fourteen. His stated intention was not to pursue steps toward the creation of an imperial railway system but to seek a limited agreement among the member states of the Reich. There is no way to measure the exact weight of this policy in the collapse of Württemberg's motion for a broad national association of German railroads. Surely the lack of a southern consensus was a factor, as noted, albeit one among several. But only after the appearance of "entirely unexpected difficulties"— meaning Budde's capitulation to the Prussian conservatives—did Bavaria suggest an alternate motion: limiting a collaboration among the states to an association for the exchange of freight cars (*Güterwagengemeinschaft*). This new proposal differed from its predecessor in two important respects. First, there would be no national headquarters (Zentralamt) in Berlin under Prussian leadership; rather, the chairmanship would be rotated from state capital to state capital every three years. And second, each state would maintain complete control of its existing fleet of locomotives as well as any future orders for rolling stock. Frauendorfer explained his intentions to Budde with disarming frankness: to hold down expenditures (by avoiding a vast national bureaucracy) and "also to restrict as little as possible the administrative and financial independence of the individual regimes."[32]

Although Budde promised to place Bavaria's motion first on the agenda of the next Berlin conference, he in fact believed it to be "scarcely acceptable in its present form." Baden also expressed reservations, and Württemberg's regime fell to blaming the failure of its initiative on Bavarian particularism. Frauendorfer professed to be "most painfully surprised" by such recriminations, assuming as he did that the German states were left with no viable option but to adopt the Bavarian plan. Otherwise, there would be neither a southern union nor a national association. Surely he was correct to suppose that the once hopeful movement for a unification of Germany's imperial railway system now lay in a shambles.[33]

Württemberg

Chief among Berlin's antagonists in the 1890s was Württemberg. In a dispute over grain rates in 1894, for instance, the Prussian regime proposed a national gathering of state delegates to discuss an "elimination of misunderstandings." Boycotted by Bavaria, a meeting in Berlin produced only further acrimony about the "arbitrary measures" of Prussia's railway administration, referring to unilateral rate reductions that applied undue pressure to the others. Thus spake Württemberg.[34] Nonetheless, common grievances against the North did not foster much harmony in the South. We already noted Stuttgart's repeated irritation with Bavaria over issues like the Bodensee beltway and the Berlin-Milan express. Exasperation with Baden was always less strident but sometimes annoying enough. One example was reported in 1895 when Karlsruhe deliberately delayed the arrival of a train at Friedrichshafen until five minutes *after* the embarkation of a steamship; when the ferry's schedule of departure was altered, so was the train's arrival, again preventing a connection. This "scandal," as a Stuttgart newspaper called it, may have been trivial, yet it served to revivify complaints about Baden's long history of protecting its railroads at Württemberg's expense.[35]

Squeezed between its more securely placed neighbors, Württemberg's railway administration had good reason to worry about its unstable finances. The state network's performance in the early 1890s was mediocre at best. But an apparent recovery netted a surplus of 6 million Marks in 1897 and 8.8 million in 1898. A report from the Ministry of Finance, however, revealed that profit was down to 1.9 million Marks in 1899 and 1.5 million in 1900. Prospects were that Württemberg's rail system would barely break even in 1901 and 1902, after which already promised wage increases to employees were sure to worsen the balance even further. The state would therefore need to defer any new construction, trim overhead costs, and seek other sources of revenue.[36]

It hardly seems coincidental that, just at this time, rumors began to percolate about the imminent possibility of Württemberg's attachment to the Prussian-Hessian railway union. Hostility to Prussia in the past now became an exercise in unctuous persuasion. First among Berlin's southern suitors was the new premier Julius von Soden, whose eager activity pushed aside concerns over the dangers of an *Anschluss*. Personalities often mattered no less in railway affairs than circumstances. And here was an illustration, highlighted by the fact that Soden's cousin Oskar was at the time Württemberg's envoy in Munich, leading to a series of "lieber Oskar" and "lieber Vetter" letters that spelled out state railway policy.[37] In the meantime, Soden continued the courtship in Berlin, where his representative Axel von Varnbüler conferred with Prussian Minister of Public Works Thielen, urging more openness between their states: "No more surprises, as has unfortunately been common in general until now."[38]

Such was the background for Württemberg's formal motion in late 1903 for an expanded railroad union of the German states. Archival records of the period show the great extent to which this development resulted from Soden's personal dynamism. As he soon explained to Baden's new premier Arthur von Brauer, negotiations with Berlin were in a preliminary stage and he therefore felt no compunction to consult with his cabinet or parliament [Brauer: "to the contrary!"]. Rather, he would take his proposal confidentially to Public Works in Berlin. If Minister Budde (after replacing Thielen) proved negative, the matter would simply be dropped.[39]

We know the rest. The matter was not dropped but forwarded to Württemberg's monarch, who turned to the Kaiser and also approved transmission of Soden's draft to Chancellor von Bülow. These political maneuvers at the highest level of government—which, if successfully concluded, would have altered the railway map of Germany—were thus executed without parliamentary consultation or collective ministerial approval. Troubling questions are thereby raised in this historical microcosm about the relationship between technology and democracy. True, passenger service was everywhere booming, evidence of a general democratization of travel. Yet Württemberg's case, not alone, suggests that rail networks presented technical problems too complex for ordinary mortals, including most politicians. It was consequently not unusual for a competent minister (in this occurrence Soden) to devise a policy and a budget, request his king to bless them, and then leave the Landtag to rubber-stamp them. Examined closely, the railway history of the nineteenth century does not present much supporting evidence for a rapid parliamentarization of the Reich.

For the eventual collapse of the Württemberg proposal Soden easily found two culprits. One was the Prussian Minister of Finance Georg von Rheinbaben, who, "to general surprise," was able to block the Heidelberg agreements and jostle Budde into abandoning them. Subsequent attempts by Stuttgart to save the day by winning over Bülow also failed. Varnbüler conceded to the chancellor that Württemberg's particularism had long precluded any genuine cooperation with Prussia, but such "petty prejudices" had been overcome, and it would be ironic if Prussian particularism were now at fault. Bülow agreed. If he were only the Prussian prime minister he might side with his colleague Rheinbaben, he admitted, but as chancellor it was his duty to think of the entire German nation. Such thoughts did not save Soden's plan from defeat.[40]

Another scoundrel, in Soden's view, was Heinrich von Frauendorfer. After inserting Bavaria's presence into the proceedings between Württemberg and Prussia, Frauendorfer repeatedly conferred with Soden and just as often came to no concurrence with him. The deterioration of rapport between their two states—after the Heidelberg and Berlin conferences—reached such a low point that Stuttgart seriously threatened to withdraw its diplomatic mission from Munich. In an attempt at some reconciliation, Frauendorfer awkwardly apologized for his regime's previous reluctance to compromise and offered Soden his hopes that "the irritation and dissatisfaction with the allegedly unfriendly Bavarian transport policy will be alleviated." Too little, too late. In the summer of 1906, his aspirations unrequited, Soden resigned.[41]

Baden

Like the other medium states, Baden had its problems with the Reichseisenbahnamt. From a military standpoint the REA's main concerns seemed legitimate enough: to build more bridges over the Rhine and to construct better rail links on the Left Bank. Yet those objectives raised at least two fundamental questions about political rights: could Berlin impose additional tracks over Karlsruhe's objection? And would the state government thereby be obligated to purchase extra locomotives to operate on them? "We hold both to be unjustifiable," Baden's Minister of Finance Moritz Ellstätter advised his cabinet.[42] If a larger issue went unspecified, it was too much an inalienable part of Baden's entire railway history to be long ignored. The state's commerce depended primarily on its key position at the head of the Rhine corridor and consequently its control of traffic on the Right Bank. Further improvement of connections across the river was certain to invite more competition from Alsace-Lorraine. As in decades past, this consideration far outweighed any possible advantages of increased east-west trade with the French, whose presence since 1870 remained at a distance removed. Despite their sharp tone, conversations about these matters in Berlin between Baden's envoy and the REA produced "a certain amicable understanding." Besides, as the former wryly commented in French, if attempts to cooperate proved unsatisfactory, Karlsruhe could always exercise an option "to deviate" (*de passer outre*).[43]

In the 1890s, like Württemberg, Baden was meanwhile undergoing some fiscal shortfalls. This discomfort explains the objections to another Rhine bridge (nonetheless agreed upon in May 1892), which according to one estimate would annually cost the state 200,000 Marks in freight revenues lost to the Left Bank. We have no means to compute the actual effect, but the Landtag was later informed that Baden's state railway network suffered a net deficit of nearly a million Marks in 1896. This ill budgetary wind was bound to agitate parliament and press in Karlsruhe, coinciding as it did with news of the Prussian-Hessian union, demands from Berlin for increased excise and inheritance taxes, and the first stirrings of Württemberg's plan for an expanded national railway association.[44]

Baden's new premier after 1900 was Arthur von Brauer, former envoy to Berlin. To some extent he shared Bavaria's apprehension about Stuttgart's "unitary tendencies," and he did not discourage talk of a union of the southern states to protect their autonomy. But we know that Baden was soon drawn into the swirl of secret contacts with Prussian agents that eventually culminated in the provisional Heidelberg accords. In these dealings, despite assurances to Württemberg that their interests were "identical," Baden was decidedly the more passive and cautious partner. On one occasion, in November 1903, Brauer expressed to Julius von Soden his "great surprise" at the latter's vigorous initiatives without sufficient consultation. Soden promised to improve, and in the months just prior to the Heidelberg meeting he took pains to do so. That the conference took place on Baden's soil can probably be attributed to Soden's attempt to mollify injured feelings in Karlsruhe. It was, in any event, Brauer who hosted the gathering in Heidelberg and who extended an opening welcome to the delegates.[45]

During the ensuing negotiations and ultimate disarray, Baden's railway policy remained balanced. On one hand, as Brauer assured his Grand Duke, the cabinet betrayed "no tendency" to forfeit the independence of the state's railroads. On the other, when the discussions were apparently moving toward an accord, he confessed to be "very pleased" at the cooperation of the medium states, which he valued as a check against Prussian domination. Indicatively, these soothing words were addressed to Dresden, since it was partly at Baden's insistence that Saxony was included among the participants. Brauer's disappearance from the premiership in early 1905 did not alter his government's conviction that a Betriebsgemeinschaft was "the only correct way" to a broader, though still federal, consortium of the nation's railway networks. Once that hope was dashed, however, the state was amenable to a more restricted arrangement covering only freight wagons. Still, Baden's Foreign Minister Marschall von Bieberstein could not suppress a postmortem speculation that it might be better after all for Prussia, Württemberg, and Baden to proceed without Saxony and Bavaria. But wishful thinking could no longer alter political reality.[46]

Low Expectations and High Finance

After 1905, the proposal of a national railway association was given a decent burial along with its chief sponsor in Berlin, Hermann Budde. The good, it seems, was interred with his bones. Metaphorically attending his funeral were some of the most gifted administrators in Germany's railway history. Budde was replaced at the Prussian Ministry of Public Works by Paul Breitenbach, a career technocrat who had capably served as president of the state's railroad directorate in Cologne. One must imagine Breitenbach as a virtual clone of Albert Maybach—without, however, a Bismarck to back him. The Kaiser's inattentive and irregular involvement in railway affairs was of little consequence, and historians who wish to make a case for the "personal regime" of Wilhelm II will find scant evidence here in support of their brief.[47] As a result, though often embattled in his own camp, Breitenbach proved during the prewar decade to be the dominant Prussian statesman in setting transportation policy. Facing him were four astute railway executives representing the medium states: Conrad Wilhelm Rüger in Saxony, Heinrich von Frauendorfer in Bavaria, Brauer's successor Alexander von Dusch in Baden, and the new premier of Württemberg, Karl von Weizsäcker. None of this formidable quartet was inclined to grovel before the big brother from the North, although each was willing to acknowledge

Berlin's right to speak for the German Reich in international affairs, no small matter prior to 1914.

It required nearly three years for the states to establish the terms of a new freight union, based on a Bavarian motion, which was a much diluted (because far less centralized) version of the original Württemberg plan for a Betriebsgemeinschaft. Even this minimalist rendition of a nationwide railway association produced its share of irritation and controversy. Its debut was embedded, moreover, in several other developments, of which we can identify four. The first was a renewed effort by the Reichseisenbahnamt to draft uniform national technological codes (*Fahrdienstvorschriften*) with standardized guidelines for rail crossings, signals, brakes, and such. After the failure of a similar initiative in the early 1890s, the REA had waited for another chance and now saw it in connection with the likely innovation of a freight union. A predictable impediment, however, was the reluctance of the states to cede authority to the Reich. Just how binding would the regulations be? That question bothered Breitenbach no less than his peers. Because Prussian rules already obtained for two-thirds of German railways, he saw no reason to allow the tail to wag the dog by adopting technical modifications to suit the medium states. Yet he could not deny the need for norms on a national basis to replace those of the superannuated Verein Deutscher Eisenbahn-Verwaltungen, whose weekly newspaper was henceforth published in Berlin. Strong support from military leaders, who considered such measures essential for their mobilization plans, helped the REA's cause. The project also earned high praise from the State Secretary of the Interior (and future Reich's chancellor) Theobald von Bethmann Hollweg as "a significant progress in the unification of a German railway system." But this hyperbole did nothing to obviate the lack of political consensus or of truly centralized administrative institutions.[48]

Second, in something of a contradiction, this period saw a push for Prussian centralization. One of the casualties in the collapse of a Betriebsgemeinschaft had been the proposal for a national railway headquarters in Berlin. That was out. But the creation of a Zentralamt in the capital for the Prussian state railway network now made perfect sense, and preparations for its organization began in 1906. Because the existing Berlin directorate was already swamped with the local problems of a large urban area, a new statewide administrative agency with broader supervisory authority would serve to coordinate the entire network in the North and to support the Ministry of Public Works in negotiations with the Reich's other member states.[49]

A third noteworthy tendency was a concomitant retrenchment of railway administrations in the other member states. Especially conspicuous, as we saw, was the inception of a Bavarian Ministry of Transportation under Heinrich von Frauendorfer. His controversial efforts to economize by streamlining the state railway bureaucracy cost several hundred office employees their jobs, as Frauendorfer enthusiastically led Munich into an age of telephones and typewriters. He also inaugurated a State Railroad Council (Landeseisenbahnrat), which brought leaders of Bavaria's business and banking community to the table with railway officials to exchange views on commercial practices. In a less ostentatious fashion, the other states followed suit. For example, Saxony (which had long had a Railroad Council) likewise took measures to reduce bureaucratic personnel even while continuing to expand operations. Steps like these may legitimately be evaluated as an implicit declaration of independence by regimes straining to survive within a state budget that deliberately eschewed financial support from Berlin. The price of autonomy may have been high, but after 1905 the medium states were willing to pay it.[50]

A fourth potential development had little real prospect of success—the effort to found, as Bavarian Crown Prince Rupprecht said, a "solid block" in the South. In times past, the mirage of southern unity had often shimmered on the horizon, and it did so again before 1914 once hopes vanished for an expanded railway union of Württemberg and Baden with Prussia and Hesse. The usual obstacles were so familiar that it appears supererogatory to review them. Frauendorfer best summarized the situation by repeating that neither Württemberg nor Baden was tempted to follow Munich's leadership, without which a genuine unity in the South was inconceivable. Truth to tell, he added in his caustic manner, the most reliable partner of Bavaria in the railway business was actually Prussia, "which cannot to the same extent be said of Baden and especially Württemberg." For his part, Karl von Weizsäcker complained that Bavaria continued to obstruct Stuttgart's ties with north-south traffic and to deny a fair share of trade around Lake Constance. Despite Frauendorfer's offer to seek "the removal of differences of opinion"—a frank admission of their existence—Weizsäcker grew "very angry" at the perceived mistreatment of his state. Among neighbors perception is everything. Hence these conflicts often tended to overshadow the cordiality of royal houses, the attraction of regional affinities, and the mutual aversion to a centralized national railway administration.[51]

A meeting at Frankfurt-am-Main in November 1908 finally marked the conclusion of protracted negotiations for a national freight union, which would only regulate the exchange of wagons and not affect the deployment of locomotives or passenger cars, nor would it control rates. By that time the German economy was booming again: freight traffic by rail increased by 8.5 percent in 1906, passenger travel by 6 percent. Yet there were already signs of a budgetary crisis that was to darken every discussion of railroads during the prewar decade. In April 1907 the REA and RSA jointly notified the chancellor's office that urgent military needs would require an additional 9.5 million Marks, of which Prussia and Hesse should bear at least 20 percent. As for the rest, the Reich ideally wanted the other member states to contribute as well in order to assure "a relatively significant increase of the potential of the German railway network in the interests of national defense." It was not long before the immensity of the Reich's appetite for funds became known. Rising public welfare costs, increased salaries for an expanding bureaucracy, and not least the enormous expense of sustaining a gigantic program of naval construction were among the major reasons for alarm in Berlin over fiscal shortfalls. New taxes would be required to increase the annual income of the imperial treasury by 80 million Marks, "a financial necessity," so the states were told. Their response was best stated in all its enigma by the Bavarian premier Clemens von Podewils: they should "render unto the Reich what is the Reich's." In short, a struggle over tax reform had begun in earnest.[52]

For our purposes, it is interesting to take special note of the central, albeit self-contradictory, role of France in German thought. Chancellor Bernhard von Bülow was convinced that French demographic growth and military prowess were in serious decline. Germany's attitude toward the Third Republic should therefore be "dilatory," as French resolve was allowed to ebb while the Reich stood firm, "since only in our strength lies a guarantee of world peace." This view was seconded by Wilhelm von Schoen, appointed in 1910 as the German ambassador to Paris, where he returned after an absence of fifteen years. In that interim, he reported back to Berlin, despite the unhealed wound of Alsace-Lorraine, the French passion for revenge had evaporated and been replaced by fears of German superiority—not only in military matters but also in industry, commerce, finance, education, science, and social welfare. "These are all sectors in which France has not remotely made the same progress as we." Even Paris, he added, had now been eclipsed by Berlin as a great capital. "Neither militarily nor otherwise," Schoen concluded, did Germany have any reason to consider France a major factor.[53]

Yet the contrary opinion was advanced by German military authorities whenever pleading for increased appropriations. In stressing the importance of building a new railway bridge over the Rhine at Bingen, for instance, the Prussian War Ministry worried in May 1908 that an added allocation of 10 to 12 million Marks was indispensable, because "in reality Germany trails France in the rapidity of mobilization and concentration" of its army. Unless Berlin found more funding, France could be expected to retain "a significant advantage." Likewise, in the autumn of 1909 Minister of War Josias von Heeringen greeted Chancellor Bethmann Hollweg with another urgent justification of the Bingen bridge, now estimated at 15 million Marks. The RSA had refused to authorize such an allocation, citing "the extraordinarily unfavorable financial situation of the Reich." But Heeringen remained undaunted, offering a compelling argument to Bethmann that "the security of the Reich against the superior structure of the French railway network absolutely requires an increase in the proficiency of our mobilization routes on the Rhine." In the point and counterpoint of these statements we should perhaps discern no more than a contest between the superiority complex (vis-à-vis France) of politicians and the special pleading of generals. Such clear civil-military lines were certain to blur, however, as the threat of a major continental war drew near.[54]

The financial distress of the Reich was also bound to pull the member states into controversy and to pose fundamental questions about their relationship to the national regime as sparring over allocations continued. The RSA estimated that from 1887 to 1909 expenses for strategic railway construction had reached 280 million Marks, that is, about 12 million annually. Maximum projections for 1910 to 1914 must be limited to about half that rate (including the bridge at Bingen), because the Reich's budget was "stretched to the limit" (*äusserst gespannt*). This comment drew a direct reply from the General Staff, now headed by Helmuth von Moltke the Younger, who acknowledged budgetary restrictions but claimed that his own funding requests were limited to "what is strictly necessary," thus implying that they should always be granted nonetheless. To no one's surprise, Heeringen agreed with Moltke "*on all points.*"[55] Caught in a bind between these powerful contestants, the chancellor temporized somewhat but listed toward the military. In spite of fiscal restraints, he said, strategic railway construction must continue, because it "depends importantly on neighboring states," meaning France and Russia.

How could the Reich make ends meet? Like his predecessors, Bethmann decided the solution was to turn to the medium states and implore them to shoulder a heavier burden. Yet he quickly encountered the same hard reality as they: while continuing to quarrel with one another, Saxony and the southern states were unanimous in evading additional fiscal responsibility for the Reich and in protecting, as Weizsäcker stated it, their "sovereign rights." In Bavaria, let it be added, this inveterate resistance was unchanged by the departure in 1912 of Heinrich von Frauendorfer (forced out in a dispute with the Roman Catholic Church and the conservative People's Party), who ended his tenure as Minister of Transportation as he had begun: "*Sempre avanti!*"[56] In Prussia, too, Paul Breitenbach stood on the principle that strategic rails should be paid from military funds, thereby refuting the contention of Reich officials that parallel lines requested by the Ministry of War were tantamount to new tracks and should be financed by the Prussian state network.[57]

The documentary record is unambiguous that German railroads were not approaching any scheme of meaningful unification in the years just before the Great War. The facts of life were patiently explained by Breitenbach to the Kaiser on Christmas Eve of 1911. Apparently Wilhelm had become enamored of a suggestion that the Reich should found a national "railway parliament" that might gather delegates from all the member states for the specific purpose of promoting harmony and greater unity among their transportation systems. But Breitenbach emphatically dismissed the notion of an Eisenbahnparlament as "impracticable." Then, appearing before the Budget Committee of the Prussian Lower House, he effectively made an identical argument, meanwhile gaining support from the Ministry of Finance against any further cession of states' rights to the

Reich. There was, as a conservative deputy correctly observed, simply "no prospect" of an imperial railway assembly.[58] The same message was delivered by a Prussian delegation to the conference of German chambers of commerce in June 1912: such a move toward a future nationalization of German railroads was "without promise of success." Thereupon, a Bavarian representative declared that he "completely shares the Prussian standpoint." Saxony, Württemberg, and Baden offered some regrets but no contradiction. This categorically negative outcome was in no way undermined by an agreement (to go into effect in May 1914) to establish norms for the circulation of locomotives and passenger cars, similar to the existing regulations on freight wagons. Two telltale features of this accord were noteworthy: that it was based on practices already coordinated among the three southern states, and that future arrangements or difficulties in operation would be settled "from case to case." A momentous victory for a national railway system it was not.[59]

By the beginning of 1914 Germany was entering a full-blown financial crisis. Prodded by Moltke, Bethmann Hollweg informed Breitenbach and the regimes of the medium states that they should press on with the planning and construction of strategic railway links, which would be "entirely decisive" in case of war. At closed sessions of the Prussian cabinet he added a second rationale for such projects: to stem the threat of unemployment with a kind of public works program. But Prussian Finance Minister August Lentze was unpersuaded, citing the "extreme difficulty" of the state's budgetary situation and therefore his "absolute inability" to find the desired funding for the present "avalanche" of fiscal requests. Moltke nevertheless insisted on the "importance and urgency" of military needs. "In my opinion no sacrifice is too great," he wrote to Bethmann; henceforth Germany had "a holy duty" to match France and to meet Russia. He enclosed a separate memo with precise quantifications. The French currently possessed fifteen main lines to the frontier, the Germans only twelve. With completion of the Bingen bridge and a concurrent French project, the count would be sixteen to thirteen, meaning that France could fully mobilize in eleven days, Germany in fifteen. Ideally, the Reich should command twenty lines to its western borders, plus three to the East. Accordingly, Moltke urged the chancellor to call a national railway conference in Berlin and to impress on Prussia and the other federated states of the Reich that increased cost-sharing was indispensable.[60]

From the REA and the RSA came a similar suggestion. Their estimates were that the Prussian-Hessian union would need to allocate 360 million Marks, Bavaria 48.6, Saxony 18.9, Württemberg 12.7, and Baden 8.3. Because the Reich was financially strapped, the states should contribute these amounts under a "unified plan," and to that end it would be useful to convene them in Munich. Although Bethmann had reservations about such a public gathering, which could not be kept secret, he agreed to approach the states. The difficulty of his task was meanwhile compounded by more exact budgetary projections from military authorities, which foresaw a total allocation of 500 million Marks for rail construction to include (besides Bingen) four more bridges over the Rhine: one near Karlsruhe at Maxau, another at Rüdesheim, and two north of Koblenz—hence directly opposite Belgium—at Neuwied and Remagen. It is worth noting that this "imperative need" to offset the "significant advantage" of the French rail system was presented to the southern states by Bethmann under the assumption that all the designated projects would be completed by 1920. Breitenbach was slightly more optimistic in setting a deadline for termination on the first day of April 1918. Not before then, in other words, would optimal conditions be attained for a war against France.[61]

These were the terms that Bethmann carried with him in the spring of 1914 on a discreet diplomatic mission to Munich and Stuttgart, where he conferred with officials of the three southern states. To no avail. Claiming that their legislatures would not ratify credits solely on the basis of estimates conceived in Berlin, leaders in the South refused to take any action until a definitive settlement was reached between Prussia and the Reich. But the snag there was that, according to the imperial treasury, the Reich would be unable to grant any more allocations for railroads until 1916, whereas Prussia categorically demanded that a budgetary commitment by that state be accompanied with a firm pledge from the Reich government "*at the same time.*"[62] Further negotiations reached the verge of collapse during the summer of 1914. Breitenbach implored Bethmann to break the impasse with the RSA, pointing out that "a very considerable participation" by the Reich was in any case "indispensable." Like the southern states, Prussia would not budge until the requisite expenditures were simultaneously assured by the national regime. Otherwise, he warned, the Prussian Landtag would balk, and the state would bring all railway construction to a halt.[63]

These differences were aired only a few weeks before the German invasion of Belgium. Moltke's efforts to stir Bethmann to continued action failed. Obviously frustrated and peeved, the chancellor could only claim that he had done everything possible to apply political pressure to the states, and if the General Staff wanted to continue to dun them, that was the job of the current Minister of War, Erich von Falkenhayn. But Falkenhayn was able to do no more than quote Moltke's plea that the matter was important and urgent.[64] Indeed it was, in the last days of July 1914, as German politicians and generals turned round and round in Berlin while their country lurched toward war.

Railroads and the German Take-Off

"The swift industrialisation of Imperial Germany is one of the commonplaces of contemporary history."[65] Written by a British scholar in a book first published in 1921, that sentence remains immutable after eight decades of statistical refinements. Only a comparison with the United

States after 1890 would do justice to the magnitude of the German expansion. The urban and industrial growth of the Reich before 1914, by whatever standard of measure, had no parallel in Europe. If ever the notion of an economic take-off has validity, it is here and now.

The pattern of growth from the 1880s to 1913 was sustained and remarkably steady (see Table 12). To be sure, it is possible to point out some occasional glitches on the economic screen—brief recessions in 1901 and 1907—but the usual tendency was decidedly upwards. For example, when surveying the aggregate of artisanal and industrial production, including mining, it is better to do so without forcing the numbers to conform to the obsolete conception of a deflationary "long swing" (*Trendperiode*) that came to an end in 1894. Instead, we see the beginnings of rapid acceleration in the mid-1880s that gathered force during the ensuing two decades and culminated like a final burst of fireworks in 1913.

Taking care not to lose our way in a blizzard of statistics, we can establish at a minimum that the progress of railroads was a mirror image of the national economy to which they so importantly contributed. One measurement is "created value" (*Wertschöpfung*) in the sector of transportation, for which railways were decisive (see Table 13). Once more we observe a running start in the 1880s, a steady climb in the two decades thereafter, and a concluding sprint in the prewar years. Like German commerce as a whole, the railway industry did not proceed without fluctuations, but these were relatively inconsequential for a leading economic sector that doubled (1880–1895) and then trebled (1895–1913) in size. As the main

TABLE 12: Total Production of German Light and Heavy Industry, 1880–1913
(1913 = 100)

Year	Value	Year	Value
1880	26.1	1900	61.4
1885	30.8	1908	78.0
1890	39.9	1913	100.0
1895	48.6		

Source: Wehler, *Deutsche Gesellschaftsgeschichte* 3: 585, 600.

TABLE 13: Total Value Created in German Transportation, 1880–1913
(Marks in 1913 prices)

Year	Value
1880	506,000,000
1886	658,000,000
1890	871,000,000
1895	1,073,000,000
1900	1,576,000,000
1907	2,410,000,000
1913	3,146,000,000

Source: Wehler, *Deutsche Gesellschaftsgeschichte* 3: 584, 599.

carrier as well as consumer of coal and metal products, the railroads obviously promoted and profited from the simultaneous expansion of those industries. Coal output more than doubled in the two decades before 1913 to about 250 million tons, half of the European total. In the same period, steel production also doubled to over 16 million tons, nearly two-thirds of Europe's aggregate. Record attainments in these staples of traditional heavy industry were accompanied by the Reich's untouchable lead in the newer branches of electronics, dyes and chemicals, and machines (notably including locomotives, to be treated later). Altogether, this was an extraordinary performance that left competitors in its wake.[66]

Although the calculations are admittedly crude, the gross income from freight deliveries is still the most reliable indicator of how the major state railway companies fared during the take-off. If the German bureaucracies were guilty of inadequate reporting, at least it was regular inadequate reporting; consequently the general pattern and scope of these statistics merit our confidence. They enable us yet again to confirm the distinctive sequence of early start, long surge, and final spurt. In round figures, the Prussian state railway system managed to treble its income between 1890 and 1913 to become a 2.5 billion Mark freight business. It dwarfed the other states, remaining proportionately ten times the size of Saxony. Bavaria and Baden also trebled, whereas Saxony grew less rapidly and began to fall substantially behind Bavaria. Despite a respectable growth rate, Württemberg continued to bring up the rear (see Table 14).[67]

The other standard measurement of growth is, of course, the length of tracks (see Table 15). But after 1890, we know, this criterion ceased to be crucial, because most of the profitable main lines had already been constructed by that time and the states became increasingly loath to invest large sums in costly secondary connections to remote areas. At least these statistics offer some impression of the relative immensity

TABLE 14: Total Gross Income from German Railway Freight, 1880–1913 (Marks)

	Prussia	Saxony	Bavaria	Württemberg	Baden
1880	341,753,000	62,514,000	79,326,000	26,186,000	29,790,000
1885	657,077,000	67,148,000	82,092,000	28,589,000	33,726,000
1890	881,212,000	86,085,000	109,055,000	34,987,000	44,987,000
1895	1,012,502,000	97,007,000	121,835,000	42,609,000	52,655,000
1900	1,392,336,000	136,985,000	171,401,000	56,215,000	78,046,000
1905	1,729,253,000	148,866,000	195,091,000	69,120,000	87,416,000
1909	2,029,595,000	167,500,000	266,413,000	78,786,000	101,153,000
1913	2,557,339,000	207,171,000	318,904,000	94,296,000	122,974,000

Source: Fremdling et al., *Statistik der Eisenbahnen in Deutschland*, pp. 400–401, 440–42, 492–502.

TABLE 15: Track Length of Major State Railway Companies, 1880–1913 (kilometers)

	Prussia	Saxony	Bavaria	Württemberg	Baden
1880	11,506	1,942	4,268	1,536	1,288
1885	21,224	2,047	4,478	1,544	1,291
1890	24,903	2,328	4,826	1,633	1,426
1895	27,227	2,455	5,323	1,689	1,525
1900	30,683	2,593	5,838	1,748	1,553
1905	34,523	2,733	6,444	1,862	1,669
1910	37,562	2,809	7,852	1,938	1,721
1913	38,791	2,815	8,034	1,998	1,757

Source: Fremdling et al., *Statistik der Eisenbahnen in Deutschland*, pp. 75, 96–97, 126–32.

of the Prussian network, which comprised almost three-fourths of the nation's entire rail system. Meanwhile, private railroads all but disappeared in Germany, leaving the Prussian administration to create a virtual state monopoly in the North, much as Bavaria, Württemberg, and Baden had separately done so in the South.

The consistency of Germany's astonishing record of growth is all the more remarkable when one takes into account the chaotic state of its rate structure. A controversy over shipments of grain and flour was illustrative. In 1891 Prussia attempted to lower the railway rates on these items, urging other regimes to do likewise, while assuring them that the measure was only "experimental and provisional." Saxony and the southern states refused on the grounds that their markets would soon be flooded by cheap imports from the North and from abroad. There was also a subsidiary issue: whether separate rates should be set for grain and for flour. Tampering with the rate structure might favor large millers clustered around northern ports at the expense of smaller inland millers in Saxony and southward. Besides, Prussia openly indicated a wish to extend its lowered rate policy to other goods that would similarly prove detrimental to the economies of the medium states. Despite long sustained pressure from Berlin, Dresden and Munich in particular stood firm, and they maintained their right to negotiate separately with Austria, thus ignoring Prussian complaints about violations, in letter or spirit, against the recent German freight association. Bavaria's new Minister of Transportation Heinrich von Frauendorfer professed his support for a simplification of rates, but, the "enviable" commercial situation of the Prussian-Hessian union notwithstanding, his office explicitly resisted adoption of its rate structure.[68]

Circulated in the newspaper press, Prussia's professed intention to coordinate national rates rather than to dominate interstate commerce went unheeded. Business leaders in the North were left to deplore the residual complexity of trade regulations. Appealing for a more uniform rate code in November 1913, the Berlin Chamber of Commerce urged adoption of the Prussian-Hessian scheme by the medium states, following the precedent of Mecklenburg and Oldenburg, which had done so; otherwise, freight shipments to the South would continue to require the use of twenty-six different rate tables! Thanks to the efforts of the REA, a compendium of German passenger fares and freight rates became available in the bookstores: only 5 Marks for a thick volume of 199 pages. In the words of one editorialist, despite Prussia's laudable efforts to achieve a rational schedule of rates throughout Germany, "the liberty of the individual states remains entirely untouched."[69]

While we know that the German railroads were thriving, it is impossible to derive a precise statistical picture of their net profits. Like freight trade considered above, we also have for passenger travel neat rows of numbers about gross income (see Table 16). These statistics leave no doubt about the democratization of railway travel in Germany before 1914, revealing a familiar pattern of growth that accelerated right up to the eve of the war, nearly trebling since 1890. However, the cost of sustaining such expanded service was immense, albeit finally incalculable because of the plethora of factors and their variability. One enormous expense was steam engines. For instance, the cumulative outlay for new locomotives by the Prussian state network doubled between 1890 and 1907, and it almost doubled again to nearly 1.4 billion Marks by the outbreak of the war.[70] The other states experienced, in smaller proportion, similar increases in their effort to meet the growing demands of the riding public. While the domestic market for these mammoth machines was strong, exports by the locomotive industry rose rapidly as well, almost tripling from 1909 to 1913 (when France became Germany's main customer). By that time, the level of annual production reached 1800 units. As Ernst von Borsig later remarked as an indisputable matter of fact, German manufacturers "dominated virtually

TABLE 16: Total Gross Income from German Passenger Fares, 1880–1913 (Marks)

	Prussia	Saxony	Bavaria	Württemberg	Baden
1880	90,024,000	17,325,000	24,564,000	9,233,000	11,216,000
1885	168,900,000	20,263,000	24,627,000	9,850,000	12,197,000
1890	228,752,000	25,927,000	31,881,000	12,181,000	15,587,000
1895	273,885,000	29,749,000	36,418,000	14,341,000	17,845,000
1900	384,021,000	40,491,000	50,945,000	19,553,000	23,165,000
1905	476,016,000	46,274,000	59,046,000	23,774,000	26,909,000
1910	605,017,000	58,481,000	86,785,000	29,492,000	30,266,000
1913	713,410,000	69,707,000	96,406,000	33,562,000	34,343,000

Source: Fremdling et al., *Statistik der Eisenbahnen in Deutschland*, pp. 314–17, 377, 380–87.

all the free markets of the world."⁷¹ Yet this good news, to reiterate, must be balanced against the heavy expenditures incurred by the state railway companies in order to acquire enough rolling stock to maintain an extraordinarily high rate of growth.

Another huge category in the budgets of all state railway companies was the cost of personnel. By 1913 German rail companies collectively employed 800,000 persons, of which 560,000 worked for the Prussian state administration. One in every three bureaucrats in the entire German Empire was a railroad employee. Given its pioneering system of social security—the accident, sickness, and pension plans of the Bismarck era—welfare costs were bound to rise precipitously as the various state networks expanded.⁷² Furthermore, the period after 1890 witnessed a steep increase in individual earnings: despite slowly climbing prices, the real wages of the total German labor force rose by more than 25 percent. Although an exact computation of the salary obligations thereby assumed by the railway companies is impossible, we know that they complained constantly about the resulting financial burden. Herein lies the best explanation for the economizing tendencies that were especially evident in the decade before 1914, such as layoffs of personnel, building rural highways to reduce pressure for more tertiary railway construction, and restricting purchases of new rolling stock. Equally indicative was the concerted opposition of the medium states, led by Saxony, to the so-called Bassermann bill, a legislative measure introduced into the Reichstag that would have limited the daily working hours of engineers, firemen, and other railway employees. It was rejected in 1911.⁷³

There is a case to be made that we are perhaps dealing here, as one historian has suggested, with "a distorted perception of reality."⁷⁴ The railway industry was booming and real wages were rising, yet dissatisfactions persisted. Some of them were stirred by the Social Democratic Party (SPD), which, once released from the anti-Socialist laws of the 1880s, began after 1890 an open campaign to unionize railway workers, while hinting ominously about the possibilities of a national railway strike. The resulting need to quell "social-revolutionary agitation," however exaggerated, was keenly felt by the regimes of both Prussia and the medium states, all the more so as they received frequent reports of labor troubles and occasional insurgencies in other countries, notably France.⁷⁵ Such events elsewhere, as Hermann Budde cautioned Bernhard von Bülow in 1904, demonstrated that augmenting wages and pensions would not suffice to suppress working-class grievances—hence, the sooner a military intervention was mounted, the more certain would be its success. Accordingly, in concurrence with the Prussian Ministry of War, Budde issued "strictly confidential" instructions for an immediate conscription of any railway workers involved in a strike attempt.⁷⁶ This initiative was elaborated by his successor at Public Works, Paul Breitenbach, who drafted a detailed set of "Basic Principles" (*Grundsätze*) for strike-busting, which were secretly distributed within Prussia and to authorities in the medium states. Exceptionally, the reaction outside of Berlin was favorable, as Saxony and Bavaria adopted similar regulations with particular zeal.[77] The Germans were thus well prepared for news of the 1910 railway strike in France, which came neither as a surprise nor as a reason for undue alarm. As employees of a public service, German railway workers possessed no right to strike nor even to join Socialist organizations upholding that right. Discipline, not to say repression, thereby prevailed on the German railroads right up to 1914, which may be counted among the factors contributing to their continued economic prosperity.[78]

It is relevant here to remark on the recruitment of female employees by the state railway companies after 1890. We earlier observed that the hiring of women was generally sooner and more frequent in France than in Germany. But one may speak of a second wave of employment that coincided with the rapid expansion of the German rail networks and the recent introduction of the typewriter. Women were now increasingly engaged by the state companies not only because they were cheap labor but also for their superior manual dexterity. In the manner of German bureaucracy, elaborate codes of behavior were framed by the several rail administrations to ensure discipline and decorum among the young unmarried girls employed in clerical positions. By 1914 their total number rose to about ten thousand in Prussia alone and not quite double that figure in all of Germany. Without them, it is unlikely that the rapid pace of prewar growth in the railway industry could have been sustained.[79]

If it is infeasible to draw a precise balance sheet of the profitability of the German state rail companies before 1914, certain generalizations are permissible. Railroads were manifestly a source of great wealth, measurable in gross income, without which Prussia, Saxony, and the southern states could not have survived with remotely the same economic élan. Conversely, the failure to create an imperial railway system explains in large measure the Reich's financial crisis—and specifically the acute shortage of military funding—during the immediate prewar decade. Railroads became the bellwether of the national economy, yet paradoxically they remained both the symbol and substance of states' rights. Little wonder, then, that the state regimes (including Prussia) jealously guarded from the Reich their practices of budgeting, fixing rates, hiring personnel, ordering rolling stock, and setting schedules. As we must imagine Sisyphus happy, we can also posit that the state rail companies remained profitable despite sharply rising overhead costs and occasional economic relapses. For example, the net profits of the Prussian-Hessian union were reported to reach slightly over a half billion Marks in 1909 and again in 1910. Bavaria meanwhile claimed a net of more than twenty million in 1911.[80] These returns were too irregular and adjustable for reliable tabulation, but there can be no question that the burgeoning of freight and passenger traffic between 1890 and 1914 brought immense sums into the coffers of Germany's member states, thus enabling them to retain the particularism of their railway networks and their ruling houses. It would take a war to cause the collapse of both.

The Consequences of Escalation

After 1890, German strategic planning was based on two simple premises: that the decisive engagement in any future European conflagration would be a land war in the West, and that the key to a swift triumph there would be the railroads. Both were embodied in the famous Schlieffen Plan—completed in 1905 and subsequently revised by Moltke the Younger—which was actually a sure recipe not for victory but for escalation. Its successful execution would require the movement of several million men by rail, along with their equipment and supplies—to date, by far, the most daunting logistical operation in history. Everything thus depended on making the maximum use of Germany's constantly expanding system of transportation.

Such an escalation would somehow have to be financed. As we have already examined the disputes and strains thereby produced, it is adequate here to establish that the military demands for increased spending for railways and bridges did not abate before 1914 and that successive Prussian war ministries continued to proclaim that further allocations for them were "absolutely necessary."[81] Nor must we recapitulate the internal tensions that resulted from the incessant *querelle d'Allemand* between the imperial regime and the member states. A sufficient illustration was the project of a railway bridge at Rüdesheim. Insistence by the Prussian Ministry of Finance that the Reich's share should be set at 80 rather than 60 percent was, not for the first time, curtly refused: "The Reich will be unable to agree to a lesser participation by Prussia." After an abrasive exchange of unpleasantries, agreement was finally reached to split costs at a rate of 75 to 25 percent. Hard feelings, too, escalated.[82]

Apart from such troublesome fiscal problems, another lingering source of internal conflict in Germany was the relationship of the civilian to the military administration of the state networks. Presumably, a sudden transition would occur at the onset of an international war. But precisely what preparations should be made, and to what extent might non-military personnel be informed of plans for the mobilization and deployment of troops? These questions never received firm answers. If Germany's fundamental strategic principles before 1914 were clear, there remained a host of uncertain bureaucratic procedures and tactical details. The result was a semantic muddle over fine distinctions among "increased danger," "imminent danger," and "immediate danger." The ostensible intention was to take precautions such that, without creating public alarm or administrative chaos, German trains would be ready to roll on the first day of mobilization. Yet the determination of what specific measures were to be taken at which exact phase of operations (prior to an official declaration of war) became extremely complex. To implement the transition, a military plenipotentiary was assigned to each railway directorate. His job was to monitor peacetime traffic patterns and to prepare their conversion to wartime functions, meanwhile keeping civilian officials informed—but only "insofar as necessary"—of the army's dispositions.[83]

In all of these highly detailed and often secret arrangements, one should not underestimate the role of the Reichseisenbahnamt. Though scorned at the time and sometimes ridiculed since, the REA was in reality an active agent in representing military interests in the minutiae of planning and preparation. It also constituted a kind of shadow bureaucracy, since everyone knew that the military plenipotentiaries would take orders and file reports through the REA in the event of war. In the meantime, the Prussian Zentralamt could handle administrative chores for the railroads in northern Germany under the supervision of the Ministry of Public Works, but that structure would be abruptly replaced at the beginning of a military conflict.[84]

Outside of the North, no surprise, the issue of military control over the railroads was even more problematical, especially in Bavaria, whose army was constitutionally exempted from the Reich's authority in peacetime. In Munich's perspective, this condition implied that an "imminent danger" could be declared only by the Bavarian king, not the Kaiser, and that the state's Ministry of Transportation would retain full administrative command of the railway network until the day of mobilization. There is no difficulty in pinpointing the irritations that grew from the REA's attempts to achieve a procedural "simplification" by melding heretofore separate peacetime and wartime regulations into a single German operational code. The REA nonetheless continued through the years to apply pressure for standardized norms and improved equipment on the railroads to enhance their military utility: signals, brakes, stations, ramps, roadbeds, grades and curves, and above all double parallel tracks. Although one cannot quantify the cumulative effect of such a cluster of technological ameliorations, it is fair to generalize that Germany, largely for military reasons, substantially closed the gap in engineering standards with France, whose generally superior (and thus more costly) construction had long been directed by the corps of Ponts-et-Chaussées, a central institution still lacking for the German territories.[85]

Reports of various delays and accidents on the rails in different parts of Germany provided the General Staff with a rationale to intervene directly to ensure the "war-readiness" (*Kriegsbereitschaft*) of the member states. This concept, first emphasized in the late 1890s, covered a secret mission of staff officers from Berlin to inspect railway installations and rolling stock throughout the land. In short order, this practice became regularized and led to the submission of annual reports on the aptitude of state networks for military action. Whereas the REA boasted of "good results" from these inquiries, Saxon and southern leaders (prodded by press leaks) began to express their usual qualms about Prussian interference.[86] "The question appears to be not without fundamental importance," observed Bavarian premier Crailsheim. But for public consumption, at least, Munich and the other provincial capitals clung to the position that they were only meeting an obligation to keep Berlin informed of preparations, and that their states' rights were in no way curtailed by doing so. As before, Crailsheim added, it would be up to Bavaria (and thus implicitly the others) to decide in peacetime whether to act alone or to cooperate with the REA in military affairs.[87] One small detail epitomized prevailing attitudes. After the Bundesrat reached an accord in 1898 on a new set of broad guidelines for military transportation, the REA offered to send multiple copies of it to the states. This gesture, however, was declined by Munich on the grounds that printed regulations would doubtless have a Reich's eagle on the cover. Lest the impression be created of a concession, Bavaria published its own.[88]

For all that static in the background, a more prominent role to be performed by the General Staff became evident by 1900. The name of Alfred von Schlieffen was not yet widely known, but his political activities noticeably increased in drafting military rules, soliciting funds for new railway construction, directing maneuvers, and cajoling the member states to participate more fully in the common effort of preparing the national defense. In fact, a more appropriate term would actually have been national offense. Shrugging off doubts of the elder Moltke about which front to face, Schlieffen foresaw a massive initial assault on France. Yet, paradoxically, a problem with the Schlieffen Plan was that its calculations depended too much on railways—not only the French and German networks that could rapidly bring their respective forces to the national frontiers, but the Belgian system that might enable the Germans to sustain their march to the English Channel and thereby turn France's left flank.

Schlieffen assumed that French fortifications on their eastern border would make a direct German assault there too costly and time-consuming. As both sides were aware, the northern front was far more porous, and the French would consequently expect an attack between Verdun and Mézières. Proud and stubborn, they would defend their redoubts, their cities, their capital, their honor. The Belgians, meanwhile, would probably offer some resistance by destroying bridges, tunnels, and railway connections south of the Maas (Meuse) River. What no one would anticipate was an extensive flanking operation by German infantry units, taking advantage of Belgian and Dutch east-west rail lines north of the Maas, skirting the northeastern sector near Verdun to penetrate French territory westward between Lille and Dunkerque. But a crucial gamble was the dependency on mainly Belgian tracks for supplies and support once German troops crossed beyond their national frontier and left their own rail lines. On that point Schlieffen remained hesitant and vague. In the 1905 draft of his Plan, he merely stated with a certain nonchalance that "the railways, insofar as they are necessary for the reinforcement of the army, must be secured." His evasion was further betrayed by the seemingly innocuous remark that "in general the available highways [in Belgium] are very good"—a prophetic suggestion that the German invaders would be forced to rely mostly on long marches, horse-drawn carriages, and the primitive technology of trucks to sweep through the Belgian countryside.[89]

Few historical figures have been more closely scrutinized or severely criticized than Schlieffen's unfortunate successor, Helmuth von Moltke the Younger, who modified the Plan and later received blame for botching the campaign. In his defense, it must be said that he correctly perceived the Plan's flaws and sensibly shortened the projected hammer stroke by deciding to respect Dutch neutrality and to confine the invasion route to Luxemburg and the southeastern corner of Belgium, moving toward Paris from the north instead of circling in a huge arc around western France. The new strategy, in other words, was both more compact and more realistic because it recognized that the reliance on railroads for logistics would be too great a risk once the German army departed its own national networks. Thus Moltke in effect conceded, more frankly than Schlieffen before him, that there would be no railway war after the initial procedures of mobilization and concentration were completed.[90]

In German military thinking before 1914, speed and mobility were of the essence. No other explanation is needed for the experiments conducted with electric locomotives on special military tracks that in 1903 produced speeds of over 200 kilometers per hour. Yet, quite apart from the dubious commercial value of such innovation (a Berlin-Hamburg express in less than two hours was dismissed for that reason as "utopian"), military leaders consistently rejected the electrification of Germany's main railway lines. Their reasons were several. First, expense. The technical possibility of electrification arose at the precise moment of Germany's financial quandary, when building a battle fleet and throwing more rail bridges across the Rhine had already been established as priorities. Second, irregularity. All of Germany's carefully plotted railway timetables would be scrambled if some trains rushed to the frontier under electrical power and unloaded troops that had to wait many hours or days for the arrival of their equipment behind plodding steam engines. Third, vulnerability. The destruction of a steam locomotive might halt the progress of a single train, but the malfunction, sabotage, or bombing of an electrical installation might entirely cripple any number of convoys. Fourth, locality. Even if the General Staff could manage to devise schemes to incorporate electric locomotives for mobilization, they would instantly become useless whenever "abroad." For military planners bent on offensive warfare, these were compelling arguments to count on conventional steam engines and to authorize designs for new railway construction accordingly. German military transports before 1914 would therefore continue to move at an average speed of 30 kilometers an hour, and orders were issued that main rail lines might be electrified only if they could be reconverted to steam power in the event of war.[91]

Although the development of air power was as yet a relatively minor distraction, it deserves mention here. The German fear, of course, was that French planes might be capable of destroying the Rhine bridges, leaving Moltke's armies stranded without adequate reinforcements or supply routes. This alarm grew especially after an air show at Reims in 1909, which demonstrated "more clearly than ever" that the French had made "astonishing progress" and reached "the peak of all nations" with their air force. The French lead was further extended by training new pilots, constructing runways in border areas, and practicing bombing sorties. Whereas German planners before 1914 regarded railway trains as vehicles of offensive warfare, they saw aircraft largely in terms of defense. Instead of mounting a large fleet of fighter planes like the French, they concentrated on zeppelins that could hover over the Rhine and protect its rail bridges. The fundamental assumption of the Schlieffen Plan thus remained essentially intact: any forthcoming struggle would be decided not by military activity in the air or at sea but by a great confrontation of ground troops in France.[92]

The military primacy of steam engines running on steel tracks therefore went without serious challenge. Strategic planning and funding requests by the German General Staff proceeded on that basis, as did army maneuvers that were, in Moltke's words, "a superb preparation for war."[93] All contingencies for a holding operation in the West and a first offensive against Russia were dropped. After the Second Moroccan Crisis of 1911, as long before, "the enemy" was in Paris. How likely was a Franco-German conflict? In late November 1912, Moltke considered that the excitement of the previous year had dissipated and that there was "no cause for concern."[94] A fortnight later this notion was elaborated in a memo to the Prussian Minister of War that was forwarded by Moltke but actually drafted by his adjutant Erich Ludendorff. It stated that Germany could presently regard the prospect of war with equanimity. "Yet I cannot extend that view [to assure] that this will also be the case in the future." With France preoccupied in Morocco and Russia still unready, the military situation currently remained favorable for the Reich. "But it can change" (*Sie kann sich aber ändern*). Fateful words. They suggested, despite a large measure of self-confidence, some deep-seated apprehensions about the sheer unpredictability of the French leadership and the growing might of the Russian army.[95]

This atmosphere of material and emotional escalation was clearly detectable in an incisive statement passed on by the former Chief of Staff, General von Waldersee, to Moltke in May 1914. There was still no evidence of bellicosity among Germany's foes, Waldersee wrote. "To the contrary, for the moment none of the major protagonists can be disposed to provoke an armed conflict." Because of its constantly evolving military preparations and its political turmoil, France was experiencing some disarray; England's chief concern was the Irish question; and Russia needed more time to pose a threat. Hence, in the normal course of events, Germany had little reason to expect an attack in the immediate future, although neither did it have "*any* grounds to *avoid* a conflict." Rather, Waldersee concluded with a flourish, "the chances of quickly and victoriously prosecuting a great European war are still very favorable for Germany [and its allies] *today*. Today. In a short while this will no longer be the case."[96]

The extant documentary record thus leaves not the slightest doubt that within the General Staff, starting with Waldersee and Ludendorff, there existed a hawkish element that was in effect urging a preemptive war with France. If he had some objections, Moltke tended increasingly to accept such reasoning (he made certain "corrections" on Ludendorff's memo but then signed it). We know all too well that this attitude reached its highest pitch in the summer of 1914 and that it was sufficient to brush aside any lingering reservations by Germany's political leadership. So it was that Chancellor Bethmann Hollweg went before the Reichstag on 4 August to announce the German army's entry into Belgium and to offer that infamous explanation: "Necessity knows no law."[97]

These climactic events in the summer of 1914 require a final comment from the vantage of railway history. The most pertinent observation is that something self-defeating and deeply irrational was transpiring in Berlin. For years, as we have amply documented, various Germany military spokesmen had urgently pleaded for greater allocations to construct railroads and bridges. By 1914 the German army had at its disposal fifteen fixed bridges over the Rhine and thirteen double-track approaches.[98] Yet for the General Staff this was not enough, and hence the need of additional funding for some projects that would not be completed before 1918. Until then, the chances to implement the modified Schlieffen Plan with success would remain less than optimal. If solely railroads were under consideration, therefore, the possibility of a swift German victory over France would be greatly enhanced by waiting at least another four years. Yet by that time, because of the growing menace from Russia, the entire Schlieffen Plan might become infeasible. In reality, then, what was the necessity that knew no law? It was that an increasing danger in the East dictated a premature strike in the West. Thus German military commanders were caught in the logical crosscurrent of demanding gigantic appropriations for future railway projects while simultaneously contending that the most propitious moment for an offensive against France had already arrived. Something had to give. And when it did in August 1914, logic mattered little.

MAP 7: Main Railways in France, 1914

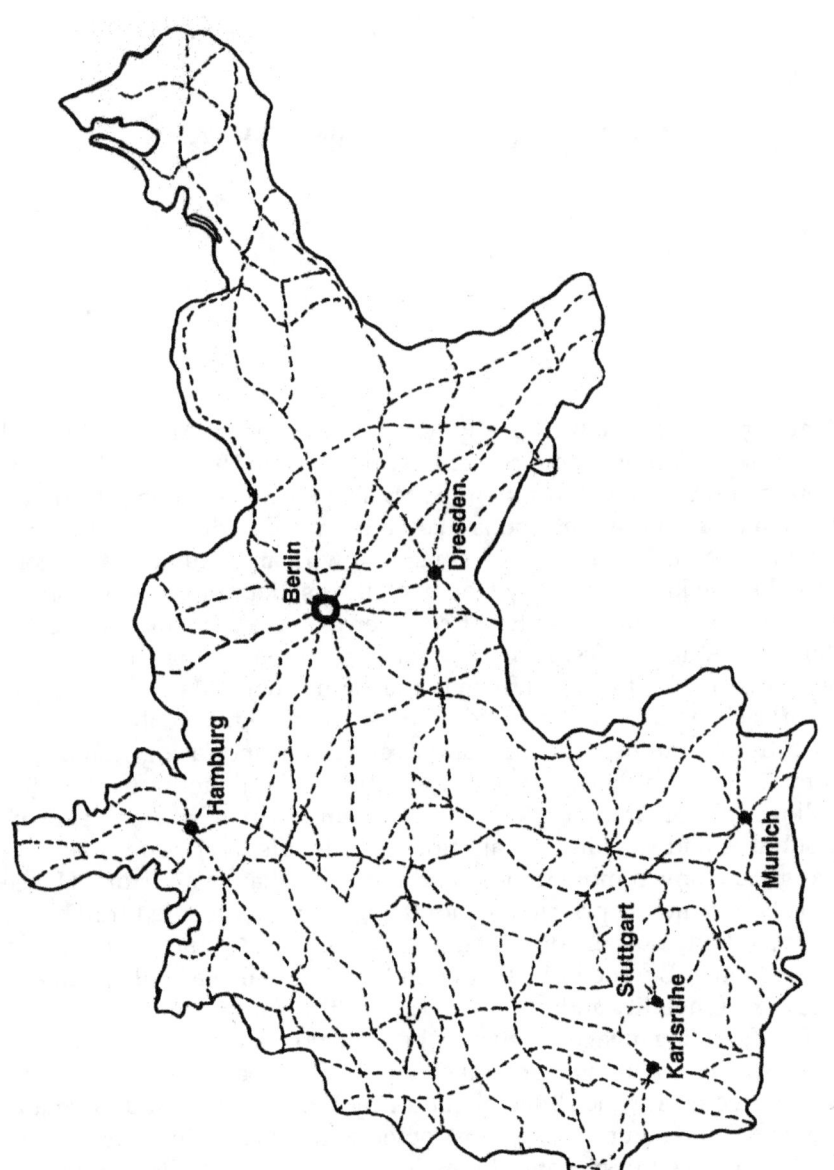

MAP 8: Main Railways in Germany, 1914

Chapter 9

COMPARISONS, 1890–1914

Throughout Europe there really was a Belle Epoque. And it coincided precisely, during the quarter of a century before 1914, with the greatest era of railway transportation. Every major and medium city had a central station, and a metropolis like London, Paris, or Berlin of course boasted several. Thousands of smaller towns and hamlets also constructed some kind of railway stop, usually a squat brick or stone structure that soon became a center of commerce and conviviality. Typically, hotels, restaurants, cafés, and shops clustered around train stations and along the street leading from them to the main square. Meanwhile, as rail networks expanded and travel became democratized, virtually everyone took a train or trolley. In population centers, an increasing number of commuters did so daily, profoundly changing the pattern of urban life by allowing a separation of domicile and employment, thereby spawning suburbs and satellite communities. Foodstuffs, fuels, and manufactured goods moved more rapidly and regularly than ever before. Hence railroads became the principal conduits of an unprecedented traffic that encouraged and sustained industrial growth. If one could have taken a cross-section of Europe in 1910, it would have revealed a civilization at a new peak of mobility and prosperity. It was the railway age.

The flattering image of such a general portrait lacks shadow and nuance. No two nations were alike, and in these pages we particularly need to account for the different routes by which France and Germany approached the summit. The most obvious distinction in their railway industries derived from opposite modes of ownership. In France the private rail companies remained largely intact right up to the Great War; the merger of a small and scattered state network with the Western Railway Company proved to be financially unsuccessful and, if anything, gave public administration a bad name. In Germany, by contrast, the number of privately operated rail lines continued to dwindle after the consolidation of the Prussian state network in the 1880s. Yet this elementary dichotomy does not begin to provide a sufficient explanation of the basic similarities and differences between the two major continental railway systems, which we must now attempt to untangle.

Administrative Organization

One similarity between France and Germany stands out: the failure before 1914 of both to achieve a nationalization of their various regional railway networks. With the collapse of the Freycinet Plan in the 1880s, that conclusion in the French case was perhaps foregone. Yet the financial woes of the private companies led to a renewed onslaught of *rachat* proposals after 1890. In whatever form, whether for partial or total acquisition by the central state of the nation's rail firms, these movements always betrayed an intention to rein in the companies and ultimately to abolish them. The fusion of the faltering Western Railway Company with the meager state network in 1909 was only a token step in that direction, which actually left the remainder of the private sector more secure than before. In Germany a similar measure, the formation of a Prussian-Hessian railway union, initially seemed to foreshadow a nationalization there. Thus the Württemberg project for a wider railway consortium gathered momentum and culminated in the accords reached at the Heidelberg conference in 1904. If implemented, this new organization would have created a central administrative office in Berlin with supervision over freight traffic, the distribution of locomotives and other rolling stock, and the structure of rates. Yet this development also stalled and left only a disappointing retrogression in the final decade before 1914.

As a result, a second similarity was the political and economic retrenchment in both cases of the periphery. Prosperity returned but slowly to France after the war of 1870, and the private companies experienced budgetary difficulty in the 1880s, when they were forced to reduce service and to lay off personnel to lower overhead costs. But they were fortified by the leadership of directors who were determined to defend their firms' autonomy from an undue intrusion of the central state. And the evidence is convincing that they succeeded after 1890 when it came to a number of specifically verifiable issues: the control of rates, the ordering of locomotives, the refusal to grant amnesty to dismissed workers, and so on. State regulatory agencies consequently had only marginal impact on the quotidian operations of the private networks, which remained the basis of the French railway system. Despite the financial turbulence of the 1870s, vigorous German growth resumed in the 1880s and continued with only brief interruptions until the eve of the Great War. In this circumstance the railroads were bound to thrive. Indeed, they became an indispensable source of revenue for the various federated German states and thus the main financial props of their bureaucracies and ruling dynasties.

Such was the case both for Prussia and the four most important medium states. The habitual quarreling among them, which eventually ended hopes for a national railway consortium, was actually a symptom of their vitality and economic viability as autonomous transportation networks. Their independence was further strengthened through internal reforms executed during the prewar years, for which Heinrich von Frauendorfer's administration in Bavaria provided the model. Particularism, not centralism, remained fundamental to German railroads.

Democratization of travel was another common element. Everywhere in Europe the volume of freight and passenger traffic vastly increased. The tendency in France and Germany alike was toward lower fares and rates, hence a thinner profit margin per unit. The resulting greater activity could not fail to increase operational costs for new equipment, fuel supplies, safety regulations, and more personnel. There was no mystery therefore in the severe budgetary constraints that accompanied the growth of railways after 1890, which helps in turn to explain the reform efforts, the disputes over cost-sharing between central and peripheral regimes, and the constant complaints from private companies in France and from state railway administrations in Germany about measures unilaterally adopted by the national government (public health and welfare programs, for example) that automatically raised the level of expenditures for the railroads.

To conduct the sprawling business of large European rail networks required an immense bureaucracy that tended to take on a life of its own. The records of French private companies and of German member states are quite similar insofar as they disclose a beehive of bureaucratic activity and also a certain arrogance among railway administrators that they alone were capable of rational decisions in the daily application of a complex technology. That attitude necessarily bred antagonisms within the political arena, where a multitude of parliamentary, extraparliamentary, and regulatory bodies presumed to control one or another aspect of the railway industry. Given their republican form of government, French politicians were especially prone to foster investigative committees, legislative inquiries, and watchdog agencies such as the CETCF and the CCCF, whose vaguely defined and often overlapping jurisdictions frequently led to conflicts of interest or, worse, to inertia.

Although the political context in imperial Germany was somewhat different, the complexity and contentiousness of would-be regulatory organizations was much the same. As a representative of the executive branch of the national regime, the REA was constantly at odds with both state administrations and parliamentary groups. It was also engaged in jostling aside the VDEV, which could now be considered an anachronistic relic of the distant era before German unification. There was ambiguity as well in the gradually shifting relationship between the Bundesrat and the Reichstag: votes in the former had originally been critical in railway affairs, but several German chancellors (starting with Bismarck) found it increasingly convenient to initiate legislative measures through the latter in order to circumvent objections from delegations of the member states. To all of which can be added the endless disputes, characteristic of France no less than Germany, among ministries competing for leverage and allocations in the normal course of cabinet politics.

The evolution of a large and organized labor force became particularly evident on the French and German railways after 1890. In both countries, the railroad was the largest single employer of workers. The unionization of labor was first legalized in France in the 1880s, and the lapsing of anti-Socialist laws in Germany in 1890 permitted the same freedom. At the same time, national social legislation began to have some visible impact. If that development came sooner and broader in Germany, France likewise began in 1893 to adopt health and welfare bills that moved toward inauguration of an obligatory national pension plan in 1910 (though it was still but partially implemented before 1914). French and German railway administrators had early anticipated the importance of securing the loyalty of their employees through medical and welfare benefits; the programs of private and state companies thus preceded national legislation and were only gradually outflanked. In the meantime, while never exceeding 10 percent of the total railway labor force and always consigned to the bottom of the pay scale, women were employed in ever increasing numbers by French and German companies before the war. Their ability to perform menial tasks at a minimum salary initially made females suitable for hiring to cut overhead, but more and more frequently they were also sought for their useful skills in supporting an expanding railway bureaucracy. In this regard, too, there was ultimately little distinction between French and German labor practices.[1]

A final similarity is worthy of special mention: the crucial role of improving technology. The hard drive of Europe's industry in the nineteenth century was of course the steam engine. But the list of what we might now call software was long and perfectible. A train in the year 1910 bore little resemblance to its precursor of eighty or even forty years earlier, and it ran on a much more extensive system of tracks. Bigger and faster locomotives, more spacious and comfortable passenger cars, sturdier freight wagons, better engineered grades and curves, compressed-air brakes, automatic coupling devices, electric signals, continuous steel rails, mightier bridges and tunnels, more opulent stations—these were some of the significant ameliorations that ensured rapid and reliable transportation to Europeans all across the Continent, regardless of nationality or the norms of railway administrations.

Nevertheless, important differences remained, and to summarize them we must begin with the already stated primary fact that the principles of ownership in France and Germany were divergent. Surely there was an element of truth in the notion that each country had chosen a modus vivendi appropriate to its national circumstance or, as the French liked to say, to the genius of its race. France's long traditions of centralized administration were offset by the instability of its republican political institutions. As one writer has well observed: "Centralization concentrates jurisdictions. It does not concentrate effective power."[2] Certainly it did not in the Third Republic, with its weak presidency, ephemeral cabinets, fractious parliament, and entrenched regional and local interests. Accordingly, liberalism continued to be quintessential to the French way of life and of doing business, an atmosphere in the public realm altogether congenial for the existence of private railway companies. In Germany, although the Kaiser's personal involvement in railway policies was inconsequential, his ceremonial presence throughout this period symbolized a greater sense of stability and continuity. The ruling establishments and bureaucracies of the large member states were relatively secure within a federal structure that left much leeway to states' rights, for which there was no parallel in the French provinces. Autonomous states with their courts and capital cities had always played a prominent role in the German territories, and it was quite fitting that they now sponsored their own state railway networks and were financially sustained by them.

In addition, viewed as national entities, France and Germany displayed a striking discrepancy in the magnitude of their railway systems before 1914. If the statistics of track length ceased to be a reliable rule of thumb for scale, they enable us to scan back across the century and to establish a crude measurement of growth (see Table 17). Prior to the mid-nineteenth century, as we see, Germany gained an early lead from a frenzy of wildcat building by private entrepreneurs and independent states at a time when more tightly enforced French engineering standards inhibited such initial rapid progress. Under the Second Empire of Napoleon III, however, the French splurged on their railroads and regained virtual parity before 1870. But thereafter the balance shifted decisively back to Germany, starting with the Reich's postwar annexation of Alsatian tracks. While legitimately boasting of better quality (a higher percentage of double tracks, for instance), the Third Republic was nonetheless incapable of matching the irrepressible vitality of imperial Germany. Most remarkable in this pattern is the almost precise correlation by 1910 of the numbers for track length and demography. One needs only to add a comma and three zeros to obtain nearly identical figures: the French nation was hovering just below forty million citizens, whereas the German population slightly exceeded sixty million. Insisting on the near equality of kilometers per capita (as some contemporaries did) is fatuous, because it obfuscates France's demographic inferiority and relative lack of dynamism. Absolute size matters, and the truth was that Germany as a whole possessed the largest railway system in Europe and, except for Belgium, also the densest.[3] An approximation of railway vehicles circulating on French and German tracks will serve to clinch the point (see Table 18).

These marked differences in the modes of ownership and the size of national rail systems importantly affected profitability. Unfortunately,

TABLE 17: Comparative Growth of National Railway Systems, 1830–1910 (kilometers)

Year	France	Germany
1830	31	—
1840	410	469
1850	2915	5856
1860	9167	11,089
1870	15,544	18,876
1880	23,089	33,838
1890	33,280	42,869
1900	38,109	51,678
1910	40,484	61,209

Source: B. R. Mitchell, *European Historical Statistics*, pp. 581–84.

TABLE 18: Total Rolling Stock, 1914

	Locomotives	Passenger Cars	Freight Wagons
France	14,000	33,000	344,000
Germany	27,040	56,030	561,250

Source: Ernest Protheroe, *The Railways of the World* (London, 1914), p. 534.

despite the episodic evidence already cited about fluctuations of the gross income, expenditures, and net earnings of separate railway firms, it is in the end impossible to calculate precisely the aggregate of their profits during many decades. There were simply too many private and state companies with various bookkeeping procedures that were too often inconsistent or altered over time.[4] Yet such infinite complexity should not preclude two observations of obvious probative value. First, it is surely unobjectionable to assume that the higher the volume of traffic per kilometer of track, the greater the profit. An advantage therefore went to the more industrialized nation, and that was unquestionably Germany. Second, the decentralized administrative organization of private railway companies favored individual stockholders to the detriment of the nation-state, a fact often pointed out by contemporary critics of the French system. By allowing and indeed guaranteeing the distribution of a major share of railway income to private investors, the French state forfeited some immediate returns, which were thereby postponed to a distant future when, the arrangement was, the companies would meekly cede their lapsed concessions to the government. Such renunciation of short-term rewards was almost unknown in Germany after 1890, because state ownership there meant that most profits were steered directly into government coffers, whence they could be promptly reallocated to bolster ruling houses, state bureaucracies, and the railway administrations themselves. The combination of this pair of structural factors makes the conclusion inescapable that Germany's railway networks rested on a more comfortable financial basis, at least when appraised as a total interlocking national system of transportation.

Labor relations, though similar in some regards, varied in France and Germany due to the unlike status of workers under the different forms of ownership. French railway employees were hired by private companies that were forever at pains to limit government regulation of their industry. The result was that French *cheminots* and office personnel were able to act like those holding jobs with other industrial firms. Specifically, they could—and after 1890 they did—affiliate in large numbers with labor syndicates, including some that hinted broadly about a forthcoming general strike. Company managers consequently found themselves in a quandary, hoping to maintain discipline in a public service crucial to national prosperity and defense, and yet wishing to guard their prerogatives as private firms in hiring and firing personnel without government interference. This ambiguity provided fertile soil for the 1910 railway strike and for the politically divisive amnesty debate that ensued from it. For German railway employees the situation was otherwise. Without ambiguity, they were hired by and worked for state agencies; moreover, the member states were decisive in adopting plans to deploy military force against any who dared to strike and thereby subject themselves to conscription and court-martial. Unlike the French, German regimes were also preemptive in forbidding the membership of railway workers in Socialist groups suspected of stirring up strike agitation. With a larger, more organized, and more disciplined labor force, German state railway companies encountered no major insurrectionary movements in the ranks before 1918.

We may conclude this survey with reference to a difference perhaps more significant than any other: the relative capacity of the French and German locomotive industries before 1914. Efforts by the republican government in France to regulate this vital sector of the nation's industry were largely ineffectual. Private railway firms remained at liberty to negotiate with suppliers, to obtain bids and sign contracts as they deemed proper, and to inform state officials whenever they chose. Erratic and often unpredictably reduced demand before 1905 retarded the growth of French manufacturers, whose average annual rate of production at that time barely reached five hundred locomotives. Not only was this level meager, it permitted no effective standardization, thereby preventing the sale of French engines at competitive prices in the European market. Hence, the exportation of locomotives from France in the prewar years was confined almost solely to its colonies. Germany capitalized meanwhile on French weakness. Within the Reich, Prussia and the medium states each had in effect their own locomotive manufacturing plants, though privately owned, which necessarily dealt on a regular basis with government regulators, and they did so within a constantly expanding economy. Steadily rising demand, techniques of mass production, lower prices per unit, higher rates of output and of export were the results. By 1913 German productive capacity rose to nearly 1800 engines a year, of which at least one-third was available for export.[5] We have already measured the consequences when French railway administrations were forced, in defiance of political pressure in Paris, to turn to German suppliers after 1905 in order to meet suddenly accelerating needs for new locomotives. It seems only logical to surmise that a difference in the structure of enterprise, rather than Germany's alleged malevolent practices of dumping, provided the real basis of an uneven commercial rivalry.[6]

Economic Competition

It is well to beware what the philosopher Alfred North Whitehead once called "the fallacy of misplaced concreteness," that is, the rhetorically convenient notion that collective nouns can become historical agents (as in a textbook: the Enlightenment produced Montesquieu, Voltaire, and Rousseau). There is a manifest danger in any label, which is evident enough in the putative contrast between France's "long stagnation" and Germany's "take-off" at the end of the nineteenth century. While they contain an obvious grain of truth, such generalizations are no substitute for an analysis that remains at the same time respectful of complexity and skeptical about the precision of statistics. Thus alerted, we may begin here with the assumption that an economic gap had opened between France and Germany by 1890 and that it widened thereafter.

In the face of this fundamental discrepancy of scale in the general performance of the two economies before 1914, similarities in the commercial role of railroads are bound to pale. Yet we may list some of them quickly. It was true everywhere in Europe, for example, that railways were by far the preferred and economically most significant mode of transportation. They received a major share of capital investment during the century, and their tonnage per kilometer outstripped roads or canals. Accordingly, in both the French and German cases, pressure emanated from the central authority of the state to make more intensive use of rails and to reduce commercial shipping rates on them. Such governmental pleas to simplify the rate structure and to lower costs of exchange could increasingly be cloaked as patriotism in the name of a growing national interest to meet international competition. In the meantime, however, elements on the respective peripheries were alarmed by the menace of encroachment on their independence. The French private companies and the German member states arose in like manner to resist curtailment of their rights (as, for instance, in the defeat of the Augagneur motion in France and the Bassermann bill in Germany). In neither circumstance, therefore, did international negotiations on economic matters have much impact on railway commerce, despite the many Bern conferences and countless diplomatic dispatches over decades. The basic reason was simple: the inability of central regimes to conclude binding accords for their constituent parts. Instead, whatever commercial regulation was achieved in Europe before 1914 resulted largely from bilateral or multilateral agreements among regional railway networks, not from agencies of national government.

Contemporaries were quite aware of the difference in magnitude between the two economies, which was clearly reflected in railway statistics. At the outset of this period, during the five years between 1892 and 1896, computations showed that the tonnage of freight shipped by rail on German tracks rose from 244,700,000 to 270,600,000, an increase of 10.6 percent; whereas for France those numbers were 103,200,000 to 108,800,000, a boost of 5.4 percent. Correspondingly, annual gross income from such traffic in Germany went from 963,000,000 to 1,071,300,000 Marks, an increment of 11.2 percent; and in France, from 554,300,000 to 576,700,000 Marks, a rise of 4 percent. When calculated per kilometer of track, Germany's total net growth was 6.6 percent, France's 1.8 percent.[7] These figures might be suspect were they not generally corroborated by more modern statisticians who have labored to work out the aggregate national output of railway services. By 1910 Germany's freight shipments by rail represented 56,400,000 tons a kilometer; France's, 21,500,000. The intensity of passenger travel was also far greater in Germany, approaching a ratio of almost two to one.[8] As noted above, the capacity of Germany's locomotive industry grew before 1914 to about four times that of France. In the meanwhile, one of the indispensable components of the railway industry, coal production, measured six times larger in Germany: 206 million tons were extracted there in 1907, only 37 million in France.[9]

In July 1914, just a few weeks before the war began, the *Revue générale des chemins de fer* attempted to draft a balance sheet of credits and debits on the railroads since 1895. It reported that the average gross annual income for all French railway companies for the years 1895 to 1910 amounted to 39 million francs, the expenses to 29 million. For Germany, those statistics were 128 million and 98 million francs. Allowances made for fluctuations in the market and for the inexactitude of these numbers, they suggest an absolute level of commercial activity in Germany nearly three times that in France, as well as a higher degree of profitability.[10] If further research is able to refine these approximations, it is unlikely to modify the conclusion that a stronger German economy was much better served by its railway system—or, inversely, that a less potent French economy set stricter limits on the expansion of its railroads. The liberal French economist Paul Leroy-Beaulieu best summed it up when he commented that, although France was actually enjoying a "rather great prosperity," his nation's performance was still modest compared to that of Germany "because the French population is less numerous and less dense, because our soil is less rich in mines, because our industry is much less active and our commerce less frequent."[11]

Inclusive as it is, that statement omits one further matter crucial for a comparison—namely, the extent to which the rail networks of the two countries were integrated into the broader European economy. Such a problem does not allow statistical precision, but we can gain a firm notion of its dimensions by observing activity on the Continent's main commercial routes. In southern Europe, the greatest influence on trade patterns was the St. Gotthard Tunnel, whose volume of freight much exceeded that of Mt. Cenis. Long and frustrating delays in the negotiations over access to a third main alpine thoroughfare via the Simplon Tunnel left that imbalance unchanged before 1914, thus assuring Germany's dominance in commerce with Italy. One qualification must be added: Marseille nonetheless remained the major port on the Mediterranean, challenged but not displaced by Genoa.[12]

Northern harbors were another issue. French ports there were losing ground year by year to Belgium, Holland, and Germany (see Table 19). Seen in a longer perspective during the three decades between the war of 1870 and the end of the century, the retardation of northern French ports is even more apparent: Hamburg increased its incoming freight by over 6 million tons, Antwerp by 5.5, and Rotterdam by 5.3; whereas Le Havre and Dunkerque each gained less than a million tons. Even Bremerhaven, with about half the tonnage of Le Havre in 1870, had drawn virtually even by 1900.[13] A single telling detail is indicative: in 1897 Bremerhaven received 1,400,000 bales of raw cotton for further shipment by rail, Le Havre but 800,000 bales.[14] In 1904, according to the *Journal des Transports*, the port of Hamburg was utilized by 14,843 ships carrying 9,610,794 tons of freight; Le Havre's count was 2219 vessels with 2,405,472 tons.[15]

This global difference in the scale of commerce, inevitably a factor for the railroads, also affected the general structure of the economy. Through its own ports and those of the Lowlands, Germany was heavily engaged in international commerce, France much less so. This suggests an important transmutation: Germany was becoming specialized in finished goods,

TABLE 19: Tonnage Entering North European Ports, 1891–1896

	1891	1895	1896
Hamburg	5,800,000	6,250,000	6,500,000
Antwerp	4,750,000	5,350,000	5,800,000
Rotterdam	3,050,000	4,200,000	4,400,000
Le Havre	3,120,000	2,800,000	2,780,000
Dunkerque	1,520,000	1,350,000	1,500,000

Source: "La situation commerciale des ports français du Nord," *Journal des Transports*, 27 Feb. 1897.

whereas the percentage of industrial products in the French export trade was declining. In the 1870s only half of German exports were manufactured articles, but by 1914 the figure was nearly three-fourths of the total. Metal products and machines had been barely 6 percent of German exports in the 1870s, but they accounted for over 20 percent in the prewar years.[16] The overwhelming German lead in the export of steam engines has already been noted. The other side of that coin was Germany's importation of lighter goods such as foodstuffs (see Table 20). These numbers confirm that France continued to possess a largely self-sufficient agriculture whose produce moved for the most part on interior railway networks. Germany was in the meantime becoming a formidable export-import nation, more highly integrated into the European economy and, as a consequence, more dependent on water and rail transportation across international boundaries.

This image is reinforced by comparing the relative growth of the French and German merchant marines. During the 1890s, Germany surpassed France in total tonnage of freight ships (not to mention its military fleet), creating a "difficult" circumstance for the French Compagnie Transatlantique. Before 1900, Germany's Hamburg-Amerika line and Norddeutscher Lloyd of Bremen were the two largest navigation firms in Europe. "As for our French companies," confessed the ever vigilant *Journal des Transports*, "they arrive well behind."[17] Once again, by statistical criteria with direct relevance to railroads, Germany was widening the gap (see Table 21). By themselves such figures may be inconclusive. But they fit into a consistent pattern of European commerce. At the climax of the railway age—in scale, in structure, and in degree of economic integration—Germany was gaining the upper hand as a large industrialized nation.

The comparative history of continental Europe's transport systems during the prewar years presents an arresting paradox. Within the Kaiserreich, patriotic groups such as the Pan-German League, their eyes fixed on international diplomatic alignments, did not cease to express

TABLE 20: Imports of Perishable Foods, 1897–1907 (tons)

	FRANCE		GERMANY	
	1897	1907	1897	1907
Butter	6,500	6,500	9,000	39,000
Eggs	13,500	31,000	107,000	148,000
Meat	5,000	2,000	15,000	14,500
Fish	17,000	34,000	43,000	128,000
Vegetables	13,000	22,000	97,000	208,000
Fruits	19,000	40,000	150,000	305,000

Source: "Le traffic international des denrées périssables," *Journal des Transports*, 5 Feb. 1910.

TABLE 21: Merchant Steamships, 1899–1914

	1899–1900		1913–1914	
	Vessels	Tons	Vessels	Tons
France	526	517,000,000	692	1,104,000,000
Germany	900	1,167,000,000	1510	2,853,000,000

Source: "La flotte commerciale du monde," *Journal des Transports*, 16 May 1914.

worried complaints about their country's "encirclement." Yet seen from the standpoint of railways, it was rather France that was isolated. Trains carrying goods to and from Germany passed all across Central Europe, traveling over trade lanes that stretched from lowland ports as well as Hamburg to Genoa, from Strasbourg to Berlin, Vienna, and beyond. Relatively speaking, France's ports and private railway companies had far less contact with the rest of the mainland. Tourism aside, by 1914 it was Berlin, not Paris, that had become the commercial center of Europe.

Military Strategy

Strategy and the deployment of railroads were synonymous for the French and German general staffs and justification enough for the huge sums spent on them by both. Apart from the common denominator of strategic construction projects on either side of the Rhine, there were many other similarities in military affairs. One was the sticky problem of transition from peacetime to wartime. French private companies and German member states had vast civilian administrations that were adamantly determined to guard their prerogatives to operate separate transportation networks without undue interference or disruption from military authorities until the day of mobilization. Yet, at the same time, the army had a stake in ensuring the readiness of railways to execute military orders and in preparing their takeover by plenipotentiaries once the ultimate signal for war was given. These competing interests often led to friction that inexorably increased as strategic planners began to press for a scheme of early warning, that is, the implementation of stages of "political tension" or "imminent danger" prior to a call for full mobilization. Whereas military leaders constantly fumbled with these details, civilian authorities complained that they were kept uninformed about the army's secret procedures that were designed to seize control of military operations at the earliest possible moment.

Everyone could agree at least that the railroads were crucial. But if so, who was to bear the expense of their construction? We have seen how this issue of cost-sharing provoked endless debates over many decades in Paris and Berlin alike. In both capitals, formulas were ceaselessly devised, modified, dropped, or revived in an effort to secure the cooperation and financial participation of the various rail companies. A fortiori, in the absence of a truly national system, they would need to build and operate whatever tracks were deemed militarily indispensable. All of which became more acutely painful as both the French and German governments experienced some budgetary constrictions in the prewar years. The fiscal difficulties in France developed largely from a sputtering economy and the felt need to keep pace with a larger and more potent neighbor. Germany's problems stemmed from a basic decision around 1900 to compete with English sea power. For the railways, the resulting strains proved to be much the same in terms of obtaining adequate investment capital; meeting cost overruns; and fulfilling demands for new equipment, improved safety, higher salaries, increased health and welfare benefits, and the rest.

Another commonality was espionage. For military planners much depended on what the other side was doing, and an inordinate amount of energy was expended on trying to discover the enemy's intentions. Worries about "highly active French spying" in Germany were closely mirrored by xenophobia in France and elaborate projects to round up or intern all suspected informers (hence the infamous enemies' lists of the Dreyfus era).[18] Both governments in fact joined in the chase after foreigners, who were often kept under surveillance and sometimes excluded from sensitive posts. The documentary record is clear that neither France nor Germany was very successful in obtaining hard data on the strategic plans of the other. French miscalculations about the Schlieffen Plan have already been noted. As for Germany's General Staff, General von Moltke admitted in 1911 that his intelligence officers were "still tapping in the dark."[19] A later study disclosed that a German spy within the directorate of the Eastern Railway Company had kept Berlin well informed until 1895, but thereafter sources were "mainly inaccurate." The Prussian military attaché in Paris was unable to supply details on the French Plan XIV in 1897, and subsequent German assumptions about General Joffre's offensive inclinations proved "largely wrong." In those days, the only reliable guide to the strategic objectives of a putative opponent, it seemed, was a direct observation of where rail connections, tunnels, and bridges were being built.[20]

One might assume that the military leadership would have been eager to take advantage of every innovation in technology in order to gain an advantage. Such was decidedly not the case before 1914; instead, it is proper to speak of technological retardation. The first hint of it was a reluctance in the 1890s to rely on field telephones, considered too complicated and unreliable to replace the telegraph.[21] Then came the possibility of electrification of rail lines, dramatized by German test runs of over 200 kilometers an hour in 1903. The French also experimented with electrical engines and meanwhile completed a few connections without any military value. As in Germany, and for the same reasons noted, French tests were usually confined to mountainous regions close to sources of water power yet far from the front. As a consequence, military convoys of both countries continued to move at a measured pace of about 30 kilometers an hour, slow but sure.[22] Likewise, air power remained in its infancy, especially after the French Minister of War Alexandre Millerand determined in 1912 that fighter planes, however thrilling their solo maneuvers, would be unsuitable to mount bombing raids on targets in Germany. They would be deployed mainly for reconnaissance. Bridges over the Rhine would thus be safe, and their principal use as before was primarily to convey trains with steam engines.[23] Also, trucks were thought too slow and clumsy, forever breaking down and frequently tearing up roadways unadapted for heavy loads. Railways were still the answer.[24]

Comparatively, what of war-readiness? That is a question, of course, to which an armed conflict is the only precise response. The military escalation had a predictable effect between 1890 and 1914: both nations were highly armed with well-equipped mass armies. In weaponry there was no technological retardation, judging from the development of rifles and machine guns, new French light artillery, and German heavy artillery.[25] Yet neither side was fully prepared, assuredly not for the protracted slaughter that was to ensue. Trains could be counted on to move men and supplies to the frontier. But then what?

That three-word query leads to a consideration of differences. First and most obvious among them was the offensive nature of German strategy versus the essentially defensive stance of France. Essentially, one must say, because allowance should be made for Joffre's belated visions of a bold stroke into Belgium or, if not, a thrust into Alsace. Yet the truth was that many years of planning and hundreds of millions of francs had already been expended for the transportation of troops from the French interior to special unloading platforms at stations in the territory of the Eastern Railway Company. What is striking about the strategic planning of the French and German general staffs was their compatibility. Both sides recognized that the line of fortifications on France's eastern frontier would make a German invasion unlikely there. No rail lines had been constructed through the Vosges mountain range. In all probability, an incursion would therefore occur north of Verdun. But for technological reasons—specifically, more powerful artillery shells and a thick webbing of recent railway connections—the redoubts in that region would be indefensible, and the French consequently moved in the prewar years to ensure the military declassification of them. In reality, French planners thereby invited the Germans to do exactly what the Schlieffen Plan prescribed: attack the French left flank. Still, the great uncertainty was the extent of the German sweep. These matters are well documented: Schlieffen's grandiose conception, Moltke's revisions, French underestimates and foolish projects for taking the offensive. All the while, a basic geographic fact remained: the assignment of French railroads would be far more delimited, whereas the greater distances required for the German army transports would stretch their capacity to the limit and beyond, once they crossed into Belgium and headed for Paris.

Numbers do not always accord, and it is usually advisable for historians to admit it when faced with statistical lacunae. Often military authorities hid allocations for railways, and finance ministers became adept at manipulating budgets. We do, however, have a record of serious attempts by the Second Bureau of the French Ministry of War to compare aggregate military expenditures by France and Germany from 1875 to 1912. According to this contemporary study, the Third Republic was actually outspending the Reich in the 1870s—at a time when the French were forced to rebuild their entire army and system of fortifications—but German increases, measured by expenditures both per capita and per unit (men and supplies), decisively tipped the balance before 1900. Thereupon the weight of German superiority mounted, and a notable gap in total combat forces (*effectifs*) and funding existed on the eve of the war.[26] This conclusion is buttressed by the Second Bureau's estimates of annual average expenditures in the three decades before 1910, which indicated that since 1890 the Germans annually invested more than twice as much as the French (see Table 22). The literal accuracy of such global figures can only be treated with caution, not to say disbelief, but we cannot overlook that their relative proportion accords with concurrent statistics of a much more vibrant German economy. In particular, the dissimilarity indicated here in military allocations matches the known differences in magnitude of track length, passenger travel, and freight loads carried by rail. If republican France were left alone to face imperial Germany, we may surmise, the French would have been outmatched.

Another gnarled issue with direct relevance to the military role of railways was the different structure of French and German high commands. Ever since the 1860s, under the first Helmuth von Moltke, the German General Staff remained a state within a state, whose chief had direct access to the Kaiser, recognized by the imperial constitution as the supreme commander. Yet in peacetime the General Staff was restricted mostly to planning and cajoling, while political and fiscal affairs rested in the hands of the Reich's chancellor and the Prussian cabinet. Thus, the Minister of War also had a key part to play before

TABLE 22: Annual Average Real Military Expenses, 1880–1910
(millions of francs)

	1881–1890	1891–1900	1901–1910
France	123.6	73.3	70.5
Germany	132.9	154.0	153.5

Source: "Comparaison des dépenses militaires des effectifs en France et en Allemagne," August 1912, SHAT Vincennes, 7 N 673.

1914 in dealing with officials of the Reich, his colleagues in the Prussian Ministry of Finance and the Ministry of Public Works, as well as the regimes of the other member states. Within this complex arrangement, railroads received attention from all sides in the bewildering combinations that we have examined. Clarity would not be achieved until the day of a declaration of war, when the General Staff (with its running dog, the Reichseisenbahnamt) would take immediate charge, civilian administrators would step aside, and all German railroads would in effect be requisitioned for the "national defense."[27]

Conditions in France were otherwise, befitting its republican form of state. There the Etat-Major was located *within* the Ministry of War, which was manifestly the seat of military authority. With the noteworthy exceptions of Freycinet and Millerand, the minister was usually a military man. However, throughout the Third Republic he sat in a civilian cabinet—including Public Works, which oversaw the nation's railway enterprises—that answered only to parliament. Moreover, unlike Germany, the fact that most railroads were owned by private companies meant that an additional layer of political negotiation with civilian administrators was necessary, further complicating the task of the central state. This configuration was such that small-group dynamics were crucial in the distribution of power, which frequently shifted with the turnover of cabinets and personalities.

No French generalissimo gained the independence of a Moltke or had such direct influence over prewar strategic decisions. We saw that a vigorous premier like Georges Clemenceau was able on occasion to face down his military cohort, and later Raymond Poincaré proved more than a match for General Joffre in blocking the latter's proposal of a surprise preemptive strike into Belgium. The consolidation of the entire French military command structure under Joffre after 1911 has led one historian to speculate that his position became "actually stronger than that of his counterpart in aristocratic, militaristic Germany, the younger Moltke"; whereas another expert has dismissed that notion as "simply ludicrous."[28] Because there is no meter for measuring the relative strength of generals, it is perhaps best to leave the question open. More important is an understanding of the complicated distinctions between the two systems of strategic planning and of the many conflicting pressures with which Joffre and Moltke had to deal. For different reasons, each was somewhat limited in his ability to control peacetime railway bureaucracies. Once the guns of August were rolled into place, nonetheless, both could take full command of all of the private and state rail networks.

One final question is inescapable. Which of the two nations was more responsible for a conflict that in its initial phase, at least, resembled nothing more than a second Franco-Prussian war?[29] The history of railways does not afford an easy response to that issue, and, of course, this is not a place to unwrap the wearisome war-guilt debate. Rather, from a military standpoint, railways may simply be added to a lengthy list of German statistical advantages—beginning with demography and the economy—as the two powers squared off for a massive duel. As the weaker of them, France understandably grasped for the support of allies and thereby contributed to a hardening of political lines and a heightening of international tensions in the decades before 1914. Yet the record gives no sign of an immediate provocation from Paris. It was not that the French could afford to wait but that their long-term railway planning left them with no realistic alternative.[30] German strategic conceptions, by contrast, were based essentially on the extensive Prussian state railway network. The logic of both geography and existing German transportation facilities dictated a northern route for any invasion of France, whereas the tracks of the southern member states were more apt for supporting defensive positions on Germany's left flank. Despite their economic prowess in Central Europe and the commercial integration of their railroads on the Continent, German commanders felt themselves encircled and feared that the balance of military power in a two-front war would soon tilt against them. Germany thus became the aggressor in the West, not because political circumstances necessitated that action but because the Schlieffen Plan posited it.[31] Accordingly, in the first days of August 1914, trains were everywhere readied for departure to the battlefields.

Epilogue

From Trains to Trenches

The railway war lasted only a few weeks in the late summer of 1914, and it was inconclusive. After a brief period of "political tension," word spread on 31 July of the German declaration of an "imminent danger of war." The French immediately began to gather freight wagons, and on that same day orders were issued by the Etat-Major for a covering operation, to go into effect the next evening, during which some troops would be moved by rail to positions on the border as a temporary forward line of defense. The signal for a general mobilization was announced on the first day of August. This action was formally to commence on the second, but in fact the French machinery of war was already set in motion: "All means of transportation ... were at that moment requisitioned by the Ministry of War and all personnel subordinated to the military command."[1] This statement by the executive committee of the Eastern Railway Company is unanimously confirmed by the records of the other large private firms. The PLM: "The service of our network was placed altogether under the authority of the Ministry of War." The PO: "From the first day of mobilization our network was transferred entirely under the authority of the Ministry of War." And, rather pathetically, the Northern Company: "In reality, operation of the network no longer belongs to us," since the military took charge "in the most absolute manner and from every point of view."[2] In sum, the administrative autonomy of the private companies ceased forthwith, and each was placed under the control of a four-man "network committee" (*commission du réseau*) composed of an officer of the Etat-Major, a regional army commander, the current director of the rail company, and one of his technical advisers.[3] If the roster suggested a military-civilian parity, that impression was false. France was divided into two strategic sectors: one on the northeastern frontier under the direct command of the generalissimo and his staff (*zone des armées*) and another to the southwest under the Ministry of War (*zone de l'intérieur*). Unambiguously, as never before, authority over the railroads now resided in the hands of the central state and military officials, a difference from the prewar years like the day before and the day after an immense explosion.[4]

In the meantime, the story in Germany was essentially the same, just as everyone knew it would be. As late as 30 July the Reich's government was still awaiting the outcome of developments in Vienna, delaying a declaration of "imminent danger" because it meant that a full mobilization was certain to follow.[5] So it did. Advanced German commando units crossed into Luxemburg and Belgium on 4 August and moved quickly to capture the fortress of Liège in the Meuse Valley. By 20 August they had entered Brussels and besieged Namur, the last major bastion before the French border. On the home front long-planned mobilization procedures were put into operation, directed by the military plenipotentiaries who effectively displaced civilian railway directorates. By 6 August 550 railway convoys a day were crossing the Rhine, carrying in all more than 3 million troops in 11,000 trains.[6] The success of the German offensive depended on rapidity of execution, and the army authorities were sometimes admittedly overzealous and overbearing. Still, according to the explanation offered to Paul Breitenbach, it was much better under the circumstances to have a single officer in charge rather than to suffer long delays because of bickering. Several complaints were lodged by state railway administrators, but they were sure to slack off as the German armies pressed forward.[7] As could be anticipated, the Reichseisenbahnamt was much more in evidence, at long last able to overrule ministers and functionaries of the member states as it attempted to implement orders from the General Staff and the Ministry of War. That the REA could truly claim to speak for the entire national transportation system, notably in demanding rate cuts for freight shipments, represented a "decisive change."[8] Like France, Germany thus experienced a sudden transformation, not a slow transition. The war had abruptly broken an impasse of decades over the issue of nationalization.

Well before the end of August, both sides had achieved a virtually complete mobilization and concentration of their combat troops. Networks of the French companies, in what became a stock phrase, performed their duties "with remarkable order and precision."[9] True, in the prewar years Germany may have outspent and outconstructed France, but the French had built well enough, and their forces were in place by 19 August, that is, within three weeks. Thereafter, aside from Joffre's abortive offensive into Alsace-Lorraine, French trains served mainly to ferry soldiers and supplies to the front, then to bring the wounded and dead back to the rear, in what soon became an interminable war of attrition.[10] The German situation was somewhat different insofar as the incursion into Belgium created logistic problems unfaced by the French. The Belgians countered the advance with disruptions, withdrawing locomotives (thereby forcing the Prussian state network to operate its own engines on foreign tracks), blocking tunnels, detonating mined bridges, destroying switches and signals at strategic railway crossings. Such hostile measures, then continued by the French, cost the German armies precious time, requiring as they did days or weeks to repair damaged installations, despite the best efforts of 26,000 German construction workers deployed for the purpose. As a consequence, distances between railheads and the front lines lengthened to as much as twenty miles before the end of August and more than a hundred miles by mid-September.[11] For the German invasionary forces, too, railways ceased after the initial weeks of warfare to be crucial except to carry provisions into the general area of combat. In France, after the German retreat from the river Ourcq in early September, the following stalemate on the Marne, and the hectic race to the sea, the front became a war of mud rather than movement. The opening planned phase of rail transport ended; the rest was immobility and improvisation. The experience of millions of men on both sides was therefore literally to pass from trains to trenches. After a few hours of journey in a railway coach and a prolonged exhausting march on foot, they were likely to spend subsequent months standing in place, facing a wall of dirt.[12]

As the war proceeded, it became ever clearer that the very existence of the private railway firms in France was in jeopardy. Their finances became chaotic and alarmingly deficitary. In the short term, the heaviest burden fell on the Eastern Railway Company, which in early August 1914 requested with "extreme urgency" a state subsidy to offset the astronomical costs of heavy military traffic incurred without any compensating commercial income. But a special allocation of 2 million francs was only an inadequate stopgap, and the budgetary pain mounted.[13] Gross receipts of the Northern Company were off 95 million francs in 1914 alone, and thereafter the German military occupation created a virtual hiatus of four years in its commercial operations.[14] A report to the transportation committee of the Chamber of Deputies in 1917 summarized the disaster of the French railway enterprises and showed that in 1912 the private companies together earned a net profit of 19 million francs, whereas the state network ran a deficit of 87 million. Thus the entire national railway system operated that year at a loss of 68 million. In 1913 it was 80 million in arrears; in 1914, 356.4 million; in 1915, 370.5 million; and in 1916, 372.5 million—over a billion francs in accumulated debts during the first three years of the war![15]

This ruinous spiral was accompanied by other symptoms that the companies were losing control of their destiny. On 3 August 1914, the eve of the German attack, the directors of all the private firms were convened in an emergency evening session at the Ministry of Public Works, where they were informed of Raymond Poincaré's personal request for the reinstatement of railway workers dismissed in the 1910 strike. In order to assure a unanimous parliamentary vote on war credits, despite their reiterated misgivings about a negative impact on discipline of the workforce, the assembled executives agreed to make "a supreme concession" to the president's wishes for amnesty.[16] Within a fortnight, moreover, it became obvious that the entire personnel of the companies had been "militarized since the beginning of mobilization" and that the companies could no longer hope to set regulations on hours or wages.[17] For his part, Minister of War Alexandre Millerand claimed in 1915 to enjoy "the most complete harmony" with the companies, but he made no secret that the basis of their cooperation with the government was a mutual recognition that "the necessities of national defense" must have "absolute priority."[18]

At the end of the war, an attempt was made to reestablish the *status quo ante bellum* of railway administration. Yet a simultaneous legislative proposal for the nationalization of the companies, introduced by the Socialist Albert Thomas, contended that the prewar crises of the French railway system were "endemic" and that the war had only revealed its inherent weakness.[19] The stinging truth of that judgment could scarcely be gainsaid, in spite of hesitations and protests to the contrary, and the interwar years consequently proved to be a time of "nationalization before the fact," as one well-informed author has appropriately entitled his treatment of the demise of the French private railway companies between 1914 and 1937.[20]

The war had similar negative effects on the rail networks of the German member states. Understandably, with the additional strain of providing free transportation for a mass army and its supplies, overhead quickly and vastly exceeded income. For state finance ministries, disaggregating military expenses from others became moot and compiling statistical tables dubious.[21] Given that the entire nation was placed under the supreme command of the German General Staff, computations of cost-sharing between the Reich and its member states also became problematical, nay impossible. Many construction projects classified in the prewar years as urgent were now deferred, though the completion of several more Rhine bridges remained a priority.[22]

It followed from the conditions of wartime that the issue of a national railway consortium should be reopened. Old political configurations soon reappeared: Württemberg and Baden adopted a "friendly position," whereas Bavaria and Saxony were "completely disinclined" and maintained that a unified national rail system was "totally excluded."[23] But the slide toward centralism in the name of national defense was inexorable. The time had finally arrived, wrote one nostalgic observer in 1916, to realize Bismarck's vision of a single imperial railway administration that would serve "the overwhelming interests of the Reich."[24] The Reichseisenbahnamt needed little further prompting to take its cue, and during the final two years of the war it moved to create a uniform national rate structure, the same goal that had been so elusive before 1914.[25] The military defeat of Germany, the armistice of November 1918, and the suppression of ensuing revolutionary insurrections left the fate of railroads to framers of the Weimar constitution. They found no difficulty in drafting an article of nationalization. Accordingly, after the first day of April 1920, all German railway networks formally passed under the Reich's new Ministry of Transportation.[26]

The Great War not only doomed the semi-autonomous railway companies of the nineteenth century to extinction, it also brought the end of the railway age. After 1914, the prewar spell of technological retardation was broken. Steam power was increasingly displaced by internal combustion and jet engines, converting the twentieth century into an epoch of automobiles and airplanes. Trains continued to roll, of course, but they no longer enjoyed a monopoly of the most advanced technology of transportation.[27] Electrification proved to be slow (only 3 percent of German rail tracks were operated with electrical current by 1930). We know that the development of high-speed electrical locomotives in the late twentieth century (the TGV in France, the ICE in Germany) has allowed a technological comeback, but trains and tracks now represent no more than one element among several in integrated national transportation systems. If some of the romance of railway travel remains, its commercial supremacy is forever gone.

Who won the Great Train Race? By almost any standard the answer is certainly Germany. Yet the irony of the First World War was that it did not matter in the outcome because railways were no longer decisive. After absorbing the initial shock of an invasion, France survived. And once the Germans had expended their superior strength as a railway power, the advantage shifted to the French, whose three major allies had in common that they were not linked by rail to the European heartland: Russia (because of its broad track gauge), Great Britain, and eventually the United States. Their combined weight was more than enough to offset Germany's military and industrial might. After a full century, the Great Train Race had finally run its course.

LIST OF ABBREVIATIONS

Archives

AN	Archives Nationales (Paris)
BA	Bundesarchiv (Berlin)
BA-MA	Bundesarchiv-Militärarchiv (Freiburg)
BHStA	Bayerisches Hauptstaatsarchiv (Munich)
CAMT	Centre des Archives du Monde du Travail (Roubaix)
GLA	General-Landesarchiv (Karlsruhe)
GStA PK	Geheimes Staatsarchiv Preussischer Kulturgut (Berlin)
SHAT	Service Historique de l'Armée de Terre (Vincennes)
SHStA	Sächsisches Hauptstaatsarchiv (Dresden)
WHStA	Württembergisches Hauptstaatsarchiv (Stuttgart)

Previous Location of German Archives

C	Coswig
D	Dahlem (Berlin)
M	Merseburg
P	Potsdam

French Railway Companies

Cie Est	Compagnie des chemins de fer de l'Est
Cie Nord	Compagnie du chemin de fer du Nord
Cie PLM	Compagnie des chemins de fer de Paris à Lyon à la Méditerranée
Cie PO	Compagnie du chemin de fer de Paris à Orléans

Agencies and Ministries

CCCF	Comité consultatif des chemins de fer
CCFA	Comité commercial franco-allemand
CETCF	Comité de l'exploitation technique des chemins de fer
CMSCF	Conseil militaire supérieur des chemins de fer
CSDN	Conseil supérieur de la défense nationale
CSG	Conseil supérieur de la guerre
MAA	Ministerium der Auswärtigen Angelegenheiten
MA	Ministerium des Äussern (Bavaria)

MdI   Ministerium des Innern (Saxony)
MInn   Ministerium des Innern (Bavaria)
REA   Reichseisenbahnamt
RKA   Reichskanzleramt
RSA   Reichsschatzamt

Journals

JT   *Journal des Transports*
RGCF   *Revue Générale des Chemins de Fer*
ZVDEV   *Zeitung des Vereins Deutscher Eisenbahn-Verwaltungen*

NOTES

Introduction

1. For a general theoretical introduction to comparative history, see Haupt and Kocka, *Geschichte und Vergleich*, especially the individual essays by Kocka, "Historische Komparatistik in Deutschland," ibid., pp. 47–60; and Haupt, "Eine schwierige Öffnung nach aussen: Die international vergleichende Geschichtswissenschaft in Frankreich," ibid., pp. 77–90. Also see Atsma and Burguière, *Marc Bloch aujourd'hui*; Breuilly, "Introduction," pp. 1–25; Van den Braembussche, "Historial Explanation," pp. 2–24; and Welskopp, "Stolpersteine auf dem Königsweg," pp. 339–67.
2. See Mitchell, *German Influence*; *Victors and Vanquished*; and *Divided Path*.
3. Hughes, *Networks of Powers*, p. 1. Hughes's emphasis, however, is on regional rather than national technological systems. For much broader and more theoretical treatments, see Bertalanffy, *General System Theory*; Gille, *Histoire des techniques*; and Ropohl, *Systemtheorie der Technik*.

Chapter 1

1. Alexis de Tocqueville, *The Old Régime and the French Revolution* (New York, 1955), pp. 19–21, 193–211. On Ponts-et-Chaussées, see Smith, "The Longest Run," pp. 657–92.
2. Amid the immense bibliography on early French railways, two recent works stand out: Ribeill, *La révolution ferroviaire*; and Caron, *Histoire des chemins de fer*. Each is intended to be the first of three volumes.
3. On Great Britain, see Parris, *Government and the Railways*; Hawke, *Railways and Economic Growth*; Aldcroft and Freeman, *Transport*; and the Anglo-German comparison of early nineteenth-century investment patterns by Then, *Eisenbahnen und Eisenbahnunternehmer*. Nearly eight thousand titles are listed in Ottley et al., *Bibliography*.
4. See Pecheux, *La naissance*, pp. 47–56, 83–87; Michel, *Chemins de fer en Lyonnais*, pp. 20–29; Ratcliffe, "Origins," pp. 197–219; and Palau, *Le rail*, pp. 2–50.
5. Compare the attack on state agencies by Leclercq, *Le réseau impossible*, pp. 13–62; and the defense of them (notably Ponts-et-Chaussées) by Ratcliffe, "Bureaucracy," pp. 331–70. Also see Fleckles, *State*, pp. 27–60.
6. See the chapter entitled "The Aegis of Liberalism" in Mitchell, *Divided Path*, pp. 3–23.
7. *Moniteur Universel*, 30 Apr. 1833. See Alfred Picard, *Les chemins de fer français* (6 vols.; Paris, 1884–1885), 1: 15–17, 286; and Fleckles, *State*, p. 437.
8. See Smith, "The Longest Run," pp. 667–71; and Caron, *Histoire des chemins de fer*, pp. 44, 113–15.
9. *Observations de la Chambre de Commerce de Besançon sur le projet de chemins de fer de Mulhouse à Dijon par Besançon et la Vallée du Doubs, et la réponse aux objections élevées contre ce projet* (Besançon, 1842). Deputies of the Haute Saône to the Ministry of Public Works, 17 Feb. and 19 March 1842, AN Paris, C 827. See Caron, *Histoire des chemins de fer*, pp. 186–88.
10. "Discours prononcé par M. Duchatel, Ministre de l'Intérieur, dans la discussion du projet de loi relatif à l'établissement des grandes lignes de chemins de fer," 7 May

1842, AN Paris, C 827. See Ribeill, *La révolution ferroviaire*, pp. 28–34. But the 1842 law is criticized by Leclercq, *Le réseau impossible*, pp. 185–93.
11. Picard, *Les chemins de fer français* 1: 241.
12. See Lefranc, "Les chemins de fer," pp. 337–64; and Dunham, "First French Railways," pp. 12–25.
13. Picard, *Les chemins de fer français* 1: 303; Edmond Teisserenc de Bort, *Examen critique du mode de concession des chemins de fer consacré par la loi du 11 juin 1842* (Paris, 1844), pp. 5–6.
14. Smith, "The Longest Run," p. 675. More critical of the "false start" afforded by the 1842 law is Caron, *Histoire des chemins de fer*, pp. 82–83, 148–50, 172–73.
15. Cie Est, Assemblée Générale (hereafter: Ass. Gén.), *rapport*, 28 Sept. 1853, CAMT Roubaix, 13 AQ, 2638.
16. "Exposé des motifs d'un projet de loi autorisant l'allocation par l'Etat d'une subvention de 10,000,000 de francs ...," 1862, AN Paris, C 1088.
17. Cie Est, Conseil d'Administration (hereafter: Cons. d'Adm.), *procès-verbal*, 7 June 1860, CAMT Roubaix, 13 AQ, 45. See Mitchell, "Le Ballon d'Alsace," pp. 125–41.
18. Cie Est, Ass. Gén., *rapport*, 28 Sept. 1853, CAMT Roubaix, 13 AQ, 2638. See Jouffroy, *La ligne de Paris à la frontière d'Allemagne*.
19. Cie Est, Comité de Direction, *procès-verbal*, 12 July 1854, 13 July 1855, CAMT Roubaix, 13 AQ, 338–39.
20. All of these archives, with those of the other French railway companies, were transferred in 1996 from AN Paris to CAMT Roubaix.
21. Cie Est, Cons. d'Adm., *procès-verbal*, 30 March 1854, 9 Sept., 25 Nov., and 23 Dec. 1858, CAMT Roubaix, 13 AQ, 41–44.
22. Cie Est, Comité de Direction, *procès-verbal*, 12 May 1854, 1 Feb. 1855, 19 Nov. 1856, ibid., 338–339, 2565.
23. Cie Est, Comité de Direction, *procès-verbal*, 21 June 1854, ibid., 338. "Without this liberty of action [to set rates], the operation of railways would be impeded or impossible." Cie Est, Ass. Gén., *rapport*, 30 Apr. 1860, ibid., 2638.
24. For example, Cie Est, Cons. d'Adm., *procès-verbal*, 31 Jan. and 13 March 1856, 21 July 1859, ibid., 42–45.
25. Cie Est, Cons. d'Adm., *procès-verbal*, 14 and 28 June, 6 Sept. 1855, 21 Feb. 1856, ibid., 42–43. See Caron, *Histoire des chemins de fer*, pp. 203–4.
26. Cie Est, Cons. d'Adm., *procès-verbal*, 11 and 14 March, 30 Apr. 1863, CAMT Roubaix, 13 AQ, 47.
27. Cie PLM, Ass. Gén., *rapport*, 20 Apr. 1854, ibid., 77 AQ, 158. See Blanchard, *Une bataille de réseaux*.
28. Cie PLM, Ass. Gén., *rapport*, 19 Apr. 1855, 26 Apr. 1856, CAMT Roubaix, 77 AQ, 47.
29. Ibid., 28 Apr. 1857. See Brunot and Coquand, *Le corps*, pp. 264–72; and Caron, *Histoire des chemins de fer*, pp. 211–23.
30. Cie PLM, Ass. Gén., *rapport*, 28 Apr. 1857, CAMT Roubaix, 77 AQ, 158.
31. Cie PLM, Cons. d'Adm., *procès-verbal*, 11 Nov. 1864, ibid., 181.
32. Cie PLM, Cons. d'Adm., *procès-verbal*, 10 Apr. 1862, ibid., 180. Cie PLM, Ass. Gén., *rapport*, 24 Apr. 1862, ibid., 158.
33. Cie PO, Ass. Gén., *rapport*, 29 Aug. 1838, ibid., 60 AQ, 173.
34. Cie PO, Cons. d'Adm., *procès-verbal*, 8 and 12 Feb., 28 May, 5 July, 24 Oct., 15 Nov., 20 Dec. 1839, ibid., 2–3.
35. Cie PO, Ass. Gén., *rapport*, 27 March 1840, ibid., 173. Cie PO, Cons. d'Adm., *procès-verbal*, 20 Aug. 1841, ibid., 4.
36. Cie PO, Cons. d'Adm., *procès-verbal*, 30 Nov. 1838, ibid., 2. Cie PO, Ass. Gén., *rapport*, 6 Oct. 1842, ibid., 173.
37. Cie PO, Cons. d'Adm., *procès-verbal*, 28 Jan. 1842, ibid., 4.
38. Cie PO, Cons. d'Adm., *procès-verbal*, 9 Feb. 1844, 27 Nov. 1846, ibid., 5–6.
39. Cie PO, Cons. d'Adm., *procès-verbal*, 1 Dec. 1843, 3 Jan. 1848, ibid., 4–6. Cie PO, Ass. Gén., *rapport*, 28 March and 27 Apr. 1848, ibid., 173.

40. Cie PO, Cons. d'Adm., *procès-verbal*, 6 July 1845, ibid., 5.
41. Cie PO, Cons. d'Adm., *procès-verbal*, 6 Aug. 1847, ibid., 6. Cie PO, Ass. Gén., *rapport*, 28 March and 27 Apr. 1848, ibid., 173.
42. Cie PO, Cons. d'Adm., *procès-verbal*, 25 Feb. to 14 July 1848, ibid., 6–7. See Ribeill, "Gestion et organisation," pp. 999–1029.
43. Cie PO, Cons. d'Adm., *procès-verbal*, 1 Sept. 1848, 4 May 1852, CAMT Roubaix, 60 AQ, 7–9. Cie PO, Ass. Gén., *rapport*, 27 March 1849, ibid., 173.
44. Cie PO, Ass. Gén., *rapport*, 30 March 1854, 30 March 1855, ibid., 174.
45. Cie PO, Ass. Gén., *rapport*, 20 Apr. 1852, ibid., 173. Cie PO, Cons. d'Adm., *procès-verbal*, 10 June 1853, 12 May 1856, ibid., 10–13.
46. See Caron, *Histoire de l'exploitation*, pp. 45–52.
47. Cie Nord, Cons. d'Adm., *procès-verbal*, 20 Sept. 1845, CAMT Roubaix, 48 AQ, 10. On the family dynasty, see Gille, *Histoire de la maison Rothschild*, a standard work now augmented by Ferguson, *World's Banker*, which capably summarizes the family's involvement with early railway companies, notably including the Northern (ibid., pp. 429–60).
48. Cie Nord, Cons. d'Adm., *procès-verbal*, 21 May and 5 June 1847, CAMT Roubaix, 48 AQ, 10.
49. Cie Nord, Cons. d'Adm., *procès-verbal*, 29 Feb. to 18 July 1848, ibid. Cie Nord, Comité de Direction, *procès-verbal*, 7 and 28 March, 25 and 28 Apr., 23 May 1848, ibid., 56–57. See Caron, *Histoire des chemins de fer*, pp. 198–201, 277–80.
50. Cie Nord, Comité de Direction, *procès-verbal*, 22 Sept. 1848, CAMT Roubaix, 48 AQ, 57. Cie Nord, Cons. d'Adm., *procès-verbal*, 8 Aug. and 22 Sept. 1848, 25 Jan. 1850, ibid., 10.
51. Cie Nord, Cons. d'Adm., *procès-verbal*, 15 Aug. 1850, 8 and 19 July 1851, ibid., 10–11.
52. Picard to Cie Amiens à Boulogne, 12 Feb. 1850, ibid., 3318. Cie Nord, Cons. d'Adm., *procès-verbal*, 30 Nov. 1850, 7 Oct. 1852, [?] Jan., 4 Apr. and 29 July 1853, 27 Jan. 1854, ibid., 10–11. On James de Rothschild's falling out with the Pereires, see Ferguson, *World's Banker*, pp. 567–68, 595–99.
53. Cie Nord, Ass. Gén., *rapport*, 30 Apr. 1855, 28 Apr. 1856, ibid., 570.
54. In general, see the chapter on "The Mobilization of Credit 1815–1852," by Cameron, *France*, pp. 105–203.
55. Cie Est, Ass. Gén., *rapport*, 28 May 1859, CAMT Roubaix, 13 AQ, 2638.
56. "Mémoire à son Exc. Monsieur le Ministre des Travaux Publics par les délégations du Conseil Municipal et du Conseil d'Arrondissement de Mayenne," 20 Nov. 1856, AN Paris, C 1066.
57. Cie Nord, Ass. Gén., *rapport*, 29 Apr. 1861, CAMT Roubaix, 48 AQ, 570. See Girard, *La politique*.
58. Cie PO, Cons. d'Adm., *procès-verbal*, 16 Aug. 1856, CAMT Roubaix, 60 AQ, 13.
59. Cie PO, Cons. d'Adm., *procès-verbal*, 6 Feb. 1857, 9 July 1858, ibid., 14–16.
60. Cie PO, Ass. Gén., *rapport*, 30 March 1860, ibid., 174. On the 1859 conventions, see Caron, *Histoire des chemins de fer*, pp. 235–42.
61. Cie PO, Ass. Gén., *rapport*, 30 March 1860, CAMT Roubaix, 60 AQ, 174.
62. "Discours prononcé par M. Plichon … sur les conventions passées entre l'Etat et les compagnies de chemins de fer," 16 May 1859, CAMT Roubaix, 48 AQ, 3349.
63. Cie PLM, Cons. d'Adm., *procès-verbal*, 11 Nov. and 9 Dec. 1864, CAMT Roubaix, 77 AQ, 181.
64. Ministry of Public Works to Cie Nord, 10 Aug. 1864, CAMT Roubaix, 48 AQ, 3318. Cie Nord, Cons. d'Adm., *procès-verbal*, 19 Aug. 1864, ibid., 14. See Merger, "La concurrence," pp. 65–94.
65. Cie PO, Cons. d'Adm., *procès-verbal*, 5 Jan. 1844, 2 Dec. 1864, 20 Jan. 1865, 2 Feb. 1866, CAMT Roubaix, 60 AQ, 5, 14–24. See Mitchell, "Mutual Aid Societies," pp. 172–89. Specifically on the PO, also see Amalric, "Une institution patronale," pp. 238–64; and Ribeill, *La révolution ferroviaire*, pp. 375–78.

66. Cie PO, Cons. d'Adm., *procès-verbal*, 30 May 1853, CAMT Roubaix, 60 AQ, 10. See Ribeill, *La révolution ferroviaire*, pp. 363–64; and Mitchell, "Weak Sisters," pp. 175–82.
67. "Réponse de la Compagnie des chemins de fer de l'Est au questionnaire de la Commission d'enquête parlementaire sur les voies de transport," 1869, CAMT Roubaix, 13 AQ, 2639. Cie Est, Ass. Gén., *rapport*, 28 Apr. 1868, ibid. Cie PLM, Cons. d'Adm., *procès-verbal*, 13 Aug. 1869, ibid., 77 AQ, 183.
68. Cie PO, Ass. Gén., *rapport*, 8 March 1847, ibid., 60 AQ, 173. Cie PO, Cons. d'Adm., *procès-verbal*, 19 June 1840, ibid., 3. See Caron, *Histoire des chemins de fer*, pp. 378–92.
69. Cie Nord, Cons. d'Adm., *procès-verbal*, 14 March 1849, 9 Jan. 1852, CAMT Roubaix, 48 AQ, 10. See Caron, *Histoire de l'exploitation*, pp. 125–42; and Mitchell, "Private Enterprise," pp. 18–41.
70. Cie PO, Cons. d'Adm., *procès-verbal*, 28 March, 13 Apr., and 13 June 1855, CAMT Roubaix, 60 AQ, 12.
71. Cie PO, Cons. d'Adm., *procès-verbal*, 14 March and 12 May 1856, 12 Jan. 1857, ibid., 13–14.
72. Cie PO, Cons. d'Adm., *procès-verbal*, 12 and 30 Jan. 1857, ibid.
73. Cie PO, Cons. d'Adm., *procès-verbal*, 31 Jan., 4 Feb., 6 March, and 11 Apr. 1857, ibid.
74. Cie Est, Ass. Gén., *rapport*, 28 Apr. 1868, ibid., 13 AQ, 2639.
75. Cie Nord, Ass. Gén., *rapport*, 28 Apr. 1862, ibid., 48 AQ, 570.
76. Cie Est, Ass. Gén., *rapport*, 23 May 1863, ibid., 13 AQ, 2639.
77. Cie PLM, Ass. Gén., *rapport*, 22 Apr. 1869, 20 Apr. 1870, ibid., 77 AQ, 158.
78. Cie PO, Ass. Gén., *rapport*, 28 March 1865, 28 March 1866, 28 March 1867, ibid., 60 AQ, 174–175.
79. Ibid., 29 March 1870.
80. Cie Nord, Cons. d'Adm., *procès-verbal*, 2 and 16 March 1860, 14 Aug. 1863, 1 Sept. 1865, 6 Nov. 1868, ibid., 48 AQ, 13–16.
81. Cie Est, Cons. d'Adm., *procès-verbal*, 11 Nov. 1869, 31 March 1870, ibid., 13 AQ, 53–54. See Miller, *Bon Marché*, pp. 36–39, 56.
82. "The year 1867 … has quite obviously proven to what extent the prosperity of the [PO] is especially linked to the prosperity of French agriculture." Cie PO, Ass. Gén., *rapport*, 28 March 1868, CAMT Roubaix, 60 AQ, 175. See Price, *Modernization*, pp. 207–59.
83. Cie PO, Cons. d'Adm., *procès-verbal*, 1 March 1865, CAMT Roubaix, 60 AQ, 23. See Weber, *Peasants into Frenchmen*, pp. 144–45.
84. Such early writings were well summarized by Pierre Charié-Marsaines, *Les chemins de fer considérés au point de vue militaire* (Paris, 1862), pp. 6–10.
85. General Pelch, "Essai sur le système défensif du Royaume modifié par la fortification de Paris et par les chemins de fer," July 1842, SHAT Vincennes, MR 1162; and Charles Collignon, *Rapport fait au Conseil Municipal de Nancy sur le tracé de Paris à Strasbourg* (Nancy, 1841), pp. 47–50.
86. "Mémoire redigé à l'époque des insurrections en Allemagne …," 1831, SHAT Vincennes, MR 1530.
87. "Compte rendu de la mission en Allemagne du Colonel de Courtiges," 4 vols. in manuscript, 1845–1846, ibid., 1514. See Jeismann, *Feinde*.
88. Paul de Bourgoing, *Tableau de l'état actuel et des progrès probables des chemins de fer d'Allemagne et du continent européen, comparés avec ce qui se prépare en France à cet égard* (Paris, 1842); "Du transport des troupes sur les chemins de fer bavarois," 2 July 1846, SHAT Vincennes, MR 1513; "Documents militaires recueillis de 1838 à 1848 par M. Paul de Bourgoing, ministre de France en Bavière," 3 vols. in manuscript, Jan. 1849, ibid., 1511.
89. Engelhand to Drouyn de Lhuys, 4 Feb. 1849, SHAT Vincennes, MR 1531.
90. Charié-Marsaines, *Les chemins de fer*, pp. 11–23.
91. "Extrait des registres de la Commission mixte des Travaux Publics," 2 Dec. 1844, AN Paris, F[14] 9359. See Picard, *Les chemins de fer français* 1:440.

92. *Observations de la Chambre de Commerce de Besançon....* (Besançon, 1842). Deputies of the Haute Saône to the Ministry of Public Works, 17 Feb. and 19 March 1842, AN Paris, C 827. Representatives of the Société du chemin de fer d'Orléans à Tours to Lamartine (president of the Commission des chemins de fer), 12 March 1842, ibid.
93. "Chemins de fer de petite ceinture et de grande ceinture de Paris: recueil de documents," 10 Dec. 1851, AN Paris, F[14] 12478. "Exposé des motifs d'un projet de loi approuvant les stipulations financières ...," 7 May 1868, ibid., C 1125.
94. Cie PO, Cons. d'Adm., *procès-verbal*, 21 Dec. 1855, CAMT Roubaix, 60 AQ, 13. Cie Nord, Cons. d'Adm., *procès-verbal*, 21 June, 7 Sept., and 18 Oct. 1861, ibid., 48 AQ, 13. Cie Est, Cons. d'Adm., *procès-verbal*, 26 Nov. 1863, ibid., 13 AQ, 47.
95. Cie Est, Cons. d'Adm., *procès-verbal*, 31 Jan. and 13 March 1856, ibid., 13 AQ, 43. Cie Est, Ass. Gén., *rapport*, 27 May 1858, 28 Apr. 1865, ibid., 2638–2639. "Chemins de fer d'intérêt local dans le département des Ardennes: rapport sur les avant-projets de ces chemins de fer," 25 March 1867, AN Paris, F[14] 15083. Niel to the Ministry of Public Works, 28 Jan. 1868, ibid.
96. Clemont-Tounerre to Randon, 27 Jan. 1864, SHAT Vincennes, MR 1535.
97. Cie Nord, Comité de Direction, *procès-verbal*, 3 March 1868, 16 March and 16 Nov. 1869, 11 Feb. and 19 July 1870, CAMT Roubaix, 48 AQ, 95–102. See Mitchell, *Victors and Vanquished*, pp. 3–15.
98. François Jacqmin, *Les chemins de fer pendant la guerre de 1870–1871* (Paris, 1872), p. ii.

Chapter 2
1. Friedrich List, *Le monde marche* (Paris, 1837). The later German edition has been reprinted as *Die Welt bewegt sich* (Göttingen, 1985). List's first major treatise, *Über ein sächsiches Eisenbahn-System als Grundlage eines allgemeinen deutschen Eisenbahn-Systems* (Leipzig, 1833), has also been recently reissued (Mainz, 1984).
2. C. Grote, *Über ein Eisenbahnsystem für Deutschland* (Göttingen, 1834), p. 2.
3. "Auszug aus einer Depêche des Grafen von Dönhoff," 27 Jan. 1836, GStA PK Berlin, III. HA (2.4.1.), II, Nr. 6963 (M). Dönhoff to MAA, 2 Feb. 1836, ibid.
4. Ludolf Camphausen, *Zur Eisenbahn von Köln nach Antwerpen* (Cologne, 1835), pp. 96–97.
5. David Hansemann, *Preussens wichtigste Eisenbahn-Frage* (Leipzig and Halle, 1837), p. 3; *Kritik des preussischen Eisenbahngesetzes vom 3. November 1838* (Aachen and Leipzig, 1841), pp. 21–24; and *Über die Ausführung des preussischen Eisenbahn-Systems* (Berlin, 1843), pp. 1–2, 83–84. However, Hansemann has been described as "an energetic proponent of state railway construction" by Klee, *Preussische Eisenbahngeschichte*, p. 27.
6. "Protokolls-Auszug der 2ten Bundestags-Sitzung," 13 Jan. 1848, BHStA Munich, MH 12947. See Carr, *History*, pp. 34–63.
7. Carr, *History*, pp. 23–24; and *Origins*, p. 104.
8. The journal, at first called simply the *Eisenbahnzeitung*, was later renamed the *Zeitung des Vereins Deutscher Eisenbahn-Verwaltungen* (hereafter: *ZVDEV*). Extensive but incomplete files are held in the Berlin Staatsbibliothek.
9. Dunlavy, *Politics and Industrialization*, p. 196.
10. "Das Vereinsgebiet deutscher Eisenbahn-Verwaltungen am 1. Januar 1864," *ZVDEV*, 2 Jan. 1864. See Helmuth Seidenfus, "Eisenbahnwesen," in Jeserich et al., *Deutsche Verwaltungsgeschichte* 2: 255–57.
11. "Beiträge zu einer Reform im Eisenbahn-Güter Transportwesen: Eisenbahn-Verbände," *ZVDEV*, 12 Apr. 1862.
12. "Die Verkehrs-Resultate der Eisenbahn-Verbände," ibid., 1 Oct. 1864. "Bericht, betreffend die Verkehrsbeziehungen ...," 10 June 1867, BHStA Munich, Gesandtschaft Stuttgart 549.
13. "Deutsche Eisenbahn-Statistik für das Betriebsjahr 1851," *Eisenbahnzeitung*, 8 May 1853. "Deutsche Eisenbahn-Statistik für das Betriebsjahr 1856," ibid., 19 Aug. 1858. "Preussische Eisenbahnen," ibid., 8 Sept. 1860. See Kocka, "Eisenbahnverwaltung," pp. 259–77.

14. See Klee, *Preussische Eisenbahngeschichte*, pp. 17–19, 114–31; Stern, *Gold and Iron*, pp. 62–64; Tilly, " Political Economy," pp. 484–97; Brose, *Politics*, pp. 209–40; Kocka, "Management," pp. 136–41; and Lothar Gall, "Eisenbahn in Deutschland: Von den Anfängen bis zum Ersten Weltkrieg," in Gall and Pohl, *Die Eisenbahn in Deutschland*, pp. 19–23. On early investment patterns in Prussia, also see the recent monographs by Then, *Eisenbahnen*; and Brophy, *Capitalism*.
15. See Gisevius, *Vorgeschichte*.
16. See Preuss, *Sächsische Staatseisenbahnen*, pp. 13–14.
17. Finanzministerium to MdI, 6 Aug. 1859, SHStA Dresden, MdI 13748. See Preuss, *Sächsische Staatseisenbahnen*, pp. 15–18, 35–41.
18. Abel to Gise, 20 Oct. 1843, BHStA Munich, MF 58632. See Bernt Mester, "Partikularismus der Schiene. Die Entwicklung einzelstaatlicher Eisenbahnsysteme bis 1870," in *Zug der Zeit* 1: 202–204; and Liebl, *Aufgeh'n wird die Erde in Rauch*, pp. 14–15, 62–70, 148–67.
19. See Hugo Marggraff, *Die Kgl. Bayerishcen Staatsbahn in geschichtlicher und statistischer Beziehung* (Munich, 1894), pp. 20–30.
20. Bavarian MA to Oberkamp, 15 and 25 Feb. 1838, BHStA Munich, Gesandtschaft Karlsruhe 1052.
21. Gise to Malzen, 30 March 1846, ibid., Gesandtschaft Stuttgart 551.
22. Bavarian MA to Degenfeld, 7 Sept. 1848, ibid., Verkehrsarchiv 6079. Von der Pfordten to Verger, 12 March 1850, ibid., Gesandtschaft Karlsruhe 1052. "Staats-Vertrag zwischen Württemberg und Baden über die Verbindung der beiderseitigen Eisenbahnen," 4 Dec. 1850, WHStA Stuttgart, E 46, Bü 213.
23. See Supper, *Entwicklung*, pp. 47–51. This volume is a reprint of the original 1895 edition.
24. Beroldingen to Bismark, 6 May 1841, WHStA Stuttgart, E 70 f, 353.
25. Beroldingen to Bismark, 29 Dec. 1840, ibid. See Supper, *Entwicklung*, pp. 8–9; and Kobschätzky, *Württembergische Staatseisenbahn*, pp. 9–11.
26. Supper, *Entwicklung*, pp. 14–26.
27. Hügel to Degenfeld, 4 Sept. 1858, 28 Nov. 1861, 11 Feb. 1864, WHStA Stuttgart, E 75, 402. Varnbüler to Degenfeld, 12 Oct. 1864, ibid. Von der Pfordten to Degenfeld, 20 Feb. 1865, ibid.
28. "Leopold, von Gottes Gnaden Grossherzog von Baden …," 12 March 1838, GLA Karlsruhe, 233/32943.
29. Rüdt von Collenberg to Leopold, 17 May 1841, ibid., 32959.
30. See Mester, "Partikularismus der Schiene," in *Zug der Zeit* 1: 204.
31. Memo from Rob. Stephenson and Co. (London), 26 Apr. 1842, GLA Karlsruhe, 421/121. Yet Baden's adoption of a wider gauge is called "incomprehensible" by Mester, "Partikularismus der Schiene," *Zug der Zeit* 1: 204.
32. Direktion der Posten und Eisenbahnen, "Mündl. Vortrag, die Abänderung der badischen Spurweite betr.," 29 Apr. 1846, GLA Karlsruhe, 421/28. Rüdt von Collenberg to the Regent, 21 June 1853, ibid., 233/33049. Yet Baden maintained left-hand rail traffic until 1888. See Mühl, *Staateisenbahnen*, pp. 7–9.
33. Blittersdorff to Böckh, 15 Apr. 1843, GLA Karlsruhe, 237/16655. Marschall, "Über die Eisenbahnverbindung mit Würtemberg [sic]," 21 Dec. 1843, ibid., 233/32959. Klüber to the Grand Duke, 16 Sept. 1850, ibid., 32961. "Staatsvertrag zwischen Baden und Württemberg über die Verbindung der beiderseitigen Eisenbahnen," 4 Dec. 1850, ibid.
34. Weizel to the Grand Duke, 11 March 1862, ibid., 32946.
35. *Statistische Übersichten der im Jahre 1862 in Deutschland, der Schweiz, Frankreich, Belgien, den Niederlanden und Russland im Betriebe gewesenen Eisenbahnen* (Cologne, 1864), in GStA PK Berlin, I. HA Rep. 89, Nr. 29528 (M). "Übersicht über den Fortgang des Baues, beziehungsweise die Ergebnisse des Betriebes der Preussischen Staats-Eisenbahnen im Jahre 1864," 10 Apr. 1865, ibid., Rep. 93 E, Nr. 3283 (M).
36. See Ziegler, *Eisenbahnen und Staat*, p. 74.

37. See Klee, *Preussische Eisenbahngeschichte*, pp. 148–56; and Stern, *Gold and Iron*, pp. 357–69. By claiming that Strousberg's heyday came after 1871, his career is put out of focus by Bernd Breitfeld, "Von der Privat- zur Staatsbahn. Zur Finanzierung der deutschen Eisenbahnen," in *Zug der Zeit* 1: 185–92. See Ohlsen, *Eisenbahnkönig*. On American counterparts, see Jones, *Robber Barons*. But that designation is rejected in favor of "powerful captains ... and their able lieutenants" by Chandler, *Strategy and Structure*, p. 36.
38. The fundamental work is by Fremdling, *Eisenbahnen*. Also see Sheehan, *German History*, pp. 466–70; and Wehler, *Deutsche Gesellschaftsgeschichte* 3: 66–74.
39. Nevertheless, it is senseless to continue to include the statistics of Austrian railways with those of Germany, as if the war of 1866 had decided nothing. For instance, see Wehler, *Deutsche Gesellschaftsgeschichte* 3: 69–70.
40. Hohenlohe to Montgelas, 24 Feb. 1867, BHStA Munich, Gesandtschaft Berlin 1036.
41. "Verfassung des Norddeutschen Bundes," 26 July 1867, GStA PK Berlin, I. HA Rep. 90, Nr. 1676 (D). See Pflanze, *Bismarck* 1: 388–401.
42. For example, petitions to the Prussian Lower House from the districts of Biedenkopf and Neu-Stettin, 1 and 5 Dec. 1867, GStA PK Berlin, I. HA Rep. 169 C, Nr. 4 (D).
43. "Reichstag des Norddeutschen Bundes: Antrag vom 16. März 1869," ibid., Rep. 90, Nr. 1676 (D). "Reichstag des Norddeutschen Bundes: Antrag Miquel und Genossen," 4 Apr. 1870, ibid.
44. Bismarck to Itzenplitz, 11 Dec. 1869, ibid. Itzenplitz to Bismarck, 19 Dec. 1869, ibid.
45. Weishaupt to Bismarck, 12 March 1870, ibid. Bismarck to Weishaupt, 1 Apr. 1870, ibid.
46. See Fogel, *Railroads*, pp. 11–13.
47. See Rostow, *Stages*, amplified by papers contained in Rostow, *Economics of Take-Off*. The notion of a take-off is dubiously applied to the two decades before 1870 by Carr, *History*, p. 69. See Ville, *Transport*, pp. 1–12.
48. Landes, *Unbound Prometheus*, pp. 193–96. However, Landes does indicate how France and Germany were in the process before 1873 of working out "the core innovations of the [British] Industrial Revolution" (ibid., p. 210). On comparative national economic growth, see B. R. Mitchell, *Statistics*, pp. 485–86. For regional railway networks in Central Europe (maps of 1840, 1845, 1850, and 1860), see Kobschätzky, *Streckenatlas*, pp. 93–96.
49. Julius Michaelis, *Deutschlands Eisenbahnen. Ein Handbuch für Geschäftsleute, Capitalisten und Spekulanten* (2nd ed.; Leipzig, 1859), pp. v–xi.
50. An example of such reasoning was Maximilian Arzberger, *Eisenbahnen als Staats- und als Gesellschaftsunternehmungen* (Hamburg and Gotha, 1842), p. 5 and passim. See Tipton, *Regional Variations*, pp. 63–80.
51. E.g., Rüdt von Collenberg to Dusch, 27 Oct. 1846, GLA Karlsruhe, 233/11299. Degenfeld to Hügel, 12 Sept. 1857, WHStA Stuttgart, E 46, Bü 216.
52. Freiherr von Schrenk, quoted in cabinet minutes of 29 March 1860, BHStA Munich, MA 99508. Schrenk to the Generaldirektion der k. Verkehrs-Anstalten, ibid., MF 58842.
53. See Wagenblass, *Eisenbahnbau*, pp. 237–75; Henning, "Eisenbahn und Entwicklung," pp. 1–20; and Fremdling, "Industrialisierung und Eisenbahn," in *Zug der Zeit* 1: 121–33.
54. "Deutsche Eisenbahn-Statistik für das Betriebsjahr 1855," *Eisenbahnzeitung*, 16 July 1857. "Deutsche Eisenbahn-Statistik für das Betriebsjahr 1859," *ZVDEV*, 6 Aug. 1862.
55. "Die deutschen Locomotivfabriken," *ZVDEV*, 7 June 1867. See Wagenblass, *Eisenbahnbau*, pp. 88–108, 203–20.
56. Carr, *History*, p. 69.
57. See Fremdling, "Modernisierung und Wachstum," pp. 201–27.
58. Kindleberger, *Economic Growth*, p. 324.
59. See Reeken, *Lahusen*, p. 12; and Fremdling et al., *Statistik*, pp. 11–18.

60. See Tipton, *Regional Variations*, pp. 130–32; and Ziegler, *Eisenbahnen und Staat*, pp. 302–18, 504–33.
61. Rüdt von Collenberg, "Die von der Grossherzoglichen Badischen Regierung verlangte Garantie behufs der Erbauung einer Eisenbahn durch die Schweiz ...," 8 Jan. 1847, GLA Karlsruhe, 233/11300. Dusch to the Grand Duke, 24 Feb. 1847, ibid., 32985.
62. For example, "Ausland: Schweiz," *Eisenbahnzeitung*, 7 Aug. 1853.
63. "Eisenbahnvertrag zwischen Frankreich und dem Königreich Italien," *ZVDEV*, 28 June 1862. "Gotthardbahn," ibid., 24 Sept. 1862. "Alpenbahn-Projekte," ibid., 25 Oct. 1862. "Note des Finanzministeriums an das k. Ministerium der Auswärtigen Angelegenheiten betreffend die Gotthard-Eisenbahn," 22 Apr. 1864, WHStA Stuttgart, E 49, Verz. 18, II/4. Mathy to the Grand Duke, 14 Nov. 1865, GLA Karlsruhe, 233/32985.
64. Edelsheim to the Grand Duke, 18 Jan. 1866, GLA Karlsruhe, 233/32985. Dusch to the Baden Ministry of Finance, 27 March 1869, ibid., 421/2181. "Gutachten der badischen Gotthard-Commission erstattet von Ministerialrath Nicolai," 15 Aug. 1869, ibid., 237/32114.
65. "Protocole final des conférences internationales qui ont eu lieu à Berne en septembre et octobre 1869," ibid., 233/11231.
66. "Gesetzes-Entwurf. Den Bau einer Gotthardbahn betreffend," 2 March 1870, ibid., 236/9121. "Kommissions-Bericht über den Gesetz-Entwurf ...," 15 March 1870, ibid. Bismarck to Flemming, 25 March 1870, ibid., 233/4258.
67. Delbrück to Bismarck, 5 May 1870, GStA PK Berlin, I. HA Rep. 77, Nr. 16 (M). Itzenplitz to Bismarck, 14 May 1870, ibid., Rep. 93 E, 3291/1 (M). See Wegelin-Zbinden, *Der Kampf um den Gotthardvertrag*, pp. 11–19.
68. See Marcus Junkelmann, "Die Eisenbahn im Krieg. Militärische Theorie und Kriegsgeschehen bis zum Ausbruch des Ersten Weltkriegs," in *Zug der Zeit* 1: 233–45; and Brose, *Politics*, pp. 224–34.
69. Grote, *Eisenbahnsystem*, pp. 2–4.
70. List, *Andeutung der Vortheile eines preussischen Eisenbahnsystems und insbesondere einer Eisenbahn zwischen Hamburg, Berlin, Magdeburg und Leipzig* (n.p., 1835). Carl Eduard Pönitz, *Die Eisenbahnen als militärische Operationslinien betrachtet und durch Beispiele erläutert* (Adorf, 1842). Still an excellent review of the subject is by Pratt, *Rise of Rail-Power*. Also see Showalter, *Railroads and Rifles*, pp. 19–35.
71. "Auszug aus einer Depêche des Grafen von Dönhoff," 27 Jan. 1836, GStA PK Berlin, III. HA (2.4.1.), II, Nr. 6963 (M).
72. Radowitz to Werther, 12 May 1838, ibid.
73. Canitz to Bernstorff, 6 March 1846, BHStA Munich, MH 12947.
74. "Auszug aus dem 12. Sitzungs-Protokolle der deutschen Bundesversammlung," 23 Apr. 1846, GStA PK Berlin, I. HA Rep. 77, Tit. 258, Nr. 27 (M).
75. Hansemann to Rochow, 1 Sept. 1839, ibid. "Promemoria," 31 Dec. 1841, ibid.
76. Hagens to Baur, 13 Apr. 1846, BHStA Munich, Abt. IV, D VI Bd. 13. "Auszug aus dem Berichte der Königlichen Bundestags-Gesandtschaft in Frankfurt," 24 Apr. 1846, BHStA Munich, MH 12947. Abel to MA, 1 Aug. 1846, ibid.
77. See Junkelmann, "Die Eisenbahn im Krieg," in *Zug der Zeit* 1: 234.
78. Das provisorsiche Comité zur Erbauung einer Köln-Coblenzer Eisenbahn (Mevissen, chair), *Denkschrift zur Begründung des Unternehmens einer zwischen Bonn, Coblenz und Bingen im Preussischen Gebiete auf dem linken Rheinufer anzulegenden Eisenbahn* (Cologne, 1850), pp. 8–9.
79. "Vortrag des Ausschusses in Militärangelegenheiten, betreffend die wegen der Ereignisse in Frankreich erforderlichen militärischen Massregeln," 25 March 1848, GLA Karlsruhe, 233/4250.
80. See Angelow, *Von Wien nach Königgrätz*.
81. *Sitzungs-Protokoll der deutschen Bundesversammlung*, 9th session (30 March 1854) and 11th session (27 Apr. 1854), GStA PK Berlin, III. HA (2.4.1.), II, Nr. 7590 (M).

82. "Auszug des Separat-Protkolls der 18. Sitzung der Deutschen Bundesversammlung," 5 June 1858, ibid. Braur, "Gutachten des General-Auditors," 22 June 1857, GLA Karlsruhe, 233/11268. Meysenbug to Serre, 2 July 1857, ibid.
83. Ritter, *Staatskunst und Kriegshandwerk* 1: 235. Also see Holborn, "Moltke and Schlieffen," pp. 172–205.
84. Ritter, *Staatskunst und Kriegshandwerk* 1: 155–58, 207–37.
85. See Bucholz, *Moltke*, pp. 36–42.
86. Lüder to Von der Pfordten, 26 Apr. 1859, BHStA Munich, MH 13225. Meysenbug to the Direktion der Verkehrsanstalten, 14 May 1859, GLA Karlsruhe, 421/357. "Kriegsbereitschaft der Eisenbahnen," *Eisenbahnzeitung*, 28 May 1859. "Separatprotokoll der 28. Sitzung der Deutschen Bundesversammlung," 19 Sept. 1863, BHStA Munich, MH 12948.
87. "Vortrag des Ausschusses in Militärangelegenheiten …," 24 Jan. 1861, BHStA Munich, MH 12947. Von der Pfordten to King Ludwig II, 26 Jan. 1861, ibid.
88. See Junkelmann, "Die Eisenbahn im Krieg," in *Zug der Zeit* 1: 235–36.
89. See Craig, *Battle of Königgrätz*, pp. 139–64; Howard, *Franco-Prussian War*, pp. 40–41; Holborn, "Moltke and Schlieffen," pp. 181–85; Showalter, *Railroads and Rifles*, pp. 52–72; Van Creveld, *Command in War*, pp. 103–47; and Bond, *War and Society*, p. 14. Strangely, a more recent military analysis omits any reference to railways: Wawro, *Austro-Prussian War*, pp. 181–273.
90. Sheehan, *German History*, p. 469.
91. See Pflanze, *Bismarck* 1: 298–303, 446–69; Gall, *Bismarck*, pp. 373–455; Kolb, *Kriegsausbruch*; Josef Becker, "Von Bismarcks 'spanischer Diversion' zur 'Emser Legende' des Reichsgründers," in Becker et al., *Lange und kurze Wege*, pp. 87–113; and Mitchell, *Bismarck*, pp. 37–53.
92. See Ritter, *Staatskunst und Kriegshandwerk* 1: 270–87; Howard, *Franco-Prussian War*, pp. 40–44; Bond, *War and Society*, pp. 15–19; Bucholz, *Moltke*, pp. 50–57; and Junkelmann, "Die Eisenbahn im Krieg," in *Zug der Zeit* 1: 240.
93. Delbrück to the Bundesrath, 30 Nov. 1868, BHStA Munich, Abt. IV, D VI Bd. 19. Bothmer to the Bavarian Ministry of War, 8 Feb. 1869, ibid. "Die Beförderung von Truppen u. Militäreffekten auf den Eisenbahnen betr.," 17 Apr. 1870, ibid.
94. Flemming to Freydorf, 25 Aug. 1869, GLA Karlsruhe, 233/4258. Bismarck to Flemming, 25 March 1870, ibid. Dusch to the Grand Duke, 1 Apr. 1870, ibid., 11910.
95. Taube to Soden, 30 Aug. 1869, WHStA Stuttgart, E 75, 483. Varnbüler to Soden, 19 Nov. 1869, 22 July 1870, ibid.
96. Hohenlohe to Montgelas, 21 Jan. and 24 Feb. 1867, BHStA Munich, Gesandtschaft Berlin 1036. Hohenlohe to Perglas, 26 Dec. 1868, ibid., 1038. Werthern to Daxenberger, 26 Aug. 1869, ibid., MH 12977.
97. "Reglement für die Beförderung von Truppen und Armee-Bedürfnissen …," 26 June 1870, SHStA Dresden, KA (P) 816.
98. For a brief and balanced narrative of the surrounding events, see Pflanze, *Bismarck* 1: 459–69.

Chapter 3

1. See Fremdling, *Eisenbahnen*, p. 117.
2. Tocqueville, *Old Régime*, p. 72.
3. See Mitchell, "Weak Sisters," pp. 175–77.
4. See Milward and Saul, *Development*, p. 508; and Landes, *Unbound Prometheus*, pp. 232–37.
5. Fremdling, "Industrialisierung und Eisenbahn," in *Zug der Zeit* 1: 127.
6. Landes, *Unbound Prometheus*, p. 193.
7. See Fremdling, *Eisenbahnen*, pp. 5–11, 83; and Wehler, *Deutsche Gesellschaftsgeschichte* 3: 74–75.
8. See Gerschenkron, *Economic Backwardness*, pp. 5–30.
9. Landes, *Unbound Prometheus*, p. 208.

10. Ibid., p. 203. Here Landes calls gains in the Pas-de-Calais "equally spectacular" as those in the Ruhr basin, but these statistics belie that claim.
11. See Hoffmann, *Wachstum*, pp. 200–201.
12. See Cameron, *France*, pp. 145–71; and Fremdling, *Eisenbahnen*, p. 34.
13. See Helmedach, "Grundsatzentscheidungen," pp. 11–50.
14. Jules Siegfried, *Quelques mots sur la question des chemins de fer en France* (Le Havre, 1875), pp. 4–20.
15. Caron, *Histoire de l'exploitation*, p. 139.
16. See Thomas, "Armies and the Railway Revolution," pp. 88–94. On the military plans of Napoleon III and Niel, see Mitchell, *Victors and Vanquished*, pp. 4–11.
17. See Caron, *Histoire des chemins de fer*, pp. 419–26. The notion that, in contrast to Germany, "France had in place a large-capacity, unitary railroad system under a single bureaucratic agency of the central government" is pure fantasy. Bucholz, *Moltke*, p. 52.
18. See Junkelmann, "Die Eisenbahn im Krieg," in *Zug der Zeit*, 1: 240–41; Howard, *Franco-Prussian War*, pp. 257–83; and Mitchell, *Victors and Vanquished*, pp. 15–19. Yet also see the severe critique of German operations by Van Creveld, *Supplying War*, pp. 85–108.

Chapter 4

1. For background, see Mitchell, *German Influence*, pp. 21–48.
2. Ibid., pp. 6–10.
3. Cie PO, Cons. d'Adm., *procès-verbal*, 12 Jan. 1872, CAMT Roubaix, 60 AQ, 30. Advanced by Marie-Noëlle Thibault in her thesis, "La question du rachat des chemins de fer dans l'idéologie républicaine au XIXe siècle" (University of Dijon, 1975), the notion of Thiers as an "heir of Napoleon" is seconded by Caron, *Histoire des chemins de fer*, p. 442.
4. Raudot, "Proposition de loi sur les concessions des chemins de fer," 14 June 1871, AN Paris, C 2853. Commission relative à l'enquête sur les chemins de fer, *procès-verbal*, 20 Dec. 1871, ibid., 3005.
5. M. de Jouvenel, quoted in the Commission ... des chemins de fer, *procès-verbal*, 28 Feb. 1874, ibid. The same file contains excerpts from petitions by various chambers of commerce, 1872–1874. On the challenge by advocates of smaller railway companies, see Caron, *Histoire des chemins de fer*, pp. 429–43.
6. "Projet de loi ayant pour objet la déclaration d'utilité publique à la concession des deux sections du chemin de fer d'Amiens à Dijon," May 1874, AN Paris, C 2855. Beaurepaire and Calvet-Rogniat to Raudot, 30 Nov. 1875, ibid., 3005. Commission ... des chemins de fer, *procès-verbal*, 4 Dec. 1875, ibid.
7. Commission ... des chemins de fer, *procès-verbal*, 6 Dec. 1876, ibid., 3154.
8. See Picard, *Les chemins de fer français* 3: 36–37.
9. For details, see Caron, *Histoire des chemins de fer*, pp. 469–75; and Mitchell, *German Influence*, pp. 144–76.
10. Picard, *Les chemins de fer français* 3: 718.
11. Wilson, "Rapport fait au nom de la Commission chargée d'examiner le projet de loi relatif au classement du réseau complémentaire des chemins de fer d'intérêt général," *Journal Officiel: Chambre des Députés*, 15 March 1879. Foucher de Careil, "Rapport fait au nom de la Commission chargée d'étudier et de proposer les voies et moyens nécessaires pour achever le réseau des chemins de fer d'intérêt général," *Journal Officiel: Sénat*, 24 May 1878.
12. *Discours prononcé par M. C. de Freycinet, Ministre des Travaux Publics, au Sénat, le 11 juillet 1879* (Paris, 1879). See Gonjo, "Le 'Plan Freycinet,'" pp. 49–86; Beck, *Der Plan Freycinet*, pp. 4–56; and Caron, *Histoire des chemins de fer*, pp. 475–80.
13. Cie Est, Ass. Gén., *rapport*, 4 Nov. 1871, CAMT Roubaix, 13 AQ, 2639.
14. Ibid. Jacqmin to Regray, 17 Feb. 1873, ibid., 2019.

15. Compare the annual reports by the Eastern's Administrative Council of 4 Nov. 1871 and 27 Apr. 1880, ibid., 2639–40. Additional statistics are recorded in Cie Est, Cons. d'Adm., *procès-verbal*, 25 Sept. 1873, 19 March 1874, ibid., 57, 59.
16. Cie Est, Cons. d'Adm., *procès-verbal*, 7 Sept. 1871, ibid., 55.
17. Ibid., 13 July 1871.
18. "Projet de loi" signed by Thiers and the then Minister of Public Works Marie-François de Fourtou, 5 Jan. 1873, AN Paris, C 2854. Commission pour l'examen du projet de loi ..., *procès-verbaux*, 22 Jan.-25 March 1873, ibid.
19. Jacqmin to Durbach, 2 Oct. 1879, CAMT Roubaix, 13 AQ, 2026. See Mitchell, "Private Enterprise," pp. 18–41.
20. Cie PLM, Ass. Gén., *rapport*, 3 Aug. 1871, CAMT Roubaix, 77 AQ, 159. Cie PLM, Cons. d'Adm., *procès-verbal*, 26 Aug. 1870, 13 June and 14 July 1871, ibid., 183–184.
21. Cie PLM, Ass. Gén., *rapport*, 3 Aug. 1871, 22 Apr. 1873, 4 Dec. 1875, ibid., 159. Cie PLM, Cons. d'Adm., *procès-verbal*, 14 July 1871, ibid., 184.
22. Cie PLM, Ass. Gén., *rapport*, 28 Apr. 1876 to 27 Apr. 1882, ibid., 159–160. Cie PLM, Cons. d'Adm., *procès-verbal*, 18 Aug. 1876, 10 Sept. 1880, ibid., 186–88.
23. Cie PLM, Cons. d'Adm., *procès-verbal*, 28 March 1872, 27 June and 25 July 1873, ibid., 184.
24. Cie PLM, Cons. d'Adm., *procès-verbal*, 6 Dec. 1878, 7 March 1879, 25 Apr. and 5 Dec. 1879, 3 March 1882, ibid., 187–88.
25. Cie PO, Ass. Gén., *rapport*, 2 Aug. 1871, 26 March 1872, ibid., 60 AQ, 175. Cie PO, Cons. d'Adm., *procès-verbal*, 15 July 1870, 20 March 1871, ibid., 29.
26. Cie PO, Ass. Gén., *rapport*, 26 March 1872, ibid., 175. Cie PO, Cons. d'Adm., *procès-verbal*, 23 June and 6 Oct. 1871, ibid., 29–30.
27. Cie PO, Ass. Gén., *rapport*, 25 March 1873, ibid., 175. Cie PO, Cons. d'Adm., *procès-verbal*, 25 Aug. and 22 Sept. 1871, 10 May 1872, 13 June 1873, ibid., 30–32. On pilgrimages, see Weber, *Peasants into Frenchmen*, pp. 349–55; and Mitchell, *Victors and Vanquished*, pp. 160–61.
28. Cie PO, Cons. d'Adm., *procès-verbal*, 6 Aug. 1875, 29 March, 26 May, 14 July, and 15 Dec. 1876, CAMT Roubaix, 60 AQ, 33–35. See Caron, *Histoire des chemins de fer*, pp. 443–45.
29. Cie PO, Cons. d'Adm., *procès-verbal*, 2 Aug., 25 Oct., and 6 Dec. 1878, 3 and 10 Jan. 1879, CAMT Roubaix, 60 AQ, 36.
30. Cie PO, Ass. Gén., *rapport*, 29 March 1879, ibid., 176. See Vilain, *Un siècle de matériel*.
31. Cie Nord, Ass. Gén., *rapport*, 30 June 1871, CAMT Roubaix, 48 AQ, 271. Cie Nord, Cons. d'Adm., *procès-verbal*, 14 Oct., 11 Nov., and 30 Dec. 1870, ibid., 17.
32. Cie Nord, Cons. d'Adm., *procès-verbal*, 24 Feb., 9 and 23 June 1871, ibid.
33. The sharp rise in expenses included 14.6 million francs for rolling stock. Cie Nord, Ass. Gén., *rapport*, 30 Apr. 1872, 28 Apr. 1873, 29 Apr. 1874, ibid., 571. Cie Nord, Cons. d'Adm., *procès-verbal*, 5 Apr. and 18 Oct. 1872, ibid., 17–18.
34. Cie Nord, Ass. Gén., *rapport*, 28 Apr. 1875, 26 Apr. 1876, ibid., 571. Cie Nord, Cons. d'Adm., *procès-verbal*, 2 Apr. and 6 Nov. 1874, 29 Oct. 1875, 21 July 1876, ibid., 18–19.
35. Administration des chemins de fer de Ceinture de Paris, "Observations sur le projet de loi relatif aux renseignements statistiques à fournir par les compagnies de chemins de fer," 10 March 1876, ibid., 3596. See Caron, *Histoire des chemins de fer*, pp. 500, 518–27.
36. Cie Nord, memo from the chief engineer of operations to administrators of the Company, 12 Sept. 1875, CAMT Roubaix, 48 AQ, 3592. Eugène Caillaux to administrators, 9 Nov. 1875, ibid.
37. "Note sur l'Assemblée Générale du Nord-Est tenue à Paris," 17–18 Dec. 1875, ibid., 3353. See Caron, *Histoire des chemins de fer*, pp. 447–60.
38. Cie Nord, Ass. Gén., *rapport*, 30 Apr. 1879, CAMT Roubaix, 48 AQ, 571. Cie Nord, Cons. d'Adm., *procès-verbal*, 25 Oct. 1878, 4 Apr. 1879, 18 Feb. 1881, ibid., 20–22.

39. Cameron, *France*, pp. 70–71. Also see the more recent surveys by Caron, *La France des patriotes*, pp. 299–317; Gueslin, *L'état*, pp. 69–79; Broder, *L'économie française*, pp. 125–41; and Barjot, *Histoire économique*, pp. 248–53.
40. Cie Nord, Cons. d'Adm., *procès-verbal*, 31 March 1882, CAMT Roubaix, 48 AQ, 23. See Gonjo, "Le 'Plan Freycinet,'" pp. 49–86.
41. Léon Say, "Le rachat des chemins de fer," *RGCF*, Jan. 1882. Say's comment on the Freycinet Plan is quoted by Caron, *Histoire des chemins de fer*, p. 489.
42. Commission … des chemins de fer, *procès-verbal*, 17 March 1882, AN Paris, C 3309.
43. Commission … des chemins de fer, *procès-verbal*, 23 June 1883, ibid. Cie PLM, Cons. d'Adm., *procès-verbal*, 6 to 26 Apr. 1883, CAMT Roubaix, 48 AQ, 189.
44. Commission … des chemins de fer, *procès-verbal*, 19 June 1883, AN Paris, C 3309.
45. Caron, *La France des patriotes*, p. 306.
46. Cie Est, Ass. Gén., *rapport*, 22 Dec. 1883, CAMT Roubaix, 13 AQ, 2640. Cie PLM, Ass. Gén., *rapport*, 24 Dec. 1883, ibid., 77 AQ, 160. Cie PO, Ass. Gén., *rapport*, 13 Dec. 1883, ibid., 60 AQ, 176. Cie Nord, Ass. Gén., *rapport*, 20 Dec. 1883, ibid., 48 AQ, 572.
47. "Rapport à M. Mathias," 5 Oct. 1885, ibid., 202 AQ, 1493. Félix Mathias was chief engineer of operations for the Northern.
48. Cie Est, Ass. Gén., *rapport*, 30 Apr. 1885, 29 Apr. 1886, CAMT Roubaix, 13 AQ, 2640. Cie Est, Cons. d'Adm., *procès-verbal*, 7 Aug. 1884, 30 Dec. 1885, 27 Sept. 1888, 10 Jan. 1889, ibid., 69–70. See Mitchell, "Private Enterprise," pp. 30–32.
49. Cie PLM, Ass. Gén., *rapport*, 27 Apr. 1882 to 15 Apr. 1889, CAMT Roubaix, 77 AQ, 160–61. Cie PLM, Cons. d'Adm., *procès-verbal*, 13 June and 22 Aug. 1884, 14 Jan. 1887, 3 Apr. 1890, ibid., 190–92.
50. Cie PO, Ass. Gén., *rapport*, 31 March 1885 to 28 March 1891, ibid., 60 AQ, 176–77. Cie PO, Cons. d'Adm., *procès-verbal*, 9 Jan. 1885, ibid., 42.
51. Cie Nord, Ass. Gén., *rapport*, 28 Apr. 1883 to 30 Apr. 1890, ibid., 48 AQ, 572–73. Cie Nord, Cons. d'Adm., *procès-verbal*, 27 March 1885, 27 March and 26 Oct. 1888, ibid., 25–27.
52. See Barjot, *Travaux publics*, pp. 19–20.
53. See Price, *Modernization*, pp. 207–59.
54. "Proposition de loi relative à une subvention annuelle de quatre millions à partir de 1875 pour la traversée du Simplon," 1873, AN Paris, C 2855. Commission … des chemins de fer, *procès-verbal*, 1 Feb. 1873, ibid., 3005. Broglie to Deseilligny, 7 June 1873, ibid., F^{14} 8589. Deseilligny to MAE, 17 July 1873, ibid. Ponts-et-Chaussées, Conseil Général, *procès-verbal*, 1 July 1875, 31 July 1876, 30 July 1877, ibid., 15958–66.
55. Commission relative au percement du Simplon et du Mont Blanc, *procès-verbal*, 23 March, 11 June, and 7 July 1881, ibid., C 3182.
56. Chambre de Commerce de Paris to Sadi Carnot, 16 June 1881, ibid., F^{14} 8589. Chambre de Commerce de Marseille to Tirard, 29 June 1881, ibid. Statement by Lesguillier on 9 March 1883, in *La question des chemins de fer. Procès-verbaux des séances du Comité des députés et du Comité des conseillers généraux* (Paris, 1883), pp. 29–30.
57. "Rapport au Ministre des Travaux Publics sur la demande en concession de MM. Michel Chevalier et consorte," 13 July 1874, AN Paris, F^{14} 12689. Cie Nord, Cons. d'Adm., *procès-verbal*, 22 Jan. 1875, CAMT Roubaix, 48 AQ, 19. Cie Nord, Ass. Gén., *rapport*, 29 Apr. 1876, ibid., 571. Ponts-et-Chaussées, Conseil Général, *procès-verbal*, 26 July 1880, AN Paris, F^{14} 15978. See Wilson, *Channel Tunnel Visions*, pp. 10–22; and Bonnaud, *Le tunnel sous la Manche*.
58. Ponts-et-Chaussées, Conseil Général, *procès-verbal*, 8 Aug. 1872, AN Paris, F^{14} 15946. Ernest Cézanne, "Rapport fait au nom de la Commission d'enquête sur les chemins de fer …," 3 Feb. 1873, ibid., C 2856. Commission … des chemins de fer, *procès-verbal*, 3 Feb. 1873, ibid., 3005.
59. Ponts-et-Chaussées, Conseil Général, *procès-verbal*, 11 Oct. 1875, ibid., F^{14} 15959. "Chemins de fer projeté d'Hirson à Neufchâteau …," 1875, ibid., C 3006.
60. Ponts-et-Chaussées, Conseil Général, *procès-verbal*, 17 Oct. 1878, ibid., F^{14} 15971. Gottschalk, "Rapport …," 30 May 1882, ibid., 12159. Lombard et al., "Proposition de loi

ayant pour objet l'établissement d'une grande ligne de Calais à Marseille ...," 1882, ibid., C 3309. Lesguillier et al., "Proposition de loi ayant pour objet l'établissement des lignes nécessaires pour compléter le 3e réseau ...," 1882, ibid.
61. Charles Dietz-Monnin, "Rapport préliminaire sur les réponses aux questionnaires de la 2me sous-commission," 1872, ibid., 3007. Commission ... des chemins de fer," *procès-verbal*, 3 July 1872, 25 Feb. 1874, ibid., 3005. Cie PO, Ass. Gén., *rapport*, 25 March 1873, CAMT Roubaix, 60 AQ, 175.
62. Ponts-et-Chaussées, Conseil Général, *procès-verbal*, 8 Oct. 1877, AN Paris, F^{14} 15967. "Circulaire de M. le Ministre des Travaux Publics à MM. les Inspecteurs généraux ...," *RGCF*, Sept. 1878. Cie PLM, Cons. d'Adm., *procès-verbal*, 6 Dec. 1878, CAMT Roubaix, 77 AQ, 187. Cie Est, Cons. d'Adm., *procès-verbal*, 9 June 1883, ibid., 13 AQ, 68.
63. Cie PO, Cons. d'Adm., *procès-verbal*, 13 and 20 Apr. 1883, CAMT Roubaix, 60 AQ, 40. "Rapport de M. Richard Waddington ...," cited by Picard, *Les chemins de fer français* 5: 133.
64. Introduction by the Comité d'études des questions de travaux publics, in *La question des chemins de fer. Procès-verbaux des séances du Comité des députés et du Comité des conseillers généraux* (Paris, 1883), p. 3.
65. Alphonse de Rothschild to Caillaux, 9 Dec. 1874, CAMT Roubaix, 48 AQ, 3486. Vuitry to Paris, 25 Oct. 1877, ibid.
66. Cie Est, Cons. d'Adm., *procès-verbal*, 18 and 24 Feb., 9 March 1876, ibid., 13 AQ, 61. Cie PO, Cons. d'Adm., *procès-verbal*, 12 Dec. 1879, ibid., 60 AQ, 37. Solacroup to Freycinet, 16 Dec. 1879, ibid. "Le projet de convention internationale sur le transport des marchandises par chemins de fer," *RGCF*, Jan. 1881.
67. *Procès-verbaux des délibérations de la Conférence internationale pour l'unité technique des chemins de fer* (Bern, 1882). "Conférences des chefs de service des contentieux et des réclamations des chemins de fer français," 1 Apr. 1882, CAMT Roubaix, 202 AQ, 1649. "Protocole final de la Conférence internationale pour l'unité technique des chemins de fer," 21 Oct. 1882, AN Paris, F^{14} 12868. Luuyt to Hérisson, 31 Oct. 1882, ibid.
68. CETCF, "Extrait du registre des délibérations," 23 Jan. 1883, 12 Feb. 1884, AN Paris, F^{14} 12374, 12868. Reynal to Guillebot de Merville, 18 Jan. 1884, ibid. Luuyt, "Rapport de la Commission," 22 Jan. 1884, ibid. *Procès-verbal de la seconde conférence internationale pour l'unité technique des voies ferrées* (Bern, 1886).
69. Cie Est, Cons. d'Adm., *procès-verbal*, 15 Feb. 1872, 5 March 1874, CAMT Roubaix, 13 AQ, 56–59. Cie PO, Cons. d'Adm., *procès-verbal*, 16 Feb. 1872, ibid., 60 AQ, 30. Cie PLM, Cons. d'Adm., *procès-verbal*, 30 Apr. 1875, ibid., 77 AQ, 185. Administration du chemin de fer de Ceinture de Paris, "Observations sur le projet de loi relatif aux renseignements statistiques ...," 10 March 1876, ibid., 48 AQ, 3596.
70. Vuitry to Paris, 25 Oct. 1877, ibid., 3486. Commission ... des chemins de fer, *procès-verbal*, 8 Feb. 1877, AN Paris, C 3154.
71. Caron, *Histoire des chemins de fer*, p. 498.
72. "Convention pour l'exploitation des deux chemins de fer de ceinture," 30 Dec. 1880, CAMT Roubaix, 13 AQ, 65. Cie PO, Cons. d'Adm., *procès-verbal*, 3 March and 12 May 1882, ibid., 60 AQ, 39. Jacqmin to Durbach, 9 Apr. 1885, ibid., 13 AQ, 2030. Cie Grande Ceinture, Ass. Gén., *rapport*, 20 March 1889, ibid., 75 AQ, 5.
73. Cie Est, Cons. d'Adm., *procès-verbal*, 8 Jan., 5 Aug., and 23 Sept. 1880, ibid., 13 AQ, 65. Cie PLM, Cons. d'Adm., *procès-verbal*, 3 June 1881, ibid., 77 AQ, 188. Cie PO, Cons. d'Adm., *procès-verbal*, 12 Aug. 1881, ibid., 60 AQ, 38. Cie Nord, Cons. d'Adm., *procès-verbal*, 7 Jan. 1881, ibid., 48 AQ, 22. See Caron, "Les commandes," pp. 37–76; Crouzet, "Essor," pp. 112–210; and Mitchell, "A Dangerous Game," pp. 29–45.
74. "Rapport d'une Commission spéciale nommée par le Conseil," 25 July 1889, AN Paris, F^{14} 17857.

75. Delattre et al., "Proposition de loi relative à la sécurité publique dans les chemins de fer," 6 Dec. 1884, ibid., C 5384. Directeur des chemins de fer (in the Ministry of Public Works) to M. de la Tournerie (Cie PLM), 2 Feb. 1887, ibid., F^{14} 8518.
76. Cie PO, Cons. d'Adm., *procès-verbal*, 25 May, 31 Aug., and 21 Dec. 1888, CAMT Roubaix, 60 AQ, 45. Ponts-et-Chaussées, Conseil Général, *procès-verbal*, 3 Oct. 1889, AN Paris, F^{14} 16015.
77. "Rapport fait au nom de la Commission du budget … par M. André Folliet, député," 10 June 1890, CAMT Roubaix, 48 AQ, 3321.
78. See Caron, *Histoire des chemins de fer*, pp. 499, 533.
79. Baron Ernouf, *Histoire des chemins de fer français pendant la guerre franco-prussienne* (Paris, 1874), p. 6. Commission supérieure de défense, "Réorganisation des frontières entre la mer du Nord et la Méditerranée," July 1873, SHAT Vincennes, MR 2146. "Observations présentées par M. le général de Rivières …," 11 July 1873, ibid., 2150. See Monteilhet, *Les institutions militaires*; Ralston, *Army*; and Mitchell, *Victors and Vanquished*, pp. 53–60.
80. Ponts-et-Chaussées, Conseil Général, *procès-verbal*, 5 Dec. 1878, AN Paris, F^{14} 15971. "Note à messieurs les sénateurs et à messieurs les députés …," 1879, ibid., C 3309. Major X, "Les chemins de fer allemands et les chemins de fer français au point de vue de la concentration des armées," *Journal des sciences militaires*, May 1879.
81. Ponts-et-Chaussées, Conseil Général, *procès-verbal*, 8 Apr., 16 Sept., and 16 Dec. 1872, AN Paris, F^{14} 15945–15947. Ministry of Public Works, "Rapport …," 27 June 1872, ibid., 15945. Ponts-et-Chaussées, "Rapport présenté au Conseil par une Commission de ses membres," 13 Feb. 1873, ibid., 15948. Caillaux to the president of the Commission des chemins de fer, 9 July 1875, ibid., C 2854.
82. Ponts-et-Chaussées, Conseil Général, *procès-verbal*, 29 Dec. 1873, 4 Oct. 1875, ibid., F^{14} 15951–15959.
83. See Mitchell, "Thiers," pp. 232–52; Jauffret, "Monsieur Thiers," pp. 27–45; and Fournier, "Fortifications," pp. 53–71.
84. "Règlement général pour les transports militaires par chemins de fer," 1874, AN Paris, F^{14} 8601. Fourth Bureau, "Note pour Monsieur le Chef d'Etat-major Général," 15 Jan. 1881, SHAT Vincennes, 7 N 2016. Commission militaire de l'Est, "Note," 21 Aug. 1886, ibid., 2029.
85. Andigné, "Rapport fait au nom de la Commission …," *Journal officiel: Sénat*, 2 Apr. 1878. Borel to Corps commanders, 6 Feb. 1878, SHAT Vincennes, 7 N 2016. Fourth Bureau, "Liste des travaux de chemins de fer à exécuter d'urgence dans l'intérêt de la défense du pays," 27 Jan. 1882, ibid.
86. Freycinet, "Projet de loi relatif au classement des lignes …," 4 Nov. 1878, AN Paris, C 3180. "Rapport fait au nom de la Commission chargée d'examiner le projet de loi … par M. Wilson, député," 15 March 1879, CAMT Roubaix, 48 AQ, 3602.
87. Fourth Bureau, "Note pour le 3e Bureau de l'Etat-major Général," 28 Apr. 1876, SHAT Vincennes, 7 N 2016. Fourth Bureau, "Mouvements des troupes vers la frontière," 31 Dec. 1879, ibid. Farre to Corps commanders, 20 May 1880, ibid. Farre to Sadi Carnot, 20 June 1881, ibid., 29. Farre to officers of the *Génie*, 2 July 1881, ibid., 37.
88. "Procès-verbal de la conférence …," 12 Aug. 1882, AN Paris, F^{14} 15131. Ponts-et-Chaussées, Conseil Général, *procès-verbal*, 2 July 1883, ibid., 15990.
89. Fourth Bureau, "Plan No 3 rectifié," with "Cartes des lignes de transport …," 27 July 1882, SHAT Vincennes, 7 N 29.
90. Fourth Bureau, "Note pour le Général chef d'Etat-major Général," 30 Jan. 1886, ibid., 2016. Commission … des chemins de fer, *procès-verbal*, 17 March 1886, AN Paris, C 5385. "Commission relative à la proposition de loi de M. Eugène Delattre …," 2 and 14 Dec. 1886, ibid., 5384. Boulanger to Commanding General of the Sixth Army Corps, 26 Jan. 1887, SHAT Vincennes, 7 N 99.
91. "Instruction provisoire …," 15 Nov. 1886, SHAT Vincennes, 7 N 99. Boulanger to the Second Army Corps, 22 Dec. 1886, ibid., 674. "Note pour la Direction de l'Infantrie," [?] Jan. 1887, ibid., 38. First Bureau to Fourth Bureau, 3 Jan. 1887, ibid., 99. "Extrait de

l'instruction ...," 7 Jan. 1887, ibid., 37. Sandherr, "Note de service," 7 Apr. 1887, ibid., 674. Boulanger to the Second Army Corps, 7 and 20 May 1887, ibid. See Mitchell, "Xenophobic Style," pp. 414–25.
92. Fourth Bureau, "Note pour Monsieur le Général chef d'Etat-major Général," 24 Aug. 1886, SHAT Vincennes, 7 N 1779. Commission d'études de l'Ouest, "Note relative à la transformation du rôle des commissions d'études," [?] Aug. 1886, ibid., 2029. Fourth Bureau, "Note pour le Conseil Supérieur de la Guerre ...," 30 May 1888, ibid.
93. See Mitchell, "The Freycinet Reforms," pp. 19–28.
94. Freycinet, "Rapport au Président de la République française ...," 12 May 1888, SHAT Vincennes, 1 N 4. Fourth Bureau, "Note pour le Conseil Supérieur de la Guerre ...," 30 May 1888, ibid., 7 N 2029. CSG, *procès-verbal*, 2 July and 6 Aug. 1888, ibid., 1 N 4.
95. Sandherr, "Note pour le 1er Bureau de l'Etat-major Général," 16 May 1888, ibid., 7 N 674. Freycinet to Floquet, 6 June 1888, ibid. In his memoirs Freycinet neglects to mention his complicity with Sandherr. Freycinet, *Souvenirs 1878–1893* (4th ed., Paris, 1913), pp. 403–12, 444–48.
96. CSG, *procès-verbal*, 2 July and 6 Aug. 1888, SHAT Vincennes, 1 N 4.
97. Colonel Leplus (Fourth Bureau), "Note," 17 Oct. 1889, ibid., 7 N 29.

Chapter 5

1. The legal and constitutional aspects have been carefully examined by Albrecht, *Bismarcks Eisenbahngesetzgebung*.
2. "Protokoll der am 7. und 8. März in Dresden abgehaltenen General-Konferenz der Deutschen Eisenbahn-Verwaltungen," 7–8 March 1871, BA Berlin, R 4101/333 (P). Fournier to "sämmtliche [*sic*] Eisenbahnverwaltungen im Gebiete des Deutschen Reiches," 27 March 1871, ibid.
3. Delbrück to the Bundesrat, 7 Nov. 1871, GLA Karlsruhe, 233/13394. Delbrück to Wächter, 20 and 22 Dec. 1871, WHStA Stuttgart, E 46, Bü 451, 453.
4. See Albrecht, *Bismarcks Eisenbahngesetzgebung*, pp. 122–23; and Huber, *Deutsche Verfassungsgeschichte* 4: 1060–63.
5. Delbrück to Jolly, 23 May 1872, GLA Karlsruhe, 233/13397.
6. Soden to Wächter, 22 Jan. 1872, WHStA Stuttgart, E 46, Bü 452. Friesen to Bismarck, 16 Feb. 1872, ibid. "Entwurf einer Antwort an das Reichskanzleramt," [?] Feb. 1872, ibid. Memo by Dr. Carl Mayer, 23 Jan. 1872, BHStA Munich, Verkehrsarchiv 7213. Hegnenberg to Bismarck, 2 Feb. 1872, ibid. Dusch to Jolly, 13 Feb. and 6 June 1872, GLA Karlsruhe, 233/13397.
7. Delbrück to Jolly, 18 Oct. 1872, GLA Karlsruhe, 233/11909.
8. Prussian Chamber of Deputies, *Stenographische Berichte*, 19 Dec. 1872, 14 Jan. and 7 Feb. 1873. Bismarck to Roon, 1 March 1873, GStA PK Berlin, I. HA Rep. 151 HB, Nr. 1309 (M).
9. See Albrecht, *Bismarcks Eisenbahngesetzgebung*, pp. 4–18; and Morsey, *Reichsverwaltung*, pp. 139–60.
10. Achenbach to Scheele, 18 Oct. 1873, GStA PK Berlin, I. HA Rep. 93 E, Nr. 12 (M).
11. Scheele to VDEV, 14 Oct. 1873, BA Berlin, R 4101/21 (C). Fournier (VDEV) to Scheele, 24 Oct. 1873, ibid.
12. Achenbach to Camphausen, 20 Nov. 1873, GStA PK Berlin, I. HA Rep. 90, Nr. 1678 (D). Achenbach to Camphausen, 12 Feb. 1874, ibid., Rep. 151 HB, Nr. 1309 (M).
13. Scheele to Saxony MAA, 13 March 1874, SHStA Dresden, MAA 7476. Scheele to Wächter, 18 March 1874, WHStA Stuttgart, E 46, Bü 461. See Albrecht, *Bismarcks Eisenbahngesetzgebung*, pp. 31–47.
14. Delbrück to Mittnacht, 5 May 1874, WHStA Stuttgart, E 46, Bü 461. Mittnacht to Soden, 12 May 1874, ibid., E 75, 410.
15. Prussian cabinet, *Protokoll*, 23 Oct. 1874, GStA PK Berlin, I. HA Rep. 90, Nr. 1676 (D).
16. Maybach to RKA, 4 March and 22 Apr. 1875, BA Berlin, R 4201/32 (C). See Albrecht, *Bismarcks Eisenbahngesetzgebung*, pp. 48–59.

17. *Stenographischer Bericht über die Verhandlungen, betreffend die informatorische Berathung des vorläufigen Entwurfes eines Reichs-Eisenbahn-Gesetzes,* 7–12 June 1875, GStA PK Berlin, I. HA Rep. 90, Nr. 1676 (D).
18. Rennen (Rheinische Eisenbahn) to REA, 12 July 1875, ibid. Achenbach to the Prussian cabinet, 14 Aug. 1875, ibid.
19. Nostitz to Friesen, 13 Dec. 1875, SHStA Dresden, MAA 7440. Draft of a memo from the Prussian cabinet to Kaiser Wilhelm I, [?] Jan. 1876, GStA PK Berlin, I. HA Rep. 89, Nr. 2 (D). Bismarck, "Votum des Präsidenten des Staatsministeriums, dem königlichen Staatsministerium vorzulegen," 8 Jan. 1876, ibid., Rep. 77, Tit. 258, Nr. 63, Bd. 1 (M). See Albrecht, *Bismarcks Eisenbahngesetzgebung,* pp. 86–98.
20. Camphausen, "Votum des Finanz-Ministers, dem königlichen Staats-Ministerium vorzulegen," 20 Jan. 1876, GStA PK Berlin, I. HA Rep. 89, Nr. 2 (D). Prussian cabinet, *Protokoll,* 12 Feb. 1876, ibid., Rep. 90, Nr. 1876 (D).
21. Friesen to Nostitz, 24 Jan. 1876, WHStA Stuttgart, E 130 a, 942. Spitzemberg to Mittnacht, 29 Jan. 1876, ibid., E 75, 414. Bismarck to Solms, 2 Feb. 1876, SHStA Dresden, MAA 7440.
22. Maybach to Bismarck, 14 and 27 March 1876, BA Berlin, R 4101/21 (C). Bismarck to Wilhelm I, 8 Apr. 1876, GStA PK Berlin, I. HA Rep. 89, Nr. 2 (D). Maybach to Bismarck, 20 May 1876, ibid., Rep. 90, Nr. 1676 (D). "Denkschrift, betreffend die Reichs-Aufsicht und die Reichsgesetzgebung über das Eisenbahn-Wesen," [?] May 1876, ibid. "Gesetz, betreffend die Übertragung der Eigenthums- und sonstigen Rechte des Staates an Eisenbahnen auf das Deutsche Reich," 4 June 1876, ibid. See Alfred von der Leyen, *Die Eisenbahnpolitik des Fürsten Bismarck* (Berlin, 1914), pp. 207–13.
23. "Grundzüge für die Ordnung des deutschen Eisenbahnwesens," sent by Maybach to Bismarck, 14 Feb. 1877, GStA PK Berlin, I. HA Rep. 90, Nr. 1677 (D).
24. Bismarck to Bülow, 15 Dec. 1877, BA Berlin, R 43/92 (P).
25. Achenbach to Camphausen, 7 Feb. 1878, GStA PK Berlin, I. HA Rep. 90, Nr. 1677 (D). Bismarck to Maybach, 20 May 1878, BA Berlin, R 43/92 (P). Memo by Maybach, 24 June 1878, GStA PK Berlin, I. HA Rep. 93 E, Nr. 12 (M). See Stern, *Gold and Iron,* pp. 208–17.
26. See Albrecht, *Bismarcks Eisenbahngesetzgebung,* pp. 99–102; and Huber, *Deutsche Verfassungsgeschichte* 4: 1063–66.
27. Herbert von Bismarck to Tiedemann, 12 Dec. 1878, 16 and 20 Jan. 1879, BA Berlin, R 43/81 (P). Bismarck to Maybach, 22 Jan. 1879, ibid., 92. Maybach to Hobrecht, 4 May 1879, ibid., 81.
28. Maybach to Bismarck, 26 Jan. 1879, ibid. On the shift to protectionism, see Wehler, *Deutsche Gesellschaftsgeschichte* 3: 637–61. Also see Sheehan, *German Liberalism,* pp. 179–218.
29. Maybach to Bismarck, 8 Apr. 1879, BA Berlin, R 4201/75 (C). Bismarck to Maybach, 19 June 1879, ibid.
30. Maybach to Bismarck, 31 Oct. 1879, ibid., R 43/80 (P). Italics added. See Albrecht, *Bismarcks Eisenbahngesetzgebung,* pp. 104–11.
31. Fremdling and Knieps, "Competition," p. 129. The same confusion of terminology appears in Dunlavy, *Politics and Industrialization,* p. 33; and Stern, *Gold and Iron,* p. 302.
32. See the disappointing summary of Bismarck's railway policy in the 1870s by Wehler, *Deutsche Gesellschaftsgeschichte* 3: 74. Later he attempts to set the record straight but insists that Bismarck was "ultimately successful." Ibid., p. 676.
33. Scheele to Saxony MAA, 13 March 1874, SHStA Dresden, MAA 7476. Maybach to Saxony MAA, 18 Aug. 1874, ibid. Friesen to Saxony MAA, 1 Sept. 1874, ibid. Friesen to Saxony MAA, 16 Nov. 1874, ibid. Maybach to Saxony MAA, 21 Dec. 1874, ibid., 1265. Maybach to Saxony MAA, 4 March 1875, ibid., 7476.
34. Friesen to Fabrice, 28 Feb. and 11 March 1876, WHStA Stuttgart, E 130 a, 942. Gasser to King Ludwig II, 4 March 1876, BHStA Munich, MA 2848.

35. Friesen to Solms, 11 July 1876, SHStA Dresden, MAA 7436. Solms to Friesen, 29 Sept. 1876, ibid. Solms to Nostitz, 4 Jan. 1877, ibid. "Denkschrift betreffend die zwischen den Regierungen Preussens und Sachsens wegen der Berlin-Dresdner Eisenbahn bestehende Streitigkeit," [?] May 1877, ibid., 7473. Dönhoff to Nostitz, 25 Sept. 1877, ibid.
36. Memo by Mayer, 16 Oct. 1872, BHStA Munich, Verkehrsarchiv 7213. Pfretschner to Bismarck, 5 March 1873, ibid.
37. Bismarck to Pfretschner, 5 July 1873, ibid. Pfretschner to Bismarck, 21 Aug. 1873, ibid. Bismarck to Pfretschner, 11 Feb. 1874, ibid., MAA 77247.
38. Pfretschner to Faeustle, 11 June 1874, ibid., MJu 16785. "Denkschrift über die Stellung Bayerns zum Reiche im Eisenbahnwesen," sent by Pfretschner to Bismarck, 12 July 1874, ibid., MA 77247. Pfretschner to King Ludwig II, 18 June 1875, ibid.
39. Perglas to King Ludwig II, 26 Jan. 1876, ibid., MA 2656.
40. Pfretschner to King Ludwig II, 28 Jan. 1876, ibid., 77249. Bülow to Werthern, 29 Jan. 1876, ibid. Bismarck to Werthern, 28 Feb. 1876, ibid. See Alexander Krueger, *Zur Geschichte des Bismarckschen Reichseisenbahnprojekts vom Jahre 1876* (Berlin, 1909), pp. 35–40; and Hermann Kirchhof, *Der Bismarcksche Reichseisenbahngedanke* (2nd ed.; Stuttgart and Berlin, 1916), pp. 29–39.
41. Maybach to Pfretschner, 29 Apr. 1876, BHStA Munich, Verkehrsarchiv 6083. Hookeden to Bavarian MA, 3 Oct. 1876, ibid. Pfretschner to Soden, 6 Nov. 1876, ibid.
42. Delbrück to Wächter, 1 July 1872, WHStA Stuttgart, E 46, Bü 452. Dillenius to Wächter, 30 Apr. 1873, ibid., 455.
43. Scheele to Wächter, 1 Nov. 1873, ibid., 457. "Betriebs-Reglement für die Eisenbahnen Deutschlands," 25 Nov. 1873, ibid., 453. Dillenius to Mittnacht, 26 Nov. 1873, ibid., 457.
44. Scheele to Wächter, 23 Jan. 1874, ibid., 457. Spitzemberg to Mittnacht, 27 Jan. 1874, ibid. Mittnacht to Scheele, 1 Feb. 1874, ibid. Scheele to Wächter, 6 Feb. 1874, ibid.
45. "Äusserung der Königlich Württembergischen Eisenbahndirektion …," sent by Dillenius to Mittnacht, 5 May 1874, ibid., 461. Mittnacht to King Karl, 25–26 Sept. 1874, ibid. Mittnacht to Spitzemberg, 29 Jan. 1876, ibid., E 75, 414.
46. Mittnacht to Soden, 20 Feb. 1876, ibid., E 75, 414. Spitzemberg to Mittnacht, 18 March and 2 Apr. 1876, ibid., E 130 a, 942–943. Mittnacht to Soden, 28 Oct. 1877, ibid., E 75, 414.
47. Wächter to Soden, 26 Dec. 1871, 8 May 1872, ibid., 409–10. Mittnacht to Soden, 12 May 1874, ibid.
48. Mittnacht to Soden, 22 Dec. 1875, ibid., 401.
49. Dusch to Jolly, 13 Feb. 1872, GLA Karlsruhe, 233/13397. Jolly to Bismarck, 20 March 1872, ibid. Dusch to Jolly, 6 June 1872, ibid. Turban to Jolly, 20 March 1873, ibid. Turban to Grand Duke Friedrich I, 26 July 1873, ibid., 237/16656.
50. Turban to Grand Duke Friedrich I, 2 June 1875, ibid., 233/13398.
51. Jolly to Friesen, 3 June 1875, ibid. Turban to Jolly, 7 June 1875, ibid. Bismarck to Jolly, 20 March 1876, ibid., 11283. Report by Turban to Baden's cabinet (of which he was now president, replacing Jolly), 4 Apr. 1877, ibid., 11245.
52. Turban to Mittnacht, 24 May 1879, WHStA Stuttgart, E 130 a, 944. Turban to Mittnacht, 9 July 1879, ibid., E 46, Bü 452.
53. Maybach to Bitter, 31 Aug. and 14 Oct. 1880, GStA PK Berlin, I. HA Rep. 151 HB, Nr. 1354 (M).
54. Maybach and Bitter to Bismarck, 23 Sept. 1881, BA Berlin, R 43/82 (P). Prussian cabinet, *Protokoll*, 28 Sept. 1881, ibid. "Nachweisung der für die Aktien der bereits erworbenen und noch zu erwerbenden Privat-Eisenbahnen auszugebenden Staatsschuldverschreibungen," 1885, ibid.
55. Kameke, Maybach, and Bitter to Bismarck, 12 March 1881, ibid. Prussian cabinet, *Protokoll*, 7 Apr. 1881, ibid. Maybach to Bismarck, 4 July 1882, ibid., 86. Prussian cabinet members Puttkammer, Friedberg, Maybach, and Scholz to Bismarck, 6 Aug. 1882, ibid., R 3101/7357 (P).

56. "Nachweisung der für die Aktien der bereits erworbenen und noch zu erwerbenden Privat-Eisenbahnen auszugebenden Staatsschuldverschreibungen," 1885, ibid., R 43/82 (P).
57. Auswärtiges Amt to Bitter, 20 May 1882, GStA PK Berlin, I. HA Rep. 151 HB, Nr. 1315 (M). "Nachweisung der in Frage kommenden Bezirksänderungen einzelner Staatseisenbahn-Verwaltungsbehörden," 1887, ibid., Rep. 93 E, Nr. 74 (M). Cologne actually had two district railway headquarters: one for the right bank of the Rhine, another for the left.
58. Nostitz to Dönhoff, 19 Oct. 1882, BA Berlin, R 3101/7357 (P). Werthern to Bismarck, 9 Nov. 1882, ibid.
59. Hatzfeldt to the Prussian cabinet, 22 Nov. 1882, GStA PK Berlin, I. HA Rep. 90, Nr. 1674 (D). Hatzfeldt to Kameke and Maybach, 10 Feb. 1883, BA Berlin, R 3101/7357 (P). Draft of a memo by Bismarck to the Prussian cabinet, [?] Dec. 1883, ibid. "Entwurf eines Reichsgesetzes, betreffend die Verpflichtung der Privat-Eisenbahnen zur Herstellung von Anlagen im Interesse der Landesvertheidigung," sent from Körte to Boetticher, 14 Dec. 1883, ibid.
60. Lerchenfeld to Crailsheim, 3 Aug. 1883, BHStA Munich, MA 96810.
61. Marschall to Turban, 9 Dec. 1883, 13 Feb. 1884, GLA Karlsruhe, 233/11488. Fabrice (Saxon legate in Munich) to Fabrice (Saxon MAA), 10 Dec. 1883, SHStA Dresden, MAA 7441. Crailsheim to Boetticher, 23 Apr. 1884, BA Berlin, R 3101/7357 (P). Prussian cabinet, *Protokoll*, 11 May 1884, ibid., R 43/86 (P). Crailsheim to Lerchenfeld, 16 May 1884, BHStA Munich, MA 77247. Prussian cabinet, *Protokoll*, 13 June 1884, BA Berlin, R 3101/7357 (P).
62. Maybach to Thielen, 15 June 1884, BA Berlin, R 4201/75 (C). Evidence thus contradicts a view that the VDEV "retained its vitality through the remainder of the century," as asserted by Dunlavy, *Politics and Industrialization*, p. 145.
63. Instances are too numerous to cite in full. Here a few examples may suffice: Körte to Turban, 4 June 1885, GLA Karlsruhe, 233/11488. Ellstätter to Körte, 1 Aug. 1885, ibid. Körte to Ellstätter, 9 Dec. 1885, ibid. Ellstätter to Turban, 18 Dec. 1886, ibid., 11508.
64. Mittnacht to Soden, 1 March 1884, WHStA Stuttgart, E 75, 410. Crailsheim to Soden, 13 March 1884, ibid. "Bahnschlüsse zwischen Bayern und Württemberg betreffend," sent by Crailsheim to Württemberg MAA, 8 Aug. 1875, ibid. "Entwurf: Staatsvertrag zwischen Württemberg und Bayern …," 6 Feb. 1887, ibid. "Schlussprotokoll zum Staatsvertrage," 10 Feb. 1887, BHStA Munich, Verkehrsarchiv 6085.
65. Crailsheim to Württemberg MAA, 4 Dec. 1886, GLA Karlsruhe, 233/11504. Ellstätter to Turban, 19 Jan. 1887, ibid., 11505. "Kommissarische Verhandlung, betreffend die Vervollständigung des deutschen Eisenbahnnetzes im Interesse der Vertheidung des Reichs," 21 Jan. 1887, BHStA Munich, MA 77262. "Behufs Regelung der Betheiligung des Reichs und des Königreichs Bayern …," 11 March 1887, ibid.
66. Bismarck to Verdy, 1 May 1889, BA Berlin, R 43/86 (P).
67. See Wehler, *Deutsche Gesellschaftsgeschichte* 3: 66–85. Naturally the numbers vary in detail: e.g., only 857 new German joint-stock companies are counted for the years 1870–1873 by Tilly, *Vom Zollverein zum Industriestaat*, p. 80.
68. Classic is Rosenberg, *Grosse Depression und Bismarckzeit*. His thesis was immediately challenged in a brilliant review by Gerschenkron in the *Journal of Economic History* 28 (1968): 154–56; and by Saul, *Myth*.
69. Wehler, *Deutsche Gesellschaftsgeschichte* 3: 547 and passim. Wehler relies heavily on the calculations of Spiethoff, *Wechselslagen*; and Spree, *Wachstumszyklen*.
70. See Wehler, *Deutsche Gesellschaftsgeschichte* 3: 548–77; and the long section on "Eisenbahn und Konjunktur" up to 1880 by Spree, *Wachstumszyklen*, pp. 261–316.
71. Nostitz (Saxon legate in Berlin) to Nostitz (Saxon MAA), 14 Nov. 1876, SHStA Dresden, MAA 7495. See Stern, *Gold and Iron*, pp. 200–201.
72. Nostitz to Nostitz, 17 June 1879, SHStA Dresden, MAA 7496.
73. Dillenius to Württemberg MAA, 5 Apr. and 18 Nov. 1879, WHStA Stuttgart, E 46, Bü 464.

74. Fremdling and Knieps, "Competition," p. 143. See Albrecht, *Bismarcks Eisenbahngesetzgebung*, pp. 71–85.
75. Minutes of the Süddeutscher Eisenbahn-Verband and the Südwestdeutscher Eisenbahn-Verband for the period 1874–1879, BA Berlin, R 4201/582–584 (C).
76. See Fremdling, *Eisenbahnen*, pp. 55–60, 90–91.
77. *Protocolle über die Verhandlungen der vom 13. Mai bis 4. Juni in Bern stattgefundenen internationalen Conferenzen betreffend die Vereinbarung eines internationalen Eisenbahntransportrechtes* (Bern, 1878), in BA Berlin, R 4201/457 (C). The quotation is from the sixteenth and final session on 4 June 1878.
78. "Protocole final de la conférence internationale pour l'unité technique des chemins de fer," 15–21 Oct. 1882, sent by Körte to Bismarck, 21 Dec. 1882, ibid., R 43/127 (P). Crailsheim to Lerchenfeld, 28 Dec. 1883, BHStA Munich, MJu 16677. Crailsheim to the Reichsamt des Innern, 28 Dec. 1883, ibid. Meyer, Gerstner, and Rutz to Bismarck, 18 July 1886, BA Berlin, R 4101/15 (C). *Protokolle über die Verhandlungen der III. Konferenz zur Ausbreitung eines internationalen Übereinkommens über den Eisenbahn-Frachtverkehr, Bern, Juli 1886*, ibid.
79. "Zur Gotthard-Bahn," *ZVDEV*, 18 Feb. 1884.
80. Maybach to Bismarck, 18 Feb. 1884, BA Berlin, R 901/14814 (P).
81. "Protokoll," 19 March and 28 Apr. 1872, BHStA Munich, Staatsrat 1219–20. Bavaria also placed orders from another Munich construction firm, Georg Krauss, starting in 1873. See Marggraff, *Die Kgl. Bayerischen Staatsbahnen*, pp. 98–104.
82. Maybach to Saxon MAA, 23 Oct. 1875, SHStA Dresden, MAA 1265. Maybach to Württemberg MAA, 20 Oct. 1875, WHStA Stuttgart, E 46, Bü 455. Maybach to Württemberg MAA, 13 Apr. 1876, ibid. Körte to Württemberg MAA, 8 March 1879, ibid., 452. Turban to Mittnacht, 9 July 1879, ibid.
83. Maybach to Offermann and Rennen (presidents of district railway offices in Cologne), 22 Dec. 1886, GStA PK Berlin, I. HA Rep. 93 E, Nr. 305 (M). Maybach to Bismarck, 2 March 1887, BA Berlin, R 901/14814 (P). Reichard to Prussian legates, 15 Apr. 1887, ibid. Werthern to Bismarck, 6 May 1887, ibid. Flemming to Bismarck, 17 May 1887, ibid. Solms to Bismarck, 11 July 1887, ibid. Gondraud's affiliates were listed in a "top secret" memo simply entitled "Notiz," [?] Apr. 1887, BHStA Munich, Verkehrsarchiv 6118.
84. Maybach to the Bavarian MA, 23 May 1888, BHStA Munich, Verkehrsarchiv 6126. Generaldirektion (of Bavaria's state railways) to MA, 19 June 1888, ibid. Direktion der Pfälzischen Eisenbahnen to MA, 7 Feb. 1889, ibid. Crailsheim to Maybach, 14 March 1889, ibid. Maybach to Crailsheim, 11 Apr. 1889, ibid. Generaldirektion to MA, 26 June 1889, ibid.
85. See Ritter, *Staatskunst und Kriegshandwerk* 1: 262–302; and Messerschmidt, *Militär und Politik*, pp. 75–98.
86. Bismarck to Kaiser Wilhelm I, 27 March and 12 Dec. 1873, GStA PK Berlin, I. HA Rep. 89, Nr. 29461 (M). Dillenius to Mittnacht, 8 July 1875, WHStA Stuttgart, E 46, Bü 451. Maybach to Achenbach, 9 Nov. 1875, GStA PK Berlin, I. HA Rep. 93 E, Nr. 2388 (M). On "the War Hoax of 1875," see Mitchell, *German Influence*, pp. 124–30.
87. Bülow to Tiedemann, 5 Dec. 1877, BA Berlin, R 43/86 (P). Bismarck and Kameke to Kaiser Wilhelm I, 28 Jan. 1878, GStA PK Berlin, I. HA Rep. 89, Nr. 29461 (M). Kameke and Maybach, "Votum dem königlichen Staats-Ministerium vorzulegen," 30 July 1878, ibid. Planitz to Saxon King Albert, 18 Feb. and 13 June 1879, SHStA Dresden, KA (P) 883. Kameke and Maybach, "Votum des Kriegsministers und des Ministers der öffentlichen Arbeiten dem königlichen Staats-Ministeriums ganz ergebenst vorzulegen," 20 May 1879, BA Berlin, R 43/86 (P). See Ritter, *Staatskunst und Kriegshandwerk* 1: 292–95.
88. Crailsheim to Boetticher, 23 Apr. 1884, BA Berlin, R 3101/7357 (P).
89. Bronsart, "Denkschrift, betreffend die militärische Bedeutung und Benutzung der Eisenbahnen Deutschlands," 28 June 1885, ibid., R 43/86 (P). Bronsart to Bismarck, 28 June 1885, ibid.

90. Cited by Gall, *Bismarck*, p. 671.
91. Bronsart to Bismarck, 11 Jan. 1887, BA Berlin, R 43/86 (P). Bismarck to Maybach, 23 Feb. 1887, ibid., R 4201/669 (C). Waldersee to the Auswärtiges Amt, 16 Apr. 1887, ibid. Bronsart to Maybach, 17 Nov. 1887, GStA PK Berlin, I. HA Rep. 93 E, Nr. 305 (M).
92. Lerchenfeld to MA, 13 May 1887, BHStA Munich, MA 2665. Bronsart to Maybach, 28 Dec. 1887, GStA PK Berlin, I. HA Rep. 151 HB, Nr. 1316 (M).
93. Verdy to Bismarck, 18 July 1889, BA Berlin, R 43/117 (P). Bismarck to Verdy, 21 July and 19 Nov. 1889, ibid. Verdy to Bismarck, 19 and 20 Dec. 1889, ibid.
94. Maybach, Scholz, and Verdy to Bismarck, 24 Jan. 1890, GStA PK Berlin, I. HA Rep. 90, Nr. 1674 (D). Maybach to Bismarck, 6 March 1890, BA Berlin, R 43/117 (P). Bismarck to REA, 9 March 1890, ibid.

Chapter 6

1. The great boom in French ore from the Briey region did not occur until after 1890. For background, see Gille, *La sidérurgie française*, which concludes in 1888; and Milward and Saul, *Development*, pp. 91–92. On the Nordwolle, see Reeken, *Lahusen*, pp. 67–105.
2. For an overview of innovation in locomotives, see Lamming and Marseille, *Le temps des chemins de fer*, pp. 83–85; and Schletzbaum, *Eisenbahn*, pp. 92–106.
3. See Schivelbusch, *Geschichte der Eisenbahnreise*; and Angelier, *Voyage en train*.
4. "Die geschichtliche Entwicklung der Normalien für die Betriebsmittel der preussischen Staatsbahnen in den Jahren 1871 bis 1895," *ZVDEV*, 27 March 1895. See Ribeill, *Cheminots*.
5. See Mitchell, "Subversion and Repression," pp. 409–33.
6. Maybach to Prussian railway executives, 3 June 1878, GStA PK Berlin, I. HA Rep. 77, Tit. 260, Nr. 6, Bd. 3 (M). Eulenburg to the Prussian railway directorates, 7 July 1878, ibid.
7. Paul Leroy-Beaulieu, *Le travail des femmes au XIXe siècle* (Paris, 1873), p. 342, cited by Marcel Lemercier, "De l'emploi des femmes dans les chemins de fer français et spécialement à la Compagnie de l'Est," *RGCF*, Jan. 1885.
8. "Über die Verwendung der Frauen im Dienste der Eisenbahnen, in specie bei der französischen Ostbahn," *ZVDEV*, 25 March 1885; and "Über die Verwendung der Frauen im Eisenbahndienst," ibid., 12 Sept. 1885.
9. "De l'emploi des femmes à l'ancienne Compagnie des Doubs," *RGCF*, May 1885.
10. "Weibliche Angestellte bei den französischen Bahnverwaltungen," *ZVDEV*, 25 Jan. 1888. See Ribeill, *La révolution ferroviaire*, pp. 363–64; and Mitchell, "Weak Sisters," pp. 177–81.
11. "Die Eisenbahnen der Erde 1883–1887," *ZVDEV*, 6 July 1889.
12. Compare Caron, "France," and Fremdling, "Germany," in O'Brien, *Railways*, pp. 28–48, 121–47.
13. See Caron, *Histoire des chemins de fer*, pp. 532, 587.
14. "Dépenses d'établissement au 31 décembre 1885, des lignes exploitées à cette date (y compris le matériel roulant)," 31 Dec. 1885, AN Paris, C 5384. See Broder, *L'économie française*, pp. 129–41.
15. Wehler, *Deutsche Gesellschaftsgeschichte* 3: 556.
16. "Aus Frankreich: Kohlenbedarf," *ZVDEV*, 20 Feb. 1889.
17. "Die deutschen Lokomotivfabriken," *ZVDEV*, 7 June 1867. See Messerschmidt, *Taschenbuch*, p. 237; Crouzet, "Essor," pp. 112–210; and Mitchell, "A Dangerous Game," pp. 31–33.
18. Commission … des chemins de fer, *procès-verbal*, 14 Feb. 1900, AN Paris, C 5634. See Caron, "Les commandes," p. 150.
19. See Mitchell, *German Influence*, pp. 185–93.
20. Pelletan, "Proposition de loi sur les tarifs de chemins de fer," 6 Feb. 1890, AN Paris, C 5465. Commission … des chemins de fer, *procès-verbal*, 7 March 1890, ibid., 5454.

21. "Proposition de loi concernant les tarif de chemins de fer: rapport de M. Richard Waddington. Discussion au Comité consultatif des chemins de fer," 17 Jan. 1891, ibid., 5561.
22. Pelletan and Pourquery de Boisserin, "Proposition de loi sur les tarifs de chemins de fer d'intérêt général," 19 Dec. 1893, ibid.
23. Münster to Bismarck, 23 June 1886, BA Berlin, R 4201/Tl 645 (C).
24. "Das Simplon-Tunnel-Projekt nach Marteaus Denkschrift," *ZVDEV*, 5 Jan. 1883.
25. "Aus Frankreich: Zur Frage der Simplonbahn," ibid., 20 Feb. 1889. See Benz, *Le percement du Simplon*.
26. "Die Alpenbahn-Projekte über den Simplon, Grossen St. Bernhard und Montblanc," *ZVDEV*, 9 May 1885. See Pecheux, *L'age d'or*, pp. 50–60.
27. Commission d'enquête des ports de la Manche et du Nord, "Tonnage total des navires entrés dans les ports … de 1860 à 1881," 1882, AN Paris, F^{14} 12159.
28. Gottschalk, "Rapport. Chemins de fer de l'Ouest et de l'Est: concurrence du port d'Anvers contre le port du Havre …," 30 May 1882, ibid. "Rapport supplémentaire …," 20 June 1882, ibid. "Concurrence des ports français du littoral de la Manche … contre les ports belges, hollondais et allemands …," 3 Apr. 1883, ibid.
29. Report by Lesguillier, 9 March 1883, in *La question des chemins de fer. Procès-verbaux des séances du Comité des députés et du Comité des conseillers généraux* (Paris, 1883), p. 29.
30. See Hermann Budde, *Die französischen Eisenbahnen im Kriege 1870–1871 und ihre seitherige Entwicklung in militärischer Sicht* (Berlin, 1877).
31. See Mitchell, "The Freycinet Reforms," pp. 19–28.
32. Ponts-et-Chaussées, Conseil Général, *procès-verbal*, 1 March 1886, AN Paris, F^{14} 16000.
33. "Comparaison des budgets de la Guerre en France et en Allemagne," 30 Dec. 1892, SHAT Vincennes, 7 N 665. See Mitchell, "A Situation of Inferiority," p. 52.
34. Freycinet to General de Miribel, 24 Feb. 1891, SHAT Vincennes, 5 N 2. The notion that military reforms had brought France to virtual parity with Germany by 1890 has been adopted by Kennan, *Decline*, pp. 247, 415.
35. Worries about French espionage became acute in 1883, causing Moltke to order precautionary measures. Prussian Ministry of the Interior to all Oberpräsidenten, 11 Sept. 1883, BHStA Munich, Abt. IV, Gen Stab 923. Friedberg to the Oberstaatsanwalt, 29 Oct. 1883, ibid. Moltke, "Denkschrift zu dem Eisenbahnen- und Telegraphen-Schutz in Elsass-Lothringen bei einer Mobilmachung," 13 May 1884, ibid. Maybach ordered the removal of "foreigners" from the state railway service and the directorates of private railway companies. Maybach to the Eisenbahn-Kommissariat, 12 July 1889, BA Berlin, R 43/64 (P). Maybach to REA, 20 Sept. 1889, ibid. On France, see Mitchell, "Xenophobic Style," pp. 419–25.

Chapter 7

1. See Caron, *La France des patriotes*, pp. 429–611.
2. "Statistique: Résultats obtenus en 1894 sur les réseaux des six compagnies principales des chemins de fer français," *RGCF*, Aug. 1895.
3. Ponts-et-Chaussées, Conseil Général, *procès-verbal*, 20 Oct. 1892, 16 Nov. 1893, AN Paris, F^{14} 16951–16955. See Caron, *Histoire de l'exploitation*, pp. 367–94.
4. Ponts-et-Chaussées, Conseil Général, *procès-verbal*, 25 July 1895, AN Paris, F^{14} 16962.
5. Comité d'exploitation des deux ceintures, *procès-verbal*, 30 Apr. 1902, CAMT Roubaix, 75 AQ, 29. See Eileen Sposato DeMarco, "Reading and Riding: Hachette's Railroad Bookstore Network in Nineteenth-Century France," Ph.D. dissertation, University of California, San Diego, 1996; and Angelier, *Voyage en train*, pp. 99–117.
6. "Les directeurs de chemins de fer nommés par l'Etat," *JT*, 21 Jan. 1893. Comité d'exploitation des deux ceintures, *procès-verbal*, 26 June 1901, CAMT Roubaix, 75 AQ, 29.
7. CETCF, *procès-verbal*, 2 Apr. and 18 June 1895, 28 Jan. and 19 May 1896, AN Paris, F^{14} 12362–12363. CETCF, "Avis," 18 Feb. 1902, 19 May 1903, ibid., 12367. CETCF, "Emploi des freins continus sur les chemins der fer français, année 1903: Rapport," 26 Jan. 1905, ibid., 12368.

8. "Locomotive électrique à grande vitesse de la Compagnie Paris-Lyon-Méditerranée," *RGCF*, Nov. 1898. "La traction électrique applicable aux chemins de fer," *JT*, 7 Apr. 1900. "Les chemins de fer électrique à très grandes vitesses experimentés actuellement en Allemagne," *RGCF*, March 1902. Ponts-et-Chaussées (4e section), *procès-verbal*, 26 March 1902, AN Paris, F¹⁴ 16344. See Bouneau, "La contribution des technologies étrangères," pp. 553–72; and Lanthier, "L'électrification," pp. 15–29.
9. "La fortification du Contrôle au Sénat," *JT*, 1 Apr. 1893. "La réforme du Contrôle au Sénat," ibid., 29 Apr. 1893. "Comptes ouverts entre l'Etat et les compagnies de chemins de fer," ibid., 22 July 1893.
10. Richard von Kaufmann, *Die Eisenbahnpolitik Frankreichs* (Stuttgart, 1896), translated as *La politique française en matière de chemins de fer* (Paris, 1900). Henri Bonneau, *Etudes sur les chemins de fer français* (Paris, 1896), p. 82. Frantz Hamon, *L'avenir de la politique française en matière de chemins de fer* (Paris, 1900), p. 1. See the critique of Kaufmann by Leclercq, *L'établissement*, pp. 14–16.
11. "Les caisses de retraites et de secours des compagnies de chemins de fer," *JT*, 7 Aug. 1897. See Mitchell, *Divided Path*, pp. 276–99.
12. "Les résultats de 1900: Chemin de fer du Nord," *JT*, 13 July 1901. "La loi Bertaux," ibid., 23 Nov. 1901. "La prix d'une loi," ibid., 11 Jan. 1902.
13. Ponts-et-Chaussées, Conseil Général, *procès-verbal*, 23 July 1891, 9 Oct. 1893, AN Paris, F¹⁴ 16946–16955. Guyot to administrators of the companies, 4 Nov. 1891, ibid., 17858. See Caron, *Histoire de l'exploitation*, pp. 255–56.
14. Ponts-et-Chaussées, Conseil Général, *procès-verbal*, 11 July 1892, 21 Feb. 1895, 27 Feb. 1896, 1 Apr. and 26 July 1897, AN Paris, F¹⁴ 16950–16970.
15. Ponts-et-Chaussées (4e section), *procès-verbal*, 7 Nov. 1900, AN Paris, F¹⁴ 16340. Pérouse to Cie Ouest, 29 Dec. 1902, ibid., 12383. CETCF, *procès-verbal*, 23 Sept. 1910, ibid., 12371.
16. Commission d'unification de matériel roulant, *procès-verbal*, 28 Oct. and 11 Dec. 1901, ibid., 12384. "Locomotives allemandes en France," *Le Matin*, 7 Jan. 1902. See Mitchell, "A Dangerous Game," pp. 36–38.
17. Maruéjouls to administrators of the companies, 7 Jan. 1904, AN Paris, F¹⁴ 12383. CETCF (2e commission), "Avis," 10 Jan. 1904, ibid. Maruéjouls to Lax, 19 Oct. 1904, CAMT Roubaix, 202 AQ, 1260. Sartiaux to Baume, 28 Nov. 1904, ibid.
18. "Proposition de loi portant rachat du réseau de la Compagnie des chemins de fer de l'Ouest ...," 28 Apr. 1891, AN Paris, F¹⁴ 12122. M.E. Wickelsheimer, *Etude sur le rachat des chemins de fer d'Orléans, de l'Ouest, de l'Est et du Midi* (Paris, 1892), with a preface by Camille Pelletan. Guillemet et al., "Proposition de loi ...," 19 Nov. 1895, AN Paris, F¹⁴ 12122. Vacher et al., "Projet de résolution tendant à la nationalisation des voies ferrées," 21 March 1899, ibid., C 5634. Commission ... des chemins de fer, *procès-verbal*, 18 May 1899, 14 Feb. 1900, ibid. Bourrat, "Rapport au nom de la commission des chemins de fer," [?] Feb. 1900, ibid., F¹⁴ 12122. Commission ... des chemins de fer, *procès-verbal*, 3 March 1900, ibid., C 5634. Bourrat, "Proposition de loi ...," 21 June 1900, ibid.
19. Commission ... des chemins de fer, *procès-verbal*, 3 March 1900, AN Paris, C 5634. Pérouse to Maruéjouls, 2 July 1903, ibid., F¹⁴ 12126. Commission de remaniement des réseaux Etat, Orléans et Ouest, "Rapport," 19 Dec. 1904, ibid.
20. Barabant to the Prefect of Police, 29 July 1891, in Cie Est, Cons. d'Adm., *procès-verbal*, 30 July 1891, CAMT Roubaix, 13 AQ, 76. Barabant to Durbach, 5 Aug. 1891, ibid., 2036. Weiss to Picard, 21 Oct. 1899, ibid., 2037.
21. Cie Est, Cons. d'Adm., *procès-verbal*, 12 Jan. 1893, and 8 Dec. 1898, ibid., 78–83. Cie Est, Ass. Gén., *rapport*, 28 Apr. 1902, ibid., 2642. "Les résultats de 1905: réseau de l'Est," *JT*, 14 July 1906.
22. Compare Caron, *Histoire de l'exploitation*, pp. 570–72; and Mitchell, "Private Enterprise," pp. 25–29. Statistics for all the companies on government loans and reimbursements from 1883 to 1913 are estimated by Leclercq, *L'établissement*, p. 29.

23. Cie Est, Ass. Gén., *rapport*, 24 Apr. 1896, 30 Apr. 1901, CAMT Roubaix, 13 AQ, 2641–2642. Cie Est, Cons. d'Adm., *procès-verbal*, 13 Apr. and 10 Aug. 1905, 15 Feb. 1906, ibid., 90–91.
24. Cie Est, Ass. Gén., *rapport*, 24 Apr. 1906, ibid., 2642. Cie Est, Cons. d'Adm., *procès-verbal*, 17 May 1906, ibid., 91.
25. Cie PLM, Ass. Gén. extraordinaire, *rapport*, 28 Apr. 1898, ibid., 77 AQ, 161. "La nouvelle convention entre l'Etat et la Compagnie de Lyon," *RGCF*, March 1898. Cie PLM, Ass. Gén., *rapport*, 26 Apr. 1901, 8 Apr. 1903, CAMT Roubaix, 77 AQ, 161. "Les résultats de 1903: la Compagnie P.-L.-M.," *JT*, 7 May 1904. Cie PLM, Cons. d'Adm., *procès-verbal*, 10 Feb. 1905, CAMT Roubaix, 77 AQ, 199.
26. Cie PLM, Cons. d'Adm., *procès-verbal*, 17 and 31 July 1891, 1 July 1892, 25 March and 23 Dec. 1904, 13 July 1906, CAMT Roubaix, 77 AQ, 193–200.
27. Cie PLM, Ass. Gén., *rapport*, 26 Apr. 1895, ibid., 161.
28. Cie PLM, Ass. Gén., *rapport*, 28 Apr. 1892, 22 Apr. 1904, 20 Apr. 1905, ibid. Cie PLM, Cons. d'Adm., *procès-verbal*, 7 and 21 Sept. 1906, ibid., 200.
29. Cie PO, Ass. Gén., *rapport*, 28 March 1891, ibid., 60 AQ, 177. "Compagnie d'Orléans: Résumé par ligne des dépenses d'établissement et des résultats de l'exploitation," 1892, AN Paris, F[14] 8513.
30. Cie PO, Ass. Gén., *rapport*, 28 March 1891, 30 March 1892, 28 March 1893, 30 March 1896, 30 March 1897, CAMT Roubaix, 60 AQ, 177. "Les résultats de 1897," *JT*, 14 May 1898.
31. "Proposition de résolution au rachat par l'Etat du réseau de chemins de fer de la compagnie d'Orléans," 7 July 1894, AN Paris, F[14] 12122. Cie PO, Cons. d'Adm., *procès-verbal*, 17 July 1891, 14 Apr. 1892, CAMT Roubaix, 60 AQ, 46–47. Cie PO, Ass. Gén., *rapport*, 30 March 1892, ibid., 177. "Les caisses de retraites des compagnies de chemins de fer," *JT*, 14 Nov. 1896.
32. Cie PO, Ass. Gén., *rapport*, 29 March 1899 to 27 March 1907, CAMT Roubaix, 60 AQ, 177–178.
33. Cie PO, Cons. d'Adm., *procès-verbal*, 8 Jan. 1904, 1 and 11 July 1904, 25 Oct. 1908, ibid., 54. Cie PO, Ass. Gén., *rapport*, 30 March 1904, ibid., 178. "Déclaration lue au nom du Conseil des Ministres par M. Clemenceau," 5 Nov. 1906, AN Paris, F[14] 12124. See Neiertz, "Le rachat," pp. 15–40.
34. Cie Nord, "Résumé, par lignes, des dépenses d'établissement et des résultats de l'exploitation," 1892, AN Paris, F[14] 8513. Cie Nord, Cons. d'Adm., *procès-verbal*, 25 March 1892, CAMT Roubaix, 48 AQ, 29.
35. Cie Nord, Ass. Gén., *rapport*, 30 Apr. 1890, 29 Apr. 1893, CAMT Roubaix, 48 AQ, 573. Cie Nord, Cons. d'Adm., *procès-verbal*, 24 March and 13 Oct. 1893, 16 March 1894, 29 March and 5 July 1895, 26 March 1897, 9 Sept. 1898, ibid., 29–34.
36. Cie Nord, Cons. d'Adm., *procès-verbal*, 23 March 1900, 21 March and 17 Oct. 1902, 25 March 1904, ibid., 35–40. Cie Nord, Ass. Gén., *rapport*, 29 Apr. 1905, ibid., 573. Cie Nord, Cons. d'Adm., *procès-verbal*, 27 Oct. and 22 Dec. 1905, ibid., 41.
37. Cie Nord, Ass. Gén., *rapport*, 29 Apr. 1891 to 28 Apr. 1906, ibid., 573.
38. Ponts-et-Chaussées, Conseil Général, *procès-verbal*, 2 Feb. 1905, AN Paris, F[14] 17000.
39. Caron, *Histoire de l'exploitation*, pp. 256, 272; and *Histoire des chemins de fer*, p. 667.
40. Cie Est, Ass. Gén., *rapport*, 24 Apr. 1906, CAMT Roubaix, 13 AQ, 2642. Cie Est, Cons. d'Adm., *procès-verbal*, 6 Sept. 1906, ibid., 91. Cie PO, Cons. d'Adm., *procès-verbal*, 7 Dec. 1906, ibid., 60 AQ, 54.
41. CETCF, *procès-verbal*, 7 Feb. and 14 March 1907, AN Paris, F[14] 12377.
42. Cie Est, Cons. d'Adm., *procès-verbal*, 6 March 1907, CAMT Roubaix, 13 AQ, 92. Cie PLM, Cons. d'Adm., *procès-verbal*, 15 and 28 March 1907, ibid., 77 AQ, 200. "A la compagnie P.-L.-M.," *JT*, 30 March 1907.
43. Cie Est, Cons. d'Adm., *procès-verbal*, 21 March 1907, CAMT Roubaix, 13 AQ, 92. Cie Nord, Cons. d'Adm., *procès-verbal*, 22 March 1907, ibid., 48 AQ, 43. Cie PO, Ass. Gén., *rapport*, 27 March 1907, ibid., 60 AQ, 178. CETCF, *procès-verbal*, 6 and 11 Apr. 1907, AN Paris, F[14] 12368.

44. Commission des travaux publics, chemins de fers et voies, *procès-verbal*, 11 Jan. 1908, AN Paris, C 7353.
45. CETCF, *procès-verbal*, 26 Feb., 12 March, 6 and 14 May 1908, ibid., F^{14} 12369. Cie Est, Cons. d'Adm., *procès-verbal*, 23 July 1908, CAMT Roubaix, 13 AQ, 93. Cie PLM, Cons. d'Adm., *procès-verbal*, 7 Aug. 1908, ibid., 77 AQ, 201. Cie Nord, Cons. d'Adm., *procès-verbal*, 6 Nov. 1908, ibid., 48 AQ, 45.
46. Cie PLM, Cons. d'Adm., *procès-verbal*, 9 July 1909, CAMT Roubaix, 77 AQ, 202. CETCF, *procès-verbal*, 11 Nov. 1909, AN Paris, F^{14} 12378. Cie Est, Cons. d'Adm., *procès-verbal*, 13 Jan. 1910, CAMT Roubaix, 13 AQ, 95. CETCF, *procès-verbal*, 7 and 17 March, 3 May 1910, AN Paris, F^{14} 12371.
47. CETCF, *procès-verbal*, 22 Feb. and 2 March 1911, AN Paris, F^{14} 12372. See Poidevin, *Relations économiques*, pp. 596–97.
48. Cie Nord, Cons. d'Adm., *procès-verbal*, 24 March 1911, CAMT Roubaix, 48 AQ, 48. CETCF, *procès-verbal*, 17 May and 22 June 1911, AN Paris, F^{14} 12372–12373. See Mitchell, "A Dangerous Game," pp. 41–43.
49. Cie Nord, Cons. d'Adm., *procès-verbal*, 14 Oct. 1910, CAMT Roubaix, 48 AQ, 47. Sartiaux to Millerand, 15 Oct. 1910, ibid., 202 AQ, 1213. "Note pour Monsieur A. Sartiaux: mouvements des trains pendant la grève," 25 Oct. 1910, ibid. "La grève générale des chemins de fer," *JT*, 15 Oct. 1910.
50. Cie PO, Cons. d'Adm., *procès-verbal*, 14 Oct. 1910, CAMT Roubaix, 60 AQ, 55. Cie Est, Ass. Gén., rapport, ibid., 13 AQ, 2643. Cie PLM, Cons. d'Adm., *procès-verbal*, 28 Oct. 1910, CAMT Roubaix, 77 AQ, 202.
51. Cie PLM, Cons. d'Adm., *procès-verbal*, 28 Oct. 1910, 28 Apr. 1911, CAMT Roubaix, 77 AQ, 202. Cie PLM, Ass. Gén., rapport, 27 Apr. 1911, ibid., 163. See Chaumel, *Histoire des cheminots*, pp. 73–81; Caron, "La grève des cheminots," pp. 201–19; Spuhler, *Der Generalstreik*; Stein, *Social Origins*, pp. 316–76; and Kriegel, *La grève*, pp. 29–33.
52. Cie Nord, Comité de Direction, *procès-verbal*, 11 Nov. 1910, CAMT Roubaix, 48 AQ, 277. "Projet de loi sur le statut des agents ...," 22 Dec. 1910, AN Paris, C 7432. Cie PLM, Cons. d'Adm., *procès-verbal*, 9 and 23 June 1911, CAMT Roubaix, 77 AQ, 203. Jaurès, "Proposition de loi tendant à instituer sur les réseaux des chemins de fer un Conseil Supérieur de Discipline," 11 July 1911, AN Paris, C 7432.
53. Weiss to Picard, 18 Oct. 1910, CAMT Roubaix, 13 AQ, 2039.
54. Cie PLM, Cons. d'Adm., *procès-verbal*, 27 Oct. 1911, ibid., 77 AQ, 203. Leboucq et al., "Proposition de résolution ...," 12 Feb. 1912, AN Paris, C 7432.
55. Dupuy to Sartiaux (with the draft of a reply), 11 March 1913, CAMT Roubaix, 202 AQ, 1214. "La réintégration des cheminots," *JT*, 12 Apr. 1913. See Mitchell, "Private Enterprise," pp. 33–38.
56. CETCF, *procès-verbal*, 27 Jan. 1910, AN Paris, F^{14} 12378.
57. Ibid., 27 July 1911.
58. "Note pour Monsieur Picard ...," 21 March 1911, CAMT Roubaix, 13 AQ, 2039.
59. Cie PLM, Cons. d'Adm., *procès-verbal*, 10 Nov. 1911, ibid., 77 AQ, 203.
60. See Broder, "La longue stagnation française: panorama générale," in Breton et al., *La longue stagnation*, pp. 9–58.
61. Cie Nord, Cons. d'Adm., *procès-verbal*, 29 Apr. 1892, 15 Feb. 1895, 17 July 1896, 12 March 1897, CAMT Roubaix, 48 AQ, 29–32.
62. Cie Nord, Ass. Gén., rapport, 29 Apr. 1905, ibid., 573. See Leclercq, *L'établissement*, pp. 31–33; and Caron, "France," in O'Brien, *Railways*, p. 34.
63. "Proposition de loi concernant les tarifs de chemins de fer: rapport de M. Richard Waddington ...," 17 Jan. 1891, AN Paris, C 5561. Commission ... des chemins de fer, *procès-verbal*, 15 May, 5 June, and 2 July 1891, ibid., 5454. "Tableau comparatif de divers projets ...," 1893, ibid., 5561. Pelletan and Pourquery de Boisserin, "Propositions de loi sur les tarifs de chemins de fer d'intérêt général," 19 Dec. 1893, ibid.
64. Comité d'exploitation des deux ceintures, *procès-verbal*, 8 Jan. 1896, 7 July 1897, CAMT Roubaix, 75 AQ, 28. CCCF, *procès-verbal*, 19 Jan. 1898, 15 March 1899, 4 June 1902, AN Paris, F^{14} 13580. These records do not support the undocumented assertion

that the CCCF "severely limited the liberty of action" of the companies, by Caron, *Histoire des chemins de fer*, p. 498.
65. Etienne to Mocquery, 5 Oct. 1906, AN Paris, F^{14} 12810.
66. Commission ... des chemins de fer, *procès-verbal*, 4 March 1891, ibid., C 5454. Réunion des chefs contentieux et des chefs des services commerciaux et des déclarations des compagnies de chemins de fer, *procès-verbal*, 17 and 24 June 1891, CAMT Roubaix, 202 AQ, 1649. Noblemaire to Guyot, 11 Aug. 1891, ibid.
67. CCCF, *procès-verbal*, 27 Jan. 1897, AN Paris, F^{14} 13580. CCCF, "Rapport fait au nom d'une commission ...," 20 Feb. 1911, ibid., 12872. But see Tissot, "Naissance d'une Europe ferroviaire," pp. 283–95.
68. CCCF, *procès-verbal*, 18 Nov. and 2 Dec. 1896, 13 Jan. and 12 May 1897, 16 Nov. 1898, 4 Jan. 1899, 17 July 1901, AN Paris, F^{14} 13580.
69. CCCF, *procès-verbal*, 16 Feb. and 9 March 1898, 22 May 1901, ibid.
70. Cie PLM, Ass. Gén., *rapport*, 28 Apr. 1893, 29 Apr. 1897, CAMT Roubaix, 77 AQ, 161. Cie PLM, Cons. d'Adm., *procès-verbal*, 24 Aug. 1894, ibid., 194. CCCF, *procès-verbal*, 23 March and 18 May 1898, AN Paris, F^{14} 13580. Cie Nord, Cons. d'Adm., *procès-verbal*, 28 June 1901, CAMT Roubaix, 48 AQ, 37.
71. Cie PLM, Ass. Gén., *rapport*, 28 Apr. 1891, CAMT Roubaix, 77 AQ, 161. CCCF, *procès-verbal*, 5 July 1899, 27 March 1901, AN Paris, F^{14} 13580. See Mitchell, "The Unsung Villain," pp. 447–71.
72. CCCF, *procès-verbal*, 18 March 1896, 1 Dec. 1897, AN Paris, F^{14} 13580.
73. Cie Est, Cons. d'Adm., *procès-verbal*, 14 Jan. 1892, CAMT Roubaix, 13 AQ, 77. Cie Nord, chief engineer of operations to administrators of the Company, 12 Nov. 1896, ibid., 48 AQ, 3541. CCCF, *procès-verbal*, 10 Feb. 1897, 2 Feb. 1898, AN Paris, F^{14} 13580. Cie Nord, "Note sur les plaintes des Chambres de Commerce ... à propos de la concurrence faite à leurs ports par la ligne d'Ostende à Tilbury," 24 March 1897, ibid., 12153. Boucher to Turrel, 8 Apr. 1897, ibid., 12159. "Concurrence aux ports du Nord par la ligne d'Ostende à Tilbury," 24 Oct. 1898, ibid., 12153.
74. "Exploitation des voies ferrées des quais des ports," 5 Apr. 1898, AN Paris, F^{14} 16973. CCCF, *procès-verbal*, 21 Dec. 1898, 17 May 1899, 24 Jan. 1900, 2 Oct. 1901, ibid., 13580. Baudin to Millerand, 14 Dec. 1899, ibid., 12159.
75. "Le trafic du Simplon," *JT*, 2 Dec. 1893. "Le chemin de fer de Simplon," ibid., 9 Jan. 1897. "Rapport de la Commission," 17 Dec. 1901, AN Paris, F^{14} 12811.
76. Cie PLM, Cons. d'Adm., *procès-verbal*, 18 July and 5 Dec. 1902, CAMT Roubaix, 77 AQ, 198. Cie PLM, Ass. Gén., *rapport*, 23 Jan. 1903, 20 Apr. 1905, ibid., 161. Paul-Olivier Lacroye, "Simplon, Frasne-Vallorbe et Faucille," *La revue technique*, 10 Aug. 1905; and "La question de Simplon," ibid., 25 Sept. 1905.
77. "Note historique sur la question des lignes d'accès au tunnel du Simplon," 20 Aug. 1906, AN Paris, F^{14} 12810. Cie PLM, Ass. Gén., *rapport*, 26 Apr. 1907, 29 Apr. 1910, CAMT Roubaix, 77 AQ, 162–163. Commission chargée d'étudier les conditions d'amélioration des relations par voies ferrées avec l'Europe centrale et avec le nord de l'Italie, *procès-verbal*, 26 July and 13 Dec. 1907, AN Paris, F^{14} 12813. Cie PLM, Cons. d'Adm., *procès-verbal*, 11 June 1909, CAMT Roubaix, 77 AQ, 202. Cie Est, Ass. Gén., *rapport*, 24 Apr. 1914, ibid., 13 AQ, 2643.
78. Fourth Bureau, "Note pour le Conseil Supérieur de la Guerre ...," 30 May 1888, SHAT Vincennes, 7 N 2029; and "Instruction générale pour la préparation du plan de transport," 1 Aug. 1896, ibid., 2019.
79. Georges Trouillot et al., "Proposition de loi relative au mode de nomination des administrateurs des compagnies de chemins de fer," 30 Apr. 1891, AN Paris, F^{14} 12497.
80. Cie PLM, Cons. d'Adm., *procès-verbal*, 20 March 1891, CAMT Roubaix, 77 AQ, 192. Ponts-et-Chaussées, Conseil Général, *procès-verbal*, 21 March 1892, AN Paris, F^{14} 16948. Fourth Bureau, "Note pour Messieurs les Commissaires militaires," 15 June 1892, SHAT Vincennes, 7 N 29. Colson to administrators of the companies, 6 Dec. 1894, AN Paris, F^{14} 14835. Holtz to Ponts-et-Chaussées, 18 Nov.

1895, ibid., 16963. Commission ... des chemins de fer, *procès-verbal*, 27 Feb. 1901, ibid., C 5634.
81. "Extrait du registre de la Commission mixte des Travaux Publics," 2 June 1890, AN Paris, F^{14} 15132. "Chemin de fer d'intérêt local à voie étroite ...," 23 Feb. 1894, ibid. "Rapport de l'ingénieur en chef," 9 Nov. 1894, ibid., 12678. Cie Est, Cons. d'Adm., *procès-verbal*, 15 Oct. 1896, CAMT Roubaix, 13 AQ, 81. Conseil Général du Département de la Meuse, *procès-verbal* (excerpt), 23 Aug. 1900, AN Paris, F^{14} 15131. "Chemin de fer d'intérêt local à voie de O m 80 ...," 24 Jan. 1902, ibid., 15086. Ponts-et-Chaussées, Conseil Général, *procès-verbal*, 10 Dec. 1903, ibid., 16995. General Picquart to Barthou, 13 June 1908, ibid., 12840. Grosdidier, "Rapport ...," 25 Nov. 1908, ibid., 15084.
82. "Avis de l'ingénieur en chef" (Department of the Vosges), 28 Apr. 1905, AN Paris, F^{14} 12680. Berteaux to Gauthier, 29 Nov. 1905, ibid. Picquart to Barthou, 2 Apr. 1909, ibid. "La percée des Vosges," *JT*, 26 March 1910. General Goiran to Dumont, 17 June 1912, AN Paris, F^{14} 12680. See Poidevin, *Relations économiques*, pp. 450–57, 784–86; and Mitchell, "Le Ballon d'Alsace," pp. 125–41.
83. Third Bureau, "Considérations générales sur le système défensif du Nord," 1899, SHAT Vincennes, 7 N 1812; and "Note au sujet du classement des places fortes ...," [?] Jan. 1899, ibid., 1804. "Rapport de la Commission des places fortes ...," 18 Nov. 1899, ibid. "Etat indiquant le montant des travaux des fortifications ...," 7 Apr. 1909, ibid., 1806. CSG, "Rapport des présentations au sujet du déclassement de la place de Longwy," [?] May 1914, ibid., 1969. See Fournier, "Fortifications," pp. 53–71; and Mitchell, *Victors and Vanquished*, pp. 111–17.
84. CETCF, *procès-verbal*, 9 May and 9 June 1896, 9 Feb. 1897, AN Paris, F^{14} 12377. "Note du Colonel d'artillerie Péchot ...," 19 Nov. 1902, ibid., 12367. CETCF, *procès-verbal*, 19 Jan. 1904, 25 July 1905, 19 June 1906, 14 May 1908, ibid., 12377–78.
85. Freycinet to General de Gallifet, [?] May 1892, SHAT Vincennes, 7 N 1939. "La Commission Militaire Supérieure des Chemins de Fer," *JT*, 3 Dec. 1898. Gallifet, "Au sujet de la constitution de la Commission des places fortes," 6 July 1899, SHAT Vincennes, 7 N 1804. Second Bureau (section allemande), "Note au sujet du service des chemins de fer au 2e Bureau," 18 March 1902, ibid., 669.
86. Billot to President Félix Faure, [?] Jan. 1897, SHAT Vincennes, 2 N 1. Etienne, "Rapport au Président de la République," 5 Apr. 1906, ibid. CSDN, *procès-verbal*, 6 and 31 Dec. 1906, ibid. Third Bureau, "Note au sujet des renseignements qui doivent servir de bases d'établissement d'un plan de guerre," 11 Oct. 1911, ibid.
87. Second Bureau, "Note pour le 4e Bureau de l'Etat-Major de l'Armée," 13 Jan. 1902, ibid., 7 N 669; and "Note sommaire sur la couverture et la concentration allemandes à la frontière française," [?] May 1907, ibid., 672.
88. Commandant Haillot to the Second Bureau, 16 March 1901, ibid., 1155. Lt. Colonel Gallet to the Second Bureau, 18 July 1903, ibid. Commandant Siben to the Second Bureau, 27 Jan. 1907, ibid. Captain Fournier (Second Bureau), "Les chemins de fer allemands à la fin de 1909," [?] Dec. 1909, ibid., 672. Second Bureau, "Note sur les chemins de fer allemands à la fin de 1910," [?] Dec. 1910, ibid. On the weakness of French intelligence, see Liddell Hart, *Real War*, pp. 49–50; and Porch, *March to the Marne*, pp. 229–31.
89. Freycinet to the Ministry of the Interior (*sûreté générale*), 30 Nov. 1891, AN Paris, F^{14} 12350. Ribot to the prefects, 31 Jan. 1893, SHAT Vincennes, 7 N 674. Sandherr, "Note pour le 4e Bureau," 12 May 1893, ibid. Mercier, "Note au sujet des mesures à prendre à la mobilisation contre les étrangers et les suspects," [?] Dec. 1893, ibid. Freycinet to the corps commanders, 6 Dec. 1898, ibid. Second Bureau, "Note pour le 1er Bureau," 20 Apr. 1906, ibid., 676. Third Bureau to the First Bureau, 19 Dec. 1912, ibid., 1969. Third Bureau to Joffre, 1 Aug. 1913, ibid., 1967. See Mitchell, "Xenophobic Style," pp. 423–25.
90. First Bureau, "Note pour le cabinet du Ministre," 27 July 1901, SHAT Vincennes, 7 N 100. General André to the corps commanders, 3 Aug., 22 Oct., and 27 Dec. 1901, ibid.

First Bureau to the Fourth Bureau, 21 Feb. 1902, ibid. "Instructions sur les grèves," 1912, AN Paris, F¹⁴ 12350. Steeg to prefects, 16 Oct. 1912, ibid. See Becker, *Carnet B*.
91. CSDN, *procès-verbal*, 21 Feb. 1912, SHAT Vincennes, 2 N 1. This document is overlooked by Williamson, *Politics of Grand Strategy*, pp. 205–6. Thus he incorrectly states that the participants of this meeting were gathered as an "informal group," whereas they were in fact at a session of the CSDN.
92. Porch, *March to the Marne*, p. 218.
93. "Etude des possibilités d'accélération de la concentration," 1912, SHAT Vincennes, 7 N 1775. CSDN, *procès-verbal*, 9 Jan. 1912, ibid., 2 N 1. Joffre, "Manoeuvres d'armée en 1912," 15 May 1912, ibid., 7 N 1965; "Instruction confidentielle sur l'utilisation en temps de guerre des fils télégraphiques et téléphoniques des chemins de fer," 17 Oct. 1912, ibid.; and "Note du Général Chef d'Etat-Major Général de l'Armée," 29 Jan. 1913, ibid., 30. Third Bureau, "Rapport fait au Ministre," 2 May 1913, ibid., 1 N 11. Etienne, "Instruction générale ...," 14 May 1913, ibid., 7 N 1779. Joffre, "Instructions générales ...," 6 Sept. 1913, ibid., 1967; and "Instruction de couverture: 2e partie," 6 Sept. 1913, ibid. Fourth Bureau, "Instruction générale ...," 10 Jan. 1914, ibid., 30. "Note pour Monsieur le Commissaire militaire du réseau de l'Est," 14 March 1914, ibid., 2045. See Lepage, "De la mobilisation à la concentration," pp. 73–87.
94. Cie Nord, Cons. d'Adm., *procès-verbal*, 23 Jan. 1914, CAMT Roubaix, 48 AQ, 51. "Nouveau matériels d'artillerie," [?] July 1914, SHAT Vincennes, 7 N 1806. "Ravitaillement des places fortes," 20 July 1914, ibid. See Contamine, *Victoire*, pp. 82–102; Williamson, *Politics of Grand Strategy*, pp. 205–26; and Mitchell, "A Situation of Inferiority," pp. 49–62.

Chapter 8

1. "Entwurf eines Gesetzes, betreffend die Erweiterung, Vervollständigung und bessere Ausrüstung des Staatseisenbahnnetzes," 9 Feb. 1891, BA Berlin, R 43/118 (P). Caprivi to Kaiser Wilhelm II, 10 Apr. 1891, ibid., R 4101/186 (C). For brief critical sketches of Bismarck's successors, see Wehler, *Deutsche Gesellschaftsgeschichte* 3: 1000–1016.
2. Kaltenborn to Caprivi, 7 Jan. and 23 May 1891, BA Berlin, R 43/118 (P). Caprivi to Kaltenborn, 27 and 28 Feb. 1892, ibid.
3. Schulz, *"aide mémoire,"* 4 July 1891, ibid. Thielen to Caprivi, 1 Oct. 1891, ibid. Schulz to Caprivi, 6 Oct. 1891, ibid. Caprivi to Thielen, 11 Oct. 1891, ibid. "Sitzung des Königlichen Staatsministeriums," 16 Oct. 1891, ibid., 64. Schulz to Caprivi, 3 Nov. 1891, ibid., 118. Thielen to Caprivi, 9 Nov. 1891, GStA PK Berlin, I. HA Rep. 90, Nr. 1689 (D).
4. Kaltenborn to Caprivi, 10 May 1892, BA Berlin, R 43/118 (P).
5. "Auszug aus einer Aufzeichnung des Herrn Reichskanzlers," 16 May 1892, ibid. Caprivi to Kaltenborn, 30 May 1892, ibid. Gossler to Caprivi, 16 July 1892, ibid., R 4101/100 (C).
6. "Die Einführung der Mitteleuropäischen Zeit in Deutschland," *ZVDEV*, 15 March 1893. "Sitzung des Königlichen Staatsministeriums," 15 Jan. 1894, GStA PK Berlin, III. HA (2.4.1.), Nr. 7076 (M). "Die geschichtliche Entwicklung der Normalien für die Betriebsmittel der preussischen Staatsbahnen in den Jahren 1871 bis 1895," *ZVDEV*, 27 March 1895. "Rückblick auf die Verwaltungsordnungen der preussischen Staatseisenbahnverwaltung," ibid., 3 Apr. 1895.
7. "Sitzung des Königlichen Staatsministeriums," 12 and 19 Oct. 1894, GStA PK Berlin, I. HA Rep. 77, Tit. 258, Nr. 73 (M). Posadowsky to Schulz, 30 May 1895, BA Berlin, R 4101/206 (C). Posadowsky to Miquel, 3, 18, and 23 Oct. 1895, GStA PK Berlin, I. HA, Rep. 151 HB, Nr. 1317 (M). Hohenlohe, "Votum des Ministers der auswärtigen Angelegenheiten dem königlichen Staatsministerium ergebenst vorzulegen," 13 Nov. 1895, ibid. Miquel, "Votum dem königlichen Staatsministeriums vorzulegen," 17 Nov. 1895, ibid., Rep. 90, Nr. 1675 (D). "Sitzung des Königlichen Staatsministeriums," 18 Nov. 1895, ibid.

8. "Die preussisch-hessische Eisenbahngemeinschaft," *ZVDEV*, 10 Nov. 1900. "Die Betriebsergebnisse deutscher und ausländischer Eisenbahnen in den Jahren 1897 und 1898," ibid., 14 Nov. 1900.
9. "Preussisch-hessische Eisenbahngemeinschaft," ibid., 8 Apr. 1899. "Aus dem Württembergischen Landtage," ibid., 12 Apr. 1899.
10. Monts to Hohenlohe, 21 Apr. 1899, GStA PK Berlin, I. HA Rep. 93 E, Nr. 131/1 (M). "Die Eisenbahnpolitik auf dem sozialdemokratischen Parteitage," *ZVDEV*, 3 Oct. 1900.
11. Prussian Chamber of Deputies, *Stenographische Berichte*, 17 Jan. 1898. Thielen to Schulz, 19 Feb. 1900, BA Berlin, R 43/85 (P). Rheinbaben to Thielen, 21 June 1901, GStA PK Berlin, I. HA Rep. 93 E, Nr. 131/1 (M). Thielen to Rheinbaben, 13 May 1902, ibid.
12. "Deutsche Eisenbahngemeinschaft," *ZVDEV*, 17 Apr. 1901. "Die Einheitsbestrebungen im deutschen Eisenbahnwesen," ibid., 15 May 1901. "In der Frage der sogen. Eisenbahngemeinschaft," ibid., 2 Oct. 1901.
13. Monts to Bülow, 21 Apr. 1901, GStA PK Berlin, I. HA Rep. 93 E, Nr. 131/1 (M).
14. "Bericht über einen Ende September und Anfang Oktober d.J. in Luzern stattgehabten Meinungsaustausch ...," 1902, ibid. Schulz to Bülow, 6 Dec. 1903, BA Berlin, R 43/68 (P). Budde to Soden, 6 and 31 Dec. 1903, ibid.
15. King Wilhelm II (Württemberg) to Kaiser Wilhelm II, 10 Apr. 1904, GStA PK Berlin, I. HA Rep. 89 (2.2.1), Nr. 2 (D). Kaiser Wilhelm II to King Wilhelm II, 4 June 1904, ibid. Bülow and Budde to Kaiser Wilhelm II, 30 June 1904, ibid.
16. Budde to Bülow, 7 Oct. and 2 Nov. 1904, BA Berlin, R 43/68 (P), including "Registratur über die Ministerkonferenz in Heidelberg am 29. September 1904 ...," ibid.
17. "Sitzung des Königlichen Staatsministeriums," 17 Nov. 1904, ibid.
18. "Rückblick auf das Jahr 1904," *ZVDEV*, 4 Jan. 1905. Clipping from the *Frankfurter Zeitung*, 14 Jan. 1905, GStA PK, I. HA Rep. 89 (2.2.1), Nr. 2 (D). "Deutsche Eisenbahn-Betriebsgemeinschaft," *ZVDEV*, 18 Jan. 1905.
19. "Die Betriebsmittelgemeinschaft im Reichstag," *ZVDEV*, 25 Jan. 1905. "Süddeutsche Bedenken zu den Eisenbahnreformen," ibid., 4 March 1905. "Die Betriebsergebnisse deutscher und ausländischer Eisenbahnen im Jahre 1902," ibid., 18 March 1905. "Beschaffung von Lokomotiven für die preussisch-hessischen Staatsbahnen," ibid., 1 Apr. 1905. "Sitzung des Königlichen Staatsministeriums," 26 June 1905, BA Berlin, R 43/68 (P).
20. Soden to Varnbüler, 20 Nov. 1905, BA Berlin, R 43/68 (P).
21. Schulz to Saxon MAA, 17 March and 8 Sept. 1893, SHStA Dresden, MAA 7484. Saxon Ministry of Finance to Saxon MAA, 24 May 1893, ibid. Stieglitz to Saxon MAA, 13 Aug. 1896, ibid., 7452. "Sächsisch-preussisch-südfranzösischer Güterverkehr: Kommissionsbericht," 15 May 1900, GStA PK Berlin, I. HA Rep. 93 E, Nr. 2339 (M). "[Potsdam] Konferenz Protokoll Nr. 3," 21 May 1900, ibid. "Deutsch-südfranzösischer Eisenbahnverband: Protokoll," 6 June 1900, ibid.
22. Saxon Ministry of Finance to Saxon MAA, 25 Aug. 1900, SHStA Dresden, MAA 7454. Thielen to Saxon Ministry of Finance, 11 Sept. 1900, ibid. This issue festered for years: "Auszugsweise Abschrift aus der Landtags-Beilage zum Dresdner Journal," 27 Feb. 1914, ibid.
23. "Falsche Gerüchte," *ZVDEV*, 7 Nov. 1900. Hohenthal to Metzsch, 25 Jan. 1901, SHStA Dresden, MAA 7454. Seydewitz to Hohenthal, 5 Feb. 1901, ibid. Seydewitz to Saxon MAA, 15 and 17 Feb. 1901, ibid.
24. "Über den Etat des Reichseisenbahnamts," *ZVDEV*, 19 March 1902. "Eisenbahn- und Finanzfragen in Sachsen," ibid., 27 Jan. 1904. "Umleitung des Güterverkehrs," ibid., 2 March 1904.
25. "Registratur über die Ministerkonferenz in Heidelberg ...," 29 Sept. 1904, SHStA Dresden, MAA 7522. Friesen to Rüger, 5 Oct. 1904, ibid. Rüger to Saxon MAA, 12 Oct. 1904, ibid. Hohenthal to Metsch, 25 Oct. 1904, ibid. Rüger to Budde, 10 Nov. 1904, ibid. Rüger to Saxon MAA, 23 Nov. 1904, ibid.

26. Bavarian consulate in Dresden to Montgelas, 8 Dec. 1904, BHStA Munich, Verkehrsarchiv 7130. "4. Sitzung der Organisationskommission," 22 Feb. 1905, SHStA Dresden, DR 24880.
27. "Denkschrift ...," 16 May 1895, WHStA Stuttgart, E 130 a, 324. "Staatsvertrag zwischen Württemberg und Bayern ...," 31 Oct. 1895, ibid. "Niederschrift über die Verhandlungen ...," 28 Jan. 1898, ibid., E 75, 401. Mittnacht to Soden, 5 Feb. 1898, ibid.
28. Thielen to Saxon Ministry of Finance, 11 Sept. 1900, SHStA Dresden, MAA 7454. Crailsheim to Saxon Ministry of Finance, 16 Sept. 1900, ibid. "Protokoll über die Verhandlungen des Finanzausschusses der Kammer der Abgeordneten," 4 July 1904, BHStA Munich, MA 77265. Pichler, "Mündlicher Bericht ...," 11 July 1904, ibid., Kammer der Reichsräte 1625.
29. Crailsheim to Von der Pfordten, 10 and 23 Apr. 1901, BHStA Munich, Verkehrsarchiv 7129. Von der Pfordten to Crailsheim, 18 Apr. 1901, ibid.
30. Von der Pfordten to Crailsheim, 5 and 12 May 1901, ibid. Crailsheim to Von der Pfordten, 8 May 1901, ibid. Crailsheim to Friesen, 9 June 1901, ibid., MA 96818.
31. "Eröffnung des bayerischen Verkehrsministeriums," *ZVDEV*, 6 Jan. 1904. Frauendorfer to MA, 19 Jan. 1904, BHStA Munich, Verkehrsarchiv 7055. Frauendorfer to MA, 10 July 1904, ibid., MA 77265. Frauendorfer, "Zur Frage der Eisenbahn-Betriebsmittelgemeinschaft," 21 July 1904, ibid. "Stenographischer Bericht über die Verhandlungen der bayerischen Kammer der Abgeordneten," 23 and 25 July 1904, ibid., MA 96818. "Protokoll des II. Ausschusses der Kammer der Reichsräte," 4 Aug. 1904, ibid., 77265.
32. Soden to Frauendorfer, 4 Aug. 1904, BHStA Munich, MA 77265. Lerchenfeld to MA, 14 Aug. 1904, ibid. Budde to Podewils, 19 Aug. 1904, ibid. Memo by Gasterstädt (Saxon railway administration), 6 Oct. 1904, SHStA Dresden, MAA 7522. Frauendorfer to Podewils, 28 Dec. 1904, BHStA Munich, MA 77265. Budde to Frauendorfer, 8 Aug. 1905, ibid., Verkehrsarchiv 7130. "Antrag der Bayerischen Kommissare ...," [?] Sept. 1905, ibid., Gesandtschaft Stuttgart 550.
33. Frauendorfer to Podewils, 5 Oct. 1905, BHStA Munich, MA 77265. "Protokoll der Kommission" [in Berlin], 11 Oct. 1905, ibid., Verkehrsarchiv 7130. Lerchenfeld to MA, 6 Nov. 1905, ibid. Frauendorfer to MA, 20 March 1906, ibid.
34. Holleben to Mittnacht, 28 Jan. 1894, WHStA Stuttgart, E 130 a, 945. "Bericht betreffend: die Erörterung über die preussischen Staffeltarife für Getreide und Mehlfabrikate," 28 Feb. 1894, ibid.
35. "Unsere badischen Nachbarn," *Der Beobachter* [Stuttgart], 5 June 1895, clipping in WHStA Stuttgart, E 70 f, 634.
36. Zeyer to the Württemberg cabinet, 19 June 1901, ibid., E 130 a, 328.
37. "Deutsche Eisenbahngemeinschaft," *ZVDEV*, 17 Apr. 1901. Crailsheim to Von der Pfordten, 23 Apr. 1901, WHStA Stuttgart, E 75, 419. Von der Pfordten to Crailsheim, 12 May 1901, BHStA Munich, Verkehrsarchiv 7129. Julius von Soden to Oskar von Soden, 15 Oct. and 28 Nov. 1901, WHStA Stuttgart, E 75, 419.
38. Varnbüler to Soden, 11 Jan. 1902, WHStA Stuttgart, E 75, 419. "Die Umleitung des württembergischen Eisenbahnverkehrs durch die Nachbarstaaten," *Münchner Neueste Nachrichten*, 26 June 1903, ibid.
39. Soden to Brauer, 26 Jan. and 10 Apr. 1904, GLA Karlsruhe, 233/11524.
40. Soden to Varnbüler, 17 Jan. 1905, WHStA Stuttgart, E 75, 419. Varnbüler to Soden, 1 Feb. 1905, ibid., E 49, Verz. 18, Ia/1.
41. Soden to Frauendorfer, 4 Aug. 1904, BHStA Munich, MA 77265. Soden to Frauendorfer, 16 Feb. 1905, WHStA Stuttgart, E 75, 412. Frauendorfer to Soden, 3 Apr. 1906, ibid., 420.
42. Ellstätter to Turban, 11 Nov. 1891, GLA Karlsruhe, 233/11511.
43. Brauer to Turban, 7 Jan. 1892, ibid.
44. Ellstätter to Baden cabinet, 6 Aug. 1891, ibid., 11512. Ellstätter to Grand Duke Friedrich I, 3 Feb. 1892, ibid., 33094. Die Karlsruher Sektionen des Süddeutschen Eisenbahnreform-Vereins, "An die beiden hohen Kammern der Landstände," [?] Dec. 1893, ibid., 237/16675. "Interpellation," 12 Apr. 1899, ibid., 233/33126.

45. Jagemann to Brauer, 7 Feb. 1902, ibid., 233/34808. Berckheim to Brauer, 13 Nov. 1903, ibid., 34809. Brauer to Soden, 16 Nov. 1903, ibid., 11524. Soden to Brauer, 10 Apr. 1904, ibid.
46. Brauer to Grand Duke Friedrich I, 3 June 1904, ibid., 11521. Brauer to Berckheim, 21 Oct. 1904, SHStA Dresden, MAA 7522. Marschall von Bieberstein, "Denkschrift über eine grössere Vereinheitlichung des deutschen Verkehrswesens," 9 May 1906, GStA PK Berlin, I. HA Rep. 89 (2.2.1), Nr. 2 (D).
47. The classical account is Eyck, *Das persönliche Regiment*. In the same vein, see also Röhl, *Germany without Bismarck*; and Röhl and Sombart, *Kaiser Wilhelm II: New Interpretations*.
48. Schulz to Saxon Ministry of Finance, 4 March 1906, SHStA Dresden, MAA 7487. Schulz to Breitenbach, 18 Aug. 1906, GStA PK Berlin, I. HA Rep. 93 E, Nr. 12 (M). Breitenbach to Schulz, 17 Sept. 1906, ibid. Schulz to Bülow, 24 Oct. 1907, BA Berlin, R 43/89 (P). Bethmann Hollweg and Schoen to Bülow, 5 Dec. 1907, ibid.
49. Breitenbach to the presidents of Prussian railway directorates, 14 Apr. 1906, 14 Feb. 1907, GStA PK Berlin, I. HA Rep. 93 E, Nr. 206, 2748 (M). Breitenbach to Kaiser Wilhelm II, 5 March 1907, ibid., Rep. 89 (2.2.1), Nr. 2 (D).
50. Rüger to the General Direction of Saxon state railways, 20 July 1906, SHStA Dresden, DR 24880. Hauck to Frauendorfer, 30 Oct. 1908, BHStA Munich, Verkehrsarchiv 7208.
51. Rupprecht to Podewils, 18 Nov. 1906, BHStA Munich, MA 96818. Podewils to Rupprecht, 19 Nov. 1906, ibid. Frauendorfer to Weizsäcker, 3 Dec. 1906, WHStA Stuttgart, E 75, 420. Weizsäcker to Frauendorfer, 14 Jan. 1907, ibid. Weizsäcker to Moser, 16 Jan. 1907, ibid. Podewils to Grünstein, 20 Nov. 1907, 18 June 1908, BHStA Munich, Gesandtschaft Stuttgart 550–553. See "Die Regierungszeit des Ministerpräsidenten Karl von Weizsäcker," in Schwarzmaier, *Handbuch* 3: 405–8.
52. "Rückblick auf das Jahr 1906," *ZVDEV*, 5 Jan. 1907. Schulz (REA) and Stengel (RSA) to Bülow, 12 Apr. 1907, BA Berlin, R 43/107 (P). "Niederschriften über Sitzungen des [Württemberg] Staatsministeriums," 4 Jan. and 5 March 1908, WHStA Stuttgart, E 130 b, 207. Reck to Marschall, 27 Sept. 1908, GLA Karlsruhe, 233/9324. Burkhard to Frauendorfer, 24 and 27 Oct. 1908, BHStA Munich, Verkehrsarchiv 7210. See Witt, *Finanzpolitik*, pp. 165–99; Berghahn, *Der Tirpitz-Plan*, pp. 129–57; and Förster, *Der doppelte Militarismus*, pp. 112–16, 129–34.
53. Hohenthal to Saxon MAA, 11 July 1908, SHStA Dresden, MAA 1733. Schoen to Bethmann Hollweg, 5 Jan. 1911, ibid., 1740.
54. Lydow (RSA) and Schulz (REA) to Bülow, 27 May 1908, BA Berlin, R 43/107 (P). Heeringen and Schulz to Bülow, 10 Oct. 1909, ibid.
55. Wermuth (RSA) to Bethmann Hollweg, 30 Nov. 1909, ibid. Moltke to Bethmann Hollweg, 21 Dec. 1909, ibid. Heeringen to Bethmann Hollweg, 12 Jan. 1910, ibid.
56. Weizsäcker to Moser, 24 Feb. 1910, WHStA Stuttgart, E 70 f, 633. Reichskanzlei to RSA, 18 Apr. 1910, BA Berlin, R 43/107 (P). "Staatsminister von Frauendorfer," *ZVDEV*, 24 Feb. 1912.
57. Breitenbach to Wackerzapp (REA), 11 May 1910, BA Berlin, R 4201/352 (C). Breitenbach to Wermuth, 27 Oct. 1911, ibid.
58. Breitenbach to Kaiser Wilhelm II, 24 Dec. 1911, GStA PK Berlin, I. HA Rep. 89 (2.2.1), Nr. 2 (D). "Der preussische Minister der öffentlichen Arbeiten und die deutsche Eisenbahngemeinschaft," *ZVDEV*, 27 March 1912. "Die Frage der Reichseisenbahngemeinschaft," ibid., 11 May 1912.
59. "Ausschnitt aus dem Protokoll der Regierungskonferenz," 21–22 June 1912, BA Berlin, R 4201/61 (P). "Das deutsche Fahrdienstübereinkommen," *ZVDEV*, 3 Dec. 1913.
60. Bethmann Hollweg to Breitenbach and governments of the medium states, 24 Apr. 1913, BA Berlin, R 43/107 (P). "Sitzung des Königlichen Staatsministeriums," 16 Oct. 1913, ibid., 69. Moltke to Bethmann Hollweg, 8 Jan. and 9 March 1914, ibid., 107.
61. Wackerzapp to Bethmann Hollweg, 6 March 1914, ibid., 107. Bethmann Hollweg to Moltke, 13 March 1914, ibid. Reichskanzlei to Lentze, 23 March 1914, GStA PK Berlin, I.

HA Rep. 151 HB, Nr. 1320 (M). Wackerzapp to Lentze, 24 March 1914, ibid. Draft of memo from Bethmann Hollweg to Hertling, Weizsäcker, and Dusch, 2 Apr. 1914, BA Berlin, R 43/107 (P). Breitenbach to Lentze, 20 Apr. 1914, GStA PK Berlin, I. HA Rep. 151 HB, Nr. 1320 (M).

62. Bethmann Hollweg to Hertling, 21 May 1914, BA Berlin, R 43/107 (P). Bethmann Hollweg to RSA, 21 May 1914, ibid. Lentze to Bethmann Hollweg, 28 May 1914, ibid.
63. Breitenbach to Bethmann Hollweg, 30 May 1914, ibid. Breitenbach to RSA, 13 June 1914, GStA PK Berlin, I. HA Rep. 151 HB, Nr. 1320 (M). Breitenbach to RSA, 8 July 1914, ibid. On the budgetary crisis, see Witt, *Finanzpolitik*, pp. 356–76.
64. Moltke to Bethmann Hollweg, 13 June 1914, BA Berlin, R 43/107 (P). Bethmann Hollweg to Moltke, 18 June 1914, ibid. "Äusserung des Kriegsministers [Falkenhayn] ...," 27 June 1914, GStA PK Berlin, I. HA Rep. 151 HB, Nr. 1320 (M). See Ferguson, "Public Finance and National Security," pp. 141–68.
65. Clapham, *Economic Development*, p. 278.
66. See Hoffmann, *Wachstum*, pp. 81–85; Fremdling, "Les frets et le transport," pp. 33–60; and Wehler, *Deutsche Gesellschaftsgeschichte* 3: 579–607.
67. Prussia also improved the canals of northern Germany. See Kunz, "La modernisation d'un transport," pp. 19–32.
68. Boetticher (RKA) to Mittnacht, 17 Aug. 1891, WHStA Stuttgart, E 130 a, 945. "Note des Staatsministers des Innern ...," 3 Sept. 1891, ibid. Mittnacht to Soden, 18 June 1893, ibid., E 75, 417. Julius von Soden to Oskar von Soden, 2 Dec. 1902, ibid., 401. "Protokoll (55. Sitzung des Eisenbahnrathes)," 7 Feb. 1907, SHStA Dresden, MdI 13760. "Protokoll des II. Ausschusses der Kammer der Reichsräte," 17 June 1910, BHStA Munich, Kammer der Reichsräte 1929. "Protokoll (65. Sitzung des Eisenbahnrathes)," 1 Feb. 1912, SHStA Dresden, MdI 13752.
69. Holleben to Mittnacht, 28 Jan. 1894, WHStA Stuttgart, E 130 a, 945. Crailsheim to Soden, 12 June 1895, ibid., E 75, 417. "Einheitliche Form der deutschen Eisenbahntarife," *ZVDEV*, 13 Nov. 1912. "Rückblick auf das Jahr 1912," ibid., 4 Jan. 1913. "Tarifverzeichnis," ibid., 5 Feb. 1913.
70. Fremdling et al., *Statistik*, p. 141.
71. Borsig to Schreiber, 7 July 1928, GStA PK Berlin, I. HA Rep. 120, C.VIII.1, Nr. 102, Adh. 2 (M). See Mitchell, "A Dangerous Game," pp. 44–45.
72. Artur Fürst, *Die Welt auf Schienen* (Munich, 1918), p. 16. See Gall, "Eisenbahn in Deutschland," in Gall and Pohl, *Die Eisenbahn in Deutschland*, pp. 46–55.
73. Marschall to Weizsäcker, 7 March 1908, GLA Karlsruhe, 237/16580. Rüger to Saxon MAA, 5 Jan. 1910, SHStA Dresden, MAA 7521. Podewils to Lerchenfeld, 26 Apr. 1910, ibid. "Bundesrath: Protokoll der sechsten Sitzung," 9 Feb. 1911, GLA Karlsruhe, 233/11508. Völcker to Ganzmüller, 13 Dec. 1911, BHStA Munich, Verkehrsarchiv 7209. Baden Ministry of Finance to Dusch, 27 Dec. 1912, GLA Karlsruhe, 233/11508.
74. Wehler, *Deutsche Gesellschaftsgeschichte* 3: 593.
75. Thielen to Jungnickel, 28 Jan. 1897, WHStA Stuttgart, E 49, Verz. 18, Ia/1. Thielen to Prussian railway directorates, 6 Sept. 1897, ibid. "Gegen die sozialdemokratische Agitation im Eisenbahnpersonal," *ZVDEV*, 19 Jan. 1898. "Drohender Streik der französischen Eisenbahnarbeiter," ibid., 22 June 1898. "Zur Eisenbahnbewegung in Frankreich," ibid., 3 May 1899.
76. Budde to Bülow, 29 June 1904, BA Berlin, R 4201/A 7640 (C). Budde to Bülow, 11 Dec. 1905, ibid., R 43/134 (P). Budde to Einem, 12 Dec. 1905, ibid., R 4201/A 7640 (C).
77. Breitenbach, "Grundsätze ...," 10 Apr. 1907, ibid. Marschall to Grand Duke Friedrich II, 17 May 1907, GLA Karlsruhe, 233/12237. Frauendorfer to Miltner, 11 Feb. 1908, BHStA Munich, MJu 16700. Frauendorfer to Bavarian Ministry of War, 16 July 1908, ibid. "Verbot der Zugehörigkeit zu sozialdemokratischen Vereinigungen," *ZVDEV*, 8 May 1909.
78. "Ministerrat-Protokoll" (Bavaria), 26 Feb. and 29 July 1912, BHStA Munich, MA 99511. Friesen to Vitzthum, 16 Apr. 1913, SHStA Dresden, MAA 7456. "Eisenbahnbeamte

und Sozialdemokratie," *ZVDEV*, 12 June 1914. See Gall, "Eisenbahn in Deutschland," in Gall and Pohl, *Die Eisenbahn in Deutschland*, pp. 64–68.
79. "Beschäftigung weiblicher Personen bei der preussischen Staatseisenbahnverwaltung," *ZVDEV*, 10 July 1901. "Verwendung weiblicher Personen im württembergischen Eisenbahndienst," ibid., 22 Jan. 1902. "Über Berufsorganisationen der deutschen Verkehrsbeamtinnen," ibid., 21 Oct. 1908. "Weibliches Bureaupersonal in Sachsen," ibid. 14 Nov. 1908. "Annahme weiblicher Arbeitskräfte," ibid., 3 Sept. 1913. For statistics, see the Reichsverkehrsministerium, *Die deutschen Eisenbahnen 1910 bis 1920* (Berlin, 1923), pp. 31–34. Also see Adams, *Women Clerks*, pp. 6–19; and Mitchell, "Weak Sisters," pp. 179–81.
80. "Der Etat der preussisch-hessischen Eisenbahnverwaltung für 1910," *ZVDEV*, 26 Jan. 1910. Frauendorfer to the Prince Regent, 25 Jan. 1912, BHStA Munich, MInn 66592.
81. Bronsart to Eulenburg, 29 Sept. 1894, GStA PK Berlin, I. HA Rep. 77, Tit. 258, Nr. 73 (M).
82. "Zu einer weiteren Besprechung über die Beteiligung der preussisch-hessischen Staatseisenbahnverwaltung ...," 21 Feb. 1912, BA-MA Freiburg, PH 3/745.
83. Thielen to REA, 9 Nov. 1891, BA Berlin, R 4101/200 (C). Caprivi to Schulz, 20 Nov. 1891, ibid. Schulz to Thielen, 8 Apr. 1892, ibid., R 4201/6593. Thielen, "Geschäftsanweisung für die Bearbeitung der eisenbahnmilitärischen Angelegenheiten," 26 Jan. 1895, ibid., MI 658. "Niederschrift" (of a conference on mobilization plans at Elberfeld), 25 Sept. 1902, SHStA Dresden, MAA 7537. "Niederschift" (of a conference on mobilization plans at Oldenburg), 28–29 Sept. 1903, ibid. "Bericht über die Mobilmachungsvorbereitungen deutscher Eisenbahnverwaltungen," 31 Dec. 1903, ibid., 7536. Breitenbach to Einem, 21 Dec. 1906, BA Berlin, R 4201/MI 658 (C). Heeringen, "Massnahmen bei drohender Kriegsgefahr," 20 Sept. 1910, ibid.
84. Unfortunately, no history of the Reichseisenbahnamt exists. Here a few examples of REA activity in military affairs must suffice: Caprivi to the Prussian cabinet, 10 Feb. 1892, GStA PK Berlin, I. HA Rep. 151 HB, Nr. 1316 (M). Schulz to Saxon MAA, 17 March and 8 Sept. 1893, SHStA Dresden, MAA 7484. Schulz to Thielen, 15 July 1898, GStA PK Berlin, I. HA Rep. 93 E, Nr. 12 (M). Schulz to Bülow, 24 Oct. 1907, 22 June 1908, BA Berlin, R 43/88–89 (P). Wackerzapp to Heeringen, 13, 24, and 26 Jan. 1910, BA-MA Freiburg, PH 3/743–750.
85. Brandt to Asch, 30 Jan. 1897, BHStA Munich, Abt. IV, D VI Bd. 18. Reuhlin to Asch, 17, 22, and 24 Oct. 1898, ibid. Crailsheim to Lerchenfeld, 28 Oct. 1898, ibid.
86. Hohenlohe to Crailsheim, 18 Nov. 1897, ibid., MKr 6649. Hohenlohe to Kaiser Wilhelm II, 20 Nov. 1897, BA Berlin, R 43/93 (P). "Auszug aus dem Bericht über die Kriegsbereitschaft der Eisenbahnen Deutschlands," 30 Apr. 1898, SHStA Dresden, MAA 7536. Schulz to Hohenlohe, 13 May 1898, BA Berlin, R 43/67 (P). Schulz to Bülow, 9 Jan. 1901, 4 Feb. 1904, ibid., 93.
87. Crailsheim to Lerchenfeld, 23 Nov. 1898, BHStA Munich, Abt. IV, D VI Bd. 18. Reuhlin to Asch, 2 Dec. 1898, ibid. Crailsheim to Asch, 5 Apr. 1899, 1 Dec. 1900, ibid., MKr 6638.
88. Crailsheim to Asch, 16 Dec. 1898, ibid., D VI Bd. 18.
89. See Ritter, *Der Schlieffenplan*, pp. 47–68, 145–60; and Keegan, *First World War*, pp. 28– 36. Surely Keegan errs in asserting that the capacity of railways became "irrelevant" to Schlieffen's way of thinking, because trains "were to carry the attackers no further than the German frontier with Belgium and France" (ibid., p. 35).
90. See Ritter, *Der Schlieffenplan*, pp. 68–71, 179–80. Also see Van Creveld, *Supplying War*, pp. 109–41; and Wehler, *Deutsche Gesellschaftsgeschichte* 3: 1114–20.
91. "Elektrischer Betrieb auf Vollbahnen," *ZVDEV*, 17 March 1900. "Die Schnellfahrversuche der Studiengesellschaft für elektrische Schnellbahnen," *Zentralblatt der Bauverwaltung*, 23 Nov. 1901, BA-MA Freiburg, MSg 105/13. "Zweihundert Kilometer Fahrgeschwindigkeit," ibid., 7 Oct. 1903. "Zu den Schnellfahren," ibid., 28 Oct. 1903. "Rückblick auf das Jahr 1903," *ZVDEV*, 2 Jan. 1904. Frauendorfer to Freilitzsch, 12 Nov. 1905, BHStA Munich, Abt. IV, Gen Stab 371. Generalstab (Eisenbahn-Abteilung),

"Jahresbericht 1906," 8 Dec. 1906; and "Jahresbericht 1910," 4 Dec. 1910, ibid., 360. "Denkschrift über die Verwendung von Elektrizität zur Zugförderung ...," 1912, SHStA Dresden, KA (P) 13926. Regarding the "new technology" after 1900, this prewar retardation is ignored by Radkau, *Technik in Deutschland*, pp. 222–39.
92. Generalstab (2. Abteilung), "Luftschiffsfahrt" and "Flugmaschinen," [?] Oct. 1909, BA-MA Freiburg, PH 3/215. Generalstab (3. Abteilung), "Zusammenstellung der wichtigsten Veränderungen im Heerwesen Frankreichs 1910," 15 Feb. 1911, ibid., 216. Winterfeldt to the Generalstab, 23 Nov. 1911, 9 June 1912, ibid. Generalstab (3. Abteilung), "Notizen ... über den ... Ausbau der französischen Luftflotte," 25 Nov. 1913, ibid., N 78/28. Moltke, "Die Lage des französischen Luftfahrtwesens am Anfange des Jahres 1914," ibid., PH 3/218.
93. Moltke to Krafft von Dalmensingen (Bavarian General Staff), 14 Jan. 1913, BHStA Munich, Abt. IV, Gen Stab 576.
94. Moltke, "Nachrichten über die militärische Lage in Frankreich," 21 Nov. 1912, ibid., 925.
95. Moltke to Heeringen ["Konzept von der Hand des Obersts Ludendorff mit einzelnen Korrekturen von der Hand des Generals von Moltke"], 2 Dec. 1912, BA-MA Freiburg, W 10/50279. On German apprehensions, see Ferguson, *Pity of War*, pp. 87–101.
96. Waldersee to Moltke, 18 May 1914, ibid. See Röhl, "Germany," in Wilson, *Decisions*, pp. 27–54.
97. Among scores of secondary accounts, see especially Fischer, *Griff nach der Weltmacht*, pp. 46–85; Mommsen, *Grossmachtstellung*, pp. 293–321; and Wehler, *Deutsche Gesellschaftsgeschichte* 3: 1152–68.
98. Reichsarchiv, *Der Weltkrieg* 1: 3–6.

Chapter 9

1. The widespread employment of women thus preceded the war; its impact on their status should therefore not be exaggerated. See Daniel, "Fiktionen," pp. 530–62.
2. Suleiman, *Private Power and Centralization*, p. 17. Also see Mitchell, *Divided Path*, pp. 17–19.
3. See Caron, "Le dynamisme, pp. 25–36; and Ville, *Transport*, pp. 114–71.
4. "Unfortunately, changes in definition occur in the published statistics of every country with very great frequency, and to produce consistent and comparable series for even one country is a considerable enterprise." B. R. Mitchell, *Statistics*, pp. 485–86.
5. Contemporary estimates varied. In 1909 the annual French production of locomotives was estimated at 400, the German at 2000, in a study by Marcel Bloch (an administrator with the PO), "Note sur les conditions de construction des locomotives aux Etats-Unis, en Allemagne et en France," *RGCF*, Apr. 1909. But by 1914 the total national capacity was placed at 950 for France, 3750 for Germany, by Freiherr von Röll (ed.), *Enzyklopädie des Eisenbahnwesens* (2nd ed.; Berlin and Vienna, 1915) 7: 173–74. In either event, the size of German output reached four to five times that of the French in the prewar years. See Mitchell, "A Dangerous Game," pp. 41–45.
6. This is not to deny a "kernel" of truth in allegations of German dumping pointed out by Tilly, *Vom Zollverein zum Industriestaat*, pp. 109–10.
7. Otto de Terra, *Im Zeichen des Verkehrs. Kritische Streifzüge und Reformgedanken* (Berlin, 1899), pp. 8–11.
8. B. R. Mitchell, *Statistics*, pp. 591–612.
9. "Les résultats de l'exploitation des chemins de fer en 1907 en France, en Angleterre et en Allemagne," *RGCF*, July 1909.
10. "Les résultats de l'exploitation des chemins de fer d'intérêt général pendant les années 1912 et 1913 en France, en Angleterre et en Allemagne," ibid., July 1914.
11. Cited in "Les chemins de fer français en 1905," ibid., Oct. 1906. See Poidevin, *Relations économiques*, p. 393.

12. "Gênes et Marseille," *JT*, 25 Jan. 1896. "Marseille et Gênes," ibid., 15 June 1901. "Les effets du Gothard," ibid., 21 March 1903. "Marseille et Gênes," ibid., 15 Aug. 1903. "Marseille et Gênes," ibid., 5 Aug. 1905.
13. "Les grands ports européens de 1870 à 1899," ibid., 9 Feb. 1901. "Les grands ports du Nord de l'Europe continentale," ibid., 18 June 1904.
14. CCCF, *procès-verbal*, 9 March 1898, AN Paris, F[14] 13580.
15. "Les grands ports européens," *JT*, 7 July 1906. See Poidevin, *Relations économiques*, pp. 132–37.
16. See Kuznets, "Quantitative Aspects," pp. 96–111.
17. "Nos transatlantiques," *JT*, 13 June 1896. "La situation commerciale des ports français du Nord," ibid., 27 Feb. 1897. "L'extension de la ligne Hamburg-Amerika," ibid., 4 March 1899. "La marine marchande française en 1912," ibid., 4 July 1914.
18. General von Horn to the Bavarian General Staff, 1 Feb. 1908, BHStA Munich, Abt. IV, Gen Stab 923.
19. Moltke to Bethmann Hollweg, 2 Dec. 1911, BA-MA Freiburg, W 10/50279.
20. Report by Archivrat Greiner, 1914, ibid., 50267.
21. For example, Colonel Michel, at a session of the CETCF, *procès-verbal*, 21 July 1896, AN Paris, F[14] 12377.
22. "Projet de chemin de fer électrique marchant à la vitesse d'au moins 200 kilometres à l'heure," *La revue technique*, 10 Oct. 1901. Weisgerber report to Ponts-et-Chaussées (4e section), *procès-verbal*, 21 March 1902, AN Paris, F[14] 16344. Excerpt from Ponts-et-Chaussées (4e section), *procès-verbal*, 3 Apr. 1912, ibid., 16374. Georges Allix, "Chemins de fer électriques," *JT*, 3 Jan. 1914. See Brunot and Coquand, *Le corps*, pp. 481–95; and Caron and Cardot, *Histoire de l'électricité* 1: 529–31.
23. Millerand, "Instruction sur l'organisation et l'emploi de l'aéronautique en temps de guerre," 27 Nov. 1912, SHAT Vincennes, 1 N 17. In general, see Albert, *La victoire*.
24. Colonel Fix, "L'avenir de l'automobilisme dans l'armée," *La revue technique*, 10 Jan. and 25 Feb. 1897. R. Bonnin, "Considérations sur l'avenir de la traction électrique sur les grandes lignes de chemins de fer," ibid., 10 Jan. 1904. "Rapport présenté au nom de la 1ère section du Conseil Général des Ponts-et-Chaussées, fonctionnant comme une commission," 31 July 1913, AN Paris, F[14] 17036.
25. See Porch, *March to the Marne*, pp. 226–27, 232–45; Stevenson, *Armaments*; and Herrmann, *Arming*.
26. "Comparaison des dépenses militaires des effectifs en France et en Allemagne," Aug. 1912, SHAT Vincennes, 7 N 673.
27. See Ritter, *Staatskunst und Kriegshandwerk* 2: 153; Huber, *Deutsche Verfassungsgeschichte* 3: 530–32; and Förster, *Der doppelte Militarismus*, pp. 18–20.
28. Compare Ralston, *Army*, pp. 338–40; and Porch, *March to the Marne*, p. 190.
29. See Maurer, *Outbreak*, pp. 3–15, 116–25. Also compare the essays on Germany and France respectively by Röhl and John F. V. Keiger in Wilson, *Decisions*, pp. 27–54, 121–49.
30. Outstanding is Becker, *1914*. Also see Soutou, *L'or et le sang*, pp. 141–92.
31. Despite his exaggeration of German intentions since 1911 to seek a war, the work of one historian deserves to be cited here: Fischer, *Krieg der Illusionen*.

Epilogue

1. Cie Est, Cons. d'Adm., *procès-verbal*, 6 Aug. 1914, CAMT Roubaix, 13 AQ, 99.
2. Cie PO, Ass. Gén., *rapport*, 31 March 1915, ibid., 60 AQ, 179. Cie PLM, Ass. Gén., *rapport*, 30 Apr. 1915, ibid., 77 AQ, 163. Cie Nord, Ass. Gén., *rapport*, 24 June 1915, ibid., 48 AQ, 594.
3. Fourth Bureau, "Chemins de fer," 1916, SHAT Vincennes, 7 N 2044.
4. See Marcel Peschaud, "Les chemins de fer pendant la guerre," *RGCF*, June 1919 ("numéro spécial"). Still unsurpassed are the twin volumes later published in the Carnegie series by Peschaud, *Politique et fonctionnement*; and *Les chemins de fer allemands*. Now also see Pedrocini, "L'armée française," pp. 161–201.

5. Lerchenfeld to Hertling, 30 July 1914, BHStA Munich, MA 3076.
6. See Liddell Hart, *Real War*, pp. 54–55.
7. Imperial railway directorate in Alsace-Lorraine to Breitenbach, 6 Apr. 1915, BA Berlin, R 4201, MI 658 (C).
8. Saxon Railway Council (*Eisenbahnrat*), *Protokoll*, 4 Feb. 1915, SHStA Dresden, MdI 13753.
9. Cie PO, Ass. Gén., *rapport*, 31 March 1915, CAMT Roubaix, 60 AQ, 179. Cie PLM, Ass. Gén., *rapport*, 30 Apr. 1915, ibid., 77 AQ, 163. Ministère de la Guerre, *Les armées françaises* 11: v.
10. Cie PO, Cons. d'Adm., *procès-verbal*, 28 Aug. 1914, CAMT Roubaix, 60 AQ, 56.
11. See Gilbert, *First World War*, p. 69.
12. See Fussell, *Great War*, pp. 36–51; and Keegan, *First World War*, pp. 71–137.
13. Gérardin to Renoult, 3 Aug. 1914, AN Paris, F^{14} 12845. Renoult to Noulens, 25 Aug. 1914, ibid. Noulens to Renoult, 28 Aug. 1914, ibid.
14. Cie Nord, Cons. d'Adm., *procès-verbal*, 28 May 1915, 25 Oct. 1917, 28 March 1919, CAMT Roubaix, 48 AQ, 52–53. See Caron, *Histoire de l'exploitation*, pp. 427–41.
15. Henri Roy, "Rapport fait au nom de la Commission des travaux publics, des chemins de fer et des voies de communication ...," 17 July 1917, AN Paris, C 7638.
16. Cie PLM, Cons. d'Adm., *procès-verbal*, 14 Aug. 1914, CAMT Roubaix, 77 AQ, 204.
17. Weiss to Descubes, 19 Aug. 1914, ibid., 13 AQ, 2040.
18. Commission des travaux publics, des chemins de fer et des voies de communication, *procès-verbal*, 24 March 1915, AN Paris, C 7639.
19. Albert Thomas, "Proposition de loi tendant à la nationalisation de tous les réseaux de chemins de fer d'intérêt général, secondaire ou local," 19 Apr. 1919, ibid., 7641. This motion was consistent with his earlier statement, *L'état et les compagnies de chemins de fer* (Paris, 1914).
20. Caron, "La nationalisation avant la lettre," *Histoire de l'exploitation*, pp. 425–560.
21. In reference to rolling stock, "beginning in 1916 data are lacking because of the war." Fremdling et al., *Statistik*, pp. 141, 163, 193, 196, 198.
22. Falkenhayn to Breitenbach, 25 Aug. 1914, BA Berlin, R 43/107 (P).
23. Seydewitz to Vitzthum, 26 Apr. 1915, SHStA Dresden, MdI 13746. Stieglitz to Vitzthum, 6 Dec. 1915, ibid. Seydewitz to Vitzthum, 12 Dec. 1915, ibid., MAA 7452.
24. Kirchhoff, *Reichseisenbahngedanke*, pp. 29–30.
25. Memos by Breitenbach to state railway administrations, 11 June 1917, 13 June 1918, BA Berlin, R 4201/33 (C).
26. For example, memo by Groener to state railway adminstrations, 25 Nov. 1920, GStA PK Berlin, I. HA, Rep. 93 E, Nr. 3 (D). Until 1933 a "Gruppenverwaltung Bayern" attempted to resist the nationalization of German railroads, but to little effect. See Witt, "Anpassung," pp. 392–432; Gottwaldt, *Deutsche Reichsbahn*, pp. 28–29; Manfred Pohl, "Von den Staatsbahnen zur Reichsbahn 1918–1924," in Gall and Pohl, *Die Eisenbahn in Deutschland*, pp. 71–92; and Mierzejewski, *Most Valuable Asset*, pp. 3–80.
27. On postwar developments, see Radkau, *Technik in Deutschland*, pp. 239–53.

BIBLIOGRAPHY

Manuscript Sources

FRANCE

Archives Nationales, Paris
C   Assemblées Nationales
F¹⁴   Travaux Publics

Centre des Archives du Monde du Travail, Roubaix
13 AQ   Compagnie des chemins de fer de l'Est
48 AQ   Compagnie du chemin de fer du Nord
60 AQ   Compagnie du chemin de fer de Paris à Orléans
75 AQ   Syndicat des chemins de fer de ceinture
77 AQ   Compagnie des chemins de fer de Paris à Lyon et à la Méditerranée
202 AQ   Chemins de fer du Nord: Secrétariat de l'exploitation

Service Historique de l'Armée de Terre, Vincennes
MR   Mémoires et reconnaissances
1 N   Conseil supérieur de la guerre
2 N   Conseil supérieur de la défense nationale
7 N   Etat-major de l'armée
9 N   Directions, commissions et inspections

GERMANY

Bundesarchiv, Berlin
R 43 (alt 07.01)   Reichskanzlei
R 901 (alt R 85)   Auswärtiges Amt
R 1401   Reichskanzleramt
R 3101 (alt R 7)   Reichswirtschaftsministerium
R 4101   Reichseisenbahnamt
R 4201   Verwaltung der Reichseisenbahnen

Geheimes Staatsarchiv Preussischer Kulturbesitz, Berlin
I. HA Rep. 77   Ministerium des Innern
I. HA Rep. 89   Geheimes Zivilkabinett, Jüngere Periode
I. HA Rep. 90   Staatsministerium
I. HA Rep. 93 E   Ministerium der öffentlichen Arbeiten
I. HA Rep. 120   Ministerium für Handel und Gewerbe
I. HA Rep. 151 HB   Finanzministerium
I. HA Rep. 169 C   Abgeordnetenhaus
III. HA (2.4.1)   Ministerium der auswärtigen Angelegenheiten

Sächsisches Hauptstaatsarchiv, Dresden
DR   Deutsche Reichsbahn (Reichsbahndirektion Dresden)
FM   Finanzministerium
KA (P) Kriegsarchiv
MAA   Ministerium der auswärtigen Angelegenheiten
MdI   Ministerium des Innern
SV   Ständeversammlung

Bayerisches Hauptstaatsarchiv, Munich
MA   Ministerium des Äussern
MF   Finanzministerium
MH   Handelsministerium
MInn   Ministerium des Innern
MJu   Justizministerium
Gesandtschaft Berlin
Gesandtschaft Karlsruhe
Gesandtschaft Stuttgart
Kammer der Reichsräte
Ministerrat
Staatsrat
Verkehrsarchiv

Bayerisches Hauptsstaatsarchiv, Abteilung IV (Kriegsarchiv), Munich
D VI   Administration (Alter Bestand)
Gen Stab   Generalstab
MKr   Akten Kriegsministerium

Württembergisches Hauptstaatsarchiv, Stuttgart
E 46   Ministerium der auswärtigen Angelegenheiten, III
E 49   Ministerium der auswärtigen Angelegenheiten, IV
E 57   Ministerium der auswärtigen Angelegenheiten, Verkehrsabteilung
E 70 f   Württembergische Gesandtschaft in Baden
E 70 h   Württembergisches Konsulat in Dresden
E 74   Württembergische Gesandtschaft in Berlin
E 75   Württembergische Gesandtschaft in München
E 130 a,b   Staatsministerium

General-Landesarchiv, Karlsruhe
Abt. 233   Staatsministerium
Abt. 236   Innenministerium
Abt. 237   Finanzministerium
Abt. 421   Eisenbahndirektion

Bundesarchiv-Militärarchiv, Freiburg
MSg 105   Materialien zur Geschichte der Eisenbahntruppen
PH 2   Kriegsministerium
PH 3   Generalstab
PH 15   Eisenbahntruppen und -dienststellen
N 16   Nachlass Moltke (Elder)
N 46   Nachlass Groener
N 78   Nachlass Moltke (Younger)
W 10   Kriegsgeschichtliche Forschungsanstalt des Heeres

Secondary Sources: Books

Adams, Carole Elizabeth. *Women Clerks in Wilhelmine Germany*. Cambridge, 1988.
Albert, Etève. *La victoire des cocardes. L'aviation française avant et pendant la Première Guerre mondiale*. Paris, 1970.
Albrecht, Claudia. *Bismarcks Eisenbahngesetzgebung. Ein Beitrag zur 'inneren' Reichsgründung in den Jahren 1871–1879*. Cologne, 1994.
Aldcroft, Derek H., and Michael J. Freeman (eds.). *Transport in the Industrial Revolution*. Manchester, 1983.
Angelier, Maryse. *Voyage en train au temps des compagnies (1832–1937)*. Paris, 1998.
Angelow, Jürgen. *Von Wien nach Königgrätz. Die Sicherheitspolitik des Deutschen Bundes im europäischen Gleichgewicht 1815–1866*. Munich, 1996.
Atsma, Hartmut, and André Burguière (eds.), *Marc Bloch aujourd'hui. Histoire comparée et sciences sociales*. Paris, 1990.
Barjot, Dominique. *Histoire économique de la France au XIXe siècle*. Paris, 1995.
———. *Travaux publics en France. Un siècle d'entrepreneurs et d'entreprises (1883–1992)*. Paris, 1993.
Beck, Robert. *Der Plan Freycinet und die Provinzen. Aspekte der infrastrukturellen Entwicklung der französischen Provinzen durch die Dritte Republik*. Frankfurt-am-Main, 1986.
Becker, Jean-Jacques. *Le Carnet B. Les pouvoirs public et l'antimilitarisme avant la guerre de 1914*. Paris, 1973.
———. *1914: Comment les Français sont entrés dans la guerre*. Paris, 1977.
Becker, Josef, et al. (eds.). *Lange und kurze Wege in den Ersten Weltkrieg*. Munich, 1996.
Benz, Gérard. *Le percement du Simplon: 50 ans de négociations en faveur de l'Europe*. Geneva, 1983.
Berghahn, Volker R. *Der Tirpitz-Plan. Genesis und Verfall einer innenpolitischen Krisenstrategie unter Wilhelm II*. Düsseldorf, 1971.
Bertalanffy, Ludwig von. *General System Theory: Foundations, Development, Applications*. New York, 1968.
Blanchard, Marcel. *Une bataille de réseau: Besançon, l'Est et le PLM (1842–1860)*. Paris, 1938.
Bond, Brian. *War and Society in Europe 1870–1970*. New York, 1986.
Bonnaud, Laurent. *Le tunnel sous la Manche: deux siècles de passions*. Paris, 1994.
Breton, Yves, et al. (eds.). *La longue stagnation en France*. Paris, 1997.
Broder, Albert. *L'économie française au XIXe siècle*. Paris, 1993.
Brophy, James M. *Capitalism, Politics, and Railroads in Prussia, 1830–1870*. Columbus, 1998.
Brose, Eric Dorn. *The Politics of Technological Change in Prussia: Out of the Shadow of Antiquity, 1809–1848*. Princeton, 1993.
Brunot, André, and Roger Coquand. *Le corps des Ponts et Chaussées*. Paris, 1982.
Bucholz, Arden. *Moltke, Schlieffen, and Prussian War Planning*. New York, 1991.
Cameron, Rondo E. *France and the Economic Development of Europe, 1800–1914*. Princeton, 1961.
Caron, François. *Histoire de l'exploitation d'un grand réseau. La compagnie du chemin de fer du Nord 1856–1937*. Paris, 1973.
———. *Histoire des chemins de fer en France 1740–1883*. Paris, 1997.
———. *La France des patriotes de 1851 à 1918*. Paris, 1985.
Caron, François, and Fabienne Cardot (eds.). *Histoire de l'électricité en France. Espoirs et conquêtes 1881–1918*. Paris, 1991.
Carr, William. *A History of Germany 1815–1945*. 2nd ed. New York, 1979.
———. *The Origins of the Wars of German Unification*. London, 1991.
Chandler, Alfred D., Jr. *Strategy and Structure: Chapters in the History of the American Industrial Enterprise*. Cambridge, Mass., 1962.
Chaumel, Guy. *Histoire des cheminots et de leurs syndicats*. Paris, 1948.
Clapham, J. H. *The Economic Development of France and Germany, 1815–1914*. 4th ed. Cambridge, 1966.
Contamine, Henry. *La victoire de la Marne*. Paris, 1970.

Craig, Gordon A. *The Battle of Königgrätz. Prussia's Victory over Austria, 1866.* Philadelphia, 1964.
Dunlavy, Colleen A. *Politics and Industrialization. Early Railroads in the United States and Prussia.* Princeton, 1994.
Eyck, Erich. *Das persönliche Regiment Wilhelms II.* Zürich, 1948.
Ferguson, Niall. *The Pity of War.* New York, 1999.
———. *The World's Banker: The History of the House Rothschild.* London, 1998.
Fischer, Fritz. *Griff nach der Weltmacht. Die Kriegszielpolitik des kaiserlichen Deutschland 1914/18.* Düsseldorf, 1961.
———. *Krieg der Illusionen. Die deutsche Politik von 1911–1914.* Düsseldorf, 1969.
Fogel, Robert William. *Railroads and American Economic Growth. Essays in Econometric History.* Baltimore, 1964.
Förster, Stig. *Der doppelte Militarismus. Die deutsche Heeresrüstung zwischen Status-Quo-Sicherung und Aggression 1890–1913.* Stuttgart, 1985.
Fremdling, Rainer. *Eisenbahnen und deutsches Wirtschaftswachstum, 1840–1879.* Dortmund, 1975.
Fremdling, Rainer, et al. (eds.). *Statistik der Eisenbahnen in Deutschland 1835–1989.* St. Katharinen, 1995.
Fussell, Paul. *The Great War and Modern Memory.* Oxford, 1977.
Gall, Lothar. *Bismarck. Der weisse Revolutionär.* Frankfurt-am-Main, 1980.
Gall, Lothar, and Manfred Pohl (eds.). *Die Eisenbahn in Deutschland: Von den Anfängen bis zur Gegenwart.* Munich, 1999.
Gerschenkron, Alexander. *Economic Backwardness in Historical Perspective.* Cambridge, Mass., 1962.
Gilbert, Martin. *The First World War. A Complete History.* New York, 1994.
Gille, Bertrand. *Histoire de la maison Rothschild (1817–1870).* 2 vols. Geneva, 1965–1967.
———. *Histoire des techniques.* Paris, 1978.
———. *La sidérurgie française au XIXe siècle.* Geneva, 1968.
Girard, Louis. *La politique des travaux publics du Second Empire.* Paris, 1952.
Gisevius, Hans-Friedrich. *Zur Vorgeschichte des Preussisch-Sächsischen Eisenbahnkrieges. Verkehrspolitische Differenzen zwischen Preussen und Sachsen im Deutschen Bund.* Berlin, 1971.
Gottwaldt, Alfred. *Deutsche Reichsbahn. Kulturgeschichte und Technik.* Berlin, 1994.
Gueslin, André. *L'état, l'économie et la société française XIXe-XXe siècle.* Paris, 1992.
Haupt, Heinz-Gerhard, and Jürgen Kocka (eds.). *Geschichte und Vergleich. Ansätze und Ergebnisse international vergleichender Geschichtsschreibung.* Frankfurt-am-Main, 1996.
Hawke, G. R. *Railways and Economic Growth in England and Wales, 1840–1870.* Oxford, 1970.
Herrmann, David G. *The Arming of Europe and the Making of the First World War.* Princeton, 1996.
Hoffmann, Walther G. *Das Wachstum der deutschen Wirtschaft seit der Mitte des 19. Jahrhunderts.* Berlin, 1965.
Howard, Michael. *The Franco-Prussian War: The German Invasion of France, 1870–1871.* London, 1961.
Huber, Ernst Rudolf. *Deutsche Verfassungsgeschichte seit 1789.* 8 vols. Stuttgart, 1957–1984.
Hughes, Thomas P. *Networks of Power: Electrification in Western Society, 1880–1930.* 2nd ed. Baltimore and London, 1988.
Jeismann, Michael. *Das Vaterland der Feinde. Studien zum nationalen Feindbegriff und Selbstverständnis in Deutschland und Frankreich, 1792–1918.* Stuttgart, 1992.
Jeserich, Kurt, et al. (eds.). *Deutsche Verwaltungsgeschichte.* 6 vols. Stuttgart, 1983.
Jones, Peter d'A (ed.). *The Robber Barons Revisited.* Boston, 1968.
Jouffroy, Louis-Maurice. *La ligne de Paris à la frontière d'Allemagne (1825–1852).* 3 vols. Paris, 1932.
Keegan, John. *The First World War.* New York, 1999.
Kennan, George F. *The Decline of Bismarck's European Order: Franco-Russian Relations, 1875–1890.* Princeton, 1979.

Kindleberger, Charles P. *Economic Growth in France and Britain 1851–1950*. Cambridge, Mass., 1964.
Klee, Wolfgang. *Preussische Eisenbahngeschichte*. Stuttgart, 1982.
Kobschätzky, Hans. *Die königlich württembergische Staatseisenbahn*. Stuttgart, 1980.
———. *Streckenatlas der deutschen Eisenbahnen 1835–1892*. Düsseldorf, 1971.
Kolb, Eberhard. *Der Kriegsausbruch 1870. Politische Entscheidungsprozesse und Verantwortlichkeiten der Julikrise 1870*. Göttingen, 1970.
Kriegel, Annie. *La grève des cheminots 1920*. Paris, 1988.
Lamming, Clive, and Jacques Marseille. *Le temps des chemins de fer en France*. Paris, 1986.
Landes, David. *The Unbound Prometheus: Technological Change and Industrial Development in Western Europe from 1750 to the Present*. Cambridge, 1972.
Leclercq, Yves. *L'établissement et l'exploitation des chemins de fer en France 1833–1914*. Paris, 1983.
———. *Le réseau impossible. La résistance au système des grandes compagnies ferroviaires et la politique économique en France 1820–1852*. Geneva, 1987.
Liddell Hart, B. H. *The Real War 1914–1918*. Boston, 1930.
Liebl, Toni. *Aufgeh'n wird die Erde in Rauch. Geschichte der ersten privaten Eisenbahnen in Bayern*. Munich, 1985.
Marggraff, Hugo. *Die Kgl. Bayerischen Staatseisenbahnen in geschichtlicher und statistischer Beziehung*. 2nd ed. Munich, 1982.
Maurer, John H. *The Outbreak of the First World War: Strategic Planning, Crisis Decision Making, and Deterrence Failure*. Westport, Conn. and London, 1995.
Messerschmidt, Manfred. *Militär und Politik in der Bismarckzeit und im wilhelminischen Deutschland*. Darmstadt, 1975.
Messerschmidt, Wolfgang. *Taschenbuch Deutsche Lokomotivenfabriken*. Stuttgart, 1977.
Michel, Serge. *Chemins de fer en Lyonnais 1827–1957*. Lyon, 1986.
Mierzejewski, Alfred C. *The Most Valuable Asset of the Reich: A History of the German National Railway, 1920–1932*. Chapel Hill and London, 1999.
Miller, Michael B. *The Bon Marché: Bourgeois Culture and the Department Store, 1869–1920*. Princeton, 1981.
Milward, Alan S., and S. B. Saul. *The Development of the Economies of Continental Europe 1850–1914*. Cambridge, Mass., 1977.
Ministère de la Guerre. *Les armées françaises dans la Grande Guerre*. 11 vols. Paris,1922–1937.
Mitchell, Allan. *Bismarck and the French Nation, 1848–1890*. New York, 1971.
———. *The Divided Path: The German Influence on Social Reform in France after 1870*. Chapel Hill and London, 1991.
———. *The German Influence in France after 1870: The Formation of the French Republic*. Chapel Hill, 1979.
———. *Victors and Vanquished: The German Influence on Army and Church in France after 1870*. Chapel Hill and London, 1984.
Mitchell, B. R. *European Historical Statistics, 1750–1970*. London, 1975.
Mommsen, Wolfgang J. *Grossmachtstellung und Weltpolitik. Die Aussenpolitik des Deutschen Reiches 1870 bis 1914*. Frankfurt-am-Main, 1993.
Monteilhet, Joseph. *Les institutions militaires de la France, 1814–1924*. Paris, 1924.
Morsey, Rudolf. *Die oberste Reichsverwaltung unter Bismarck, 1867–1890*. Münster, 1957.
Mühl, Albert. *Die grossherzoglich badischen Staatseisenbahnen*. Stuttgart, 1981.
O'Brien, Patrick (ed.). *Railways and the Economic Development of Western Europe 1830–1914*. Oxford, 1983.
Ohlsen, Manfred. *Der Eisenbahnkönig Bethel Henry Strousberg. Eine preussische Gründerkarriere*. Berlin, 1987.
Ottley, George, et al. (eds.). *A Bibliography of British Railway History*. 2nd ed. London, 1983.
Palau, François, and Maguy Palau. *Le rail en France. Les 80 premières lignes 1828–1851*. Paris, 1995.
Parris, Henry. *Government and the Railways in Nineteenth-Century Britain*. London and Toronto, 1965.

Pecheux, Julien. *La naissance du rail européen (1800–1850)*. Paris, 1970.
———. *L'age d'or du rail européen (1850–1900)*. Paris, 1975.
Peschaud, Marcel. *Les chemins de fer allemands et la guerre*. Paris, 1927.
———. *Politique et fonctionnement des transports par chemin de fer pendant la guerre*. Paris, 1927.
Pflanze, Otto. *Bismarck and the Development of Germany*. 3 vols. Princeton, 1990.
Picard, Alfred. *Les chemins de fer français. Etude historique sur la constitution et le régime du réseau*. 6 vols. Paris, 1884–85.
Poidevin, Raymond. *Les relations économiques et financières entre la France et l'Allemagne de 1898 à 1914*. Paris, 1969.
Porch, Douglas. *The March to the Marne: The French Army 1871–1914*. Cambridge, 1981.
Pratt, Edwin A. *The Rise of Rail-Power in War and Conquest*. London, 1915.
Preuss, Erich, and Reiner Preuss. *Sächsische Staatseisenbahnen*. Berlin, 1991.
Price, Roger. *The Modernization of Rural France. Communications Networks and Agricultural Market Structures in Nineteenth-Century France*. London, 1983.
Radkau, Joachim. *Technik in Deutschland. Vom 18. Jahrhundert bis zur Gegenwart*. Frankfurt-am-Main, 1989.
Ralston, David B. *The Army of the Republic. The Place of the Military in the Political Evolution of France, 1871–1914*. Cambridge, Mass., 1967.
Reeken, Dietmar von. *Lahusen. Eine Bremer Unternehmerdynastie 1816–1933*. Bremen, 1996.
Reichsarchiv. *Der Weltkrieg 1914 bis 1918*. 12 vols. Berlin, 1928–1939.
Ribeill, Georges. *La révolution ferroviaire. La formation des compagnies de chemins de fer en France (1823–1870)*. Paris, 1993.
———. *Les cheminots*. Paris, 1986.
Ritter, Gerhard. *Der Schlieffenplan. Kritik eines Mythos*. Munich, 1956.
———. *Staatskunst und Kriegshandwerk. Das Problem des "Militarismus" in Deutschland*. 4 vols. Munich, 1954–1968.
Röhl, John C. G. *Germany Without Bismarck*. London, 1968.
Röhl, John C. G., and Nicholas Sombart (eds.). *Kaiser Wilhelm II: New Interpretations*. Cambridge, 1982.
Ropohl, Günter. *Eine Systemtheorie der Technik. Zur Grundlegung der allgemeinen Technologie*. Munich and Vienna, 1979.
Rosenberg, Hans. *Grosse Depression und Bismarckzeit. Wirtschaftsablauf, Gesellschaft und Politik in Mitteleuropa*. Berlin, 1967.
Rostow, W. W. (ed.). *The Economics of Take-off into Sustained Growth*. London, 1963.
Rostow, W. W. *The Stages of Economic Growth*. Cambridge, 1960.
Saul, S. B. *The Myth of the Great Depression, 1873–1896*. London, 1969.
Schivelbusch, Wolfgang. *Geschichte der Eisenbahnreise. Zur Industrialisierung von Raum und Zeit im 19. Jahrhundert*. Munich and Vienna, 1977.
Schletzbaum, Ludwig. *Eisenbahn*. Munich, 1990.
Schwarzmaier, Hansmartin (ed.). *Handbuch der Baden-Württembergischen Geschichte*. 3 vols. Stuttgart, 1992.
Sheehan, James J. *German History 1770–1866*. Oxford, 1989.
———. *German Liberalism in the Nineteenth Century*. Chicago, 1978.
Showalter, Dennis E. *Railroads and Rifles. Soldiers, Technology, and the Unification of Germany*. Hamden, Conn., 1975.
Soutou, Georges-Henri. *L'or et le sang: Les buts de guerre économiques de la Première Guerre mondiale*. Paris, 1989.
Spiethoff, Arthur. *Die wirtschaftlichen Wechsellagen: Aufschwung, Krise, Stockung*. 2 vols. Tübingen and Zürich, 1955.
Spree, Reinhard. *Die Wachstumszyklen der deutschen Wirtschaft von 1840 bis 1880*. Berlin, 1977.
Spuhler, Hans. *Der Generalstreik der Eisenbahner in Frankreich von 1910*. Berlin, 1975.
Stern, Fritz. *Gold and Iron: Bismarck, Bleichröder, and the Building of the German Empire*. New York, 1977.

Stevenson, David. *Armaments and the Coming of the War, 1904–1914.* Oxford, 1996.
Stürmer, Michael. *Das ruhelose Reich. Deutschland, 1866–1918.* Berlin, 1983.
Suleiman, Ezra N. *Private Power and Centralization in France.* Princeton, 1987.
Supper, Otto. *Die Entwicklung des Eisenbahnwesens in Königreich Württemberg.* 2nd ed. Stuttgart, 1981.
Then, Volker. *Eisenbahnen und Eisenbahnunternehmer in der Industriellen Revolution. Ein preussisch/deutsch-englischer Vergleich.* Göttingen, 1997.
Tilly, Richard H. *Vom Zollverein zum Industriestaat. Die wirtschaftlich-soziale Entwicklung Deutschlands 1834 bis 1914.* Munich, 1990.
Tipton, Frank B., Jr. *Regional Variations in the Economic Development of Germany during the Nineteenth Century.* Middletown, Conn., 1976.
Van Creveld, Martin. *Command in War.* Cambridge, Mass., 1985.
———. *Supplying War: Logistics from Wallenstein to Patton.* Cambridge, 1977.
Vilain, Lucien-Maurice. *L'évolution des locomotives à vapeur de la Compagnie des chemins de fer de l'Est 1853–1938.* Paris, 1980.
———. *Un siècle de matériel et traction sur le réseau d'Orléans (1840–1938).* 2nd ed. Paris, 1983.
Ville, Simon P. *Transport and the Development of the European Economy, 1750–1918.* London, 1990.
Wagenblass, Horst. *Der Eisenbahnbau und das Wachstum der deutschen Eisen- und Maschinenbauindustrie 1835–1860.* Stuttgart, 1973.
Wawro, Geoffrey. *The Austro-Prussian War: Austria's War with Prussia and Italy in 1866.* Cambridge, 1996.
Weber, Eugen. *Peasants into Frenchmen: The Modernization of Rural France 1870–1914.* Stanford, 1976.
Wegelin-Zbinden, Sibylle. *Der Kampf um den Gotthardvertrag. Schweizerische Selbstbestimmung am Vorabend des Ersten Weltkrieges.* Zürich, 1974.
Wehler, Hans-Ulrich. *Deutsche Gesellschaftsgeschichte.* Vol. 3: *Von der 'deutschen Doppelrevolution' bis zum Beginn des Ersten Weltkrieges 1849–1914.* Munich, 1995.
Williamson, Samuel R., Jr. *The Politics of Grand Strategy: Britain and France Prepare for War, 1904–1914.* Cambridge, Mass., 1969.
Wilson, Keith. *Channel Tunnel Visions, 1850–1945: Dreams and Nightmares.* London, 1994.
Wilson, Keith (ed.). *Decisions for War 1914.* New York, 1995.
Witt, Peter-Christian. *Die Finanzpolitik des Deutschen Reiches von 1903–1913.* Lübeck and Hamburg, 1970.
Ziegler, Dieter. *Eisenbahnen und Staat im Zeitalter der Industrialisierung. Die Eisenbahnpolitik der deutschen Staaten im Vergleich.* Stuttgart, 1996.
Zug der Zeit – Zeit der Züge. Deutsche Eisenbahn 1835–1985. 2 vols. Berlin, 1985.

Secondary Sources: Articles

Amalric, Jean Pierre. "Une institution patronale au XIXe siècle: la participation aux bénéfices dans la Société des chemins de fer de Paris-Orléans," *Revue d'histoire économique et sociale* 40 (1962): 238–64.
Bouneau, Christophe. "La contribution des technologies étrangères à l'électrification ferroviaire de la France, 1890–1940," *Histoire, économie et société* 12 (1993): 553–72.
Breuilly, John. "Introduction: Making Comparisons in History," in *Labour and Liberalism in Nineteenth-Century Europe: Essays in Comparative History* (Manchester, 1992), pp. 1–25.
Caron, François. "La grève des cheminots de 1910: une tentative d'approche," in Fernand Braudel et al. (eds.), *Conjoncture économique, structures sociales. Hommage à Ernest Labrousse* (Paris, 1974), pp. 201–19.
———. "Le dynamisme des modéles technologiques français et allemand," in Yves Cohen and Klaus Manfrass (eds.), *Frankreich und Deutschland. Forschung, Technologie und industrielle Entwicklung im 19. und 20. Jahrhundert* (Munich, 1990), pp. 25–36.

———. "Les commandes des compagnies des chemins de fer de 1850 à 1914," *Revue d'histoire de la sidérurgie* 6 (1965): 37–76.
Crouzet, François. "Essor, déclin et renaissance de l'industrie française des locomotives 1838–1914," *Revue d'histoire économique et sociale* 55 (1977): 112–210.
Daniel, Ute. "Fiktionen, Friktionen und Fakten – Frauenlohnarbeit im Ersten Weltkrieg," in Wolfgang Michalka (ed.), *Der Erste Weltkrieg. Wirkung, Wahrnehmung, Analyse* (Munich and Zürich, 1994), pp. 530–62.
Dunham, Arthur L. "How the First French Railways were Planned," *Journal of Economic History* 1 (1941): 12–25.
Ferguson, Niall. "Public Finance and National Security: The Domestic Origins of the First World War Revisited," *Past and Present* 142 (1994): 141–68.
Fournier, Pierre. "Les relations entre fortifications et chemins de fer," *Revue d'histoire des chemins de fer* 15 (1996): 53–71.
Fremdling, Rainer. "Les frets et le transport du charbon dans l'Allemagne du Nord, 1850–1913," *Histoire, économie et société* 11 (1992): 33–60.
———. "Modernisierung und Wachstum der Schwerindustrie in Deutschland 1830–1860," *Geschichte und Gesellschaft* 5 (1979): 201–27.
Fremdling, Rainer, and Günter Knieps. "Competition, Regulation, and Nationalization: The Prussian Railway System in the Nineteenth Century," *Scandinavian Economic History Review* 41 (1993): 129–54.
Gonjo, Yasuo. "Le 'Plan Freycinet,' 1878–1882: un aspect de la 'grande dépression' économique en France," *Revue historique* 248 (1972): 49–86.
Helmedach, Andreas. "Infrastrukturpolitische Grundsatzentscheidungen des 18. Jahrhunderts am Beispiel des Landverkehrswesens: Grossbritannien, Frankreich, Habsburgermonarchie," *Comparativ* 6 (1996): 11–50.
Henning, Friedrich Wilhelm. "Eisenbahn und Entwicklung der Eisenindustrie in Deutschland," *Archiv und Wissenschaft* 6 (1973): 1–20.
Holborn, Hajo. "Moltke and Schlieffen: The Prussian-German School," in Edward Mead Earle (ed.), *Makers of Modern Strategy: Military Thought from Machiavelli to Hitler* (3rd ed.; New York, 1969), pp. 172–205.
Jauffret, Jean-Charles. "Monsieur Thiers et le Comité de Défense," *Les Cahiers de Montpellier* 5 (1982): 27–45.
Kocka, Jürgen. "Eisenbahnverwaltung in der Industriellen Revolution. Deutsch-Amerikanische Vergleiche," *Vierteljahrschrift für Sozial- und Wirtschaftsgeschichte* 84 (1987): 259–77.
———. "Management in der Industrialisierung. Die Entstehung und Entwicklung des klassischen Musters," *Zeitschrift für Unternehmensgeschichte* 44 (1999): 135–49.
Kunz, Andreas. "La modernisation d'un transport encore préindustriel pendant l'ére industrielle: le cas des voies navigables de l'Allemagne impériale de 1871 à 1918," *Histoire, économie et société* 11 (1992): 19–32.
Kuznets, Simon. "Quantitative Aspects of the Growth of Nations," *Economic Development and Cultural Change* 15 (1967): 96–111.
Lanthier, Pierre. "L'électrification des chemins de fer secondaires en France: une occasion manquée?" in André Blanc (ed.), *Electricité et chemins de fer: cent ans de progrès ferroviaire en France par l'électricité* (Paris, 1997), pp. 15–29.
Leclercq, Yves. "L'état, les entreprises ferroviaires et leurs profits en France (1830–1860)," *Histoire, économie et société* 9 (1990): 39–63.
Lefranc, Georges. "Les chemins de fer devant le parlement 1833–42," *Revue d'histoire moderne* 5 (1930): 337–64.
Lepage, Pierre. "De la mobilisation à la concentration: le plan de transport français en août 1914," *Revue d'histoire des chemins de fer* 15 (1996): 73–87.
Merger, Michèle. "La concurrence rail-navigation intérieure en France 1850–1914," *Histoire, économie et société* 9 (1990): 65–94.
Mitchell, Allan. "'A Dangerous Game': The Crisis of Locomotive Manufacturing in France before 1914," *Technology and Culture* 36 (1995): 29–45.

———. "'A Sitution of Inferiority': French Military Reorganization after the Defeat of 1870," *American Historical Review* 86 (1981): 49–62.
———. "Le Ballon d'Alsace: Ein vergessenes Kapitel der deutsch-französischen Eisenbahngeschichte," in Walther L. Bernecker and Volker Dotterweich (eds.), *Deutschland in den internationalen Beziehungen des 19. und 20. Jahrhunderts* (Munich, 1996), pp. 125–41.
———. "Private Enterprise or Public Service? The Eastern Railway Company and the French State in the Nineteenth Century," *Journal of Modern History* 69 (1997): 18–41.
———. "The German Influence on Subversion and Repression during the Early Third Republic," *Francia* 13 (1969): 409–33.
———. "The Freycinet Reforms and the French Army, 1888–1893," *The Journal of Strategic Studies* 4 (1981): 19–28.
———. "The Function and Malfunction of Mutual Aid Societies in Nineteenth-Century France," in Jonathan Barry and Colin Jones (eds.), *Medicine and Charity Before the Welfare State* (London, 1991), pp. 172–89.
———. "The Unsung Villain: Alcoholism and the Emergence of Public Welfare in France, 1870–1914," *Contemporary Drug Problems* 13 (1986): 447–71.
———. "The Xenophobic Style: French Counterespionage and the Emergence of the Dreyfus Affair," *Journal of Modern History* 52 (1980): 414–25.
———. "Thiers, MacMahon, and the Conseil Supérieur de la Guerre," *French Historical Studies* 6 (1969): 232–52.
———. "Weak Sisters: The Employment of Women by French and German Railroads in the Nineteenth Century," *Francia* 22/3 (1995): 175–82.
Neiertz, Nicolas. "Le rachat des chemins de fer de l'Ouest (1908)," *Revue d'histoire des chemins de fer hors série No. 4: Le statut des chemins der fer français et leurs rapports avec l'état 1908–1982* (Paris, 1996), pp. 15–40.
Pedrocini, Guy. "L'armée française et la Grande Guerre," in André Corvisier (ed.), *Histoire militaire de la France* (3 vols.; Paris, 1992), 3:161–201.
Ratcliffe, Barrie M. "Bureaucracy and Early French Railroads: The Myth and the Reality," *The Journal of European Economic History* 18 (1989): 331–70.
———. "The Origins of the Paris-Saint Germain Railway: Some Entrepreneurial and Financial Problems in the Launching of Railways in France in the 1830s," *Journal of Transport History* 1 (1972): 197–219.
Ribeill, Georges. "Gestion et organisation du travail dans les compagnies de chemins de fer, des origines à 1860," *Annales* 42 (1987): 999–1029.
Smith, Cecil O., Jr. "The Longest Run: Public Engineers and Planning in France," *American Historical Review* 95 (1990): 657–92.
Thomas, Thomas H. "Armies and the Railway Revolution," in Jesse D. Clarkson and Thomas C. Cochran (eds.), *War as a Social Institution: The Historian's Perspective* (New York, 1941), pp. 88–94.
Tilly, Richard H. "The Political Economy of Public Finance and the Industrialization of Prussia, 1815–1866," *The Journal of Economic History* 26 (1966): 484–97.
Tissot, Laurent. "Naissance d'une Europe ferroviaire: la convention internationale de Berne (1890)," in Michèle Merger and Dominique Barjot (eds.), *Les entreprises et leurs réseaux: hommes, capitaux, techniques et pouvoirs, XIXe-XXe siècles* (Paris, 1998), pp. 283–95.
Van den Braembussche, A. A. "Historical Explanation and Comparative Method: Towards a Theory of the History of Society," *History and Theory* 28 (1989): 2–24.
Welskopp, Thomas. "Stolpersteine auf dem Königsweg. Methodenkritische Anmerkungen zum internationalen Vergleich in der Geschichtswissenschaft," *Archiv für Sozialgeschichte* 35 (1995): 339–67.
Witt, Peter-Christian. "Anpassung an die Inflation. Das Investitionsverhalten der deutschen Staatsbahnen/Reichsbahn in den Jahren 1914 bis 1923/24," in Gerald D. Feldman et al. (eds.), *Die Anpassung an die Inflation* (Berlin and New York, 1986), pp. 392–432.

Name Index

Abel, Karl von, 61
Achenbach, Heinrich von, 123–25, 127
Adriatic Sea, 49
Algeria, 12, 23, 94, 201–2
Allain-Targé, François-Henri, 88–89
Alps, 12–13, 58–59, 146, 166, 178, 211, 257
Alsace-Lorraine, 8, 85, 91–92, 127, 151, 168, 206, 209–10, 215, 218, 227, 231, 266
Alsatian Balloon, 206
Amiens, 17, 87, 97, 116, 159, 194
Amsterdam, 48
Andigné, General, 115
Andrézieux, 4
Anhalt, 42
Antwerp, 39, 55, 79, 107, 148, 167, 201–2, 257
Ardennes, 10–11, 18–19, 34, 98, 202, 206
Arles, 194
Arnhem, 48
Arras, 194
Asia, 79, 105
Augagneur, Jean Victor, 195, 197, 255
Augsburg, 37, 45–46, 70, 217, 223
Australia, 201
Austria, 9, 31–32, 40, 42, 47, 51, 55–56, 59, 62, 64–65, 73, 120, 139, 149, 151, 237
Avignon, 87

Baden, 41–43, 45–49, 59–62, 66, 64, 66, 73, 122, 133, 135–37, 140, 143, 147–48, 159, 218, 222–25, 227–28, 230, 233, 236–38, 268
Balkans, 40, 50
Banès, Antoine, 14
Barabant, Roger, 183, 185, 187, 206
Bartholony, François, 13, 15, 26–27
Barthou, Louis, 191–92, 195, 204
Basel, 4, 8, 47–48, 59, 159, 202
Bassermann, Ernst, 239, 255
Baudin, Pierre, 183
Bavaria, 32, 37, 41–47, 51, 56, 58–63, 66, 70, 72, 75, 80, 121–22, 126, 130–40, 147–48, 151–52, 154, 159, 169, 181, 184, 215–19, 221–33, 236–38, 240, 242–43, 250, 268
Bazaine, Marshal Achille, 82
Beaurepaire, Dominique de, 87–88, 92
Belfort, 34, 113, 184, 191, 207

Belgium, 6, 10, 18, 23, 25, 28–29, 43, 51, 55, 77–78, 98, 109–10, 128, 148, 165, 188, 193, 202, 209–10, 234, 244, 246, 252, 257, 261–63, 266
Bennigsen, Rudolf von, 53
Berlin, 35, 38, 44, 50–52, 55–56, 59–60, 63–66, 70–72, 74, 80, 109, 120–24, 128, 130–40, 144–48, 151–55, 157, 159, 165, 168, 170, 179, 191, 206, 209, 214–21, 223–31, 233–34, 237–38, 240, 242–43, 246, 248–49, 259–60
Bern, 59–60, 108–10, 128, 145–46, 165, 200, 204, 256
Besançon, 33
Bethmann Hollweg, Theobald von, 229, 231, 246
Billot, General Jean-Baptiste, 119, 208
Bingen, 137, 231–34
Bismarck, Otto von, 35, 50, 52–54, 60, 63–66, 72–73, 86, 91–92, 112, 120–41, 144–46, 148–56, 159, 166, 170, 213–15, 218, 228, 239, 250, 268
Black Forest, 58
Black Sea, 30, 49
Bodelschwingh, Karl von, 42
Bodensee. *See* Lake Constance
Bohemia, 64
Boirault coupling device, 196
Bon Marché, 29
Bonneau, Henri, 179
Bordeaux, 6, 13, 15, 78, 80, 95, 116, 186, 202
Borel, General Jean-Louis, 115
Borsig, Ernst von, 238
Borsig factory, 56, 191
Boulanger, General Georges, 116–19, 140, 148, 153–54, 171
Boulogne, 17, 167, 194, 203
Bourbonnais, 11–12, 26
Bourg, 11
Bourges, 11
Bourgoing, Paul de, 31–32
Bourrat, Jean, 182
Brandenburg, 55, 80
Brauer, Arthur von, 225, 227–28
Braunschweig, 42
Breitenbach, Paul, 228–29, 232–34, 239, 266
Bremen, 57, 159, 167, 201, 258
Brenner Pass, 59, 146

Breslau, 50
Brest, 203
Bretten, 49
Briand, Aristide, 195
Brie, 14
Briey, 159, 206
Britain. *See* Great Britain
Brittany, 13, 26, 30, 73
Broglie, Albert de, 86, 88, 92, 105
Bronsart von Schellendorf, General Paul, 152–54
Bruchsal, 49
Brussels, 203, 209, 266
Budde, Hermann, 218–20, 222, 224, 226, 228, 239
Bülow, Bernhard von, 217–19, 226, 231, 239
Burgundy, 4, 11, 73, 93

Cail factory, 9
Caillaux, Joseph, 195
Calais, 16, 87, 97, 107, 167, 169, 203
Camphausen, Ludolf, 39
Camphausen, Otto, 125, 127
Canitz, General Karl von, 61
Cannstatt, 46
Canrobert, Marshal François, 114
Caprivi, General Leo von, 214–16
Carnot, Sadi, 108, 179
Central Europe, 31, 40, 72, 142, 165, 259, 264
Cette, 4, 78
Châlons-sur-Marne, 34
Chalon-sur-Saône, 11, 161
Charié-Marsaines, Pierre, 32
Charleroi, 16
Cherbourg, 203
Chevalier, Michel, 106
Christophle, Charles, 88
Cissey, General Ernest de, 114
Clemenceau, Georges, 188, 208, 263
Clermont-Ferrand, 11
Cobden Treaty, 28
Cologne, 16, 39, 41–42, 55, 62, 109, 137, 146, 213, 216, 228
Colson, Clément, 193, 199, 203
Coquet, Lucien, 206
Corsica, 202
Crailsheim, Christoph Krafft von, 138–39, 148, 152, 216, 223, 243
Crampton engine, 160
Creusot, 9, 184, 192
Crimea, 32

Dauphiné, 12, 18–19
David, Eduard, 217
Delbrück, Rudolf, 121–24, 130, 132, 135, 144
Delcassé, Théophile, 210
Denmark, 35, 63
Didion, Charles, 90
Dieppe, 167
Dietz-Monnin, Charles, 108
Dijon, 6
Dillenius, Friedrich von, 123, 133–35, 144, 151

Dôle, 11
Donauwörth, 46
Dönhof, August von, 38–39, 61
Doubs River, 11
Doumer, Paul, 196
Dresden, 37, 44, 46, 52, 121, 130, 135, 221–22, 228, 237
Dreyfus, Alfred, 117–18, 175, 209, 260
Duchatel, Charles-Marie-Tanneguy, 6–7
Dumont, Charles, 197
Dunkerque, 16, 34, 87, 107, 167, 169, 194, 201–2, 243, 257
Dupuy, Jean, 195, 206
Durlach, 49
Dusch, Alexander von, 228

Elbe River, 44, 52, 55
Ellstätter, Moritz, 227
Ems dispatch, 66
England, 4, 6–7, 30, 38, 48, 57, 94, 107, 129, 158, 201, 208, 245, 260. *See also* Great Britain
English Channel, 106, 206, 243
Epernay, 98, 181, 184
Epinal, 4, 113, 207
Erlanger, Emile, 99
Erzberger, Matthias, 219
Eulenburg, Botho, 161
Europe, 6–7, 15, 43–44, 47, 49, 54–55, 58, 60, 68–69, 78–79, 81–82, 96, 105–6, 109, 146, 149, 161–62, 167, 200, 202, 235–36, 248, 250–52, 255–58. *See also* Central Europe

Falkenhayn, General Erich von, 234
Farre, General Jean, 116
Faucille Tunnel, 204
Faure, Félix, 111, 167
Ferry, Jules, 80, 89, 225, 266
Fives-Lille factory, 184
Flanders, 29
Forbach, 8
Frankfurt-am-Main, 39–40, 43, 46, 51–52, 61–62, 64, 80, 85, 109, 112, 141, 146, 148, 216, 224, 230
Frankfurt-an-der-Oder, 50
Frankfurter Zeitung, 219
Franqueville, Ernest de, 27
Frasnes, 204
Frauendorfer, Heinrich von, 221–24, 226, 228–30, 232, 237, 250
Freycinet, Charles de, 89–90, 94, 96, 108, 110–11, 115–16, 118–19, 154, 156, 158, 170, 198, 207–9, 263. *See also* Freycinet Plan
Friedrich I (of Baden), 135
Friedrichshafen, 46–47, 133–34, 136, 225
Friedrichsruh, 138, 155
Friesen, Richard von, 125–26, 130–33, 135–36
Fürth, 37–38

Gambetta, Léon, 82, 88–89, 118
Gard, 94, 104
Gare de l'Est, 94, 104
Gare du Nord, 10, 17, 189
Gauthier, Armand, 204
Geneva, 11, 13, 194, 204

Genoa, 56, 58–59, 107, 167, 201, 257, 259
Germersheim, 61
Gomel, Charles, 185
Gondraud *frères*, 148
Görlitz, 44, 50
Gossler, General Heinrich von, 215
Gottschalk, Alexandre, 107, 167
Great Britain, 4, 8, 28–29, 39, 48, 75–77, 110, 145, 165, 201, 210, 234, 269
Grenoble, 12, 59, 116
Guillemet, Gaston-Marie, 182
Guyot, Yves, 199

Habsburg Monarchy, 31, 35, 40, 51, 64–65
Hachette, Louis, 177
Halle, 50, 221
Hamburg, 38, 55, 79, 109, 138, 148, 167, 201, 257, 259
Hamburg-Amerika, 258
Hanover, 42, 50, 52, 124, 137, 159, 216
Hansemann, David, 39, 61
Harkort, Friedrich, 42
Hazebrouck, 16
Heeringen, General Josias von, 231–32
Heidelberg, 218–19, 222, 224, 226–28, 249
Heidenheim, 134
Heine, Heinrich, 39
Henschel factory, 191–92
Hergatz, 134
Hesse, 42, 52, 133, 213, 216, 218, 221, 230. See also Prussian-Hessian railway union
Heurteau, Charles, 187
Heydt, August von der, 42
Hirson, 207
Hobrecht, Arthur, 127
Hof, 44–45, 221
Hofmann, Karl von, 127
Hohenlohe, Chlodwig von, 51
Hohenzollern Monarchy, 63, 125, 213, 217
Holland. See Netherlands
Hungary, 56, 146

India, 29, 58
Ireland, 245
Italy, 45, 56, 58–60, 105–6, 109, 128, 146–48, 202, 257
Itzenplitz, Heinrich von, 50, 53, 60

Jacqmin, François, 36, 90–93, 96, 103, 108, 183
Jaurès, Jean, 195, 210
Joffre, General Joseph, 208, 210–12, 260–61, 263, 266
Jolly, Julius, 135
Journal des sciences militaires, 113
Journal des transports, 177, 179, 184, 187, 194, 203, 257–59
July Monarchy, 5, 14, 18, 21, 86
June Days, 15, 17–18, 88
Jura Mountains, 11

Kaltenborn, General Hans von, 214–15
Karlsruhe, 47–49, 51, 62, 135–36, 147, 225, 227–28, 234
Kassel, 52, 191, 216
Kaufmann, Richard von, 179

Kehl, 48–49, 62, 65–66
Kessler factory, 56
Koblenz, 234
Koechlin factory, 9
Königgrätz, 64–65
Königsberg, 42, 213
Krupp family, 56

La Chapelle, 17, 97, 194
Lahusen family, 57
Lake Constance (Bodensee), 38, 45–47, 133–34, 136, 139, 159, 223, 225, 230
Lamartine, Alphonse de, 14
Laon, 194
Larcy, Roger de, 87
Lasker, Eduard, 53
Lauenburg, 42
Laurier, Clément, 88
Lausanne, 204
Lauter River, 62
Le Chatelier, Henry-Louis, 181, 193
Legrand, Alexis Victor, 4–8, 20, 25–26, 71
Le Havre, 4–6, 29, 79, 107, 201, 203, 257
Leipzig, 37–38, 40–41, 44, 221
Le Mans, 188
Le Matin, 181
Lentze, August, 233
Leopold (of Baden), 48, 73
Leplus, Colonel, 119
Lerchenfeld, Hugo von, 138, 154
Leroy-Beaulieu, Paul, 256
Leutkirch, 133–34, 159
Liège, 16, 266
Lille, 6, 16–17, 97–98, 116, 159, 169, 194, 243
Limoges, 116
Lindau, 45–47
Lipkowski brakes, 178
List, Friedrich, 38, 43, 60, 71
Liverpool, 39
Loire River, 4, 13, 33, 94–95, 104, 113, 116, 188
London, 48, 248, 253
Longwy, 34–35, 207
Lons-le-Saunier, 161
Lötschberg Tunnel, 161
Louis Bonaparte. See Napoleon III
Louis Philippe, 14, 18
Lourdes, 96
Lübeck, 131
Lucerne, 59, 218
Ludendorff, General Erich, 245–46
Ludwig I (of Bavaria), 45
Ludwig II (of Bavaria), 131
Lukmanier, 59
Lunéville, 33
Luxemburg, 8, 65, 206, 209–10, 244, 266
Lyon, 6, 11, 14, 59, 93, 99, 116, 194

Maas. See Meuse River
MacMahon, Marshal Edne-Patrice de, 82, 86, 89, 114
Maffei factory, 45, 56, 147, 181, 192
Magne, Pierre, 33
Main River, 66
Mainz, 32, 56, 65, 148, 217
Manchester, 39

Mannheim, 47–49, 148
Marne River, 212, 267
Marschall von Bieberstein, Adolf, 49, 228
Marseille, 6, 11–12, 30, 32, 56, 78, 80, 87, 93, 106–7, 116, 159, 167, 194, 201, 204, 257
Maubeuge, 98, 207
Maxau, 234
Maybach, Albert, 124–29, 131–33, 136–41, 144–48, 151, 154, 156, 161, 214, 228
Mayenne, 21
Mayer, Emile, 207
Mecklenburg, 42, 63, 219, 238
Mediterranean Sea, 4, 6, 15, 45, 56, 78, 107, 146, 167, 257
Memmingen, 133–34, 159
Mercier, General Auguste, 209
Metz, 6, 8, 82, 115, 151, 168
Meuse (Maas) River, 16, 243, 266
Mevissen, Gustav, 62
Mexico, 81
Mézières, 243
Michel, Colonel, 106, 207
Milan, 9, 58–59, 166
Millerand, Alexandre, 210, 261, 263, 267
Minden, 42
Miquel, Johannes von, 53, 214–16
Miribel, General Marie-François-Joseph de, 118
Mittnacht, Heinrich von, 134–36, 138, 140, 216–17
Moltke, Helmuth von (Elder), 62–66, 81–82, 112, 117, 120, 149–52, 154, 160–71, 243
Moltke, Helmuth von (Younger), 232–34, 241, 244–46, 260–63
Montluçon, 11
Montmédy, 207
Montpellier, 4, 87
Morocco, 210, 245
Moselle (Mosel) River, 168, 209
Moulins, 11
Moyet-Bouvier coupling device, 196
Mt. Blanc Tunnel, 105–6
Mt. Cenis Tunnel, 59, 79, 105–6, 146, 148, 159, 166–67, 203, 257
Mulhouse (Mülhausen), 6, 8, 34, 45, 47, 191
Munich, 9, 31–32, 37–38, 45–47, 51, 56, 62, 66, 109, 121, 138, 147–48, 181, 190, 192, 217, 221, 223, 225–26, 230, 233–34, 237, 242–43
Münster, Georg von, 166

Namur, 16, 266
Nancy, 6, 8, 33
Nantes, 13, 15, 96, 116, 188, 202
Napoleon Bonaparte, 3, 29, 31, 43, 45
Napoleon III, 15, 18, 20–21, 24, 26, 35, 49, 62–63, 65–66, 72–73, 81, 86, 112, 162, 184, 252
Nassau, 42, 52
Netherlands, 40, 45, 146, 148, 257
Neustadt, 62
Neuwied, 234
Nevers, 11
Newcastle, 56
Niel, Marshal Adolphe, 35, 81
Nimes, 87

Noblemaire, Gustave, 90–91, 94, 96, 100, 148, 179–80, 185–87, 191, 199–200, 204
Noizet, General Alfred de, 34
Norddeutscher Lloyd, 258
Nördlingen, 46
Nordwolle factory, 159
Normandy, 73
North Africa, 5
North Sea, 45, 55, 148
Nürnberg, 37–38, 56, 221

Oder River, 55
Oldenburg, 159, 219, 238
Olmütz, 62
Orient Express, 9, 55
Orléans, 6–7, 19, 95, 116
Ostende, 203
Ourcq River, 267

Palatinate, 45, 61–62, 64, 80, 217, 223
Paray-le-Monial, 96
Paris, 6–10, 12, 14–18, 20, 24, 30–35, 38, 45–46, 48, 56, 62, 71, 74, 80–82, 85, 87–88, 92–99, 102–3, 106–7, 109–10, 112–13, 116–17, 140, 151, 157, 159, 161, 163, 165– 66, 168, 170, 175, 177, 180, 183, 186, 188– 89, 194, 200, 212, 215, 248, 255, 259–60, 262, 264
Pas-de-Calais, 77, 198, 201
Passau, 148
Péchot, Colonel, 207
Pelletan, Camille, 166, 199
Pereire family, 10–11
Pereire, Emile, 11, 72
Pereire, Isaac, 72
Pergler von Perglas, Max Josef, 133
Pfordten, Ludwig von der, 64
Pforzheim, 49
Pfretschner, Adolf von, 132–33
Philippart, Simon, 87, 98–99, 159
Picard, Alfred, 7, 183, 199–200, 203–4
Pillet-Will, Michel Frédéric, 13
Podewils, Clemens von, 231
Poincaré, Raymond, 210, 263, 267
Poland, 44, 55
Pönitz, Carl Eduard von, 60
Posadowsky, Arthur von, 216
Posen, 50
Potsdam, 221
Pouyer-Quertier, Auguste, 87–88
Prague, 44, 46
Probstzelle, 221
Prussia, 31, 35, 37–45, 47, 50–55, 60–66, 70–76, 80–81, 86, 97, 120, 122–23, 125– 33, 136–41, 145, 148, 151, 155–56, 166, 169–70, 213–22, 225–26, 228, 230–34, 236– 41, 250, 254, 260, 262–64, 266
Pyrenees Mountains, 178

Radowitz, Josef Maria von, 61
Randon, Marshal Jacques, 35
Ranke, Leopold von, 79
Raudot, Claude-Marie, 86, 88, 105
Regensburg, 56
Reims, 8, 10, 98, 245

Remagen, 234
Rennes, 116
Revue générale des chemins de fer, 256
Reynal, David, 100–101, 108–9
Rheinbaben, Georg von, 219, 226
Rhine River, 9, 13, 28, 39, 42, 45, 47, 49, 55, 59, 61–62, 66, 68, 135, 151, 154, 159, 168, 192, 202, 208–9, 216, 227, 231, 244–46, 259, 261, 266, 268
Rhône River, 59, 105–6, 201
Riviera, 11
Rome, 203
Roon, General Albrecht von, 63
Rothschild Bank, 16, 90, 95, 97, 146
Rothschild, Alphonse de, 108, 188
Rothschild, Edouard de, 188
Rothschild, James de, 10–11, 16–18, 99
Rotterdam, 48, 55, 148, 167, 257
Roubaix, 16, 19, 27, 184
Rouen, 4, 7, 116
Rouher, Eugène, 19–20, 26–27
Rüdesheim, 234, 241
Rüdt von Collenberg, Ludwig, 48–49
Rüger, Conrad Wilhelm, 222, 228
Ruhr, 55, 58, 77, 216
Rupprecht (of Bavaria), 230
Russia, 30, 48, 55, 60, 152, 201, 208, 232–33, 245–46, 269

Saarbrücken, 8, 137
Saarland, 42
St. Cloud, 21, 26
St.-Etienne, 4, 11–12, 116
St. Germain, General, 119
St.-Germain-en-Laye, 4
St. Gotthard Tunnel, 58–60, 66, 79, 105–8, 135, 141, 148–49, 159, 166–67, 201–3, 257
St.-Quentin, 16
Salzburg, 56
Sambre River, 207
Sandherr, Colonel Jean, 117–18, 209
Saône River, 6, 11, 33
Sartiaux, Albert, 182, 188–89, 195
Sauvage, Clément, 90, 92
Savoy, 194
Saxony, 37–38, 42–45, 47, 50–52, 66, 72, 74–75, 80, 120–23, 125–27, 130–37, 139, 143, 148, 159, 213, 219–23, 228, 230, 232–33, 236–40, 268
Say, Léon, 100, 106
Scheele, Friedrich Wilhelm, 123–24, 134
Schleswig-Holstein, 35, 52, 58, 81
Schlieffen, General Alfred von, 82, 171, 208– 10, 241, 243–46, 260–61, 264. *See also* Schlieffen Plan
Schneider factory, 9, 184, 192
Schoen, Wilhelm von, 231
Schultz, Friedrich, 214–15, 218
Scotland, 4
Sedan, 80, 82, 93, 97
Seine River, 13, 65, 71, 116
Séré de Rivières, General Raymond Adolphe, 114
Seydewitz, Paul von, 221–22
Siegfried, Jules, 78–79

Sigmaringen, 139
Silesia, 50, 58, 76
Simplon Tunnel, 59, 105, 166, 203–4, 257
Société Alsacienne factory, 184, 191
Soden, Julius von, 217–18, 220, 222–28
Soden, Oskar von, 225
Soissons, 10, 98
Solacroup, Antoine-Emile, 90
Spain, 6, 48, 202
Spitzemberg, Karl Hugo von, 134
Splügen Tunnel, 59
Spree River, 71
Stephenson, Robert, 48, 56
Strasbourg, 4, 6, 8, 32, 35, 45, 47–49, 59, 61– 62, 65–66, 115, 168, 259
Strousberg, Bethel Henry, 50, 72, 159
Stuttgart, 40–41, 46–47, 49, 51, 56, 59, 124, 133–35, 151, 216–19, 223, 225–27, 230, 234
Suez Canal, 79, 104–6, 146
Sweden, 55
Switzerland, 12, 14, 45, 47, 51, 56, 58–60, 105, 128, 139, 145–46, 148, 159, 167, 201

Talabot, Paulin, 12, 90, 94
Teisserenc de Bort, Edmond, 7
The Hague, 48
Théry, Edmond, 166
Thielen, Karl von, 214–15, 217–18, 221, 223, 225–26
Thiers, Adolphe, 5, 7, 14, 86, 89, 92, 98, 112, 114, 176
Thionville, 8
Thomas, Albert, 268
Thüringer Wald, 221
Tilbury, 203
Tocqueville, Alexis de, 3, 73
Toul, 113, 207
Toulouse, 13
Tourcoing, 16
Tours, 95, 188
Trieste, 40, 56, 148
Turban, Ludwig, 135–36, 147
Turin, 59
Turkey, 63

Ulm, 46–47
United States of America, 29, 38, 57–58, 64, 124, 190, 196, 235, 269

Vacher, Léon, 182
Valenciennes, 98
Vallorbe, 204
Van Blarenberghe, Henri, 183
Varnbühler, Axel von, 225–26
Varroy, Henry, 100, 108
Varzin, 124, 154
Vendée, 96
Verdun, 113, 115, 206–7, 243, 261
Verdy de Vernois, General Justus, 140–41, 154
Versailles, 4, 112, 129, 133, 146
Vichy, 11, 26, 117
Vienna, 9, 29, 31, 40, 45–46, 51, 64, 109, 259, 266
Viette, Jules, 177–78
Vincennes, 32, 34, 262

Vollmar, Georg von, 217
Vosges Mountains, 8, 13, 29, 151, 168, 202, 206, 261

Waddington, Richard, 108, 166, 199–200
Waldersee, General Alfred von, 152–54, 245–46
Waterloo, 31
Weichsel River, 154
Weishaupt, Theodor, 53
Weiss, Eugène, 195
Weissenburg, 62
Weizel, Gideon, 49
Weizsäcker, Karl von, 228, 230
Welti, Emil, 59
Wendel family, 56
Wenger brakes, 178
Weser River, 42, 55
Westinghouse brakes, 139, 160, 178
Westphalia, 42
Wien-Raaber Eisenbahngesellschaft, 56
Wilhelm I, Kaiser, 63–64, 120, 125–26, 132, 138, 141, 150
Wilhelm II, Kaiser, 140–41, 214, 217–18, 226, 228, 232, 242, 262
Wilhelm II (of Württemberg), 218, 226
Wilson, Daniel, 90, 115
Wittelsbach Monarchy, 45
Worms de Romilly, Paul, 193, 196
Württemberg, 41–43, 46–49, 59, 66, 72, 121–23, 130–31, 133–40, 143–45, 147, 159, 213, 216–19, 222–30, 233, 236–38, 249, 268

Zola, Emile, 36
Zorn River, 33
Zürich, 223

Subject Index

accidents, 111, 177, 194, 196, 242
accounting. *See* bookkeeping
administration, 68–75, 157–64, 248–55; French, 3, 5, 8–9, 12–14, 16, 18, 20, 34, 69, 88–92, 94, 96–97, 109, 113–14, 116, 165, 168–70, 176–78, 183–84, 187–88, 193, 195, 197, 200, 259, 265, 268; German, 41–42, 44, 47–48, 53, 56–57, 61–62, 117, 120–22, 126–29, 133, 135, 137–39, 141, 144, 148, 150, 165, 168, 170, 213, 215, 220–21, 223–25, 228–30, 237, 239–42, 259, 266, 268. *See also* civil-military relations, management
agriculture, 3, 13–14, 16, 25, 28–30, 54, 57, 82, 87, 103, 180, 186, 201, 248, 258
airplanes, 245, 261, 269
alcoholism, 30, 158, 202. *See also* wine
allocations, 168, 251, 259, 262; French, 5–6, 20, 34, 90, 107, 113, 176, 180, 186, 198, 207, 261, 267; German, 42, 49, 140, 143, 150–51, 153–55, 164, 169, 216, 220, 230–34, 240–41, 245–46
amnesty, 161, 195–96, 249, 254, 267. *See also* strikes, workers
anti-Semitism, 117
appropriations. *See* allocations
army. *See* military
artisans, 3, 29, 235
Association of German Railway Administrations, 40–42, 49, 51, 57, 61, 69, 72, 109, 123, 128, 138, 167
ateliers. See workshops

banking, 4, 10, 16, 42, 50, 70, 99, 123, 137, 142, 146, 230
Belle Epoque, 186, 248
beltway, 71; of Berlin (Ringbahn), 42, 50; of Paris (Ceinture), 17–18, 33–35, 109–10, 112–13, 177; on Lake Constance (Bodensee), 47, 134, 136, 139, 223, 225
Betriebsgemeinschaft, 218–20, 222, 224–25, 250, 268
block system, 160
Bonapartism, 20–21, 31–32, 39–40, 62, 64, 70–71, 73, 86, 88, 106, 158, 227–30. *See also* Napoleon Bonaparte, Napoleon III
bookkeeping, 21, 57, 101–2, 104, 161, 169, 178, 189, 253. *See also* finance

bookstores, 177, 238
border, 6, 31, 33, 51, 55, 65, 105, 122, 127, 130, 243, 258; Franco-Belgian, 5, 15–16, 35, 118, 210, 266; Franco-German, 8, 33, 61–63, 66, 80, 82, 91–92, 97, 112–14, 116–17, 135, 140, 151–53, 168, 171, 191, 206, 233, 245, 261, 265; of railway companies, 10–11, 18, 28, 37, 40, 45, 73, 87, 95–96, 98, 102, 112, 131, 133, 137, 159, 170, 194, 205, 221
boundary. *See* border
bourgeoisie, 3, 63
brakes, 22, 41, 111, 139, 150, 160, 171, 177–78, 196, 207, 221, 229, 242, 251
bridges, 7, 49, 62, 65–66, 91, 95, 97, 107, 132, 154, 227, 231–34, 241, 243–46, 251, 260–61, 266, 268
budget: of French companies, 13–14, 74, 97, 111, 158, 178, 180, 186, 188, 249–50, 267; of German states, 42, 48, 72, 128, 216, 226–27, 230, 239–40, 250; of national regimes, 81, 85, 107, 112, 140, 152–54, 169–70, 211, 215, 232, 234, 250, 260, 262. *See also* allocations, expenses
Bundesrat, 122, 124–25, 127–28, 131, 133, 135, 144, 215, 243, 250
bureaucracy, 250–51, 263; French, 3, 5, 12, 25, 74, 93, 111, 158, 180; German, 42, 44–45, 47–48, 53, 58, 72, 120–21, 123–24, 129, 135, 138, 150, 153, 215, 217–18, 221, 223–24, 229–31, 236, 239–42, 249, 252, 254. *See also* administration
business, 4, 69, 72, 150, 250; French, 5, 9, 12–13, 15–17, 29–30, 76, 93–94, 97, 99, 103, 106, 116, 177, 182, 186, 188, 202, 205–6, 252; German, 39, 42, 55, 58, 74, 125, 131, 142, 165, 217, 230, 236–37; Swiss, 78

cabinet, 168, 251; French, 10, 13–14, 21, 26, 33, 44, 46, 49, 61, 74, 87–89, 91–93, 100, 114–15, 118, 180–81, 196–97, 204, 252, 263; Prussian, 123–25, 127, 137–38, 141, 150–51, 214–17; Bavarian, 66, 148, 223; Württemberg's, 226; Baden's, 228. *See also* Ministry
canals, 3–4, 23, 25, 28–29, 33, 38, 56, 69, 77–79, 89, 98, 104–5, 107, 146, 166, 201, 255

Subject Index | 323

capitalism, 4–8, 13–14, 21, 37, 39, 42, 44–45, 50, 56, 69, 72, 77, 87, 142, 164, 175, 179, 186, 255. *See also* commerce, investment, profits
Catholicism, 65, 122, 232
Center Party, 122
centralism, 71, 78, 157–58, 165, 170, 255–56; French, 3, 5–6, 8, 12, 22, 69, 72–73, 86, 90, 99–104, 111, 117–18, 166, 175, 179, 207, 251–52, 263, 265; German, 37, 41, 45, 53–54, 122–24, 126, 129–30, 132, 135, 138, 215, 217, 224, 229–30, 242, 249–50, 268
Chamber of Deputies, 5–6, 89–90, 96, 107–8, 115, 122, 126, 131, 178, 182, 191, 195, 204, 267
cheminots. *See* workers
civil-military relations, 33–35, 80, 113, 150, 205, 213, 232, 241–42, 259, 263, 265–66. *See also* cost-sharing, directorates, plenipotentiaries
coal, 4, 15, 18, 23, 25, 28–30, 42, 57–58, 74, 76–77, 94, 98, 104, 146–47, 154, 165, 178, 181, 197–98, 200–2, 205, 209, 216–17, 219, 236, 256
coke, 23, 28, 77, 98, 104, 147, 200–1
combustibles, 28–29, 77, 98, 201, 248. *See also* coal, coke
commerce, 48, 75–80, 159–60, 162–68, 248, 255–59, 269; French, 4–6, 8–9, 12–13, 18, 20, 24–30, 33–34, 87, 92–94, 100, 103–13, 116, 179, 184, 188–89, 197–204, 206, 267; German, 37–43, 45–46, 49, 51–60, 65, 134–35, 141–49, 209, 214, 216, 220–21, 227, 230–31, 234–41, 264; chambers of, 58, 87, 106, 201, 217, 233, 238. *See also* economy, international trade
Comité commercial franco-allemand (CCFA), 206
Comité consultatif des chemin de fer (CCCF), 107, 157, 167, 199
Comité de l'exploitation technique des chemins de fer (CETCF), 109, 157, 177, 190
Comité des fortifications, 114
Comité supérieur de défense (CSD), 114, 118
Commission des places fortes, 207–8
Commission d'études de la guerre de siège, 208
Commission militaire supérieure des chemins de fer (CMSCF), 115
Compagnie transatlantique, 258
concessions, 4, 6–8, 10–12, 18–19, 22–23, 25, 27–28, 39, 47–48, 50, 69, 87–88, 98, 106, 108, 110, 134, 176, 180, 204, 253
Conseil d'Etat, 25, 27, 103
Conseil supérieur de la défense nationale (CSDN), 208
Conseil supérieur de la guerre (CSG), 114, 118, 208
conservatism, 42, 53, 63, 73, 81, 89, 105, 122, 188, 213, 215, 217, 219–20, 224, 232–33
constitution, 157; French, 27, 86; German, 52, 120–22, 125–26, 129, 131–32, 134–35, 137–38, 141, 144–45, 147, 149, 151, 159, 223, 242, 262, 268

construction, 80, 169, 171, 259–60, 266; French, 3–4, 6, 8–10, 12, 19–24, 27, 32–35, 72, 95, 100–101, 111–14, 118, 162, 177, 180, 183, 186–88, 204–6, 208, 211; German, 37, 39, 44, 47–48, 55–56, 61–62, 64, 69–70, 123, 127, 132, 135, 139–40, 143–44, 146, 150–55, 168, 215–16, 220, 225, 231–34, 239, 242–44, 246, 252, 268
conventions, 24, 34, 92, 100, 109, 157, 185, 200; of 1859, 21–22, 26–27, 86, 90, 101; of 1883, 22, 100–102, 111–12, 156, 162, 184, 190, 195
Corps Législatif, 20
costs. *See* expenses
cost-sharing, 111, 140, 169, 205–6, 214, 216, 233, 241, 250, 259, 268
cotton, 28–30, 57–58, 167, 201, 257
coupling devices, 196, 251
Crédit Mobilier, 99
crossings, 10, 16, 24, 74–75, 91, 160–61, 194, 207, 229, 266. *See also* gatekeepers, signals

Darmstädter Bank, 146
debts, 17, 42, 85, 104, 112, 183, 185–87, 189, 223, 227, 267
decentralization, 30, 43, 73, 253
deficits, 22, 27, 29, 165, 168–69, 183, 186–87, 189, 227, 267
deflation, 77–78, 142–43, 164, 235
democratization, 160–61, 176, 189, 226, 238, 248, 250
demography, 99, 164, 198, 231, 252, 256–57, 264
depression, 99, 102, 104, 112, 142–43
deregulation, 71, 73, 87, 89, 158
diplomacy, 55, 66, 68, 76, 109, 256, 258; French, 91, 151, 158, 170, 200, 208, 210; German, 39, 41, 43, 46–47, 62, 72, 74, 122, 134, 148, 151, 222, 226, 234. *See also* international affairs
directorates: French, 9–10, 12, 14, 36, 72, 86, 90–92, 94, 111, 113, 147, 177, 182–83, 185, 187, 191, 194–96, 200, 206, 249, 260, 265, 267; German, 47–48, 123–24, 126, 137, 139, 150, 161, 215, 228–29, 242, 266. *See also* management
Disconto Gesellschaft, 123, 137, 146
dividends, 12, 73, 164, 176
downsizing, 103–4, 164, 186, 198, 249
dumping, 181, 193, 255

earnings. *See* income
Ecole Polytechnique, 89, 118
economy, 4, 8, 16, 22–23, 25, 30, 40–41, 43, 47, 56, 58, 71, 75–80, 101, 106, 120, 149, 157, 161, 163, 167, 170, 177, 208, 240, 249, 260, 262, 264; crisis of, 14, 21, 24, 103, 110, 183, 233; growth of, 18, 27–29, 57–58, 70, 75– 76, 97, 99, 141–43, 147, 149, 164, 184, 186, 188–89, 190, 197–98, 230, 248–50, 256; recession of, 28, 102–4, 112, 128, 164–65, 176, 182, 198, 235; stagnation of, 104, 112, 142, 188, 197–204, 255; take-off of, 54, 60, 144, 234–41, 255
education, 86, 91, 231

324 | Subject Index

electricity, 94, 111, 160, 178, 196, 236, 244, 251, 260, 269
employees, 10, 14, 17, 23–24, 44, 57, 74–75, 93, 95, 103, 139, 160–61, 179, 185, 187, 194–96, 210, 223, 225, 229, 239–40, 251, 254. *See also* personnel, women, workers
engineering, 3, 5, 32, 48, 59, 71, 80, 89–91, 105–6, 109, 118, 146, 162, 242, 251–52; military (*Génie*), 33–35, 81, 114, 206. 208. *See also* Ponts-et-Chaussées
engineers (drivers), 10, 14, 74, 92–93, 179, 181, 239
engines. *See* locomotives
entrepreneurs. *See* capitalism, private enterprise
espionage, 117–18, 171, 208–9, 260
etatism, 39, 69–71, 86, 88–89, 111, 158, 182
expenses, 169, 250, 253, 256, 262; French, 5, 13, 19–20, 22–24, 29, 33–34, 75, 86, 94, 98, 100, 103–4, 110, 114, 162, 176, 178–80, 183–88, 192, 194, 198, 207, 249; German, 48, 52, 60, 140, 147, 152–53, 216, 222, 224–25, 232, 238–40, 268. *See also* allocations
exports, 57, 146–47, 165, 190, 201, 238, 254–55, 258
extraparliamentary committees, 6, 106, 108, 183, 203, 250

federalism, 38–39, 43, 64–65, 71, 73, 78, 120, 129–30, 136, 139, 141, 157, 218, 223, 228, 233, 249, 252. *See also* particularism, Reich
finance, 69, 78, 164, 168–70, 254, 260; French, 8–9, 13–14, 16–17, 19–20, 24, 34, 88–89, 95, 97, 99, 101–4, 110–11, 158, 178, 182–85, 187–88, 248–49, 267; German, 37, 42–43, 57, 59, 70, 80, 127, 137–38, 140, 146, 148, 150, 154, 213–17, 219–20, 223–25, 227–34, 239–41, 244, 252, 262. *See also* budget, taxation
firemen, 10, 74, 92–93, 179, 239
First World War. *See* war of 1914
flooding, 28, 30
flour. *See* grain
foodstuffs. *See* agriculture
fortresses, 33–34, 61, 80, 113–14, 117–18, 151, 168, 171, 206–7, 211, 243, 261–62, 266
Fourth Bureau, 115–19, 170, 205, 207, 209–11
Franco-Prussian War. *See* war of 1870
freight, 78–79, 159–60, 163–67, 250, 256–58, 262; French, 4, 10, 15, 18–19, 27, 33–34, 98, 101, 106, 108, 176, 180, 184, 187, 196, 199–201; German, 46, 51, 56–57, 133–34, 136, 143, 145, 148, 219, 221–22, 227–30, 236–38, 240, 249, 266; blockages of, 85, 87, 95, 97, 109, 194. *See also* rates
freight wagons, 9, 35, 95, 97, 145, 147, 150, 196, 205, 216, 218, 224, 228, 230, 233, 251, 253, 265
Freycinet Plan, 89–90, 94, 99–101, 104, 111, 113, 115–16, 158, 163–64, 169, 197, 203, 249
frontier. *See* border
frontier zone, 113–14, 168–69, 205, 211, 265
fruits, 30, 221, 258
funding. *See* allocations, finance

gatekeepers, 10, 24, 74–75, 161
general staff, 170, 259, 261–62; French (Etat-Major), 80–81, 114, 168, 207, 210, 263, 265; German (Generalstab), 62–65, 137, 149–52, 154, 168–69, 232, 234, 242–46, 260, 263, 266, 268. *See also* Second Bureau, Fourth Bureau
geopolitics, 6, 38, 43, 55, 60, 134, 149, 170, 261, 264
German Customs Union (Zollverein), 28, 40, 52, 69
German Confederation (Bund), 31, 39–40, 45, 49, 51, 61–64, 69–71, 73–74, 80. *See also* North German Confederation
grain, 28, 30, 56, 80, 103, 201, 224, 237. *See also* wheat
guarantees of interest, 12–13, 15–17, 22, 42, 44, 70, 95, 101, 104, 176, 185, 189. *See also* loans

harbors. *See* ports
health care, 23, 74, 179, 185, 187, 250–51, 260. *See also* social welfare
highways, 3, 7, 38, 61, 69, 239, 244, 255, 261
homologation, 26–27, 108, 181
hours (of labor), 14, 23, 75, 139, 179, 185, 194, 239, 267

imperialism, 105. *See also* Pan-German League
imports, 18, 23, 28, 30, 56–57, 76–77, 146–47, 165, 190, 201, 237
income, 14–15, 19, 21–23, 27–29, 91, 94, 97–99, 103–4, 163–64, 176, 183, 186–90, 198–99, 203, 216, 219, 223, 225, 227, 231, 236, 238–40, 249, 253, 256, 267–68. *See also* profits
industrialization, 3, 28–29, 55, 76, 234, 248, 253, 258
Industrial Revolution, 29, 54, 142
industry, 69–70, 76–77, 156, 164–65; French, 4–5, 7–11, 15, 18, 23–25, 29–30, 34, 74, 86–87, 91, 94, 103–4, 107–8, 110, 175, 184, 186, 188–93, 198–99, 201, 254, 257; German, 37–41, 46, 54–58, 120, 129, 136, 142, 146–47, 220, 231, 235–36, 238–40, 269. *See also* locomotives, manufacturing of
international relations, 4, 9, 51, 60, 91, 105, 108–10, 123, 128, 146, 200, 204, 206, 229, 256, 264. *See also* diplomacy
international trade, 4, 10, 15–16, 24–30, 37, 45, 47, 49, 55, 78–79, 105–6, 108, 145, 148, 165–66, 181, 196, 199, 202, 221, 255–57. *See also* commerce
investment, 69–70, 72, 77, 255, 260; French, 4, 7–8, 12–13, 15–16, 20–23, 87, 104, 106, 114, 186, 253; German, 37, 42, 44–45, 56, 80, 141–43, 236. *See also* banking, capitalism
iron, 4, 22–23, 56, 146–47

joint-stock companies, 42, 45–46, 69, 141–42

Kaiserreich. *See* Reich
Kleinstaaterei, 37, 43, 46, 55, 72, 158
Kondratieffs, 76, 142, 235

labor. *See* workers
law, 12, 52, 99, 124, 126–27, 130, 138, 144, 179; of 1838 (Prussian), 39, 123; of 11 June 1842, 6–8, 10, 18, 22, 86, 90, 101; of 18 April 1843, 47; of 12 March 1874, 98; of 20 December 1879, 129, 136; of 14 February 1880, 136; of 21 July 1909, 194. *See also* legislation
leagues (*Verbände*), 41, 145
legislation, 6–7, 15, 39, 47, 89–90, 97, 122–24, 127–28, 130, 137–38, 144, 161, 166, 182–83, 185, 187, 195, 197, 199–200, 234, 239, 251, 255, 268. *See also* parliament
liberalism, 4–7, 13–14, 28, 38–39, 42, 50, 53, 62–63, 70–73, 86–89, 111, 122, 124–25, 128, 137, 142, 145, 157, 182, 252, 256
lines. *See* routes, tracks
loans, 12–13, 15–17, 20–22, 24, 27–28, 42, 70, 85, 104, 176, 184–85, 187, 189. *See also* guarantees of interest
localism, 4, 6–8, 12–13, 18, 20–21, 30, 34, 37, 40, 42, 52, 54, 58, 68, 71, 78, 87, 101, 105, 118, 133, 139, 159, 186–87, 201, 207, 221, 252
locomotives, 68, 77, 79, 160, 251, 253, 261; French, 4, 9, 14–15, 18, 21–24, 35, 92, 94, 97, 99, 104, 110, 178, 180–82, 184, 186, 188–93, 196, 205, 260; German, 38, 48, 54, 57–58, 60, 65, 72, 131, 136, 147, 150, 216, 218–19, 224, 227, 230, 233, 238, 244–45, 249, 258, 261; manufacturing of, 45, 56–57, 110, 147, 159, 165, 180–81, 184, 186–87, 189–93, 220, 236, 238, 254–56
lumber. *See* wood

management, 3, 13, 17, 21, 74, 109, 142, 167, 177, 179, 185, 187–88, 190, 195, 197, 200, 255. *See also* administration
merchant marine, 167, 203, 258–59. *See also* ports, ships, waterways
metallurgy, 15, 55–58, 65, 68, 158, 192, 198, 236, 258. *See also* iron, steel
military, 68, 76, 79–82, 157–58, 168–71, 259–64; French, 5–6, 15, 17, 28, 31–36, 86–88, 91–93, 95, 97, 109, 111–19, 178, 204–12; German, 38–42, 45, 51, 60–66, 75, 120–21, 127, 133–37, 139–41, 147, 149–55, 159, 161, 214–16, 219, 221, 227, 229–34, 239–46, 254; logistics, 31, 80, 168, 170, 241, 243–44, 266, 268; maneuvers, 42, 76, 205, 214, 219, 226, 243, 245, 261; planning, 31, 33, 60–61, 63, 80–81, 112, 114–19, 132, 150, 168, 170–71, 199, 204–5, 208–11, 229, 233, 236, 241–45, 259, 261–62, 264. *See also* general staff, mobilization, Schlieffen Plan, war
mining, 4, 25, 29, 57, 60, 74, 77, 94, 104, 159, 177, 197–98, 201, 209–10, 216, 235, 257. *See also* coal, coke
Ministry: of Commerce, 3, 5, 8, 42, 48–50, 53, 59–60, 123, 135, 203; of Finance, 42, 44, 47, 81, 87, 125, 127, 130, 136, 168, 214, 219, 221–22, 225–27, 233, 241, 263; of Foreign Affairs, 45–47, 133, 146, 221, 223, 228; of the Interior, 6, 47–49, 161, 229; of Justice, 132; of the Marine, 210; of Public Works, 3, 5–6, 8, 10, 13, 16, 18–23, 26, 33, 35, 71, 81, 86–87, 89, 94, 96, 98, 100–101, 103, 105, 107–8, 110–11, 113–14, 118, 123, 127, 136, 144–46, 168, 176–78, 180–81, 183, 190–92, 195–97, 199–200, 204, 214, 217–18, 225–26, 228–29, 239, 242, 263, 267; of Transportation, 223, 229, 232, 237, 242, 268; of War, 31, 33–34, 61, 63–64, 66, 81, 113–16, 118, 132, 135, 140, 150–54, 168, 170, 194, 205–11, 214–15, 231–32, 234, 239, 241, 245, 261–63, 265–67. *See also* cabinet
mobilization, 34, 64–65, 112, 115–19, 137, 150–52, 170–71, 205, 208, 211, 229, 231, 233, 241–42, 244, 259, 265–67
monarchy, 3–5, 7, 14, 18, 21, 31, 35, 40, 43, 45, 51–53, 61, 63–65, 71, 73–74, 80, 86, 114, 120, 125, 130, 132–33, 139, 151, 213, 217–18, 226, 230, 249, 254
mutual aid societies, 23, 179, 187

national defense. *See* warfare
nationalism, 3, 5–10, 25, 31–32, 37–39, 43, 51, 54, 60, 65, 68, 71–72, 75, 105, 107–8, 112, 120, 129–30, 133, 181–82, 251, 254–55, 258–59, 261
nationalization, 88, 125–26, 129, 131–32, 135, 138, 141, 152, 156, 158–59, 175, 182–90, 205, 233, 249, 266, 268. *See also* rachat, *Verstaatlichung*
nation-state, 37–38, 43, 68, 78, 157, 176, 253
newspaper press, 21, 51, 59, 66, 92, 123, 125–26, 138, 148, 160–61, 181, 192, 216–19, 222, 225, 227, 229, 237, 242
North German Confederation, 41, 51–53, 59–60, 65–66, 73, 121, 130, 144

operations, 159, 250, 259–60; French, 5, 7, 9–13, 15, 18–19, 21, 29, 34–36, 72, 94, 96, 102–4, 111, 114–16, 162, 176–77, 183–85, 192, 205, 208, 210–11, 249, 265, 267; German, 41, 48, 62, 64, 123, 131, 137–38, 140, 143, 150, 152, 170, 215–16, 230, 233, 241, 266
Orleanism, 14, 86. *See also* July Monarchy

Pan-German League, 258
Paris Commune, 82, 85, 92–93, 95, 97, 112, 161, 175
Paris Exposition, 180; of 1878, 99; of 1889, 103, 175; of 1900, 183, 189
parliament, 250; French, 6–7, 13–14, 17, 21, 33, 71, 86–89, 91–92, 96–97, 100, 105–8, 111, 114–15, 117–18, 166, 178, 180–83, 186–87, 191–92, 195–96, 199–200, 203–4, 206, 252, 263; German, 49, 53, 125–28, 131, 153, 216, 218–19, 224, 226–27, 232. *See also* legislation, politics
particularism, 38, 43–55, 59, 61, 66, 71–72, 74, 78, 80, 121–24, 126, 128–30, 132–34, 136–38, 141, 147–48, 152, 157, 213, 215, 219–20, 222, 224, 226, 241, 250. *See also* federalism, southern Germany
passenger cars, 9, 24, 43, 71, 75, 147, 160, 218, 230, 233, 251, 253

passenger fares, 10, 18, 78, 95–98, 108, 176, 187, 189, 199, 216, 238, 250
passengers, 4, 15, 18, 27, 40, 46, 77, 85, 94–95, 97, 106, 160, 176, 180, 184, 189, 199, 219, 221, 226, 230, 238, 240, 250, 256, 262
pensions, 23, 93, 162, 179, 185, 187, 194, 223, 239, 251
personnel, 7, 10, 14, 23–24, 65, 74, 97, 100, 103, 113, 134, 138, 150, 176, 185, 187, 194, 208, 216, 222–23, 230, 239–41, 249–50, 254, 265, 267. *See also* employees, engineers, firemen, women, workers
phylloxera, 103, 186, 202
pilgrimages, 96
platforms. *See* ramps
plenipotentiaries, 150, 170, 242, 259, 266
police, 17, 75, 99, 161, 183, 185
political tension, 116–17, 171, 259, 265
politics, 68–69, 71, 76, 78, 156–57, 161, 249–51, 264; French, 5, 8–9, 16–17, 20, 23, 31, 33, 73–74, 86, 88–92, 96, 99, 109, 116–18, 164, 169, 175–76, 192, 203–4, 210, 252, 254–55, 263; German, 38–46, 49–51, 54–55, 58, 61, 64–65, 80, 120–21, 126, 128–29, 137, 141, 149–50, 152–54, 158, 170, 213–14, 220, 223–24, 226–29, 232, 234, 243, 245–46, 262, 268
Ponts-et-Chaussées, 3, 5–8, 27, 32–33, 69, 72, 81, 86, 89, 91, 96, 106–7, 109, 111, 113–14, 162, 167–69, 176, 179, 190, 200, 203, 207, 242
ports, 4, 15–16, 46, 49, 55–56, 58, 78, 88–89, 106–7, 133, 148, 159, 167, 201–4, 237, 257, 259. *See also* merchant marine, ships, waterways
postal service, 44–45, 48, 75, 121, 158
prices, 25, 30, 56, 77, 94, 111, 142, 153, 176, 181, 187, 191–93, 235, 239, 254–55
private enterprise, 68–70, 156, 159, 252; French, 5–8, 10, 12–13, 15–16, 20, 22, 24–25, 28, 35, 73, 86–87, 89–90, 93, 101, 157, 176–79, 184–85, 190–97, 255; German, 37–39, 42, 44–45, 50, 72, 152. *See also* business, private railway companies
private railway companies, 69, 81, 156–58
  French; 7–28, 30, 34–35, 73–74, 78, 86, 88, 90–100, 109–10, 112, 116, 118–19, 161, 165–66, 176–97, 200, 205, 207, 211–12, 248–55, 259, 263, 265–68
    Ardennes, 10–11, 18
    Bordeaux, 15
    Centre, 14–15
    Charentes, 87, 96
    Dauphiné, 12, 18
    Eastern (*Est*), 8–11, 13, 18, 24, 28, 30–31, 34, 36, 49, 59, 61, 85, 87–88, 90–93, 95, 97–100, 102, 104–6, 109– 10, 114, 116, 159, 161, 180–86, 188, 190–91, 193–95, 197, 199, 202–3, 205–7, 210–11, 260–61, 265, 267
    Grand Central, 11–12, 26
    Lyon-Mediterranean, 11–12
    Nantes, 15
    Northeastern, 98–99

Northern (*Nord*), 10–11, 15–19, 21–23, 25, 27–30, 88, 90, 93, 95, 97–100, 102, 104–6, 109–10, 116, 159–60, 166, 169, 176, 178, 182, 188–96, 198–99, 201–3, 207, 210, 265
Paris-Lyon, 11–12
Paris-Strasbourg, 8
PLM, 11–13, 15, 18–19, 23, 26, 28, 30, 80, 90, 93–95, 98, 101, 103, 110, 116, 147, 159, 166, 178, 182, 185–88, 190– 92, 194, 196–97, 201–2, 204, 265
PO, 11–15, 17, 19, 21–22, 26–28, 30, 76, 80, 87, 89–90, 94–97, 100, 102–4, 110, 116, 183, 186–88, 190–91, 194, 196, 201, 265
Southern (*Midi*), 18, 78, 87, 182, 192
State (*Etat*), 96, 102, 110, 178, 182–83, 188, 248–49, 267
Western (*Ouest*), 15, 18, 74, 87, 102, 110, 182–83, 188, 192, 202, 248–49
  German, 41–42, 44–45, 47–48, 50, 56–57, 60–61, 65, 72, 75, 80, 124–27, 131–32, 137–38, 151, 220, 223, 237
    Bergisch-Märkische, 137
    Berlin-Dresden, 131, 137, 151
    Berlin-Königsberg (*Ostbahn*), 42, 80
    Berlin-Potsdam-Magdeburg, 37, 137
    Berlin-Stettin, 127
    Cologne-Minden-Hanover, 42
    Hamburg-Berlin, 63
    Leipzig-Dresden, 37, 44, 131
    Magdeburg-Leipzig, 55
    Munich-Augsburg, 37, 44–46
    Nürnberg-Fürth, 37–38, 40, 44
    Ostpreussische-Südbahn, 214
    Rhenish, 124
    Rhine-Nahe, 137, 152
profit, 69, 81, 162–64; French, 5, 9, 14–16, 22–23, 25, 29, 34, 92, 94, 98, 101, 176, 183, 188, 199; German, 37, 43, 45, 53, 75, 137, 159, 216, 225, 238, 240; margin of, 29, 142, 250, 252–53, 256, 267
protectionism, 128, 145, 190, 201–2. *See also* tariffs
Protestantism, 65
Prussian-Hessian railway union, 216–19, 221, 223, 225, 227, 230, 233, 237–38, 240, 249
prussification, 126, 131, 214–20
public service, 25, 73, 90, 158, 179–80, 186, 190–97, 240, 254

quais. *See* ramps

rachat, 14, 17, 88–89, 96, 100–101, 158, 163, 188, 205, 249. *See also* nationalization
rails, 5, 10, 16, 22, 29, 32–34, 56–58, 91, 94, 97, 107, 150, 201, 203, 232, 242, 251, 255. *See also* tracks
ramps, 116, 150, 152, 203, 212, 221, 242, 261
rates, 77, 165–67, 250, 255; French, 6, 10, 22–27, 29–30, 73, 89, 100–102, 107–8, 158, 176, 182– 83, 199–204; German, 38, 40–41, 53, 56, 78, 123, 134–36, 144–46, 148–49, 216, 218, 224–25, 230, 237–38, 240, 249, 266, 268
receipts. *See* income

reform, 14, 65, 81, 90, 111, 117, 123, 126–27, 144, 156–57, 178–79, 182, 218, 223, 231, 250
regions, 74, 159, 249, 256, 261; French, 6–9, 11–12, 15, 20–23, 26, 30, 34–35, 87–88, 96, 98, 101, 103, 105, 116, 176, 198, 200–203, 206, 252; German, 37–38, 40–41, 46, 54–56, 58, 123, 137, 139, 230
regulation, 69–72, 157–59, 165, 169, 250, 256; French, 5–6, 23, 25, 27, 34–35, 101, 108, 110, 117, 179–81, 183, 190, 193, 197, 199–201, 203–4, 207, 249, 254, 267; German, 37–38, 40–41, 44, 50, 62, 66, 126, 134–35, 137–38, 145–46, 148, 150, 221, 229–30, 233, 240, 242–43, 255. *See also* state
Reich, 65, 91, 121–22, 124–29, 131–32, 134, 144, 147–48, 150, 152–57, 159, 164, 167, 169–70, 208, 210, 214, 218, 226, 229–35, 240–43, 245, 252, 258, 262–63, 265, 268; medium states of, 130–33, 135–39, 141, 143–45, 147, 149, 151, 159, 165, 216–17, 219, 222–23, 227–30, 232–33, 237–39, 250, 254; member states of, 31, 38, 40, 52, 70–71, 73–74, 78, 121–22, 124–26, 128–29, 135, 138, 140–41, 144, 150–51, 154, 157, 169–70, 213, 215, 219–20, 224, 229–30, 240–43, 251–52, 254–55, 259, 263–64, 266, 268; unification of, 31, 38–41, 43, 49–54, 56, 60, 62, 73, 78, 112, 120, 129–30, 135–36, 139, 141, 145–46, 149, 158, 162, 250
Reicheisenbahnamt (REA), 122–24, 126–27, 130–31, 133–35, 138–40, 144–45, 147, 150, 214–15, 217–18, 221, 227, 229–30, 233, 238, 242–43, 250, 263, 266, 268
Reichskanzleramt (RKA), 121–22, 126–27
Reichsschatzamt (RSA), 214–16, 230–34
Reichstag, 52–53, 122, 124–25, 127, 222, 239, 246, 250
reimbursements, 34, 184, 187
reparations, 85–86, 91, 112, 142, 169
revenue. *See* income
revolution, 31, 54, 104–5, 136; of 1789, 3, 29, 175; of 1848, 14–15, 17–18, 23, 32, 40, 43, 49, 58, 61–62, 72, 74, 92, 164, 195; of 1918, 268. *See also* Industrial Revolution, Paris Commune
rights-of-way, 15, 38, 41, 133, 159, 183
rivers, 4, 9, 11, 28, 33, 42, 55, 62, 71, 107, 148, 154, 209, 227, 243, 267
roadbeds, 7, 51, 151, 242
roads. *See* highways
robber barons, 50, 72, 87, 159
rolling stock, 165, 253; French, 7, 9–10, 16, 35, 92, 94–95, 97, 99–101, 104, 110–11, 158, 176, 180–82, 186, 196, 205, 207; German, 49, 121, 136, 147, 153, 219, 224, 239–40, 242, 249. *See also* freight wagons, locomotives, passenger cars
routes, 162, 171, 257; French, 5–8, 10–12, 15–16, 20, 30, 32–34, 87–88, 96, 98, 101, 107, 112–14, 116, 177, 201–4, 206, 211; German, 37, 39, 42, 44–47, 51, 58–59, 61–62, 66, 137, 139, 146, 167, 214–15, 221, 231, 233, 244–45, 264. *See also* tracks
royalism. *See* monarchy

safety, 16, 75, 101, 103, 111, 158–60, 176, 178, 183, 196, 221, 250, 260. *See also* brakes, signals
salary. *See* wages
schedules, 10, 25, 51, 66, 103, 109, 116, 194, 208, 221, 215, 225, 240, 244
Schlieffen Plan, 82, 171, 208–9, 241, 243, 245–46, 260–61, 264
Second Bureau, 117–18, 208–9, 262
Second Empire, 15, 17–19, 24–25, 28, 32, 70, 73, 88, 95, 198, 252
Second Republic, 15, 17–18, 20, 25
Senate, 89–90, 177–78
ships, 78–79, 167, 203, 213, 225, 244, 257–60. *See also* merchant marine, ports, waterways
signals, 16, 22, 41, 94, 111, 150, 159–60, 171, 194, 196–97, 207, 221, 229, 242, 251, 266
silk, 29
Social Democratic Party, 217, 239
socialism, 161, 177, 195, 217, 239–40, 251, 254, 268
social welfare, 10, 74, 179, 183, 185, 187, 194–95, 231, 239, 250–51, 260. *See also* health care, mutual aid societies, pensions
southern Germany, 9, 38–39, 41–43, 46, 48, 50–52, 55, 58–59, 61–62, 65–66, 74, 120–23, 126–27, 130, 133–35, 139–40, 144–45, 150, 152, 154, 170, 213, 216–20, 224–25, 227, 230, 232–34, 237–38, 240, 242, 264. *See also* federalism, particularism, Reich
state: controls by, 5, 8, 10, 13, 18, 22, 24, 28, 40, 42, 45, 50, 61, 70, 73, 86, 89–90, 93–94, 96, 98, 100, 108, 111, 121, 131–34, 158, 169, 177, 179–81, 192–93, 197, 199, 220, 224, 230, 250, 263, 265; intervention by, 5–6, 10, 13, 16, 21, 23, 25, 27, 69, 71, 87, 94, 124, 133, 144, 147, 166, 178, 183, 210, 215, 239, 242, 249, 254, 259; ownership by, 38, 42, 44, 47, 53, 72, 88, 137, 183, 248, 253; supervision by, 5, 23, 40, 88, 122, 124, 136, 156, 242, 249. *See also* nationalization, regulation
state networks, 45, 49, 56, 61, 73, 102, 122–23, 136, 143, 148, 160–61, 166, 213, 215, 220, 222, 225, 229, 232, 236–39, 248–49, 264, 266–67
states' rights, 43, 72–73, 123–25, 129–36, 138, 144, 147, 149, 151–52, 157, 233, 240, 243, 252. *See also* federalism, particularism
stationmasters, 10, 74
stations, 9–10, 17, 24, 35, 42, 58, 71, 75, 87, 91, 94–95, 101–2, 116, 118, 148, 150, 160–61, 165, 176–77, 180, 183, 194, 205, 211–12, 242, 248, 251, 261
statistics, 9, 18, 21, 46, 54, 56–58, 68, 70, 77–79, 102, 104, 111, 130, 141–43, 146, 160, 162–64, 166–67, 176–77, 186, 188–89, 192–93, 197–98, 204, 219, 233, 235–36, 238, 252–53, 255–58, 262, 264, 268
steam, 4, 18, 28–29, 31, 38, 54, 60, 68, 72, 79, 158, 160, 189–90, 203, 225, 238, 244–45, 251, 258–59, 261, 268
steel, 22, 56, 77, 94, 97, 113, 150, 171, 236, 245, 251

stockholders, 9–10, 13, 15–16, 22, 26–28, 44, 72–73, 101, 104, 164, 176, 184, 186, 188, 190, 253
stock market, 21, 24, 42, 44, 60, 99, 102, 127, 142, 164, 197
strategy. *See* military, warfare
stone, 202, 248
strikes, 17, 103, 183, 185, 187, 193–96, 198, 209–10, 239–40, 254, 267. *See also* workers
subsidies, 7, 12, 15, 22–23, 27, 34, 42, 58–60, 70, 78, 88, 95, 98, 105, 146, 186, 203, 267
sugar beets, 16, 80, 198
switches, 171, 207, 266

tariffs, 28, 40, 78, 128, 145, 148, 202. *See also* protectionism, rates
taxation, 95, 97, 101, 108, 145, 159, 176, 227, 231
technology, 31, 54–55, 68–69, 72, 75–76, 78, 109, 158–60, 171, 250–51, 269; French, 4, 20, 22, 32–33, 90, 98, 106, 110, 177–78, 196–97, 207, 265; German, 39–40, 48, 56, 70, 128, 149, 226, 229, 242, 244; retardation of, 260–61, 268–69. *See also* engineering
telegraph, 31, 160, 194, 260
telephone, 160, 211, 230, 260
terminals. *See* stations
textiles, 28–30, 57–58, 76, 159, 167, 201, 206. *See also* cotton, silk, wool
Third Republic, 86, 93, 99, 112, 118, 149, 156, 163, 167, 169, 196, 231, 252, 262–63
tourism, 16, 96, 209, 223, 259
tracks, 3–4, 6, 9, 13, 15–16, 21–22, 27, 30–33, 35, 39–40, 46, 50, 54–56, 65, 68–69, 71, 80, 89, 91, 94, 96, 98, 100–101, 115, 133–34, 166–67, 170, 178, 180, 186, 188, 194, 199, 201, 205, 207, 210, 219, 227, 243, 245, 251, 256, 260–61, 264, 266; gauge of, 41, 48–49, 60–61, 109, 159, 162, 206, 269; length of, 18–19, 28, 37, 152, 162, 164, 189, 236–37, 252–53, 262; parallel (double), 64, 114, 116, 127, 131, 134, 137, 139–40, 148, 152–54, 162, 168–69, 204, 209, 212, 221, 232, 242, 246, 252, 269; spur, 8, 18, 20, 34, 48, 58, 87, 150, 159, 162; transversal, 32, 64, 87, 203, 211. *See also* routes
trade. *See* commerce, international trade
trade unions, 74, 161, 254. *See also* workers
trolleys, 139, 162, 248
trucks, 244, 261
tunnels, 7, 9, 24, 56, 58–60, 66, 79, 91, 95, 97, 105–7, 132, 135, 146, 159, 166–67, 201–4, 206, 243, 260, 266
typewriters, 162, 230, 240

urbanism, 3, 29, 46, 71, 159, 194, 229, 235, 248

vegetables, 30, 258
Verpreussung, 40, 72, 216
Verstaatlichung, 127–29, 136, 152, 158, 223. *See also* nationalization
victuals, 28. *See also* agriculture, grain, wine

wages, 10, 14, 23, 75, 103, 142, 179, 185, 187, 194–95, 223, 225, 231, 239, 251, 260, 267
warfare, 82, 267; defensive, 31–32, 34, 38, 52, 60, 79, 93, 95, 112–16, 118–19, 121, 132, 147, 149–50, 152–53, 168, 170–71, 205–7, 231, 243, 245, 254, 261, 263–65, 268; offensive, 31–32, 61, 80, 115, 152, 168, 170–71, 208–11, 243–46, 260–61, 264, 266. *See also* military planning
war, 29, 38, 40, 49, 86, 117, 143, 171, 242; of 1864, 35, 63, 81; of 1866, 28, 35, 51–52, 54, 57, 59, 64–65, 73, 81–82, 164; of 1870, 9, 30, 35–36, 50, 52, 57, 60, 66, 68, 71, 76, 81–82, 85, 89–95, 97, 105, 109, 111–12, 121, 130, 137, 141–42, 156, 158, 162, 164, 175, 198, 207–8, 249, 257, 263; of 1914, 142, 175, 190, 212, 214, 232–34, 238, 244–46, 248–49, 251, 256, 261–69. *See also* military
war-readiness, 242, 259, 261
war scare: of 1875, 116, 151, 153; of 1887, 153–54
waterways, 4, 22, 28, 33, 45, 56, 58, 68, 78, 80, 103, 105, 201, 258. *See also* canals, ports, rivers
weather, 25, 62, 78, 201
wheat, 57, 201
wine, 11, 28, 30, 57, 94–95, 103, 186, 202. *See also* phylloxera
women, 10, 23–24, 75, 161–62, 187, 240, 251
wood, 57, 147, 202
wool, 28–29, 57, 201
workers, 74–75, 160, 164; French, 14–15, 17, 23, 62, 92–93, 95, 97, 103, 179, 181, 183–85, 187, 194–95, 209–10, 249, 267; German, 44, 57, 77, 240, 266; unionization of, 161, 239, 251, 254. *See also* socialism, strikes, women
workshops (*ateliers*), 9, 17, 35, 92, 94, 97, 110, 181, 184, 186, 189, 194, 219

xenophobia, 117, 171, 209, 260. *See also* anti-Semitism

zeppelins, 245

www.ingramcontent.com/pod-product-compliance
Lightning Source LLC
Chambersburg PA
CBHW071216080526
44587CB00013BA/1396